Date: 9/7/21

THE INTERNATIONAL
BRIGADES

ALSO BY GILES TREMLETT
Ghosts of Spain
Catherine of Aragon
Isabella of Castile

THE INTERNATIONAL BRIGADES

Fascism, Freedom and the Spanish Civil War

GILES TREMLETT

BLOOMSBURY PUBLISHING

LONDON · OXFORD · NEW YORK · NEW DELHI · SYDNEY

BLOOMSBURY PUBLISHING
Bloomsbury Publishing Plc
50 Bedford Square, London, WC1B 3DP, UK
29 Earlsfort Terrace, Dublin 2, Ireland

BLOOMSBURY, BLOOMSBURY PUBLISHING and the Diana logo are trademarks of
Bloomsbury Publishing Plc

First published in Great Britain 2020

A catalogue record for this book is available from the British Library

Library of Congress Cataloguing-in-Publication data has been applied for

ISBN: HB: 978-1-4088-5398-6; TPB: 978-1-4088-5399-3;
EBOOK: 978-1-4088-6877-5

4 6 8 10 9 7 5

Typeset by Newgen KnowledgeWorks Pvt. Ltd., Chennai, India
Printed and bound in Great Britain by CPI Group (UK) Ltd, Croydon CR0 4YY

MIX
Paper from
responsible sources
FSC
www.fsc.org   FSC® C020471

To find out more about our authors and books visit www.bloomsbury.com
and sign up for our newsletters

For my mother, Berenice Tremlett,
and dedicated to the memory of my father, Edward Tremlett

Contents

THE INTERNATIONAL BRIGADES, SPANISH CIVIL WAR 1936–39

COUNTRIES OF ORIGIN

In 1936, many of today's countries were colonies or part of larger sovereign entities. Volunteers in the International Brigades came from some four-fifths of the fewer than eighty sovereign countries and dominions then in existence. It is impossible to calculate how many non-sovereign countries, colonies and other territories were represented, but there were at least twenty-five.

SOVEREIGN NATIONS AND DOMINIONS

Albania	Egypt	Peru
Andorra	Finland	Philippines
Argentina	France	Poland
Australia	Germany	Portugal
Austria	Greece	Romania
Belgium	Hungary	Russia (USSR)
Bolivia	Iraq	San Marino
Brazil	Iran	South Africa
Bulgaria	Iceland	Spain
Canada	Ireland	Sweden
Czechoslovakia	Italy	Switzerland
Chile	Latvia	Syria
China	Lithuania	Turkey
Colombia	Luxembourg	United Kingdom
Costa Rica	Mexico	United States of America
Cuba	Netherlands	Uruguay
Denmark	New Zealand	Venezuela
Dominican Republic	Nicaragua	Yugoslavia
Ecuador	Norway	
El Salvador	Panama	
Estonia	Paraguay	

NON-SOVEREIGN NATIONS, COLONIES, PROTECTORATES, INTERNATIONAL ZONES, SOVIET REPUBLICS AND OTHERS

Algeria	Indonesia	Scotland
Armenia	Lebanon	Slovakia
Belarus	Macedonia	Slovenia
Croatia	Montenegro	Tangier
Cyprus	Morocco (French)	Ukraine
Danzig	Morocco (Spanish)	Vietnam
Ethiopia	Pakistan	Wales
India	Palestine	West Indies
French Indochina	Puerto Rico	

Sources: RGASPI 545.6.1–66 and 545.2.108, with thanks to Severiano Montero

Introduction

Virgilio Fernández del Real came through the doorway to my Madrid apartment in his wheelchair dressed as theatrically as always. A thick, black, maroon-lined Salamanca cape was wrapped around his upper body, keeping out the March chill. Pinned onto his black beret were a ribbon bearing the purple, red and yellow stripes of Spain's lost Second Republic and a badge in the same colours carrying the triangular symbol of the International Brigades. A luxurious white beard, topped by rheumy blue eyes and bushy white eyebrows, occupied much of the space between beret and cape. First reactions to him differed. Some saw a stern sort of gravitas, others an adorable *abuelo*, or grandfather. Either way, he impressed.

On this day in 2018, however, Virgilio was a shadow of the vigorous nonagenarian I had met just three weeks earlier. He looked pallid, pained and listless. Two weeks of illness and hospitalisation are debilitating at any time, but more so at ninety-nine years old. I had offered him a place to recover from the after-effects of a virus until he felt well enough to return home to Mexico. Despite the constant reassurances of his wife Estela Cordero, I found myself silently panicking that he might never recover. The next morning Virgilio, now dressed in a soft scarlet leisure suit, still looked wan, but when I offered him breakfast he asked me to fry two eggs with *chistorra* sausage. Clearly, he was feeling better.

Virgilio lived in Guanajuato, a quaint, former silver-mining city built atop a criss-cross of tunnels in a steep-sided river valley. A retired paediatrician, he had made his home in a colonial-era hacienda with a walled garden full of exotic plants. It also serves as an arts centre named after his deceased former wife, the Canadian-born artist Gene Byron. Virgilio returned to Madrid every year or so, answering the call of those seeking to remember the more than 35,000 foreign volunteers who came to Spain to fight in a war that pitted fascist troops and weapons – provided to the reactionary general Francisco Franco by Hitler and Mussolini – against those defending the democratic Republic. To some, Virgilio was a hero. The queue of people traipsing through our kitchen to pay homage over the next few days was remarkable. To others in my conservative neighbourhood, where a deep-seated suspicion of the political left has passed through the generations, he may have seemed like an elderly devil.

More than a year later, in May 2019, Virgilio sent me a message after Madrid's city elections saw conservatives take power with the backing of a new far-right party, Vox. 'We have to prove that we are the immense majority, and those fascists can start getting ready to *ir a tomar por culo* [stick it up their arse],' he said. Virgilio, by then a centenarian and still an avowed communist, had lost none of the political indignation that saw him join the International Brigades as an eighteen-year-old ad hoc anaesthetist.

Earlier that same month I had planned to visit Geoffrey Servante, the only remaining British Brigader, at his retirement home in the Forest of Dean. Servante's Spanish experience began with a bet in a Soho pub in the summer of 1937, where he overheard someone saying that it was no longer possible to join the International Brigades. They told him that the politics of fascist appeasement (masked as 'non-intervention' in the Spanish Civil War), had forced the French to close the land border while warships from Britain and elsewhere patrolled the coasts. 'I bet you a hundred quid I can do it,' said Servante. The former Royal Marine, educated by Jesuits and uninterested in politics, beat the blockade.

Unlike the fifth of British volunteers who died,[1] and the considerable number who were injured, Servante survived the war unscathed.[2] In fact, his small artillery unit took part in no major battles and his stories suggest that Spain was mostly fun and games. Perhaps everything was like that to him. A mischievous grin crosses his face in photographs from those days, but also in more recent ones. He never collected his bet money, however, since the man who offered the wager died before he returned home. I had just obtained Servante's daughter's email and was composing a message to her when I typed the family surname into an online search engine to check the spelling (remarkably close to the Spanish Cervantes, but on Forest of Dean records for several centuries). That is how I discovered Servante had died two weeks earlier, aged ninety-nine. I had spoken to other Brigaders from Britain, the United States, and elsewhere, before – and was always impressed by the intensity with which they recalled their experiences – but was particularly sad to miss Servante. He had been one of the few vocal survivors who openly fitted a description that more piously political Brigaders, who were sometimes known as '100 percenters', called 'adventurers'. Such men wore their experience more lightly, and were rarely heard from afterwards. He was probably more representative than we imagine.

Virgilio did not return to Spain. In November 2019 he sent me a video of what, in his now wheezing voice, sounded much like a last public proclamation. 'I will be 101 on 26 December,' he said, before calling for Mexican domestic servants to be given proper labour rights, and declaring '¡Viva la República Española!', 'Long Live the Spanish Republic!' He never did celebrate that birthday, dying just nine days before the date. 'I hug him and it is as if he is still here, but also far away,' Estela wrote in a message sent fifteen minutes after his death.

Only two other veterans of the International Brigades, living in France and Spain (since the Brigades, in a largely ignored part of their history, also recruited locally – with Virgilio one of the first Spaniards to join, becoming part of the diaspora of Republican exiles after the war), are now known to be alive. Even they may well not be with us by the time this history of the International Brigades reaches readers' hands. In a way, that is a relief. There is no one to offend or argue with, and the Brigaders were a strong-willed, disputatious lot. It also makes this an apt moment to write their history. Apart from their historical relevance, they deserve to be remembered not just by those who sympathise with their mostly leftist politics but by anyone who believes Western democracies were right to fight fascism in the Second World War. The great Republican senator and Vietnam veteran John McCain – hardly a radical leftist – noted shortly before his own death in 2018, that many Brigaders had 'just come to fight fascists and defend a democracy … I have always harbored admiration for their courage and sacrifice'.[3]

War is often binary. You win or lose, are victorious or defeated. There are usually only two sides, forcing a choice between often imperfect opponents. The volunteers who joined the International Brigades formed a veritable Tower of Babel, speaking a cacophony of languages from around the world. All the nations of Europe and the Americas, bar the occasional archipelago or island state, were represented. No single nationality can claim predominance.

More than half the foreign volunteers were communists and their well-structured national parties were crucial for organisation and recruitment. Yet this does not define the Brigaders. Volunteers did not pledge allegiance to the communist cause. Nor should they be called an exclusively 'Comintern army', with the implication that they were run directly from Moscow by the Communist International – even if this, again, oversaw both the creation and organisation of the Brigades. In political terms they saw themselves, like the Republic they came to defend, as a broad popular front force of the kind that voters in both Spain and France had recently placed in government. Within their ranks there were left-wingers of all kinds, centrists, Catholics, Protestants, atheists, practising and secular Jews, Moslems and, also, agnostic adventurers. Given that people from China, Vietnam, Indonesia, Syria, Abyssinia, Turkey and Latin Americans of mixed, indigenous or black African roots also joined their ranks, there were many other belief systems too.[4] Jews from across the world were so numerous that they provide an alternative narrative to the traditional lament for a people passive in the face of the coming Holocaust. In Spain they consciously fought against fascism, bravely and well.

Most Brigaders fitted into one of two overlapping categories: the devout and the displaced. The former were highly politicised, while the latter belonged to a first or second generation migrant diaspora in Europe and the Americas that had suffered the hardship of economic or political exile. These were not uniformly 'good people', as this history makes clear. That is too much to expect from 35,000 soldiers, however idealistic their task. Desertion was frequent. Prisoners were shot. There were cowards, psychopaths and rapists in their ranks. Nor did that idealism – which was extraordinary in terms of race (providing, for example, the first black American commanders of white troops) and the attempt to unite people across national and cultural boundaries – extend to everything. Stalinism lurked, and not just in the wings. Homosexuality was punishable. Women were looked down upon or mistreated by, amongst others, the misogynistic International

Brigades chief André Marty. Those women who joined the Brigades mostly served as doctors, nurses, translators or propagandists. The front line was reserved almost exclusively for men. Yet the writing of these women and of other female observers is often more revealing than the dutiful memoirs of the men who fought or, in an organisation obsessed with its own narrative, were employed to write. Separating truth from wishful-thinking and propaganda is the greatest challenge for anyone investigating the International Brigades.

Although the International Brigades are often referred to as a 'transnational army', they never formed, in the operational sense, an independent, self-sufficient 'army' or any other kind of autonomous unit. Instead, they were a provider of frontline shock units to the Republican army (and also of smaller artillery, anti-aircraft and medical units). The half-dozen brigades mostly operated as separate units, and the three to six battalions in each one (and, occasionally, smaller companies) were sometimes deployed independently, or loaned out to Spanish brigades or divisions. The International Brigades, in other words, were grouped together for recruitment, training and administration – and sometimes fought side-by-side – but took their orders from the Republican government. At full strength, the Brigades numbered more than 42,000 men, according to paymaster records from December 1937.[5] Some 32,500 foreign volunteers passed through their ranks, according to the Brigades' own records, while Spanish recruits like Virgilio made up the rest (and often became exiles after the war). Given the early chaos in record-keeping, however, I estimate the overall total of foreign Brigaders at 35,000.

Despite the outpouring of literature by, or about, the International Brigaders (and one incomplete bibliography contains 2,317 books in dozens of languages[6]), there has been no comprehensive, global history in English for four decades.[7] Even in Spanish, and with the exception of Rémi Skoutelsky's French-coloured but excellent *Novedad en El Frente*, the 1974 edition of Andreu Castells's *Las Brigadas Internacionales de la Guerra de España* remains the most complete study. Almost all published books concentrate on individual experiences, or on volunteers of a single nationality. A wealth of primary sources has become available since then, especially with the opening of the surviving parts of the International Brigades' own archive in Moscow. I am fortunate to be the first historian of the Brigades to have unlimited access, since a digitised version of these records became available shortly before I began my research six years ago. This narrative history uses that archive extensively, and others in places as far east as Warsaw, Poland, and as far west as Stanford, California, to retell their story and reassess the Brigades' role and impact – which extends far beyond Spain and the civil war years.

As a result, the number of countries that sent volunteers must be revised upwards. The standard figure is fifty-two, but the Comintern files reveal sixty-five named countries.[8] While five of these – Palestine, Armenia, Cyprus, Ethiopia and Puerto Rico – were not fully or properly independent, many of today's sovereign states either did not exist or were in those parts of a world still dominated by large empires. In fact, men and women from almost four-fifths of the world's sovereign countries or empires were present. Volunteers from within empires were often listed by their metropole. Algerians, Vietnamese and some Moroccans, for example, were registered as French. The half-dozen Indian volunteers mostly appear as British (though 35-year-old Gopal Mukund Huddar from Nagpur, who used the nom de guerre John Smith, is also being listed as coming from Iraq). Indonesian-Chinese doctor Tio Oen Bik was counted amongst the Dutch.[9] The Ethiopians (then Abyssinians) mentioned by some Brigaders were mostly registered as Italian. The story of black volunteers, indeed, is wider than the Americans and Cubans who are usually cited – and includes Yvan Dinah, a 23-year-old French law student and battalion commander from Martinique.

Some volunteers are impossible to pin down by nationality. Who is the single 'Moor' who crosses the frontier late in 1937 – maybe Palestinian communist Najati Sidqi, who 'went to defend Jerusalem in Cordoba'?[10] Where should we place those who arrived from Free City of Danzig, or from internationally administered Tangier, at the same time? In today's terms, too, we would have to divide up Yugoslav volunteers into seven different countries, or those from Czechoslovakia into two. Even the Indian recruits included men like Doctor Ayub Ahmed Khan Naqshbandi, from Lahore, now in Pakistan. I have been unable to ascertain how many of the roughly two hundred 'Russian' exile volunteers were originally from what today is Russia, and how many from other parts of the Soviet Union.[11] It would be surprising if some were not Georgian, or from elsewhere. Volunteers came, then, from sixty sovereign (or mostly independent) states in 1936, and more than eighty of today's countries.

How many died? By the end of March 1938, with the carnage of the Ebro Battle still awaiting, the Brigades counted 4,575 foreign volunteers dead, or fifteen percent. The overall figure is much higher, since another eighteen percent were missing – either lost in action, or having deserted, and the Ebro accounted for between ten and fifteen percent of the total number of dead. In fact, more than half of the volunteers were out of action by then, since a further sixteen percent had been repatriated (usually wounded or unfit) and seven percent were in hospital in Spain. The most reliable national studies, for France, Canada and the United Kingdom, show up to a quarter dead – depending on nationality. My final, conservative estimate is that one in five volunteers died and became, in the words of Hemingway's eulogy to the lost Americans, 'part of the earth of Spain'.[12]

Only one political and moral category fits almost all the Brigaders. They were anti-fascists. The crucial binary choice for foreigners in the Spanish Civil War – which stretched over most of the three years prior to the outbreak of the Second World War – was between fascism and anti-fascism. This choice was explicit at the time, made obvious by the units sent by Hitler and Mussolini, and often expressed as fear for the future. Although few could foresee the full ghastliness of that, it was effectively a choice between the coming fascist aggression of the Second World War, including the Holocaust, and its most elemental opposite – the absence of fascist rule, genocide, and wars of racial superiority in Western Europe. As Western democracies would eventually realise, this fight required the help of Soviet Russia.

For Spaniards, the war was a far more complex clash – fuelled by both national history and ideology. Franco and the generals who destroyed Spanish democracy were not all pure-bred 'fascists', though they belonged to the wider family of violent, far-right regimes inspired and backed by the dictatorships in Germany and Italy. Their hybrid ideology mixed the extreme intolerance of entitled, reactionary Spain with the stiff-armed ceremonial and new beliefs espoused by Mussolini and Hitler. Franco incorporated fascist parties and ideas to reinforce an otherwise flimsy set of political beliefs and, crucially, would have lost the war without Hitler and Mussolini's armed forces.

Franklin Roosevelt was amongst those to recognise the violent, dangerous and ruthless nature of a fascistic Spanish ideology built 'along totalitarian lines' and locked into a mutual embrace with Nazis and fascists.[13] It was Hitler's Luftwaffe which, on the Führer's personal orders, flew Spain's most potent and experienced fighting force – the Army of Africa, with its hardened legionnaires and colonial mercenaries – to the mainland. Otherwise, Franco's side would have been defeated within weeks. Some 90,000 well-trained troops sent by Hitler and Mussolini (more than twice the total number of Brigaders and other foreign volunteers in the Republic), helped tilt the balance after that. They provided two-thirds of an air force that eventually dominated Spanish skies. It is not surprising, then, that the word 'fascist' was used by Brigaders, other Republicans and supporters abroad to describe Franco's army. The Republic, abandoned by other democracies, was left to rely on the distant and unreliable Soviet Union of Joseph Stalin.

The dictators used Spain to train soldiers, hone strategy, test weapons and, above all, see how far Britain, France and the United States were ready to appease them. The greatest lesson, indeed, was that these countries were prepared to go a long way. They also discovered the brilliance of 'blitzkrieg' and became convinced of the tactical benefits of blanket-bombing cities and spreading terror amongst civilians. The Spanish Civil War was, in many ways, the opening engagement of the Second World War. Most of those who volunteered came to see it as a 'dry run' for the much bigger battle against fascism that followed.

With the recent experiences in Afghanistan and Syria, it no longer seems quite so remarkable that 'volunteer' international armies can suddenly emerge – however much these may diverge in their origins and ideals from the International Brigades. In the 1930s, however, only the medieval Crusades seemed a relevant comparison. As then, the Brigades were formed at a time when people rarely travelled beyond their own nation's borders. Those who chose to enlist were doing something that seemed remarkable – even if many were already migrants and some were sailors. Jobs, families and safe futures were abandoned (though unemployment was also escaped).

The Brigaders fascinated contemporaries, especially those drawn to witness a war whose impact on global public debate outstripped even that of the conflict, three decades later, in Vietnam. Writers like Ernest Hemingway, André Malraux, George Orwell and John Dos Passos came to gawk, or join in. Just as Spain was the most important lifetime experience of many International Brigade veterans – eclipsing even their later fight against fascism in the Second World War – so it became the inspiration for major works of literature. Hemingway's *For Whom the Bell Tolls*, Peter Weiss's *Aesthetics of Resistance* and – in a different way – Orwell's *Homage to Catalonia*, were all inspired by the experiences of foreign volunteers in Spain. The war itself became, in the words of the British poet Stephen Spender, 'the centre for the struggle of the soul of Europe' and 'a poet's war'.[14] This was also hailed as the first 'photographers' war' – where the likes of Robert Capa and Gerda Taro would make their names and produce iconic images of the Brigaders. Great future politicians and intellectuals such as future German chancellor Willy Brandt, the first prime minister of independent India, Jawaharlal Nehru, and the French philosopher Simone Weil also came to look, learn or participate.

The Brigaders would not have identified themselves as individual history-makers, but their future impact was considerable. Two of my favourite examples come from Britain, where by 1974 one veteran, Sir Alfred Sherman, had become future prime minister Margaret Thatcher's free market guru, while another, the Transport and General Workers' Union leader Jack Jones, was deemed in a nationwide poll 'Britain's most powerful man'.[15] The final chapter of this book explains their considerable future impact as resistance fighters, partisan leaders, spies, generals, police chiefs, ambassadors, politicians, ministers, prime ministers and, especially behind the Iron Curtain, senior communists. In that sense, they were as potent a generator of elites as any Ivy League university, Oxbridge college or French *grande école*.

The Brigaders are normally viewed as experiencing defeat, rather than victory. I disagree, since this ignores the full nature of what they were fighting for: the destruction of world fascism. It is true that Franco was victorious on the battlefield and remained in power as the vengeful dictator of Spain until 1975. No one captured the poignancy of that quite as well as W. H. Auden in his prescient 1937 poem 'Spain', which not only saw the urgency of 'today the struggle', but also recognised that history 'cannot help or pardon' the defeated. The Brigaders, however, saw the fight against fascism in broader, global terms. They continued their struggle when the Second World War broke out five months after the war in Spain ended, playing a remarkably important role in resistance movements across Europe. Most decent citizens of the Western world (and many other places) joined them as avowed anti-fascists and the defeat of Hitler and Mussolini became their final victory. Indeed, the International Brigaders and those foreigners who volunteered to defend the Spanish Republic without joining their ranks (some of whom are also mentioned here) can claim the moral virtue of having begun that fight long before others realised that it was necessary.

In order to stop a destructive or corrupting idea from spreading, it must first be identified as such. The men and women in this book did exactly that with fascism – taking up arms against an ideology that went on to systematically murder over 6 million Jews as well as an unknown number of gypsies, homosexuals, people with disabilities, and others, while provoking a world war that claimed 50 million dead outside the Far East. They were amongst the few prepared to risk their lives to halt the descent into all of that. This does not make them saints or excuse the later political choices or behaviour of some of them in Soviet-dominated central and eastern Europe, which this book also explores. Some individuals, indeed, fail badly on any reasonable test of decency, or of the desire to promote liberty and democracy. We should not fool ourselves about that. Final judgement, however, is best left to the free and democratic Spain that re-emerged in the late 1970s after Franco's death. A law approved by all parties in the Madrid parliament in 1996 awarded Brigade veterans Spanish nationality, praised their defence of democracy and formally offered them the nation's gratitude.[16] It is a fitting way for them to go down in history.

Madrid, June 2020

Welcome to the Games: Barcelona, 19 July 1936

In the summer of 1936 Muriel Rukeyser, a young American poet and writer on her first magazine assignment outside the United States or Britain, spent the night in a cheap, windowless hotel room in Perpignan, south-east France, before taking a train towards the Spanish border.[1] After changing to a train with hard wooden bench seats at the frontier station of Port Bou on 19 July, she travelled through undulating groves of olive trees and almonds, occasional flashes of sparkling blue in the distance announcing to her the presence of the Mediterranean Sea. In towns and villages, small boys hung from the branches of yellow-flowered trees, whistling and watching the train chug by. Tall, full-faced and intense, twenty-two-year-old Rukeyser jotted down brief, telegraphic impressions in her notebook: cork oaks, olive trees, peasant women in her third-class carriage and, everywhere, 'politics' and 'discussion'.[2] Nearby sat Otto Boch, an exiled young German cabinet-maker with a 'gazing Brueghel face, square forehead and eyes, strong square breast ... narrow runner's hips'.[3]

Rukeyser soon found herself deep in conversation with Boch, and other international travellers on the train, who ranged from a troupe of peroxide-blonde English dancers, on their way to perform in Barcelona, to a Hollywood film director and his cameraman.[4] It was useful that her editor at the London magazine *Life and Letters To-day* had equipped her with a 'Guide to 25 Languages in Europe', since, apart from the expected passage of Spaniards and French, the train was full of young Swiss and Hungarian athletes, all heading towards Barcelona for the so-called 'People's Olympiad', an alternative Olympics, that was due to start with a torch-lit procession later that day.[5] The phrase book covered everything from Finnish to Esperanto but, annoyingly, left out the language of the provincial towns and small villages they were travelling through: Catalan.

The train was travelling into a country where the ideological fires that would soon consume the Europe of Hitler, Mussolini, Stalin, and those who stood in fear of them, threatened to burst into life at any moment. Indeed, as it trundled through the countryside of northern Catalonia, the train slowed gradually and then came to a stop at the station in the small industrial town of Montcada i Reixac, just twenty-four kilometres short of Barcelona. Armed men appeared: something was afoot in the city. In a Spain already used to periodic eruptions of political violence, speculation ran rife. An anarchist rebellion? A fascist coup? A communist revolution? Or, someone suggested, it might be an attempt to stop the leftist People's Olympiad itself.

Spain had its own particular and sluggish history of emergence into the industrial era and of the political passions it had unleashed. In a century soon to be dominated by the violent clashes provoked by the all-encompassing, quasi-religious ideologies of radical left and radical right, Spain also served as a large, experimental crucible where everything might spontaneously erupt at any moment. One lucid observer would compare it to a 'cockpit'. The author was referring primarily to the underlying conflict between Spaniards, but his metaphor also serves to describe Spain as a place where the great ideologues could send their strutting, plumed champions (and lesser, disposable fowl) to fight while the rest of the world watched from the barriers, placing bets on the winners.

While Rukeyser, Boch and the other sporting travel mates were making their way across the Spanish frontier, Barcelona was buzzing with rumour and intrigue. The great Mediterranean port, squeezed between steep hills and the sea, was a cauldron of tightly packed humanity – from the neatly ordered fishermen's quarter and laundry-adorned streets of its Gothic centre, to the mathematical grid of bourgeois nineteenth-century apartment blocks. These, in turn, were ringed by smokestack industries and textile sweatshops, punctuated by rural smallholdings and grand mansions creeping up the scrubby slopes of the surrounding hills. As if by weight of gravity, the city's central nervous system and energy seemed to run down towards its older quarters and along the busy Ramblas to the port – the great mercantile centre built on centuries of Mediterranean trade, later expanded to Cuba and Latin America. This was currently paralysed by a dockers' strike.[6] The city's morning newspaper, *La Vanguardia*, carried other reminders of brewing trouble: an anarchist gang had been arrested on suspicion of wounding three Civil Guards in a shoot-out, while a collection of pistols, rifles and a sabre had been confiscated from the homes of two militant right-wingers. The regional Catalan government, meanwhile, had been forced to deny that it was arming workers' militias against the threat of a military coup.

Barcelona had grown rapidly in the early twentieth century, with the First World War providing a boost for a non-combatant country happy to feed and fuel those slaughtering one another for land or national pride. It now hosted a volatile social structure: a wealthy, Francophile bourgeoisie rubbed shoulders with idealistic or chauvinistic middle-class Catalan nationalists, while anarchists plotted the downfall of both. The latter's philosophy, imported from Russia via Italy, had attracted the city's industrial masses as well as landless, jobbing labourers across the country, making Spain the global capital of political anarchism. Broken-backed immigrants from poorer parts of the country scrabbled to make a living amongst the shacks and shanties on the hills and beaches. Shot through with the lifeblood of trade, Barcelona boasted that it was more cosmopolitan than the distant capital, Madrid, 500 kilometres away in the middle of the high, thin-aired *meseta* plain of central Spain.

It was a relatively benign summer, but even at night the temperatures remained stubbornly in their twenties while daytime humidity sat at a shirt-drenching 65 per cent.[7] At night, when temperatures cooled, the Ramblas boulevard bustled with people. Subtitled Hollywood films filled the cinemas – with Johnny Weissmuller as Tarzan of the Apes while Clark Gable and Joan Crawford pursued their on-and-off-screen romance in *Chained*.[8] But that afternoon it was the 'Ode to Joy' from Beethoven's Ninth Symphony which rang out from the Palau de la Música – a wedding-cake, art-nouveau opera house dripping in elaborate, glazed ceramics. The great Catalan cellist Pau Casals held the baton. His symphony orchestra was practising for the opening ceremony of the People's Olympiad – a counterpoint to the Summer

Olympics to be held in Berlin that August, which Hitler was already preparing as a propaganda exercise for an emboldened Nazi regime that had extinguished democracy in a matter of weeks in 1933.

On the other side of the Atlantic a black American athlete, Jesse Owens, was training for the Berlin Games in Cleveland, Ohio. Under international pressure, Hitler had reversed a decision to prevent blacks and Jews from taking part. Earlier that summer, Berlin police had been told to take down signs reading 'No Jews' that had proliferated ever since the 1935 Nuremberg Laws had declared them non-citizens and banned Jews from marrying 'pure' Germans. Back in Cleveland, Owens himself was no stranger to race laws. The previous year he had set three world track and field records in the space of just forty-five minutes – a feat that will likely remain unmatched for ever – yet he was still forced to eat in 'black only' restaurants and sleep in 'black only' hotels. No one yet knew that it would be his legs, muscles and flowing stride[9] that would ridicule Hitler's dream of using the Olympics to prove the superiority of the Aryan master race. Mostly, however, the world stood by and let the Führer realise his grandiose fantasies – with Rukeyser already detecting, on her way through London: 'The feeling of Hitler in the sky, very highly regarded by many, [and] the feeling of Mussolini.'[10]

In contrast, the official poster for the People's Olympiad bore, as one of three faces, that of a black athlete. Organisers specifically requested that the US team include 'negro sportsmen' because 'we are defending the real Olympic spirit, which stands for brotherhood between races and peoples ... Our Olympics will give an opportunity to those races who are being outlawed or discriminated against, such as Negroes, Jews and Arabs.'[11] The US team duly included Charles Burley, a talented black nineteen-year-old Golden Gloves champion boxer from Pittsburgh (49 fights, 43 wins – including 13 knockouts – and 6 losses) who had refused to try out for the US Olympic team in protest at 'racial and religious discrimination in Nazi Germany'.[12] Black trade unionist, sprinter and hurdler Dorothy 'Dot' Tucker also travelled across the Atlantic with the ten-person team.[13] Dressed in their white singlets, Burley and Irv Jenkins, a Cornell University heavyweight, had sparred on the deck of the liner that took them to Europe. It was still strikingly unusual in both the Americas and Europe for the lines separating race, education and class to be so roundly ignored.

Rukeyser's German friend – and, soon, never-to-be-forgotten lover – Otto Boch, and the Swiss and Hungarian athletes on her train were coming to take part in an event which was due to start that same Sunday afternoon, with a ceremony welcoming 6,000 athletes at the hilltop Montjuïc stadium. A British team had been assembled and was staying in a hotel in the portside Barrio Chino, the infamous red-light district.[14] Nat Cohen and Sam Masters, two East End Londoners from the Clarion Cycling Club (their wittily ironic motto: 'We have nothing to lose but our chains'), were pedalling across France to join the spectators. In the city itself, idealistic young men and women had been drawn into organising the games, including a handful of foreigners. One of the most striking was the tall, hard-smoking twenty-four-year-old Dutch freelance journalist Fanny Schoonheyt. Spanish volunteers were amazed by the towering blonde Schoonheyt, who seemed to them like some Nordic screen siren.[15]

For locals, the Olympiad was a chance to meet new people and learn about other cultures. In Barcelona, streets were plastered with posters proclaiming: 'A week of people's sport and folklore.' Catalonia's curious and sometimes incompatible mixture of ideological radicalism and local nationalism meant that these games doubled as an internationalist proclamation of left-wing solidarity while also being billed as a celebration of local tradition. Some of the world's smallest, colonised, and even non-existent, nations were invited: teams from Alsace, Algeria and Palestine were to be there – representing, like the Basque country and Catalonia itself – places where people still only dreamt of being independent. Teams of 'Moroccans' and 'Jews' were also due, according to one leaflet calling on people to offer rooms.[16] The raised fist, the delicate-but-dull Catalan *sardana* dance and the gravity-defying Catalan *castells*, the human towers built from people perched on each other's shoulders, were all to be symbols of this mixed bag of sporting events. Even Swiss yodellers – some of whom were on Rukeyser's train – were expected to take part.

In public, at least, this was about returning to ideas of 'fair play' and true sportsmanship in the face of Hitler's belligerent, bullying use of the Olympics. 'Sport is war minus the shooting,' is how the writer George Orwell, who appeared in the city a few months later, summed up the increasingly nationalistic use of sport.[17] Opponents routinely denounced the Olympiad – which some called the Spartakiada – as a celebration of communism, anarchism and separatism – or all three at the same time. 'While they are all busy playing with balls, boxing, swimming and running around, we can at least be sure that they won't be carrying out the revolution,' snorted Barcelona's conservative *Veu de Catalunya* newspaper.[18]

Hotels were full, especially around the Plaza de España at the foot of Montjuïc where the grand buildings put up for the 1929 International Expo still stood. Visitors wandered idly down the Ramblas boulevard, past stands hawking flowers, books and postcards. Others were attracted to the Barrio Chino red-light district. US gymnast Bernie Danchik would take home a photograph of a smiling prostitute posing on a shiny Citroën car, her breasts enveloping the vehicle's double chevron bonnet ornament; and a card for an establishment run by Madam Albina, promising 'modern comfort' and 'discretion'.[19] Meanwhile, some athletes climbed the steep hill to the Montjuïc stadium to attend last-minute training sessions. Elsewhere in the city, and across Spain, others were preparing for a different, bloodier sort of public spectacle: a military-led, fascist-backed coup d'état.

As locals and tourists strolled through the streets, the tension of that hot and humid night grew. After decades of infighting, which had seen the left split into a multicoloured array of social democrats, republicans, socialists, Trotskyites, Soviet-style communists and anarchists, the sportsmen and women gathering in Barcelona were an expression of a new, if brittle, peace reigning across the left. This had only recently begun to unite against the threat of fascism, with broad popular front governments being formed in both Spain and France over the previous five months.

Barcelona had long been a city of sporadic political violence. Twenty-seven years earlier it had gone through the convulsion of the Tragic Week, when workers' organisations rebelled against a mass call-up of military reservists destined for Spain's troubled colonies in North Africa. 'Down with war! Send the rich instead!' they had shouted as some eighty churches and religious buildings were burned, amid popular belief in the Roman Catholic Church's role as a pillar of the exploitative elite. The army was called in, and seventy-five people were killed. In the early 1920s violent anarchists had filled factory owners and managers with fear. They, in turn, hired gun-wielding *pistoleros* to kill union leaders and shootings had become common. When miners in northern Asturias launched a revolutionary strike in 1934, the regional government of Catalonia took the opportunity to declare a new 'Catalan State within the Federal Republic of Spain' (although Spain was not, and never had been, a federation). There were barricades in the street, rebels on the Ramblas and machine guns in the broad, square Plaza de Cataluña. Forty-six people died across Catalonia.

In the weeks running up to the Olympiad, police discovered small stockpiles of arms being hoarded by suspected fascists. A long-running dispute between a British factory manager, Joseph Mitchell, and his employees at the L'Escocesa textile factory, had seen him gunned down.[20] Rumours circulated that generals, backed by right-wing parties, were preparing a coup. Barcelona had been the focal point for the country's last successful putsch, when Catalan elites and conservatives enthusiastically sent local military commander General Miguel Primo de Rivera off to Madrid to install a dictatorship backed by the monarch (who hailed him as 'my Mussolini') in 1923. It seemed logical, therefore, that the city should once more be a prime target.

Max Friedemann, a political exile from Nazi Germany, found himself both helping to prepare the Olympiad and taking part in unarmed workers' patrols, keeping an eye on the port and on army barracks. The city had become a modest gathering point for exiles from Germany, Italy, Poland and other places where left-wingers were being pursued. While France, Switzerland and, to a certain extent, Czechoslovakia, remained the favoured refuges, a significant number of social democrats, anarchists, communists and socialists had found safety in Barcelona, forming support groups based on nationality or political inclination. Nazi persecution in Germany had seen several thousand Jews arrive in the city. Some spent their first few nights huddled together on the benches of the Ramblas, which they ironically referred to as 'Hotel Catalonia'. One of the attractions was that, under Spain's five-year-old Republic, Jews were once more able to openly practise their religion.[21] A left-wing group called the Jewish Cultural Association had more than a hundred members and was involved in preparing the Olympiad, their activities watched closely by Nazi agents, who were also active in the city.[22]

On 18 July news began to trickle through of events elsewhere in Spain. In the Canary Islands and Spanish-controlled Morocco, army units had rebelled against the elected government. More worryingly, they had done the same in Seville and appeared to be gaining control of the biggest city in the south. Some kind of military *pronunciamiento*, normally a relatively bloodless coup, of the kind Spain had suffered dozens of times in the previous century, appeared to be underway. This time, it was the reactionary right – a coalition of authoritarian Catholics, landowners and army officers – that was rebelling. In the Palau de la Música, a frantic messenger rushed into the rehearsals. 'We have been warned that tonight there will be a coup attempt. The concert and games have been suspended. Everyone must leave immediately,' he said.[23] But the balding, bespectacled Casals – a man of well-shined shoes and gaiters – raised his baton for the last time, insisting they play Beethoven's 'Ode to Joy' once more.[24] 'There we were, singing the immortal hymn of brotherhood while in the streets of Barcelona, and elsewhere, a bloody battle was being prepared,' he later recalled. The 'Ode to Joy', repeated on the radio, would form part of the soundtrack to events over the coming days.[25]

That evening, Barcelona's usually bustling nightlife was dimmed by anxiety. An anonymous Dutch woman journalist – perhaps Schoonheyt's freelance rival, the sometime actress and writer Marijke van Tooren – arranged to meet friends at a seaside restaurant, which she found half-empty. Waiters, chefs, barmen and the cigarette boy clustered around the radio, listening to news of the distant uprising. The atmosphere, she said, was 'high voltage'. The foreign guests at the dinner party made world-weary small talk about the regular outbursts of violence and agreed that trouble had been brewing for months. The group tried to go dancing, but found the singer at the chandeliered Miramar club crooning to just a handful of people, while only the in-house dancers shuffled across the floor. The foreigners downed their whiskies and left after an hour. 'It's just as boring as in the rest of Europe,' one of the party complained. 'Barcelona is the only city left with a decent nightlife. What a pity!'[26]

While some partied, others were preparing for the worst. Several of Friedemann's group of Germans – along with a handful of Polish, Hungarian and Czech exiles – had spent two hours the previous day visiting hunting shops in the city centre, buying up shotguns, plus a solitary revolver.[27] 'These were our first trophies,' Polish exile Jozef Winkler recalled later.[28] Friedemann and his wife Golda were exhausted after two days with little sleep. That evening, they took a suburban train back to their home in Sarrià, a neighbourhood on the hillside above the city.

Around 4 a.m. the next morning Max and Golda were awoken as violence erupted. Military units from barracks on the outskirts of the city were heading towards the centre with horses, armoured cars and artillery. The troops themselves were not all aware of what they were doing – some, for instance, thought they were being roused to protect the Olympiad.[29] They were soon met by gunfire from loyalist police units, who had been expecting trouble and were quickly backed by armed trades unionists.[30] Athletes woke to the sounds of barked orders and marching feet, followed by volleys of rifle fire and the boom of artillery pieces. Black American sprinter Frank Payton heard what seemed like 'several thousand machine guns and rifles'.[31] As the sun rose over the harbour, fierce fighting continued. *New York Times* correspondent Lawrence Fernsworth saw how 'riderless horses galloped over the bodies of the dead and the dying. From windows and rooftops everywhere spat more rifle and machine-gun fire ... shells tore through the length of the streets, slicing off trees, exploding against a building or blowing a street car or an automobile to bits.'[32] He was exaggerating, but not much.

There were fierce clashes outside the hotels in the Plaza de España, where many of the athletes were staying. Some rebel troops made it into buildings around the Plaza de Cataluña, which sits at the top end of the Ramblas and acts as a gateway between the old and new quarters of the city. These and other key buildings occupied by the rebels were cleared, floor-by-floor, in ugly hand-to-hand combat. In those first, few, early morning hours, the fighting was intense.[33]

The city's trains, buses and trams stopped running, so Max and Golda walked back into the city before separating on the broad Diagonal boulevard so that she could go to the Plaza de España to check on the visiting athletes. Max, meanwhile, headed towards the Communist Party offices – running from doorway to doorway, and seeking cover behind trees – where he had been told there would be guns. At the offices he was informed that none were left. If he wanted a weapon, they said, he would have to seize one from somewhere. Nobody seemed to find it a strange piece of advice to give a man with a German accent. Later that morning, despite the continued fighting at various spots around the city, US consul Lynn Franklin felt safe enough to walk to his office on the Plaza de Cataluña. He found the square littered with empty trams and the corpses of mules. A dead man lay prostrate beside a machine gun on the pavement.

Barcelona spent much of that hot, bright day in a state of eerie paralysis, punctuated by occasional battles that erupted at crossroads or in major buildings. Most people hid indoors. At midday on 19 July, General Manuel Goded, who was meant to be leading the uprising in Barcelona, landed in the harbour in a military seaplane and went straight to the nearby Capitanía, or regional military headquarters – a large, converted convent near the port.

The building was already surrounded by militiamen, with Max Friedemann amongst those taking cover behind trees and in nearby buildings. A tense stand-off saw pro-fascist soldiers take up positions behind sandbagged windows, while the motley crowd outside – only a minority of them armed with pistols, hunting rifles and carbines – wore cotton neckerchiefs with the colours or stripes of trades unions and political parties. A loyal army unit then arrived and, with a single cannon shot, blew open the Capitanía's gates. Friedemann was amongst those who rushed inside: 'The soldiers did not even shoot at us. Only a few officers resisted. They were overwhelmed. We pushed forward into the armoury and confiscated the whole stock of weapons and ammunition.'[34] The munitions were immediately transferred to the headquarters of trades unions and political parties.

To the amazement of some observers, and to many of those taking part, the street-fighting that day was not just a man's business. Fanny Schoonheyt, dressed in a bright yellow short-sleeved shirt, joined a mixed group that crept over nearby roofs into the building. 'I had to steal my first weapon,' she wrote excitedly in a letter to a girlfriend in Rotterdam, adding that her 'rather conspicuous' shirt made her an easy target. 'It is a miracle they didn't shoot me. Perhaps they were so surprised that they forgot to react.' [35]

With the streets empty, shops closed and the shooting mostly sporadic, only the curious or foolhardy stepped out to see what was going on. Felicia Browne, a young British graduate from the Slade School of Art who had travelled to Spain a few days earlier seeking artistic inspiration, only avoided walking into the Plaza de Cataluña 'battlefield' because a policeman hiding in a doorway blew his whistle at her. 'Between the firing you could hear the wind going through the trees, peaceful as hell,' she wrote in a letter home.[36] For Browne, peering out from underneath a pudding-bowl haircut, through round-framed glasses, it was a thrilling contrast to a comfortable London upbringing where she had feared she might 'drown in the well-upholstered family household'.[37]

By the end of the day the rebels had been pinned back and were holed up in a few barracks, a convent and a handful of other buildings scattered around the city. Loyal air force planes bombed them. General Goded was captured, admitted failure and ordered the few troops who still backed him to desist. 'Luck has gone against me and I am now a prisoner; if you wish to avoid further bloodshed, I release you from your pledge to me,' he said on a radio broadcast that was heard across Spain.[38]

Franklin had little doubt about the political leanings of the military rebels. 'Fascist uprising in Barcelona' was how he headed his cabled report that afternoon. 'At six o'clock [p.m.] five fires in the city could be counted, three of them reliably reported as churches,' was his final update.[39] Although Franklin saw Goded's anti-government reactionaries as 'fascists', that did not mean he approved of those fighting against them. In fact, it soon became clear that the streets no longer belonged to the government, but to the unions and left-wing parties who were arming their people. Some of these returned to one of the perennial activities of Barcelona's enraged working class, church-burning.

A day that had started with a fascist coup was now producing something very different: a left-wing counter-revolution led by a hotchpotch of radical workers' groups and trades union militants (or *sindicalistas*). 'Many of the Sindicalists' automobiles have rough-looking women in them accompanied by armed men and the sign given by those who pass, on foot or in automobiles, is the raised fist,' Franklin reported. Felicia Browne was impressed. 'The women are fine,' she wrote to a friend.[40]

Some athletes thought, initially, that the explosions and gunfire were part of a fireworks display for the games. The US athletes largely hid in their hotel by the Boquería food market, 400 metres from the Plaza de Cataluña. 'They don't do things by halves out here,' wrote Bernie Danchik. 'Every time we shove our heads out of the windows, we are shot at.' From this privileged position in the centre of the city, he soon realised that the rightist uprising had mutated into something completely different. 'Sunday – Comes the revolution!' he jotted in his papers.[41]

* * *

German Gerhard Wohlrath had camped overnight with his Swiss girlfriend Käthe Hempel on the beach at Arenys de Mar, 40 kilometres north of Barcelona, after finishing what they thought would be the penultimate leg of their bicycle trip to watch the People's Olympiad. They awoke to what sounded like a thunderstorm breaking over Barcelona. Plumes of black smoke were visible in the distance. In small towns like Arenys and Montcada – where Muriel Rukeyser and her lover Otto Boch were stuck – the counter-revolution began immediately. 'Houses along the coastal road were decorated with Catalan or red flags. People were crowded on the streets around loudspeakers. Some wore rifles on their shoulders or pistols in their belts,' Wohlrath recalled.[42]

That evening a relative calm settled in the Catalan capital. Armed militias daubed requisitioned vehicles with their acronyms – guns jutting out of windows 'like porcupines', according to Rukeyser – and raced around the city at high speed. These militias rounded up real or imaginary rebels and their supporters, while, in the first few hours of chaos, others took advantage of the situation to pillage or burn churches. One of the more macabre entertainments was to open the tombs of nuns and monks and display the desiccated corpses to the public. The city's main arsenal, at a barracks in the neighbourhood of San Andrés, was in anarchist hands that evening and some 30,000 rifles were distributed. Armed anarchists, Franklin reported, were now the greatest danger.

At some stage Dutch athletes were surprised to find their mentor, Fanny Schoonheyt, stride into the Hotel Olympic with a weapon slung over her shoulder. This was a trophy from the previous day's raid on the Capitanía. She informed them that she, and the armed men with her, were there to 'inspect' their quarters. Rukeyser and Boch, meanwhile, had been driven into town. Machine-gun nests stood at crossroads, overlooking the corpses of dead animals and the skeletons of burned-out cars, many of which had simply smashed into each other as excitable youngsters sped around the city. White sheets hung from balconies and windows – a way of proclaiming one's home non-belligerent territory and of keeping the people with weapons away. Even those civilians out on the streets made sure to carry white handkerchiefs. So-called *pacos*, or pro-rebel snipers, were still a problem. 'Shooting is heard, again and again – not cannons or machine guns (except once), but guns. My teeth feel the shots,' described Rukeyser. 'Ahead of us a man falls, and our truck swerves and turns, taking a detour as some street corner battle opens up.' Later, she surveyed the city from the rooftop of the Hotel Olympic. 'Overturned cars, dead animals, coils and spires of smoke rising from churches,' she wrote. 'In the streets, there are no cars that are not armed and painted with [political] initials or titles.'[43]

That evening Rukeyser was transported up the hill to a dinner at the Olympic stadium in a car pockmarked by bullet holes and stained with blood.[44] The shooting was not just from fascist snipers. In some quarters the violence was already being used for revenge attacks on small businesses, Church property, priests and conservatives, or to carry out personal vendettas. Anarchists opened the gates to the Modelo prison, releasing its population of common criminals back into the city, where, as a prison official dutifully recorded it in his paperwork, some appear to have taken advantage of the chaos to return to their ways: 'Today this prisoner effected a violent escape ... along with all the others.'[45]

Schoonheyt was not the only foreigner to be caught up in the fighting. An American athlete found himself using a crowbar to help lift flagstones and build barricades.[46] French long distance-runner Ange Cassar, meanwhile, claimed to have seen three athletes fall to rebel bullets, though he did not provide names.[47] And an Austrian athlete, known only as Mechter, was said to have died during an attack on an army barracks.[48] Yet those who tried to help the militias were often reprimanded. This was not their business, they were told.[49]

After an emotive goodbye march and ceremony in the cobbled Plaza San Jaume, the Olympiad athletes were shepherded down the Ramblas towards the docks and under the figure of Christopher Columbus atop his towering column. Even the snipers seemed to respect their passage. 'When we get to a corner, they stop the war so that we can pass,' commented Danchik.[50] The facades of buildings along the way were scarred with bullet marks, and small flags or bunches of flowers marked the places where people had died during the fighting. The fighting had been particularly intense around the artillery barracks housed in the medieval Drassanes shipbuilding yard, at the end of the Ramblas. A small passenger vessel, the *Ciudad de Ibiza*, waited to take Rukeyser and the Belgian and Hungarian teams to Sète, across the border into south-east France. The *ship* travelled overnight, since submarines from fascist Italy were already rumoured to be patrolling the coast, ready to sink Republican shipping. 'You came to see the games; and have remained to witness the triumph of our Popular Front,' the athletes were told in one of the many send-off speeches. 'Now your task is clear. You will go back to your countries and spread through the world the news of what you have seen in Spain.'[51]

Not everyone, however, boarded the boat. Emmanuel Mink, a twenty-three-year-old Polish amateur soccer player exiled in Belgium, had already agreed with Abrasha Krasnowieski, an agile, terrier-like Hungarian friend, that they would stay. They had bumped into Winkler's gang of armed exiles and been invited to join them.[52] Of those who boarded the evacuation vessels, several – including French distance runner Jules Burgot and American wrestling coach Alfred 'Chick' Chakin – would return to Spain months later after news began to spread that an extraordinary foreign volunteer army, the so-called 'International Brigades', was being formed.[53]

Some of those who decided to stay and fight were women. Kate Hempel and her boyfriend Wohlrath remained, as did Clara Thälmann, a Swiss anarchist sympathiser and swimmer attracted by the 'revolutionary tone' of the city. 'I don't want to leave this country,' Felicia Browne wrote in a letter home, and she also avoided the exodus that was overseen by the various consulates.[54] Indeed, in these early days it was common to see women bearing arms. German photographer Hans Guttman had already taken an iconic picture of the coming war, with Schoonheyt's seventeen-year-old friend from the Olympiad organisation, Marina Ginestà, smiling on a roof overlooking the Plaza de Cataluña. This was to be the first great war for press photographers and looked as though, rather like the Russian revolution, it would also be one of the first for women fighters in Europe. Ginestà's face broadcast a smiling, naïve image of defiance – that of a beautiful, daring young woman, apparently ready to fight for life and freedom. In fact, this was the only day Ginestà, a French-speaking translator and interpreter, carried a gun. At this stage she was still convinced that, rather than a coup, the violence was simply an attempt to stop the People's Olympiad. She was by no means alone.

Amongst the handful of athletes who ignored the instructions to leave was Otto Boch. From the very first day, when their train had ground to halt in Montcada, he had felt liberated. 'You don't know how much joy that Sunday brought, to be able to raise my fist [to give the German Red Front salute] after three years without being allowed to,' he explained.[55] After years of political exile in France and Italy, the young Bavarian finally had a chance to fight fascism. Boch told Rukeyser that he was not going to miss it. 'Otto, on the dock, looked deep into me. "You will do what you can in America," he said, "and I in Spain." He smiled, with his own happiness ... We spoke of my coming back to Spain, but it was not very real. These days were all we could look at. "Gifts of the revolution," he said. He had been waiting to fight against fascism since Hitler came to power,' she wrote.[56]

Many of the exiles already in Spain had nowhere else to go, or shared the political idealism of those imposing a new, revolutionary spirit on the city. They were already part of the worldwide tumult provoked by what the Anglo-German historian Eric Hobsbawm, then a student at Cambridge, later called 'the Age of Extremes'. That spirit was increasingly visible on the streets, where people were abandoning ties and jackets for blue workers'-style cotton overalls. These were often topped with the colours of a favoured political faction – be it the red of socialists and communists, the red and black of the anarchists, or the gold and red of Catalan nationalism. Some foreigners had found their way to the Hotel Falcón on the Ramblas, sleeping on the chequered-tiled floors and damask-covered sofas in its art nouveau 'reading room'. The Falcón was where those whose politics did not fit that of the anarchists or Stalin's Soviet communism were brought together by the influential POUM – the Workers' Party of Marxist Unification, a local anti-Stalinist communist group – under the leadership of Austrian Kurt Landau. They included German Socialist Workers' Party (SAP) members such as the chisel-faced future Chancellor of Germany, twenty-two-year-old Willy Brandt,[57] or members and sympathisers of the Britain's Independent Labour Party (ILP). They would eventually include the writer George Orwell – Eric Arthur Blair – who joined the militia in December.[58] American Mark Sharron, who later became Leon Trotsky's bodyguard, snored so loudly that the reading-room lodgers tried to stick plasters over his mouth.[59]

By the time Rukeyser and the athletes boarded the *Ciudad de Ibiza*, Barcelona had been saved from the generals. Apart from later bombing of civilian neighbourhoods by Italian aircraft sent by Mussolini, and as a place for violent factionalism, the city would see relatively little fighting in the coming war. Yet here in Spain's second city, a young Jewish-American woman from New York and a German from Bavaria had, in their own way, already defied the fanatical intolerance of fascism. The mixture of love, sex, war and revolution, all kaleidoscoped into a few days, had proved intoxicating. The young lovers would never meet again, since Boch was one of the first foreigners to pick up arms in defence of Spain, and was also amongst the many to die. Rukeyser would never forget him, returning time and time again to that single week in her poetry. It represented, she wrote, the 'beginning of pride' and a moment when she 'saw the future stand up/ free and alive'.[60]

Spain was about to become much more than a poet's inspiration or the romantic backdrop for a young couple thrown together by exciting, exotic circumstance. News of the attempted coup was spreading quickly across the world. For people in faraway places, Spain's civil war would be the burning political issue of the next three years. It was soon to be a magnet for idealists, adventurers, journalists, artists, writers and, above all, those who felt sure that this was the first part of a much bigger battle, against the dark and destructive ideals of fascism. From factory floors and intellectual soirées across Europe, to the White House in Washington and the Kremlin in Moscow, Spain was already the subject of heated debate. For most of the estimated 40,000 foreign volunteers who eventually came to fight in defence of the Republic it was, when not their grave, the defining experience of a lifetime.

2

The Workers and the Army: Madrid,
20 July 1936

Mika Etchebéhère had arrived in Madrid just a few days before the generals and their fascist allies rebelled. A thirty-four-year-old Argentine, whose Jewish parents had fled the Tsarist regime in Russia, the dark-haired, broad-smiling Mika had come to join her French-Argentine husband Hipólito. He suffered from recurring bouts of tuberculosis but had been in the capital for two months, writing about Spain's novel experiment in broad, left-wing coalition government for the Paris-based magazine *Que Faire*. Immediately she had noticed the political strains that wracked the five-year-old Republic and its latest iteration under the popular front government elected just five months previously. 'An agonising tension kept everyone awake,' she observed. 'It was as if they were watching over a dying man.'[1] Within four days of arriving in the Spanish capital Mika found herself joining crowds of workers as, with news of events in Barcelona and elsewhere spilling in, they wandered from place to place, demanding that the government arm them.

Rumours of a coup had been sweeping through Madrid for weeks. They had started, indeed, on the very same day that the left won elections in February.[2] So, too, had the plotting. Reactionaries on the political right, parts of the Church, some wealthy businessmen and, above all, army officers – especially those in the Army of Africa – were all ready to join.

Armed men cruised Madrid's streets in their cars at night. Political or police killings were resulting in an average of one corpse in the city every two days,[3] with some seventy people a month dying in the political or police violence across Spain. This was not enough to make people fear for their personal safety but allowed the plotters to paint a picture of a collapse into chaos, anarchy and disorder. The underlying battle pitched the ordered, timeless hierarchies of Church, army and landowners against the large urban proletariats of modern industrial Spain and their peasant allies in the poverty-stricken countryside.

The moderate left-wingers who led the popular front government refused to believe the army would rebel. A failed coup against the Republic, led by General José Sanjurjo in 1932, had put the army off such adventures, they thought. When officers brought Prime Minister Santiago Casares Quiroga proof of an imminent uprising on 16 July, he sent them away.[4] The prime minister came from President Manuel Azaña's moderate Republican Left party and led what the well-informed British journalist Henry Buckley – probably the only foreign correspondent to fully comprehend the complexities of Spain at that time – saw as a government of 'quiet, middle-class liberals' (since the Socialists had refused to join) who made British liberal David Lloyd George appear radical. They thought they had guaranteed peace by sending potentially troublesome generals to far-flung garrisons. The young, ruthless and successful General Francisco Franco was in the Canary Islands, on Tenerife; and General Sanjurjo, the former coup leader, was in exile in neighbouring Portugal. Azaña had commuted his death sentence, ignoring a warning by Mexican president Plutarco Elías Calles that 'to avoid a bloodbath' he must execute Sanjurjo.[5]

A classic coup d'état takes place in a capital city, with the seizure of the most important government buildings. The plotters, however, were planning something very different. Their coup would begin outside the capital and be followed by a quick, short war as rebel columns fell on Madrid. The growing strength of Madrid's working class, which had been displaying its muscle with strikes, made it a difficult place to launch a right-wing revolt.[6] The Spanish capital had grown rapidly over the previous fifty years, doubling in size to vie with Barcelona as the country's most populous city. What it lacked in ancient architecture, it made up for in street life. Madrid was reputed to have cafeterias that simply never closed. At Chicote, a new bar with art deco interiors on the central Gran Vía boulevard, bow-tied waiters served what were deemed the best cocktails in southern Europe. Workers, bureaucrats, aristocrats and foreign visitors, meanwhile, flocked to the global mecca of bullfighting – a brand-new, neo-Mudejar bullring at Las Ventas that boasted horseshoe arches, coloured tiling and geometrical brick patterns. The mostly conservative bullfighters, however, were currently also on strike to protest against Mexican matadors competing with them.

A booming construction industry and timid industrialisation had increased the size of the city's working class and seen it become increasingly well-organised. The Communist Party, though much smaller than the Socialists, had quadrupled their membership to 83,000 in just four months and the two parties had recently fused their youth organisations, which totalled 140,000 members.[7] Santiago Carrillo, a pudgy-faced twenty-one-year-old revolutionary socialist who had returned enthused from a recent visit to Moscow, was the leader of the booming youth wing. Meanwhile, the head of the Socialists' powerful radical wing, Francisco Largo Caballero, was on record as claiming that 'the revolution we want can be achieved only through violence'.[8] Talk like that saw the sixty-seven-year-old former stucco worker dubbed 'the Lenin of Spain'. It also divided the party, with the moderate Indalecio Prieto warning against the rise of 'revolutionary infantilism' on May Day in 1936.[9] The communists were equally critical. For months they had fretted that strikes, talk of revolution and violence – especially by anarchists, whose CNT union had seven times as many members as the Communist Party – would provoke a coup.[10] Indeed, the line dictated from Moscow from 1935 onwards was that democratic popular front governments were the best response to fascist growth in Western Europe. This made the communists a voice of relative moderation and reason.[11] Revolution could – indeed must – wait.[12] With their disciplined, impressive May Day marches, however, the communists had added to the growing fears expressed by those in Madrid who supported a coup.

Crucial to the projected coup was the Army of Africa. Its base in Spanish Morocco was so far away that Madrid barely contemplated it as a threat. 'This is where the idea of rescuing Spain was born,' Franco declared later. 'Without Africa I can barely explain who I am to myself.'[13] This 35,000-strong army was a world of its own, consumed by conspiracy theories and resentful over reforms that had seen some officers downgraded. It saw itself as the standard-bearer of national pride, having maintained Spain's protectorate against ferocious local resistance. At its core lay the Spanish Legion, founded in 1920 by the battle-scarred, irascible and (eventually) one-armed Colonel José Millán-Astray, with the help of the then young *comandante* Francisco Franco. The latter was widely admired as a brilliant and fearless officer, despite his priggish nature, short stature, high-pitched voice and a broad bottom that had seen him dubbed 'Paca la Culona', or 'fat-arsed Fanny' by a hard-drinking colleague, Gonzalo Queipo de Llano. The *legionarios* expressed a virile disdain for danger in their suicidal battle cry 'Long live death!'

General Emilio Mola, an embittered Army of Africa veteran who signed his secret instructions as 'the Director', became the chief architect of a plot that originally aimed to install General Sanjurjo as dictator.[14] Mola was based in Pamplona, in the Navarre region of northern Spain, where – usefully for his purposes – the ultra-conservative Carlist monarchists were strongest. These had their own candidate for king and a 25,000-strong militia, the *requetés*.[15] Majority support for a coup amongst Spain's outsized officer corps was also crucial. This formed a state-subsidised, conservative middle class of 21,000 men who, until recently, had provided 800 generals for just eighty posts. Backing could also be found amongst most of the country's 115,000 churchmen and churchwomen, who accounted for almost one in every 200 Spaniards.[16]

The Casares Quiroga government missed several opportunities to quash the coup before it could be launched. The prime minister personally interviewed one of the main plotters, Lieutenant Colonel Juan Yagüe Blanco, to test his loyalty in June. 'He has given me his word ... and men like Yagüe keep their word,' he said afterwards.[17] A request to arrest Mola while he was holed up in secret enclave with the heads of various northern garrisons that same month was similarly dismissed. 'General Mola is a loyal Republican who deserves the respect of the authorities,' Casares Quiroga insisted.[18] A rambling letter of 23 June from Franco expressed loyalty but warned of a 'serious state of unhappiness' amongst the officer class. 'Those who paint the army as being against the Republic are not telling the truth,' he claimed. 'Those who portray the concern, dignity and patriotism of officers as evidence of conspiration and disaffection are rendering wretched service to the nation.'[19] He was, in effect, muddying the waters in order to play both sides of the game until it suited him. The conspirators, indeed, were still not sure whether he would back them, complaining of his 'hesitations and parsimony'.[20]

As the plot advanced, Mola began to issue precise instructions. He demanded the use of extreme violence and the arrest or punishment of all opposing politicians. In the Ketama region of Morocco's Rif Mountains, during manoeuvres shortly before the coup, Yagüe's tent was a centre of plotting for what he already called 'the Crusade'.[21] At a farewell dinner, drunken young officers shouted secret Falangist greetings like 'CAFÉ!' (an acronym for '¡Camaradas! ¡Arriba Falange Española!', or 'Comrades, up with the Spanish Falange!').[22]

While the plotters prepared to launch their coup, the Falange was stoking tensions on the streets of Madrid. This tiny party – backed by, amongst others, Mussolini – had gained no parliamentary seats in February.[23] The Falange's leader was José Antonio Primo de Rivera – the tall, cultured and good-looking son of the last man to launch a successful coup in Spain, General Miguel Primo de Rivera. His father had run the previous dictatorship under the monarchy between 1923 and 1930. Guarded by armed toughs and adored by his followers, Primo de Rivera gave rousing speeches attacking everything from socialism and anarchism to unfettered capitalism. While an authoritarian Catholic party, the Spanish Confederation of the Autonomous Right (CEDA), led Spain's right-wing opposition in parliament, the Falange led it in street-fighting and assassination. Above all, the Falange was nationalist, pledging to pursue 'holy civil war to rescue the Fatherland'. Its militants were meant to be 'half-monk, half-soldier'.[24] To foreign observers, and many at home, though, they were simply 'fascists'. In the weeks before the uprising, the Falange had murdered liberally. Journalists, a judge, police officers and workers were targeted, with a machine-gun attack on striking construction workers especially provocative.

On 12 July, just six days before the coup attempt, Falange gunmen killed José del Castillo, a left-leaning lieutenant from the Assault Guards police force (which had been set up as an urban counterweight to the conservative, rural Civil Guard). Married three weeks earlier, Castillo's bride had apparently received a letter saying: 'Why marry a man who will soon be a corpse?'[25] In a fit of fury, Castillo's colleagues detained and shot one of the country's most prominent and reactionary right-wing politicians, José Calvo Sotelo. Many blamed this murder for sparking rebellion amongst the generals. In fact, it served as what Henry Buckley – a supporter of the Republic, and then writing for the

Daily Telegraph – called the 'big dramatic act on which to hinge the coup which had been constantly postponed since February'.[26]

Logistics had been prepared as far away as Rome, Lisbon and London. Orders for forty-three Italian aircraft, and 220 tons of bombs, had been placed in Rome on 1 July.[27] The industrialist Juan March, a former tobacco smuggler who had become one of Spain's wealthiest men, stood surety. Over lunch at Simpson's restaurant in London's Strand, plotters had asked the right-wing Catholic publisher Douglas Jerrold to charter an aircraft that could fly to the Canary Islands and transport Franco to Morocco, so that he could take control of the Army of Africa once the coup had started. They requested that the aircraft take some English 'platinum blondes' to the Canary Islands, so that it would look like a tourist trip. Jerrold rang a pilot called Captain Cecil Bebb, whose passengers eventually included retired army major Hugh Pollard, his daughter Diana and her friend, Dorothy. They set off from Croydon airport in a de Havilland Dragon Rapide on 11 July, two days before Calvo Sotelo was killed.[28]

Six days later news reached the government in Madrid that a rebellion of some kind had started in the Spanish North African city of Melilla. Plotters in the enclave had launched their revolt a day early after their plan was discovered by local commander General Manuel Romerales Quintero (described by one historian as 'the fattest of Spain's 400 generals and one of the easiest to trick'),[29] who then dithered about how to respond. They followed Mola's instructions to use extreme violence.[30] Some 225 soldiers and civilians were shot that night in a town of 62,000 inhabitants. This was three times that year's 'monthly' toll of victims across the whole of Spain in the political violence from which the plotters now claimed to be saving their countrymen. The same fate awaited Romerales, who was deemed an 'extremist' for opposing the coup.[31] The entire plot had to be pushed forward, with Franco seizing control of the Canary Islands before flying off in the Dragon Rapide to take command of the Army of Africa as it rose in cities such as Tetuán, Ceuta and Larache.[32]

Few people in Madrid were told of the uprising. Government censors banned the press from reporting on it even though, by midnight, every journalist in the city knew. Eduardo de Guzmán, from the anarchist newspaper *Libertad*, was amazed by the patina of normality, with most people completely unaware of the approaching storm.[33] 'A fine bourgeois gentleman would not have noticed anything amiss. He would not have realised that, moving amongst the street clowns and musicians who occupy the pavements in the Plaza de Sol most nights, are a handful of workers. They chat and stroll around peacefully, but they have a hand in their pocket. And in that pocket they have a gun, lovingly oiled just a few minutes earlier,'[34] he said.

The following morning the government continued to negate the obvious. Radio broadcasts claimed that no one on the mainland had rebelled. Casares Quiroga assured people that Franco was 'safely in storage in the Canary Islands' and told a friend that 'this coup is guaranteed to fail. The government is master of the situation. It will all be over soon.'[35] Government spokesmen continued to claim that General Mola and others remained loyal at the same time that news drifted in that Mola had rebelled and that northern cities were falling to his men. As the situation worsened, Casares Quiroga remained paralysed.

The rebellion was, nevertheless, slower to take off in Madrid than almost anywhere else. A key Madrid plotter, Colonel Valentín Galarza, had been arrested the week before and other co-conspirators were in hiding. In barracks around Madrid officers stayed up late into the night arguing about whether to rebel, or not.[36] This was fortunate, for the government was also wracked with indecision. Crowds had gathered in the streets crying '¡Armas! ¡Armas! ¡Armas!' and the government had to decide whether to arm them.[37] 'There was not a single minister, from the Premier down, who did not hate the idea of arming the masses and know the dangers involved,' wrote Buckley.[38] If the coup succeeded, however, the other choice was military dictatorship. So Casares Quiroga bent, and then resigned. Over just fourteen hours, Spain had three governments, as a replacement cabinet was appointed (and tried, but failed, to negotiate with the rebels), then dissolved, before a third government led by the mild-mannered, bespectacled chemistry professor José Giral[39] was formed. Yet there was still no sign of a coup in Madrid. The city remained in a state of suspense.

On Sunday 19 July, the fifty-seven-year-old reactionary general, Joaquín Fanjul, dressed in civilian clothes and sneaked into the huge Montaña barracks that lay just beyond the Plaza de España square, at the end of the Gran Vía, Madrid's central street.[40] He had come to lead the rebellion in Madrid. The imposing, three-storey-high, oblong fortress was perched at the top of a slope that ran down towards the river Manzanares to the spot where the city's washerwomen laboured. Two huge interior patios served as parade grounds. High walls and the reduced number of entranceways made it a perfect place for rebels to gather and await the arrival of the relief columns that were meant to descend on the capital from elsewhere. It was, however, the height of summer and half of the men were on holiday (as were many of Madrid's diplomats, newspaper correspondents and government officials). Only about 1,400 troops were inside, though armed Falangists, retired military officers and other supporters slipped in to join them. Machine guns were set up in the main doorway of the barracks as a motley crowd gathered in nearby streets. They included Assault Guards and militiamen, most of whom still had no weapons. Some rifles had already been handed out, but many lacked bolts – 47,000 of which reportedly sat inside Montaña barracks.[41] A beer truck helped pull two artillery pieces into position nearby and leaflets were dropped calling for a surrender.[42]

Mika and Hipo Etchebéhère, meanwhile, followed the crowds that milled around the city, searching for guns. They began at the Socialist Youth headquarters, where a young man told them it had only received two rifles and five pistols, but more were expected. 'We hope to get them tomorrow,' they were told. In the chaos of the first days, some militia units were ready to accept any volunteer. 'No one asked if we belonged to the party,' explained Mika. 'It was seen as a revolutionary right, whoever wanted arms should have them.' At a dingy, smoke-filled hall taken over by the POUM, Mika came across 'a hundred people packed onto benches or sitting on the ground, including a group of strange-looking women. Someone told me they were prostitutes from a nearby brothel who wanted to join the militia.'[43] In her middle-class way, Mika found them more frightening than the generals.

It was not until the morning of 20 July that proper fighting started and the Montaña barracks was stormed. By that stage other barracks around the city had either declared, or been won, for the government. Some units had simply turned against their treacherous officers.[44] The attack on the barracks provided an early warning of just how ramshackle the Republic's military machine was to be in the first months of the coming war. When a white sheet appeared in one window, a group of militiamen rushed towards the gates, only to be mown down by machine-gun fire from elsewhere. Artillery fire eventually opened up breaches in the walls and a few hours later soldiers and militiamen stormed in. While loyal regular army units took prisoners, others did not. The writer Arturo Barea saw a giant militiaman hurling soldiers down, one by one, from the upper galleries overlooking a courtyard. One of them 'fell through the air like a rag doll, and crashed onto the stones with a dull thud'.[45] Soon the ground was littered with corpses of soldiers, many of whom appeared to have been indiscriminately machine-gunned; others had committed suicide. One Republican soldier came across a mess table surrounded by more than a dozen dead officers and NCOs. 'At the head was a major with a bullet hole through his heart; all the others were slumped with similar bullet holes,' he said.[46]

An English nurse, Mary Bingham, saw a ten-year-old boy save his father by begging with the militiamen and telling them that his family were Republicans.[47] Virgilio Fernández, a seventeen-year-old medical orderly, waved his Communist Party card in the face of anarchist gunmen who wanted to shoot some of the wounded at his hospital. 'I told them they had to be healed first. Then they could be put on trial and shot,' he said.[48] Most of the Falangists and officers were killed. Many of those who survived would be executed within days or murdered by militias at Paracuellos de Jarama, just outside Madrid, several months later. Some hid in foreign embassies, along with other coup supporters and scared members of the upper-class or right-wing elites. An armoured car had to be brought into the barracks to prevent Fanjul – 'a rather pompous little man', according to Buckley – from being lynched. Instead, he was court-martialled and shot. The armoury was sacked, the 47,000 bolts distributed and, in effect, the coup was over in Madrid. Enthusiastic crowds brandished their newly captured weapons or paraded their prisoners. This, some claimed, was Madrid's equivalent of the storming of the Winter Palace in Saint Petersburg. Revolution was in the air.

There had been fighting at barracks elsewhere but with most of the police and the air force remaining loyal, the rest of the city remained largely untouched.[49] Madrid was euphoric. The coup, it seemed, was bound to fail. Buckley, having dizzily compared the taking of the Montaña barracks to the fall of La Bastille, felt sure that the revolt would not work: 'A military coup which does not succeed in the first twenty-four hours has failed,' he typed confidently. In historical terms, he was mostly right. But Spain was to prove an exception. In fact, Mola's plans make it clear that the plotters had always known it would be almost impossible to succeed in Madrid. He blamed 'the working class' and gave instructions for rebel columns from other cities to converge on the capital. The rebel generals, in other words, expected civil war.[50]

By the third week of July at least forty-six religious buildings had been subjected to arson attacks, great or small.[51] Groups of anarchists piled up pews, pictures and statues, before setting light to them. Mika Etchebéhère found a crowd cheering and singing outside one burning church. Buckley passed by the Covadonga church in Plaza Manuel Becerra after it had been set on fire by militiamen, who claimed that priests had fired on them. A worker ran down the street in pursuit of a boy who had stolen a chair from the same church, confiscated it from him and then smashed it to pieces. 'This,' he told the boy, 'is revolution, not robbery.'[52] Everywhere militiamen claimed that priests – or someone – had been shooting at them from church towers.[53] Buckley could find no proof of that, but he found evidence that other church buildings, including one in the Calle Ayala, were being used as sniper emplacements. Barea saw his white-haired, eighty-year-old former chemistry teacher, Father Fulgencio, being taken away on a stretcher from the flame-licked Escuelas Pías school. He was certain that the church was an evil force, but found himself worrying about the illuminated manuscripts and fine science books he had previously perused in the library.[54]

Some of the seized weapons, including a machine gun with no tripod, eventually arrived at the POUM hall where Mika and Hipo Etchebéhère had established themselves. The militia members had little idea what to do with them, so Hipo offered to instruct them. This was enough for them to appoint him their chief as they formed an independent militia group of around a hundred men and women (including Mika, who would later lead the unit herself), two lorries, three cars, the machine gun and thirty rifles. It was just one of the many inexperienced and ill-coordinated groups that appeared in the city almost overnight.

On 21 July, their militia set off blindly looking for – and failing to find – General Mola's column as it marched on Madrid from Pamplona. On the way back, they stopped at a school that had been turned into Communist Party barracks and met the legendary firebrand Dolores Ibárruri, the forty-year-old member of the party leadership who used the pseudonym 'La Pasionaria', or Passionflower (though it was also a reference, ironic or not, to Easter Week and Christ's Passion). They reminded her that their POUM group's sympathies lay with Stalin's arch-enemy, Trotsky. 'That doesn't matter,' she replied. 'Because we are fighting for the same cause.' The next day the small troop joined a larger ad hoc column of all political colours led by a regular army captain, and caught a train to the front near Sigüenza, 120 kilometres to the east.[55]

The French–Argentine couple were now fully integrated into the fight – like dozens, quite possibly hundreds, of foreigners who had been swept up by the wave of enthusiasm which engulfed those cities that, by reacting quickly and arming workers' groups, had quashed the first attempts at overthrowing the government. More foreigners were already on their way, either individually or in small groups, heading for the French frontier by train, truck, bus or, even, bicycle. Already, to them, this seemed like a fight that was about much more than Spain and its internal politics.

Those early volunteers, like Mika and Hipo Etchebéhère in Madrid, and Otto Boch, Felicia Browne and Fanny Schoonheyt in Barcelona, or the mixed band of Mussolini-opponents who gathered together in 'an Italian column'[56] felt sure that the war would be over in weeks. Victory seemed certain. And when that victory was achieved, some also hoped that the revolutionaries who now swarmed around the streets of Barcelona and Madrid would run the country.

3

Amateur Warriors: Tardienta, August–September 1936

Through the sight of her machine gun, Fanny Schoonheyt watched as a single file of armed, blue-uniformed Falangists made their way through a wheat field towards her position on top of a small hillock outside Tardienta, in the north of Aragon. A peasant farmer, frantically whipping the horse that drew his cart, had warned her small machine-gun team that the enemy were on their way, giving the group time to prepare to fight on a front where neither side had much idea about how to conduct a war. 'With those blue uniforms you could see them in the wheat fields from miles away,' she recalled. A burst of fire mowed down the first line of soldiers. The others turned and fled, but rather than splitting up, they stayed in a neat line. 'Easy prey!' she remembered later.[1] A bullet had punctured her metal canteen, but that was the worst that happened to her.

At some stage a young Spanish photographer called Agustí Centelles spotted Schoonheyt outside the headquarters of the Unified Socialist Party of Catalonia (PSUC), a brand new party which had brought together Catalan socialists and communists, at the Hotel Colón in the Plaza de Cataluña. He took out his Leica and snapped a picture of the tall, blonde Dutch woman in uniform. A smiling, unarmed Fanny stands beside the sandbags at the columned doorway with her tasselled forage cap set jauntily to one side and a khaki shirt hanging baggily from her shoulders. As a young, sporty, upper-middle-class girl in Rotterdam, it seems that Schoonheyt had been taught to shoot. She was also strong, with an athlete's build and broad back. That made her valuable to those now patrolling the city with guns they barely knew how to use. In the first few days Fanny helped hunt down snipers, crawling over rooftops and firing up from the streets.[2]

Schoonheyt's real baptism of fire, however, came after she joined a PSUC armoured column of 2,000 men and women that left Barcelona on 24 July, as it made its way towards Tardienta and the northern city of Huesca which, like Zaragoza, had been taken by the rebel generals.[3] Bridges had been blown up along the way, slowing progress, and, as they waited to cross one, enemy bombers appeared. Most of the bombs fell wide of the target but a man near her, who had just lit a cigarette, had his head blown off. Immediately after the air attack, the column diminished in number, as many volunteers simply turned around and went home. Fanny was not one of them. Instead, she was seconded to a machine-gun unit of fifty people where she soon impressed with her cool, stamina and skill. Legend would give her the ability to shoot aircraft out of the sky and to walk for miles carrying a heavy gun on her back. She admitted, however, that her feats were often exaggerated by others. A visitor to the front found her sheltering in a self-built straw hut, nut-brown and wearing shorts and a man's singlet. Schoonheyt declared that she was not just there to fight for the Republic, but also to show Spanish women how they could carry out their duties in a country 'where men and women will have the same independent rights'.[4]

Schoonheyt was by no means the only foreigner on the chaotic Huesca front, which was little more than a series of loosely connected positions in the vicinity of Tardienta. Muriel Rukeyser's boyfriend Otto Boch served as a machine-gunner with the same column.[5] In a postcard from the front on 31 July, he told Rukeyser that he was with ten fellow Germans.[6] Many of the other athletes and Barcelona-based exiles who had volunteered 'to fight the fascists' were on the same front. Schoonheyt recalled a group of Italians who took part in an attack on the town of Almudévar while she laid down machine-gun fire.[7] They were led by a man wearing 'grey pants, jacket and a hat, as if he was walking down the Ramblas'. As the attack failed and the group retreated, he walked calmly back behind the group, even though the enemy were now aiming their fire directly at him. This could easily have been Carlo Rosselli, a leader of the anti-fascist Giustizia e Libertà movement that brought together Mussolini opponents of various political colours. He had helped form an Italian column of several hundred fighters. At least ten Italians would die here over the next two months.[8]

In early August, after being turned down several times because she did not speak Spanish or Catalan, artist Felicia Browne joined the column with a new batch of volunteers whose mismatched uniforms made them look, she wrote, 'like pirates'.[9] Doubtful and insecure in her earlier letters, the war infused her with purpose. One journalist claimed that he had heard Felicia boldly insist that she was unafraid and could 'fight as well as any man'.[10] As if to prove it, she volunteered to join a ten-strong unit who, on 22 August, went behind enemy lines to sabotage a munitions train, only to see the train run straight over their dynamite charge without it exploding; the blasting cap merely produced a tiny puff of smoke.[11] They were then attacked by an enemy patrol and Browne rushed to the aid of a wounded Italian fighter, dragging him behind a rock and drawing their fire until, according to one of the party, 'with several wounds in the breast and one in the back, Felicia ... sank dead to the ground'.[12]

Women were a celebrated part of the hotchpotch army that was emerging spontaneously from the combined ranks of army loyalists, workers' groups and ordinary volunteers. Golda Friedemann was also nearby in Tardienta, having helped her husband form one of the first all-foreign units. Their Thälmann Group[13] was named after the German communist politician Ernst Thälmann, who had gained 13 per cent of the vote in presidential elections in 1932, before being arrested by the Gestapo and imprisoned. (He remained in solitary confinement until he was executed at Buchenwald in 1944, on Hitler's personal orders.) Although initially only fifteen-strong, the Thälmann Group included three couples when it joined the Carlos Marx column that headed north-west from Barcelona towards Huesca.[14] A photograph from these weeks shows the Thälmanns marching three abreast through a square, their mismatched uniforms, weaponry and differing heights fitting perfectly Felicia Browne's description of the Republic's 'pirate' army. At a time when militia units were refusing to adopt the 'bourgeois' trappings of rank, discipline and – sometimes – orders, their attempt at marching must have made a strange sight. Indeed, one of the onlookers appears to be scratching his head in disbelief.[15]

Unlike many of the Spanish fighters, the Thälmanns did not disappear home in the evening in the belief that war was a daytime activity. This was just one of several international volunteer groups. Browne reported seeing 'a lot of French chaps' and was very impressed by what she called, in the terminology of the times, 'three Yiddish tailors from Stepney'. In those early months, a *Manchester Guardian* newspaper correspondent reported coming across volunteers from Italy, France, Belgium, Germany and a young woman who was described as half-Czech, half-British. The latter was, in fact, the British-based German exile and translator Liesel Carritt, who had insisted to the Thälmann Group that she wanted to fight with a gun in her hands, rather than work as a nurse. After some discussion, she was allowed into the unit, where she was deemed 'well-prepared and showing fine initiative'.[16] Elsewhere in Spain, foreign volunteers appeared either on their own or in small groups. At the Basque border town of Irun, French police counted 226 international volunteers crossing the border before it was closed on 5 September. A section of Polish machine-gunners fought bravely there, though most would be killed.[17] An armed battle against fascism had appeared in Europe and, for varying reasons, many non-Spaniards felt an urgent need to be there.

A number of women attained legendary status during this stage of the war. The French journalist Louis Delaprée dubbed one famous militiawoman from Granada, whom he encountered with a cavalry unit while he was accompanying a group of British MPs on a tour, as 'Amalia the Amazon' (real name Amalia Bonilla). 'My two daughters were militiawomen. The youngest was killed,' Amalia explained, as a recently captured dapple-grey thoroughbred wheeled around nervously underneath her. 'This woman, who has killed five men, turned out to be an excellent introduction to the Spanish war for the English visitors,' Delaprée commented.[18] The German ambassador at Franco's headquarters was shocked to see him approve the execution of a group of captured militiawomen with only minimal interruption to his lunch.[19]

The official enthusiasm for militiawomen did not last long. By the end of August, the Socialist Youth newspaper *Juventud* was proclaiming that 'in these moments the role of a woman is to help men, not supplant them'.[20] The women fighters (including foreigners) lasted longer in the anarchist and POUM units, not least because these were less concerned with hierarchy. Mika Etchebéhère, for example, defined herself as a 'captain-mother who watches over her soldier-children', and claimed that she did not know how to command. 'Or, rather, I don't have to impose myself,' she added. 'When an order arrives, I inform my company and between us we carry it out.' Etchebéhère eventually recruited two women from a communist column, where they had been cleaning dishes and clothes.[21] 'I did not come to the front to die with a dish cloth in my hand,' one protested.[22] Even then, Etchebéhère rowed furiously with her anarchist commander, Cipriano Mera, after he chastised her for weeping over a mortally wounded young boy in her unit. 'Weeping, when you are so courageous? Of course, you're a woman after all,' he sneered. 'And you, for all your anarchism, are nothing more than another man, as rotten with prejudice as any other,' Mika replied.[23]

The Republic soon decided it did not want women at the front and began to issue instructions for them to withdraw after just three months.[24] Exceptions would remain, including Fanny Schoonheyt and Mika Etchebéhère, but the several hundred women who arrived from abroad later would find it almost impossible to join a fighting unit.[25] Those who got closest were as medical staff tending to the wounded near the front. Two such volunteers, German nurses Augusta Marx and Georgette Kokoeznynsgy, followed Felicia Browne to the grave in October after being burned to death while hiding in a haystack – and thus, in the words of La Vanguardia newspaper, being subjected to an 'act of fascist barbarism'.[26] Margarita Zimbal, a nineteen-year-old German who had already taken part in a failed landing on the island of Majorca, also died that month: she was described as a 'fighter and nurse'.[27]

As the dust settled on the first week of war, it seemed probable that the reactionary generals and their backers were heading for a quick defeat. Their most important fighting unit was the Army of Africa, but that was mostly stuck on the wrong side of the Mediterranean. This was because the lower ranks of the Spanish navy had lived up to European sailors' reputation as the most rebelliously left wing of military men. A low-ranking navy telegraphist in Madrid, Benjamin Balboa, had intercepted Franco's message announcing the rising and immediately arrested his own commander for being part of the plot. He then warned all signals operators in the Spanish navy to 'watch their officers, a gang of fascists'.[28] A gunboat, the *Dato*, was the only major vessel to end up in rebel hands in North Africa. In a celebrated message, the crew of the battleship *Jaime I*, which had been ordered to sail south from the major navy base at Ferrol, signalled the navy ministry: 'We have had serious resistance from the commanders and officers on board and have subdued them by force ... Urgently request instructions as to bodies.' They were ordered to lower the rebel officers' corpses overboard 'with respectful solemnity'.[29] In Ferrol, rival warships had exchanged fire before the rebels seized control.[30]

So far, whenever local workers' groups had been instantly armed, they had almost always held out against the plotters. Spain's forty-six provincial capitals, where major army units were often based, were crucial and could dominate the surrounding region.[31] That put the reactionary rebels in charge of a small corner of the south-west, where Queipo de Llano had seized the city of Seville and was carrying out his threat to 'hunt down troublemakers like vermin'.[32] Nearby, Córdoba and the southern ports of Cádiz, Algeciras and Huelva were also in the coup leaders' hands, though Republicans held many of the populous towns and villages between them. The city of Granada was initially divided, but coup supporters gained the upper hand there and the celebrated local poet and playwright Federico García Lorca, author of *Blood Wedding* and *The House of Bernarda Alba*, would be shot and killed. A swathe of northern and central Spain, running from Teruel, Zaragoza and Huesca in the east, to the Portuguese border and the western Atlantic coast of Galicia, also lay in rebel hands. To the north of that, the big industrial and port cities on the Bay of Biscay – including Santander, Bilbao and Gijón (where several hundred rebels would, nevertheless, hold out in their barracks for a month) – and their provincial hinterlands, remained loyal to the rightful government.

On 20 July, in a field in Portugal, the coup's nominal leader, General Sanjurjo, had excitedly jumped into a little de Havilland Puss Moth with a suitcase stuffed full of uniforms and medals in order to fly to Spain. Either the weight of his medals, or something else, meant that the aircraft failed to clear the pine trees at the edge of the field. The pilot was thrown out and survived. Sanjurjo, the planned *caudillo* of a new Spanish dictatorship, burned to death.[33]

It was by no means clear who would take over Sanjurjo's role. In Seville, Queipo de Llano took to the radio to bully and terrorise with words, while the troops under his command carried out his threats. In the first of his regular broadcasts, when he promised that the Army of Africa was on its way, he both highlighted where the rebels' real power lay and identified its greatest problem.[34] For if Franco could not transport his army across the sea from Morocco, it would be of little use. Nor would he, personally, be in a position to take over from Sanjurjo.

4

The Fascists Are Here: Seville, August 1936

Adolf Hitler first concentrated on events in Spain after attending a performance of Richard Wagner's *Siegfried* at the Bayreuth Festival on the evening of 25 July.[1] He was staying, for the duration of the festival, at the Wahnfried estate that had belonged to the deeply anti-Semitic composer whose music so enthralled and inspired him. The Führer was, as ever, uplifted by the opera and when emissaries from Franco arrived asking for transport aircraft, fighters, anti-aircraft guns and rifles, Hitler cast aside his initial doubts about the plotters' slipshod planning. Instead, he ranted about the global menace of Bolshevism and dubbed his future operation against the Spanish Republic 'Operation Magic Fire'. Having thus named it after the passage in Wagner's opera in which Siegfried battles his way through flames to rescue Brünnhilde, he sent twenty large Junkers Ju 52 transport aircraft to carry the Army of Africa to mainland Spain. His decision turned a failing military coup into a lengthy civil war.[2] It also changed a local war into an international one.

The German Führer had not been consulted before the uprising. Mussolini, on the other hand, had pledged to provide the plotters with aid in the form of aircraft, though he was hesitant about delivering it. He wanted to see whether France, Britain or Russia would help the Spanish Republic, in which case he might have found himself dragged into an as yet unwanted European-wide war. Within a week, however, he became convinced that France and Britain were not going to intervene, in part because the Conservative-led government in London preferred the reactionary generals to the left-wing counter-revolution on the streets of Barcelona, Madrid and elsewhere. The Soviet Union, meanwhile, also seemed unwilling – at least initially – to be dragged into a messy counter-revolution that it did not control and which threatened the alliances it sought against Germany. Mussolini signed off on the dispatch of a first batch of Savoia SM.81 bombers on 27 July. A dozen of these took off for Morocco the following day, though strong headwinds saw two crash and another was forced to land in French Morocco – thereby alerting the world to Mussolini's decision to join the fight.

The world's first major military airlift started on 28 July and, together with sea crossings protected by German warships, some 15,000 troops from the Army of Africa were in and around Seville ten days later.[3] Most of the work was done by Hitler's Ju 52s. This single action, together with the constant flow of arms and ammunition that both Hitler and Mussolini now provided, saved the generals. The coup could now be turned into a civil war, and only one of the two sides boasted an experienced, efficiently led and well-supplied army.[4]

Amongst the first troops to arrive were those of the Spanish Legion. A reputation for ruthlessness preceded them. Arturo Barea, while serving as a sergeant in the engineers, had accompanied the Legion as it razed villages in the Beni Arós region in 1921. 'There was no limit to its lust for revenge. When it left a village, all that remained were burning buildings and the corpses of men, women and children,' he wrote.[5] Most soldiers in the Army of Africa, however, were Moroccan mercenaries, gathered into colonial regiments commanded by Spanish officers. The infamous cruelty of the Army of Africa's officer class was, perhaps, most obviously displayed by Lieutenant Colonel Juan Yagüe Blanco. He had been Franco's right-hand man during the miners' rising in Asturias in 1934, operating with such sadistic glee that the officer in overall command, General Eduardo López Ochoa, withdrew his men after discovering that they were carving up captive miners with knives. 'They cut off their feet, their hands, their ears, their tongues, even their genitals! A few days later, one of my most trusted officers told me that there were *legionarios* wearing wire necklaces from which dangled human ears from the victims,' he reported. 'I also had to deal with the deeds of the *regulares* of the *tabor* [a battalion of Moroccan troops] from Ceuta: rapes, murders, looting. I ordered the execution of six Moors.'[6]

Franco himself flew from Morocco to Seville on 6 August. Bluster and brutality had so far allowed the rebels to hold on to the small part of Andalusia they ran. Now Franco was able to be far more ambitious and he split his forces in two as they set off towards Madrid. One force under the infamous Yagüe went north towards Badajoz – where the sight of hundreds of unarmed prisoners being slaughtered in the bullring drove the Portuguese journalist Mario Neves close to madness – before swinging east towards Madrid. A second column under Colonel José Enrique Varela swept through much of Andalusia, consolidating the nationalist zone by joining up the rebel garrisons at Córdoba, Granada and Huelva. Mola, meanwhile, concentrated his forces on keeping the eastern front in Aragon stable while trying to shrink the large, northern Republican pocket that contained Bilbao and much of Spain's heavy industry.

Air power provided by Italian and German air force pilots would be vital. Two merchant marine ships, indeed, soon arrived with twelve Fiat CR.32 fighters, together with their crews, support personnel and munitions.[7] They were the first of 377 such aircraft that accounted for the bulk of the fighters in Franco's air force.[8]

French prime minister Léon Blum, as the head of a popular front government, initially wanted to help the Republic. A visit to London ten days after the fighting started put paid to that, probably because British prime minister Stanley Baldwin said he would not help if Italy declared war on France. Britain was unprepared for another great European war, though it did not want Spain to become a fascist territory if that war did break out. When Blum proposed a non-intervention agreement early in August, Britain was quick to back it.[9] Other governments soon joined non-intervention, thereby sabotaging the Republic's chances of snuffing out the rebellion before it could spread.

While the British and French governments helped set up a formal committee to oversee non-intervention, Hitler and Mussolini both paid lip service to the initiative and openly flouted it. Mussolini's unpunished invasion of Abyssinia in 1935 had already provided proof that fascist expansionism would be appeased outside Europe. The Non-Intervention Agreement, signed in August 1936, was an early indication that the fascist powers might also be permitted to act with relative impunity inside continental Europe. In the meantime, the Non-Intervention Committee set up to oversee and, eventually police, non-intervention became what an American ambassador called 'the most cynical and lamentably dishonest group that history has known'.[10]

Hitler and Mussolini continued to pretend that they had nothing to do with the reactionary military uprising. At the end of August, the multilingual Hungarian writer and journalist Arthur Koestler, another Comintern man, used his press credentials to travel to Seville. He wanted to find out whether the reports that Hitler and Mussolini's airmen were helping the rebel generals were true. Koestler had originally asked to join the Republican army, but was instead told to use his journalistic cover to spy. Given his political affiliation, Koestler was, in effect, acting as a secret agent for the Republic. In Seville, he soon found a group of Luftwaffe officers drinking sherry and enjoying lunch at one of the city's grandest hotels, the Cristina, with the pro-Nazi journalist Hans Strindberg. The son of the great Swedish playwright August Strindberg, Hans knew Koestler because they had once worked together on a German newspaper. He was also aware of the latter's strong left-wing views. The encounter almost turned out badly for Koestler:

> Hitler was denying having dispatched aircraft to Spain, and Franco was denying having received them, while there before my very eyes fat, blond German pilots, living proof to the contrary, were consuming vast quantities of Spanish fish, and, monocles clamped into their eyes, reading the 'Völkischer Beobachter'. There were four of these gentlemen in the Hotel Cristina in Seville at about lunchtime on 28 August 1936 ... As I entered the lounge, the four pilots were sitting at a table, drinking sherry. The fish came later. Their uniforms consisted of the white overall worn by Spanish airmen; on their breasts were two embroidered wings with a small swastika in a circle ...
>
> The five gentlemen put their heads together. Then followed a strategic manoeuvre: two of the airmen strolled towards the door – obviously to cut off my retreat; the third went to the porter's lodge and telephoned – obviously to the police; the fourth pilot and Strindberg paced up and down the room ... his friend, airman number four, joined in the fray. With a stiff little bow he told me his name, von Bernhardt, and demanded to see my papers. The little scene was carried on entirely in German.
>
> I asked by what right Herr von Bernhardt, as a foreigner, demanded to see my papers. Herr von Bernhardt said that as an officer in the Spanish Army he had a right to ask 'every suspicious

character' for his papers. Had I not been so agitated, I should have pounced upon this statement as a toothsome morsel. That a man with a swastika on his breast should acknowledge himself in German to be an officer in Franco's army, would have been a positive tit-bit ...'[11]

The only countries that appeared willing to help the beleaguered Republic were Mexico and the Soviet Union, though Stalin was wary of getting too involved in a far-off war. Arms, fuel and other support were shipped from both countries. Stalin sent military advisors to help organise the Republican army. Several hundred Russians would also fight as pilots, anti-aircraft gunners or tank drivers, until the Republicans were able to train their own men. This was, however, a far smaller contingent of regular, professional soldiers than those supplied later by Hitler, with his Luftwaffe 'Condor Legion', or by Mussolini, who eventually sent entire army divisions.

The number of foreign volunteer *centurias* continued to grow. The Italians, used to coordinating between opposition parties who had operated in exile for a decade, were amongst the most active – with more than 300 of the 650 who eventually joined Rosselli's Italian column already in Spain.[12] In what served as a test run for later recruitment, a group of 400 volunteers of various nationalities – including many German, Italian and Polish political exiles – had reached Barcelona from France on 31 August. It was the biggest single contingent of foreign volunteers yet and had been coordinated by the communists, who made sure they scored a propaganda victory. Cheering crowds gathered at each of the stations they passed through and the president of Catalonia, Lluís Companys, awaited them on the platform. 'Overwhelmed by the shouting, flowers and hugs, we formed into a tight marching column and, led by a military orchestra, went down the main streets of the city to their Karl Marx barracks,' recalled Antoni Mrowiec, a Polish exile who had been living in Alès, France.[13] By this time, however, the Republic was more worried about Madrid than the stagnant front in Aragon, which was fed by troops from Barcelona. Mrowiec and three dozen other Poles and Hungarians found themselves drafted to the Libertad column that was about to set out for the Spanish capital.

It was now very clear, from the flow of people already crossing the border independently into Spain, that numerous foreign volunteers were willing to defend the Republic. By this stage, indeed, they numbered well over a thousand. If the deep well of sympathy for the Republic could be tapped and organised, then an entire new army might come to its defence.

That idea was beginning to gain support in Moscow. Stalin did not want to commit the Red Army, but Soviet-style international communism had a well-structured global organisation that was used to operating clandestinely and with disciplined efficiency – the Comintern. Its recent policy of pursuing popular front alliances with other more moderate left-wing groups in Europe and elsewhere had earned it goodwill and gave it a wide range of friends prepared to follow its lead.

5

A Professional View: Huesca,
mid-September 1936

Tom Wintringham looked out at the city of Huesca – small but clearly delineated in the distance by the bright September sunshine.[1] In the background, the silvery-grey Pyrenees rose up 'abrupt and fantastic, as if painted on the back-cloth of a theatre-scene'.[2] Bald, fit and moustachioed, the thirty-eight-year-old former British army officer and Oxford-educated barrister had been brought to the front line by another kind of volunteer – a student doctor from St Bartholomew's Hospital, London, called Kenneth Sinclair-Loutit, who, ignoring a warning from his father that he would be disinherited if he left for Spain,[3] led a medical aid unit to the front from Britain.[4] This was the first properly organised aid from Britain to the Spanish Republic, enthusiastically backed by left-wing and literary luminaries such as Rebecca West and Victor Gollancz.

Two months had gone by since the generals launched their coup. Fanny Schoonheyt was back in Barcelona, recovering from either 'nervous exhaustion' (as one newspaper called it) or, more likely, a long-running kidney complaint. She had become a minor celebrity in Barcelona, where local journalists claimed the hospital room she occupied felt like 'a *vedette*'s dressing room'. Schoonheyt does not seem to have returned to the front line, but her machine-gun skills were too good to waste so she was sent as an instructor and political commissar to a training camp outside Barcelona.[5]

By now groups of all political colours were welcoming foreigners. Signs at Barcelona's railway station pointed them towards recruiting offices. Anarchists and others were joining the two major columns organised by the Federation of Iberian Anarchists and their National Labour Confederation trades union (CNT-FAI) which were led, on the one hand, by Buenaventura Durruti and, on the other hand, by members of the Ascaso family. They included the twenty-six-year-old French philosopher Simone Weil, who joined a twenty-two-strong international section of the Durruti Column but had to be sent home after, on being asked to cook, scalding her foot with red-hot olive oil.[6] Like many who travelled to Spain, Weil had found herself struggling to jettison the pacifist ideals that the left held during and post the First World War. This was viewed by many on the left as an 'imperialist war', engineered by greedy European elites and paid for with working-class blood. 'I don't like war,' Weil explained, but 'when I realised that, despite all my efforts, I could not avoid taking part morally in this war, by which I mean that every day, at all hours, desiring the victory of one side over the other, I told myself that Paris was like being in the rearguard and took a train to Barcelona.'[7] She was shocked, though, by the casual way in which the anarchists shot priests and other people who were simply assumed to be sympathetic to the fascists. The death of a fifteen-year-old Falangist fighter captured by her volunteer colleagues, who had chosen to be executed by firing squad rather than repent, weighed heavily on her conscience, 'even though I didn't know about it until afterwards'.[8]

Tom Wintringham had come to Huesca to visit the Thälmann Group – which is why he now found himself being served a plate of hot, pungent beans by the bantering cook and former People's Olympiad athlete Abrasha Krasnowieski, whose cheerful demeanour made him the heart and soul of the group. 'Eat your bloody breakfast!' Krasnowieski mock-commanded, using up what appeared to be his entire reserve of English, while a Spanish sub-chef chuckled. Sam Masters – one of the Jewish tailors from Stepney alluded to by Felicia Browne – had joined this group of fifteen where German, Spanish and Yiddish were the main languages for communication.[9] With serious fighting a rarity at their position near Grañen in these weeks, Masters gained a reputation for being 'not always very interested in war', while showing a rare talent for raiding vineyards and orchards that lay between the lines. Wintringham was himself invited to gorge on a bunch of sticky, blue grapes.

Wintringham was impressed by the camaraderie, but shocked by much else. During the First World War front-line trenches could be just fifty metres apart. But here in Huesca, they were 800 metres distant, making the machine-gun fire that greeted his dash between two Republican positions a matter of random luck and wasted ammunition.[10] Both sides operated like this. Real fighting required daring raids across the wide no-man's-land, but such engagements were rare. That did not stop Wintringham from instinctively diving into a hollow as soon as he heard gunfire: however badly aimed, he reasoned, real bullets were flying in his direction. As he ran from hollow to hollow he both worried about whether his bald pate would glisten in the sun, attracting fire, and became quietly furious at the casual way in which these foreign volunteers were putting themselves at risk.

The Spaniards whom Wintringham observed seemed even more blasé. One kept walking slowly across the field, half a hundredweight of tomatoes and fruit on his shoulders, ignoring sniper fire. It was, Wintringham soon found out, not considered 'manly' for a Spaniard to throw himself into a hole just because someone was shooting at him. 'Was I afraid? Of course, I was afraid. It is a soldier's job to feel afraid at the right time,' wrote Wintringham. It was also a soldier's job to dig trenches, fortify positions and stand watch, but this was done only in a lacklustre fashion, if at all. Positions that should have been joined up by trenches long ago still required dashes across open land. Those trenches that existed were too shallow or had been dug in a straight line that could easily be overrun. This was, in other words, still an amateur war where taking unnecessary risks was part of the 'excitement'. Wintringham argued with Wohlrath, Friedemann and the other foreign volunteers, who shared an unrealistic belief that, despite two months with only minor advances, Huesca would soon fall to the Republicans. 'We all hate digging. As well, we shan't be here much longer,' one of them reasoned. Wintringham's only consolation was that the other side was equally amateurish. This 'was not the kind of war I liked', he concluded.[11]

There were other problems. For most militiamen, discipline was something that the fascist army in front of them used to oppress its working-class soldiers. In the militias there was no saluting superiors and little recognition of rank or hierarchy. Militiamen demanded that military decisions be debated and taken jointly. Those professional army officers who had stayed loyal to the government were mistrusted; they were often blamed for failures, and sometimes shot by their own men.

A newer, much larger German-speaking unit of 120 people had just established itself beside them. Confusingly, it called itself the Thälmann Centuria, and would later absorb some members of the more ad hoc Thälmann Group. This was mostly filled with communist exiles from the Nazi regime, who were arriving from across Europe. The *centuria* was, at least in comparative terms, a model of Prussian discipline and tidiness, provoking mirth amongst the anarchic Spanish militiamen. Wintringham, however, was admiring and believed a much larger international 'legion' ought to be recruited so that it could set an example to the militias. Those Germans who knew Spain – people like Friedemann and Wohlrath – disagreed, saying they learned from the Spaniards too. 'We have to be close to them, mixed in with them, to do this,' they argued.[12]

At around the same time that Wintringham was throwing himself into the hollows of Grañen's dusty fields, another balding, experienced ex-army officer visited the same lines. Ludwig Renn was a Saxon writer and soldier, who no longer used his aristocratic name of Arnold Friedrich Vieth von Golßenau. He had sat on the opposite side of the trenches to Wintringham in the Great War. That war, with its ten million dead, mindless nationalism and savage humiliation of defeated Germany, had continued to poison European politics and democracy in the years since the peace treaty was signed at Versailles in 1919. It had also brought old enemies like Renn and Wintringham together. The First World War was part of the cocktail of personal experience, along with the financial crash, depression and rampant unemployment of previous years, that had driven people towards more extreme political options on both left and right. Renn had written *War*, a celebrated autobiographical account of life on the Western front and, after watching dozens of socialist demonstrators being attacked and killed by police in Vienna in 1927, veered to the political left and embraced communism – vowing never to sit by passively again.[13] Tall, skinny and with a schoolteacher's wire-framed glasses, he was, according to one observer, 'an ascetic warrior, a soldier-monk'.[14] Others simply found him stiff and humourless.

In Grañen, Renn had been surprised to find Fernando Trueba, the union official commanding the Carlos Marx column – equivalent, in his mind, to a general – in a pair of grey dungarees. Since everyone else wore similar garb, he was unsure who of those sitting down to lunch with him were also in charge. The commander admitted that the largely self-formed units in his column were a hotchpotch of sizes and that he himself had little military knowledge. Renn asked if he had placed his units all in one long (and easily overrun) line. 'Of course, just like the fascists,' came the reply. Renn was even more scandalised at the lack of reserves to fill gaps that might appear during an attack, or to fight anyone who broke through.

Renn shared his worries with Hans Beimler, the jug-eared former German communist Reichstag deputy who had helped set up the *centuria* and was already famous for being the only escapee from one of the new concentration camps being set up in Hitler's Germany at Dachau.[15] 'Every unit must have reserves, however big or small. Any officer with even the smallest knowledge of modern warfare knows that,' an indignant Renn told him. The fascists might be making the same mistakes, he pointed out, but their new German and Italian advisors would soon correct them. 'Yet here the leader of the column, although he is a good man, didn't even understand [the reasons for] my question,' he complained. [16] That night, as if to confirm his diagnosis of a disastrously ill-prepared army, another aristocratic former German army officer turned communist who had volunteered to help organise and train the *centuria*, Hubert von Ranke,[17] explained why a neighbouring anarchist unit could be heard blasting away at invisible targets in the dark. 'They always get these night panics. Then they fire madly until they run out of ammunition and ask for more, threatening to leave if they don't get it,' he said.[18] This, he sneered, was typical of anarchists. He does not seem to have told Renn that one of the few early victories around Huesca had been won by a column including up to a hundred Italians and other international volunteers, many of them anarchists, who took the Monte Pelado hill at the end of August. Mutual scorn and mistrust between communists, anarchists and other factions was already weakening the Republican response.

Renn's view of this chaotic army was coloured not just by his Saxon upbringing and military past, but also by his attraction to the discipline of communism (which, as a prominent party member, had seen him imprisoned by Hitler for eighteen months in 1933, following the Reichstag fire).[19] He liked things to be ordered, thought out and done properly. Indeed, he had already disapproved of the British hospital set up by Sinclair-Loutit and his team of doctors, nurses and ambulance drivers in Grañen. Renn saw medical staff smoking in the wards while, given the lack of doors in the building, stray dogs sniffed around the patients. 'The nurses are bored petit-bourgeois who want to experience something different,' Beimler explained. They were fine nurses, he added, and good people but they needed 'political education'. This attitude irritated the volunteer nurses and doctors, who were by no means all communists. Beimler probably did not know that the British Medical Aid Unit's treasurer was Winston Churchill's cousin, Viscount Peter Churchill.[20] Some of those first medical volunteers, whose numbers swelled as they were joined by doctors and nurses from around the world, would remain in Spain for the next three years, outlasting the majority of armed volunteers.

Renn and Wintringham may have fought against each other twenty years earlier, but they were both keen students of military tactics and now saw eye to eye on the Republic's need for help on the ground. In fact, the two men had made similar political journeys over the previous fifteen years. Wintringham was nominally visiting as a correspondent for the communist *Daily Worker* (newspaper credentials were one of the easiest ways to get into war-torn Spain) but he had long been an operative for the Comintern, the international arm of Soviet-style communism. He had studied at the Lenin School in Moscow, where national parties sent their most promising cadres. Many of Wintringham's fellow alumni would soon appear in Spain. It can have been no coincidence that both he and Renn were reconnoitring the front lines, for the Comintern was already thinking about whether it should do more to prevent a fascist triumph in the Iberian peninsula.[21] Wintringham had argued with friends in England about the need to organise a legion of international volunteers to join the battle. They had warned that Clement Attlee's Labour Party, although deeply sympathetic to the Republic (while being, as a later commentator observed, 'more Methodist than Marxist'), would never back such a thing. 'They will think of the Catholic vote and the pacifists,' he had been told. 'And such a legion would be sure to be labelled Red and communist. We must avoid those labels being stuck on the war in Spain, which is a defence of democracy, of a democratic republic, against fascism.'[22]

Yet, Wintringham remained convinced that the Republic's 'amateur-anarchist' way of fighting would bring certain defeat. Even the Thälmann Centuria, whose discipline he admired, worried him, since

its volunteers appeared to have adopted the Spanish militiaman's
disdain for danger. One set of attacks on a hilltop hermitage
dedicated to Santa Quiteria saw the Thälmann Centuria run blindly
and willingly into enemy fire on repeated occasions, suffering heavy
losses. Hardened by their encounter with Nazism, these volunteers
were 'strong men who proved and overproved their courage',
according to the future American volunteer fighter and historian
Robert Colodny.[23] In a bold, night-time attack they had clambered
up the terraced farmland in front of the hermitage and taken it, only
to be forced out by enemy reinforcements, including experienced
Moroccan colonial soldiers, coming down the hill in the opposite
direction.[24] With little support, apart from a similarly courageous
group of young Spanish anarchists, and even less information about
how heavily fortified their objective was, the attack had been doomed
to failure. Three Danish brothers who had cycled to Spain – Harald,
Kaj and Aage Nielsen – were the last to flee. 'They set an early example
of what shock troops could be like. They tried to do the impossible,
and paid for it,' said Colodny.[25]

Wintringham was not impressed by an action that had seen the
125-strong *centuria* – by now bolstered by a handful of Austrians, Poles,
Danes and Belgians – lose nineteen dead and fifty-two wounded before
being sent back to Barcelona to reorganise.[26] 'An army that consists of
troops who are willing to do nothing much except at intervals find graves
and glory – such an army needs an example and training of exactly the
opposite sort given by the Thälmann Centuria,' Wintringham observed
afterwards. 'How could these incredibly valiant Spaniards get hold of
the art, the science, the discipline of war? By example and by training,
given them by foreigners, but not in this hopelessly slipshod, casual,
unscientific way,'[27] agreed Renn.

The sight of Hitler's Ju 52s flying above the lines at Huesca confirmed
to Wintringham that the often shambolic enemy had already realised
that foreign help was crucial, and he was cast down by the thought
that his earlier proposals for recruiting men to defend the Republic had
been so badly received in Britain. By the time he returned to England,
however, he found that his friends 'had already seen the need'. So, too,
had Joseph Stalin. Wintringham had dreamed of recruiting fifty men
for Spain. 'I did not know that four months later I would be helping to
organise 500.'[28]

6

Creating the Brigades: Madrid, Moscow, Albacete, October 1936

Francisco Largo Caballero made it obvious that he did not like the foreigners who walked through his door on 17 October 1936. The Italian, the Pole and the Frenchman had come to offer help, but the man who was now both the prime minister and war minister of Spain was suspicious of their aims and methods. Luigi Longo, Pierre Rebière and Stephan Wisnieski were all Comintern officials. They had been ushered through the door by another Italian, Vittorio Vidali, a Comintern man who was already a senior figure in the communist branch of the Republican army and called himself Carlos Contreras. They had been forced to wait for the meeting overnight and Vidali had to explain to the frustrated foreigners that 'mañana was a very Spanish thing and that we shouldn't despair'.[1]

Largo Caballero walked towards them but declined to sit down, suggesting that this was to be a very short meeting. He did not like the idea of foreign-run units in his army, especially if they were organised by communists.[2] But these were Stalin's men. Russia was sending weapons, advisors and instructors. Stalin was determined not to upset Britain and France (who were already terrified of Hitler's Germany) by sending troops of his own from the Red Army, but he still wanted international communism (or the part of it controlled by Moscow) to be present. The nearest thing he could offer to an army was the proposal now laid out by Longo. It included helping to organise several brigades of international volunteers, with tens of thousands of men who would come from a broad range of anti-fascist parties and movements. These International Brigades would tap into a widespread desire across the left – and amongst others who simply feared the rise of Hitler and Mussolini – to fight fascism directly. It was obvious, however, that the organisation would largely be in communist hands.

Largo Caballero had taken charge of the government early in September after Giral proved incapable of organising an efficient defence against Franco's skilled troops. These were now sweeping towards Madrid from the west, rolling over the undisciplined and poorly armed militia units that stood in their way. The latest disaster had come the day before Largo Caballero became prime minister with the fall, on 3 September, of Talavera de la Reina, 110 kilometres from the capital and the last major city on the road to Madrid.

This was as chaotic as the Aragon front, but faster moving. Trying to find the front to the west of Madrid, the German writer and First World War veteran Gustav Regler was told by his driver that it would be 'wherever they start shooting at us'.[3] When they found Republican troops positioned along a road, ignoring the open countryside around them, they refused to discuss whether they risked being outflanked. 'It's not the custom. We only fight on the roads,' the soldiers informed him. Polish volunteer Antoni Mrowiec was amongst a group of foreign machine-gunners rushed to this front from Barcelona – together with the hundred-strong, mostly Italian Gastone Sozzi Centuria – to slow the advance just outside Talavera.[4] Under the guidance of regular army officers, they successfully held their positions for a month and helped to buy time for the Spanish capital. The reckless bravado of an anarchist unit with a dozen trucks which appeared out of nowhere summed up what, to the more disciplined communists, was the basic problem of the Republican army. 'They drove cars through our lines towards the fascists, and soon disappeared from sight. After a dozen minutes we heard the sound of violent shooting, and a moment later we saw some retreating cars and silhouettes of anarchists fleeing in panic,' described Mrowiec. They then refused to dig in and help defend the line, charging back 'to wherever they had come from'. Largo Caballero himself – often dressed in the boiler suit costume of the militias – promoted this kind of behaviour, claiming that Spanish troops would never dig into defensive positions because their pride would not allow them to. They preferred to fight *a pecho descubierto* (literally bare-chested or like a fighting bull, head on and without hiding), he claimed. That made Renn, who recalled the German army's suicidal 'buffalo strategy' in 1914, wince.[5]

Largo Caballero clearly saw the International Brigades as a communist invention. In Republican Spain, with the professional army mostly on the other side and the newly formed units already almost largely based on political or union affiliation, there was nothing especially sinister or strange about that. The Spanish communists were efficient organisers and their vast Fifth Regiment – which served as an umbrella organisation for their own brigades[6] – was acquiring a reputation as one of the most effective parts of the ragtag army that emerged during the first weeks of fighting. He listened in silence to the visitors, who tried to guess whether his occasional nods meant that he understood what they had said, or approved. 'Do you have arms?' he asked, after Longo had presented the plan. 'Of course,' Longo lied. It would be a vast popular front army, he explained, made up of workers from around the world of (almost) all left-wing persuasions. 'It is good that you come to our aid, given that this way you will be defending yourselves,' Largo Caballero said, referring to the regimes in Italy and Germany. 'Since you wish to fight, the Spanish government accepts your help, though it must be clear that you will provide your own arms. They will be paid ten pesetas a day, like our own militiamen.'[7] This was more than many militiamen earned in civilian life, and equivalent to four British shillings, or a fifth of a pound.[8] The interview was over and the group was offended by its brevity. Largo Caballero, they thought, looked annoyed that it had lasted for more than five minutes. Was that his temperament, or proof of his unrestrained hostility to the volunteers? Both, they were told. Longo blamed Caballero's military advisors for persuading him that the volunteers were 'the devil's tail', but Vidali laughed the episode off. 'That's it!' he explained. 'We've achieved the most important thing – and can now form a brigade.'[9]

In fact, this meeting was really about rubber-stamping something that had been agreed earlier. The International Brigades, indeed, were already being formed. Popular pressure, Moscow strategising and Republican politics had combined to create them. On 28 August the Comintern's Bulgarian secretary general Georgi Dimitrov – based in Moscow – wrote in his diary that discussions were under way for a 'possible organisation of an international corps'.[10] The strands were coming together, and the Communist Party was doing the stitching. At a meeting of the Comintern Presidium on 18 September, various measures were approved for helping Republican Spain, such as sending specialists to help its army but also to 'recruit, amongst the workers from all countries, volunteers with military experience, with a view to sending them to Spain'.[11] The following day, the senior French communist André Marty – a cantankerous, walrus-moustached, former leader of a French navy mutiny – began work on a general operations plan for Spain with the help of Comintern military advisors. The moody, blustering and insecure Marty was famous for his explosive temper and ability, in the words of one of those advisors, 'to turn a molehill into a mountain'.[12] He was also one of Comintern's seven secretaries, and his involvement was a sign of how seriously the organisation took this new project. The plan recommended a foreign legion of shock troops, some 4,000 to 5,000 strong.[13] By 10 October, a week before the meeting with Largo Caballero, around 500 of these were already sitting in the old fort in the northern Catalan city of Figueres, waiting for somewhere to go.

Two days later, very late in the evening, Longo knocked on the door of the communist Fifth Regiment's offices in Albacete, but was told to come back in the morning. He slept on a bench until the local commander arrived in the morning, and then warned the surprised man that not only was Albacete to be the International Brigades' headquarters, but that hundreds of men were on their way from Figueres. Another 800 were on a boat that had already sailed from Marseille and was due to dock at Alicante.[14] 'They looked at me as if I was mad,' Longo recalled.[15] In less than thirty-six hours buildings were found, leaking roofs hurriedly patched up and floors covered with straw for the first contingent. Beds, food, kitchens and latrines were still lacking, however.[16] From 14 October onwards, several hundred men a day would reach this charmless rural city in the flat farmland of La Mancha – which was conveniently situated on the roads and railways that led to Barcelona, Valencia, Madrid or Andalusia. They included many of those who were already fighting or training in the various foreign units that emerged spontaneously in the opening weeks of the war. These included the Thälmann Centuria, the mostly Italian Gastone Sozzi Centuria, Rosselli's Italian column, a French-speaking Commune de Paris Centuria, as well as the dozen British and Irish who, under the leadership of the Stepney cyclist Nat Cohen and his girlfriend (and future wife) Ramona Siles García, had formed the untested Tom Mann Centuria in Barcelona.[17] They hoped that this foreign 'army within an army' would prove to be a more effective fighting force than the militia units with which they had served so far.

7

The Tower of Babel: Albacete,
October 1936

The journey to Albacete was one of contrasts. As the men rode down from Figueres by train, villagers cheered, bands played, flowers were thrown and alcohol was consumed in liberal quantities. Few of those foreign volunteers who made the trip in these early days forgot the wild enthusiasm with which they were greeted everywhere. Only the more disciplined – typically the most serious-minded and dedicated communists – remained completely sober. Political and national strains were already apparent, exacerbated by petty jealousies and the rowdy squabbling of overexcited and inebriated men, though these were mostly drowned out by the ecstatic reception and the shared sense of both purpose and potential glory. The volunteers were a mixture of intense, ideological young men, city toughs, manual workers from factory floors and mines, adventurers, and those with nothing better to do. They were also, disproportionately, exiles and migrants (or the children of migrants). Most were passionate left-wingers. Together they formed an army of the devout and the displaced.

Paris became the main recruiting point for the new Brigades, with organisation mostly in the hands of the French Communist Party, the Confédération Générale du Travail (CGT) trades union and various spin-off committees.[1] Economic and political exiles from elsewhere drifted towards the Main-d'oeuvre immigrée (MOI) offices in the communist headquarters in Rue La Fayette, with a union building in the Avenue Mathurin-Moreau acting as a marshalling point for men who initially arrived from across Europe.[2] On trains heading south from Paris and boats leaving the harbour at Marseille, men began to learn to communicate with people who spoke languages they could not begin to understand. The *Ciudad de Barcelona*, a requisitioned passenger boat, had slipped silently out of Marseille on 11 October, a lone sailor singing plaintive snatches of what passengers assumed was flamenco – 'sounding of southern grief on lonely arid hills', according to one of the more imaginative and poetically minded passengers.[3]

A few days later a British Labour Party member called Esmond Romilly found himself wandering the Marseille docks, having lost his passport and most of his money while cycling across France from Dieppe fuelled by cognac and black coffee. Romilly was by no means typical of the recruits, since his father had been the British military governor of Galilee and his Aunt Clementine was married to Winston Churchill. The latter was now in his wilderness years and arguing vehemently for rearmament in the face of Germany's growing military machine, but had refused to shake the hand of the Republic's new ambassador in London, Pablo de Azcárate, instead muttering 'blood, blood, blood' in response to behind-the-line killings by anarchists and others.[4] Romilly had run away from a notoriously philistine public school, Wellington College, where he declared himself a pacifist and set up a radical magazine called *Out of Bounds: Public Schools' Journal against Fascism, Militarism and Reaction*.[5] He was also an adventurer who described himself as belonging 'to that very large class of unskilled labourers with a public-school accent'.[6]

Romilly had no idea that the International Brigades were being formed, but he was determined to fight in Spain. After a few days sleeping in a church hostel in Marseille, he was rowed out to the Spanish steamship SS *Mar Caspio*, where around 600 men from across Europe were slowly being gathered together. They were, he noted, nearly all working class. A notice pinned outside the dining room gave an idea of just how mixed the passengers were: 'Guard duties: 7–9 French, 9–11 Germans, 11–13 Italians, 13–15 Yugoslavs, 15–17 Belgians, 17–19 Poles, 19–21 Flemish, 21–23 Russians, 23–1 French, 1–3 Germans, 3–5 Poles, 5–7 Belgians.' When Romilly told the serious young French official from the Communist Youth International who was in charge that he was not actually a communist, the latter was 'delighted and treated me with extra consideration to emphasise the *Front Populaire* spirit'.[7] Not everyone was so welcoming. Another group of Frenchmen wanted him to explain how Britain's Labour Party squared the idea of 'non-intervention' in Spain with socialist principles. 'That, of course, I could not tell them,' he admitted.[8] The subject was hard to dismiss, since they could see British warships standing off Spanish ports and monitoring the shipping that went in and out of them.[9] In fact, the Labour Party and the powerful trades unions which backed them were initially mistrustful of the International Brigades because of the role played by the same communists who, until the switch to supporting popular front alliances, had accused them of being 'social fascists'.[10]

In Valencia, Romilly's detachment of recruits was welcomed by huge, cheering crowds and entertained with dinner and a music-hall show. A merry, if chaotic, column of men eventually arrived at the railway station. 'We learned new slogans: *"Viva las señoritas españolas"* and *"Viva vino Blanco"*,' Romilly remembered.[11] '*Viva Rusia!*' some people shouted back, reflecting a common belief that the foreign soldiers reaching Spain must all be from the Soviet Union. A bumpy eight-hour journey amongst a 'garlicky mass of men, sprawling on the floor under seats and sleeping on racks' was made more painful by his attacks of diarrhoea and slower by the fact that the train stopped at each little station, where 'there was the same crowds, the same friendly words, the same forest of clenched fists'.[12] Fortified by sweet muscatel wine and potent *anis*, they were also bombarded with gifts of flowers, fruit and bread. A French volunteer remembered the haughty girls. 'Young women laughed nervously, making their beautiful eyes even more enchanting,' he recalled. 'Despite the great modesty they impose on themselves, it seemed as if their beautiful lips burned with kisses for us. When a comrade showed his desire to kiss one of these pretty girls, her father exhorted her to accept the kiss as an honour.'[13]

Some of these would-be soldiers had never travelled out of their home countries before and the nerves caused by their mission – to fight in a foreign army – were heightened by being out of their natural environment. Some sang away their fear and excitement with tunes from home. As often as not, someone then started on the one song that almost everybody knew, even if the words came out in different languages – the left-wing anthem 'The Internationale'. 'Here were we, all young men from really all the nations in Europe, and some from outside Europe as well, joining in this one song in their own language which seemed to express a yearning for the unity of mankind. I find it extremely difficult to explain how exhilarating this was. I don't think I've ever felt the same feeling at any other time in my life,' a British volunteer who arrived later recalled.[14] The enthusiasm shown by Spaniards as the trainloads of foreigners trundled south remained undimmed over the coming months. 'I'll never forget that journey,' said Frenchwoman Lise London after she was recruited by Marty to work at Albacete and experienced the station-by-station welcomes, where crowds of well-wishers offered 'arms full of flowers, fruit, food, jugs of fresh water, and bottles or goatskins full of wine'.[15]

For those who were not already exiles, the journey to Spain was one of the most remarkable of their lives. Few countries approved of men fighting in a foreign army – especially a 'Red' one – and non-intervention rules turned many journeys to Paris into clandestine or semi-clandestine adventures. Comintern and other organisers did their best, but chaotic improvisation was to the fore. Frontiers were crossed at night, rivers swum, trains clung on to and border guards dodged. Hungarian István Bakallár set out on foot with two *pengös* (about two shillings, or £5 today) in his pocket and made his way through Italy, Switzerland and France. He rode on the back of hay carts, hitched rides on lorries, jumped onto slow-moving trains, foraged for food, was arrested in Italy, and eventually – two months later – he reached Paris. Pole Julius Hibner was smuggled into Czechoslovakia with no passport and twenty *zlotys* stashed inside a false shoe heel while his eighteen-year-old compatriot, nurse Rachel Schwartzman (known as 'Angèle') stayed with communist families as she passed through four different countries.[16] British volunteers would eventually be given tickets to Dunkirk or Paris, nominally to spend the day or the weekend.[17] The evening trains from the Gare de Lyon in Paris to Perpignan[18] or from the Quai q'Orsay to Marseille were soon full of small groups of young men from around Europe, mostly wearing working men's flat caps, carrying backpacks and nonchalantly pretending not to have anything in common. Many different routes opened up, as some travelled on specially fleeted trains, or convoys of buses and trucks.[19]

Volunteers were usually interviewed by a Communist Party or union official before departure, though there were so many routes to Spain that no single system existed. Military training and some kind of political background were the best guarantees to acceptance, but the filters did not always work and some of those who got through were completely unsuitable. Late in October an angry Marty rebuked his party colleagues in Paris for sending a 'deficient selection' of 515 men, of whom nearly half had not done military service and many were old, sick or were simply unemployed and looking for something to do. 'It will be extremely dangerous if you keep sending us such people,' he said.[20] Half the Swiss recruits came from the ranks of the unemployed and the mayor of Lyon was believed to have sent dozens of beggars as a way of getting them off his streets. As a result, several groups of men had to be sent back.[21]

The knots of young men who stood around the Quai d'Orsay when the first batch of recruits left early in October included a twenty-eight-year-old Londoner called John Sommerfield, who had left school at sixteen, jobbed as a stagehand and merchant seaman, shown a talent for writing, published in the communist press and composed three novels. His group of up to a dozen English speakers was the least typical of all, for it had been put together by twenty-year-old (Rupert) John Cornford, a Cambridge poet and communist who had already fought with a POUM unit on the Aragon front.[22] Cornford was Charles Darwin's great-grandson and had decided not to use the first name given to him in honour of the family friend and First World War poet Rupert Brooke. Trying to keep up with this energetic, convinced and sports-mad militant was, in his brother's words, 'like standing on a railway embankment and trying to grab an express train'.[23]

The tall, stooping Cornford had initially recruited these men to fight in Aragon, before being redirected in Paris to the new International Brigades. His group included not just the writer Sommerfield but two Cambridge graduates (including the future Yale and Harvard classics professor Bernard Knox[24]), an Oxford graduate studying medicine in Edinburgh, a London university graduate, an actor, three ex-servicemen and two unemployed workmen. Knox and Cornford had visited the latter's father, a Greek scholar at Cambridge, who handed over his First World War officer's pistol. Knox had smuggled it through French customs, because Cornford's passport already had Spanish entry and exit stamps 'and his bags were likely to be given a thorough going-over'.[25] Standing on the platform, watching the other groups arrive, it slowly dawned on them that this was a much bigger affair than they had expected. Sommerfield felt 'delighted, not quite understanding, but full of hope'[26] before someone stepped forward and proclaimed himself to be in charge. Railway union officials were on hand to smooth their path, but few had any idea about where they were going.

Cornford's group still hoped they would be taken to Barcelona and the Aragon front. They had been recently joined by an English-speaking German exile, Jan Kurzke, adding a painter to their unrepresentatively intellectual and artistic group. Cornford's tales of the leisurely warfare on the Aragonese front and his insistence that both sides lacked the weapons for a proper 'modern' war convinced the volunteers that they were heading towards something far more benign than trenches akin to those of the Western front. In Cornford's telling, both Spanish armies sounded more like those led by the revolutionary Pancho Villa, who fought against regimes in Mexico at the time of the First World War, than those which had soaked the mud of the Somme and Verdun with the blood of young men. Along the way, his group idly debated whether prisoners should be shot.[27] Most agreed with a Catholic Irishman who joined the group and argued that they should not, but Kurzke reminded them that the other side would not be so generous.

Many volunteers arrived in a state of total ignorance about both Spain and war. 'Men like myself did not speak a word of Spanish,' admitted James Yates, an African-American from Mississippi who would join the US contingent that arrived the following year. 'To order a glass of milk, we would moo like a cow. We cackled like chickens to order eggs, and we touched our bodies in order to indicate that we wanted to use the toilet.'[28] Northern Europeans were alternately delighted or dismayed by their first sight of a Mediterranean country. 'How beautiful Spain is! I had never seen olive trees and orange groves where golden fruit hung from tree branches and the ground was covered with a golden carpet of oranges,' Aleksander Szurek, a Polish exile who had been living in rainy Normandy, recalled.[29]

If alcohol often smoothed the transition, waking up the following morning was a different matter. Albacete is cold for most of the year, with October night temperatures sinking to an average 8 degrees centigrade (and as low as minus twenty at the height of winter). Conditions were rough. Somehow more than a thousand men were stuffed into a former convent school, a police barracks designed for eighty families and one of the larger houses in the city.[30] For the first two weeks volunteers slept on cement and straw-covered floors. By morning the latrines were stinking and overflowing. There were two taps for 800 men to wash from. Plates and cutlery had to be shared. Water was scarce and men spent all morning queuing for lunch, and then all afternoon queuing for supper[31] – which consisted of 'a plate of soup, a plate of hash, and sometimes a pomegranate'.[32] Spanish food, fried in olive oil, was, at best, unfamiliar. 'For those of us who were used to Polish, Jewish or French cuisine, all we could do was hold our noses and swallow,' said one France-based Polish exile.[33] They soon discovered that war was as squalid as it was heroic. 'The Latin type of latrine, at which you have to squat, is bad enough at its best, but these were made of some kind of polished stone so slippery that it was all you could do to keep on your feet,' Orwell wrote later after joining a POUM unit in Aragon. 'In addition they were always blocked ... these latrines first brought home to me the thought, so often to recur: "Here we are, soldiers of a revolutionary army, defending Democracy against Fascism, fighting a war which is ABOUT something, and the detail of our lives is just as sordid and degrading as it could be in prison." '[34] Olive oil, powdered peppers and chickpeas wrought havoc on northern stomachs. Diarrhoea swept through the ranks.[35]

As hundreds more volunteers arrived daily, men were billeted in the arches under the bullring while towns and villages in the region were told to expect to receive the units that were being hastily formed every day. All this was organised by a headquarters staff crammed into a few rooms of the former Bank of Spain branch in Albacete.[36] A sleepy provincial farming capital suddenly found itself hosting a large and chaotic military detachment which exchanged instructions, greetings and insults in a dozen or more languages. 'It was impossible to ask the comrades not to go into town, or to drink,' observed Pierre Rebière, who jostled with another Frenchman for control of their large contingent.[37] The rowdiness of some upset the local people, he said, 'making them look badly on the rest of us, as if we were undesirables'. Several days later, after his trip to Madrid to see Largo Caballero, Rebière returned to find the situation little better. Volunteers were being allowed to wander around town, seeking ways to entertain, or simply look after, themselves. 'That was not the best way to instil the discipline needed by an army,' he admitted. Makeshift kitchens were set up at the bullring, with the men eating on the arena's sand.[38]

The early arrivals almost all came from the countries which would provide most volunteers over the next two years. They were mostly French speakers from France and Belgium, or exiles from Italy, Germany and Poland – which explains why the first four battalions were based around their languages. Three out of every five Italians arrived from France, while only about one in fifteen came straight from Italy, with the rest from a million-strong community of Italian emigrants around the world.[39] Within a dozen days[40] of the first men arriving, a number of nearby towns and villages had been identified as places where the individual battalions of up to 600 men that were being formed around the main language groups could be based, reducing pressure on Albacete itself.[41] The French speakers went thirty-five kilometres away to La Roda, where they took over a convent and an aristocrat's palace – improving their living conditions instantly. Other battalions went to Mahora, Madrigueras and Tarazona de la Mancha.[42]

When the already experienced volunteers from the Commune de Paris Centuria (who had mostly fought at either the Basque frontier town of Irun or in the failed Majorca landing) joined them with their leader Jules Dumont, command of the new French battalion was handed over to him.[43] Dumont was a decorated First World War officer who had already fought as a volunteer in Abyssinia against the invading troops sent by Mussolini in 1935. A ragbag of uniforms and rifles arrived, leaving Rebière to muse whether the sans-culottes of 1789 might have looked smarter. They were forever being told that things would arrive *mañana*, he complained, and some of the volunteers began to look down their noses at 'Spanish indolence'.[44] Ambition and envy within the ranks also made things difficult. The first commander of the Albacete camp, a former French regular army officer called Jean Marie who had already helped defend Irun, left after just a few days when he realised that he was not going to be given command of the first brigade to go into battle. He was replaced by a senior French communist, Vital Gayman (aka Vidal), who had been working for the party for over a decade.[45]

In theory, the volunteers were meant to do three hours of military training each morning and two more hours in the afternoon. But that rarely happened. Units were still being formed, instructors were few and guns mostly ancient. The first batch of three to four hundred rifles, donated from across Europe, included at least a dozen models, often without the right calibre ammunition, and contained Chinese, Japanese, Turkish and Russian guns. It was, Gayman said, 'like the collection from a weapons museum'.[46] Even the arms being sent by Stalin were, initially, antique weapons that the Red Army was keen to offload.[47] So much time was spent just dealing with the basic requirements of feeding and organising provisions or housing, that there was barely any time left for training. Wintringham became a machine-gun instructor, and was given ten days to learn what he said would normally take year – before then trying to teach others. An additional problem was that the men themselves often simply failed to turn up.[48] Marching and saluting, for example, were anathema to some. 'We have come here to fight fascists, not to march through the streets of Albacete,' some complained. Others claimed that their experience on either side during the First World War, in the Balkans or in Italy's expeditionary force in North Africa meant they were already fully trained and prepared.

The fact that many had years of political militancy behind them was another problem. They wanted officers who were comrades and a revolutionary army 'built on free principles, without order, without military discipline' and with orders debated and voted on at assemblies.[49] Some officers were reluctant to issue orders, fearing that they would be seen as behaving like factory bosses. This 'absurd democratisation' was what Longo called 'the weak point of the Spanish militias',[50] but many of those who had arrived from the Aragonese front wanted to maintain the tradition. 'Introducing the daily routine and organising the most elementary drill quite often required a great deal of energy and frequently only succeeded after the suppression of opposition not just from the soldiers, but also from a significant portion of the officer corps,' one senior officer complained.[51] They did not realise that the International Brigades were meant to be Red Army-inspired units, based on discipline and absolute obedience.[52] Romilly came to accept that this was best. 'What matters is that the rank and file should volunteer, and that their officers should have military experience,' he said.[53]

'Units were created literally within the course of one or two days from those volunteers who were on hand at the time,' reported Polish officer Karol Świerczewski, who became one of the senior field commanders. 'There were subunits that contained dozens of nationalities (one of the companies ... had fourteen); furthermore, all of these people were absolutely unacquainted, not accustomed to one another ... Representatives of the world's numerous nationalities, including blacks, Japanese, and Chinese, had to agree among themselves, found a common language, suffered the same adversities.'[54] Volunteers swore an oath to fight for the liberty of Spain and the world: 'My eternal enemies are, like the enemies of Spain, the fascists. I know that if fascism is victorious in Spain, tomorrow it will come to my country and destroy my land ... I prefer to die than live under its yoke.'[55]

Some of the organisational work was done by a handful of regular, non-Russian Red Army officers sent by Moscow as 'volunteers' and destined to become senior field commanders. Most used aliases: János Gálicz became General Gal; Máté Zalka took the name of General Lukács; Manfred Stern became Emilio Kléber; and Świerczewski was Walter. Their non-Russian status allowed Stalin to maintain that he was not breaking non-intervention rules. Soviet 'advisors' were often at the elbows of many senior Republican army commanders, and Red Army tank drivers and pilots were also already in Spain. In all, 2,105 Russians passed through Spain in short rotations, and they probably numbered no more than 500 at any one time.[56] This remains modest beside the Luftwaffe's 19,000 men or the 76,000[57] Italians sent by Mussolini.[58]

In practice, Comintern officials held most of the important posts and the International Brigades would arouse suspicions that they were at the service of Joseph Stalin himself. For the purposes of this war, however, even the communist Brigaders were, first and foremost, popular front anti-fascists and members of Spain's Republican army.[59] Political motivation was, in any case, seen as the crucial motivating factor that could turn this largely inexperienced rabble into efficient 'shock troops', willing to fight in the hardest and bloodiest fronts of the war. 'The morale of the Brigades is strong. Lacking are automatic weapons and artillery; one-third have insufficient military training. The command staff is extremely small and insufficiently qualified,' Marty reported early in November, as the first 3,000 volunteers were being organised.[60]

Since equipment and training was poor, Marty tried to maintain the men's morale with rousing speeches that praised the courage of Spain's militias while explaining why they had not yet won. 'There are three things that they have lacked, three things essential for victory, three things we must have – which we will have. The first is political unity; the second is military leaders; the third is discipline,'[61] he roared at the volunteers due to form the first International Brigade, in a speech delivered from a balcony at the Albacete barracks. They were no longer communists, socialists, republicans or radicals, he insisted, but a group of 'anti-fascists'. He then introduced the man who would lead them into battle, General Emilio Kléber, a Red Army veteran who had been a senior Comintern military advisor in China.[62] Kléber stepped forward, promised them proper training and warned against impetuousness. 'We are preparing for war, not massacre. When the first International Brigade goes into action, they will be properly trained men, with good rifles, a well-equipped corps.'[63]

The flow of recruits continued as the pent-up demand, which had even seen some French communists disciplined for travelling to Spain as 'freelance' fighters, was released and organised. French police reported that discreet instructions had gone out within the Communist Party to find 'the most thoughtful, those best suited to take command under fire, and those willing to sacrifice their life for the Spanish Republic'.[64] Fresh batches of recruits arrived once or twice a week.[65] Each trainload of new arrivals – several hundred men at a time – was marched to the outskirts of Albacete. There they were divided up into language groups, while specialists (from interpreters and mechanics, to cooks and typists) were identified and anyone with military experience who had not been a lowly private could be expected to be given a group to command. Experienced officers were few and those who had previously commanded troops often found themselves in positions beyond their previous rank and ability.[66]

Overall, experience was more important than political affiliation – except when it came to choosing the commissars in each unit, who were charged with maintaining both morale and discipline.[67] The commissars were major figures, almost as important as the commanding officers, whose job mirrored that of the Red Army commissars and, before that, of the *commissaires politiques* in the French Revolutionary Army at the end of the eighteenth century. They played a pastoral role but also wielded considerable power and did much to shape the attitudes and culture within an individual battalion or company. 'His first job is welfare. He serves as a buffer between officers and soldiers. He endeavours to fulfil these tasks without possessing any kind of power. He cannot give orders but must operate almost entirely by persuasion,' one British volunteer explained later.[68] At its worst, however, the role of the political commissar was more sinister. 'In practice, he may be something approaching a Secret Police spy, of whom everyone is terrified.'[69] Unsurprisingly, they provoked intense feelings – of both love and hate – amongst the men.

There were few volunteers for office jobs. 'They said they had come to fight, not to work as bureaucrats,' explained Gayman.[70] Even at this stage it was obvious that some of the volunteers were not fit for the task, with 'malingerers, vagrants, the lumpen proletariat as well as the puny, sick and old' weeded out. This was done on first impressions only, since there was insufficient time for a proper selection process.[71] Early attempts to maintain the popular front spirit saw the Italian battalion of the first International Brigade commanded by a Republican, with a socialist and a communist as his political commissars while the first artillery battery was commanded by a French socialist.[72]

This mismatch of experience and inexperience, of clashing national military cultures and the remainders of an 'anti-military' culture amongst some of the volunteers (many of whom, responding to the senseless butchery of the First World War, had been proud pacifists just a few months or years earlier) produced moments of incomprehension that ranged from comic to lethal. The proud commander of the Balkan battalion, for example, spoke to Spanish officers in his native Bulgarian. This was then translated by a Sephardic Jewish volunteer called César Covo who spoke *ladino* – a version of the fifteenth-century Spanish taken into exile by the Jews expelled in 1492; passwords in Spanish sometimes proved unpronounceable for those unaccustomed to the language.

The Spanish crowds who shouted '¡Viva Rusia!' when they saw the International Brigaders were not completely amiss, given that the first Soviet military advisors had already arrived in Spain. Pilots and tank commanders were also appearing with Polikarpov I-15 biplane fighters, known as '*chatos*' (literally 'snub-nosed') and T-26 light tanks that Stalin began to sell to the Republic.[73] Two Russians, indeed, liaised with the army headquarters in Madrid and reviewed all the operational plans. Given that they were not supposed to be in Spain (because of the non-intervention pact), they were always referred to, like other Russian advisors, as either 'Mexicans' or – for GRU military intelligence operatives – 'preachers'. They generally used noms de guerre, with the senior of the two, Colonel Simonov, known as Valois, while his sidekick was referred to as Petrovitch.[74] A military council headed by Marty was in overall charge, but even he admitted that any decisions on military operations were 'placed in a report to the Mexican comrades' and that it was 'only after their examination' that army headquarters in Madrid was contacted.[75] Confusingly, those volunteers from other countries who had been living in exile in Russia or studying at the International Lenin School in Moscow were often also known as 'Mexicans'. The true sign of a deep-level, long-term communist was often that he or she would be known by a single name, usually an alias. This was a tic from their often clandestine pasts, though the telltale prefix of 'comrade' was dropped.[76]

Fewer than three weeks had gone by since the first men arrived in Albacete when instructions came to send a brigade to the front. Those were received on the evening of 30 October and the first hastily put together brigade left two days later.[77] Weapons had only recently arrived – the French battalion marching straight to the railroad yard and excitedly tearing open the huge wooden crates containing theirs. 'There were stamps and bills of lading and brand marks on the cases that showed they had made the rounds of the international arms markets; some were in Arabic and one case was branded with the letters IRA,' recalled Bernard Knox. 'They contained American '03 Springfields, the rifle carried by the Doughboys in the Great War.'[78]

There had been little or no time to learn how to use them.[79] Four battalions had been hurriedly formed. This was enough, in theory, for a brigade of around 2,400 men. The Republican Army was now organising itself around so-called 'mixed' brigades that carried rifles and machine guns and often included small cavalry units. Each brigade was given a number, with XI to XV reserved for the internationals – and this first brigade was known as XI International Brigade. Each battalion was organised around one of the main languages of the early Brigaders: German, French, Italian and Polish.[80] They were named, respectively, Edgar André, Commune de Paris, Garibaldi and Dabrowski (or Dombrowski). Those who did not speak those languages were shoehorned into the battalions, forming small 'national' units with a translator. There was no proper brigade staff and only a handful of people who could speak the five languages (including Spanish) necessary to make them gel.[81] 'We calculated that we needed at least another ten to fifteen days to be able to organise them into a brigade,' said Longo. Improvisation and haste, however, were to mark the International Brigades' first few months.

'We left in a kind of rout,' admitted John Sommerfield. 'On the afternoon of our departure we began to get some equipment. Some got extraordinary dark-blue short coats, some ammunition belts, some caps, some vests, some boots, some bayonet frogs, some scarves, some gloves. Everyone got something and no one everything. We marched off looking like a lot of scarecrows, and in filthy tempers.'[82]

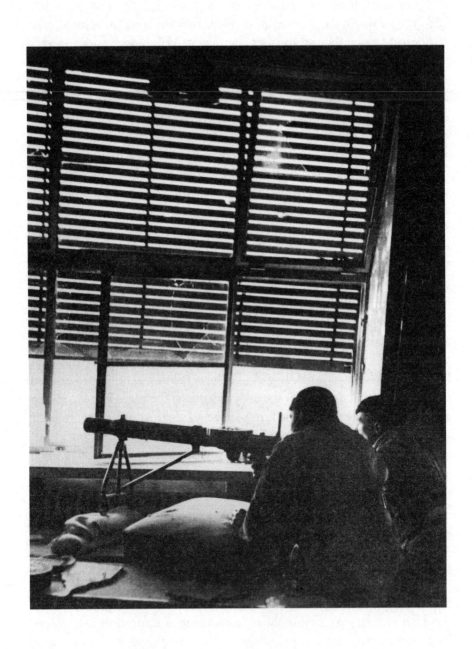

8

The First Brigade: Gran Vía, Madrid, 8 November 1936

On 8 November 1936, Jan Kurzke found himself shivering in the cold dawn at the Mediodía railway station in Madrid's Atocha neighbourhood. The weather was remarkably similar to the damp London mist which had swallowed him up when he had walked towards a tram stop three weeks earlier, wearing a felt hat and carrying a small bag that contained little more than overalls, woollen underwear and a copy of *Hamlet*. The commuters making their way to offices in the City of London could not have suspected he was heading for war. On that occasion, the thirty-one-year-old exiled German painter had kissed goodbye to his girlfriend – artist and sometime model Kate Mangan – who had stood in her dressing gown and watched his departure from the top-storey window of the unfurnished, uncurtained house they had been loaned. He did not yet know it, but at that moment Mangan had vowed that she, too, would go to Spain.

It was a grey morning in Madrid, the drabness made worse by fine, icy drizzle.[1] Even as it prepared to become the hub of a war on this grim Sunday, the city assumed an air of languid acceptance. Cafes slowly filled as people warmed themselves with coffee and *churros*, deep-fried bars of ribbed dough. At the lounge bar of the Hotel Gran Vía, a correspondents' hang-out housed in the block bounded by Madrid's central avenue and the broad Montera street, waiters and a handful of clients were suddenly drawn outside by the noise of shouting and clapping, underscored by the rhythmic beat of marching feet and the clatter of horses' hooves. 'Up the street from the direction of the Ministry of War came a long column of marching men. They wore a kind of khaki corduroy uniform, and loose brown Glengarry caps like those of the British tank corps. They were marching in excellent formation. The tramp, tramp of their boots sounded in perfect unison,' recalled Geoffrey Cox, a young journalist from New Zealand who tumbled out of the hotel to watch them march by. 'Many had scarred tin helmets hanging from their belts. Some were young; others carried themselves like trained, experienced soldiers.'[2] Their uniforms still did not match, but it was clear that this was no ordinary militia unit. Officers were visibly in command, revolvers at their waists.

They clearly were not Spaniards either, but nobody seemed to know who they were or where they had appeared from. People rushed up from side streets or leaned out of windows to cheer. A barman turned to Cox and excitedly proclaimed: 'The Russians have come! The Russians have come!' Some Madrileños wept, convinced that a foreign army had arrived to help, while others up at this early hour shouted 'Salud! Salud!' The soldiers raised a fist and replied in the same manner. 'But when I heard a clipped Prussian voice shout an order in German, followed by other shouts in French and Italian, I knew they were not Russians,' said Cox. 'The International Column of anti-fascists had arrived in Madrid. We were watching the first brigade of what was to develop into the most truly international army the world has seen since the Crusades.'[3]

The Madrid into which the International Brigaders marched that November morning was in dire need of cheer. Seventeen weeks after a failed coup d'état had turned into a vicious, full-blown civil war, the Republican army remained so badly organised that, despite their lack of experience and training, these disciplined foreign troops caused a fine impression. Some thirty-six hours earlier, on 6 November, a long black limousine had slipped out through the gates of the war ministry into the late afternoon gloom, rounded the walled-up and sandbag-covered Cibeles fountain (now sardonically nicknamed 'the Hidden Beauty'[4]) and turned towards the road leading to the eastern coastal city of Valencia. In the back sat Largo Caballero. The Spanish prime minister was fleeing the country's capital,[5] as were the rest of his government and most of the staff and paraphernalia that went with it. Suddenly Madrid, a bureaucratic city par excellence, had no government apparatus, no senior civil servants. All that was left were its people, the refugees

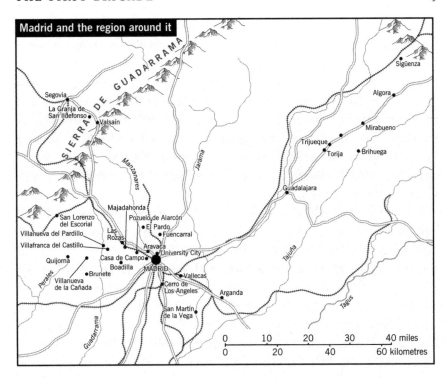

Madrid and the region around it

who had flooded in during the previous weeks, and the soldiers and militiamen whose task was to defend it. Madrid was a city preparing for a siege – or for a defence that many, including Largo Caballero, expected to end swiftly in bloody defeat.

Amongst those to abandon the city was Ludwig Renn, who had been drafted in to write training booklets by the military command and was stopped in the street by the British communist journalist Claud Cockburn, driving an official car.[6] 'Get in!' he shouted. Renn asked where he was going and Cockburn admitted he had no idea. 'Anywhere but Madrid. The city may well be surrounded at any minute,' he answered. When Renn protested, he was informed that these were the orders given by both the government and their Russian advisors. Communist discipline was expected from both of them. He squeezed himself into the car – feeling guilty about leaving – and they drove to Cuenca, spending the night in a town hall lit only by the kind of thin-flamed, clay or metal oil lamps that had existed in Spain for at least ten centuries. General José Asensio, Caballero's undersecretary of war, also left. General José Miaja, a pudgy, balding and bespectacled fifty-eight-year-old who had remained loyal to the government, and General Sebastián Pozas were given two envelopes and ordered not to open them until the morning. They disobeyed, breaking the seals and immediately discovering that their instructions had been placed in the wrong envelopes. Miaja, taking his instructions from Pozas's envelope, was to 'defend the capital all costs'.[7] Pozas, whose brother Gabriel had joined the military uprising, was his superior, but in charge of a wider zone and would prepare a possible retreat eastwards towards Guadalajara or Cuenca.[8]

General Kléber, whose job it was to lead the first group of international volunteers into battle, had been in Madrid for the previous two days, chivvying supplies out of the communist Fifth Regiment. He found the war ministry curiously empty, with just Miaja and his deputy, Lieutenant Colonel Vicente Rojo, in charge of the units that had remained to defend the city. Caballero's departure had confirmed many people's worst fear – that the capital was about to fall. Franco's forces had been drawing ever closer over the previous few days and Madrid had become the first European city ever to sustain prolonged aerial bombardment.[9] German Ju 52s and the infamous Italian 'Black Bird' Capronis[10] were gradually intensifying a bombing campaign that, later in the month, would see them fly up to four sorties every twenty-four hours.[11] Civilians cowered in metro stations; others were killed in their homes or in the street, victims of shrapnel and collapsing buildings. It was a new, unexpected and terrifying side of war – indiscriminate of age, sex, or uniform. Already in this, photography's first major war, the images of gutted homes – spilling mattresses, furniture, children's toys – were appearing in the world's press.

After one night-time bombardment some days later, the *France-Soir* correspondent Louis Delaprée tripped over a dying young woman amid the rubble on the corner of Gran Vía and Alcalá, while 'under a pile of glass, her small, flattened child' lay. He accused his newspaper of not showing nearly enough of the suffering in Madrid because, adding bitterly: 'the massacre of a hundred Spanish children is less interesting than a sigh from the royal tart, Mrs [Wallis] Simpson [whom Edward VIII would soon marry]'.[12] Within a few years, many European newspaper readers would learn from personal experience that this terrifying new threat from the skies was the future of warfare.

Such was the pace of Franco's advance that many press correspondents, especially those following his assault columns, assumed the capital would fall within hours. Some newsrooms believed that this had already happened and the Hearst newspaper group's star foreign correspondent, the orange-haired Hubert Renfro 'Red' Knickerbocker, even filed a description in colourful prose of Franco leading his triumphant troops into Madrid – a barking dog trotting behind them.[13] This was based on reports broadcast by Francoist radio stations in Lisbon and elsewhere. Meanwhile, as the Brigaders marched through the city, the London *Times* was preparing its pages for the following day. The headline on its piece from Spain's capital city read 'Last Hours of Madrid'.[14]

General Kléber was a forty-year-old Red Army veteran with a generous shock of grey-flecked hair, a strong-boned face, thick eyebrows and pinched eyes. He had a bullish look and an impatient, no-nonsense air which, mixed with his unspoken vanity, soon created enemies. A Ukrainian Jew, born Manfred Stern, he, like many men attracted to the International Brigades, grew up within the now-shattered frontiers of the Austro-Hungarian Empire. Kléber was also a distinguished former spy who had worked for Russia's GRU military intelligence in China and the United States (where he had organised the stealing of tank designs). He had passed himself off as a Canadian and travelled to Spain under the guise of a fur dealer,[15] although his English was heavily accented and, as he himself admitted, 'there were a limited number of generals in Canada, and it would hardly seem possible for any of them to be on the side of the communists'.[16] A moderately informed student of European military history might have realised that this nom de guerre was identical to that of one of Napoleon's favourite generals. Kléber had studied medicine in Vienna and then joined the Austro-Hungarian army during the First World War, where he was captured by the Russians and taken to Siberia. Freed after the revolution, he had joined the Bolsheviks and fought with partisans in Mongolia.[17] As a trusted Russian agent, he was then sent to take part in an unsuccessful uprising in Hamburg in 1923, one of several failed attempts to spark a communist revolution across Germany.[18]

Kléber had arrived in Madrid in mid-September 1936, initially to reinforce the Spanish Communist Party's military structure, which was still based around the large and growing Fifth Regiment.[19] Even the

Spaniards were not entirely sure of Kléber's proper identity and he had to pretend that he had never before met the Russian advisors whom he bumped into at the war ministry, where he became one of five senior communists (two of them foreign, including Vital Gayman) assigned to the high command. He seemed both pleased and embarrassed to be given the rank of general, a ruse invented by the Spanish communists in order to convince the war ministry that Kléber was important, experienced and useful. 'This leap upstairs was excessive,' he himself admitted. 'It would have been more fitting to have become a colonel or a major ... But the step had already been taken.'

That did not stop him from proudly sporting a general's hat. Kléber was prone to falling out with superiors and had initially been expected to organise a behind-the-lines guerrilla army,[20] but was otherwise well suited to the task ahead. He battled with the Albacete commanders over the number of battalions he could take to Madrid, eventually losing in a tussle over the Italians – whose original leader, the US-based lawyer Annibale 'Umberto' Galleani, he considered 'a romantic windbag'. Galleani had been replaced by the Italian Republican Randolfo Pacciardi, who insisted on a few more days training and getting to know his troops. Pacciardi was clearly suspicious. 'Who is this Kléber?' he asked. 'They say he is Canadian, yet he speaks Russian. But he is not Russian. And who has made him a general?'[21]

Kléber's new brigade had been meant to take part in a flanking manoeuvre against Franco's approaching forces and, on reaching Madrid two days earlier, after a long, bumpy journey – first by train and then in Russian-made trucks – was deployed around the outlying areas of Vallecas and Vicálvaro.[22] Kurzke, Cornford, Sommerfield and the rest of the group who travelled together from London had all joined a machine-gun unit with the French battalion. They spent a damp, cold, pitch-black first night on the hills above Vallecas waiting for an attack that never happened. The brigade nevertheless suffered its first injury when one man accidentally shot himself.[23] They met retreating Spanish troops in tattered overalls and rope-soled canvas shoes from which their toes poked out, who somehow still found the strength to sing despite being 'wet, shivering, utterly exhausted, huddled together for warmth'.[24] Some of the volunteers looked little better. The Germans and their subsection of Czechs had procured decent khaki uniforms, but the impeccable French commander Jules Dumont deemed his own men distinctly *loqueteux*, or 'ragged'.[25]

While Kurzke and the section of twenty-six mostly English-speaking volunteers (with Bernard Knox as political commissar)[26] tried to puzzle out how to use some antiquated French St Etienne machine guns, Franco was travelling to a country palace just fifteen kilometres away in San José de Valderas. From there, he planned to await the conquest of Madrid.[27] In Seville, Francoist newspapers were boasting that he was a 4.60 peseta taxi ride from the Gran Vía and that he expected to celebrate Sunday Mass in the capital that week. Reviewing the maps of the front lines, Franco could see that the city lay on the western side of a large bulge of Republican land which his troops blocked to the west and north.

In the evening, as they tussled with the machine guns in an oat-strewn farmhouse attic, Kurzke's section was surprised by the arrival of a cape-wearing general (Kléber), who greeted them in American-accented English with a short 'Hullo boys!'[28] Sommerfield idealised men like this, and was easily impressed. 'He was a remarkable-looking man, large, with an easy manner, tremendously strong face, humorous eyes, deep voice, face like a rock; a man that exhaled a sense of power and reliability,' he wrote. They complained about the complex French machine guns, which were famous for breaking down, and asked for more reliable British Lewis guns. Kléber promised to find some and, sure enough, these arrived the following day. It was only after Kléber had left that they found out who they had been speaking to. 'No one knew his nationality or where he had come from: there were only rumours and stories,' Sommerfield recalled.[29]

During his six weeks in Madrid at the start of the war, Kléber had watched with despair as Franco's troops bulldozed their way towards the capital. He blamed Largo Caballero and his military chief José Asensio for the Republican army's failures.[30] Only Franco's determination to capture Toledo, where Civil Guardsmen and others had been holding out in a besieged Alcazar fortress since the July coup, had bought Spain's capital city the time it needed to start digging trenches and erecting barricades. The victory at Toledo finally allowed Franco to claim leadership of the rebel side and he was duly proclaimed its *caudillo* on 1 October.[31] It also gave the Russians time to start sending tanks, planes and other arms to the Republic.[32] Kléber had himself fled Toledo shortly before it fell, driving across the last open bridge with his translator, the elegant, blue-eyed Spanish composer Gustavo Durán, at such a speed that their car tumbled off the road, rolling down an embankment into a vineyard. They scrambled out, bruised and battered but relatively unharmed.[33]

By 7 November, Franco's troops had fought their way into the outer suburbs to the south-west of Madrid. A light Italian Fiat-Ansaldo tank – barely big enough to squeeze two men into and armed only with machine guns – clanked its way into the streets near the baroque Puente de Toledo bridge over the river Manzanares. A counter-attack was launched by the Carabineros, the well-armed former customs force of the finance ministry, who had set up defensive positions behind the bridge's semi-circular stone balconies and the rococo statues of the city's patron saints, Isidoro the Farm Labourer and his wife María de la Cabeza. A soldier crawled up to the tank and hurled grenades to disable its tracks. The crew members were killed. Documents of vital importance were found on the corpse of one of them, Captain Guillermo Vidal-Quadras,[34] including the plan of attack for Madrid over the next few days.

The documents revealed that, far from concentrating on the south, Franco's troops planned to enter from the west, traversing a large, walled expanse of parkland known as the Casa de Campo, crossing the river Manzanares and climbing the steep hillside up to the half-built University City.[35] That same evening, the volunteers found themselves heading towards the train station at Vallecas as a mass of troops and weaponry was shifted across the Spanish capital. As dawn broke and the drizzle stopped, they left the Mediodía railway station at Atocha and began their march up the Gran Vía.[36] A giant poster warned the people of Madrid what would happen to them if Franco's troops entered the city: 'At Badajoz the fascists shot 2,000 people; if they capture Madrid they will shoot half the city.'[37]

While Madrileños were undoubtedly glad to see the 2,100 international volunteers from the three battalions that made up this first version of XI International Brigade, Cox's earlier vivid description exaggerated the enthusiasm of the onlookers that morning. Those who made the march later recalled, variously, that the atmosphere was of sadness, silence and defeat, or that people seemed 'serious-faced' and the city 'muted'.[38] Sommerfield felt that the city folk watched them march by 'like people who go to the theatre to forget some calamity in their own lives'.³⁹ It was, Rebière said, as if they were yet another 'straw plug brought in to stem the flow of water into a ship that had already been ripped open'. He felt proud, nevertheless, of his ragtag outfit, and as his men marched to war he forgave them 'the grudges, the wine, abuses and excesses' of previous days.⁴⁰

Eventually, they reached the edge of the city, close by the unfinished university, with the snow-covered Guadarrama mountains forming a gentle arc in the distance. By now the sun was shining and they trudged along the as-yet unsurfaced roads in University City – a bulky, unfinished showpiece of contemporary architecture – with the Commune de Paris battalion reaching a large, ugly red-brick building. This was the Faculty of Philosophy and Letters, where Kléber was setting up his headquarters. To the west it overlooked, below a steep incline, ploughed fields, the wooded valley of the shallow river Manzanares, and the Casa de Campo.

Once inside the faculty building, the volunteers were struck by the contrast between their own filthiness and 'the richness of panelling and glass, of lifts housed behind ornamental doors, chromium outlined radiators, glistening door knobs, and graceful hanging lights'. There were washrooms with 'shining taps, white tiles, wooden seats, shower-baths, and crystal globes filled with green, translucent liquid soap'.⁴¹ It was only now that the Lewis guns arrived (the French baptised the circular discs that fed ammunition into them 'Camemberts'). It was also when they first heard the deep-throated growl of the Italian Caproni bombers and the 'splitting roar' of exploding bombs dropped close by, shaking the ground and sending blasts of hot air towards them. Those who had not yet felt fear, suddenly found it striking at their guts. Every morning from then on, the bombers passed overhead, dropping their bombs on Madrid and returning calmly until the small, snub-nosed Russian biplanes appeared, buzzing around the lumbering black Capronis as they made their way back to base. Sommerfield recalled seeing one of the latter in flames, before it hit the ground with a 'tremendous roar', and thinking that this, at least, was one less fascist bomber that might eventually target London.⁴²

While most of their comrades fell asleep, Sommerfield and Cornford managed a wash in cold water before they were hurriedly told to form up and then set up their machine guns on the ridge overlooking the Manzanares and, on the far side, the large, walled Casa de Campo park. That morning Franco's troops had entered the park, and were rapidly pushing towards them. After minimal training, and with weapons they did not yet fully understand, the first International Brigade volunteers were about to go into action. Their role was to be front-line shock troops – to attack and be attacked, to kill or be killed. Their main qualification for carrying out this task in a foreign land whose language few of them spoke was the simple, idealistic conviction that they were doing the right thing.

9

No Pasarán: Parque del Oeste, Madrid,
9 November 1936

The damp soaked into the men's boots. Across from the Republican trenches, on the other side of the Manzanares, lay a narrow stretch of land bordered by a flint and stone wall. Built in the eighteenth century around the old royal hunting ground of the Casa de Campo, this seven-foot-high wall was punctured at intervals by broad metal gates. Somewhere beyond that was the enemy, though exactly where they did not know.[1] On the day that they arrived Rebière estimated they were still four or five kilometres away, but the shells that greeted them on their first morning – showering them with earth – proved that Franco's forces were getting closer. The Republicans' forward lines were inside the park itself, manned by Spanish units.[2]

Behind their positions lay the university buildings and, looming at the top of the hill on the edge of town, the imposing bulk of the Modelo prison on the corner of Moncloa Square, where hundreds of pro-Francoist army officers and supporters were being held.[3] Both sides now knew that this was the most important sector of the front, as the legionnaires and Moroccans pushed through the park towards the final barrier that blocked them from the city itself, the shallow river Manzanares. The untried troops of this first International Brigade had been given the task of helping to defend the exact stretch where Franco wanted his men to cross. This began in the parkland on either side of the railway crossing at the Puente de los Franceses (and, beside it, the low Puente Nuevo road bridge) and stretched north to the road crossing at the Puente de San Fernando.[4]

The first enemy attempt to cross the river happened sooner than expected. By early morning on 9 November, and apparently confused about their orders, one of the companies of the Edgar André Battalion had placed itself close to the river in the Parque del Oeste, or West Park. This was a mixed company of Hungarians, Yugoslavs and others who did not fit into the otherwise German-speaking parts of the brigade.[5] The frightened volunteers mostly had no idea where the enemy was, or where the bullets that whistled around at intervals might have come from. Much of that shooting came from their own side. Shrubs and bushes took on ominous shapes in the dark – and were often shot at.[6]

As another grey, misty dawn broke and enemy shells flew through the branches of the trees above them in the park, the Hungarians spotted a unit of Moroccan troops (who often wore red fez hats, or turbans) gathered on the far side of the river. With no orders to follow, but an obvious desire for action, the Hungarians' commander told them to charge down the hill and wade across the river by the railway bridge.[7] On the far bank, however, they ran straight into a wall of machine-gun fire and retreated quickly. The Moroccans charged after them across the Manzanares, wading through the thigh-high water as the Brigaders fled over the railway tracks on the narrow valley floor into the steeply inclined West Park.[8] Madrid's first streets lay a few hundred metres away up the hill, and it was around here that the fleeing Edgar André volunteers encountered Spanish Republican militiamen.[9] A momentary stand-off saw both sets of Republicans wondering whether the other was friend or foe – a judgement made more difficult by language and the fact that both sides in the war wore identical helmets. Then the Moroccans appeared.

The inexperienced Brigaders and their equally novice Spanish comrades appear to have left large gaps between their sections, allowing some of the attackers through. Equipment and organisation failed them. Machine guns jammed after firing just fifteen to thirty rounds and there were no hand grenades. The First World War Remington rifles also jammed: volunteers spent as much time struggling to loosen the bolts as actually firing. 'It is despairing to pull the trigger but realise that you haven't shot … The comrades' gestures showed profound consternation and impotence,' recalled one of those present.[10] With no telephones and runners often disorientated or injured, commanders lost control and small groups of men had to make their own plans.[11] With their clandestine and revolutionary street-fighting pasts in Germany,

Austria or Hungary, this came naturally to some volunteers. Confusion, nevertheless, reigned.[12]

To the Spaniards, however, these international volunteers already seemed special. Rafael Bañuls, a young Spanish militiaman who reached the West Park later that morning with a group whose officers had abandoned them, recalled being greeted by an International Brigade lieutenant who wept with joy and shouted '*¡Avanti camaradas!*', mixing up Italian and Spanish. 'Those men in their thick corduroy uniforms seemed bigger than us,' Bañuls recalled. 'They were close to being overrun and we were reinforcements that they didn't expect.'[13] With their short training, few hours of fighting and smattering of First World War veterans, the Brigaders were already more experienced than Bañuls's unit. This was a war where most soldiers on the Republican side, including the Brigaders, learned only as they fought. Many did not even know when, or how, to take cover. 'We were like a pack of wild animals, with no one in command,' recalled Bañuls. 'Fortunately, the *Internacionales* made us hit the ground.'[14]

What happened next remains confusing. As the attackers crossed the West Park, the Spanish militia unit that was defending the rail and road bridges failed to detonate the charges designed to blow them up – leaving a potentially clear path for any tanks and other vehicles to cross. A handful of Francoist soldiers appear to have made it into the city streets, reaching as far as the corner of Princesa and Marqués de Urquijo streets, just 800 metres from the start of the central Gran Vía.[15] At some stage a tank clanked noisily towards the square before stopping beside a fire engine that was fighting a blaze in a bombed school building on Princesa Street, where artillery shells and bombing raids were causing damage, and then turned back. Nobody knew which side it belonged to, but it was just a few hundred metres from the Plaza de España.[16]

Panic, meanwhile, was spreading up the Gran Vía. Miaja and his staff bolted from the war ministry, fearing that a section of the city was about to fall. Some attackers appear to have been aiming for the Modelo prison, where they probably hoped to free the hundreds of pro-Francoist officers.[17] Rumours spread of ordinary Madrileños arming themselves with sharpened knives and, in imitation of their forebears who turned on Napoleon's occupying troops to start the Peninsula Wars in 1808, killing at least one of the small number of Moroccan soldiers who had reached the outskirts of the Argüelles neighbourhood. Perhaps they, or the rumour-mongers, were inspired by slogans placed in newspapers which urged: 'People of Madrid. However high the sacrifice, we must prevent the mercenaries and professional assassins from satisfying their base instincts and savage lust with our wives and daughters.'[18]

At the headquarters of the Motorised Brigade – a group of leather-clad socialist motorcyclists whose low-slung Harley Davidsons and other motorbikes were based in the Plaza de Chamberí – a panicked messenger rushed in carrying, incongruously, a piglet under his arm. 'They're in the Calle de Ferraz,' he shouted. This street ran parallel to the West Park, just one block away from it. 'I didn't know what to do. If they'd given me a machine gun I would have used it,' said Victoria Román, a student who was working there. 'Everything was obliterated except a passionate desire to defend the city.'[19]

In the West Park itself, however, the tide had already turned. As the Moroccan troops prepared to push forwards again, the volunteers once more acted on instinct, adrenaline and a pent-up desire for battle. Nobody was issuing orders, but parts of the remaining two companies of the Edgar André suddenly stood up and charged down the hill, accompanied by some Spaniards. It was a moment of collective madness. 'We were all suddenly possessed by the same drunken spirit,' recalled one of them.[20] As the only political commissar present, and the closest thing this group had to a commander, the German volunteer Fritz Rettmann was amazed – reflecting later that there is nothing more foolish than to charge an enemy whose condition and strength are unknown. He knew, however, that he could not stop them. 'All you can do is jump up in the same fashion, put yourself in front of them and rush forwards,' he reflected.[21]

The Moroccans were even more surprised by this impromptu attack, and they now turned and fled into a cluster of buildings on the other side of the Manzanares. The ragtag group of volunteers and Spaniards crossed the river in pursuit. Later that day, however, it became clear that they risked being marooned on the far bank and orders arrived for them to turn around and cross the Manzanares again. Rettmann had to cajole the proud Spaniards, who were determined to stay. As night fell and the enemy set up machine guns to cover the railway bridge and the low Puente Nuevo road bridge beside it, the last men waded back through the cold water, before hastily digging themselves foxholes and falling, exhausted, into them.[22]

The first seven men to die in the uniform of the International Brigades fell during that rush across the Manzanares and in the fighting around the Puente de los Franceses, the Puente Nuevo road bridge and in the West Park.[23] They were a typical mixture of the political exiles who made up most of the early recruits – four Hungarians, a Greek, a Yugoslav and one of a number of volunteers who were deemed 'stateless'.[24] Most had given home addresses in France. Another four men – including a Belgian and two Spaniards who had joined the Edgar André Battalion – died over the same period in the Casa de Campo, perhaps on a patrol. A further thirty-six men, mostly Hungarians, were injured, meaning that a good part of one of the battalion's four companies had been put out of action within forty-eight hours of their arrival.[25] They had contributed to a vital moment in the defence of Madrid. It was, after all, one thing for the enemy to be driving through the poor, less densely populated outskirts across the Manzanares – as it had over the previous few days – and quite another for it to be fighting below the balconies of people living just up the street from the Plaza de España. Chicote's cocktail bar and the Hotel Gran Vía, where correspondents stayed, were little more than a twenty-minute walk away.

Yet the attackers had been driven back. The International Brigades and several equally inexperienced Spanish brigades had arrived just in time. Franco's troops, used to rolling straight through poorly prepared militia groups, had discovered over the previous days that Madrid's defenders were far better organised and more tenacious. This first International Brigade was made up of men who had only reached Albacete two or three weeks earlier and were still learning, but they had proved their worth. As tales began to spread and propagandists stepped in to magnify these achievements, a legend was born. The *brigadistas* were the saviours of Madrid. They were the men who had delivered on La Pasionaria's famous, fist-raised pledge of '¡*No Pasarán!*' – 'They shall not pass!'

This was not really true, given that the people of Madrid and Republican units who had come here from as far away as northern Asturias were doing most of the fighting. It was, however, not completely false either. Franco's advance units had momentarily breached the great defensive line of Madrid along the river, but they had been thrown back. That had happened in the sector defended, in part, by the International Brigades. It had taken just forty-eight hours for them to be proclaimed Madrid's heroes.

10

Death in the Park: Casa de Campo, November 1936

The Casa de Campo's seventeen square kilometres of rolling, rustic terrain was punctuated by the occasional man-made lake, ornamental pavilion, farmhouse, lodge or labourer's hut, but was mostly covered in holm oaks, pines and thick clumps of evergreen rockrose, broom and gorse. To one English volunteer it was like 'the bare parts of Sussex, only wilder and without houses'.[1] Patrols and counter-patrols wandered through it, including those sent in by Kléber as soon as the Brigaders arrived.[2] Small detachments of a half-a-dozen men sat – alone, alert and frightened – waiting for something to happen, shooting at their own shadows. Some regular soldiers of the Republican army still wore the same uniforms as their opponents, bringing occasional mix-ups.[3] Snipers climbed trees and waited silently for targets to walk into sight. The stealthy troops of Franco's Army of Africa were especially feared. Led by Moroccans and legionnaires, these forces soon occupied a thick wedge of parkland, with the blunt point almost touching the river Manzanares.[4] As the first Brigaders took up positions, panic broke out just five kilometres across the river in the town of Pozuelo after a false sighting of Moroccan cavalry.[5]

It was into this hunting ground that, on 10 November, Kléber was ordered to send a company of men on the volunteers' first major attacking sortie,[6] joining a Spanish unit that set out from Húmera, a village across the river on the far side of the park. It became, in the words of the veteran French battalion commander Jules Dumont, 'a veritable disaster'. A company of 115 men, led by a hard-drinking, old-fashioned but experienced French officer called Lieutenant Blanche, sneaked through one of the perimeter wall's metal gates at 2 a.m. The Brigaders were warned to watch out for green or white turbans and soon captured two Moroccan sentries, but then let one escape – who sounded the alarm. Instead of withdrawing before enemy reinforcements arrived, Blanche chose to make a stand and when the entire company eventually tried to retreat through the same narrow gate they were mown down by a single machine gun. A former Spanish bullfighter known as Chaparro ferried twenty-three of the dead and injured back after his fellow stretch-bearer was shot in the head. Blanche had taken with him a group of four machine-gunners from the English section. Only one, a veteran of colonial campaigns in Asia called Joe Hinks, survived, firing his heavy Lewis gun from the hip and then lying hidden under a mound of fallen leaves for several hours.[7] Blanche was one of the fourteen dead. All the platoon commanders were put out of action and the fifty-four uninjured survivors had to be sent back to the faculty building to recover and reorganise.[8] Rebière blamed Blanche and 'the *eau-de-vie* he drank to give him courage'.[9]

As Franco's troops settled into their part of the park, Miaja sent the Brigaders to counter-attack and join the flanking moves designed to cut the advancing enemy units off from their rearguard on 13 November. First the Poles, and then the whole battalion were thrown into the attacks. The former were badly mauled and many Brigaders now experienced their first sight of dead or seriously wounded comrades. Fear, as a result, began to seep through the ranks. That night Kurzke heard someone near him shout in pain and start crying. 'I asked who it was but nobody knew,' he said. 'We heard later that is one of our gun crew who had shot himself through the hand by holding it in front of his rifle.'[10] Such self-mutilation (known as 'Blighty wounds' to British troops) had been a common feature of the First World War, since it guaranteed a trip away from the front line to hospital. It was another way of running away.

Perhaps this was also the moment when a pro-Francoist journalist, Víctor Ruiz, who wrote under the name El Tebib Arrumi, claimed to have spotted two Moroccan soldiers picking through the bodies of the dead for booty. The fallen Spanish militiamen 'had nothing on them but lice', while the 'large, well-built men' and the 'round-faced blonds' of the International Brigades provided much better fare.[11] José María Permán, a Falangist poet with a rich imagination, claimed to have witnessed the Casa de Campo 'covered with the corpses of Russian, Jews and Senegalese'. It was proof, he said, that the savage peoples of Asia were on their way. 'Once again the barbarians, once again the attack from the East.'[12]

Republican attempts to push the enemy back out of the Casa de Campo all failed, not least because Franco's forces occupied the Garabitas Hill, which overlooked the rest of the park and gave a clear view of University City and the western fringes of Madrid, including the Royal Palace. Pinned back by artillery fire, the French battalion's commander Dumont watched from the top of an abandoned windmill as a huge build-up of enemy troops took place in the distance. Franco clearly remained convinced that this was the best route into the city.

The brigade was still in, or on the edge of, the Casa de Campo park on 15 November. It was preparing for a new attack – to be led by the famous anarchist Buenaventura Durruti, who had arrived with his troops at the same time as a column of Catalan socialists and communists – when news arrived of a disaster. While Durruti and the Catalans had been preparing to launch their offensive from University City, they had been surprised by a Francoist assault. Durruti's troops either had not occupied, or did not know how to hold, the defensive trenches that the International Brigaders had helped dig and handed over to them.[13] The Durruti anarchists had come from the more leisurely Aragonese front and were not used to the intense warfare with heavy bombardments and close-up firefights that was becoming the norm around Madrid. Nor had they come across the experienced and professional Army of Africa before.

Even then, the Francoist attack almost stalled. It was not until late in the afternoon, after several failed attempts to cross the Manzanares, that the task of making a breakthrough was given to the most senior Moroccan officer in the Army of Africa, Comandante Mohammed Ben Mizzian. *New York Herald Tribune* correspondent John T. Whitaker had previously witnessed him handing two, supposedly leftist, young women over to a group of forty of his men in Navalcarnero and predicting they would survive only a few hours. Once again, militarily, it was the Moroccans who tipped the balance as first one unit, and then several more, waded across and fought their way into the nearest buildings in the university campus.[14] Darkness and the next day's mist allowed more of Franco's men to cross and their progress was mapped in the names of the faculty buildings they took, starting that day with Architecture, Agriculture and two other key buildings – a former, two-storey country palace with an attached model farm, known as the Palacete, and an elegant, turreted French cultural centre, the Casa de Velázquez.[15]

The Brigaders had been busily stocking up on cigarettes and brandy during what was meant to be a short rest in nearby Aravaca, but were suddenly bundled into trucks and ordered back to help contain the advance.[16] In a swift manoeuvre, they retook the lightly defended Philosophy Faculty and began a drawn-out, floor-by-floor fight for the nearby medical faculties, though by now other parts of the campus were lost.[17] At times the fighting was fierce, with bayonets fixed. Opposing fighters found themselves in neighbouring classrooms or lecture halls. Pickaxes were used to open holes in walls so that rooms could be quickly sprayed with machine-gun fire. Grenades with their pins pulled were sent up to other floors in the lifts. One group of Moroccan soldiers was later found dead in a laboratory where it was assumed they had eaten rabbits and other animals that were being used for experiments with poisons.[18]

For the next week, this two-square-kilometre wedge of ground became the most important spot in the defence of Madrid and, hence, the war. This was Franco's bridgehead. The Republicans needed to either drive Franco's men back across the river or make this small patch of land at the gates of Madrid unserviceable as a point from which to organise the capture of the city itself – else, the Spanish capital would be lost. Many felt that was inevitable. From the safety of Valencia, Largo Caballero was already proclaiming that Madrid was not so important and that it would be a morale-boosting, rather than strategic, victory for Franco if he took it.[19] Much would depend on how the volunteers fought over the coming days.

11

Bulletproof Books: University City, Madrid, November 1936

The fourth-floor library of the Philosophy Faculty was new and, as yet, the tomes that lined its shelves remained unused – at least in this building, where nobody had ever attended a lecture. Jan Kurzke and his band of intellectual machine-gunners searched for sandbags to protect their positions, but failed to find them. Instead, they found a new use for the thick, learned volumes on the library shelves.

The large glass windows of the building had long been knocked out and the south-facing rooms were in sight of the snipers. So now the thickest volumes in the library were taken out and stacked along the windowsills. 'They were better than sand-bags. We packed them tight against each other in double rows. The Maxim [machine gun] was put on the table in front of the first window with books on both sides to protect the men who were feeding the gun ...,' Kurzke recalled. 'Quantity came before quality. The small volumes were found to be too light. A prolific writer was preferred because he filled a large, heavy volume which did not crumple before a bullet.'[1] Indian metaphysics and early nineteenth-century German philosophy proved the densest of all. 'They protected us well; those old, wise men, with their long beards and busy pens,' he added.[2] After studying the impact of snipers' bullets on the books, they discovered that these rarely got past page 350 and began to believe the old stories about soldiers' lives being saved by Bibles in shirt pockets.[3]

Days were bright but cold and nights were freezing – framed by spectacular sunsets and dawns on the snow-clad sierras.[4] Nevertheless this, for now, was a relatively comfortable form of warfare. The enemy was some 600 metres away and, except when its artillery targeted them, fairly innocuous.[5] The sniping on both sides was largely ineffectual and the machine-gun company decorated the walls of the room it occupied with posters they found of Segovia's cathedral and one inviting visitors to 'Sunny Spain!' These former pacifists were already discovering a certain frisson in the anonymous killing of the enemy. 'There was a movement and you fired and the movement stopped: you felt a momentary thrill of accomplishment, but it was impersonal, clay-pigeon shooting; you did not think that you were making widows and orphans, robbing mothers of their children,' said one of the company.[6] 'I think I killed a fascist,' an excited Cornford, formerly the proud member of an anti-war committee,[7] wrote to his scholarly girlfriend, Margot Heinemann. 'Fifteen or sixteen of them were running from a bombardment. I and two Frenchmen were firing from our barricade with the sights at 90: We got one, and both said it was I that hit him ..., though I couldn't be sure. If it is true, it's a fluke.'[8] Two donkeys ignored the firing and wandered backwards and forwards, grazing on the grass until one of them was killed by jittery night-time sentries who imagined they were under attack. The battalion cook sneaked out, retrieved the animal's corpse and served it for lunch.

While this atypical group of volunteers reviewed the great classical tomes, pored over illustrations of Goya and Velázquez, and found themselves engrossed in Shakespeare or Wordsworth, the occasional bullet found its way harmlessly into the wall above them. They did not know that the worst danger lay in their own lines, where artillery units fired shells that often behaved erratically. One of these hit their room. It spattered the walls with shrapnel but, miraculously, did not kill anyone. Shaken young French volunteers trembled and wept. Several of the wounded had been taken to hospital before an apologetic German volunteer artillery officer appeared. 'I hope nobody has been killed,' he told Kurzke. 'We have a lot of old ammunition and the timing is very bad.' Kurzke wanted to know why the International Brigades had not been provided with their own artillery unit yet. 'Hell knows,' the German replied. 'Everything is made difficult and I don't know who is responsible, I think it's Miaja, but you can't say it aloud. They are afraid the [International] Brigade is getting too influential. They don't like the Fifth Regiment [with whom the Brigade was intimately associated] because it's communist.'[9]

It was a truism of twentieth-century warfare that the soldiers at the front often knew less about the progress of war than newspaper readers or radio audiences sitting comfortably in their armchairs at home. In fact, the Brigades were just beginning to obtain their own small artillery weapons – even if few people knew how to use them. With the front line just a short, five-*céntimo* tram-ride away from the city centre, however, it was not difficult to find Spanish recruits with a knowledge of mathematics who could be trained up quickly.

Madrid schoolteacher José Mera had been called up by his trade union to join a group of teachers, university lecturers and school porters who, as Franco's forces threatened the city, gathered in a building on the grand Castellana boulevard without weapons. Only the sound of the number 8 tram ringing its bell the next morning reassured him that Franco's men had not yet broken through. Setting out for the front in his raincoat, collar and tie, with a blanket under his arm, Mera bumped into a doctor friend whose knowledge of mathematics had seen him put in charge of the artillery battery now attached to Jules Dumont's battalion. He had persuaded Mera to join him, and a short while later he was with the International Brigades as one of the first of its Spanish recruits. The young teacher had been upset by the random murders by anarchist gangs of alleged enemies of the Republic (whose bodies Rebière saw daily in the city's parks, convinced that they included 'good companions ... victims of the hatred between parties that divides and weakens poor Spain').[10] He would have been even more upset if he had known that groups of prisoners were being taken out almost daily from the Modelo prison, which was clearly visible from University City, and murdered on the outskirts of town. Mera was impressed by the volunteers, however. 'I saw them lying in the rain night and day, completely silent, just waiting for the enemy. All of us who had suffered from the lack of discipline on our side and from the ghastly assassinations, who had become convinced that a war couldn't be won like that, saw in the Brigaders what a real army should be like.'[11]

From their spot in the Philosophy building on the north side of the Francoist pocket, the machine-gun crew and a company of the French battalion had a privileged view of the fighting that raged over the coming days. A few hundred metres separated their comparatively safe berth from the ferocious fighting into which the other two battalions – Polish and German – were plunged as they tried to force their way

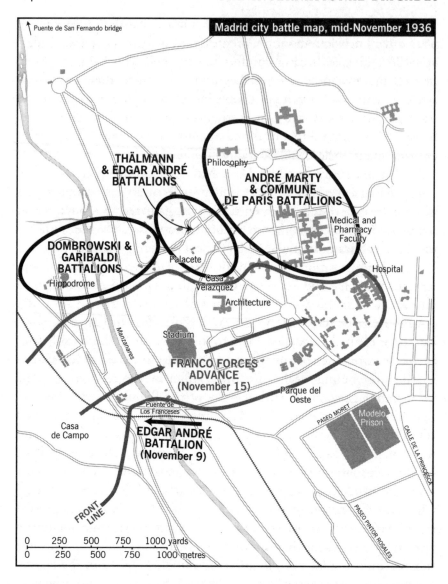

↑ Puente de San Fernando bridge

Madrid city battle map, mid-November 1936

THÄLMANN
& EDGAR ANDRÉ
BATTALIONS

Philosophy

ANDRÉ MARTY
& COMMUNE
DE PARIS BATTALIONS

Medical and
Pharmacy
Faculty

DOMBROWSKI &
GARIBALDI
BATTALIONS

Palacete

Hospital

Hippodrome

Casa
Velázquez

Architecture

Manzanares

Stadium

FRANCO FORCES
ADVANCE
(November 15)

Parque del
Oeste

Puente de
Los Franceses

Casa
de Campo

EDGAR ANDRÉ
BATTALION
(November 9)

PASEO MORET

Modelo
Prison

CALLE DE LA PRINCESA

FRONT
LINE

PASEO PINTOR ROSALES

0	250	500	750	1000 yards
0	250	500	750	1000 metres

south towards the Puente de los Franceses railway bridge. Their field of combat was the narrow valley floor and the steep stretch of land leading up to the main university complex. If they could reach the bridge, which lay just over a kilometre away, then the enemy forces on this side of the river would be cut off and could, eventually, be captured.[12]

Francoist forces had taken and occupied Casa Velázquez, the elegant, twin-turreted mansion that had served as the French cultural centre, which was now targeted with incendiary shells, lighting up the night as it burned to a shell.[13] All the modern campus buildings were shelled by one side or another, but new building techniques seemed to make them virtually indestructible. 'I saw the walls crumbling ... but the structure was steel and the floors were strengthened with steel mesh,' Kurzke said after the Medical Faculty had been shelled. 'After months and even years of bombardment the structure still remained, though nothing else was left, and in the ground floors and cellars of the skeletons, men were still living and fighting.'[14]

At the Palacete model farm, starving livestock bellowed and screeched in fright as German and Polish volunteers attacked, were thrown back and counter-attacked. The front line moved backwards and forwards a mere 300 metres as barns, outhouses and the main building itself – or parts of it – changed hands continuously. The elegant salons and grand sweeping staircase inside the palace were slowly destroyed. Entire sections of men were all but wiped out as they either attacked the building, or tried to hold it against the Moroccans and legionnaires. Franco's small German and Italian tanks created havoc, driving into the buildings and machine-gunning anyone in their way. With no anti-tank weapons, Brigaders were forced to improvise, trying to stop them with primitive Molotov cocktails or by crawling up to them and throwing grenades, sticks of dynamite or even iron bars into their tracks.[15] The cannon on the Russian T-26 tanks – which had arrived a few weeks earlier and were still mostly driven by Red Army soldiers – were far more potent, but rarely available.[16]

In actions which saw relatively small groups of volunteers pitted against a handful of attackers, acts of personal bravery often made a considerable difference. Communists claimed that the ideological convictions of the men made them better fighters. This was more than just vacuous propaganda. Although some volunteers were adventure-seekers, conviction of some kind had brought most to Spain. Hardcore communists, raised on tales of workers' bravery during the Russian revolution, were sometimes courageous to the point of suicidal. Otto Stank, a German volunteer, was one such example. His extraordinary behaviour during a fight over one of the Palacete farm buildings was both brave and foolish but, most importantly in a fight involving relatively few men, it was also inspiring for his comrades. With his unit pinned down, Stank rushed at the enemy tanks, hurling Molotov cocktails. After the tanks turned around, he had then stepped out to hurl insults at them. 'He couldn't control himself any more. He cursed the fascists,' one of his comrades recalled. 'He said: "You rogues, you cowardly dogs, come on!" Then they turned their weapons around and shot at Otto. Otto was blinded for life.'[17]

Despite the injuries he sustained in this moment of battle-madness, Stank encouraged his colleagues on, lying in a corner of the farm building loudly singing 'The Internationale'. This stirred his men into continuing the fight, though he may also have been trying to protect his own life as they had already agreed to shoot him themselves if the Army of Africa troops – who had a reputation for hacking off the genitals of living men – overran them.[18] Singing was, at least, a way of proving that he was not so badly injured that he needed to be put out of his misery.

The number of dead and injured climbed alarmingly. In one attack all but six out of a section of thirty-six Balkan volunteers from the Dombrowski Battalion were killed or wounded, while the company commander appointed the previous day – a French speaker called Vernier who Kléber described as 'bourgeois, but an honest anti-fascist' and known only to his men as André – shot himself through the head. He had been in Spain for just three days.[19] The International Brigades still did not yet have a full record of their own volunteers and he was one of many anonymous victims in the early fighting.

Again, the German artillery officer told Kurzke that this level of casualties could not be normal. He had been through the entire First World War, including the Battle of Verdun, which had been one of the most senseless and bloodiest slaughters in history. Many of the Brigaders in the French- and German-speaking battalions had been on opposing sides in that war. Two such veterans were battalion commanders Jules Dumont and the Edgar André's Hans Kahle, who had lain in trenches across from one another near the infamous Dead Man's Hill at Verdun.[20] 'This is slaughter in comparison … There is something very wrong here,' the artillery officer said.[21] Senseless losses, the volunteers had been repeatedly told in Albacete, would be avoided by virtue of their good discipline and training. It was turning out not to be true. Some wondered whether the Spanish high command thought of them as disposable – a group of lunatics, radicals, or both, whose loss would not provoke problems amongst the rest of the army or amongst the populace. 'There was Verdun, but I never had this feeling of being doomed,' said Kahle. 'I am afraid I'm getting very sentimental, but you shake hands with comrades in the morning and they are dead before the evening.'[22][23]

12

A New Brigade: Albacete, Chinchón, Cerro de los Angeles, 9 November 1936

On the same day that the first International Brigade was marching up Madrid's Gran Vía, those in charge at Albacete were trying to obey an order that left them flabbergasted. They were to send a second brigade to the capital immediately. They did not have one. A brigade was meant to have three or four battalions of 600 men each, organised into companies and sections, with various supporting units and officers or non-commissioned officers in charge of each of them. The Italian battalion that Kléber had wanted to take with him was the only one to have been properly organised. Two others were being formed – a second German battalion, which followed the now well-established pattern of naming itself after Ernst Thälmann, and another one named after André Marty himself that was mostly made up of Belgians and French. Half the men in these last two battalions had only arrived over the previous forty-eight hours. Arms and uniforms had not been distributed and basics such as kitchens and transport were not ready.[1]

After the rapid departure of the previous brigade, Marty and his staff had decided that in future everything must be done more calmly and carefully. 'Not even four days had gone by ... since we solemnly pledged that we wouldn't allow another brigade to go until it was perfectly trained and prepared,' recalled Longo, who demanded that he be allowed to go with the Italians as their commissar.[2] 'Everything was improvised in even more of a rush and amid greater confusion than the previous time.'[3] Ludwig Renn arrived from Madrid that morning and was immediately told that he was in command of the German battalion. This still had no company commanders and was actually only half German, with many men speaking no German at all. They included a company of Poles, another of Yugoslavs, Bulgarians, Turks, Greeks and Armenians and small sections of Hungarians, Flemish and English speakers.[4] The medical unit spoke French.

Winston Churchill's rebellious nephew, Esmond Romilly, initially attached himself to a group of fourteen White Russians from Paris. Overall, the International Brigaders were an ethnically diverse group for their time – including everyone from Syrians and Armenians to Chinese and semi-indigenous South Americans – but these, the White Russians, were possibly the most incongruous recruits to the Brigades.[5] They or their families had fought against communism, gone into exile and now sought a way to get home. Membership of the Brigades, they explained to Romilly, was one of the few ways that could be achieved, which was why more than 250 volunteered to fight in Spain.[6] They were mostly middle-aged, taciturn men, often given to drink and nostalgia – and they received Romilly, one of the few native English speakers to have arrived at the International Brigades HQ, with warmth.

While the various national groups attempted to march or do physical exercises to get fit, Romilly found himself 'in an almost hysterical state of giggles' as his uncoordinated Russian comrades 'panted and heaved and sweated … like pieces of rusty old machinery'.[7] Eventually, he came across a group of a dozen or so English speakers – mostly British, but including some Irishmen, an American, an Australian tramp, and a man with six passports, five languages and few front teeth who appeared to be Latvian.[8] Some of these men were originally from the English-speaking Tom Mann Centuria, raised with the help of Tom Wintringham, which had spent the previous few weeks in Barcelona, waiting for somewhere to go. Since both the French and Germans were forming battalions, the English-speaking group voted to join the Germans, who now included veterans from the Thälmann Centuria on the Aragon front.[9] Together with a dozen Flemings and a handful of Germans, they now formed a thirty-man *Zug*, as the Germans called their platoons, led by a gangster-faced Prussian known as Paul.[10]

The last recruits to be incorporated into this new brigade arrived the day before the unit disembarked.[11] These men were hurriedly lined up and a loud voice called for those who had attended military schools – a common option for middle-class sons in the fractured remains of the Austro-Hungarian Empire – to come forward. Hours later a thirty-one-year-old Russian called Alexei Eisner found himself automatically stepping out on his left foot and swinging his arms as he marched through the muddy field, counting forty paces in French, towards the imposing figures of André Marty and Vidal. He knew how to march because he had been forced to enter a military academy in Sarajevo after his stepfather removed the family from revolutionary Russia when Eisner was fourteen.[12]

'Are you German?' asked Vidal.

'No, I'm Russian,' Alexei answered.

'You have to say that you are *White* Russian!' said Vidal menacingly.

Eisner was furious. 'I'm too young to be a White Russian,' he remonstrated.

Vidal ignored the reply. 'Birthplace?' he asked.

'Saint Petersburg.'

When Eisner added that he was now thirty-one years old, Vidal told him that he did not seem serious enough to be that old. 'Make him a platoon commander!' he shouted to someone standing behind him.[13]

As one of the shortest officers in his mostly Polish company, Eisner found himself given a dozen of the smallest men for his platoon. Eleven of his unit identified themselves as Jews. Most were originally from Poland, but were now studying in Belgium or working as artisans in Paris. Only two had ever fired a weapon. Unlike Eisner, who nevertheless dreamed of returning to his native Russia, most were communists.

That same afternoon the new brigade was equipped with khaki coats, blankets, rifles, belts, boots, socks, plates, knives, spoons and 'every sort of underwear'.[14] The corduroy trousers came in one size – extra large – requiring some people to hack off the leg ends. Then the men were told to pack their bags, because they were to move on that evening. Eisner assumed this meant they were being taken to a training ground, but his political commissar admitted that they were heading straight for the battlefront in Madrid. There was no time for training. They would have to learn as they fought. That, the commissar lied, was the most efficient way anyway. When Eisner asked whether it was really wise to take a group of largely untrained men straight to the front, he was publicly bawled out. If some people didn't know how to shoot, that was their fault! Didn't he know that they had come to Spain to fight, rather than to train? Or that the best soldiers were not those who had trained, but those whose political motivations were purest? Eisner controlled his anger. 'I realised that this desperate reply meant that, deep down, he felt pretty much the same as I did,' he wrote. The commander of the brigade's French-speaking battalion, Captain Yves Le Goux, was so vociferously forthright in the same opinion that Marty had him arrested. He had held his job for just two hours.[15]

After supper the brigade marched out into a courtyard and Eisner studied his platoon, which was dwarfed by giant Germans and Poles. 'None of them knows how to shoot,' he thought. 'How will we react under fire?' Marty stood looking out at the 1,500 or so men with his large Basque beret slanting backwards on his head. 'I know that you are not all properly trained to fight at the front,' he said. 'Anyone who feels unsure of himself can step out. You won't be accused of weaknesses. You can join the next brigade to leave.' Nobody moved.[16]

Marty then introduced them to an elegantly dressed officer with blond hair and grey-blue eyes, wearing a carefully pressed huntsman's suit and long, shiny boots. 'He seemed only to be lacking a Tirolese hat with a feather sticking out of it in order to complete the picture of an Austrian landowner preparing for a pheasant shoot,' recalled Eisner. The same man had aroused the curiosity (and suspicions) of other volunteers when he boarded the first-class section of a train in France wearing a fitted grey jacket and striped woollen tie fastened into place with a pearl pin, with a smart gabardine over his arm. When they reached Port Bou, however, the man was greeted effusively by a woman wearing a distinctive Ukrainian-style embroidered linen dress and a small pistol hanging from her belt. The awed volunteers recognised her as none other than the Russian journalist Elisabeta Ratmanova, wife of the famous writer Mikhail Koltsov.[17]

The dapper officer with the trimmed moustache rapidly won their respect, not least because Marty introduced him as 'the Hungarian revolutionary general Paul Lukács'. 'It was not common to meet revolutionaries who were generals, or generals who were revolutionaries,' said Eisner.[18] Nobody had ever heard of him. In fact, as only Renn and a few others knew, this was really Máté Zalka, a Hungarian who (like Kléber) had turned communist after being captured by the Russians during the First World War. An innkeeper's son, and born Bela Frankl, Zalka had fought for the Bolsheviks and become a writer – taking his nom de plume from the town of Mátészalka.[19] He already had experience of organising foreign volunteer units, having led the section of his prisoner-of-war camp which decided to join the Russian revolution. He had also run a Moscow theatre and been a trusted diplomatic courier.[20] First in German and then in Russian, Lukács told them he was proud to command their brigade, adding that both artillery and cavalry units would join them soon.[21] Most of his troops spoke Italian, French or Polish, and did not understand him, but just the sound of Russian – the language of romance, revolution and resistance – was inspiring to many.

That night the new brigade marched to the railway station, spent a sleepless night on the train and waited wearily in the town of Villacañas for trucks to take them to Chinchón, forty-five kilometres south of Madrid. Eisner looked in at the town church, where the images of saints and virgins had been smashed while paintings hung in tatters from their frames. He knew anarchists were to blame, but felt a shared guilt. 'Numerically they were an important part of the Popular Front,' he said later. 'So their errors must inevitably be accepted as belonging to all of us.'[22]

Romilly's company managed two hours of chaotic training outside the town. He now learned to fire a rifle – something he had refused to do as a rebellious pacifist at his public school. An attempt at practising manoeuvres was interrupted when, a couple hours later, a motorcycle messenger tore up the road towards them. 'I am sorry. I wanted all of you to have a thorough training, for sixteen days at least,' their company commander said. 'We are leaving at once for the front.' The men were bundled into sturdy Russian ZIS-5 trucks with wooden sides, many of them clutching bottles of the rough local wine that they knew simply as 'vino' and which routinely also found its way into water bottles. Northern Europeans swigged this as if it was weak beer. They were informed that from now on anyone found drunk would be shot, but that did not stop the Flemish volunteers drinking so much that 'a handsome, blue-eyed blond young man' passed out.[23]

The brigade reached Chinchón, with its sunken circular central plaza forming a natural theatre overlooked by balconies, at around 7 p.m.

It was due to take part in an early morning attack on the Cerro de Los Angeles (literally the Hills of Angels, recently re-baptised as the Red Hills),[24] but Chinchón was chaos. Some units got lost, the civilian drivers disappeared into the warmth of local houses and there were not enough trucks to transport them to the attack. Drunken members of the André Marty Battalion had to be rounded up by their commissar.[25] Renn glumly accompanied Longo (also known as Gallo), who insisted on keeping the exhausted volunteers awake by making stirring speeches. The attack was eventually postponed by twenty-four hours, so that this new XII International Brigade and others taking part could organise themselves properly. Lukács told his men that this had been a deliberate test to check the volunteers' readiness to scramble into action. It was a useful lie.

The following day's attack revealed just how shambolic the new brigade was. A request for grenades had seen them supplied with pomegranates instead – since these shared the same word, *granada*, in Spanish.[26] Renn caught one of his soldiers loading a bullet into his rifle back to front and asked whether he had ever fired one before. 'Not even in a fairground,' the volunteer replied.[27] When Romilly tried to fire his own weapon, it did not work.

Supported by tanks driven by Russian Red Army 'advisors', the brigade advanced up the broad, dome-like hill towards a high-walled hermitage and its accompanying buildings – from where Franco's troops dominated the surrounding countryside. It was a bright sunny day and the enemy machine guns had a clear view of the attackers as they struggled uphill, and the first casualties began to fall as the volunteers peppered the hermitage's thick walls with ineffectual fire. When ordered to fix bayonets, some volunteers looked up the steep, rocky approach slopes to the sturdy buildings and refused to move.[28] The Italian volunteers had brought ladders, but they were of little use.[29] With the tanks gone, night falling and the battalion commanders unable to communicate with Lukács, the French and Italians retreated. Renn could not stop his men from following them. They argued that, in Spain, everybody went home at night. Some French volunteers, meanwhile, began to run back in panic, convinced that they were surrounded – an idea that appeared to have come from their own commander.[30] A random group of around a hundred volunteers stayed near to the hermitage, exposing themselves to possible capture, while Lukács wandered the battlefield trying to find his men.[31]

Eisner was one of the last to leave, after bumping into two Frenchmen. 'Come on. The Fascists have gone to bed, and our guys are having supper in a restaurant,' they joked.[32] In the dark, many lost their bearings and argued with each other about what they should do next.[33] Heavy, wheeled machine guns with metal defensive plates were lugged this way and that by exhausted volunteers. So, too, were the wounded, as people tried and failed to find the medical services in the dark.[34] Even Renn was not sure where to go.[35] The author of *War* was crestfallen. 'We arrogantly looked down on the Spaniards, calling them weak, but now the famous internationals had taken the first opportunity to turn around and go back to eat and sleep,' wrote Renn.[36] Things took a turn for the worse when some of his men had to dig in using their bayonets – since no one had thought of providing shovels – and spent a freezing night in the open countryside, kept awake by an elderly Czech volunteer groaning in the cold. Some had already dragged their heavy, wheeled machine guns for almost twenty kilometres.[37] In the morning, they buried their first dead.[38] Eisner's platoon wandered the countryside all day long until they bumped into Lukács himself, who found them satiating their thirst in a village fountain.[39]

The following day a similar attack had to be called off because much of the brigade, along with some other units, could not be found. By this time Renn had lost his voice and was so exhausted that, after shepherding his men onto a transport bus (requisitioned from a smart hotel and boasting luxuriously soft, leather seats) he sat and wept in front of them. 'I felt thoroughly ashamed, found myself a seat and wrapped my face in a scarf. I tried to stop my sobbing, but could barely manage it,' the First World War veteran admitted.[40] The brand new but exhausted XII International Brigade, after five days without proper rest and having failed to do anything remotely useful, slept deeply in Chinchón that night.

Like many failed attacks, the attempt to take the Cerro de los Angeles was soon pronounced to have been 'diversionary' and, therefore, to have succeeded.[41] The men did not believe that, and some rebelled. A dozen Flemish volunteers refused to go any further and twenty Frenchmen, blaming their officers, were rumoured to have declared themselves anarchists, saying they would not follow orders any more.[42] The French battalion's commander, Moulin, disappeared – there were rumours that he had deserted. He had only been appointed a couple of days earlier.[43] Another, more junior officer was said to have been either shot for repeatedly abandoning his men or, at best, sent back to Albacete (this was rumour, but Marty later recognised that a Belgian captain was shot for 'sabotage' in Madrid in November).[44] Lukács was angry at having to carry out an attack with no artillery. 'If this had happened in Russia I should have called it sabotage, but here it seems to be nothing more than stupidity,' he complained.[45]

It did not always help that many of the lower ranking officers, along with the political commissars, were so-called 'Mexicans' – international Communist Party officials who had travelled to Spain straight from the USSR. Other volunteers spoke admiringly of the men who had travelled from 'over there' and thought of them as 'supermen, the beacons who would guide us to victory'.[46] Many boasted mysterious noms de guerre. The 'Mexicans', however, were clubbish and secretive, talking to each other in imperfect Russian and showing that, even across national groupings, they had a separate bond.[47]

Amongst those who viewed them suspiciously was the Ladino-speaking French-Bulgarian César Covo – whose family spoke a language based on the ancient Spanish of the Sephardic Jews expelled from Spain in 1492. Although he was a faithful Communist Party member, Covo viewed the 'Mexicans' as a mafia. 'They had a taste for mystery and all their conversations were secret,' he said. 'Most had come to Spain in the same spirit in which, in other times, civil servants had gone to the colonies.'[48] In practice, they fell into two groups: those who simply felt superior; and those who displayed calm, courageous conviction. The latter made excellent leaders, but were often too keen to lead from the front and expose themselves to danger. As a result, there were soon serious concerns that Europe's communist parties were sacrificing their most capable and promising young men.[49] The former group, meanwhile, could prove disastrous, as a section from Renn's battalion, who had been marched back twenty-five kilometres by a panicked officer, would soon realise.[50]

By this time Eisner, who was able to translate into French for Lukács, had been appointed head of his personal guard.[51] He soon discovered that Lukács spoke to both his chief of staff, the Bulgarian known as Belov,[52] and to the mysterious man who had originally been introduced to them all as 'the German worker Fritz', in Russian.[53] The latter did not, in fact, speak German at all – and was the Red Army officer (and future, distinguished Second World War general) Pavel Batov, who was the unit's Russian advisor. Belov, meanwhile, was the son of two famous Bulgarian revolutionaries who had fled to the Soviet Union in the 1920s.[54] His real name was Karlo Lukanov and he would later become Bulgaria's foreign minister. All three of them, Eisner noted, came from 'over there'.[55]

The following night was much shorter. They were woken at 3 a.m. and bussed into Madrid.[56] As they were driven towards the city, members of the Balkan company – where the languages ranged from Bulgarian and Serbo-Croatian to Turkish, Greek and Armenian – tried to learn to pronounce the Madrid front's password '*Vivir-Vencer*' which proved an almost impossible tongue-twister.

The city, now fortified for war, proved for many a disappointment. It was 'mostly tramlines and barricades', noted Romilly.[57] 'They had made it look like a part of London where the road is up and street mending is going on in a lot of places, with braziers heating the workmen's meals.' Gustav Regler joined them at the barracks, having just been appointed as a political commissar in the French-speaking André Marty Battalion, which was more commonly known as the Franco-Belgian Battalion.[58] This was already proving itself to be a troublesome battalion, not least because it had had four, mostly incompetent, commanders in ten days.[59] The French volunteers were as good as any others at fighting, but they also prided themselves on a Gallic form of cheekiness when out of the line and a period spent waiting in a perfume factory saw them come out, 'smelling wonderfully'.[60] Many went absent, catching trams into the city to sightsee, drink, or both. Patrols had to be sent out to find them and when they were threatened with punishment a significant part of the battalion came close to mutiny and demanded to be sent home. Such was the protest, that the only way to impose discipline was to invite those who wished to leave to put their names on a list. Eighty of them did so, according to the disciplined – and disapproving – communist Raymond Hantz, who said they were sent home immediately. A harsh Hungarian disciplinarian called Bikis was eventually handed command and took to giving his orders with a pistol in his hand, in case anybody argued.[61]

On arrival, the first thing Gustav Regler found was a group muttering rebelliously about their officers and interrupted them:

I said casually: 'When I'm afraid, the first thing I mistrust is my
own arguments.' Ten pairs of eyes glared at me.
    'Who says anyone's afraid?'

'Well, I certainly should be, if I were part of a civilian army and had had to put up with this kind of stupidity.'

'Who are you, anyway?'

'I'll tell you that later. First, I want to explain what is different about our army. We aren't tied to any one commander. We get rid of the inefficient ones and look for better ones. Our discipline is voluntary, not enforced. That is why we have Commissars, advisers, who don't let anyone get above himself.'

'Well, but where's our Commissar? We haven't seen anyone who might have saved us from that mess?'

At this moment, stretcher-bearers appeared bringing the dead into the barrack yard. There were three, if I remember rightly. The rain had stopped. The wind blew back the groundsheet that covered one of the dead men. His face was already yellow; there was an exactly recognisable distance between us and him. His state of homelessness might at any moment overtake us. But there was a good safeguard against that kind of infection – to march on, to go forward. I saw that the whole troop was now standing round me, noting my reactions. Did they expect me to show revulsion or become voiceless in the presence of those silent forms? I pulled the groundsheet back from another face and said:

'They can say no more. It is for us to speak and to act for them. These dead men must have a reason. A mutiny among their comrades would make fools of them, meaningless sacrifices. I must also tell you that I am your Commissar, and that I want each company to choose a man who will keep me informed of your doubts and fears, your wishes and your complaints.'[62]

Marty had made it clear to Regler that he could use any kind of force to maintain discipline, even though these men were volunteers. 'You will have *full* powers,' Marty had emphasised. 'I knew exactly what he meant, and resolved never to use the powers in the sense that he intended,' said Regler.[63]

The following day, Lukács's men were driven further around Madrid and then to the elegant surroundings of the Puerta de Hierro country club on the north side of University City, close to the Casa de Campo.[64] This was where Madrid's aristocrats had, until recently, played polo and where Kléber's XI Brigade now had its headquarters. From here they

were to go into the front line at University City for their real baptism
of fire. After the dismal performance at the Cerro de los Angeles, there
were good reasons to doubt whether this rapidly thrown together
group of untrained amateurs were equal to the task of fighting against
experienced, professional opponents. It was too late, however, to dwell
on that, since they were now heading for the most important and
sensitive spot on any front in Spain.

13

Save Madrid: University City, November 1936

After just ten days fighting to contain the Francoist advance into Madrid, XI Brigade's new and charismatic commander, Hans Kahle, contacted the headquarters at Albacete demanding reinforcements. He had already lost 'almost one third of my men', with at least forty dead and more than 120 injured.[1] A quarter of the men from the German- and French-speaking battalions were out of action and the Polish battalion had suffered losses of up to 50 per cent.[2] Almost all officers and commissars in the Hungarian company were dead. Many of the more seriously wounded had shrapnel wounds to the head, he said, and steel helmets would have reduced the numbers considerably. He worried, too, that the Spanish earth was swallowing up the flower of German communist youth. 'Spanish land has been paid for with the blood of some of our party's best cadres. We can't sacrifice the best,' he said.[3]

Kahle had been promoted to replace Kléber because the latter was now in command of a wider sector of the front.[4] The six-foot tall, Spanish-speaking, easy-mannered German proved a popular brigade commander. 'He was a communist ... was precise in his orders, understood the unstable Spaniards, mingled the methods of Potsdam with those of Alcazar, obeyed his party, because obedience flowed down to the troops, but leavened it at staff meetings and conferences with an almost French irony,' Gustav Regler wrote.[5] He also wanted 230 replacements for 160 dead or injured, apparently because at least fifty volunteers were either physically or morally unable to fight. Some had already deserted. They were probably *provocateurs* or police informants, he said, revealing a communist tendency to see enemies within. Such was the chaos in which the battalion had been put together that not all the dead could be named. Indeed, half of the first thirty graves in a cemetery for the volunteers set up the following week at Fuencarral, on the outskirts of Madrid, would carry the inscription 'Unknown'.[6] Overall, however, the individual bravery of the volunteers was proving to be both remarkable and lethal.

Kléber was desperate to relieve Kahle's men and, as soon as Lukács's XII Brigade was ready on 19 November, he ordered a handover. It was the start of a falling-out between the two commanders who, despite their similar backgrounds, were very different men. Kléber seemed to delight in his status as 'general' and resided in the glorious clubhouse of the polo club, while Lukács chose to be both closer to the front line and a less conspicuous target for bombardment by setting up his small headquarters in a dingy, roadside labourers' house near the San Fernando bridge.[7] A poorly coordinated handover took place over the next forty-eight hours.[8] Lukács was furious that some of his men had been forced to take over in broad daylight, when the Francoists could both see them arriving and attack before they became accustomed to the terrain. To make things worse, Kléber styled himself 'head of the International Brigades' on the orders sent to Lukács. He later blamed his chief of staff for the error but he had not asked for it to be changed. When the normally good-humoured Lukács received the instructions, he was furious. 'You must have translated that wrong,' he reprimanded Eisner.[9]

The International Brigades' first 'general' hoped his spat with Lukács would blow over, but his attitude alarmed Marty and he now sensed that in Albacete they were beginning 'to record Kléber's sins of commission and omission'.[10] The handover period was inauspicious for other reasons. In one of the more mysterious episodes of the war in Madrid, the charismatic Buenaventura Durruti was shot at University City on 19 November: a bullet entered his chest and he died later in hospital. Some speculated that this had been a revenge attack by rival anarchists, though it was probably a stray bullet or a wound he clumsily inflicted on himself after mishandling his own weapon.[11] Although they detested anarchism, men like Lukács admired Durruti for his energy, sincerity and lack of personal ambition. They believed he had been preparing to apply stricter discipline in his units and closer coordination with the other Republican forces.

Lukács had barely finished setting up his XII Brigade headquarters, when a Citroën car with a cracked windscreen drew up belching blue exhaust fumes. A small, scruffy, dark-haired Hungarian-speaking photographer stepped out and introduced himself as Robert Capa.[12] Endre Ernö Friedmann was the twenty-three-year-old son of a Jewish-Hungarian dressmaker who had only recently taken on the byline of Robert Capa.[13] Still relatively impoverished, he was just beginning to make a mark in Paris as a news photographer

Originally Lukács wanted to send him away, but Capa turned out to be charming, self-deprecating company.[14] 'Just tell him that he can't photograph me,' he ordered.[15] Armed with nothing more than a Baedeker's map, Lukács sent Regler and another officer out to scout no-man's-land, saying they could take Capa with them.[16] At this stage, Capa had still not encountered real combat, and was happy not to get too close. 'If shooting can be avoided, I don't mind,' he told Regler, as they crept along the banks of the Manzanares, below frost-trimmed mossy branches, frightening a hare and bumping into Hans Beimler as he tramped around through the undergrowth, also looking for the front line. Regler was delighted by 'this small beautiful boy who everyone loved'.[17] When bullets and shells began to fly overhead, Capa excused himself, saying he needed to change his trousers. 'My guts aren't as brave as my camera,' he explained.[18] That did not stop him returning several times to photograph the Brigaders in University City – a place where, he later said, 'the abnormal ... had become normal', and which Delaprée described as 'a good approximation of hell'.[19]

Spread over a dozen pages of the magazine *Regards* a few weeks later, Capa's pictures of volunteers in the trenches, huddled behind machine guns at University City, and helping women with their laundry, helped create the glamorous narrative of the International Brigades. The text praised the 'volunteers for liberty' and spoke of solidarity between 'our young people and the young people of Spain'.[20] It was the first of many pieces of photojournalistic reportage and film that he and his partner, Gerta Pohorylle – who had taken on the byline 'Gerda Taro' – would devote to the Brigades. He had met the small, stylish Polish woman from a well-off Stuttgart family two years earlier and they had formed a dynamic partnership that was both professional and romantic.

Self-confident and vivacious, Taro was three years older and added a dose of organised ambition to the duo.

With her green eyes, carefully plucked, arched eyebrows and copper-coloured hair cut boyishly short, the elegant Taro had more political baggage than the jocular Capa. She had been close to Willy Brandt's Socialist Workers' Party (SAP) and fled to Paris in 1933 after being arrested for distributing anti-Nazi leaflets. She was also a gifted photographer and between them they were determined to turn 'Robert Capa' into one of the great names in photography, even if she took some of 'his' photographs. They had literally crash-landed into Spain early in August 1936, after being sent to Barcelona by *Vu* magazine in an aircraft that had to make an emergency landing. By September they had already produced one of the iconic photographs of the war, the 'Falling Soldier' – an image of a white-clad militiaman allegedly dying on the Córdoba front, but actually a posed shot taken miles away from the fighting. Although they liked to get as close to the action as possible, they did not worry too much about authenticity. If their pictures helped highlight the Republican cause as well, then even better. In fact, the two photographers – along with journalists such as Louis Delaprée, Geoffrey Cox and the *New York Times*'s Herbert Matthews[21] – were amongst the International Brigades' keenest international cheerleaders, lavishing them with praise and enlarging their mystique.

The battalions of XII Brigade walked through the rain towards the still poorly defined front line, unsure of exactly where the enemy was positioned. The handover had been badly managed, with some troops withdrawing before others arrived, leaving the newcomers to discover the front line for themselves, sometimes by moving forward until they were shot at.[22] As they advanced towards their ill-defined new positions, some of the newly arrived Italian volunteers, who were positioned closest to the river, began to run and had to be turned around by their officers and commissars.[23] Again, the fighting concentrated on a few hundred metres of rough, damp land and around the buildings closest to the Manzanares, some of which had been lost during the handover.[24] As rain fell, Romilly's English unit attacked and retreated constantly. Fierce fighting broke out over the smallest of buildings – huts, barns and outhouses – often known simply as 'the red house', 'the white house' or 'the green house'.[25]

The front once more was fragile, and the potential prize of the Spanish capital was both so great and so close that Franco insisted on repeated attempts at breaking through the Republican lines. Lukács was amazed that this never happened. 'Do you know why we can't see Moroccan *chilabas* outside our window?' he mused out loud. 'Because the enemy cannot even begin to imagine that we are just a wafer-thin line, and that there isn't a single reserve battalion between here and El Pardo [six-and-a-half kilometres upstream].'[26]

On their second day at the front, Covo's Balkan company retreated after seeing a building that had been occupied by their Polish company destroyed, while the commander ran from the rubble, covered in dust, stammering: 'There is no ... There is no company ... There is no Polish company left!'[27] Some men did not stop running until they reached the outer suburbs of Madrid. Others stayed where they were, but found themselves at a loss about what to do. They had little ammunition, no food and no officers. The enemy had given up for the day, but Covo was sure that one more determined attack would see the Francoists drive straight through them into Madrid.[28] The Polish company had already lost all its officers and platoon commanders, so Ludwig Renn ordered the soldiers to choose new men to lead them.[29] Their new commander appeared the following morning and requested that they be tasked with recapturing the buildings they had just been ejected from. Renn asked why. 'It's like this,' he explained. 'We ran. When the [Polish Communist] Party's [exiled] organisation in Paris finds out, they will feel ashamed of us.'[30] As a result, yet more Poles died. In two days, the new brigade lost 20 per cent of its strength. Longo found that 'too high, not just because of the blood spilled but because of the disorganisation it provokes in each unit'.[31]

Covo was intrigued by the different fighting styles of the enemy. The Moroccan colonial troops rushed them head on, urged forward by pistol-wielding Spanish officers who threatened to shoot anyone who turned back; the legionnaires (who, like the French Foreign Legion, also included some foreigners) came more surreptitiously, advancing from cover to cover. The formers' lives were valued more cheaply, he concluded, making them dispensable.[32] When one Moroccan soldier became lost and ran backwards and forwards, terrified, in front of the faculty buildings occupied by Regler's men, there was a debate amongst those manning the windows about whether to kill him. 'The majority were against it, because one does not shoot a man in the back and after all he was only a man, a victim of colonialism,' said Regler. They killed him anyway. 'The volunteers did not shoot less well because they had hesitated.'[33]

Each time the Brigaders entered a building they found it draped with the dead and dying of the previous occupants – Spanish militiamen, Moroccans, legionnaires or men from their own units – though bodies could not always be identified.[34] They became used to the smell of burning flesh and what Sommerfield called 'the faces of men dying and not knowing it, greenish, livid, with impersonal, gasping mouths ... a whole dance of shudderings and writhings and convulsions, an opera of moans and howls and whimpers'.[35]

The volunteers remained absurdly brave. Amongst their most ingenuous beliefs was that, although they had not been provided with armour-piercing rounds for their rifles and machine guns, they could defeat tanks. When the supplies of hand grenades arrived, the Brigaders found these were tin cans filled with sticks of dynamite. A wick protruded from them, which was lit by a burning cigarette. They were, at least, plentiful. Many men had by now seen the Soviet film released that year, *We Are from Kronstadt*, in which brave Russian sailors run up to tanks and disable them with grenades. The technique worked occasionally with these handmade grenades, but mostly saw people machine-gunned or trampled to death.[36] A Spaniard called Antonio Col[37] gained a reputation as a Kronstadt-style tank-killer and Willi Wille, a German Brigader who had travelled to Spain before the International Brigades were formed, was another skilled practitioner of this suicidal art,[38] though he would soon die in action.[39] This sense of suicidal bravado was even more pronounced amongst the officers, who were mostly either enthusiastic young idealists or dogged veterans of clandestine activism, police beatings and prison cells.

Often the results of the volunteers' efforts depended not on how they fought, but on which side had the support of artillery or tanks that day. The latter were, compared to today's tanks, little more than tracked armoured cars with small guns, though the Russian T-26s that backed the Brigaders were far superior to the minuscule Italian and German machines. The same could be said for the *chatos*, the Polikarpov I-15 biplane fighters[40] brought from the Soviet Union that began to triumph in the sky above them.

Renn's disciplined Germans generally fought more sensibly. Within their ranks, Esmond Romilly's English group survived unscathed. Renn liked his 'diligent' English speakers. He was especially pleased that, when his aristocratic family began sending messages that urged him to go home, Romilly declared he 'liked the reds, and wanted to stay'.[41] His group nevertheless felt guilty that they had suffered so little compared to, say, their Balkan and Polish colleagues in the other non-German companies of the Thälmann Battalion.

While fighting raged daily in the waterlogged land beside the river and around the Palacete and Casa Velázquez buildings, part of the Franco-Belgian André Marty Battalion stayed in the relative comfort of the Philosophy Faculty. From there, they took potshots at a mostly distant enemy and watched as the buildings being fought over by their comrades went up in smoke. The rest of the battalion, however, were caught up in the bloodier floor-to-floor fighting in the Medical Faculty, though positions there soon became solidly established and their regular early evening attacks did little to upset the enemy. Frank Thomas, a Welsh mercenary who was one of a small number of British volunteers on the Francoist side, said the attacks always came an hour after nightfall. 'The attacks failed quite as regularly, with heavy losses to the enemy … their only effect was the useful practice it gave us with our rifles and [hand] bombs,' he wrote later. 'The sight of matches [used to light hand bombs] was the warning that attacks were starting.'[42] Artillery and trench mortars caused his unit far more annoyance, Thomas concluded. This insistence on repeated, futile attacks saw the André Marty Battalion's losses rise to 280 out of 420 men, while their officers continued to perform poorly, even phoning Lukács to complain that they were being shelled. He informed them curtly that, in war, this was normal. After several days of furious fighting, however, the front began to stabilise.[43]

Franco was beginning to run out of reserves to throw at the defenders' lines, and relentless rain dampened the ardour of both sides. Eventually they fought themselves to a halt, and the University City lines would remain almost unchanged for the rest of the war. Lukács's men began to be pulled out overnight on 25/26 November and, over the next few days, were replaced once more by battalions from XI Brigade.[44] Eisner was struck by what five days of fighting had done to his exhausted, pallid comrades in their filthy uniforms. 'The playful rowdiness had gone,' he observed. 'The danger, suffering and deaths of their companions had wiped away the layers of cockiness, removing the slight, unconscious theatricality in their words and gestures which were the inevitable result of the Brigaders' special situation and the grateful attention and torrent of praise that they had been receiving from the Spanish people.'[45] The trucks which took them away at dawn were now eerily roomy, but as they passed a mass grave, some still raised a fist and shouted: 'Rot [Red] Front!'[46]

The two International Brigades took it in turns to hold this line until early December.[47] As they tried to shore up their numbers with new arrivals from Albacete (some of whom arrived still in civilian clothes, carrying suitcases as if they had just stepped off a train[48]) and returnees from hospital, they also swapped battalions. The German-speaking Thälmann and Edgar André Battalions were placed together in XI Brigade under Hans Kahle while the mostly Polish-speaking Dombrowski Battalion joined Lukács in XII Brigade.[49] This was sensible, since orders were being mangled by interpreters and different nationalities had learned different fighting styles during military service, but it was also a sign that the national groups did not always get on well.[50] 'To the German soldiers it seemed, without basis or sometimes with basis, that the French chief of supplies was favouring his own Frenchmen, and vice versa. The Poles and others considered themselves badly treated by both sides,' Kléber explained.[51] It also meant that virtually all of Lukács's Brigade, except for their commander, spoke French, since the Poles were mostly exiles from France and Belgium.

Nobody knew, yet, that the lines established at University City would remain fixed. Attacks were still launched, but almost always failed as the lines of defence on both sides became firmly established, bolstered by a maze of trench networks. Expensive tapestries, towels and carpets taken from the Puerta de Hierro country club provided the Brigaders with colourful, if rain-drenched, canopies.[52] Artillery bombardments, mortar shells, bombs and sniper bullets continued to claim victims. As the death toll mounted, Kléber complained that his men were being sent on useless missions that simply brought more losses. On 27 November a group of fifteen French communists held a meeting of their own in the Philosophy Faculty. Such meetings were often held discreetly, so that the 50 per cent or so of non-communists did not feel excluded or ignored.[53] 'All those present agreed that our colleagues are demoralised and that there is flagrant incompetency in the military command, which means that they have twice been sent out to be butchered,' the communists wrote in a report. 'This explains why many companions are now asking to go home. Naturally, we disapprove of that … Our battalion left Albacete with 420 men in three companies, and we have around 140 left.'[54]

Some deaths were caused by sheer carelessness. On 1 December, as evening fell and the usual daily exchange of fire between the now static lines came to a stop, Covo saw the tell-tale pale sheepskin jackets of three officers or political commissars walking down the steep slope towards his position near the river Manzanares. The setting sun picked out their figures as they strolled nonchalantly over a crest and down the hill towards them. The bulky profile of Hans Kahle was instantly recognisable and the smaller man beside him was, evidently, his political commissar, the likeable Fritz Vehlow, who called himself 'Louis Schuster'.[55] Both were listening attentively to an even larger figure, an older man wearing a cap with ear flaps and a red star adorned with the hammer and sickle. This was Hans Beimler.

Covo watched transfixed as they wandered towards what everyone in the front line knew was a danger spot covered by enemy snipers. 'We tried to warn them by waving our arms and calling out, each in their own language,' he explained. A group of Frenchmen shouted themselves hoarse, but the three men simply waved back before returning to their all-absorbing conversation. As soon as they reached the sniper's box, the patch of land covered by the sharpshooter, several shots rang out. Beimler was hit first, grabbing his chest and shouting: '*Rot front! Rot front!*' All three men then tumbled out of sight down the side of the hill. It seemed impossible to get to them. 'No one moves!' barked Covo's Bulgarian commander, followed by his translators. But two Brigade stretcher-bearers – including a twenty-four-year-old, rugby-playing Parisian factory worker and army reserve sergeant called Théophile Rol – had already thrown themselves down the hill after the injured men.[56]

Both Beimler – the former Reichstag deputy, who had escaped from Dachau – and political commissar Vehlow died of their wounds. Lukács was furious, blaming the pale sheepskin coats, since these both stood out in the countryside and identified their wearers as senior officers or commissars. 'What idiot thought of handing those out?' he asked. 'At this rate we won't have a single officer or commissar left.' He banned the sheepskins from the front line, though Regler disobeyed him and wore Beimler's coat himself for the next four years[57] (a newspaper cutting of Stalin promising aid to Spain was the only item found in the coat's pockets[58]).

A death notice signed by Lukács and Kléber claimed that Beimler died 'heroically' in an area that had not previously been under enemy fire.[59] He was now not just a hero, but a martyr, and his legend would continue to swell after his death. Everybody now competed to claim a part of the new 'hero' and Marty was enraged when an honour guard formed to greet the body on its way through Albacete was roundly ignored. The body was taken to Barcelona – a city with spare time for ceremonial – and buried after a multitudinous funeral procession down the Ramblas, behind a banner that proclaimed: 'Vengeance for the Death of Hans Beimler!'[60]

There was little that could be done about this exhortation in a city as far from the front as Barcelona. In Madrid, however, the sensation was that the Francoist advance had finally been halted. It was an act of heroic resistance, stretching over the month of November, in which the militias and people of Madrid had played the main part, and to which the International Brigades had contributed with courage, blood and a morale-boosting message that, despite the feeble response of the Great Powers, the world had not turned its back and forgotten them. Up to 4,000 volunteers had held a two-kilometre stretch of the crucial front around the Francoist bulge on the city side of the river Manzanares, which was just six kilometres long.[61]

'Madrid had not fallen. It has resisted, and will continue to resist,' said Luigi Longo.[62] Franco disagreed, but realised he would have to find a different way to choke the Spanish capital. The volunteers of the International Brigades would stay in, or near, Madrid, for the next six months. Their fame was spreading and more men were now setting out from across the oceans to join them.

14

Hail, the Saviour of Madrid!: Cinema Monumental, Madrid, November–December 1936

On the evening of 11 November, the Monumental, a vast, state-of-the art cinema for 4,200 movie-goers on Madrid's Calle Atocha, had been packed with a noisy crowd. There was nothing strange about this. Little more than a kilometre from the battlefront, despite the bombing and shelling, restaurants and cafes remained open and many militiamen could catch the metro or tram straight from the front into the centre of Madrid. More importantly, the Francoist boast that their army would be sipping coffee or attending Mass in Madrid that week had proved empty.

There was no film at the Monumental this night, but rather the crowd had gathered to see Madrid's military commanders make their first public appearance. Italian Giuseppe Di Vittorio took the stage and presented himself as the voice of the international volunteers. He was amongst the senior communists who had set up the Brigades and was now Kléber's commissar in XI Brigade.[1] Di Vittorio reminded the boisterous audience that the world was watching events in Madrid. The past few days, with the forward march of global fascism finally being halted, represented the start of what he hoped would eventually lead to 'the liberation of the Italian people and of all the peoples of the world'. The speaker who followed answered with a phrase that, along with the famous '*No Pasarán!*', 'They shall not pass', was becoming common currency: 'Madrid will be the tomb of Fascism', he pledged.[2]

Italy's left was as demoralised as Germany's. It was, however, less monolithic, with volunteer fighters in Spain coming from a broad spread of parties. The Italian experience of fascism and exile was longer, since Mussolini had come to power in 1922.[3] Wider anti-fascist coalitions, bringing together Republicans, anarchists, socialists and others, had been in existence since 1931, with Carlo Rosselli's moderate 'liberal socialist' Giustizia e Libertà one of the most prominent groupings. Socialists and communists, meanwhile, did not have the same history of antagonism as in Germany and had also begun working together in exile in 1934.[4] The other parties, indeed, had been faster than the communists in recruiting volunteers for Spain, with the mixed but mostly anarchist Colonna Italiana providing several hundred fighters to the Francisco Ascaso column[5] before the communist Gastone Sozzi Centuria was formed.[6] The Colonna's shared leadership – with a social-liberal *repubblicano*, an anarchist and Rosselli jointly in charge – proved that anti-fascism was its sole unifying force.[7] In fact, at the same time as the Comintern was overseeing the creation of the International Brigades, various Italian parties had already agreed to form a large Italian anti-fascist legion that would be at the service of the Spanish Republic.[8] The idea was abandoned once the Brigades were formed and the Italian legion became, in essence, the Garibaldi Battalion. Not everyone was delighted. 'Arriving here, I found myself faced with a completely different situation from the one I was expecting,' complained one senior socialist, Amedeo Azzi.[9] In order to maintain balance, the Garibaldi Battalion became the only one with two chief political commissars – Azzi and the communist Antonio Roasi[10] – as well as a *repubblicano* commander in Randolfo Pacciardi.[11]

Di Vittorio had belonged to several parties himself, but was now a communist who went by the alias Nicoletti. His flamboyant style of oratory, jutting out his chin with each defiant statement, reminded at least one onlooker of Mussolini (himself a former socialist).[12] Di Vittorio had escaped the round-up of communist leaders in 1926, unlike his philosopher colleague Antonio Gramsci, who was slowly dying from various illnesses suffered during a decade of imprisonment. Like Gramsci, Di Vittorio knew about the importance of publicity and propaganda. He was convinced that people across the world needed to be persuaded that the International Brigades were living proof that the world's left could unite against fascism. Back in Moscow, the Comintern leadership agreed. This message of left-wing unity had been the great U-turn performed at the Seventh World Congress in 1935, but that was an age ago in terms of the fast-moving politics of the 1930s. The other senior Italian communist in Spain, Luigi Longo, found himself having to explain to both Spaniards and volunteers exactly who these foreign soldiers really were. 'We are an expression of the Popular Front and make ourselves available to the Spanish people and government. The military units formed by our volunteers are an integral part of the Spanish army and are under its command, without interference from any other organisation,' said Longo, who would become Commissar Inspector General of the International Brigades. 'The Spanish flag is the flag of all of us, and we fight for its victory.'[13]

It was Di Vittorio's task to persuade the world that this contribution was proving valuable. Propaganda is best when contained in a well-told and mostly truthful story. It is even better with a hero. He chose Kléber. The false 'general' would have to be made 'the saviour of Madrid'. Towards the end of November, Di Vittorio organised a press campaign designed to achieve exactly that. Soon Kléber's name was on the front page of Madrid newspapers, being hailed as 'the formidable general in charge of the [entire] international column'.[14] In order to make him even more attractive to the press, Di Vittorio blew Kléber's cover, broadcasting and embellishing on his colourful past as a hardened, heroic fighter and veteran of revolutions – or attempted ones – in Russia, China and Germany. Soon Kléber was being lionised everywhere. The poet Rafael Alberti, who had turned a sequestered aristocrat's palace near the Retiro Park into the headquarters of his 'Alliance of Anti-Fascist Intellectuals',[15] was especially gushing: 'Kléber, my general ... with my voice, which is blood and memory/ I salute you/ ¡Salud! Spain is ours!'[16]

The embellishments grew and grew. Rumours even circulated that Kléber had personally captured the Russian tsar's family. The general was, as usual, both furious about someone else deciding for him and delighted by the popularity. 'A simply scandalous history resulted,' he admitted later, claiming that he had tried to fight off the journalists and 'blur over and deflect interest in my past in the USSR'.[17] Sections of his first interview, published in the popular weekly *Estampa* magazine, were reprinted by several Madrid dailies. He declared that victory would have been won already if 'we had been better organised'. This was unlikely to win him friends amongst the Spanish military command. 'It is vital that anti-fascist fighters stop behaving as they have done in certain sectors, where some fight while the others remain where they are and loudly applaud those who act,' he added.[18]

Kléber was photographed meeting a foreign delegation in boots, khaki riding britches and high-collared grey jersey and, separately, wearing a general's hat. The accompanying write-up called Russia 'his homeland' and compared him to both the Italian general Giuseppe Garibaldi and a military hero of both the American and French revolutions, the Marquis de Lafayette.[19] With Di Vittorio's help, Kléber convinced the great *New York Times* correspondent Herbert Matthews that he had once commanded an army of 56,000 men in China, taking them on an eight-month retreat over 5,500 kilometres. He also claimed to have spent most of his recent years in Canada, rather than as a Soviet spy in the USA. He was 'the man of the hour in Madrid', said Matthews, adding that 'in the troubled and anxious times that face the world it would surprise no one here if Emil Kléber were to prove an important factor'. Matthews even claimed, quite wrongly, that Kléber led his troops from the front 'shooting a rifle with remarkable accuracy and demonstrating a courage that proved contagious'.[20]

Kléber's gruff charm, common touch and gift for languages made him popular not just with journalists but also with the lower ranks. At the top end of the command chain, however, he riled people by criticising the high command while blaming his own mishaps on underlings.[21] Senior Russians warned Kléber that he was straying into the dangerous arena of sensationalism.[22] With Stalin purging the military, it was not the time to be drawing attention to oneself. At military headquarters, meanwhile, Miaja and his chief of staff, Lieutenant Colonel Vicente Rojo, seethed with irritation and envy. They accused him of lying about his victories, positions, the strengths of his battalions and, even, of refusing to join attacks or arriving late for them. What they really hated, however, was Kléber being awarded the credit for saving Madrid.

Rojo spelled all this out in an angry report sent to his superiors on 26 November (just eighteen days after the volunteers reached Madrid). 'The press is indulging in a false and highly exaggerated bout of exaltation of this general,' he railed. 'It is true that his men fight well, but no more than that, and that is something which a lot of men who are not under his command also do. As for his supposed capabilities as a commander, since these seem to need the prop of false popularity, they are also false,'[23] Rojo complained. 'This general tends to try to dominate everything, both politically and militarily ... [and] he has become a military idol to some of our political parties and that is extremely damaging,' he continued. All this added up, he claimed, to a deliberate and disgraceful attempt to undermine his own and Miaja's authority.[24]

Kléber also fell out with some of the Soviet advisors. One came to inspect Kléber's command post, found that he had withdrawn two battalions into reserve and flew into a rage. 'Wrecker! I will arrest you and send you home under guard!' he threatened, while Kléber's own staff looked menacingly at the intruder. 'Who do you think you are? Who appointed you chief of this sector? I wouldn't even entrust you with a company!'[25] Kléber did not realise that Rojo and Miaja hated him. He was also convinced, too, that his staff loved him, although both Lukács and his 'bourgeois'[26] French chief of staff, Colonel Vincent, clearly did not.

Unfortunately for Kléber he had, by now, also made an enemy of André Marty. In December a meeting was held in Albacete about the 'problems he [Kléber] causes'. These included his insistence that more Spaniards be brought into the Brigades, in part to save the lives of valuable communist cadres from numerous national parties who were dying on the battlefield and in part so that the Brigades were closer to the Spanish people. By now, however, a specific sort of deviance was being identified – known as *Kléberismo*. It was, according to Marty, a problem of commanders who 'did not realise that the prestige of the units they commanded in this period was due to the ... quality of their soldiers'.[27] It could just as well have been defined as an attempt to outshine others, particularly Marty himself, but also Miaja and Rojo. By the end of the month Kléber had been sent off to an inconspicuous 'advisory' job on the Mediterranean coast, far from the front line. Even his rival Lukács could see that Kléber was being mistreated. 'They have behaved badly towards him, without gratitude or loyalty,' he commented. 'He is a strange man. If only he could add a bit of modesty to his other abilities – intelligence, courage, quick-wittedness and command of languages.'[28]

This was not the end of Kléber's career in Spain – he was too valuable for that – but he would be given more discreet tasks from now on. Before he left, Lukács went to visit Kléber at El Pardo. 'I started off by telling him all the disagreeable things: that I disapproved of his behaviour towards our Brigade and that he had been wrong to give up command of his own. And then I told him that it is not completely false to call him the "saviour of Madrid", though no one deserves that honour individually,' he told Eisner. 'The people saved themselves. But there can be no doubt that at the crucial moment nobody did more to defend the city than Kléber.'[29]

While enemies circled around Kléber, the men of the Brigades found themselves hailed as heroes wherever they went. On short furloughs into Madrid, they would be waved past controls, let off tram fares and welcomed into any military canteen, including by the anarchists, wherever they stopped. The German writer Alfred Kantorowicz, who had just reached the city, was amazed at their reception when a colleague called Kurt drove him to XI Brigade headquarters, where he was to produce the unit's newspaper. 'Kurt's shout to the sentries: "International Brigade!" is a phrase to conjure with here. It acts as a universal password and Open Sesame. The glamour and affection that clings to this battalion of French, Italian, German, Polish, Hungarian, Yugoslav, Belgian, English, American and Czech anti-fascists make one flush with pride and pleasure at being allowed to belong to it. To be able to say, "I'm one of the Eleventh [International] Brigade," makes one much more respected hereabouts at the present time than any other rank, distinction or reputation in the world,' he wrote.[30]

Women, bartenders and newspapermen also loved them. The Spanish women were sometimes a mystery to the foreign volunteers, however, especially in rural or middle-class areas where tradition required them to be carefully chaperoned. Where that was not the case, the other nationalities were furious to discover that the Italians proved to be the most popular. Other volunteers either abstained from sex or ignored the warnings about the sexually transmitted diseases that sent many soldiers to hospital and queued up outside brothels (on the Francoist side, Hitler's Condor Legion set up its own brothels where men waited in disciplined lines, to the mirth of the Spaniards).

Correspondents who cultivated Brigaders could garner quotes without risking the front line and – since the latter had access to alcohol, cigarettes and decent food – the attraction was mutual, though sometimes strained. 'At first they were delighted to see us; not only were English volunteers "news", but we could give them a lot of information about the fighting in the University City,' Romilly admitted. 'But the limits of their generosity were severely tested, as we all lived off them.'[31] Visiting dignitaries also sought them out. When a delegation of British MPs visited, John Cornford and others ended up sleeping on the floor of Conservative MP Jack Macnamara's hotel room. Macnamara's parliamentary secretary and partner on trips abroad, where they were freer to enjoy their homosexuality, was the Soviet spy Guy Burgess. Both Burgess and Cornford had been part of the influential communist groups that emerged from Trinity College, Cambridge during the early 1930s.[32]

More thoughtful newspaper correspondents saw the Brigaders' presence in Madrid as a sign of a wider, deeper phenomenon. At the *New York Times*, Herbert Matthews had decided by the end of December that, in the words of one headline: 'Spain's war is international'. While the volunteers accounted for no more than one in ten troops in the capital, he told the newspaper's readers, they symbolised something far greater. 'It is quite possible that the influx of what may well be termed idealists from all over the world will increase apace, for one of the most striking things about this war is the depth of feeling which it has aroused among anti-fascists everywhere. They, as well as Hitler and Mussolini, are turning the Spanish Civil War into a world war.'[33]

15

The Battle of the Mist: Boadilla, 14–23 December 1936

As people back home counted down the five days left until Christmas, Esmond Romilly found himself stuck in crossfire in the woods outside Boadilla del Monte, a tiny village in the wooded countryside twenty kilometres west of Madrid. A Spanish Republican unit had retreated through the lines of his mostly German company of the Thälmann Battalion as Franco's forces, having failed to conquer Madrid with frontal attacks, tried to encircle the city. It was the fourth day of a fierce battle which pitted the two International Brigades and a number of Spanish Republican units against Francoist rebels backed by German tanks. The Thälmann volunteers remained dug in but, in the general confusion, Romilly's group of ten British volunteers from the same *Zug* (platoon) thought they had received an order to advance. A ragged group of Spanish anarchists went forward with them. 'I had no idea where we were going or what was happening,' Romilly admitted. But as the crossfire intensified and they scrambled for shelter, the eighteen-year-old looked around and saw his close friend Joe Gough – an 'unemployed Luton humourist' with whom he had made a pact of mutual protection – kneeling on the grass, his head hanging unnaturally forward and his gun pointed to the ground between his hands. 'I tried not to look at his head – it was sunk forward on to his chest. I felt I was in the presence of something horrifying. I didn't think about where we were, or the bullets – I didn't think about Joe being dead – I just thought it was all wrong Joe's head being like that.'[1]

The survivors of Romilly's small *Zug* of English speakers ran back through the woods, turning to fire at their pursuers, taking cover every few metres behind the short, wide-canopied pine trees. Small Italian- or German-made tanks were driving along the trenches, machine-gunning those who had stayed. Romilly could see enemy soldiers walking along behind them, shooting the injured.[2] Bombers sent shrapnel up behind them as they rushed from ridge to ridge. Romilly and his band of English speakers were not the only ones running. That night the German company commander read through the first seven English names on the roll call of Romilly's *Zug* – 'Avener, Birch, Cox, Gillan, Gough, Jeans, Messer …' All but one was greeted with the word *gefallen*, 'dead'. Six of the section had died, and one more was injured.[3] It had, in effect, ceased to exist. The three survivors would soon be shipped home.

This was the first time that the first two International Brigades – XI and XII Brigades – had fought side by side. Despite the lessons learned at University City and elsewhere, their 3,000 volunteers – or however many were left – were unable to hold their line. Days of fog had been followed by rain; to Jan Kurzke the landscape looked 'brown and dismal, like Hampstead Heath in December'.[4] It was here that the only English-speaking units in the Brigades, the machine-gun section of the French Commune de Paris (also now referred to as the Dumont Battalion)[5] and Romilly's *Zug*, finally met. Amongst the radical public schoolboys this was something of a reunion, since Romilly already knew Cornford and had a remarkably similar background to David Mackenzie, a rear admiral's son who had been schooled at Marlborough College.[6] 'I've come here to deny the report that I have been killed,' Romilly would hear Mackenzie tell a journalist in Madrid shortly after this battle was over.

The International Brigades had moved to Boadilla hurriedly after deserters revealed that Franco intended to make a second attempt at blocking the road that ran north-west out of Madrid towards Galicia and La Coruña.[7] It followed a failed attempt to cut the road two weeks earlier and isolate the capital from those defending the mountain ranges to the north-west. With the combined use of aerial bombardment, tanks and infantry by both sides, Renn saw this as the first proper battle of the war. Kurzke's unit had arrived in a bad mood, since they had been planning to spend the first afternoon on leave in Madrid. 'We were already climbing on the trucks when the alarm came through. One truck had already left and they had to chase it half way to Madrid with a motor-bike, and caught up with it just as the boys were sighting the first pub,' he said.[8] Even then they had to wait for hours for the transport to arrive, huddled in the rain and stamping their feet to keep warm. The mist and rain constantly frustrated plans and disoriented troops on both sides. The Republican army was still chaotically organised and basic defensive tactics, like digging proper trenches, were routinely disregarded.[9] Eventually, almost the whole of the first two International Brigades, the 'saviours of Madrid', found themselves fleeing through the low pines in the sparsely wooded, sandy-soiled countryside around Boadilla del Monte. Kurzke's commissar, Rebière, called it a moment of 'sauve qui peut', or 'every man for himself'.

Boadilla was one of the key points and it was just in front of the village that Kurzke and his company set up their two machine guns early in the battle. Like many of the villages that the Brigaders were encountering, Boadilla reflected the social realities of life in the countryside around Madrid. The largest buildings were the church and Palace of Infante Don Luis – a three-storey, neoclassical country house built for a member of the royal family in the eighteenth century. Apart from that, according to one Brigader, all the other buildings were 'hovels'.

It was political commissar Bernard Knox's final day: 'Soon we saw the milicianos in front of us in full retreat,' he wrote:

> as they came toward Boadilla and the main road our orders were to cover their retreat and hold our position until further orders. The order to withdraw soon came; we did so by sections, one covering the other with fire as it came back. As our section was moving back, dragging the gun, I felt a shocking blow [from a bullet] and a burning pain through my neck and right shoulder and fell to the ground on my back with blood spurting up like a fountain. John came back, with David, our Oxford man who had been a medical student. I heard him say, 'I can't do anything about that,' and John bent down and said, 'God bless you, Bernard,' and left. They had to go; they had to set up the gun and cover the withdrawal of our other crew. And they were sure that I was dying.
>
> So was I. As the blood continued to spurt I could feel my consciousness slipping fast away. I have since then read many

accounts by people who, like me, were sure they were dying but survived. Many of them speak of a feeling of heavenly peace, others of visions of angels welcoming them to heaven. I had no such feelings or visions; I was consumed with rage – furious, violent rage. Why me? I was just twenty-one and had barely begun living my life. Why should I have to die? It was unjust.[10]

In later life, as a Harvard classics professor, Knox discovered this reaction was not untypical. Hector, in Homer's *Iliad*, had gone 'winging down to the House of Death, wailing his fate, leaving his manhood far behind, his young and supple strength', while Virgil's Turnus 'fled angry to the shades below' causing the commentator Servi to remark that he was 'angry. Because he was young.'[11] Many other young men died the same way that day, on both sides.

Jan Kurzke recalled watching Knox's face turn 'a frightful white colour' as shrapnel shredded the scrub and pine trees around them. Then Kurzke himself was hit: 'I must have roared with pain as my leg shot into the air and I thought it had been torn off though I was clutching it with my hands and it was shaking as if jerked by strings. I was lying on my back though I did not remember having fallen and I was conscious. John [Cornford] and someone else were bending over me and the other man was cutting my trouser leg open and tying a string round my leg to stop the bleeding ... I could not, at the moment, remember where I was or where I was going.'[12] He tipped wine down his throat in an attempt to quench the sudden thirst brought on by shock and the loss of blood and – with his leg bent, paralysed and bleeding heavily – he was alternately dragged and carried back by Cornford and the others.

Injured men were routinely transported back on mules, but even this option was no longer available. Leon, the aged grey mule that had been carrying the machine guns (named after either Trotsky or Blum, presumably because of his bony head), was too decrepit. A young jenny they had found to accompany him had been caught in the crossfire (the French cooks, nevertheless, found a use for her).

When the machine-gun crew bumped into the stocky figure of their commissar, Rebière, the latter threw the injured Kurzke across his shoulder. Kurzke was eventually strapped to the front of a tank, from where he could see the retreating troops as they pushed past the officers who were trying to stop them. 'Once an anarchist runs there is no stopping him,' he scoffed.[13] After a long, bumpy and painful ride to Madrid, both Knox and Kurzke were carried into one of the city's grandest hotels, the Palace, which was now a hospital. The ballroom, lined with gold mirrors, had been turned into an operating theatre, with eight tables under the enormous crystal chandeliers; individual rooms had been turned into wards.[14] Kurzke found himself in Room 360, being tucked into white linen sheets under a yellow bedspread and looking bemusedly at a shiny, polished wardrobe.[15] As with Romilly's section, there was now little left of the English-speaking machine-gun unit of the French Brigade. To the dismay of those who had fought with them, the survivors were sent back to HQ Albacete to join a new brigade.[16]

Boadilla, or the so-called 'Battle of the Mist', was the first operation in which a majority of the first two International Brigades had fought together. The encounter revealed that while the volunteers could fight more or less efficiently at close quarters on the fringes of Madrid, manoeuvring in wider spaces exposed the inadequacies of both the International Brigades and the Republican army as a whole. Raw courage and political conviction were clearly not enough, especially when attacking an entrenched enemy.

By the time it was all over, Rebière was furious. He knew who to blame, or thought he did. Anarchists were the prime culprits, followed by the Germans. The former were a standard scapegoat and little was expected of them; the latter were his own companions in arms and included Romilly's now decimated *Zug*. The vitriol in Rebière's post-battle report reveals just how hard the dream of a Tower of Babel version of internationalism was to put into practice in a Europe where most workers had barely travelled beyond their home towns. Since any failure of coordination put lives at risk, this was an important issue and one which aroused nationalistic and chauvinistic passions.

At the start of the Battle of the Mist, the Thälmann Battalion had reached their position too late because their captain had gone to lunch and left the order on his desk, or so Rebière claimed.[17] That had allowed Franco's troops to take the village of Boadilla (along with the fact that the French battalion was already 152 men, or around 20 per cent, short).[18] The fighting over the following days had been all about trying to stop the enemy advancing further and then pushing it back into the village.[19] A furious Dumont demanded, but failed to get, an apology, while his men muttered about 'treason' and betrayal.[20] Whatever the truth, the consequences were undoubtedly grave. Had the village been held, the numerous casualties – the corpses of volunteers strewn amongst the scrub and pine needles in the woodland to its north – would not have occurred. Many belonged to the Thälmann Battalion itself. The dead from Romilly's *Zug* were finally collected and taken to the new International Brigades' cemetery in the village of Fuencarral, to be buried alongside eighteen German volunteers who died in the same battle.[21]

Esmond Romilly returned to England soon after, publishing a well-received account of his experiences, *Boadilla*. In his write-up of the battle in the newspaper *Todos Unidos*, one of the many newspapers that would be edited by the International Brigades themselves, Thälmann commander Richard Staimer (who had taken over from Renn[22]) mentioned twenty model German proletarians 'aged between twenty-two and twenty-four'. In fact, their average age was twenty-nine. He failed completely to mention the English dead, or the Poles, Belgians, French, Swiss and other nationalities in his battalion who had been killed.[23] Even had he wanted to acknowledge these deaths, Staimer might have found it hard to discover all their names. The small, stiff sepia cards used to record those buried at Fuencarral – recycled from office use, with the previous annotations scribbled out – reveal the difficulties in identifying the dead. This was either because there was not yet a proper register, or the bodies were unrecognisable. Where names were not available, the cards offer up clues such as 'he has black skin' (maybe a volunteer from Cuba, the United States or Africa), 'monogrammed red socks', or 'tattooed chest reads *"souvenir du Maroc"*.' Other tattoos on unidentified corpses included 'a serpent coiled around a dagger', 'a wrist-watch', and 'a young man with hat'.[24]

The Germans' error of arriving late was made, in Rebière's eyes, more outrageous by the fact that they apparently looked down on the other volunteers. Ever since the Thälmann Battalion had replaced the Polish-led Dombrowski, the Germans had tightened their control over XI Brigade as a whole, and treated it as their own. 'A certain imperialism reigns amongst them,' Rebière claimed. 'This spirit of domination is, without doubt, the result of the education imposed on the German people by the country's bourgeoisie. They only trust themselves. They spoil the [German-speaking] Edgar André and Thälmann Battalions, while the French battalion remains the poor cousin.' Dressed in their smart khaki uniforms, he added, they considered the French, in their motley clothes, to be inferior soldiers.[25]

Rebière deemed the Germans' behaviour 'childish' and claimed the French were above that sort of thing, but he was voicing a sensation that was more apparent to the French than to others. It certainly was not true amongst XI Brigade's senior officers – where news that Dumont's French were retreating 'for the first time ever' had been taken as a sign of just how grave the situation must be. In one of the hagiographical and heavily censored 'official' Brigade histories, written by German volunteer (and, later, Thälmann Battalion commander) Gustav Szinda, he claimed that: 'If you wanted to find Dumont, you only needed to go where the fight was the hardest. His name and the battalion were so popular among all the units, and when the French battalion was on the right or left wing, the battalions immediately whispered: "Today we need not be afraid, Dumont is to our right or left!" '[26] If the Germans thought they were superior, Rebière clearly held to an even older prejudice. A German-Jewish mafia had installed itself in Brigade headquarters, he claimed, making sure that they kept the most comfortable and least dangerous jobs for themselves.[27]

Stalin Was Still a Saint: Albacete, November–December 1936

Many years later Gustav Regler, the German writer who had become a political commissar in Lukács's brigade, would recall his first meeting with André Marty at the International Brigades' HQ in Albacete. Regler had left Madrid at Koltsov's urging during the panicky days of early November 1936, when it looked as though Franco would enter the city, and decided to enlist in the International Brigades.[1] He came to Albacete with impressive credentials. Koltsov, after all, was considered to be Stalin's eyes and ears in Spain. Regler could also boast of a long friendship with the French writer André Malraux. The latter was not a communist, but his España squadron of a dozen pilots and old Potez bombers had been one of the first volunteer outfits to help the Republic.[2]

Regler had expected a warm reception. Instead, he found himself under interrogation as Marty tried to work out whether he was a double agent for any of the multiple enemies who populated his paranoid Stalinist world view:

As he invited me to be seated in his office, I felt that he had decided upon a cat-and-mouse game.

'Where have you been?' he asked. 'What do you think of General Miaja? Are the Republicans going to win?' And then suddenly: 'When did you leave Germany? Whom do you know in Paris? Malraux? Aha! Where is he now? Did you also meet any anarchists?' Then abruptly, this time like a pistol-shot: '*Show me your membership card of the POUM!*'[3]

Regler had not yet paid much attention to the POUM (Workers' Party of Marxist Unification) – the breakaway Catalan-based communists led by Andreu Nin who would welcome 600 foreign fighters into their ranks. It was viewed by Marty as Trotskyist, a hated rival to Stalinist-style communism and, so, a deadly foe (even if, in Spain, it backed the Republic). In fact, Nin's party was organisationally independent, although it shared Trotsky's view that Stalin's tactical pragmatism was a cynical manoeuvre away from pure and proper communism.[4]

The meeting with Marty proved depressing confirmation of what Regler eventually saw as the unstoppable decline of his beloved communism, which was starting to turn into 'a world of hypocrisy which left me crippled in spirit'.[5] Unlike most of the working-class recruits to the International Brigades, Regler's elevated position as an intellectual had given him a privileged view of the increasingly cruel machinations of Stalinism. He had begun to suspect that something was going wrong the previous year, when he took part in a left-wing writers convention in Paris. There the French author André Gide had publicly offered his allegiance to the Soviet Union. Gide was not a party member, but the communists were delighted to have one of Europe's greatest intellectuals (who would win the Nobel Prize for Literature in 1947) as a so-called 'fellow-traveller'. Regler himself had led the crowd of 5,000 into singing a communist anthem, but then been scolded for making a 'popular front' moment look like a party event. While receiving this reprimand, Regler noticed how the other writers present in the room 'sat like schoolchildren who have been reminded that the cane is always in readiness behind the blackboard'.[6]

On a recent visit to the Soviet Union, Regler had seen how the cult of Stalinism, and its obsession with 'enemies' of all kinds, was beginning to take hold. A friend had been arrested under new laws against homosexuality – even while Gide, a noted homosexual himself, was being paraded around the country like a public trophy. After seeing a factory worker taken off by an armed guard ('a robot leading off a robot') for twice breaking a machine tool, Regler realised that mere negligence was now considered criminal. 'A failure of nerve, a slip in a calculation, a defect of raw material, a trick of wind or weather – it was all the same, all sabotage,' he said.[7] Suspicion and fear were spreading rapidly, leading people to think one way but act and talk another. 'This psychosis, the daily possibility of a lapse into sin, was fostered on the highest level. Any act of kindness was to be viewed with suspicion, and there was no such thing as mercy, so that too was ruled out.'[8]

The most shocking purges of all had been announced the previous summer, while Regler was with the African American singer Paul Robeson at a Moscow radio station. Robeson was giving a talk on Russia's own mixed-race poet, Pushkin (whose great-grandfather had been an African slave, freed by Peter the Great), and had just pronounced the Soviet Union to be: 'The only country in the world where we can feel at home. Here there is no segregation, no foolish ban – we are all brothers'.[9] He was then expected to sing, but instead an announcer read out in a shaky voice the news that the legendary old Bolsheviks Grigory Zinoviev, Lev Kamenev and a dozen others were to be tried. Robeson was as shocked as Regler that these founders of the revolution were now enemies. 'It must not be!' he cried out, and refused to sing.[10]

In August, Regler had watched Kamenev and the others enter the monumental House of the Unions for the show trials that saw them confess in order to protect their families and be rapidly executed in the Lubyanka basement.[11] He was reminded of similar trials in Nazi Germany and imagined 'the founders of the State ... being consigned blood-stained to their coffins, while in the Kremlin a man who would let no other man near him sat sipping vodka and poring over the next list of victims'.[12] Regler began to have nightmares in which he himself was being persecuted, and would wake up sweating.

While all this was happening in Moscow, Regler followed the news from Spain. He was both alarmed and thrilled. 'Spain was the threatened friend in 1936, after Russia had proved to be the friend fallen into evil ways,' he said.[13] His excitement increased when he discovered that the USSR was backing the Republic and that his friend Koltsov was now the *Pravda* correspondent in Spain. 'We shall support the Spanish Republicans ... Stalin believes in revolutions – when they don't happen at home,' a friend quipped.[14]

Regler had enjoyed a privileged, if depressing, view of the events in Moscow. Ordinary, working-class communists across Europe could not be expected to share anything like that depth of knowledge. For them, the basic credo remained pure. Proof of that had come while they were fighting at the University City, when the Eighth Extraordinary Session of the Soviets met in Moscow to approve a new constitution for the USSR.[15] This was Stalin's constitution, or so the Brigaders read in their own *Peuple en Armes* newspaper, which was overseen by the commissars. 'It starts from the viewpoint that all nations and races have equal rights ... that differences of colour, language, cultural level, level of development, or any other difference between peoples and races cannot be used to justify inequality,' the newspaper reported.[16] The aim was 'the abolition of misery for the majority, and of luxury for the minority'. The success of the previous stage of communism meant that they had now reached a promised land where, finally, 'from everyone according to his abilities, for everyone according to their needs'. Here were a set of ideals with which even those who were not communists could sympathise.[17]

To many volunteers, in the words of a Canadian who later turned his back on communism, 'Stalin was still a saint.'[18] To people in Republican Spain, this was mostly unquestionable. He was, after all, the only world leader of any standing – apart from Mexico's president, Lázaro Cárdenas – prepared to defend the Republic against the fascist-backed generals. Some of those who travelled to Spain with no political affiliation soon came to appreciate the party's disciplined approach to warfare and joined the Spanish Communist Party.[19] For many, in any case, the goings-on in Moscow were irrelevant. They were in Spain, and the fight here was against fascism. That was far more important.

Regler did nothing to disabuse his fellow volunteers of the idea that Stalin was, indeed, a saint. After his stormy meeting with Marty in Albacete, he bumped into André Malraux. Sitting in the corner of a shabby, fly-infested cafe, they read through the manuscript of *Return from the USSR*, which Gide had sent to Malraux so that he could help him decide whether to publish this evisceration of Soviet Russia, after a visit which had shattered his illusions. It was one of the first anti-Soviet tracts by an intellectual voice supposedly sympathetic to communism. Gide's messenger stood at the cafe doorway, talking to the boot-boy and waiting to carry the reply back to France. The manuscript was like an unexploded bomb. 'I doubt whether in any other country in the world, even Hitler's Germany, thought be less free, more bowed down, more fearful (terrorised), more vassalised,' it read. 'We were promised a proletarian dictatorship. We are far from the mark. A dictatorship, yes, obviously; but the dictatorship of a man.'[20]

Both Regler and Malraux (who had visited the Soviet Union in 1934) increasingly shared Gide's opinions, but they also thought it best if the book remained unpublished until after the Spanish war. Hitler was an even worse threat. The rest of Europe, especially Spain, needed Stalin's Russia too badly. Gide ignored their advice and published with Gallimard later that month in Paris, unleashing a storm of criticism. His final line – possibly added because of the response from his friends at the International Brigades' base in Albacete – held out the hope that Spain would somehow inspire the USSR to rescue itself, rather than the other way around: 'The help that the Soviet Union is giving to Spain shows us what fine capabilities of recovery it still possesses,' he said.[21]

As if to stoke the drama further, Marty sent for Regler again and was unctuous in his friendliness. It was all part of what one French volunteer would call Marty's 'baggage of inconsistencies'.[22] Marty led Regler up to his wife's room and left him there. The tall, green-eyed, dark-haired Pauline Taurinya – who reportedly also controlled the camp's accounts, ran the International Brigades' incipient medical service and kept firm control of her husband[23] – spread a collection of pistols across her bed and invited Regler to choose one. 'I did so with deliberate coolness, bowed to the very good-looking woman and withdrew, scenting a suspicious mixture of politics and sex,' he wrote.[24]

Marty was not wrong to suspect that the International Brigades might have been infiltrated by spies. He was just looking in the wrong place, for at least one of these was often by his side. Like many of the volunteers, Marty's quartermaster, Henri Dupré, had lived much of his adult life in a world of radical politics, coloured by violence. Unlike the vast majority of others, he was a fascist. In the summer of 1936, the forty-one-year-old had helped found the secret Cagoule fascist group in France.[25] Like other European countries, France had an array of fascist-leaning groups, but this one was especially dangerous because it both planned to overthrow the government and enjoyed the backing of the L'Oréal cosmetics company owner, Eugène Schueller, and other wealthy industrialists. Some of the French volunteers had probably spent the previous couple of years involved in street fights with its members. If it was surprising to find a fascist in the ranks of the volunteers, then it was even more surprising that soon after HQ Albacete was set up, Dupré was appointed quartermaster-general, responsible for all supplies.[26] The reason for that, quite simply, was that André Marty liked him. Marty did not of course know he was a fascist and, paranoid as he was, was quite incapable of seeing that the biggest spy and saboteur of all was someone he himself had appointed to one of the most important positions in the Brigades. Before Dumont appeared, indeed, he had wanted Dupré to take command of the Commune de Paris Battalion.[27] He even appears to have tasked him with spying on other military commanders and keeping an eye on anarchists and other potential troublemakers in the first French units.[28]

Dupré claims to have joined the Brigades with twenty other undercover Cagoule members, all of whom were part of the group of 300 who left Gare d'Austerlitz train station in Paris on 4 October 1936. It is possible that he knew the communist world well, since, in the political turbulence of the time, a sector of the French far left had swung to the far right, following former communists (and future collaborationists with Hitler) like Jacques Doriot or Marcel Gitton. Dupré ingratiated himself with Marty, and fooled others, by outdoing them in his harshness and expressions of mistrust. 'If I was the general in charge I would immediately execute the entire headquarters staff of the first [XI] Brigade for "sabotage",' he told an astonished Giuseppe di Vittorio at one stage, after that brigade went into action low on munitions, with faulty machine guns and short of food. After Dupré's men had injected a mixture of oil and black sand – or 'emery grit' – into the gearboxes of several trucks, he angrily demanded that the drivers be placed before a firing squad 'without trial'.[29]

The impact of Dupré's malign influence is impossible to track. A boastful biography he wrote several years later is both unreliable and unspecific, talking of 'the sabotage of arms, munitions and transport' between October 1936 and August 1937.[30] Dupré claims that the success of the sabotage which his group of twenty infiltrators perpetrated was seen most clearly during the bigger battles. He exaggerated wildly, but his testimony suggests that the word 'treachery' may help resolve several otherwise unanswerable questions. Why had so many machine guns and rifles jammed in the first few days of fighting in Madrid? He certainly claimed that the same 'emery grit' had been applied to the Russian Maxims carried by some of the first machine-gun groups. His later grandstanding is so outrageous that it is impossible to divine truth from lies. The only thing that remains clear are his beliefs: that he hated 'Slavs'; that Bonaparte had been right to identify Russia and the 'Barbarians from the east' as the enemy; that only 'continental soldiers' could keep 'the flame of intelligence and human dignity' alive; and, lastly, that Mussolini was the only one doing that.[31]

The impact of Dupré's treachery may be difficult to evaluate, but it cannot have helped when the brand new XIII International Brigade set out from Albacete in December.[32] Organisation and training were still rudimentary. One of the battalions, the Chapaev, broke all Tower of Babel records with people from twenty-one nations in it. They included twenty 'Palestinians', who were mostly left-wing Jews from British-run Mandatory Palestine, five men from Luxembourg, and one Brazilian.[33]

Thirteenth International Brigade was part of a larger force, which included the anarchist Iron Column, tasked with conquering the city of Teruel. This snowbound provincial capital sat just 160 kilometres from the Mediterranean coast and there were fears that Franco might use it as a springboard to push east and split Republican Spain in two. The battle was to be planned and overseen by two Russian advisors called Voronov and Kolpakchi. The ground attack was launched on 27 December, with the aim of separating Teruel from the rest of the Francoist forces, and starving it into submission.

Shortly after the three battalions of this new brigade launched their attack, they were surprised to hear the voice of one of their own battalion commanders haranguing them on a loudspeaker. He had crossed the line to the enemy side and was now encouraging others to follow him. He may have been one of the twenty Cagoule men who had allegedly joined the Brigades with Dupré. As if this was not disheartening enough, his substitute proved incompetent and the battalion of 490 men ended up being commanded by a lowly sergeant.[34] Once more, and despite 'professional' Russian planning, the Republican army failed to mount a properly joined-up attack. Artillery fire proved ineffectual, various Russian tanks were knocked out, at least two of Malraux's planes[35] were downed, the railway was not cut and enemy reinforcements arrived from as far away as Madrid. Losses, in dead and captured, were so large that after a few days the three battalions were merged into two.[36]

The Chapaev battalion, named after the Red Army's celebrated Russian Civil War commander Vasily Chapaev, carried the brunt of the fighting at Teruel. It launched seven attacks up the terraced vineyards in order to take a strategically positioned cemetery, but was forced back each time.[37] The battalion may have been chosen to lead the attack because their commander, Hans Klaus Becker,[38] had made them look so smart and disciplined on the parade ground or simply because they were mostly German and mostly communists, like XIII Brigade's Moscow-trained commander, the outwardly jovial and phlegmatic Wilhelm Zaisser, known as 'General Gómez'.[39]

Becker was a communist who had been in exile in France. He was also a former German army officer, which may explain why some commissars, who deemed him 'a bad communist', mistrusted him.[40] To his critics, Becker was a poor leader. His moods swung violently. One moment he was physically attacking members of the French battalion because they refused to move without a French commander, the next he was moping and complaining, demoralising his men by telling them they had been given an impossible task and arguing that they should return to Valencia (where they had spent a week awaiting an Italian beach-landing that never happened). He argued with his political commissars, who opposed his constant orders to withdraw and disliked his tendency to blame junior officers. He had led his men unnecessarily through a valley covered by enemy machine guns, before insisting on giving a rousing pre-attack speech in a gravel pit that was known to be targeted by enemy artillery. Shells fell and, amid scenes of panic, eight of his men died. By the end of a week of failed attacks Becker appeared to have given up, was barely present on the battlefield and had left the political commissars and company commanders to lead the men. Eventually, attempts at advancing were abandoned and, instead, the men dug a vast network of defensive trenches. Rather than concentrate on their own poor officers, however, the Brigade leadership blamed the anarchists, claiming that they had deliberately tried to demoralise the volunteers.[41]

Anarchists were always the easy scapegoat. They were especially disliked by senior officers and communists because some volunteers clearly found their ideals attractive. 'After the first attack, a campaign was begun amongst the volunteers to sow discontent and reduce their confidence in their officers, blaming them for the losses suffered,' wrote Luigi Longo.[42] 'The volunteers were invited to desert and join the anarchist column where – the agents of discontent claimed – there were better physical conditions, frequent leave and no need to be continually throwing oneself into such bloody attacks.' Fifteen of them, indeed, ran off with the anarchists when they withdrew.[43] The volunteers were hardly to blame for being attracted by the creature comforts offered by the anarchists. Their own officers, after all, required them to cope with temperatures as low as minus fifteen Celsius over several weeks.[44] Marty blamed 'the sectarianism' of a communist cabal led by a commissar called Souchnec for the fact that up to 250 had deserted on their way through Valencia.

The Francoist side was delighted by XIII Brigade's early problems. It claimed to have put 250 volunteers out of action and captured five Russian tanks in a single day. Overall losses were worse than that, since the Chapaev Battalion alone lost more than three hundred men. The Teruel attack ended in failure, and the Brigade (having lost 800 of the 1,900 men it set out with) had to be sent 100 kilometres south to Utiel to reorganise.

A pattern, however, had now been established. On the one hand, failure needed a scapegoat, in this case Becker, whose political purity was deemed suspect. On the other hand, and more dramatically for the vast majority of volunteers who had nothing to do with the political posturing and infighting amongst the upper ranks, it was becoming clear that new International Brigade units were routinely suffering serious losses in their first combat operation. This was, perhaps, inevitable, given the lack of training, their use as shock troops and the fact that these men were being forced to learn how to fight on the battlefield itself. In the chaos of the Republican army, however, there was nothing strange about that.[45]

17

Sans Nom and the Poles: Southern front, Andalusia, Christmas Eve, 1936

From the outbreak of the war in Spain, Aleksander and Berta Szurek had spent many of their free hours listening intently to their radio set. At their home in Rouen, they followed the progress of the battles and fretted about the victories of Franco's troops. Few people in the capital of Normandy shared their enthusiasm. None of their fellow Poles in the city were, like the Szureks, members of the Communist Party. Most saw communism as a threat to their Catholic religion. Even amongst the town's émigré Jews, more attuned to the horrors of fascism, there was a deep scepticism about far-left politics. Some also saw communism as a threat to their religion and, hence, identity.[1] Aleksander Szurek, however, sought freedom, sacrifice and the kind of adventure that could satisfy his desire to experience both action and the romance of revolution.[2]

Poverty, rather than politics, had driven a large number of Polish Jews to France and Belgium over the previous decades. A visiting British Jew, Neville Laski, was shocked two years earlier by the 'poverty, squalor and filth' he found in the Jewish quarter of Warsaw, which he deemed 'a teeming city of wretchedness'.[3] Millions of non-Jews were equally as poor. 'It made me despair of civilisation,' Laski wrote. 'I have heard much of Poland. But nothing that I have seen or heard in any degree pictures what I saw with my own eyes.' Few parts of Europe were poorer than this and 'misery' drove many Jews towards communism, according to one enlightened government minister Laski met.

While Germany began its journey towards genocide and the Holocaust, anti-Semitism was on the rise all across Central and Eastern Europe after the First World War. Countries with large Jewish populations like Hungary, Romania and, above all, Austria became increasingly aggressive.[4] In the words of one historian: 'In the 1920s and 1930s Central and Eastern European Jewry nearly everywhere faced the threat of communal degradation or dissolution, if not of physical uprooting and destruction, well before the "Final Solution" was launched.'[5] The authoritarian government of Marshal Józef Piłsudski that ruled the Poland which had emerged, once more, as an independent nation in 1918, was by no means the worst.

As the head of a country with large Jewish, Ukrainian and Byelorussian minorities, Pilsudski could not completely ignore its varied cultures. By 1936, however, his successors were actively promoting anti-Semitic legislation and violence against Jews appears to have claimed several hundred lives between 1935 and 1939.[6] All this helped push a section of Poland's Jews further towards the socialist Jewish Labour Bund or to communism.[7] Those who left the country often found a willing audience for their ideas among immigrant factory workers in France and elsewhere. As a result, only about 20 per cent of Polish International Brigade volunteers came directly from their own country: most were economic migrants living in France, Argentina and Belgium; almost a third were Jewish (against 10 per cent of the population) and 15 per cent identified as Ukrainian or Byelorussian rather than straightforwardly Polish. Ninety-two per cent were working class, much like the volunteers from other countries.[8]

Berta Szurek did not argue, but she grew restless as the time for her husband's departure drew near. They had been through much already. To begin with she had agreed that, as an active party member, it was Aleksander's duty to heed the call for volunteers. She, too, was devoted to the party. It had guided their lives since before they left Poland. Now, however, she sighed and suffered. 'Maybe I should go with you,' she said. But the couple had a child, a young daughter named Helena.[9] Who would look after her? A Latvian, an Armenian and two German refugees from Rouen had agreed to go with Szurek. They were the only recruits he could find. Their goodbye party was, despite the political differences, held at the town's Zionist club, loaned to them for the occasion ('You could say,' Szurek noted later, 'that, faced with war, they joined us like they did later in the Warsaw Ghetto uprising.'). They drank wine, but this was no celebration. Berta gave the only speech, holding back tears. 'Go fight for humanity and our children,' she said, and, 'Come back!' Some in the audience cried.[10]

Szurek's group followed the now familiar route across the border, stopping first at the run-down castle in Figueres until there were enough volunteers gathered there to fill all the carriages of a train, which villagers still came out to cheer. Gathered in the bullring in Albacete, the new arrivals were again asked to separate themselves into groups of former officers, non-commissioned officers and ordinary soldiers. Szurek was amongst the latter. Watching from above was a shaven-headed officer with blue eyes and scars across his skull. His pasty white complexion and pale eyes suggested that he must come from Northern or Eastern Europe. He wore high cavalry boots, breeches and a leather jacket. There were no insignia on his cap to explain who this man – referred to as 'Walter' – was, except that everybody knew he was commander of the new brigade that they were expected to join: XIV International Brigade.

At Albacete, Szurek soon ran into people he knew. Amongst them was an old colleague from the Geserd, or 'Society to Settle Working Jews on the Land in the USSR'.[11] The Geserd had helped organise emigration from Europe and the Americas to the specially created Jewish settlement land around Birobidzhan – in the USSR's far east, towards the end of the Trans-Siberian Railway. The town was situated just eighty kilometres from the southern border with China and lay closer to Alaska than to the Holy Land. The first settlers here had had to contend with terrible floods, while bears and tigers roamed the nearby forests. It was, nevertheless, a Jewish homeland of some kind. Nobody could imagine that, in the future, the Birobidzhan Jews would also face purges.

The training procedures at Albacete had barely improved during the first months of the war. By the time Szurek left for the front, heading with the rest of his battalion towards southern Andalusia, he had still not fired a live round. Most others had only been given the opportunity to fire off six bullets from a handful of antique rifles that were kept for training purposes.[12]

Although XIV Brigade was mostly French-speaking, one of its four battalions, known as the Slavic Battalion, was made up of thirty-two different nationalities.[13] This was the so-called 'Sans Nom', the 'Nameless'

Battalion – formally known as the 9th Battalion, International Brigades – and Szurek had been sent to its Polish company. Its creation was so rapid that it could not even join the other three battalions when they first paraded in front of their commanders. Szurek soon discovered that his new commander, 'General Walter', was a fellow Pole who, as he proved when showing his company how to dismantle their weapons, was obviously comfortable with guns. He was also perfectly fluent in Russian, and was beginning to have a workable command of both Spanish and French.[14] Walter's brigade staff – a mixture of Poles, Italians, Germans and Bulgarians and French – spoke to each other in Russian. That this should be their lingua franca was another sign of how important the 'Mexicans' were in the International Brigades' upper ranks, though a fifty-year-old French socialist was in charge of its artillery.[15]

The Red Army, once more, was providing the leadership. Walter was Karol Świerczewski – a forty-six-year-old veteran of several wars and a former military instructor at a Comintern school in Moscow. Some of the 'Mexicans' had almost certainly studied under him. Even more than Lukács or Kléber, who had interspersed their military activity with spying or writing, he was a full-time soldier, shaped entirely by the culture of barrack room and battlefield. His role in the Comintern school had been as commander of a training centre for guerrilla fighters from communist parties around the world.[16] He was both the best and probably the harshest commander the Brigaders would have – a man of considerable personal courage, but one who showed no mercy when it came to shooting prisoners or those deemed cowardly in battle.

Len Crome, a Latvian-born volunteer who had moved to Edinburgh aged seventeen and qualified as a doctor, recalled meeting Walter for the first time and wondering why he had been so distant. Crome suspected the problem was that he was not a communist; in fact, Walter's scorn reflected a different way of ranking people. 'You dress and behave like a civilian,' a fellow medic explained to Crome. The next morning, Crome stood nervously in a Madrid tailor's shop being measured for a uniform.

Although Walter was not intellectual, Crome found his grasp of situations, and of people, 'uncannily accurate, crisp and sophisticated':

> While his loyalty to communism and the Spanish Republican cause was unquestionable, his view of superior officers and hierarchy was

often sceptical, not to say cynical. His remarks about people at the base, in Albacete and elsewhere, men like Marty and others, were caustic, scathing and often unprintable. Personally, I never learned to predict his reactions. His impact was always forceful, both at rest and in action. I don't think that I ever stopped being afraid of him ...[17]

Crome recalled several occasions when Walter had ordered the shooting of his own men or officers for cowardice, while also showing 'short shrift to spies and diversionists planted among us'. He claimed to love the rank and file, however, stating that there were 'no bad soldiers – only bad officers'.[18] He forced his men to train hard, but also made sure they had the best possible food, clothes, footwear and quarters.

Walter marvelled at the way a brigade could be conjured up out of nothing. One of his battalions, he later reported, had been 'gathered, staffed, and armed in one day'.[19]

The order that formally created XIV International Brigade was issued on 23 December, and that same afternoon, at four o'clock, 'the first echelon took to the southern front' in Andalusia.[20] Despite this rush, the brigade was, in some ways, the best prepared unit to have left Albacete. It was the fourth of the International Brigades – and the fact that a further 3,000-odd men could be put together in four battalions was a sign of just how many volunteers were pouring across the border into Spain.[21] Some 14,000 men had arrived in just ten weeks, at an average rate of 200 per day. The Sans Nom Battalion boasted thirty-six machine guns, giving it a firepower that previous battalions could scarcely dream of. Armament, however, is no replacement for training. Nor does it turn bad officers into good ones.

There had been some conspicuously incongruous appointments. Major Gaston Delasalle, a dandified former French military intelligence officer who had allegedly taken part in the attempts to squash the navy mutiny led by Marty in the Black Sea in 1919, was given command of the Marseillaise Battalion.[22] He was a straightforward mercenary, a soldier who enjoyed his profession and was happy to exercise it on behalf of people who might appreciate his talents, and pay him. In the Republican army and the International Brigades, he could expect, too, to be promoted to positions of responsibility more rapidly than in another army. Within the Marseillaise Battalion, former Great War British army officer George Nathan, a Jewish Londoner, was given the rank of captain and put in charge of the first all-English-speaking company in the Brigades. The five remaining members of Cornford's machine-gun unit were also sent there, where they were joined by another prominent British writer and historian, Ralph Fox. British communist leader Harry Pollitt was delighted, since he had wanted a writer to present as a new Lord Byron, imitating the latter's exploits in Greece. He had even been disappointed with the poet Stephen Spender for declining to play the role.[23] This company also included the well-known IRA leader Frank Ryan, who had led a group of thirteen Irishmen into Spain as a counterweight to a separate column of Catholic volunteers who had gone to fight for Franco.[24]

The ex-British army officer Nathan arrived in Albacete in a mismatched outfit – half military and half civilian – cheap shoes and an old sweater.[25] He had clearly been through hard times. Though raised as an Anglican by his Church of England mother, he now defined himself as Jewish, since his butcher father came from an East London working-class Jewish family. He had lied his way into the British army just before the First World War at the age of sixteen, after adding two years to his age. By the end of that war he had been commissioned as an officer, holding the rank of lieutenant. He was captured and, as part of a group who continually tried to escape, was sent to a remote Baltic island. 'As they are five rattling good men they will not mind,' a former camp colleague observed.[26] Nathan left the army after being posted to India, apparently bored by the colonial life. Even more remarkably, given that he now had former IRA men under his command, he then spent time with an infamous auxiliary police unit in Ireland that served as a paramilitary group and worked closely with the British army as it tussled with the IRA. While there he had almost certainly taken part in the murder of the Sinn Féin mayor of Limerick, his predecessor and a city clerk.[27] The wife of one victim identified him as the plain-clothes officer in charge of the group of soldiers who had knocked on their door. He rejoined the British army twice but was eventually court-martialled, perhaps because he was a homosexual. After various failed attempts to get ahead as a civilian, Nathan tried to make a life for himself in Canada as either a farmer or salesman. This had gone so badly that the previous year he had been forced to ask for help from the British Legion.

In Albacete, Nathan was given command of the English company only because there was no one else suitable to do the job. This produced a sudden and remarkable personal transformation. '[His] boots, given a spit and polish brush-up … glittered in the sunlight … His army greatcoat looked as though it had been tailored for him. His collar and tie were neatly set, and even his helmet had been cleaned. The chin-strap was at the correct angle,' recalled one of his company.[28] In a cut-glass upper-class British accent he confidently issued orders that his men automatically followed. He also soon began to carry a swagger stick and, with his neat moustache, looked and behaved like the quintessential British infantry officer. It was not a look generally favoured by the proletarian fighters of the Brigades and some instinctively disliked him, considering him snobbish. Most soon agreed, however, that he was an exceptional leader of men.

Fourteenth Brigade's mission was to help stop an enemy advance that was pushing east from Córdoba. Aleksander Szurek's Sans Nom Battalion was the first to arrive, beating the others by a day.[29] As soon as the men descended from the camouflaged train with its smashed windows into Andújar, in Jaén province, the local army commander ordered them to occupy a hilltop position known as Telegraph Hill, equidistant from two whitewashed country towns, Villa del Río and Montoro, on the southern side of a loop in the river Guadalquivir.[30] Córdoba lay fifty kilometres to the west.

The weather was cool but sunny that Christmas and the newly arrived Central Europeans marvelled at their first sight of palms and pomegranate trees. To Szurek, the countryside on the way to Andalusia seemed as exotic as the Arabian desert. Lemon and orange groves painted the landscape with bright, unusual colours. Flat, open fields of wheat and cotton spread across the valley floor.[31] Endless rows of olive trees ran up the hillsides, sagging under the weight of fat, purply-black fruit bloated by the same winter rains that had swelled the normally placid Guadalquivir.[32] One reason that Franco's forces had chosen to advance in this direction from Córdoba was because it wanted the rich olive crop that was almost ready to collect; as a result, this attack became known as the Olive Offensive. Another was that the road here led to Madrid and the narrow Despeñaperros pass that divided this part of Andalusia from the flat plains of La Mancha and central Spain.[33]

The Sans Nom spent the night of 23/24 December in Villa del Río, where Szurek first came across a typical tableaux of the war in Spain. In a square, he looked on aghast as local people burned church paintings and smashed an altar, and imagined how shocking this would be in his native Poland. In another square he saw his first dead 'fascist', lying with a bullet hole through his forehead. He noted with puzzlement how handsome the man was, and wondered: 'Could he have left relatives?'[34] It was the naive observation of an as yet unbloodied soldier.

The corpse Szurek saw probably belonged to one of the handful of Franco supporters shot in cold blood by militiamen as villagers began to flee into the countryside. As in much of Andalusia, where the almost feudal division between landowners and peasants was starkest, villagers had backed the Republic but concentrated on collectivising or managing the land, rather than defending it. They had also settled old grudges left over from rural strikes in previous years and from centuries of humiliation. Landowners, rightists and clergymen were amongst those shot or sent to prison in Madrid and elsewhere. Local *caciques* (land-owning strongmen), meanwhile, had formed armed bands to defend their estates and had been surprisingly effective at preparing Andalusia for a swift takeover by the rebels. Other landowners, such as those from Villa del Río, had fled or were hiding in foreign embassies in Madrid. In a miniature version of the Alcázar at Toledo, a group of almost a thousand Civil Guards, Falangists, rightists and their families had holed up in a remote hermitage, the Sanctuary of the Virgen de la Cabeza near Andújar, where, despite being supplied by air, they were eventually starved and bombed out.

With its 700 men, thirty-six machine guns, twenty-two trucks and 150 boxes of grenades, the Sans Nom was the best equipped International Brigade battalion to have been sent into battle so far. This probably owed much to the Brigades' contacts in the Communist Party and also the goodwill generated by the Brigaders' performance in the defence of Madrid. Supplies of second-hand weapons and munitions remained, however, as diverse in origin as the volunteers themselves. Overnight the men had discovered that only four of their thirty-six machine guns worked; that may have been because the 1915 Colt guns were famously prone to overheating and jamming, or this could have been the work of Quartermaster Dupré and his band of saboteurs. A volunteer mechanic and a watchsmith managed to hastily repair all but six of them, but only two were considered completely reliable. It was then discovered that the ammunition belts were empty, and there was only one machine to load them; the rest had to be done by hand.[35]

Franco's army, while usually far better armed and always more professional, had some logistical problems of its own: the units heading in the direction of the Sans Nom had, for example, so few vehicles that they often had to move on foot. Unlike the Brigaders, however – with just, at best, five days of training and six shots each – the approaching Francoist column had spent five months fighting in southern Spain and, in some cases, had been through years of colonial wars in Morocco. In all likelihood, they also had something that the Sans Nom lacked completely – maps. The battalion had to rely instead on local guides and Republican army officers who appeared to know very little about what was happening on the ground. 'They could say nothing concrete at all: not where the enemy was; nor how far away; nor on what side of us; nor how strong they were,' recalled Dusan Petrovitch, a Serbian political commissar with XIV Brigade.[36]

The local guides disappeared on the morning of the 24th as soon as the battalion found itself in a firefight. This began when a Francoist column ran into one of the four companies at a crossroads. The volunteers were caught milling around trucks that they had just started unloading. Some, indeed, still had not managed to get down from them. Lorries, munitions, ambulances and tins of Russian food had to be abandoned as Brigaders were captured or killed.[37] But this was just the start.

As the surviving volunteers desperately sought cover, Italian Fiat CR-32 biplanes strafed their positions, and two hundred Moroccan cavalrymen joined the attack. In one of the few successful cavalry actions of the war, the Moroccans and other Francoist troops trapped the Brigaders in a pocket of land that backed onto the meandering Guadalquivir.[38]

Part of Szurek's Polish company, which had taken up a separate position, managed to cross a bridge and escape, but very few others did.[39] An initially disciplined retreat, which began late in the afternoon, with the volunteers holding on to their heavy-machine guns, turned into a rout, with men fleeing towards the marshy banks of the wide, swollen Guadalquivir river, even though they did not know how to swim. Some drowned. The

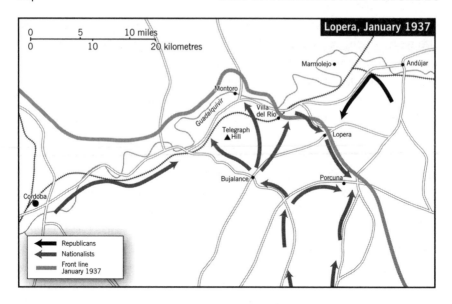

battalion commander, a Bulgarian 'Mexican' known as Stomatov (real name Atanas Georgiev Dolaptchiev) was the first to cross on a makeshift raft, abandoning his men[40] and leaving them stranded on the wrong side of the river. Without maps and with few officers, they had no idea where to go. They broke up into ever smaller groups, independently seeking ways to escape. Some tried building their own rafts. Others went downstream to the bridge at Montoro. By now, both Montoro and Villa del Río had been taken and the Brigaders were met by machine-gun fire.[41] Undulating Andalusian olive groves proved almost impossible to navigate, as the neat rows of trees played tricks on their eyes. The Moroccan cavalry galloped through the groves, hunting down volunteers. One group of Brigaders was attacked at close range by Francoist soldiers who tricked them with raised fists and cries of '*¡Salud camaradas!*'[42]

Nightfall on Christmas Eve brought only relative respite. 'By night the Andalusian countryside is of a devilish uniformity,' observed Nick Gillain, a self-confessed Belgian 'mercenary' who commanded a cavalry platoon. 'On all sides there are endless interminable rows of olive trees and white-walled oil presses that glow in the dark.'[43] Groups of Brigaders formed and split up, sometimes mistaking each other for the enemy. Many fell asleep, exhausted, hungry and shivering, in the thickets by the river. In the dawn river mist of Christmas Day, some managed to cross the Guadalquivir on makeshift rafts, leaving their weapons behind or tossing them into the water. Others swam, making it across to the other side of the river. Euphoria at their timely escape was short-lived, as the Moroccan cavalry were now patrolling the far bank. One by one, or in their small bands, the men were picked off as they came out of the water. A party who took refuge in a *cortijo*, a country farmhouse, and sought comfort in its wine, were found drunk and fast asleep when taken prisoner hours later. Unarmed groups and individuals wandered the countryside for days, their clothes in tatters, driven mad by thirst, hunger and the cold. The lucky ones stumbled upon the scattered farm buildings where local villagers fed them. Others unable to find shelter scavenged on bitter olives and grass.[44] Of the 700 men of the Sans Nom Battalion, only half made it back.[45]

Franco's forces later claimed that they had 'found' 300 corpses, piles of arms and had taken many prisoners that night, 24 December, while a Francoist newspaper boasted of the work of the *Moritos*, or 'little Moors'. The column's Jesuit chaplain, Bernabé Copado, declared it to have been an 'unforgettable' day. Their units had lost just twenty killed and sixteen wounded. They spent the next day dragging the corpses of dead Brigaders into a mass grave and counting their war booty.[46]

Many Brigaders who survived the rout were in no condition to continue: according to a secret report written by political commissar Petrovitch, their morale was broken and, blaming their officers, some refused ever to fight again.[47] All were clear that they would never follow Stomatov into battle.

Once more, an International Brigades unit had been thrown into the front line without training and had suffered heavily on its first combat operation. The result did not surprise Walter, who arrived with the rest of the brigade just as the disaster was unfolding. 'All of these people were absolutely unacquainted, not accustomed to one another, and right off found themselves in battle,' he explained later. Bedraggled, semi-naked survivors were sent to a hotel in the small town of Marmolejo, where they dressed in whatever clothes they could find in the hastily abandoned rooms. 'Some men found only women's clothes which they put on and then began dancing. Our laughter at their antics dispelled our sullen mood,' recalled Szurek.[48] None of this diminished the hatred for Stomatov, who had been met on his return by a furious Walter demanding to know what he had done with his battalion.

18

Men in Rubber Coats: Lopera,
25 December 1936

The rest of Walter's new brigade reached Andújar by train from Albacete on Christmas Day, though they heard little or nothing about the rout at the Guadalquivir river.[1] Sans Nom survivors were kept apart, so that they could not tell their tales of disarray and defeat.[2] The story of the International Brigades was meant to be radically different: they were the saviours of Madrid and the elite of the Republican army. Walter demanded to know why the Sans Nom had been so hastily deployed, and without reserves, before his arrival. He was told that the front had been crumbling and this had been an emergency. His ire was not calmed by the fact that the local army headquarters could only give him a vague idea about where that front line might now be. It might be three kilometres away or, maybe, fifteen.

News soon arrived that Franco's forces were heading towards the town of Lopera – and may have taken it already, since this was the next logical target – so Walter was instructed to take his remaining three battalions there. He still had no concrete information on the enemy's whereabouts and was struggling to discover what had actually happened to the Sans Nom. As the size of the previous day's disaster became apparent, he sent out cavalry patrols of a dozen or more men to scout both Villa del Río and Lopera.[3] In the former location they ran into gunfire and even the lightweight FA-I armoured car[4] supporting them tried to flee, its driver forced back at gunpoint by one of the cavalrymen. At Lopera, however, they found a ghost town. The few remaining inhabitants were locked inside their houses and the patrol does not seem to have seen the bodies of half-a-dozen rightist civilians, including the sixteen-year-old son of the town clerk, who had been executed earlier that same day, before the last militiamen fled.

Walter, meanwhile, was waiting for Spanish reinforcements to arrive as a reserve. These did not appear until 26 December, a day he used to survey the terrain himself, setting out at night in his large black Matford car. An accompanying Spanish Republican colonel, stricken by fear, questioned if he was really needed for such an outing, especially after they were met by a hail of bullets – almost certainly from friendly militiamen – as they walked up a hill outside Lopera.[5] When his companions threw themselves to the ground, Walter told them not to bother. 'Don't worry. If you've had time to hear the whistle, you know that one's not going to get you,' he said.[6] The phrase was part of the 'common knowledge' that veteran volunteers passed on to newcomers.

The three battalions moved off towards Lopera at 10 a.m. on Sunday 27 December. A small Spanish militia unit drafted in to replace the Sans Nom brought their numbers up to 3,000 men. Slightly earlier, after attending Sunday Mass in the local market,[7] a Francoist column of 4,000 men left Villa del Río to cover the much shorter distance from there to Lopera. The enemy arrived 'firstest with the mostest', as the Irish volunteer Joe Monks remarked, and claimed the empty town and the surrounding hills that looked over open countryside.[8] This was a huge advantage in the run-up to what was set to be one of the crucial civil war battles in Andalusia.[9] For centuries, southern Spaniards had lived in tightly packed towns and villages that were easy to defend, working the fields during the day and returning to them at night. Many, like Lopera, had church towers or castles whose crenellated battlements made excellent machine-gun emplacements.

While the Army of Africa veterans and some 2,000 Andalusian *requetés* – the ultraconservative, Catholic paramilitary group whose members across Spain had been in training for years – settled in, the volunteers puffed and wheezed their way along rough tracks and across the soft-earthed olive groves.[10] Many had previously shed their blankets and greatcoats, not thinking the southern nights would be so cold.[11] Fourteenth Brigade's task was to attack a superior force which enjoyed the advantages of height, cover and spotter planes. Walter chose to attack on a narrow front from the north-east. The terrain was heavy-going, with the final stretch towards Lopera requiring the attackers to cross open land and establish themselves on barren hilltops before rushing the town itself. But these hills did at least offer the opportunity of a successful attack, and the town of Porcuna sat on higher land only four kilometres to the south, allowing the Republican artillery guns positioned there to target the defenders.[12] This was to be a hammer blow, concentrated against a single spot in the defences. It was the best possible plan, but success depended on courage and discipline under fire by untested, untrained soldiers.

The attack began in the afternoon, five hours after the enemy had walked into the town and begun settling themselves on neighbouring hilltops.[13] As the volunteers approached, they could see groups of Moroccans in dark cloaks running into positions from where they could produce lethal crossfire.[14] Nathan's English-speaking company led the attack, charging up the bare Andalusian hillsides (one of them appropriately named Calvario, or Calvary[15]). On each occasion Nathan waved his swagger stick above his head and the men ran behind him, reassured, as Monks described it, by his serenity and 'the steadiness of Nathan's splendid shoulders'.[16] As Nathan's men set out on the upwards rush to top of Cerro Calvario hill, he urged them to: 'Cheer! Give them something to be afraid of!'[17] His plan to storm their way into the town had to be quickly abandoned, however, because their rifles and machine guns jammed and they received constant fire from the neighbouring Cerro San Cristóbal hill. Amongst those to die that day was thirty-six-year-old Yorkshireman and writer Ralph Fox.[18] The company named the hill they were attempting to take after him and tried again, repeatedly, the following day. Above them, Fokker aircraft strafed and bombed freely in the absence of the Republican air force.[19] As the attack progressed, chaos grew and things increasingly went wrong. At one stage, one volunteer battalion began firing on another. Casualties mounted, attacking companies became jumbled and men began to run away or, simply, gave up on the attempt to advance. A French machine-gunner called Collange found that, when ordered to clamber up to the crest of a hill, his two assistants remained at the bottom.[20]

In the confusion, some officers urged units to flee, while others turned them back at pistol point. Large groups of men abandoned the front together and at least 150 men had to be brought back from Andújar.[21] One company disappeared altogether and the Marseillaise Battalion's commander, Delasalle, could not be found. Eventually Gillain's cavalry platoon was given the full-time task of hunting down deserters and turning them around.[22] The attack, inevitably, had to be called off again for the evening.[23]

Aleksander Szurek, who had been waiting in reserve with the remnants of the Sans Nom in Marmolejo, was unexpectedly called upon to join Walter's personal guard.[24] This felt like a promotion and he was inordinately proud (though he disgraced himself early on by accidentally firing his pistol into the roof during a visit by Marty). Szurek accompanied Walter to the British trenches after yet another failed attack. The Polish general already had an affectionate relationship with the company, and had been thrilled to meet Irish veterans from two battles that he had studied carefully in Moscow – the fighting in O'Connell Street during the Easter Uprising of 1916 and, again, in 1922. 'What could the General offer? Valour,' Szurek wrote of Walter.[25] 'He stood above their trench and watched the enemy shoot. That made the soldiers nervous and they pulled him down. The general laughed, and so did they. Once again the general stood on a small elevation near the trench and observed the enemy's position through binoculars as bullets whistled by him more frequently.' A terrified Szurek decided it was his duty to stand there too, beside the commanding officer. Walter ordered him to sit down. 'If the Comrade General sits down, then I will too. Bullets aren't choosy about their targets,' he noted. Walter sat down, and in that moment a close bond was formed between the two men that would last for much of the war.

Any 'malingerers' attempting to drift away from the front line were met by an incandescent Walter.[26] At one stage, he found himself being approached by a horde of Frenchmen, led by Delasalle and his political commissar, who had left the line together. They were, in effect, on strike and refusing to fight unless they were fed. Delasalle, meanwhile, complained that the men were impossible to command.[27] Walter harangued them. 'Did you come to Spain to desert the front? What kind of anti-fascists are you?' he demanded. A fifty-year-old former Cossack and white Russian exile called Karchevski, Walter's cold-blooded 'security' chief, walked up to his boss and asked him in Russian: 'Comrade general, do you want me to shoot them? I've everything ready.' Walter shook his head, and instead organised food and made sure the men got on trucks to take them back to the front. First though, he took the commissar, a former union official, aside and told him he was 'a shit of an anti-fascist'. The man returned to the line weeping.[28]

The following day, after part of the Francoist forces defending the town had set off to try to take Porcuna, a joined-up attack involving most of what was left of Walter's battalions made it into the outskirts of Lopera.[29] One French volunteer on a motorbike made several daring runs through the town's streets, spraying it with bullets from a sub-machine gun before circling around and roaring back.[30] When what seems to have been the same rider stalled his motorbike outside the town, Szurek watched, amazed, while he 'elegantly and haughtily, pulled on a pair of white gloves' before 'smiling mischievously' at Walter, who was watching from a ditch. On another trip, however, the man was caught by a bullet and killed.

A handful of other volunteers also fought their way into buildings on the edge of Lopera.[31] A larger section of the attacking force had reached within fifty metres of the town when the defenders who had left for Porcuna returned and a surprise bayonet charge pushed them back. When the attackers tried again, they were met by machine-gun fire that littered the hillside with dead and wounded. They were forced to withdraw. That night even the seemingly indomitable George Nathan sat hunched and exhausted under a blanket against an olive tree. The attack had failed and he had lost most of his company.[32]

The next morning, as he surveyed the carnage through his binoculars, Walter realised that the battle was lost and his men continued to retreat.[33] Gillain described this as being 'carried out with joyous abandon'.[34] In fact, Nathan's company withdrew in impeccable order, section by section, his men providing covering fire as they went. When some looked to be running too fast, he barked out a command: 'Dress your files! Retire in proper formation!' It was enough to stop any attempt at flight. 'It was an exhibition of cool leadership,' commented one observer.[35] Unfortunately, there were not many volunteers left. At least nineteen men from the all English-speaking company had died, including the writer Ralph Fox and John Cornford, the latter having turned twenty-one just hours before his death. The Irish were hardest hit. Of the thirteen men who had accompanied Frank Ryan across the Spanish border, six were dead and three more, including Joe Monks, were injured.[36]

A third of the volunteers were by now out of action, with some 300 dead, many injured and a considerable number of deserters. 'I have to admit that the International Brigade has suffered 30 per cent losses, and is crushed,'[37] the front's commander reported back to the Republican army headquarters.[38] This message was intercepted and published by the Francoist press, which was both horrified by and in awe of the International Brigades. Only between one and two hundred of the rightist defenders died. The losses included the famous bullfighter and notorious Falangist, José García, Pepe 'El Algabeño', who had joined a volunteer force of Seville *señoritos*, who – like the *hidalgos*, the 'sons of someone' of medieval Spain – each came with two horses and a man. They had played a terrifying role in the rearguard, exacting revenge on peasants who had ousted the local *señoritos* from their lands.

Fourteenth International Brigade, formed in just a week, had failed to take Lopera, but this was by no means a disaster. Over the previous eighteen days, the enemy had captured 1,500 square kilometres of land east of Córdoba. That advance had been stopped at Lopera[39] and the road to the Despeñaperros pass remained in Republican government hands for the rest of the war. The International Brigades may have brought the advance to a halt, but the cost in lives over a single week had been high. The acts of extraordinary bravery performed by some Brigaders – whose corpses now littered the Andalusian countryside – contrasted with the cowardice and bungling of others.

A few days after Franco's forces withdrew, a group of villagers were recruited to gather the corpses of the dead volunteers and pile them up beside the road running from Andújar into Lopera. Some were found still hugging the trunks or the thick, exposed roots of the olive trees that they had tried to use for cover.[40] The gruesome task of picking up bodies already half destroyed by bullets, shrapnel or bayonets, made some of the villagers repeatedly vomit.[41] Intact corpses were dragged down the hillside on ropes tied behind mules. The locals were amazed by the quality of the volunteers' boots and the rubberised black coats worn by commissars like Ralph Fox,[42] which were quickly removed and taken home.

Three piles of bodies were now heaped high in stacks bordering the Andújar–Lopera road. Gasoline was thrown over them and, as they crackled in the flames and dense black smoke billowed above the olive groves, the smell of burning flesh made the peasants retch once more. When the flames eventually died out, lime was poured on top, followed by a layer of earth. By the following spring the mounds had been covered over by luscious green grass. Years later children were still playing with the skulls that slowly emerged from the ground, lining them up along the road to scare passing travellers.[43]

19

Justice and a Different Kind of Army: Lopera, January 1937

The two failed Republican attacks at Lopera and Teruel, which overlapped in time, provoked consternation amongst the Brigades' leadership. The narrative so successfully built at Madrid appeared to have been shattered: the International Brigades were not invincible and the pro-Franco press wallowed in accounts of the number of dead and wounded and the large haul of captured munitions and equipment. In propaganda terms, the Francoist objective was to rid the Brigades of their mystique and embolden their own troops, who had come to respect and fear the foreign volunteers, while demonising them as murderous 'Reds'.

More worrying than the narrative, however, were the weaknesses that had been exposed in the Brigades. Their successes in Madrid had much to do with the fact that they had been mostly required to defend. That was usually much easier to do, in terms of both men and munitions needed by the two sides; the ratio needed by an attacking force was always more than one to one and often required forces that were several times larger. The attacks at Teruel and Lopera demanded a separate set of skills, as well as considerable individual courage. It takes a different mindset to charge towards guns than it does to hide behind a wall or pile of sandbags and shoot at someone running towards you.

It could be argued that the volunteers had been sent on impossible missions. Future attacks on Teruel would involve much larger forces. The problems, however, went deeper than that. Training, communications, leadership and armaments had all failed. At crucial moments the attackers found themselves with jammed weapons or without ammunition.[1] Even the basic task of keeping men fed, watered and warm had been inadequately carried out. For a hardened military man like Walter, the worst thing had been the lack of discipline. He had been personally constantly engaged in chasing men back into their lines at Lopera, while his cavalry and commissars hunted down malingerers and deserters. The Belgian mercenary Gillain estimated that some 500 men out of 3,000 had abandoned the line. Even amongst the well-led and disciplined English-speaking company, at least one volunteer deserted, declaring: 'This isn't war. This is bloody madness. I've had enough!'[2]

All this coalesced with a tenet of Stalinist communism – that if something has gone badly wrong, someone is to blame and that person is, at best, a saboteur or, at worst, an outright traitor. 'In war, treason is an invention the losers use to justify themselves,' wrote Gillain. 'Treason explains everything. Who should be blamed?'[3] He claimed it was Mieczyslaw Domanski Dubois, the communist Polish medical chief, who first pointed the finger at Major Gaston Delasalle. After the battle, the commander of the Marseillaise Battalion had been arrested in the nurses' quarters at a nearby field hospital.[4] This, apparently, was where Delasalle had been spending his nights. A girlfriend had followed him from Barcelona as a volunteer nurse, and had brought her friends with her. This added further weight to growing suspicions about the former intelligence officer.[5] Those volunteers who thought they had joined an army which they were free to leave, whenever they wanted, and where strict military justice would not be applied, were now to find out that this was not the case.

A court martial was set up to try Delasalle in a classroom in Arjonilla, where Walter had his headquarters. Marty, schooled in paranoia and mistrust, was in his element and soon arrived with a bulging file of his own and his mind already made up. A tribunal of three officers listened to the evidence, while emissaries from each company watched what one witness later called a 'show trial'. The dry and unsympathetic political commissar André Heussler, who would later be deemed a traitor by French Resistance colleagues during the Second World War, acted as prosecutor. Some of the allegations were absurd. Marty's rich imagination conjured up a network of fascist informants, all headed by Delasalle. He was in cahoots with anarchists and fascists in Catalonia, had worked for both the Bulgarian and Romanian governments, and was linked to other spies in Albacete. This conflation of fascists and anarchists, as if they were natural allies, was typical of Marty. He also claimed that Delasalle had ordered his own men to fire on another Brigades battalion; deliberately sent them on a suicidal charge with empty weapons; abandoned the English-speaking company; and had taken part in a feint by the defenders, who raised a red flag and tricked a group of volunteers, who were then met with gunfire.[6]

An abject Delasalle leapt into a frenzy when he heard that he was being accused of treason, and had to be wrestled back into place by his guards. Nobody dared contradict Marty's thesis, and by the time the prosecutor had finished, some in the audience already knew what would happen next. As Delasalle received the sentence that he was to be shot, he began shouting at Marty: 'You know that you are lying! Why have you condemned me to death?'[7] Delasalle was marched away by Karchevski looking, according to Szurek, 'as pale as the day he marched from the front with his battalion'. Dr Domanski Dubois, inseparable at Walter's side, followed. Moments later two or three shots rang out.[8]

Command of the Marseillaise Battalion passed, exceptionally, to a French anarchist, Demouzin.[9] Although Delasalle's death later became a cause célèbre in France, few volunteers mourned him. 'The sentence was what any army would have handed down on charges like that,' commented one junior officer.[10] Yet neither Stomatov, who had abandoned his battalion, nor a Luxembourger company commander called Rasquin, who had also abandoned his men at Lopera (while his second-in-command fled to Andújar) were tried.[11] Unlike Delasalle, however, Stomatov, for one, was a communist. His punishment was to be sent to the front line as an ordinary soldier.[12]

The senior French officer Joseph Putz later suggested to Nick Gillain that Delasalle had been shot, not because of his cowardice and failure, but because of his relations with anarchists in Barcelona. 'Well, given that the anarchists are part of the Republic, that does not count as treason,' retorted Gillain.[13] The Belgian concluded that it had all been designed as a warning to those amongst the often strong-minded and individualistic volunteers tempted to follow the men of XIII Brigade who had joined the anarchist ranks at Teruel. That, in itself, spoke to the growing rivalry between communists and anarchists in Spain, as the former expanded rapidly and threatened the position of what had become one of the two principal leftist forces in the country, along with the socialists.[14] Such was the paranoia about anarchists amongst the Brigades, that one shell-shocked tank driver, a Russian called Soloviev, ranted and hallucinated continually about them from his hospital bed at the Palace Hotel, in Madrid, where Jan Kurzke and others were being treated. 'Anarchists will slaughter us all, they came for me, they told me about it last night!' he would shout.[15]

Either way, the volunteers were now aware that their only moment of absolute free will had been the decision to join the Brigades. The army they had joined was just like any other, in that it did not tolerate deserters or cowards, executing them or putting them in punishment 'Pioneer' or 'Labour' units. This was not a decision of the International Brigades' chiefs or of the Comintern, but of the Spanish Republican government who they now served. Whatever their motive for joining – ideology, moral imperative, adventure, unemployment or a rush of blood to the head – they were now stuck. Many had assumed they would be in Spain for the few months that it took to win the war over fascism, or that home leave would be granted generously. They were wrong on both counts.[16]

20

Mothers and Jews: Algora,
1 January 1937

Bluma Akkerman can only have wept after reading the letter that arrived from her youngest son, Piet, telling her that he had followed his older brother Emiel to Spain on 27 October 1936. Bluma was a Jewish woman of Polish origin; her family, the Klippers, had moved to Belgium from Kraków in 1896 after her mother died. So, too, had many other impoverished Polish Jews. Amongst them had been her husband Joseph's family, the Akkermans from Radom. The couple met in Antwerp and Judaism rooted their identity, with Yiddish as the tongue in their family home. Bluma had given birth to two sons, Emiel and Israel, during the prosperous decade before Europe was torn asunder by a continental war.

The family's history was full of misfortune. When Belgium became a battlefield during the First World War, they fled to Holland. Not long after their return, Joseph died. The boys found themselves entering adulthood in a country which had succumbed to the scourge of early 1930s Europe, rampant unemployment. However, like Bluma, Emiel and Israel were strong characters. They made it through the hard times, working in mines and the diamond-cutting business. The boys joined Hashomer Hatzaïr, a Marxist Zionist group that originally sought to set up progressive kibbutzim in Palestine. They went on to become labour organisers, giving speeches and organising strikes. Both were natural leaders, despite their youth.[1]

The boys had also abandoned Judaism and the family's religious identity, though culturally they still referred to themselves as Jews. The youngest, Israel, changed his name to the Flemish-sounding Piet. Slight and short, with a pale, childish face marked by thin lips and topped by black hair, the twenty-three-year-old looked even younger than his years. Piet, however, had a way with words and men followed him: he had already marched at the head of Antwerp's diamond workers earlier in the year, when they went on strike to protest against the murder of two socialists by local fascists. That could be seen as part of the years of skirmishing across Europe that had now come to a head in Spain. Soon Piet had a police file. 'An excellent orator, who appears to have an honourable profession but, as soon as anything happens in the street, he is there,' it noted.[2]

In October 1936, both Piet and Emiel joined the International Brigades in Spain. Their mother by this time had remarried and moved to Britain. The boys did not inform her of their plans – they knew she would have tried to stop them. They were amongst the first wave of recruits, leaving separately along with many other 'foreigners' (including second-generation immigrants, some of whom, like Piet, had trouble gaining nationality) living in Belgium. Some 800 immigrants would volunteer from Belgium, including 350 Poles, 131 of them Jewish. Many of those, like Piet, had found a safe harbour in left-wing politics, where they could work on an equal footing with other Belgians.[3] A further sixty-five Jews with Hungarian, Romanian, Czech, Belgian or other nationalities would also travel to Spain, bringing the total to 200, or one for every 250 members of the overall Jewish community in Belgium.[4] Jews, then, were far more likely to travel to Spain than other Belgians, who accounted for some 1,700 Brigaders. This was part of a much wider tendency, since Jews were proportionally over-represented in almost all national groups in Spain. They eventually accounted for at least one in ten of the International Brigaders (with less reliable estimates reaching as high as one in five).[5]

On 27 October, Piet wrote to his mother to explain why he and his brother had volunteered to fight in Spain. His letter reveals a raw and painful inner battle between filial love and idealism, in which the latter had won out. 'My dear mother,' he opened. 'I beg your forgiveness for the displeasure that I have caused you. I ask that you forgive me for following the voice that called me, which is so much stronger than my own personal welfare and which has overridden everything related to that.' The experiences and battles of the Jews, he argued, were akin to that of the idealists who travelled with him to fight fascism – even if it took them on different paths:

I don't know if one day you will understand all that I would have done to try to avoid you this suffering; but I have found it impossible. I know mother, all that you have done for us, and all that you have sacrificed. Between your opinions and mine lies an unbridgeable gulf. We never agree. This gulf is not just between youth and age, or between faith and atheism. The two of us, you and I, are both Jews; but we are separated by an ocean of contradictions. One of us declared herself to be in favour of one thing, and the other rebelled, obstinately placing himself against that. What separates us is my need for action. If only those last words could explain to you fully what drove me, what came over me!

Both of your sons have stayed on a straight, pure path through life. I never stole, mother, that you do know. You know, too, that I have never exploited my neighbour. I've never prayed. I have never spoken to God only to renounce him five minutes later. I helped people when, where and however I could. Not all mothers can say that about their sons. I grew up in a society rife with injustice and oppression. I have suffered both as a worker and as a Jew. I was downtrodden, but I never bowed to those terrible blows, unlike so many of my childhood friends, and I never tried to find happiness through money.

I was very young, as I'm sure you will remember, when I began to see the state of our society with clarity. There is one trait that I have developed clearly; that Jewish stubbornness when it comes to holding on to an idea. Do you recall, mother, how they promised to buy me a bicycle if I left the Hashomer Hazaïr group? I was twelve! A bicycle! My dream, my ideal. But I turned it down. And do you remember the vast piles of money they promised me if I learned to cut a diamond? They tried to take me to a diamond workshop with Samuel where I could earn a lot of money. But I was never interested; I had sworn to myself that I would never bow to the power of money, because I knew that the quest for money is one of the main causes of misery and oppression, not just of the working classes, but of all oppressed peoples.[6]

Piet's letter explains perhaps better than any other source why so many Brigaders were Jews. Their experience of historical bigotry and the forthright anti-Semitism of fascism meant that their knowledge of oppression was greater than that of other working-class people who travelled with them, and with deeper roots.

> The pursuit of money is also the pursuit of power. Have not 99 per cent of the pogroms in the world been organised to distract attention from the misery of the people by provoking hatred towards the Jews, while those who are really responsible, the authors of misery, laugh in secret because instead of attacking their power, people slaughter the Jews? Your children, however, have not tolerated this, have not stooped, have not stayed silent.[7]

Over the previous fifty years, Europe's Jews had experienced waves of pogroms of increasing ferocity. These had begun on the western edge of the Russian empire – the so-called Pale of Settlement – in the parts of Poland, Ukraine, Byelorussia, Moldovia and Lithuania acquired by Imperial Russia, as it ate up bits of the Ottoman Empire, the Polish-Lithuanian Commonwealth and the Cossack Hetmanate. Before acquiring these territories, Russia itself had had relatively few Jews, and it now ordered most of them to convert to orthodoxy or stay in the broad stretch of land occupied by the Pale of Settlement that ran, south to north, from the Black Sea almost to the Baltic, with the lands of Germany, Prussia and Austro-Hungary marking its western border. As a result, the Pale was home to an estimated 40 per cent of the world's Jews.

A first round of pogroms had been sparked when Jews were blamed for the assassination of Tsar Alexander II in 1881, with a second wave following in 1903 and a final bloodbath that saw up to 100,000 Jews murdered during the turmoil of the Russian revolution (the majority killed by the revolution's opponents). Nothing on this scale had been seen in Europe since the mid-seventeenth century, and by the time bloodshed was over in 1921, the movement for a Jewish homeland in Palestine was growing strongly. Even places such as Limerick in Ireland or Tredegar in Wales had turned on their small Jewish communities, attacking property or driving them out. A more extreme British example came from Esmond Romilly's future sister-in-law, the Hitler-adoring Unity Mitford, who insisted that her name be spelled out in full ('for everyone should know that I am a Jew hater') when she wrote to the newspaper *Der Stürmer* to say that, 'As a British woman Fascist ... the English have no notion of the Jewish danger ... We think with joy of the day when we shall be able to say with might and authority: England for the English! Out with the Jews!'[8]

With the previous year's Nuremberg laws stripping German Jews of their citizenship, it was clear that Nazis and fascists were preparing to do far greater damage. Even then, as the Israeli statesman Chaim Weizmann said, the world often appeared divided into two parts: 'Places where the Jews could not live and those where they could not enter.' Zionism and left-wing radicalism were the main two political outlets for the growing sense of frustration and fear.

It was this attraction towards the far left, especially amongst recent city-based migrants, that explained the high representation of Jews within the International Brigades. Part of that attraction was what one observer called 'the moral affirmativeness, longing for justice, and universalist ethos shared by the Marxist vision and Jewish tradition'.[9] In Belgium, particularly, the far left won Jewish converts precisely because it worked hard to highlight the relationship between anti-Semitism and fascism. That is what the athletes from left-wing Jewish sports clubs who had travelled to the Barcelona Olympiad in July 1936, such as Emmanuel Mink, had consciously aimed to point out.[10] It is also what Piet Akkerman sought to describe in the final sentences of his letter home.

Please understand, mother. You need to know, that I have not come to Spain out of selfish interest. I just had no right NOT to come – on seeing that in Spain lay the powder keg that was about to set fire to the entire world, that would perpetuate oppression, scientifically institute mass murder, and trample and animalize the whole of humanity. Once I'd seen THAT, how could I NOT go? How could I hesitate, even with my scarce abilities, to help prevent another world war and to defeat fascism?

Don't cry mother, don't cry. And if you do so, please don't cry out of sorrow. Your son tries to be a man who both thinks and acts humanely.[11]

If Bluma Akkerman did not weep when she received this letter from Piet at her new home in London, then she surely cried towards the end of November when she was informed that, during fierce, hand-to-hand fighting in the Medical Faculty of Madrid's University City, Emiel had been killed.

Her elder son had had an easy charisma and seductive personality – bringing him a series of glamorous girlfriends, and roles in the local theatre club – that contrasted with Piet's need to be forceful in order to overcome his natural timidity. Emiel had by this stage left the Communist Party, though this had not dampened his hatred of fascism or his desire to go to Spain. This kind of zeal was often shared within families, or small friendship groups in Belgium and elsewhere who took up the cause of Republican Spain and volunteered together. That same enthusiasm, indeed, would eventually drive the partners of both Akkerman brothers – Emiel's widow Vera Luftig, and Piet's girlfriend Lya Berger – to join a group of a dozen volunteer Jewish nurses who travelled from Belgium to a hospital for Brigaders in Ontinyent, Valencia.[12]

The battalion Piet Akkerman found himself assigned to, the French-speaking André Marty Battalion, was probably one of the worst formed to date. It had proved incompetent at Cerro de los Angeles and chaotic in University City. In both places its men had proved undisciplined and liable to rebel. Much of that could be blamed on its commanders: they had included an argumentative drunk, a panicky coward, a charlatan and a pistol-wielding Hungarian disciplinarian.[13] All were removed in succession before the battalion was finally given a commander – 'Bernard' – who knew what he was doing. Unfortunately, this was a brief interlude; Bernard was injured at Boadilla and replaced by 'Geoffroy', another alcoholic.[14] Under such circumstances, political commissars were crucial to maintaining both morale and discipline. At Boadilla, Piet's company's commissar accidentally shot himself, and Piet was appointed in his place.[15] He was one of the few capable of transmitting the calm, courage and conviction that volunteers expected and needed to see amongst their senior ranks.

The battalion was sent with the Italian Garibaldis and the Polish Dombrowski to attack a series of small towns along the road to Zaragoza. They arrived damp and shivering and spent the night in a church, which had been not been ransacked and remained just as it was when the local priests fled. Unlike some other volunteers, who expressed

shock at the sight of anarchists destroying church goods, the men of
the André Marty seemed fairly unperturbed, burning whatever they
could find. 'There was no fuel other than paintings, frames [and] parts
of the altar. All this burned during the night,' recalled one machine-
gunner. 'Tragically, many things were burned, including antiques of
great value. When we left two days later and the people discovered what
state we had left the church in, we felt distinctly odd. I and many other
comrades have always regretted what happened.'[16]

On New Year's Eve – the same day that the Belgian government passed
a law banning its citizens from fighting in Spain[17] – Piet was preparing
his men for an advance on the small town of Algora, on the still poorly
established front 110 kilometres east of Madrid, near the city of Sigüenza.
The following day the André Marty Battalion did better than expected,
taking Algora two hours ahead of schedule in an impeccably planned
and executed attack. Their commander Geoffroy, however, failed to
communicate this to his own side's artillery and air force. As a result,
the volunteers were strafed by Republican fighter aircraft and targeted
by an International Brigade artillery unit. The Russian pilots paid no
attention to the desperate waving of Piet's companions, wounding
several of them before flying on to neighbouring Mirabueno – where
the Garibaldis had also scored a quick victory – and accidentally killing
seven Italian Brigaders.[18]

The new year, however, had started with victory. Some of the André
Marty Battalion celebrated by getting drunk, washing down the cured
hams and sausages left behind by the enemy with wine and brandy.[19]
Unsurprisingly perhaps, Geoffroy also turned to the bottle rather than
organise defensive positions against a counter-attack.

Late that afternoon, enemy troops approached Algora but, when
informed several times that this was happening, Geoffroy dismissed the
idea. His men were seeing Italians, not Moroccans, he insisted. Earlier
victory was soon tinged by tragedy. Piet Akkerman and a group of men
walked up to what they assumed was a group of Republican troops,
only to find themselves in an ambush.[20] Piet was badly wounded and
struggled through the night. The twenty-three-year-old died of his
wounds the following day, just as reinforcements helped chase the
enemy away.[21]

Bluma Akkerman lost her only remaining son just one month after
Emiel had been killed. Some would later see, in their deaths and that of

other Jewish Brigaders, proof that Jews had not sat by passively as the Holocaust was prepared. These deaths were part of what one historian of the Jewish Brigaders has called 'a prehistory of the Holocaust, essential to the story of Jewish resistance to fascism', though another notes that they mostly viewed themselves as 'cosmopolitans and universalists'.[22] Piet was buried hurriedly, with nothing to mark his grave. His companions wrote his name on a piece of paper and placed it in a glass bottle beside him, in case somebody found the grave one day. Nobody ever did.

21

The Final Battle for Madrid: Las Rozas, Aravaca, Villanueva, January 1937

There was little time for Piet Akkerman's comrades to grieve. While XII Brigade was conquering a line of modest towns and villages along the road to Zaragoza, Franco was preparing another mass assault to the north-west of Madrid. The aim, once more, was to cut off the road to La Coruña as a step towards surrounding the Spanish capital. The previous attack had been beaten back to Boadilla, leading Franco to conclude that any further advance would need a much bigger army. This he increased from 10,000 to 20,000 men. Again, these were the best he had, with sixteen out of twenty-three battalions made up of legionnaires and Moroccan colonial troops from the Army of Africa.[1] If the previous battle at Boadilla had been the first 'real' modern battle, bringing together air power, artillery, tanks and infantry, this was the first major confrontation of its kind across open ground.[2]

With XII Brigade fighting in Algora and other towns to the east, only XI Brigade was available to take part in the initial defensive action. The brigade was thrown into the line near Las Rozas and Villanueva del Pardillo.[3] With the aid of half-a-dozen Russian T-26 tanks, which claimed to have destroyed twenty-five of the tiny German Panzer I tanks, the French Commune de Paris Battalion helped bring one of the attacking columns to a virtual halt near Pozuelo de Alarcón.[4] When a second advancing column ran into the two German Brigades' battalions, however, it ploughed straight through them. Condor Legion observers, looking for clues about how to improve their techniques, took note of that. One of their pilots, however, was downed and his corpse identified by a Thälmann company commander as being an airman called Walter, who had served with him in the Luftwaffe.[5]

The Thälmann Battalion had quickly earned a reputation as the toughest, most disciplined and bravest of the seven volunteer battalions. In its earliest days, claimed Marty, the battalion was almost entirely communist and 60 per cent of its volunteers had already 'taken part in the revolutionary battles' in their home countries.[6] Those men had provided 'inspiration and leadership' during the chaotic first days in Madrid.[7] Its new commander, Richard Staimer, was a dogmatic, unimaginitive communist who expected his men to show courage and absolute obedience. He had even created within what was already a shock battalion, small 'shock groups' for the most dangerous tasks. Staimer himself tended to disappear in the heat of battle and was missing once more at Las Rozas as his battalion was almost encircled and fought its way to safety under the command of a captain, Max Hornung.[8] Staimer had gone to Madrid, leaving strict instructions that his battalion should not move. It obediently remained in place, at least initially, even after its flanks were left exposed because units on either side had retreated. 'Had the enemy been a bit quicker, they would have been annihilated,' commented Marty.[9] The battalion may have enhanced its reputation as a fearless, disciplined fighting force, but it had failed to learn that wisdom can be better than valour.

Proof of that came three days later in the same battle, when the Thälmann were defending a line along the edge of some woods near Aravaca. Once more Staimer disappeared (now feeling ill) and handed command to a lieutenant. This time, it was a disaster. 'The result,' Marty wrote later, 'was that the battalion was virtually exterminated.'[10] Of the 200 men who went into battle, just forty-eight came out able to fight again, the rest were dead, injured or missing. When orders came for them to launch an attack, the reply was: 'Impossible. The Thälmann Battalion has been destroyed.'[11] Only the quick thinking of a sergeant in the machine-gun company, who ordered his men to concentrate their fire on two enemy groups who were threatening their flanks, prevented an even worse rout. Staimer, a rigid communist who clearly preferred a disciplined defeat to an imaginative retreat, attempted to have the sergeant court-martialled for disobedience. It was as if the Thälmann volunteers had to compensate for Staimer's own failings by ensuring that the battalion, even without him, was the most courageous of them all.

Under Staimer, the Thälmann Battalion increasingly saw itself as a fighting force ruled by and belonging to the German Communist Party. He himself was a true Stalinist, having joined the party aged fifteen, passed through the Comintern schools and spent the previous three years in Moscow.[12] While other units sought to turn the popular front project into a social reality (or, at least pay lip service to it), Staimer's battalion sneered at both non-communists and other international battalions, which it regarded as inferior.

Staimer's rigidity and need to conceal his cowardice turned him into a bullying and sometimes splenetic demagogue. Those who did not obey orders to the last letter were treated as dangerous 'wreckers' or saboteurs. His men were the best, he would boast, and they were right to feel superior to everyone else. That included even their German comrades in the Edgar André Battalion (now that the Thälmann had switched to Hans Kahle's XI Brigade), which also began to feel looked down upon. Marty worried that the Thälmanns were becoming as stubborn and disdainful in their attitudes as their sworn enemy, the Nazis.[13]

Perhaps Staimer's worst trait was scapegoating. The sergeant who saved the battalion from an even bigger disaster was a typical example. Only the evidence given by an observer who was actually on the battlefield, praising the man's quick-thinking, had saved him from punishment. 'The impression is that Staimer always tends to present the things that happen in his absence in the following manner: if things go well he indulges in a round of propaganda for himself and his battalion; but if things go wrong he blames the person who had to replace him, as if saying: "This would never have happened if I had been there. What a pity that I was ill," ' said Marty, who was himself displaying a growing Germanophobia.[14]

Other International Brigades arrived to help on the front at Las Rozas. General Walter's XIV Brigade was hurried north from Lopera and was soon in position beside the Garibaldi and Dombrowski Battalions and fighting, for the first time, with the support of tanks.[15] It enjoyed some success, but the brigade was still learning. Walter found himself faced with a rebellion when an exhausted German company refused to go any further without rest and food, sending a delegation that demanded[16] to know why they were getting so little sleep and being rushed to another front so soon after Lopera. Walter was furious. They were part of an army now, he told them; it was a place where hierarchy was not just permissible, but necessary. 'There are no delegations in the army!' he shouted.[17] (Even his faithful aide-de-camp, Szurek, wondered whether that was historically correct: 'Had not the Russian revolution begun with soldier delegations?' he mused.) Walter knew he had no choice and invited the entire company to meet him in a wine cellar in the market at Galapagar. He patiently explained where they were, showed them maps by candlelight, and told them that the battle was crucial. 'The government of Republican Spain has turned to its best soldiers! Could it be that it made a mistake with XIV Brigade?' he asked.[18] The Germans assured him it had not, but they still wanted food and a few hours' rest on the cellar floor, having spent the previous day squeezed into trucks that had been caught in a huge snarl-up of military traffic.[19]

By the time this third and final failed attempt at blocking the main route between Madrid and La Coruña was over, the entire XI Brigade was down to 600 men, almost a third of its strength.[20] It had to be sent away, to Murcia, to reorganise and rebuild. The International Brigades involved in the battle had, once more, fulfilled their role as shock troops by plugging gaps in the hardest sections of the line. A ten-kilometre stretch of the main La Coruña road that reached the outskirts of Madrid at Puerta de Hierro was now cut. The front had been about to give way and, in the words of one historian, 'the capital had not lived such a critical moment since 15 November',[21] when the Francoists crossed the river Manzanares into University City. Franco's army had strengthened its hold on almost all the land immediately to the west of Madrid.[22]

The defenders, however, had done just enough to prevent this fresh offensive from achieving its aim, and there were plenty of back roads leading north into the mountains that were still in Republican hands. Franco's commanders put their failure to advance any further down to the Republic's 'professional foreign commanders'.[23] The price had been enormous. Many of the Brigaders who had arrived in Madrid in October or early November – just two long months earlier – were now dead or out of action. Few would see the war out.

22

Bethune, Blood and Bombing: The coast between Málaga and Almería, February 1937

Norman Bethune was – as so often happened – in a hurry. The mercurial Canadian physician was not famous for his patience, nor his sense of discipline. The son of an uncompromising backwoods evangelical pastor, Bethune had found his own form of religion, and pastoral mission, in medicine and socialism. Pale-skinned, with a strong-boned face and receding hairline, the forty-six-year-old doctor was tough, energetic and erratic in his enthusiasms, but nobody could doubt his passion for either medicine or the Republican cause.

For two months Dr Bethune had been running an innovative mobile blood transfusion service, which carried refrigerated blood to front-line hospitals around Madrid. His Canadian Blood Transfusion Service was just one of a patchwork of international volunteer medical services provided by Quakers, anti-fascist groups, communist organisations like International Red Aid and others. Queues of Madrileños could be found at his doors every morning waiting to give blood, while two battered but specially adapted vans transported the vital supplies to front-line Republican hospitals and casualty centres. In a war where many things had to be made up on the spot, this was one of a handful of groundbreaking initiatives to refrigerate blood – the miraculous saviour of soldiers, but previously only available at rearguard hospitals – and transport it close to the front, where it saved many lives.

Bethune had been a brilliant and ambitious chest surgeon at the Sacré Coeur and two other hospitals in Montreal, but was forever restless. His wide-reaching interests stretched to art, war – he had served in the First World War as a stretcher-bearer and then as a Royal Navy surgeon-lieutenant – and the socialisation of medicine in an age when almost all doctors outside the USSR charged for their services. A wild and oscillating character, he could swing from charismatic to capricious to cold-heartedly cruel. In Montreal, he saw himself as 'a big frog in a small pond'.[1] Although Bethune was only a recent adoptee of left-wing ideas, he had embraced these with typical, obsessive enthusiasm. Spain beckoned strongly.

With the backing of the recently founded to Aid Spanish Democracy in Canada (similar to committees that were being set up in many other countries), he reached Madrid in early November, during the intense fighting at University City, to set up a Canadian medical relief organisation. Within twenty-four hours of arriving, police had burst into his hotel room and begun to interrogate him. They thought that the combination of his military bearing, thin moustache, suit, tie, and porkpie hat gave him the look of a fascist. The fact that he had been chatting to Austrian journalist Ilse Kulcsar, whose boyfriend was the writer Arturo Barea, at the bar in the Hotel Gran Vía had, apparently, helped arouse suspicion. Why had he been grilling her for information?[2] Immediately afterwards he swapped his bourgeois-looking jacket and tie for a yellow turtleneck and shaved off the moustache.[3]

A chance meeting with the Italian communist Tina Modotti – a former model, Hollywood actress and talented photographer, who was now an official at Socorro Rojo (as International Red Aid, a sort of Comintern Red Cross, was known in Spanish[4]) – allowed Bethune to contact the International Brigades. He soon met, and got on with, Kléber and other volunteer officers. In typical fashion, however, Bethune impatiently rejected the advances of a Brigades medical chief whom he disliked and was then turned down by the one he did like.[5] In the end, he had to invent his own role, setting up his transfusion service in a luxurious eleven-room apartment in the Salamanca district of Madrid, where the city's wealthy had traditionally lived and which was being spared by Franco's bombers. The place soon became famous as a refuge for newspaper correspondents and other hard drinkers. Some guests, including the British scientist J. B. S. Haldane and *Daily Worker* correspondent Claud Cockburn, stayed for days or weeks on end. Various young women traipsed through the bedroom of the magnetic Bethune, drawn by his energy and flamboyant intellect.

Bethune himself drank heavily and would occasionally disappear to bed for long stretches of time with his girlfriend, the Swedish former marathon dancer and war reporter Kajsa Rothman.[6] Described as a 'giantess with red-gold flowing hair', she doubled as an occasional administrative assistant for the transfusion service.[7] Her father had co-owned the liberal *Karlstads-Tidningen* newspaper, for which she wrote. Kajsa was one of more than a dozen female war correspondents, mostly from Scandinavia, Britain, Germany and the United States, whose work in Spain established that this was now also a woman's profession. Like many of the journalists who had stayed in Madrid, she was also an ardent Republican supporter. Such was the anarchic and occasionally raucous nature of his independent outfit, that Bethune, his team and various hangers-on, were eventually arrested as suspected spies. All were released, except an Austrian named Hermann Hartung, who was believed to have been shot, but actually survived the war.[8]

Bethune was not the first doctor to set up mobile transfusions in Spain, nor did he develop the best technique, but he was one of several pioneers who separately devised ways to take blood to the front-line hospitals where it was needed most. During his time as a stretcher-bearer in the Great War, he had seen many soldiers lose blood, go into shock and die. He knew that rapid transfusions (as opposed to the arm-to-arm ones often delivered much later in hospitals a long way from the front) would save lives.[9] Bethune explained his process in a letter to his backers in Canada: 'We collect ½ to ¾ gallon daily, mix it with Sodium Citrate (3.8%) and keep it just above freezing in the refrigerator in sterile milk and wine bottles. This blood will keep for about a week.' Already arranged by blood types, the bottles were delivered to front-line medics in two refrigerated vehicles.[10] Volunteers from the Brigades were amongst the chief beneficiaries. Bethune called this 'a glorified milk-delivery system', but it would save many lives over the coming weeks. Indeed, with the battles around Madrid raging through the early part of 1937, this soon – briefly – became the world's busiest mobile transfusion service. 'After I had given a transfusion to a French soldier who had lost his arm, he raised the other to me as I left the room in the Casualty Clearing Station, and with his raised clenched fist exclaimed "Viva la Revolution [sic]",' Bethune recalled. 'He recovered.'[11] Such experiences thrilled the restless doctor and fulfilled his desire to be both important and close to the action.

Early in February 1937, Bethune found himself in Spain's temporary capital, Valencia, visiting officials as he sought to extend his service and they tried to work out how his unit and, more importantly Bethune himself, fitted with similar initiatives. It was here that he first heard talk of a devastating attack on the southern port city of Málaga. This was the largest city in a narrow corridor of Republican land that stretched along the southern coast from Estepona (45 kilometres from Gibraltar) to the foothills of the Sierra Nevada mountain chain, south of Granada.[12] A winding road that ran east along the increasingly narrow coastal plain towards Almería, more than 200 kilometres from Málaga, provided the only route in and out. This was where Bethune, 'part adventurer, part humanitarian'[13] as one colleague described him, and his two-man team decided to head in the mobile improvised blood vans (an old, wood-sided Ford station wagon and a 2.5 ton Renault truck). They were excited by the thought of being near the front again. 'Madrid was the hotspot in November. We were there! Now Málaga, and we'll be there!' one of Bethune's assistants exclaimed.[14]

The team left Valencia late at night on 7 February, just as resistance in Málaga was crumbling, and motored down the coast towards Spain's south-eastern corner near Almería. As they drove, Francoist gunboats pounded Málaga from the sea and two separate columns advanced on the city. One of these columns was made up of 10,000 Italian troops from Mussolini's so-called Corpo Truppe Volontarie (CTV) – a fascist militia army which would soon outnumber the International Brigades[15] – which had landed in Cádiz the previous month and was about to enter Málaga's largely defenceless streets. In the almost total absence of government aircraft, the so-called Legionary Air Force provided by the Italians was also free to do as it wished. 'The first sentence we shall pass in Málaga is the death sentence,' the Francoist general Queipo de Llano had pronounced in one of his drunken, inflammatory radio broadcasts.[16] He remained true to his word.

Amongst the first to flee the city were those in charge of Málaga's defence. Kléber, the now semi-disgraced 'saviour of Madrid', was hastily drafted in to help reorganise this but his demands that local military commanders be sacked were ignored.[17] Kléber now modestly referred to himself as a lieutenant colonel (several steps down from his controversial Madrid title of general), and could do little more than accompany the Spanish officer in charge as he also moved east, having lost all control.[18] Panicked militiamen from anarchist and other units were left leaderless, outgunned and undersupplied.

The militias encouraged people to abandon the city and surrounding villages, warning of an imminent massacre on a scale of the one perpetrated in Badajoz. There was nothing unreasonable about this, since some 20,000 citizens would eventually be executed in Málaga (many after being prosecuted by Franco's future prime minister, Carlos Arias Navarro).[19] The anarchists' own history of assassinations almost certainly increased the fear of indiscriminate revenge and terror. Over 200,000 people were suddenly on the move, streaming out of the city and nearby villages in cars, trucks, buses or on mules and horses, but mostly on foot, in thin, rope-soled shoes that provided scant protection from the sharp stones on the dirt road.

A sandstorm slowed down Bethune and his team, and they were still in Alicante when news reached them the following morning that Málaga had fallen. This only increased Bethune's determination. What he did not know was quite how many were now fleeing the city, or that at eight that morning, fighter aircraft had begun strafing civilians on the ground, or that, two hours later, the great guns on the *Canarias* warship started to target the refugees. This was to become the routine of the next five days, as unarmed people were strafed and bombed while crews on the vessels just offshore could be seen celebrating their best hits. Eventually, the refugees took to walking by night and hiding by day. Lost, frightened children desperately sought mothers, fathers and siblings amongst the mass of people marching, or limping, through the dark.

Unaware of this, Bethune left Almería with his two assistants that afternoon (leaving behind one of their blood vans, which had broken down), and soon ran into the first few groups that had fled Málaga. As they travelled west the density of human beings grew until they crested a rise and saw a solid column of people crossing the wide plain below them like meandering black ants. As they drove down the road, beeping their horn to clear the way, they could see that many were barefooted or had simple rags tied around their feet. Children outnumbered adults, with each family typically comprising between three and six offspring. They also passed retreating soldiers, who muttered about 'fascists' somewhere behind them. Bethune's team urged him to turn around before they ran into Mussolini's Italian troops, but he decided to plough on. He pointed to the sign on the edge of the Renault truck which read 'Servicio Canadiense de transfusión de sangre al frente' (the Canadian Blood Transfusion Service for the Front), and declared: 'See that boys? To the front we go.'[20]

Around them was one of the largest refugee columns seen in Western Europe since the First World War. While Bethune put their number at 150,000, historians have since suggested up to twice that number.[21] They needed transport, food or water, rather than blood. In yet another prelude to events across the continent a few years later, it was the first European refugee column ever to be systematically strafed and bombarded.[22] As one of the few foreign witnesses to what became the worst single atrocity of this war, Bethune later published his own account of what he saw, accompanied by photographs of young children, including those lying down to recover or die beside the road. 'Imagine one hundred and fifty thousand men, women and children setting out for safety to the town situated over a hundred miles away,' he wrote:

> There is only one road they can take. There is no other way of
> escape. This road, bordered on one side by the high Sierra Nevada
> mountains and on the other by the sea, is cut into the side of the
> cliffs and climbs up and down from sea level to over 500 feet.
> The city they must reach is Almería, and it is over 200 kilometres
> away. A strong, healthy young man can walk on foot forty or fifty
> kilometres a day. The journey these women, children and old
> people must face will take five days and five nights at least. There
> will be no food to be found in the villages, no trains, no buses to
> transport them. They must walk and as they walked, staggered and
> stumbled with cut, bruised feet along that flint, white road the
> fascists bombed them from the air and fired at them from their
> ships at sea.[23]

The medics pressed on through the mass of people in their large Renault, and slowly made their way to the town of Motril, where they believed the front line to be.[24] As they drove, Bethune counted around 5,000 children under the age of ten, 'at least 1,000 of them barefoot and many of them clad only in a single garment', though temperatures plummeted at night.[25] Twenty kilometres short of Motril, Bethune could go no further. He turned the truck around, opened the doors, and within minutes it was full of children and pregnant women. Bethune ordered his men to drive the refugees to Almería and come straight back for more. Meanwhile he and his assistant, Thomas Worsley, stayed behind and spent the night in a cowshed, sharing an open fire with refugees. The following day, he walked on seventeen kilometres to investigate conditions, as the Renault ferried people back and forth. Government aircraft were noticeably scarce, but one of those that did arrive – a Republican bomber – crashed into the sea beside the beach and Bethune ran down the rocks to help rescue the aircrew, making tourniquets out of wires he pulled from the wreckage.

The bombardments and strafing left families scared and traumatised: under terrifying assault from both sea and sky, and nowhere to run, they threw themselves into ditches, scrabbled in the dirt, fled into the sugar-cane fields or simply panicked – losing children and other family members. One group tried to hide beneath a carob tree, but found it already occupied by the corpses of another family. 'One child had turned black, another was also coloured … and a small boy had neatly combed hair … the parents were dead too,' a survivor recalled.[26] Elsewhere, a dead young woman was found propped upright against a roadside tree, a child still trying to suckle at her breast; a desperate father was seen to shoot his two children and wife before turning the gun on himself; and a young man riding on a donkey carried his sister's corpse in front of him, determined to bury her properly when he reached Almería. The road was so littered with corpses that, at night, it was difficult not to step on them.

After finishing an exhausting series of sorties in the now-struggling Renault, the team returned to Almería. There things worsened, with what Bethune called a 'final [act of] barbarism'. Air-raid warnings suddenly rang out and thirty seconds later bombs began to fall on streets clogged with refugees. The attack came as Bethune sat in a garage, watching the engine on the Renault being repaired, and he was showered with stones and glass. 'They deliberately dropped ten great bombs in the very centre of the town where on the main street [exhausted refugees] were sleeping huddled together on the pavement,' he reported.[27] He dusted himself off and ran outside, picking up what he found to be the lifeless bodies of three young children who had been in a bread queue. 'The street was a shambles of the dead and the dying, lit only by the orange glare of burning buildings. In the darkness the moans of wounded children, shrieks of agonised mothers, the curses of the men rose in a massed cry higher and higher to a pitch of intolerable intensity.'[28] He estimated the dead in this attack at fifty civilians and two soldiers, with a similar number of wounded.

According to Jan Kurzke, Bethune returned to Madrid from Almería 'a changed man ... looking like a biblical prophet, his face burned, making his dishevelled white, wispy hair the more striking'.[29] The Canadian was a regular visitor to Kurzke's room, Room 360, in the improvised hospital in the Palace Hotel (Madrid's other grand hotel, the Ritz, had also been made into a hospital: Buenaventura Durruti had died there, in Room 27, in November). Bethune's ambitions to extend the transfusion service, however, were soon dashed. He could not speak Spanish, was not prepared to follow orders and had rival Spanish doctors offering similar and better services. During this time he wrote his pamphlet, entitled 'The Crime on the Road: Málaga to Almería', which did much to win sympathy for the Republican cause in France and North America. He was also encouraged to leave Spain, where his mercurial personality had made too many waves. His services as a medical expert would, however, soon be welcomed by the Chinese army as it fought Japan. When Bethune died two years later, from blood-poisoning, Mao Tse-tung himself wrote the eulogy, praising his 'absolute selflessness'.[30]

In mid-February, the remnants of XIII Brigade arrived in the city. Orders had been issued on 6 February for an International Brigade to travel to Málaga's defence, but it was far too late for that now. Almería's streets were packed with famished and orphaned children and some Brigaders secretly chose to give up their rations to the locals they encountered, hiding from their own quartermasters and cooks as they did so.

Thirteenth Brigade followed the same route that had been taken by Bethune's blood transfusion team, along the infamous coast road, looking to engage an approaching enemy. 'As far as we could see, the road was full of people,' German volunteer Ewald Munschke recalled. 'A torrent of human beings: men, women, children, old people and youths, ragged, their shoes torn or bare-footed.'[31] A rousing version of events (almost certainly vetted by commissars) had the Chapaev Battalion and others flying their flags and singing marching songs as they made their way along the coastal road. Some 250 unarmed 'militiamen', many of them young boys, turned around and joined them. This allowed XIII Brigade, which had received few reinforcements after the debacle at Teruel, to bring itself almost back up to strength.[32]

The international volunteers helped to establish a new front line by taking a series of towns and villages, starting with a small fishing village overlooked by a Moorish fort, Castell de Ferro. This feat sounded better in the telling than in reality: they had found the fort empty; Queipo de Llano's troops and the Italians had not yet arrived here. A notice pinned to the local police chief's door, addressed to the Francoist troops, explained that the chief was also a Francoist and asked if they could please avoid sacking his home since he would be back as soon as possible.[33]

The Brigaders handed over the coastal section to Spanish Republican soldiers and moved up into the mountains, where they 'recaptured' another seven towns and villages.[34] In fact, they mainly found themselves moving in unopposed. In Pitres, high up the mountain, the enemy simply abandoned its positions; the Brigaders took over their headquarters and answered phone calls from the Francoist command in Granada, asking what was going on.[35]

The Republican line now stretched up to Spain's highest town, Trevélez, and to its tallest mainland peak, the Mulhacén. It was easy defensive terrain, where potential attackers had to navigate deep ravines and winding mountain tracks. British writer Gerald Brenan, who later published *South from Granada* and *The Spanish Labyrinth*, had established himself here in the village of Yegen in the 1920s, enjoying the isolation while greeting the likes of Virginia Woolf, Lytton Strachey and Dora Carrington as occasional visitors.[36]

For the Tirolese volunteers of XIII Brigade, it was a delightful return to mountains, precipitous valleys and snow, while rugged Hungarians enthusiastically set off up to the highest spots. The less hardy city folk and industrial workers, however, remembered the intense cold and the hunger, with the French practising the tradition of 'organising' (Republican army jargon for fixing, scavenging or pilfering supplies) from amongst the local orchards. Many of the young militiamen who had joined the Brigades on the coast road were illiterate Spanish farm boys who now had to be taught both to shoot and to read and write. Most were used to resupply the small outposts of half-a-dozen men positioned in spots overlooking the narrow mountain tracks, where mule trains picked their way along paths carved into the steep mountainsides, which made the Brigaders giddy with vertigo.[37]

In military terms, there was little to do during this time. Enemy lines were too far away, and only the occasional artillery shell produced casualties. Freezing night-time temperatures were the volunteers' worst enemy. Not surprisingly, most remember this period with relative fondness. On clear days, they found the views looking south, over the glittering Mediterranean, spectacular. From the mountaintop, Berliner Rudolf Engel thought he could see the far-off coast of Africa through his binoculars 'and to the north-west you could sense the splendid city of Granada, not too far away'.[38]

Around this time Bernard Knox – who had seen himself 'winging down to the House of Death' after taking a bullet to his carotid artery at Boadilla – was told he was well enough to leave the Ritz hotel hospital (there, a Spanish volunteer nurse took his temperature by feeling his forehead, a skill she claimed to have learned 'from watching American films'). He too had been making occasional visits to Kurzke's room and had witnessed Jan's temporary room-mate – known only as '74', the number scribbled on a piece of paper stuck to the man's forehead – cry out for his mother, '¡Ay mi madre! ¡Ay mi madre!' as he passed away.

Knox could now move freely and decided it was time to go home to Britain and be properly treated. On the first leg of the journey, from Madrid to Albacete, his train pulled over to let another one pass and the future Harvard and Yale classics professor saw what he deemed an 'encouraging sight': 'As it rattled past, I saw men waving and giving us the salute with the clenched fist; evidently, these were reinforcements for Madrid. As the coach passed, I saw that it displayed a long white banner that read "THE YANKS ARE COMING".'[39]

23

A Valley Called Jarama: Pindoque railway bridge, 11 February 1937

The muddy waters of the Jarama churned their way past the concrete piers of the iron railway bridge over the river at El Pindoque, twenty-five kilometres south-east of Madrid.[1] Fierce rain had swollen the river and, of all the places where Franco's army might choose to cross, this seemed the least likely. The bridge was long and narrow, designed only to carry wagons of beet to a large sugar refinery, near the town of Arganda del Rey. Sleepers were bolted directly onto the bridge's iron structure and the river was clearly visible through the large gaps between them. A narrow metal workman's walkway provided the only reliable, footsure path, but this was 200 metres long and very exposed. It appeared almost impossible to attack.[2]

By now, 11 February, everybody knew that Franco would need his armies to cross the Jarama river at some point, as he launched yet another attempt to surround and throttle Madrid, but nobody knew where the main thrust would come. Some of his troops had pushed towards the far bank of the Jarama over the previous four days, sweeping aside the mostly untried Spanish conscripts who were unable to stop the strongest attacking army yet seen in this war: some 20,000 men – three columns – backed by new weapons developed in Hitler's and Mussolini's factories.

A large part of the International Brigades – ten of the sixteen battalions[3] – found themselves either at the river's edge, held nearby in reserve, or on their way to a battlefield that would soon be dubbed 'the Verdun of Spain'.[4] Behind them, just ten kilometres away, sat Franco's target: the road connecting Madrid to the temporary capital, Valencia.[5] Franco's commanders were aware of the difficulty of their task. 'Of all the acts of war, the most risky and difficult is always to cross a river, and more so when it is as large as the Jarama,' said Víctor Ruiz, the pro-Francoist journalist who accompanied them. Just as daunting were the steep walls of the valley on the other side. The aim, nevertheless, was to cross the Jarama, capture the road and, so, 'strangle Madrid'.[6]

Tasked with guarding the Pindoque railway bridge, and in command of a company of fresh recruits, was a young officer known only as Lieutenant Martin.[7] He had just arrived from Albacete, and many fellow officers in the Franco-Belgian André Marty Battalion had not yet met him.[8] On 8 February Martin's men had marched through rain and mud to replace a Polish company,[9] and take up defensive positions on and around the bridge.[10] Cables dangled off the bridge's metal structure attached to sticks of dynamite and ran to a nearby farm shed, from where they could be detonated by the Brigaders if necessary. Machine-gun posts were placed in the middle of the bridge and on the near side. No one, however, was posted to watch the far bank.[11] Although it was known that Franco's forces were somewhere on the other side, they were still largely invisible – except from the air, where the Republic's air force of Russian planes launched raids when the weather permitted.

In fact, the enemy was not far away.[12] On clear days, from hills and ridges with names such as La Marañosa and El Espolón de Vaciamadrid, Francoist artillery and spotters enjoyed a magnificent view of the bridge defended by Martin and the flat valley land around. They were also free to bombard a five-kilometre stretch of the main Madrid to Valencia road at will, forcing any traffic to divert.[13] Supplying Martin's company was difficult in these circumstances, made worse by the atrocious weather, meaning that his men received their food cold and only by night.[14] The young lieutenant had set up his three machine guns and posted sentries. That night, the men fell asleep in huddled groups, confident that they would have due warning if Franco's men attempted to cross the bridge. For two nights, as the rain poured down and the paths and tracks turned to mud, they were undisturbed.

In the small hours of 11 February, however, a platoon of Moroccan *regulares* (full-time soldiers from the Army of Africa) slid silently down the Jarama's clay riverbanks to a fordable stretch of water one kilometre upstream.[15] Brigade commander Lukács had left the Republican side unguarded along most of the twelve-kilometre sector between the two main bridges, believing that the river here was impassable. The *regulares* crept up to the guards with their curved *koummya* knives, slitting throats and hurling grenades. In a matter of minutes, most of Martin's sentries were dead or out of action. The cables leading to the bridge were also cut before the dynamite could be detonated, though a single, loud blast sent the final section of the metal bridge up in the air, only for it to come to rest at a twisted but useable angle.

Meanwhile the rest of the André Marty Battalion were finding their way through the dark from the north, wading through the slippery mud, towards high ground above Pindoque bridge. They had been due to march to their new positions through the small hours, leaving at three in the morning, but the Garibaldis, who were replacing them at a road bridge near Arganda del Rey, were late and so they set off at 5.30 a.m. The aim was to occupy a series of hilltop positions behind Martin's company before daylight, and so give the Republicans command of the valley floor.[16] For three days they had watched as the enemy tried to approach the bigger road bridge – a solid, iron construction that was Franco's expected target – near Arganda, but Republican artillery had kept them pinned back.[17]

The bad weather began to clear.[18] After an hour of walking, the men of the André Marty Battalion heard the noise of rifle and machine-gun fire, grenades, mortars and the loud blast of dynamite being detonated, coming from the direction of the Pindoque bridge.[19] Violent flashes of light bounced off the water, though the Brigaders could only guess at what was actually happening.[20] As dawn approached and the volunteers got closer, the sound of firing diminished. By the time the battalion's commanders made it to the crest of a hill and peered down in the early morning light into the valley, they were met by the desperate sight of Lieutenant Martin's men on a hillock below them, trying to hold out against hundreds of Moroccan soldiers.[21] They looked on hopelessly as the volunteers were gradually overrun and killed. Another band of Martin's men in buildings nearby were just as efficiently eliminated, though at some cost to the Moroccans.

At first, the newly arrived André Marty men assumed that the Pindoque bridge had been blown up.[22] But, as the morning river mist lifted off the valley, they looked on in horror as fascist trucks arrived piled high with iron plates, which, once laid across the tracks, made the bridge passable again for the invaders. The bridge was beyond the range of the battalion's machine guns; there was nothing the volunteers could do about it. Four wounded soldiers from a Spanish section of Martin's company managed to escape and were able, in stumbling French, to explain what had happened. In essence the André Marty Battalion, XII Brigade, had let the enemy in.[23] Franco now had his route across the Jarama.[24]

Suddenly the remainder of the André Marty were spotted by Franco's artillery observers on hilltops across the river, who then directed a continuous barrage at their positions, forcing them back off the ridges. A few observers stayed behind to watch as Moroccan cavalry units poured onto the bridge and down its final, steep section. The horses had to be led by their reins, shying and slipping on the wet, muddy metal plates. Some of the animals fell into the river; one was left dangling from the metal structure, its head submerged in the flooded waters.[25]

For over three hours Franco's forces continued to cross the bridge, all the while under attack from Republican aircraft, which in turn were targeted by rapid, accurate anti-aircraft fire from the new German 88mm flak guns.[26] Soon there were more than 2,000 cavalry and infantrymen on the Jarama valley floor, or hidden in the thickets along the river. 'It was a sign,' one of the observers commented later, 'of just how meticulously planned the attack had been.'[27] A young brigade intelligence officer jumped on his motorbike and, negotiating the mud and artillery shells, set off to inform XII Brigade commander Lukács.

Peering through his binoculars, the battalion's French commissar Armand Maniou spotted a Spanish officer on a grey mount harangue his Moroccan cavalrymen, who then set off on a charge at the ridge occupied by another group of André Marty men. 'Whoever has never witnessed a cavalry charge cannot really have a proper idea of the grandeur of this act of war,' wrote Ruiz, as he praised Franco's 'Moors' and 'Saracens'. 'The Moor is always a fine, even magnificent, soldier; but he is at his singular best when mounted on a good horse … Unlike other cavalrymen who use their horse's body as defence, the Moor likes to rise up on his stirrups, grab the saddle pommel and stand tall with his torso stretched out, leaning forward as if to protect his mount from bullets with his own chest. They charge off with no second thoughts, in a marvellous race to be the first to reach the enemy.'[28]

The Moroccan soldiers charged the ridges in waves of 500 men, their high-pitched battle cries terrifying the defenders.[29] Over a hundred international volunteers of a second André Marty company, commanded by Raymond Hantz, set up four machine guns on the ridge and gazed down in amazement. Apart from the Garibaldi Battalion – who were trying to make their way along the valley floor from the north, but were kept away by an intense, pinpoint artillery barrage[30] – the André Martys were on their own. They were all that stood between Franco's forces and the crucial road linking Valencia and Madrid. 'We knew we had to hold out, even if we were all slain. If we didn't hold on … there was nobody else behind us to stop them,' said Maniou.[31] The only reinforcements to reach them were three Russian T-26b tanks, which dashed towards the bridge.[32] However, two of these were soon disabled by German anti-tank guns on the other side of the river.[33] Despite being unable to move their machines, and with Moroccan soldiers banging on the hatches, the two-man Russian crews refused to leave their tanks, which sat in the middle of the Jarama battlefield for hours. Led by the bald-headed Russian 'advisor' Dimitri Pavlov, and still mostly manned by Russians while Spaniards and international volunteers trained to take over from them, this tank brigade would nevertheless play an important role in the coming battle.

With limited munitions and little chance of resupply, the André Martys delayed opening fire until the dismounted Moroccan cavalry were halfway up the slope, some 500 metres away.[34] Though this was probably a little early, there was scant cover available to the attackers. Soon the hillside was littered with wave upon wave of Moroccan dead and wounded. The same scenario was repeated several times, until the fascist commanding officers realised that the sparse remains of the International Brigade battalion could only cover part of the ridge, and that they could easily be outflanked. Meanwhile, the ravine behind the ridge filled with injured French, Belgian and other volunteers, deposited there by stretcher bearers since the brigade's medical unit had not been alerted in time to join the battalion. Fortunately for those volunteers, the Moroccans approaching them were mistakenly shelled by their own side.[35]

Armed mainly with grenades and knives, more Moroccan soldiers crept through the thick bushes until they were just a few metres away from the André Marty positions. After half an hour of close fighting, the order was given for the battalion to retreat. The Brigaders gave up their positions early that afternoon and fled into the ravines, leaving their wounded behind.[36]

Werner Heilbrun, XII Brigade's popular chief doctor, watched it all unfolding through his field glasses, frustrated that he could not get to the injured men left in the ravine. The doctor was like a 'beggar-monk', who wore his cap tilted across black hair, emphasising a gaunt face and deep-set eyes – Regler described him as 'the embodiment of kindness, prudence and courage'.[37] An exiled German Jewish psychiatrist, Heilbrun was one of the 200 volunteers who had travelled to Spain from the fast-growing Jewish communities in Mandatory Palestine.[38] He was not a communist, but believed Hitler had to be stopped somewhere. 'He regarded the Führer as a fool who knew nothing whatever about the Jews and had been successful only because the masses were so immeasurably uneducated,' said Gustav Regler. He was also much loved by the new Spanish recruits who were now joining the battalion as its international volunteers were killed or wounded.[39]

That evening Heilbrun described how he watched the André Marty Battalion – hitherto the most disappointing, notoriously troublesome and ill-disciplined of all the early battalions – bravely trying to hold out against Franco's armies. 'They were better than any creed deserves. Schaefer, the Alsatian, stood firm until a shell-splinter got him in the stomach. Bouman went on firing his machine-gun until he ran out of ammunition,' Heilbrun told Regler. 'Bouman went on using his revolver until he was bayoneted. He was lucky that he didn't live to see what happened at the end. The wounded were lying on stretchers on the road to Chinchón. I wanted to get them away, but at the last minute I was warned not to try. The Moors slaughtered the lot. I saw it happen! One or two tried to crawl away …'[40]

Franco had now gained a foothold in the Pajares hills that rose up from the valley on the east side of the river. His soldiers reported 'finding' 140 bodies (André Marty men) and taking just seventeen prisoners, some of them French.[41] The attackers went little further, however, as they were immediately bombed and strafed by Russian aircraft.[42] Franco's commanders were, nevertheless, delighted. One entire column and half of another had crossed the Jarama during the day, and the rest would follow over the next twenty-four hours. Víctor Ruiz rode down the muddy tracks to a house fifty metres from the river and could scarcely believe that Franco's men were on the far bank and fighting their way up the hillsides. He claimed that a lack of artillery support for the thin line of defending volunteers had been crucial. It had been 'a crime', he declared, 'to leave the [International] Brigades, who still have orders to oppose our attack, without this attacking and defensive weapon that is today so absolutely necessary, the artillery gun.'[43]

A wounded Maniou was mocked for exaggerating when he made it back to the battalion headquarters with some stragglers, protesting that this was a major offensive. 'Over the following days I would be proved right,' he said later, blaming his commanders for their poor knowledge of enemy plans.[44] Maniou was indignant when the André Marty Battalion was then accused of having fallen asleep on the job. 'Those accusations are unacceptable,' he said. In fact, brigade commander Lukács bore much of the responsibility. He had sent the first company to the Pindoque bridge on its own, four kilometres from any support. It was an isolated and vulnerable target that had been easily destroyed. Once Franco's troops were across the river in such numbers, there was little that the André Marty Battalion could do beyond slowing them down.

The André Marty Battalion had been decimated, but they had managed to buy time for others to arrive. The Polish Dombrowski Battalion now moved into position behind them and linked up with the Garibaldis.[45] The Dombrowski also joined the first of a series of tank raids against the attackers. The Poles followed a group of fourteen Russian tanks that burst onto the plain, firing at Franco's men from their flank and behind.[46] Once more, however, the new German anti-tank guns came into their own, taking out five of the vehicles. It was, nevertheless, an effective way of disrupting the attackers' plans and such tank sorties would be used repeatedly over the coming days.

The situation was still dynamic. While the Dombrowskis were being pushed back, they were at least maintaining a defensive line in the northern part of the Francoist bulge on their side of the river. To their south, however, the hills rising from the plain were poorly defended and there was little to prevent the enemy marching across them to the Valencia road. During the day Hans Kahle's XI Brigade began to arrive and stretch the line south – though only the Commune de Paris Battalion arrived during daylight on 11 February, while the Thälmann appeared that night and the Edgar André on the 12th.[47] Like the other brigades, XI Brigade had been training to take part in a Republican offensive and were now somewhat confused to find themselves forced to defend.[48] Indeed, one Thälmann company made up of keen new volunteers from Scandinavia started off with an overenthusiastic charge that saw several killed on their first day of action.

Overnight, the situation worsened. The next bridge downstream, at San Martín de la Vega, was taken on 12/13 February in a repeat of the Pindoque railway bridge incident – with Moroccan soldiers again fording the river at night and this time catching a Spanish Republican guard unit unawares. Once more, attempts to sabotage the bridge failed, leaving just an easily avoided hole halfway across. As this was a more substantial road bridge, a greater volume of troops were able to cross quickly, who then fought their way towards a soon-to-be infamous hill known as El Pingarrón. If the previous day Franco had seen one and a half columns cross the Jarama, he now had all three columns there, and he could push towards the Valencia road, which lay just ten kilometres away.[49]

The brand new XV International Brigade was also on its way. This included a mostly Bulgarian and Yugoslav battalion – the Dimitrov – recruited in part by the senior Yugoslav communist Josip Broz, also known as Tito (who, despite numerous alleged sightings, never did travel to Spain).[50] Yet another mainly French-speaking battalion, the Six Février, and the American Abraham Lincoln Battalion had also been formed, but the latter did not arrive at the front for several days. Instead, the defenders were joined by a battalion based around the survivors from the British company who had fought at Lopera with XIV Brigade. This initially bore the name 'Saklatvala', after one of Britain's first communist MPs, Mumbai-born Shapurji Saklatvala, who represented Battersea North – though it would become better known as the British Battalion.[51]

24

The British: San Martín road, Jarama valley, 12 February 1937

Six months earlier, Tom Wintringham had stared out at the mountains behind Huesca and imagined what it would be like to have an army of international volunteers supporting the ragged Republican militiamen fighting there. His idea had originally been scoffed at in Britain, but now he commanded a whole battalion of British volunteers. Wintringham was proud of the men he led onto hills above the San Martín bridge road early on 12 February, though he had no idea that this had been taken by Franco overnight. Like the men under his command, he believed they were joining a Republican offensive. In fact, as he was soon to find out, the British Battalion was now at the southern end of a line of poorly connected international battalions – half of which had arrived over the previous hours – in the hills overlooking the river Jarama. Fulfilling their role as shock troops, these were required to be the first buffer against a Francoist offensive that, with the conquest of the second bridge, had just grown considerably in intensity.

If a British battalion in Spain had been formed relatively late, this was mostly because the Communist Party of Great Britain had been slow to organise. By the end of 1936, however, the sight of groups of suspicious-looking young men gathering at London's Victoria Station had become commonplace.[1] When questioned by plain-clothes police officers from Special Branch, they claimed – fairly implausibly – to be going to spend a few days in Paris, or to be day-tripping to Dunkirk.[2] Few of these men had passports or had ever been abroad in their lives;

many belonged to an unemployment-hardened British working class (though a number also came from Australia, New Zealand and other dominions or colonies). Some already carried the memories and scars of fighting Oswald Mosley's fascist Blackshirts on London's streets or blocking their path as they tried to march through the city's East End at Cable Street. Others had taken part in hunger marches or the mass trespasses at Kinder Scout, in the Derbyshire Peak District. Although it was possible to travel to Spain independently, recruitment was mostly through the Communist Party offices in King Street, London – where volunteers could be expected to be quizzed not just on their suitability for warfare, but on their politics too.

None of this background, however, had prepared the nine-stone amateur boxer Walter Gregory, a volunteer from Nottingham, for the squalor he witnessed in Madrigueras, where the battalion's training camp was based. Gregory, who had gone through periods of unemployment, was shocked by the 'almost unbelievable' poverty. 'I felt myself to be no stranger to hardship,' he said, but 'compared to the poor peasants of this part of Spain, the unemployed of Nottingham were affluent.'[3]

It took time, however, to get used to the local habits. The British volunteers shared, and grumbled about, the diet of 'bean and beans and beans'. They downed coarse red wine in the local cafes as if it was beer, often ending up asleep under the tables, and had to be reminded that their hosts, the Spaniards, rarely got drunk. Most of the Irish volunteers who joined them were keen drinkers – and this became a point of contention when tensions flared up between the two groups, provoking at least one fist fight and ending in a stormy meeting, during which the Irish debated whether to move to the new American Abraham Lincoln Battalion. Most of the new Irish volunteers were Republicans and, like their leader Frank Ryan, some were experienced IRA men who viewed the British as their historic enemy and oppressor. 'I can understand that,' said one British volunteer, before an Irish communist argued that 'distinctions must be made between anti-fascist working-class comrades from Britain and British imperialism'. Most decided to leave anyway. Marty was furious and future Irish recruits were directed back to the British 'Saklatvala' battalion.[4]

An additional problem was the quality of some of the recruits. 'About ten per cent of the men are drunks and flunkers. I can't understand why you've sent out such useless material,' Wintringham wrote to Harry

Pollitt, head of the British Communist Party. 'We call them "Harry's anarchists".'[5] A proportion were rumoured to be tramps or unemployed men who had been recruited from the Embankment in London and had 'no enthusiasm for the war', according to one political commissar.[6]

The battalion's original commander, Scottish journalist Wilfred Macartney, was deemed to have 'impeccable revolutionary credentials', having spent ten years in Parkhurst jail for a clumsy attempt at spying for the USSR. He was also a wealthy man with a generous inheritance which he spent, when not in Spain, on high-living and expensive hotels.[7] With a Lenin School-trained political commissar, Londoner Dave Springhall, this was, nevertheless, a highly politicised and motivated group of men. Two-thirds were communists, from a Great Britain party with a total membership of just 11,500 members in December – though a significant, if uncountable, proportion had simply joined in order to ease their path to Spain, helping to raise membership by a further 900 over four months.[8] One of the best company commanders was a London bus driver.[9] The core of the battalion were the survivors of Nathan's company at Lopera which, in turn, contained several of those who had marched up Madrid's Gran Vía with the first International Brigade three months earlier. Most of the others had some sort of military training, as First World War veterans or army reservists.[10] Their five weeks of training at Madrigueras, with just fifteen or so rounds of ammunition fired by each man, was ridiculously inadequate by the standards of a normal army, but a luxury in Spain. There was every reason to expect them to be good.[11]

Those expectations were about to be put to the test. The men were glad that the enthusiastic and unpretentious Wintringham – a keen student of military history – had replaced Macartney. They did not know that Marty and others were beginning to look at the Scot with suspicion, or that Marty had arrested Wintringham's new American girlfriend, the 'petite and vivacious' (as Kurzke's girlfriend Kate Mangan described her) journalist Kitty Bowler, when she appeared in Madrigueras with information about how to maintain the battalion's machine guns.

A grumpy, rumpled Marty interrogated Bowler personally. 'Behind a rolltop desk sat an old man with a first-class walrus moustache,' she recalled. 'He was sleepy and irritable and had pulled a coat on over his pyjamas. He reminded me of a petty French bureaucrat ... To my surprise my mass of Spanish papers did not interest him in the least. Even my UGT [socialist trades union] card and pass were thrown back in my face, contemptuously. My past was all that interested him … at the end of an hour he read out the charges and they shocked me out of my certainty. 1) Travelled from Albacete to Madrigueras by truck without pass. 2) Penetrated (literal trans. of the French) into a military establishment. 3) Interested yourself in the functioning (bad) of machine guns. 4) Visited Italy and Germany in 1933. THEREFORE YOU ARE A SPY.'[12]

Bowler had been released after several nights of interrogation, claiming that 'they were furious because I didn't break down and weep as they expected a woman would'.[13] Neither she nor Wintringham, who was already married to a fellow British communist whom he planned to leave for Bowler, knew that she was the subject of a secret expulsion order. Above Wintringham, as commander of the new XV Brigade, was the ambitious 'Mexican' János Gálicz, known simply as General Gal. He was yet another Austro-Hungarian who had joined the Red Army.[14] Gal quickly earned a reputation as one of the toughest, most ruthless officers in the International Brigades. 'For him, anyone who committed a mistake deserved the firing squad, so that they could not repeat the mistake again,' recalled one volunteer.[15] The high command liked him, however, and within three days he would be put in charge of the entire division, with his political commissar, the Yugoslav Vladimir Ćopić – a gifted baritone who serenaded visitors with revolutionary songs[16] and rode a handsome charger[17] 'with the elegant composure of a consummate aristocrat' – taking over XV Brigade.[18]

Three days earlier, weeping villagers had waved the British off from Madrigueras, the tears of one local particularly affecting a young recruit. 'For all my education and her lack of it, she knew more about life and death than I did,' he wrote afterwards about the tearful local woman who sent him off with a pocketful of mandarins. 'She foresaw what I did not: that many of us would not come back.'[19]

The final day before the British took up their positions at Jarama was spent practising with their weapons – for the first time for some newcomers – before being moved towards their start point at 7 a.m., given a hearty breakfast at the cookhouse and told they were about to fight 'for all the peoples of the world'.[20] They were well armed, the weather was dry and they felt confident. As they clambered up towards a plateau covered by olive groves, the sun grew warmer and their legs heavier. They began to jettison anything that was not strictly necessary, leaving the olive grove 'like an abandoned fairground', according to Jason Gurney, a South African sculptor.[21]

'There was an extraordinary variety of objects amongst the debris – hand grenades, ammunition, machine-gun spare parts and clothes and equipment of all kinds. But the personal items which had been jettisoned provided the strangest part of the collection. Books of all kinds – though Marxist textbooks, which were large and heavy, lay fairly near the bottom of the hill. The rest were an amazing variety, ranging from third-rate pornography to the sort of books which normally fill the shelves of the more serious type of undergraduate. There were copies of the works of Nietzsche, and Spinoza, Spanish language textbooks, Rhys Davids's *Early Buddhism* and every kind of taste in poetry'.[22] Some things had not been discarded. One volunteer still carried with him his mandolin. Another was equipped with Shakespeare's *Tragedies*.[23]

Soon the British were on the plateau. Ahead of and below them, not yet visible, lay the Jarama river itself and the valley. Far off to the right Wintringham thought he could discern the distant shape of Madrid and, beyond that, the snow-clad peaks of the Sierra.[24] They could hear the newly created Six Février Battalion already fighting on their right. Some, less accustomed to the sounds of war, mistook the sound of distant machine- gun fire for that of cicadas. In the skies above them, a dogfight played out: five of the sluggish, twin-winged German Heinkel 51s had turned to fight seven of the nimble, single-winged Russian Polikarpov I-16s. The men cheered as three of the German-manufactured aircraft dived into the ground. The Russian planes were still outperforming their German and Italian counterparts, though the latter were introducing newer and better models while both sides were also now using anti-aircraft guns which left puffs of white smoke in the sky.[25]

It was, however, still relatively peaceful by the time the 400 men of the British Battalion reached the crest of the escarpment at the edge of the plateau. Three hillocks sat just below them: one was covered by short, thorny trees and topped by a small white farmhouse; a second was conical and almost bald of vegetation; and the third, which was closest to the Six Février Battalion on their right, was little more than a sharp-pointed, symmetrical knoll.[26] Beyond that the land dipped down into a valley and a road ran towards the bridge near San Martín that Franco's men had taken a few days before.[27] Approaching briskly up the slope towards the British volunteers came the familiar figure of an immaculately dressed, pipe-smoking officer, nonchalantly swinging his cane. George Nathan, the hero of Lopera, was now a senior brigade staff officer. 'Your battalion's a bit late,' he informed Wintringham matter-of-factly.[28] It was only now that Wintringham realised that this was not the big attack they had all been expecting to take part in, but a defensive counter-attack.[29] They could see enemy troops in the distance, heading towards them on this side of the river.[30] Six hundred Moroccans, supported by a thousand legionnaires, were approaching. His battalion was outnumbered three-to-one.[31]

The advance companies had not gone far down the hill towards the valley when the shooting started, and Wintringham decided to defend from atop the two larger hillocks. The machine-gun company, when and if it was ready, would occupy the ridge above and behind them. His men were now, however, in perfect view of Franco's artillery spotters, with very little cover and no entrenching equipment. As they retreated back up the hill, their inexperience showed. Some men stood up to shoot, or left themselves silhouetted (from below) against the skyline behind them, and were swiftly mowed down by machine-gun fire or caught by Moroccan snipers. An experienced Scottish sergeant sobbed out loud as he shouted at the younger men, 'Get them off the skyline!'[32]

The ensuing battle between professional Moroccan troops and 'city bred young men with no experience of war ... and no competence as marksmen' was brutal.[33] Without maps, and with communication difficult, each company had to fight for itself.[34] Bayonets and helmets were all they had to scrape at the ground with as they hurriedly tried to construct parapets. Soon dead bodies were being used, bullets thudding into them. For the next three hours the battalion experienced the sort of intense bombardment familiar to veterans of the First World War. The sound of shrapnel tearing through the air was terrifying. 'Your stomach just turns to water,' said one, putting the reaction down to beginners' nerves.[35] Those who made the mistake of gathering at the white farmhouse – an easy artillery target – were amongst the first casualties. It was, a First World War veteran claimed, 'worse than the Somme'.[36] One shell-shocked company commander was found weeping uncontrollably behind the hillocks while his men fought on the other side.[37]

Soon they would baptise this place as 'Suicide Hill', and, against Wintringham's wishes, they were ordered to cling on at all costs even though they risked being surrounded. In front of them, the soldiers of the Army of Africa used their skills to approach silently through the gulleys and thick underbrush, with only the small puffs of smoke from their rifles giving them away.[38] They were followed by legionnaires, one of whom later recalled the shock of running into the Brigaders. 'We were advancing virtually without losses, and it all seemed like a walk in the park, until we bumped into XV International Brigade,' he recalled. 'Those guys were well prepared, especially ideologically, and were not at all the type to run at the first sound of war.'[39]

The British also enjoyed the advantage of occupying higher ground. This was considerably reduced, however, by a lack of proper ammunition for their machine guns. The heavy, wheeled Maxim guns had been dragged up the hill and through the thick, crumbling soil beneath the olive trees.[40] The machine-gun company commander, Harry Fry, had already realised they had been provided with the wrong ammunition. Attempts to remedy the situation, however, were held up by a drunken British driver who ran the ammunition truck off the road.[41] This reduced the battalion's firepower considerably, since the five[42] Maxims on the ridge overlooking the three hillocks could jointly fire 2,500 rounds a minute. That was slightly more than the battalion's several hundred riflemen could manage with their Russian Mosin-Nagant rifles,[43] whose clips needed reloading after five shots. Without the machine guns, the chances of holding on to their positions were considerably reduced.[44]

One of the most formidable characters in the battalion was Fred Copeman. Born in a Suffolk workhouse and raised with his fists before him, he had joined the Royal Navy and become a heavyweight boxer. He was dismissed from the navy in 1931 after taking part in the Invergordon Mutiny and then joined the Communist Party. Copeman had spent six months in prison for biting a policeman's bottom during a demonstration and signed up for the International Brigades the day after his Scottish girlfriend asked him why he wasn't going to Spain. Foul-mouthed, quick-tempered and prone to bullying, some thought 'Bloody Fred' was certifiably mad. He was, nevertheless, made an officer.[45] Furious at the lack of machine-gun support, the thirty-year-old charged off to shout at Fry and, then, at Wintringham. By this stage a bullet had scraped Copeman's head and a piece of shrapnel was lodged in his thumb, but he was so maddened by rage he barely noticed. A trip to the dressing station to have his wounds tended to saw him come across the crashed ammunition truck. Somehow, he and a political commissar managed to carry two boxes up the hill to the line, just as a reserve truck also appeared with ammunition. 'Of course there's fucking, blinding, sodding ammunition,' he told Wintringham.[46]

The machine-gun ammunition belts had to be loaded bullet by bullet (by Copeman and others) which meant they still could not provide covering fire as the enemy crept ever closer and the men in the advanced companies began to retire.[47] The latter were killed or wounded by their dozens as the Moroccans surged onto the hillocks above them. Men ran blindly in panic and those who survived often became lost. One overwrought rifleman recalled that he 'did a bit of squealing [and] screaming for' his mother, before being found by a Spanish Republican unit.[48]

Ironically, the lack of machine guns eventually played to the British Battalion's advantage. The Spanish officer leading the Moroccans was now convinced that only a thin line of riflemen stood between them and a breakthrough that would take them to the Valencia road. He ordered his men to charge up the open slopes towards the ridge, just as Copeman's machine-gun company finally loaded its weapons. Dusk was creeping across the valley as the Moroccans clambered up the slope, in four long lines. Mounted officers in blue and red cloaks waved them forward with sabres.[49] 'You'll never see how many men you can kill in a short time,' Copeman told the machine-gunners after ordering them to rake the hillside from right to left and back again. 'But don't fire until I say so because if you do there's anti-tank guns over there. They'll blow us right out of the bloody ground. They don't know we are here at the moment, so good luck, you haven't been noticed up to now.'[50]

It was hard to make the men hold their fire until the Moroccans, who were still killing stragglers from the advance companies, were just fifty metres away. They waited, nevertheless, with dry mouths and trembling fingers.[51] Copeman steeled their nerves, using his sailor's experienced fists when necessary. 'One young Irishman … threatened to open fire and to hell with Fred Copeman,' he recalled. 'There was no time to argue the point. I sailed into him and laid him out.'[52] Someone else quickly replaced the dazed machine-gunner. Then they opened fire.

Copeman had been right. It was like 'mowing down wheat', as he recalled. 'You might think to see men mown down as if a scythe was going through them wouldn't be possible, but this is literally what happened,' another remembered.[53] Up to half a battalion of Moroccans – some 250 men – were put out of action in just three minutes. The rest scrambled for cover, scurried back down the hill or fell, feigning death. Copeman ordered his men to fire behind them so that the enemy could not retreat and then had them systematically rake the ground where soldiers were playing dead. By now the machine guns were beginning to overheat and, with no water supplies, the men urinated into their helmets and poured the contents into guns' cooling jackets and over red hot barrels.[54] It was a desperate, miraculous, last-minute victory.

Further up the as-yet-incomplete line and unaware that a second bridge crossing had taken place, Hans Kahle's XI Brigade was trying to occupy the central space between the other two International Brigades. At first he concentrated on trying to link up with Lukács's men and the Dombrowski Battalion to the north. Soon, however, his three battalions found themselves fighting the new enemy column that had appeared to their south as it tried to advance through the vast olive groves. The interminable rows of trees proved disorientating for attackers, while the defenders were able to use the thick, gnarled olive trunks as cover for machine-gun emplacements. Amidst the trees, Francoist artillery spotters found it difficult to distinguish between friend and foe, or even see where Pavlov's tanks were hiding. From his command post at a hilltop military radio telegraphy station, Kahle watched as his battalions ran out to attack from behind Pavlov's tanks, or retreated slowly in a backwards and forwards game that cost many lives, but favoured his men more than the attackers. The main problem was to make sure that all the battalions linked up and that Franco's men did not spot the gaps between them.[55]

Losses mounted and almost all battalions suffered moments of confusion. Spanish troops in the new mixed brigades, many of them new or poorly commanded, proved erratic. Rather than dig in to hold a newly conquered position, they frequently ran back when Pavlov's T-26b tanks turned around to refuel. These were discovering that, while they were still far superior to the small German Mark 1 Panzers (whose crews were trained by the future Second World War tank commander Wilhelm Von Thoma[56]) and Italian Fiat-Ansaldos, they had a serious opponent in the new German 37mm Pak 36 anti-tank gun.[57]

Night-time on 12 February, and the usually abstemious Lukács drained a glass of brandy under the olive trees to celebrate the

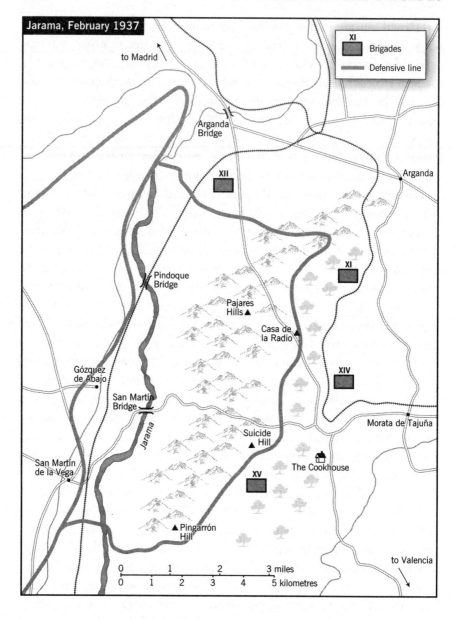

fact that his XII Brigade had held on. He had chosen his favoured
toast: 'War is such a terrible mess!' The survivors of his André Marty
Battalion – 130 men out of a unit that had boasted some 350 three
days earlier – had been withdrawn and, embracing their former
reputation, rampaged angrily through Arganda, raiding its cellars

for alcohol.[58] They were eventually given the task of guarding the Arganda bridge again.

A disconnected line of International Brigade battalions looped through the hills to the British Battalion's position. The latter's last-gasp victory, meanwhile, had allowed it to hold on until night fell and the battle ended. Most of the men retired to eat and sleep in a sunken road that sat a hundred metres from the ridge, which was now their forward line, while the enemy established its line on the hillocks just below them.[59] Attempts were made to collect any remaining dead or wounded. Some men managed to haul themselves back out of no-man's-land in the dark, but that night Jason Gurney discovered dozens of men with shrapnel wounds lying on stretchers at an abandoned field-dressing station:

> Many of the men had already died and most of the others would die before the morning. They were chiefly artillery casualties with appalling wounds from which they could have little hope of recovery. They were all men whom I had known well, and some of them intimately – one little Jewish kid of about eighteen whose particular blend of Cockney and Jewish humour had given him a capacity for clowning around and getting a laugh out of everyone even during the most depressing period, now lay on his back with a wound that appeared to have entirely cut away the muscle structure of his stomach so that his bowels were exposed from his navel to his genitals. His intestines lay in loops of ghastly pinkish brown, twitching slightly as the flies searched around over them. He was perfectly conscious, unable to speak, but judging from his eyes he was not in pain or even particularly distressed. [This was almost certainly Maurice Davidovitch, a courageous young stretcher-bearer who had helped bring many of the wounded here before being hit himself.[60]] One man of whom I was particularly fond was clearly dying from about nine bullet wounds through his chest. He asked me to hold his hand and we talked for a few minutes until his hand went limp in mine and I knew he was dead. I went from one to the other but was absolutely powerless to do anything other than to hold a hand or light a cigarette. Nobody cried out or screamed or made other tragic gestures. I did what I could to comfort them and promised to try to get some ambulances. Of course, I failed, which left me with a feeling of guilt which I never entirely shed.[61]

After just eight hours of fighting, the British Battalion had been reduced to half-strength.[62] Stragglers were forced back to the line at gunpoint, with Copeman and the Anglo-Egyptian Andre Diamant – who had taken command of one of the companies – finding almost a hundred men in the wine vaults of a farmhouse; they had to threaten to throw a grenade in before the men agreed to leave.[63] Only two of the original company commanders were left, and one of those was the nerve-wracked former Welsh Guardsman Bert Overton, who was prone to breaking into tears and was fast becoming a liability. A company of young Spaniards clad in rope-soled shoes and with no blankets to protect themselves from the night cold now joined them. They had become separated from their own unit and – accepting the British Battalion's Filipino translator Manuel Lizarraga as their commander – stood shoulder to shoulder with the British over the coming days.[64]

The thirteenth of February dawned another bright day. Elsewhere on the front, almost all the volunteer battalions had been fighting, though some were just coming into the line. From north to south, there was now an almost continuous line of volunteers – with the Garibaldis, the remains of the André Marty, Dombrowski, Commune de Paris, Thälmann, Edgar André, Dimitrov, British and Six Février ranged along the crests and through the olive groves. At full strength, that would have accounted for 5,000 men. A further 2,000 or so volunteers from the Abraham Lincoln battalion and XIV Brigade were about to arrive. It was in their hands, largely, to stop the Francoist offensive. In simple terms the aim was, once more, to save Madrid.

For men like Marty, this was the internationalist dream come true. Volunteers from almost a quarter of the world's countries were here together, fighting under the banner of anti-fascism. Equally as important, to Marty and the founders, was that all this had been organised and led by communists. To the men waiting to engage with the enemy as the sun rose over the Jarama valley on 13 February, that was the least important point. In terms of dead and wounded, the previous day had been the worst in the International Brigades' short, if intense, history. There was nothing to suggest that this day's fighting would be any different.

25

Disobeying Orders: Jarama valley, 13 February 1937

The survivors of the British Battalion crept back into position while a sickle moon still hung in the sky.[1] In the valley below, a brigade-sized detachment of enemy troops was at rest. Wintringham had placed Fry's machine-gun company out ahead, with a magnificent field of fire across the conical hill and neighbouring slopes. His five machine guns were able to keep attackers at bay for several hours. Wintringham knew, however, that their weakness lay on their flanks. His men had still not joined up with the Franco-Belgian Six Février Battalion across the main road on their right. To his left the line defended by the International Brigades was reinforced by Spanish troops from the communist Fifth Regiment led by Enrique Líster, a gifted, twenty-nine-year-old military leader who had studied at the Frunze Academy in Moscow.[2] Further to his right he could also see that the Dimitrov Battalion was under fierce attack.[3] Wintringham was ordered to relieve pressure on the other battalions by sending his men charging 600 metres down towards enemy machine-gun positions. He refused. Instead, he led a fake attack with forty men, which managed to distract the enemy for a short time.[4]

At three o'clock that afternoon Wintringham was once more ordered to launch a frontal attack. Once again, he disobeyed. He believed that commanders in the field should have the freedom to 'snatch at opportunity, alter plans rapidly, bluff, use surprise, switch forces and transport from one line to another'.[5] This was a personal interpretation of a 'democratic' army, and not one his seniors shared. He did not know that, to his right, the French and Belgians of the Six Février were also refusing to advance.[6] An early attempt to follow similar orders had seen their commander and political commissar killed. The burned-out husks of two Russian tanks, just thirty metres in front of their lines, were a reminder that the other side now had highly effective anti-tank guns. 'It seems they were at the limit of their physical and moral resistance,' XV Brigade's own historians admitted in a draft – but accurate – version of events that day which would be taken to the Comintern archive in Moscow.[7] Wintringham's refusal to move was, at best, insubordination. At worst, it was viewed as a form of rebellion or cowardice. However sensible it may have seemed, it was also a sign that those in command of the thin, irregular line of units defending the hills that led to the Valencia road had lost control. Neither Gal nor Ćopić could sway battalion commanders like Wintringham.

The British Battalion's own defensive line crumbled when company commander Bert Overton panicked during an artillery bombardment and ordered his men to run, thereby exposing the machine-gun company's flank. It was now that the attackers repeated an old trick. A group approached, giving the fist-to-forehead anti-fascist salute and shouting '¡Vivan las Brigadas Internacionales!' and '¡Camaradas!'[8] Once more, the similarities in the uniforms worn by both sides allowed them to sow confusion and the British thought they were either Republican soldiers or deserters from the other side. It was not until they were thirty metres away that Fry recognised the officers' uniforms as being those of the Spanish Legion. Fierce hand-to-hand fighting ensued, but Fry and much of his company were captured. They were marched 400 metres down the valley, where a Spanish officer ordered the Australian-born volunteer Ted Dickenson, who had looked scornfully at his captors,[9] to step in front of the firing squad that many assumed would now kill them all. Fifteenth Brigade's own historians recorded what happened next:

> Dickenson, knowing what was coming, displayed marvellous
> courage. He stepped smartly out of the ranks, marched toward
> the trees indicated by the fascist officer, turned about, and with
> the words 'Salud Comrades', fell with fascist bullets in him. Then
> suddenly a German officer appeared [German advisors were
> increasingly present, much like the Russians on the other side],

whispered to the Spanish officer, and they were moved further up the valley. Thus, in that moment their lives were saved. The reason is obvious – the political value in British prisoners as a means of propaganda were apparent.[10]

They were lucky. 'Red opponents before Madrid' – Condor Legion commander Wolfram von Richthofen noted down later – 'French, Belgian and English prisoners are taken. All shot except for the English.'[11]

Wintringham himself received a bullet in the knee soon afterwards. The British were rescued, once again, by nightfall, when they retreated back towards the sunken road. This may have been when some British volunteers were embarrassed to discover that, as they retreated, a group of militia women remained firmly at their machine-gun post. 'We'd gone back a bit, and some of them were actually running. And here we came across three women sitting behind a machine gun just past where we were, Spanish women. I saw them looking at us. You know, I don't know whether it shamed us or what. But these women, they stayed there,' recalled Scottish volunteer Tom Clarke.[12]

To the right of the British both the Six Février and the Dimitrov Battalions received the setting sun with similar relief. None of them were at more than half-strength by now. Further north, the Dombrowski were similarly demoralised after having obeyed orders and left their trenches to charge across a valley behind Pavlov's T-26b tanks before being chased by Moroccan cavalry in the closing daylight hours.[13] A Francoist cavalryman remembered the excitement of pursuing them across country. 'It was an amazing spectacle to see how all the squadrons set out on a frenzied gallop, in perfect lines that were four-deep, treading on the heels of the internationals,' he recalled.[14] The Dombrowski paid dearly. As they scrambled back towards their original defensive line, enemy units circled behind them. The Poles ran out of ammunition and fought with bayonets[15] before retiring to new positions that, nevertheless, still stood between the enemy and the Valencia road.[16] At least fifty Dombrowski were dead and another hundred had been wounded, though the other side had also suffered heavily.[17]

That night, by complete accident, a Very flare launched by the enemy landed on top of the British ammunition dump in the middle of the sunken road. Panic broke out. Some thought it was a gas attack and fumbled with the masks they had been given. The same jittery company commander who had provoked earlier panics now ran off shouting 'liquid fire!' and urging his men to follow. Only the reappearance of Jock Cunningham – a tough, experienced Scot who had fought alongside Cornford, Kurzke and Knox at University City and had dragged himself out of the bed where he was recovering from flu – with sixty stragglers, allowed order to be restored.[18]

The next day the British Battalion crept back into position. Many still had not eaten since they began fighting two days earlier, but Cunningham provided a fresh input of energy and morale. The thirty-three-year-old Scot was a natural leader who had served in the Argyll and Sutherland Highlanders and been jailed for organising a mutiny over the conditions the regiment encountered when stationed in Jamaica in 1929. In the early hours the British charged the position where Fry's men had been taken, forcing the enemy back and recapturing some machine guns. Only 215 of the original 400 men were left.[19]

Supplies, including water, were scarce and the sun beat down. Machine-gunners had to run up and down the line, asking men to give urine for the Maxims' cooling-jackets.[20] Little happened until early afternoon, when they had been told that Russian T26 tanks would be coming up on either side of them. When the rumble of tanks was finally heard, they were heading towards them from enemy lines. Behind them, according the XV Brigade chronicler 'swarmed Moors'.[21]

It soon turned into a rout. 'The slaughter was terrible. One would see five men running abreast, and four of them suddenly crumple up,' one survivor recalled.[22] Small groups, including one led by the so-called 'Boxing Parson from Killarney' – a lapsed Church of Ireland priest called Reverend Robert Hilliard – held out briefly. Hilliard was an ex-evangelical, Cambridge-educated, Olympic bantamweight who, when drunk, had entertained his comrades by putting on his best parson's voice to deliver a benediction in the name of Marx. Although injured, the thirty-three-year-old managed to escape, only to be killed days later when a bomb fell on his hospital.[23] One volunteer watched as his wounded comrades were bayoneted to death by the attacking Moroccans. Often it took more than one man to complete the task. 'The first [would] … let fly with his bayonet … and the chap would grab [it] … as it came down, but then another would … get him in the side.' A group led by Andre Diamant stopped several times to turn and hold the enemy back, but even this was eventually forced to withdraw from the final ridge.[24]

Many men fled back to the cookhouse, where Frank Ryan was amongst those who heard a rumour that the entire front line had been ordered to retreat. 'Now there was no line, nothing between the Madrid road and the fascists but disorganised groups of weary, war-wrecked men,' said Ryan.[25] Trucks full of able-bodied soldiers were racing away, while the wounded and dying from the dressing station lay around 'moaning and screaming'. A panicked British doctor urged his people to 'go while the going was good', jumped on to a passing truck and shouted at the cooks: 'The Fascists are coming! Poison the soup! Poison the soup!' Defeat, and its consequences, seemed to be staring them in the face. 'I thought the war was over,' one New Zealand volunteer recalled, as he made plans to grab as much ammunition as he could and disappear into the woods to wage solitary guerrilla warfare.[26]

Hungry men crammed into the cookhouse, from where they had set off two and half days earlier, grabbing tins of garlicky sausages. Across the slopes and fields, groups of weary Spaniards and lost Slavs or French speakers from the Dimitrov and Six Février (which had both lost around two-thirds of their men[27]) had collapsed in utter exhaustion and shock. Cunningham and Ryan tried to raise their morale. There was now a gap in the line, they said, and it needed to be filled again. Each persuaded a group of several dozen men to follow them back up to the last defensive ridge. The two groups merged together in the early evening gloom and began to make their way along the road that had separated the British and Six Février positions. By now there were 140 of them. Suddenly Ryan shouted: 'Sing up, ye sons o' guns!' It was, he said, the sort of thing he had previously shouted to raise morale before banned Irish Republican demonstrations. Slowly the men began to sing a tune whose English words may not have been intelligible to everyone, but whose melody was instantly recognisable.

So comrades, come rally,
And the last fight let us face.
The Internationale
Unites the human race.[28]

This was 'The Internationale', the anthem of leftists across the world. For those present, it was one of the most remarkable moments of the war. 'Stragglers still in retreat down the slopes stopped in amazement, changed direction and ran to join us; men lying exhausted on the roadside jumped up, cheered, and joined the ranks,' recalled Ryan.[29] 'I looked back. Beneath the forest of upraised fists, what a strange band! Unshaven, unkempt, bloodstained, grimy. But full of fight again, and marching on the road back.'[30] A large group of Spaniards and others also joined them. By now there was at least half a battalion's worth of men. One of those present still struggled to believe it when he retold the story decades later. 'We were stone mad when I think about it,' he said. 'We found ourselves in a small army! Going forward, with Cunningham in front.'[31]

A single, brooding figure stood by the road waiting for them as they advanced. This was their divisional commander, the usually cantankerous Colonel Gal. He ordered them to stop for a moment while he talked, quietly but seriously. 'He said that the decisive moment of the battle had come ... that the battalion had shown a quality of endurance that he had rarely seen in many years of warfare [and] that our retreat had left a gap in his line he could not fill with any other unit,' one Brigader remembered.[32] They believed him.

Cunningham led them along the road, which he had not walked before. He inadvertently passed the forward posts of the enemy's fragile front line before swinging the men off the road and up towards the positions previously held by the British. As darkness fell, pandemonium broke out. Neither side knew where the other was. The Moroccans in the forward posts in front of their line panicked and ran, convinced that they were being surrounded and unable to work out how many men were now attacking. Individually or in small groups the Brigaders moved through the dark, attacking machine-gun posts, charging with bayonets and sowing panic. Commands were shouted in English, French and Filipino-accented Spanish. Eventually Ryan, realising they were back in one of their old lines, ordered the men to dig in. Cunningham and others had to be persuaded to turn back and join them.

The line was re-established and the hole was plugged. The Dimitrovs had managed a similar feat to their right and during the night Spanish units began to arrive to fill other gaps.[33] Only eighty of the 630 men in the British Battalion had escaped unscathed, but here – and all along the front, whether defended by International Brigaders or Spaniards – the Valencia–Madrid road was safe.[34] Even those on the other side recognised the bravery of the Brigaders. 'It must be candidly admitted, with some national pride, although I still consider their cause a false one, that the latter presented us with more solid opposition than we were accustomed to,' wrote Frank Thomas, the Welsh mercenary fighting for Franco.[35]

By 19 February, XV Brigade estimated that the British, Six Février and Dimitrov were jointly down to 490 men. At least 450 were dead or wounded and a similar number were missing – lost, captured or had deserted. In terms of manpower, three battalions had effectively been reduced to just one. Reinforcements were needed desperately. Fortunately, the brigade had another whole battalion waiting in reserve. It was the same outfit that Bernard Knox had seen from his hospital train – the Abraham Lincoln Battalion.

26

The Yanks Are Coming!: Jarama valley, 16 February 1937

To those who had watched them training, there was something quaint and old-fashioned about the Americans. Some struggled to work out why, until they realised what they were wearing: matching 'doughboy' uniforms worn by the servicemen who fought in Europe during the First World War, mixed with thick blue shirts.[1] It was rather like watching a newsreel from twenty years earlier.

Unlike the sometimes middle-aged veterans of the Garibaldi Battalion, or the hardened political and economic exiles from Germany, Poland and elsewhere, there were many younger men amongst the volunteers arriving from the United States. Almost 40 per cent were aged twenty-five or less, and a surprisingly high number were students, with the City College of New York (CCNY)[2] a particularly rich source of recruits. One later American arrival, thirty-three-year-old Brooklyn writer Alvah Bessie, would find himself nicknamed 'Papa' because of his age.[3] Like the Canadian recruits who joined them, many also had first- or second-hand experience of migration. One in five were not yet US citizens. The proportion of 'foreigners' rises to one-third if those who thought of themselves as dual nationals are included. Three-quarters of Italian-Americans had migrated as adults.[4] Not surprisingly, a good number had Spanish surnames, suggesting that they also came from immigrant communities.

With so many immigrants, and some 70 per cent of them Communist Party members,[5] the Americans were another group of the 'devout and the displaced'. As in other battalions, too, a disproportionately high

number of their volunteers were Jews. At least 17 per cent of those
with US citizenship declared themselves Jewish, and a reasonable
overall estimate is at least one in five, while the US volunteers historian
Peter Carroll estimates more than a third.[6] The battalion also absorbed
volunteers who had arrived from other countries – with Cubans,
Canadians and Irish accounting for almost an entire company.
Meaningful military experience was, sadly, often lacking.[7] So too were
obvious leaders. James Harris, their first battalion commander,[8] was a
former army sergeant who could often be found in a drunken heap.[9]
One early political commissar was so ideologically driven that he began
castigating the mayor of Villanueva de la Jara, the town sixty kilometres
from Albacete where they were sent to train, for not collectivising his
land.[10] To begin with, the townsfolk there had kept away from them,
lowering their shutters and, if they were women, running away when
approached. The Brigaders blamed this hostility on 'a few undesirable
elements among the French who preceded the Americans', and who
'became constantly drunk, caused nuisances, molested the townspeople
and even went so far as to attack the local women'.[11]

The battalion had a section of sixty Cuban-led Hispanics, many
recruited at the leftist Julio A. Mella club in Harlem and headed by the
charismatic, capable student leader and exile Rodolfo de Armas. Their
Caribbean charm and shared language helped win over the townsfolk.
The forty-odd Irish who had left the British Battalion, and who now
wore green handkerchiefs around their necks, were even bigger drinkers
than the French, but less aggressive. Villagers deposited those who could
no longer walk unassisted at the barrack gates every evening.[12]

Twenty-seven-year-old university economics professor Robert
Merriman would soon stand out as a natural leader, and not just because
of his broad and imposing 6ft 2 frame. Merriman had had two years'
experience with the Reserve Officers Corps at the University of Nevada
and, like Tom Wintringham and Ludwig Renn, was genuinely attracted
to the military life. His steadying presence would become essential,
since the lack of effective command and discipline in the battalion's
early days clearly exacerbated problems such as drunkenness, talk of
leaving to join other parts of the Republican army and outbursts of
anti-Semitism amongst some former sailors.[13]

By the time the Americans assembled in Albacete's bullring to be
harangued by Marty and told they were going to the front, some still

had not fired a weapon. A convoy of mismatched trucks arrived and
began to unload greased 1914 rifles and helmets. By now a meeting of
volunteers – from which a drunk Harris was absent[14] – had confirmed
the name of the battalion. It was one that avoided any suggestion
of radicalism,[15] and was bound to garner sympathy back home: the
Abraham Lincoln Battalion.

Nonetheless, these were profoundly politically motivated men.
According to Merriman, they were 'strong individuals with strong
beliefs'.[16] They even sent a political delegation to the International
Brigade commanders to lodge a series of complaints, and were chastised
for behaving like 'naughty children'.[17] It is not clear whether, at this
stage, Merriman was a Communist Party member or not.[18] He had
previously lived in the USSR, where a diplomat deemed him 'the type
of person who values too much his own freedom of speech and action
to subordinate himself to any organization which maintains rigorous
discipline'.[19] Merriman had travelled on his own to Spain and had
begged his way into the Brigades just as more organised groups of
Americans arrived. After sailing across the Atlantic, the other Americans
had sat, wide-eyed, on the trains going south from Paris listening to
tales of derring-do from European volunteers who had swum rivers,
sneaked across frontiers in the middle of the night, dodged police and
hitched rides on hay carts in order to join them. Merriman jotted his
own thoughts down in a diary: 'Men may die but let them die in a
working-class cause. Men die and mean to die (if necessary) so that
the revolution may live on.'[20] His wife Marion, a University of Nevada
graduate who had also lived in the Soviet Union, shared those ideals,
and soon travelled to Spain to be with him.

The men of the Abraham Lincoln Battalion started dying even before
they could go into the line. Sent in trucks towards the front on the cold,
moonless night of 16/17 February, the French drivers of the leading two
vehicles took a wrong turning.[21] Amongst those riding in the first truck
was Walter Grant, a twenty-five-year-old pastor's son from Marion,
Indiana, whose conversion to left-wing causes had been accelerated
when the Ku Klux Klan lynched three men in his home town.[22] The two
trucks, driving without headlights, crested a rise and then drove down
the hill towards the San Martín bridge and straight into the enemy
lines. They were machine-gunned off the road by a group of *legionarios*
and all seventeen men were killed. The legionnaires later claimed that

all but one of the Americans had died during a brief exchange of fire after the sleepy men scrambled from their crashed trucks, while one wounded prisoner was meant to be sent to hospital but had his throat slit by Moroccan troops who later scavenged through the wreckage.[23] In fact, the legionnaires (with just one of their own men injured) were not interested in taking prisoners and almost certainly executed them. The rest of the battalion might have met a similar fate if one of the doctors, William Pike, had not decided to double-check which turning to take – and led them in the right direction.[24]

Ordered to dig in to a reserve position in the second line, the Lincolns experienced their first bombardment the following morning.[25] 'What the hell are they trying to do – kill us?' somebody quipped. Nobody seems to have laughed.[26] As the sun rose, artillery, enemy aircraft and heavy machine guns began to target their positions. For the first time, they saw comrades killed or wounded.[27] Fortunately, they were not yet needed in the front line and the next few days revealed that leadership remained an almost crippling problem. Their drunken, erratic commander Harris repeatedly disappeared, then reappeared after a few days, leading the men on a shambolic, moonlit training manoeuvre that placed them perilously close to the enemy's front lines. He had to be replaced by Merriman.[28]

It was not until the 23rd that the Lincolns received their full baptism of fire. By now the two sides were fortifying their positions into permanent lines, but the Republican commanders thought they had a chance of trapping the entire attacking army – now without reserves – on their side of the Jarama. Late in the afternoon, the Lincolns were sent on an attack through a field of widely spaced olive trees and low vines. Two tanks led the way, but one was hit, shooting flames high into the sky, and the other one turned around. The Cuban section charged close up to the enemy trenches, where grenade attacks put a number of machine guns out of action, but Rodolfo de Armas and many others were killed or wounded.[29]

Many of the Lincolns were stranded in no-man's-land during daylight, while others tried to dig new positions. All of their eight machine guns either failed to work or broke down.[30] The Dimitrov battalion and Spanish 24 Brigade, on either side, had not moved forward with them as expected – and they later complained that the Franco-Belgian Six Février had simply 'refused to advance' during the same attack. Enemy machine guns, mortars and snipers picked away at anyone who moved. Many volunteers stayed where they were until dark, hiding behind olive trees or trying to dig some cover for themselves, while listening to the moans of the injured. Eventually, the firing stopped and they were ordered back. Up to twenty men were dead, and another forty or fifty were injured in the action.[31]

Four days later, after seventy-three poorly trained men arrived (some still in civilian clothes), the Lincolns were sent out to support an attack on the hill called El Pingarrón.[32] Forty of the newcomers had never shot a rifle and the attack itself, which had been intended to be in support of the Spanish 24 Brigade, became a suicidal assault. They had still failed to make their machine guns function properly. More seasoned units along the front were by now openly ignoring orders from commanders who seemed determined to imitate the worst strategies of the First World War by throwing men against machine guns and well-entrenched rifle companies. Others scrambled forward cautiously a dozen metres or so, but stopped when pinned down by machine-gun fire. After the attack effectively failed to start across the rest of the front, the Lincolns were nevertheless ordered to go forward anyway.[33] They were the only ones to do so. The promised tanks and aircraft appeared only briefly.

A colourful, roughly edited report lodged in the International Brigades' archives tells the story of the disastrous 27 February attack:

About noon the men went into the attack. The sun was hot.
Group by group hopped the trenches, charging the fascists who
were only about 250 metres away. A few groups got over with
scarcely any casualties. The enemy machine guns began their ugly
work. They grazed the sandbags all along the line in a constant
staccato. Heavy firing came from both sides. Bullets sprayed in
the direction of the Lincoln battalion like the heavy pounding of
a riveting machine. Cross-fire from many machine guns made an
impenetrable stone wall against advance. More groups and sections
went over. Many got wounded as they climbed the parapets to go
over. Some comrades from amongst the recent arrivals, uninformed
and inexperienced went over the top with full packs on their backs.
They charged like a cyclone toward the fascists. Many wounded

men crawled back to the trenches safely; many were killed in the attempt.

[XV Brigade commander] Ćopić had received this order from the Commander of the Division [Gal][34] who demanded categorically that the Lincoln Battalion advance immediately and occupy the enemy positions at all costs. All Merriman's messengers had been wounded and just as Comrade [Dave] Springhall [a humourless Londoner who was one of the brigade's political commissars] was approaching, Merriman personally went over the top of the trenches to give the signal for a more energetic advance. At the same instant Springhall and Merriman were wounded. Merriman got a bullet through the right shoulder.[35]

In the ensuing chaos, command passed through several people's hands quickly.[36] One volunteer, appointed mid-battle, admitted: 'I don't know about military things a fuck!'[37] Of 263 men who went into battle, only 150 were left in the line the following day.[38]

By now it appeared that almost all of this section of the front was on strike, and even battalions in the same brigade were no longer supporting one another. Fifteenth Brigade's own historians admitted that the Dimitrov (one-third of whose Italian company had already died) had refused to join the Lincolns' advance while only a dozen men from the British Battalion did so (and were mowed down).[39] 'The Americans showed discipline and great courage, not a single man remaining in the trenches. The attack failed, but it was not the fault of the Lincoln Battalion,' they said, before adding 'the entire XV Brigade is now demoralised.'[40]

The brigade's new commissar, Frenchman Jean Chaintron-Barthel (who had already lost a brother in earlier fighting), met the International Brigades' chief commissar Luigi Longo a few days later and complained that the demands made of XV International Brigade had been too hard for such undertrained troops.[41] 'Our Brigade had been through a harsh baptism and now lacks the impetus to go on the attack. It has reached the limit of physical endurance ... In my opinion the order to attack given by the general staff on the 23rd and 24th was impossible, but was carried out anyway. We have suffered heavy losses and damage to the morale of the comrades.'[42] Chaintron-Barthel blamed a lack of training. 'I have seen volunteers weep because they did not know how to use their rifles or machine guns,' he said. To make things worse, it had begun to rain heavily, adding further misery to the already cold and blustery weather as the wounded struggled back or were carried by stretcher-bearers who constantly slipped in the mud. Some died of exposure in no-man's-land.

When all the Lincoln survivors were moved into a reserve position the following day, there was, in the words of their own historians, 'almost an insurrection' amongst the American volunteers.[43] They angrily demanded a meeting with Commissar Chaintron-Barthel. This was held in the courtyard of the same cookhouse where Frank Ryan and others had, two weeks earlier, led a group of weary men singing back into battle to the tune of 'The Internationale'. Now the tone was bitter and suspicious. The Americans claimed that 'fascists' on the brigade staff had deliberately plotted to have them wiped out.

In poorly translated French, Chaintron-Barthel tried to point out that they were breaking the rules of the army they had joined. Madrid was in danger, they were expected to follow orders and meetings like this were simply not allowed. The 'rugged individualists' who, according to the International Brigades' own scribes, had supposedly been knocked into shape during training, refused to believe him. That, he was told, applied in a capitalist army, not in a people's army. The Americans' own commissar, Samuel Stember, who had stayed safely back in the cookhouse during the fighting, later accused those 'who challenge the military or political authority' of being 'self-seekers who are no less guilty than the deserters who have been sentenced to hard labour in the Labour Battalion'. The meeting had proceeded 'as if they were framing demands against the Capitalist class', he complained. 'We have learned by bitter experience that wherever committees dominate and endless discussion follow there the gates are open for the fascists to enter. The disruptive elements hide within such committees,' he added, slipping into clichéd Stalinist rhetoric. 'There was no punishment meted out, but if these disruptive elements try to do their nefarious work again, severe measures will have to be taken.'[44] Stember was removed shortly afterwards. The 'rugged individualists' won that battle, at least.

The Jarama line had now been stabilised. It was not, however, the end of the Lincolns' stay at Jarama, where desultory fighting punctuated long stretches of calm for months and First World War-style trench warfare brought occasional flurries of action. During this period of stalemate their chief obsession, along with combating lice, boredom, the cold, and lamenting the absence of women and tobacco, was food. The Lincolns came to worship their Japanese chef, Jack Shirai, who found alternatives to the tough mule meat that made their mouths feel as if they were 'full of rubber bands'.[45]

The Lincolns would not leave the front until 17 June. By then a Scottish volunteer called Alex McDade had written them a song that, set to the tune of the cowboy's lament 'Red River Valley', soon became their anthem.[46]

There's a valley in Spain called Jarama,
It's a place that we all know so well,
For 'tis there that we wasted our manhood,
And most of our old age as well …

Oh, we're proud of our Lincoln Battalion,
And the marathon record it's made,
Please do us this little favour,
And take this last word to Brigade:

'You will never be happy with strangers
They would not understand you as we,
So remember the Jarama valley
And the old men who wait patiently.'

The long wait in the trenches of Jarama over the next few months was a sign that Franco had accepted he could not break through here. It meant, too, that the defence of this crucial line had been a victory. Madrid remained free and the route to Valencia was open. The International Brigades could claim much, of the glory.

27

Mussolini at Guadalajara: Brihuega, Torija, Trijueque, 9 March 1937

Giovanni Pesce had read the newspapers. So had most of the Garibaldi Battalion, now at rest in barracks just outside Madrid at El Pardo, having finally been withdrawn from the tedium of the Jarama front five days earlier. They knew that a fresh Francoist offensive had been launched in the province of Guadalajara, sixty kilometres east of Madrid, and that the bulk of the unprecedented 41,000-strong attacking army was made up of fellow Italians, so-called 'volunteers' from Mussolini's fascist militia expeditionary force, the Corpo Truppe Volontarie (CTV). So when they were ordered to pack their kit, check their weapons and prepare for departure on the afternoon of Tuesday 9 March, Pesce knew they were probably going to fight their countrymen. The Garibaldini were frustrated, however, to see other battalions, such as the Thälmann, Commune de Paris and Edgar André, pile into trucks before them. Then their brigade commander, Lukács, arrived in a large green motor car and enquired if they were really prepared to battle fellow Italians. 'If there is a single battle that we should fight in, it is this one,' the anarchist adjutant Giorgio Braccialarghe replied. 'Italy is not Mussolini. We must prove that.' Lukács asked whether they would treat Italian prisoners properly. 'We're anti-fascists, not assassins,' came the reply.[1]

Whilst the Garibaldis had waited in the courtyard for the trucks to take them to the front, their temporary commander – former railwayman and communist activist Ilio Barontini – had warned them that the enemy was well armed and numerous. It was, however, a chance to avenge their comrades in Mussolini's jails, he told them: 'You must be worthy of these fighters … of the Italy that struggles and fights, that does not bow to the arrogance and the tyranny of fascism.'[2] It was still remarkable that men like Giovanni Pesce – who had grown up in a single-room shack by the coal mines at La Grand-Combe, south-east France – were setting out to kill, and try not to be killed by, other Italians on Spanish soil.[3]

After dark, as they drove off towards the front into the cold, damp night, Pesce and his companions took swigs of brandy and loudly bawled verses of the 'Bandiera Rossa' ('Red Flag') to keep up their spirits.[4] The German-speaking Edgar André Battalion and the French Commune de Paris of Hans Kahle's XI Brigade had been the first to arrive in the rush to halt the Italian thrust towards Madrid. Other international battalions were just beginning the task of gathering their men and equipment in order to join them. Everyone recognised, however, that this battle had special meaning to the Garibaldini. Italy's own civil war was about to start on the stony, wooded and, above all, bitterly cold stretch of Spain's central *meseta* plain that is known as the Alcarria.

The previous day, three divisions of Mussolini's CTV had launched a surprise attack, striking west along the main highway towards Guadalajara and Madrid from Algora (where the body of the young Belgian Jewish volunteer Piet Akkerman lay buried beside a bottle containing a scrap of paper with his name on it). This broad, well-kept road – popularly known as the 'French Highway' – linked Spain's capital city to Zaragoza and, eventually, Barcelona. The Italians had gained some twenty kilometres of this road on the first day – a sixth of the distance to Madrid from their starting point. Their belief that they could reach the capital in a week did not seem unfounded, especially as they advanced a further twenty kilometres down the same road, which followed an almost straight line through gently undulating countryside, on the day that Pesce and the Garibaldini set off to join the defensive line. A second prong of the attack, meanwhile, was already at the gates of Brihuega. This strategic town lay in the bowl of a deep valley at the centre of the Alcarria region. The third, entirely Spanish division was pushing along the broad valley of the river Badiel to the north and, beyond that, down the valley of the river Henares.

This was the start of Franco's fourth major attempt at taking or encircling Madrid, after the offensives at University City, La Coruña

The People's Olympiad: Barcelona's left-wing alternative to Hitler's Olympics was halted by the coup attempt that sparked the Spanish Civil War, with some foreign athletes staying to fight and defend the Republic.

Some Republicans, especially in anarchist areas, were suspicious of the communist-backed Brigades. Propaganda posters tried to create support, in this case proclaiming: 'The International Brigades of the Republican Army help defend your land and goods'.

Muriel Rukeyser: the American poet who lived and loved through the first week of war in Barcelona. Her German lover, Otto Boch, joined the militia and died fighting in 1938.

Fanny Schoonheyt: the Dutch militiawoman and machine-gunner who fought in Barcelona and Aragon in the first months of the war.

Thälmann Group: a column made up mostly of exiled Germans and Poles formed in the first days of the war and led by Max Friedemann (probably far left). Several women were members, including Golda Friedemann and British-based German exile and translator Liesel Carritt (both possibly in second row).

The Tom Mann English Centuria was formed in Barcelona but never fought, and members mostly joined the International Brigades. Left to right are Sid Avner, Nat Cohen, his future wife Ramona García Siles, Tom Wintringham (kneeling in white), Italian Georgio Tioli, Australian Jack Barry and David Marshall.

Three Red Army International Brigade 'generals' and a German commander: Hungarian General Paul Lukács (aka Máté Zalka or Bela Frankl), on the left – possibly with Russian advisor and future hero of Leningrad, Kirill Meretskov; Austro-Hungarian General Emilio Kléber (Manfred Stern), centre, in his button-up jersey; Pole General Walter (Karol Świerczewski), walking with Communist commander Juan Modesto (left) and 35 Division commissar Julián Muñoz Lizcano; and the popular German commander Hans Kahle (on the right), with Ludwig Renn (in glasses on the left).

Brigaders fighting
in the University
City in Madrid,
November 1937

Gustav Regler: German writer, commissar and close friend of French Nobel André Gide. Regler's disenchantment with Soviet communism saw him hope that Spain might provide a new model of solidarity.

Ludwig Renn: the German aristocrat, First World War officer, homosexual, writer and convinced communist was one of the most senior and cool-headed field officers in the International Brigades.

General Franco's Moroccan troops from the Army of Africa being transported by German Luftwaffe aircraft to mainland Spain. The airlift ordered by Hitler prevented the coup led by reactionary generals from failing, and turned it into a civil war.

Prisoners from the machine-gun battalion of the Littorio Division in Mussolini's 40,000-strong Corpo Truppe Volontarie (CTV), captured by Italian Brigaders from the Garibaldi battalion at Guadalajara in March 1937. The balding figure, with scarf and single star, must be Major Antonio Luciano, whose early capture helped bring the defeat and humiliation of Mussolini's army.

Polish exile Gerta Pohorylle was the world's first great woman war photographer. She published under the byline 'Gerda Taro', and also as part of 'Robert Capa'. She died, aged twenty-six, after being run over by a tank at Brunete.

Hungarian photographer Endre Ernö Friedmann (right) created the 'Robert Capa' byline with partner Gerda Taro (left), and together they helped make the International Brigades famous. Capa became the world's greatest war photographer and died, aged forty, after stepping on a landmine in Vietnam in 1954.

highway and Jarama. The war had grown in dimension with each major offensive and, in terms of the number of attacking troops, this was the biggest so far.[5] Just as the shock troops of the International Brigades had played a crucial role in the previous major battles, so it quickly became their task to absorb the initial shock of the attack launched by Mussolini's men. The latter were experimenting with what they called *guerra celere* – 'fast war' – which would soon be better known in its German version as blitzkrieg. This involved the rapid conquest of land in assaults spearheaded by tanks, supported by artillery or aviation and followed by motorised infantry, who, in Spain, were moved swiftly in the hundreds of trucks that the Italians had shipped with them.

With the Republic caught unprepared, every extra hour that could be gained by slowing down Mussolini's men was potentially invaluable. Over the next few days, a large part of this task would fall to the International Brigades who, between the start of the war and the end of March 1937, had registered a total of 18,714 foreign volunteers as having joined their ranks, including 2,124 Italians. More than a thousand volunteers were already dead, and many more were injured or missing. The level of loss was already making it difficult to maintain five full brigades of up to 3,000 men each, along with an increasing number of smaller international artillery and tank units as well as the training camps, hospitals and logistical bases they now needed.[6]

While Mussolini had been preparing his troops to fight a large land battle on Spanish soil, the process of appeasement had been continuing apace around the rest of Europe. Over the previous weeks countries including Britain, France, Portugal, Hungary, Ireland and Canada had all approved some kind of ban on joining the International Brigades. American passports were stamped 'Not valid for travel to Spain' and the multinational Non-Intervention Committee had begun the process of setting up controls on the Spanish border. On 8 March, the International Board of Non-Intervention had formally come into being, with hundreds of land- and sea-based observation officers operating under a Dutch vice-admiral. A Danish officer, Colonel Lunn, was in charge of watching over the French border. This took the non-intervention farce to another level, since Germany, Italy and Russia were all board members. Maritime patrols were also initiated, with Germany and Italy given the task of patrolling the entire eastern seaboard. The latter simply used this as cover while their own invisible 'pirate' submarines set about sinking Republican shipping. This made passing the frontier somewhat more difficult, but boats, and sometimes buses, still carried people into Spain. Volunteers also began to use routes that involved hiking over the Pyrenees at night, and more than a thousand were now arriving every month. The French authorities closed their eyes a little, since the government was, according to Jean Chaintron-Barthel, 'under pressure from the workers'.[7]

The attack by Mussolini's troops had originally been planned as the second part of a pincer movement coinciding with the Jarama offensive. Given the size of the Italian army in Spain, that plan might well have worked, but it was not ready in time for Jarama. The International Brigades claimed some of the credit for that, since XIII Brigade had helped slow the Italians down by harassing them on the Motril front. Despite the vast convoys of vehicles needed to transport Mussolini's army, Republican intelligence had failed to realise what was being planned. Two Italian divisions had been moved nearby in mid-February, yet the Republican command was convinced that the next attack would come near El Pardo or at Jarama.[8]

Mussolini's generals had concluded that the failure to break through at Jarama proved that Franco was too cautious and conservative. They had already practised their *guerra celere* in Abyssinia and were determined to prove that they were the true masters of modern mechanised warfare. Spain was an ideal stage for that. Mussolini's wider ambition was to control a large swathe of the Mediterranean – the *mare nostrum* of the Roman Empire – with Spain as a lesser ally.[9] If his men could conquer Madrid, where Franco's men had failed, that would establish him even more firmly as the leader of the greatest power in the Mediterranean basin.

The Italians had detailed plans, over 40,000 well-armed troops, their own air force and an exaggerated sense of self-confidence. Their army was made up of three 'Blackshirt divisions' drawn from the fascist militias – nominally 'volunteer' units that acted as part of Italy's military reserve – with names (Dio lo Vuole/'God Wills It', Fiamme Nere/'Black Flames', and Penne Nere/'Black Feathers') heavily laden with fascist symbolism. Though commanded by regular army officers they were mostly made up of reservists from the Milizia Volontaria per la Sicurezza Nazionale (MVSN), many of whom came from the poor peasantry of southern Italy, enticed by the regular salaries and other promised rewards. Their ethos, nonetheless, was fascist and they saw themselves as participating in a glorious crusade to spread Mussolini's credo around the Mediterranean.[10] Completing Mussolini's army in Spain was the Littorio division of regular soldiers, led by the white-bearded General Annibale Bergonzoli (also known as 'Barba Elettrica', or 'Electric Whiskers').[11]

More than 85 per cent of Franco's attacking army for this new offensive, then, were Italian, the only other direct Francoist support on the ground coming from the 6,000-strong Spanish-Moroccan Soria division. On the Republican side, the bulk of the troops remained Spanish, but some 3,500 volunteers from XI and XII International Brigades would do much of the fighting over the first few days.

The Italians' shared victory in Málaga had persuaded them that they were vastly superior to the Republican army, if not to Spanish soldiers in general. Their previous campaign in Abyssinia had been the bullying of a poor, underdeveloped country by a modern, industrialised power, but to Mussolini it was proof of fascist Italy's glorious future. The Italian dictator, who was sailing towards Libya on the recently built Italian navy flagship *Pola*, was following the campaign intently.[12]

The Russian 'advisor' Kirill Meretskov, a twenty-seven-year Red Army veteran and future Marshal of the Soviet Union who went by the nom de guerre of Pavlovich, visited the Guadalajara front on the first day of the Francoist attack and was shocked to find no real defensive line. Instead, a largely imaginary eighty kilometre-long front was defended by scattered units of the Republic's largely untested 12th Division, who were positioned on hilltops and at road junctions. In other words, the gently undulating woodland and clay fields of the Alcarria region lay wide open to attack.[13] Beyond lay Guadalajara and the road into Madrid.

The main thrust of Mussolini's men was along two roads that ran west across a ten-kilometre-wide plain. This was bordered on one side by the river Tajuña – with the main crossing point at Brihuega – and on the other by the steep escarpment that overlooked the valley of the river Badiel, where the Soria division was advancing. The French Highway ran parallel to the escarpment, almost touching it at some points. A string of small, dirt-poor villages, populated by one and two-storey peasant houses[14] stretched along it from Almadrones (where the first day's advance halted) to the town of Torija. A solid, square medieval castle was a sign of the latter's strategic importance overlooking both the plain and the entrance to a narrow valley where the French Highway dipped down towards Guadalajara.

The attackers – four Italian divisions and the Soria division – outnumbered the original, inexperienced defensive force by six to one in men and by much more than that in tanks, artillery and machine guns, according to a report drawn up later by the gaunt and bespectacled Red Army advisor to the International Brigades known as Simonov, aka Valois, whose real name was Boris Samoylov. He exaggerated the ratios (which were probably five to one in men), but thousands of trucks and some 140 armoured cars and tanks mounted with heavy machine guns and flamethrowers accompanied the fascist armies. In terms of the most important infantry weapon – the machine gun – the imbalance was even more stark: the Republicans were outnumbered twenty to one.[15]

Detailed plans had been drawn up: the Italian aim was to punch through this front and, within a week, link up with the Jarama forces to complete an encirclement of Madrid. That, they believed, would bring a swift end to the war. By 8 March the four divisions were in place near Sigüenza, and ready to advance. Republican spotter planes arrived in the afternoon and were amazed to see a tail of trucks and Fiat-Ansaldo tanks stretching back for ten kilometres along the French Highway, as several hundred Italian vehicles readied to push further forwards.[16] A unit of seven Republican T-26b tanks was not far away and reached the front line by midday. Together with a Spanish infantry unit, they slowed the Italian progress by launching a series of daring, lightning raids – copying the tactics that had proved so effective at breaking up much smaller attacks at Jarama. The superior firepower, armour and manoeuvrability of the Russian tanks proved crucial once more, with just seven T-26s capable of stiffening the resolve of the inexperienced Republican infantry by slowing the progress of an Italian division of 10,000 men, who ended the day five kilometres short of their target. The Republican command, however, still did not believe that this was the big attack they had been expecting somewhere near Madrid and took only limited measures to reinforce the front.[17] They decided, instead, to wait.

The next day Mussolini's men continued their rapid advance before running into sustained resistance from the International Brigaders and others, late in the afternoon, at a crossroads on Kilometre 83 of the

French Highway. They were already more than halfway to Guadalajara and had covered a third of the distance to Madrid in thirty-six hours. If they continued at the same pace, they would be in Madrid in four days. This did not quite live up to the boast of General Roatta that, by the end of 9 March, 'we will be in Guadalajara ... and within two days in Madrid', but it was still a serious threat to the capital. The Republican command had belatedly realised that the attack was serious and Hans Kahle's Edgar André (accompanied by a Russian advisor known as Alberti) and Commune de Paris Battalions reached the crucial crossroads at Kilometre 83 late in the day. Ludwig Renn recalled a desolate plain, 'barren and shrouded in mist', where the damp chilled the men's bones and the slightest breeze cut through them like a sharpened knife.[18] The Brigaders appeared as the inexperienced Republican troops who had faced the enemy over the previous thirty-six hours retreated once more, having seen their own half-a-dozen tanks turn around to refuel. In the distance, two dozen Italian tanks were rumbling slowly down the road.[19]

Earlier in the day, Kirill Meretskov had visited Colonel Lacalle, the sapper officer in charge of the 12th Division, and found 'an unshaven man in a dirty undershirt, woollen socks and night shoes'. Colonel Lacalle now arrived at the crossroads and was shocked to see two dozen fascist tanks trundling towards him. 'What are they doing?' he asked. 'Heading for Brihuega', came the reply. Lacalle immediately ordered his driver to hurry back to the town, shouting: 'I have family there!' According to a disgusted Meretskov: 'He raced past the German [Edgar André] battalion from the XI [International Brigade], without even stopping to find out who they were or where they were going.'[20] As a result, it was the Red Army veteran Meretskov, Renn, Kahle and Líster (whose men were also on their way) who huddled over a map together and decided to make a stand at the crossroads.

This was an important junction, with a ruler-straight country road leading south-east to Brihuega, just eight kilometres away. Two huge poplars had been felled to block the road.[21] These and a single trench line were the only existing fortifications. Strangely, the Italian advance ground to a halt after a shell set fire to the Edgar André's ammunition truck. While everyone waited to see whether this would explode and devastate everything around it (it didn't), night fell, drawing the curtain on the day's activity. In the meantime, the last of Kahle's battalions, the Thälmanns, arrived and were told to install themselves in woodland south-east of the crossroads. In the darkness, they immediately became disorientated and disorganised.[22]

Though the Republican army was still chaotic, it had learned much over the previous six months. Teams of trench diggers were now brought in during the night, allowing those due to fight the following day to rest. That felt like luxury to the International Brigaders. It was, however, impossible to dig more than a few feet before hitting solid rock.[23] This meant less protection not just from enemy bullets but also from the icy winds and stinging rain that swept across the plain. On the right-hand side of the road, scrubby woodland and some gentle undulations in the land provided the only real cover. While the Thälmanns tried to reorganise themselves in the damp, dark woods behind them, the other two battalions spent a calmer night waiting to see what the morning would bring. Their line was barely two kilometres wide and could be easily outflanked, but there were no other units available to extend it further.[24]

The balance of force, then, was heavily tilted towards Mussolini's Italians. The weight of experience, however, lay on the other side. By now, all six volunteer battalions in XI and XII International Brigades had been fighting for five months, Franco's three previous attempts at taking Madrid having served as their training schools. The officers and men who had survived the offensives at University City, La Coruña highway and Jarama had learned much: they could defend; they knew, in theory, how to attack; and, above all, they could maintain their weapons and manage on scarce resources. They had no anti-tank guns, but had learned how to use special, armour-piercing ammunition in rifles and machine guns. In the middle of the night on 9 March, two armoured cars appeared, bringing them a stock of these precious, red-tipped bullets.[25] These, they knew, were usually given only to the best marksmen.

They received word too that some of the better Spanish units in the Republican army were also being hurried to the Guadalajara front. Most of these men were experienced, reliable – no longer prone to panic and equal in ability to the best International Brigades. None had arrived yet, but the knowledge that they were on their way was a reassurance since those Spanish units already based in the Alcarria could not be relied on. 'We call those [units] "positional",' explained Meretskov, meaning that they might hold a position they were familiar with, but could do little else.[26]

Under the guidance of the Russian advisors, a neatly defined triangle of land was turned into the defensive battlefield. It was bounded by three

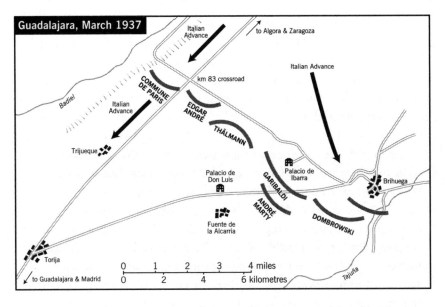

Guadalajara, March 1937

unusually straight roads and had Torija, Brihuega and the crossroads at Kilometre 83 of the French Highway at its points. A first defensive line was meant to stretch between the latter two points. Behind that, the rest of the triangle was made up of mostly flat, rain-soaked fields and forest. It was a risky strategy. Torija was the only reliable escape route for the defenders, encirclement was a real danger and the longest side of the triangle measured just fifteen kilometres. The tanks and trucks of the Italian fascist expeditionary force could cover that distance in under an hour. The Republicans still had only a vague idea, however, of how large the approaching army was.[27] Nor did they know exactly where to find it. In fact, one of General Roatta's divisions, advancing down another road, was already at the gates of Brihuega. Two corners of the triangle – Brihuega and the crossroads at Kilometre 83 on the French Highway – were under immediate threat and only thinly defended. The rest had no defence at all.

When a grey, cold day dawned on 10 March, the volunteers peering through the drizzle from the crossroads could see what to expect. Just three kilometres down the road ahead of them, artillery batteries were being drawn up into firing positions and Fiat-Ansaldo tanks were rumbling towards them. Mussolini's confidence in these tiny tanks, armed just with machine guns, was misplaced. So, too, was his generals' inability to see the importance of having anti-aircraft and anti-tank weapons that could match the German guns that had been so successful at Jarama. Swedish volunteer Sixten Olsson (also known as Rogeby) recalled witnessing his company commander, a grumpy, forty-year-old manual worker from Berlin called Emil Wendt,[28] exhorting Spanish tank commander Ernesto Ferrer, who led a platoon of just two T-26 tanks, to engage with them:

> The damned line of tanks up on the road starts filling the forest with shrapnel and noise, but now Emil loses his patience, runs over to our tanks and half begs, half forces one of them into action … He stands tall on the tank, shouting his orders at the driver, with shrapnel flying all around him. The first shot hits too far away. Emil goes mad with rage. 'Damned saboteur, you damn hillbilly … haven't you ever seen a cannon before? Well shoot, you blubbering idiot!!!' Bulls-eye! Emil goes mad again, but for the opposite reason this time. '*Ombri, beloved ombri … ona mas* [one more] … *bueno … bueno!*' Not far enough. In an instant he changes temper again, showering the unfortunate Spaniard in the worst verbal abuse of five different languages imaginable … Another bulls-eye! Emil has lost every sense of civilised behaviour, dancing a wild war-dance up on the roof, while one ball of fire after the other points out the idiocy of the Italian boldness.[29]

Needing little more encouragement, Ferrer raced forwards to disable two more tanks before spotting a group of twenty being refuelled further down the road. Charging towards them, he opened fire and disabled several while setting several fuel trucks ablaze. In the chaos, the two-man tank crews ran for cover and Ferrer was able to retire, blowing up or machine-gunning some fifteen infantry trucks along the way. For close on two hours, he had almost single-handedly held off the fascist advance.

This remarkable act of daring, on its own, was enough to oblige the Italians to reorganise, gaining precious time for the defenders. When the next attack came it was not supported by tanks and was easily repulsed, allowing XI International Brigade to hold the crossroads all day. That night Rogeby and the Edgar André men toasted Wendt 'in either cognac or black wine, and never before has a company commander been so celebrated in such an unconventional way'.[30] They were toasting a man who would die the following day.

28

The Italian Civil War: Brihuega, 10 March 1937

At much the same time as Emil Wendt was performing his war dance and Ernesto Ferrer was driving his tank at the enemy on the morning of 10 March, Giovanni Pesce and the Garibaldi Battalion were struggling through the mud on either side of the undulating road that led from Torija to Brihuega.[1] Lukács had set up his command post in a square, four-storey aristocrat's country house, the Palace of Don Luis, two-thirds of the way to Brihuega. From there, they had spread out into a line on either side of the road – forming the southern edge of the defensive 'triangle' – and walked towards Brihuega. They were still not sure whether the town remained in Republican hands. In fact, the Italian fascist expeditionary troops had marched into Brihuega that morning.[2] An angry Renn claimed it had been taken without a shot being fired.[3]

Already a veteran of several battles, Pesce had celebrated his nineteenth birthday just over a fortnight earlier. His company dragged their heavy Maxim machine guns through clay-like mud and puddles of icy water into the fields beside the road, having been told not to dismantle them into smaller, lighter parts: they might be needed at any moment, they were reminded.[4] When the Maxims sank almost as far as their axles, they were hauled onto the stronger men's shoulders (the Russian version of this gun weighed 60 kilos, though the iron protection plate was often carried separately). The Garibaldis' orders were to block the road to Torija and work their way into the hills north-west of Brihuega. They were due to be joined, during the day, by the rest of XII Brigade – the

Polish Dombrowski and a rebuilt André Marty which now had so many
Spaniards in it that it was often called the French-Spanish Battalion. All
were still under the command of the ever-elegant Lukács. When they
were just three kilometres short of Brihuega, Pesce saw a motorcycle
heading towards them. As soon as he spotted them, the rider screeched
to a halt, backed up and raced off in the opposite direction. They had
seen, briefly, their first Italian enemy.

The enemy had also seen them. As they continued forward, troops
appeared walking towards them. Before they could distinguish whether
they were friend or foe, machine guns opened fire. The Garibaldis found
themselves face down in the freezing mud and puddles, being shot
at by fellow Italians. It was now obvious to them that Brihuega had
already been taken and that this was where they must make their stand.
Pesce was aware of the size of the task. 'On this line, in front of the
Guadalajara road, there is only our battalion, a few hundred men, when
thousands would be needed,' he wrote later. The first group of advancing
troops then disappeared, giving the Garibaldi time to move three of its five
companies into the woods overlooking the road, while Pesce's machine-
gun crew and two other companies dug themselves in to the quagmire
of mud in the open land on either side of it. Barontini produced a flash
of the morale-raising gravitas expected of a former political commissar.
'At this moment, on this line defended by the Garibaldis, Madrid's fate
will be decided,' he told his men.[5] Soon the CTV's light Fiat-Ansaldo
tanks were clanking down the road towards them, spraying men and
mud with bullets and this miniature Italian civil war claimed its first
victims. When Pesce and the other heavy machine-gunners returned
fire, however, the thinly armoured tanks turned around.

Lukács's other battalions reached the Palace of Don Luis and the
village of Fuentes de la Alcarria later on 10 March. The Dombrowski
were immediately ordered to deploy on the right of the Garibaldi, just
as the attackers built up what might have been a dangerous flanking
manoeuvre. Crucially, ten T-26 tanks now arrived to support the
brigade. When another attack began on their left flank, threatening the
wide, empty space that separated them from Kahle's XI Brigade, the
André Marty Battalion was deployed and, with help from the tanks,
brought it to a halt. 'It's hard to say how events would have unfolded
if the XII Brigade had arrived a few hours later,' Samoylov observed in
his report.[6]

Lukács now had no reserves. Meanwhile the Italians were planning a much stronger attack from Brihuega for 4 p.m. with a force four times as large as XII Brigade. By the time this happened, however, another three Spanish battalions had appeared and one was sent to him. The Spaniards arrived just in time, allowing him to place them beside the Dombrowski and thwart yet another flanking attempt. A large gap still existed, however, between the two International Brigades. When Renn and Kahle visited Lukács that evening, driving down a road clogged with refugees, they agreed that if more reinforcements did not arrive soon the Italians would 'turn us into sausage meat'.[7] Fortunately, there was a series of delays: the weather was still too bad for either side to fly reconnaissance aircraft; it also reduced visibility on the ground, making it difficult to explore terrain. Both sides were often confused about where the front was, especially in the forests where patrols wandered about blindly, and a number of prisoners were taken when they simply walked into Republican lines by mistake. It was not always clear, either, whether the Italians they met were friend or foe. 'Don't shoot, we are Italians!' one side would shout. 'So are we!' the others would reply. The first Garibaldi volunteers to die at the hands of their countrymen were four members of a patrol who were captured, tied to a tree and executed.[8]

Pesce was part of an overnight forest patrol that found itself with a particularly magnificent prize – the entire headquarters staff of one of the Littorio division battalions. To begin with, neither side was sure who had captured whom. '¡Arrendetevi! [Surrender!],' the Italian CTV soldiers shouted. '¡Arrendetevi voi! [You surrender!],'[9] Pesce's companions replied. Eventually, it became obvious that the regular army soldiers of the Littorio division were surrounded. Their battalion commander, Major Antonio Luciano, surrendered with two other officers and forty-six men from his machine-gun group. 'He told us that he had been called up [for Spain], and had simply obeyed orders,' Pesce recalled. He also requested that, if they were going to shoot him, they do so quickly. Under interrogation that night, Major Luciano became the first reliable source of intelligence about the size of the approaching army.

A skeleton defensive line was now in place, but the Italians had numerous reserves to throw at it and XII Brigade's right flank was, as Samoylov described it, 'hanging in the air'.[10] There were also plenty of other routes available that would enable the fascists to march on

Torija and bring defeat. 'The results of the first stage of the operation … should be recognised as quite favourable for the Italians,' said Samoylov. 'Almost half of their forces had yet to enter the battle and they had the possibility of launching manoeuvres on both flanks.'[11]

The following day, 11 March, Pesce and his companions, though soaked to the skin and frozen, were still in place. So too were the five other international battalions. More importantly, there was now frenzied activity behind them. Major Luciano's sensational information about the size of the enemy army had, overnight, forced the Republican command to recognise the extent of the threat. A new army corps was being rapidly organised to counter it, with two divisions to cover the flanks and one division to defend the crucial triangle. The latter division was to be built around the two International Brigades and would include many of the Republic's very best troops, led by Líster and the equally legendary, if unpredictable, Valentín González, known as El Campesino ('the Peasant'). Líster himself was placed in charge of the whole division. His men, however, would not arrive until the following night.[12] Until then, the six international battalions would have to do much of the fighting.

By now the rest of Republican Spain had also woken up to the fact that an Italian army was fighting its way towards Madrid. A clever Republican slogan – 'Spain is not Abyssinia' – had been coined, and proved hugely popular. It tapped into Spanish pride and became a rallying call for defence.[13] The might of the Italian expeditionary force was, however, about to be launched at what all sides now recognised as the Republican weak spot – Torija. If what Renn called 'this large *pueblo* with its miserable houses'[14] could be taken, the fascists would be at the gates of Guadalajara and the International Brigaders would struggle to escape.

At 10.30 a.m. on the morning of the 11th, an artillery barrage announced the beginning of a day-long attempt to dislodge the Garibaldis and destroy the defensive triangle from the Brihuega corner. Icy rain was falling and the men were soon shivering, fingers numb against barrels of guns and rifles, in their wet, frozen uniforms. It was a challenging start to their most difficult day yet. Mussolini's forces, however, were still confused about exactly where the Garibaldis and the rest of Lukács's brigade were situated. They seemed to have assumed that they would all be hidden in the forest and that the road from Brihuega to Torija formed a sort of no-man's-land. The following morning two disorientated Italian trucks drove along the road up to the Brigaders' lines and only stopped when Pesce machine-gunned their tyres from his foxhole beside the road. They had been carrying supplies, including letters, newspapers and parcels, to Italian officers in Brihuega. Leafing through the newspapers, Pesce read that Mussolini was now boasting about a rearmament campaign that would provide Italy with '8 million bayonets [armed men]'. Il Duce was sure that 'the courage and tenacity of our legionaries will overcome all enemy resistance. Crushing the international forces [International Brigades] will provide us with a hugely important political and military success. I inform the legionaries that I am following their progress minute-by-minute and that this will be crowned with victory.'[15]

Shortly afterwards another two trucks drove up, apparently believing that the first two simply needed towing back. The Garibaldis were so well dug in that, even though they were just a few metres away, the new arrivals could not see them as they descended from their cabs, lit cigarettes, chatted and tried to attach chains to the other vehicles. A short burst of fire encouraged them to surrender.[16] Two Italians fell to their knees, weeping and begging for mercy. Their officers had told them that captured troops were routinely shot. It took them a while to understand that this would not be the case.

Fiat-Ansaldo tanks appeared once more, turned around and then returned with artillery support. As attacks continued during the day, Pesce began to fear that they could not hold the position. The attrition and cold conditions sapped the men's morale. The occasional shout of '*No Pasarán!*' provided only momentary cheer as the fascists advanced through the forest to their left and took an old hunting lodge known as the Palace of Ibarra.[17] On the road, however, the red-tipped, armour-piercing rounds being used by the Garibaldi volunteers caused havoc with the lightweight Italian tanks, which Pesce deemed 'easy to perforate'.[18]

The fighting on the French Highway was much harder and the Edgar André and Commune de Paris eventually lost control of the crossroads. That afternoon, for the first time, General Roatta put his flame-throwing tanks at the front of the advance. These appeared by surprise, spitting twenty-metre-long bursts of flame, turning anything in their path to charcoal and leaving behind puffs of oily black smoke. As a killing weapon, the flamethrower may have been less effective than a machine gun, but this was more than compensated for by its ability to strike terror into the hearts of even the most battle-hardened soldiers. 'The truth is that they were frightening – the tank advanced, spewing flames at us from its tube. But when we realised that the flame only travelled fifteen or twenty metres and that it then immediately went out, we realised that if we protected ourselves well the tank wasn't that dangerous,' one commissar told Alexander Rodimstev a thirty-two-year-old, beret-wearing Russian advisor who was to play a major role in the defence of Stalingrad.[19] By then it was too late. The Italians had found a way through. The Edgar André Battalion, positioned on the right side of the highway, suffered worst; they were eventually left with just one out of seven machine guns functioning, before their positions were overrun by fascist infantry and much of the battalion was wiped out.[20]

Platoon commander Sixten Rogeby was one of a handful of Edgar André walking wounded who limped back along the French Highway, convinced that there were no reserves behind them and the battle was lost: 'In my section, there were two of us left. The Company Commander [Emil Wendt] had been killed by a dumdum to his head. So we moved backwards, those of us who could move,' Rogeby recalled.

> I tried to gather up abandoned weapons – a light machine gun, two rifles and three heavy hand grenades. Then I felt a blow to my hip. A bullet had gone clean through, just a few decimetres in from the widest part of my body. But it didn't break any bones.
>
> I could walk, barely. After a while I had to drop the grenades, then the rifles. It was too heavy, carrying it all. I saw a big German walking there. That's the picture I remember the most clearly. He wasn't carrying anything, which I thought was wrong. You should make use of everything you can. So I asked him if he couldn't help carry something. Then he lifted his shirt, and I saw the blood pulsating from a hole in his chest. Someone else took care of the machine gun. Some Spaniards gave me a hand, so I could limp on. Then suddenly we saw the second line. It was there, after all.[21]

The reinforcements Rogeby saw were probably from the Spanish 50 Brigade who were positioned at around Kilometre 77 on the French

Highway, near Trijueque, with a platoon of tanks and an artillery battery. This is also where Mussolini's men halted for the night. They were now just four kilometres from Torija and the defensive triangle had been squeezed to almost a quarter of its original size, occupying a sliver of land measuring no more than fourteen square kilometres. More dangerously, there was still a large undefended gap between the main bloc of Kahle's XI Brigade men on the right-hand side of the French Highway and Lukács's XII Brigade. If the attacking troops found the gap, then Torija would likely fall soon after. For Samoylov this was the moment of maximum jeopardy. 'A crisis situation had developed again,' he admitted. 'It was even worse than the evening of 9 March.' Then the snow, which had already appeared sporadically, started to fall solidly.[22]

When dawn broke on Friday 12 March, the battlefield was dusted with snow, which soon began to melt into pools of muddy slush. The fascist advance was four days old and poised just short of a crucial target at Torija. This must have been the night when Pesce, who wrote a memoir of the battle sixteen years later but was unsure of dates, walked north-east into the forest with four men to reconnoitre the fascists' positions. At times they were just a few metres from other Italians, though these soldiers were mostly concentrating on staying warm and, if possible, dry. Crawling through the mud to a spot where they could look out over the highways that curled down the hillsides into Brihuega, the party saw the headlights of numerous trucks entering the town. Some were towing artillery and groups of men were marching through the dark. Four hours later they reported back to Barontini: the CTV was preparing for another push.[23]

Roatta had decided to throw the last of his divisions into the battle. Some twenty-four battalions were now quartered in or around Brihuega. These were to be sent against the Garibaldis and the other three battalions commanded by Lukács (including, now, a reserve battalion of Spaniards). At the same time, the fresh regular army Littorio division was expected to smash its way through on the French Highway, take Torija and drive a wedge between the two International Brigades.[24] The situation was increasingly critical and, with the Italians looking likely to break through, the following day Lukács received orders to sacrifice his entire brigade if necessary.[25]

On the French Highway, the Republican aim now was to recover Trijueque, the last village before Torija, which had been taken by

Mussolini's soldiers the night before. The task was given to Líster's newly arrived men, while the Thälmann and Kahle's borrowed Spanish battalion, named 'La Pasionaria', tried to widen the front towards XII International Brigade. A gap still existed between them, and a tank unit was ordered to guard it.

Bad weather and organisational chaos prevented the Italians from launching their own attack until midday. The snow and rain were beginning to wreak havoc with their mechanised divisions, which were now restricted to the main roads. Engines would not start, the snow blinded drivers, covered the roads with slush and caused vehicles to slip off the road. Then, suddenly, the clouds lifted. The Republican air force, stationed nearby, finally took off. Airfields were still waterlogged, so only a dozen light fighters could take to the air but these quickly found an entire Littorio regiment backed up in trucks over a five-kilometre stretch of the French Highway. Arrayed in a continuous long line, they made a perfect target. The fighters strafed at will, provoking chaos. Trucks blew up, ran into each other and threw men, machinery and munitions into the snow. Some stood blazing in the middle of the highway, while shocked Italian fascist soldiers shivered in the cold.

This meant the Littorio division did not reach Trijueque until midday, by which time Líster's men, accompanied by two companies of tanks, were counter-attacking towards the village. They now found themselves forced to cope with the full Italian offensive and were pushed back to within a kilometre of Torija. At the same time, Italian infantry and tanks streamed out of Brihuega to attack Lukács's men, while a CTV battalion slogged through the mud into the gap that separated them from XI Brigade.

The commander of the Republican air squadron had flown a reconnaissance mission over Brihuega that morning and found it overflowing with Italian fascist soldiers. He calculated that at least 800 vehicles were in the area, 400 of them squeezed into Brihuega itself. At 2.30 p.m., just an hour after the Italian attack began, he reappeared with his entire squadron. The troops packed into the narrow streets of Brihuega or gathered in their starting positions for the attack were an even easier target than the trucks on the French Highway. Soon the streets of Brihuega were littered with burning vehicles and the corpses of men and animals.

Líster chose to counter-attack at the moment when Italian morale was beginning to ebb. He was heavily outnumbered in men, machine guns and rifles, but the balance of tanks was now just two to one against him. The superior quality of the Russian vehicles turned that into an overall advantage, with one observer boasting that 'our tanks were driven right over their tankettes, which just crunched'.[26] Líster's infantry also waded into the muddy fields of the defensive triangle from the French Highway. This was now so small that tanks could avoid the mud and drive along the roads that marked its edges to fire at will on the enemy. Trapped in the mud, with tanks bombarding them, the Italian infantry lasted just twenty minutes before fleeing. That saved Lukács's men from being cut off and El Campesino's troops arrived after dark, closing the gap that separated them from Kahle's men.

For the first time in Spain, Mussolini's men had been pushed back. The distance was not great, but the momentum had changed. The tide had begun to turn in the Italian civil war being fought on Spanish soil and, to the satisfaction of Pesce and the Garibaldi volunteers, Mussolini's swaggering fascism looked set for its first major defeat in over a decade. Not a single Republican tank or aircraft had been lost that day. The capacity of the International Brigades to resist attack had, once more, proved vital.

29

The Battle of the Loudspeakers: Palace of Ibarra, Brihuega, 13 March 1937

The armoured truck that pulled up in the forest by the Palace of Ibarra near Brihuega looked nothing like a weapon of war. In fact, there was something monstrously comical about it. Lying on its side, with its giant square mouth hanging off the trailer and its point balanced above the driver's cab, lay a bizarre machine that looked vaguely like a slumbering Eiffel Tower. This was, in fact, a giant loudspeaker known as the 'Altavoz del Frente', big enough to bellow Italian phrases at the men crouched behind their weapons inside the hunting lodge's thick, low walls. One of the Garibaldis' propaganda team was talking into it:

> *Allò, Allò,* Italians, peasants, soldiers, officers, listen to the voice of the country. Return to your homes.
>
> Your wives and children are waiting for you. Return to your homes: you do not have to die.
>
> Young people aged eighteen, who together with the over fifties were sent to Spain as cattle to the slaughter house! They told you that you were going to Abyssinia but they took you to Spain; they promised that you would work, but they brought you to a massacre.[1]

First employed at Jarama, the loudspeakers had quickly become one of the political commissars' favourite tools to weaken the enemy's morale. Amongst those writing the propagandists' scripts, together with leaflets dropped on Mussolini's men, were the International Brigades' Commissar Inspector General Luigi Longo, and his wife Teresa Noce, who edited the Italian Brigaders' newspaper, *Il volontario della libertà*. Day and night, the commissars blasted out slogans warning the Italian militia 'volunteers' in front of them of their mistake and promising them a warm reception if they deserted. Central to the message was the idea that Mussolini had tricked them into coming to Spain against their will.

This was mostly a lie. Like the groups of Portuguese and Irish volunteers who had also joined Franco's side, the vast majority of the CTV militia had known exactly where they were going.[2] A small number probably did not, or not until it was too late for them to abandon their unit without punishment. More importantly, however, this story of Mussolini's wicked trickery guaranteed them decent treatment when captured. It was also the story that the Garibaldis and the Spanish Republic wanted the world to hear. The only true 'volunteers' were meant to be in the International Brigades, who were on the right side of history, politics and morality. The only way, therefore, that the working classes could have been recruited by the other side was through lies and deceit.

Listening to the loudspeaker broadcasts, Giovanni Pesce reflected that this was what he himself wished to believe since, like most Garibaldini, he felt no joy in killing ordinary fellow Italians. 'We must not tire of enlightening them,' he said.[3] Gustav Regler agreed. 'That was what I had come for – to point out the new frontiers and abolish the old. The revolution in ideas. The true civil war in all its tremendous novelty – to bring about the disintegration of the enemy, to unmask the lying propaganda. To restore humanity in the midst of murder.'[4]

This was, unsurprisingly, the tale many captured fascist prisoners told their interrogators, repeating the stories broadcast by the 'Altavoz del Frente' or read in Republican leaflets. They had thought they were going to Abyssinia to police Italy's new colonial conquests in return for land to work, they claimed, and had only been told they were going to Spain to shoot at fellow southern European peasants after they had boarded ships at Gaeta. Instead of disembarking in Africa, they had found themselves put ashore at Cádiz and then moved north to the freezing Alcarria plain. 'We protested to our officers, but they threatened us. Then they promised the war would be over in a few days, that it would be easy,' one of them told Pesce after he was taken prisoner. Others admitted they had known they were coming to Spain, but it was simply a way to escape unemployment.[5]

Proof that the propaganda was having some impact came from the Italian artillery, which tried constantly to put the loudspeaker car out of action. According to Pesce, prisoners were soon telling them 'how enormous the impression produced by the speeches pronounced in Italian was, as many soldiers have then begun to reflect and became convinced we were right'.[6] Nobody appears to have worried that their excuses suggested that they would have happily killed Africans in Abyssinia instead.

The exception to that were the Abyssinian volunteers in the International Brigades themselves, a handful of whom had joined the Garibaldi. When Regler arrived here, he came across one of them, whose father had been hanged by Mussolini. He was delighted at the opportunity to take revenge and greeted Regler by drawing a finger across his throat. 'Mio giorno – my day,' he announced. The Dombrowski Poles, positioned beside the Garibaldis, also had little patience with Mussolini's troops and bridled at being ordered to scatter leaflets near their lines. Like the Abyssinians, the Poles simply saw men who wished to kill them. 'If the Italians on the other side are so ready to desert, why aren't they shooting their officers? We aren't the Salvation Army!' one of them protested to Regler.[7]

Whatever the truth about the CTV militiamen's motivations, when the Garibaldis prepared to storm the Palace of Ibarra the following day, 14 March, Ilio Barontini warned them not to believe their own propaganda about facing innocent, weak-willed fools. The hunting lodge and forest around it were defended by highly driven soldiers from the ardently fascist Lupi Battalion, the 'Wolves', he reminded them. 'Keep in mind that it is a fortified place, commanded by officers who are fanatical fascists. They will resist and shoot until the last man,' he told them. 'You know that we can't match the superiority of their arms. We only have our courage.'[8]

In the assault that followed, he was proved right. The sturdy shooting lodge had to be reduced almost to rubble by tank and machine-gun fire. Then it was stormed. The defenders were eventually surrounded, but when Garibaldi officer Nunzio Guerrini invited them to surrender the answer came in the form of a hand grenade, which killed him instantly.

In the bloody battle which followed, the Garibaldis were helped by men from the André Marty Battalion and Asturian miners armed with explosives. Eventually, the palace was conquered and a further 262 Italians captured.[9] This helped ensure the Garibaldis' control of the forest, whose edges now became their line of defence. Any attack would have to advance over open ground towards troops, artillery and tanks hidden amongst the low oaks and thick scrub.

There was, in any case, little chance of that happening. General Roatta had decided the previous day, when his forces had first been obliged to retreat, that the offensive stage of the battle was over. He blamed the weather, but his inability to foresee how this might trap his army on narrow, slushy roads while it was attacked by aircraft, tanks and infantry was mostly to blame. The stubborn defence of the two International Brigades, the courageous attack of Líster's men and, above all, the skirmishing tanks and roaming, low-level aircraft, had stopped the Italian advance. So, too, had the commissars' comical loudspeakers. As Roatta tried to hold on to the land conquered so far and set about establishing a defensive line on 14 and 15 March, the Republican army began to prepare a proper counter-attack.[10]

Roatta's army corps still had more men and weapons than the three Republican divisions that had been created to attack it, but morale and Russian hardware evened out the balance. The major Republican attack came on 18 March, with Lukács's brigade given the task of occupying Brihuega itself. That afternoon, after the clouds parted, a wave of seventy aircraft launched a devastating attack on the town and positions around it. Next the Brigaders discovered how difficult it was to attack across the water-logged fields and the clinging, clay mud of the Alcarria, with several tanks becoming stuck. Lukács's men moved slowly but, by the end of the day, the Italian division in Brihuega was almost surrounded. The Republican commanders would later rue the fact that, on other side of the town, the inexperienced Republican 70 Brigade failed to shut off the one remaining exit route. Brihuega itself was by now so cluttered with burning vehicles and panicked men that the only way out was on foot. The motorised units around it, meanwhile, fled down the only open road.

At nightfall the first International Brigade units entered the town, finding the Italian 1st Division's hastily abandoned headquarters, with all its paperwork. More than 300 fascist soldiers had fallen captive, along with 150 machine guns, six tanks, thirty artillery pieces and a vast stock of munitions. Over five hundred Italians lay dead in the forests, on the muddy fields or in the rubble and twisted metal in the streets of Brihuega, which Samoylov described as looking like 'an entire cemetery of burned and destroyed vehicles'.[11] As the town's inhabitants emerged from basements and cellars, the Brigaders experienced – for the very first time – the joy of being received as liberators. This moment would be attributed to the Garibaldis, but members of the Polish Dombrowski later complained that their role in the victory had been deliberately suppressed for propaganda purposes.

Having defeated one of the four Italian divisions, the Republicans aimed to destroy another the following day, 19 March. The target was the regular army Littorio division deployed on and around the French Highway. The aim was to carry out a pincer movement that would force it back past the crossroads at Kilometre 83 and trap it on the next few kilometres of road. The attack was timed to start at 2 p.m. Before it began, however, Roatta decided to withdraw his army. Reserves were drawn in from other fronts to create a line of defence, and by 11.30 that morning intelligence from the Republican air force reported that trucks from the Littorio division were driving back up the French Highway. Looking down on the trucks' canvas canopies, the pilots were unable to say whether these were empty or full of retreating men. When the Edgar André Battalion eventually confirmed that a full retreat was under way, the pursuit began. The Littorio division was strafed from the air and chased by tanks. The Edgar André, joining Líster's troops, advanced unopposed past the crucial crossroads at Kilometres 83 where so many of its men had died a week earlier. Líster's tanks charged on another twelve kilometres before meeting the Italians' new defensive line while, elsewhere, the infantry units that had proved so adaptable over small stretches of terrain, found it much harder to maintain the momentum of a long pursuit over unfamiliar countryside. By night-time it was clear that the Littorio division had been thrown back, leaving large amounts of war materiel behind, but also that it had managed to escape.[12]

Once again, it became clear that the Republican army's impressive ability to improvise effective defence did not mean it could also attack well. The following day, 20 March, the Republican pursuit continued, but stalled when it met a strong defensive line that had been set up at Kilometre 95 on the French Highway. Republican spotter planes, however, found Italian convoys on the road behind it. Trucks stood two or three abreast, moving slowly or standing still in traffic jams. Sixty-seven Republican aircraft took part in what a later generation of English-speaking military pilots would have called a 'turkey shoot'. Trucks crashed into one another, men ran into the fields, and the convoys ground to halt. A ten-kilometre stretch of the highway became one continuous target, which for twenty minutes the planes strafed in long, straight runs. Soon the road was choked with burning vehicles, exploding fuel trucks and wounded, dead, dazed or panicked soldiers. Algora was full of Italian corpses. The aircraft returned soon afterwards, repeating their assault on the convoy. Several hundred vehicles had been destroyed and Samoylov calculated that this one day's destruction added an extra month to the time the Italians would need to rebuild their forces.[13]

When the Republican infantry attacked that afternoon, expecting to join the pursuit, it found a stubborn wall of resistance. The few prisoners taken that day turned out not to be Italians, but Spaniards. With the Italian attack crumbling, Franco had brought in his own troops to shore up the front. This was still thirty kilometres further forward than before the original Italian advance, but, to the chagrin of Mussolini, the Italian army corps had been defeated. It was a huge blow to Il Duce's reputation. For the first time, his chest-puffing arrogance looked like hubris. Even Franco's Spanish generals now laughed at their pompous Italian counterparts. Officers at Franco's headquarters in Salamanca reportedly stopped saluting their Italian superiors. Frank Thomas, the Welsh mercenary who had joined Franco's Legion (and would soon desert), found the German ground troops just as delighted as his Spanish comrades. 'Being friendly with several Germans in a nearby tank corps, I had heard the news about Guadalajara quickly, and the Germans were, paradoxically, since they are Italian allies, as pleased as we were,' he said.[14] Franco's officers composed a song with the line: 'Guadalajara is not Abyssinia; here the reds are chucking bombs which actually explode.' The Italians would stay, and play a major part in the war, but from now on Franco increasingly took his advice from Hitler's commanders.

For the Republic, the battle of Guadalajara had been a resounding victory. The world heard about it soon enough. Herbert Matthews of the *New York Times* claimed that 'Guadalajara is for fascism what Bailén was for Napoleon' – referring to the Spanish War of Independence in 1808 and the first major defeat of a Napoleonic army. He also pointed out, however, that whenever it looked like the Republic might be winning, Hitler and Mussolini stepped up their aid. 'It is all very logical and very obvious, but sooner or later it must either stop or be made so overwhelming so as to ensure a quick victory for Franco. The other alternative is a European war,' he wrote.[15]

The men of the Garibaldi Battalion, meanwhile, had won their miniature civil war, even if they had taken little satisfaction in killing and capturing so many fellow Italians. That seemed tragic.[16] For those who had been waiting for the Republic to recover the initiative and begin the process of defeating Franco's fascist uprising, the battle provided a first injection of optimism. The tide, they believed, had finally turned. It was no longer a question of '*¡No pasarán!*' ('They shall not pass!') but of '*¡Avanzaremos!*' ('We will advance!').

30

Blue Nose and the Deserters: Valencia, 20 April 1937

Auguste Lecoeur slept overnight in a park in Valencia in the warm late spring, pretending to be a deserter from the International Brigades. The following day he began his search for the man known only as Nez Bleu – 'Blue Nose'. This was the nickname of the man who acted as the chief conduit for those French volunteers wishing to escape Spain and return home. Lecoeur, a political commissar who was on a special mission for André Marty, carried a fake ID card identifying him as a French volunteer called Paul Rohart. The commander of the International Brigades' headquarters had briefed him personally, ranting about suspected traitors. 'Marty, as everybody knew, saw spies and saboteurs everywhere,' Lecoeur observed later. 'It is true that there were some of these, but they were far cleverer than him.'[1]

In the morning, after spending the night in the park, Lecoeur loitered by the gates to the French consulate in Valencia and approached two young men who were carrying a large cauldron of food from there to the neighbouring French School, which enjoyed diplomatic protection and was known to be where deserters were housed.[2] They advised him to go to the Café des Français in the port and ask for Blue Nose. There, he met two French deserters who had arranged to see Blue Nose in the consulate that afternoon, and tagged along to the meeting. Blue Nose, he discovered, was the same Captain Yves Le Goux who had briefly been given command of the André Marty Battalion but had been sacked before it had even gone in to action. After carrying out various tasks in the rearguard, the forty-nine-year-old former notary's clerk and French army reserve officer had abandoned the International Brigades at the end of January,[3] and now worked with the consulate.

Lecoeur was then taken to the French School where a group of at least seventeen deserters had been gathered together, and were being fed, prior to repatriation. Some had been here for two months. 'It was no paradise. Most men slept on the floor,' he wrote.[4] A single fountain provided water and somewhere to wash. The volunteers did not go out, since they faced arrest by police and feared being shot for cowardice. He listened to the men's stories and decided that they were not the dangerous bunch of Trotskyists or fascist spies that Marty had told him to expect. 'I soon realised that these were neither communists, nor Trotskyists, nor anarchists, but mostly adventurers who had come for a change of scenery rather than in pursuit of any ideal,' he said. 'Once they realised that they were involved in a real war, that was being fought with real bullets, with all the crudity of Spain and its civil war, they wanted to put an end to such a risky enterprise.'[5]

When it came to punishing the men, Lecoeur preferred leniency. He even felt sorry for some of them. One wanted to return home to look after his sick parents, another appeared to be clinically depressed about not having heard from his family for months, while yet another was seriously ill.[6] 'I concluded that even if we momentarily brought these men back to their senses, even if they agreed to return to the Brigades, they would always remain, with some exceptions, undesirable and even dangerous elements by their example, and in my opinion it was better for us to decide ourselves to repatriate them,' he said.[7] This would be done by expelling them from the International Brigades and from Spain, and also informing the trade union or political party they belonged to of what had happened as a way of shaming them in front of their peers and home communities.

When he revealed himself, however, and made this offer to the men Lecoeur found himself 'preaching in the desert'.[8] The deserters worried that they were being tricked and would be shot, and so demanded official confirmation of the offer. This came the next day on a piece of paper signed by Marty, but when the men saw his signature they turned on the Brigader who had brought it. Lecoeur had to draw his revolver, Republican militiamen rushed in to help him and a scuffle broke out. The men, who later blamed Blue Nose for their reaction, were taken off to jail (or hospital) and the following day

Lecoeur repeated the offer, adding that those who wished to rejoin their units could do so without punishment. To his amazement, they all now opted to stay. He knew why. 'They pictured themselves lying abandoned in the countryside with a bullet in the back of the head,' he said.[9] Rumours that deserters were being quietly shot were rife in the Brigades. Documents show, however, that those who fled the enemy and were subjected to court martial were, at this time, receiving six-month prison sentences.[10] Only Le Goux, arrested the following day, and a fifty-year-old artillery commander called Jean Chevallot were actually sent to prison. The former passed through the International Brigade prisons for the next two years – despite his pleas that he had only signed on for three months' service and had been employed by the French consulate when arrested.[11]

Documents found on the deserters revealed a deeper current of dismay and disillusion. Chevallot carried two letters from former comrades in his artillery section who had abandoned the Brigades to join, in one case, an anarchist unit and, in the other, a Republican army artillery school. Both men were relieved that their letters would not be read by a military censor. 'At last I can write freely,' starts the letter from Alphonse Guichard,[12] who added that he was still proud to be fighting fascism by working at the artillery school. 'Here I have learnt what politics is. I shall never be a communist or a supporter of the Soviet regime ... I was almost put before the firing squad because of a letter that Papa sent to Spain.'

The other letter-writer, Marcel Neury, asked his family not to broadcast the news he was about to give them, since he did not want it used against the Republican cause. 'I have left the International Brigades,' he announced. 'I came to Spain full of enthusiasm. It was the crowning moment of our revolutionary life ... [but] now we have witnessed the end of our dream. Progressively, the army of comrades has disappeared to make way for harsh militarism, with ever-increasing favouritism imposed for the Germans and Russians [he appears to mean both Red Army advisors and the White Russians in his artillery unit]. We Belgians, Italians and French have realised that we are now submitted to the will of a German-Russian high command with a Prussian mindset that we do not share.'[13] The verbal humiliation of their beloved commander Chevallot – a professional artilleryman and former First World War officer – by the choleric General Gal during the

Jarama battle had finally persuaded Neury to desert the Brigades for an anarchist unit. 'I repeat, I am still a Bolshevik!' he insisted.

Gal's temper was infamous. British volunteer Jack Shaw recalled how the general had jumped out of his staff car on spotting Shaw and his comrades – a group of dirty, unwashed and starving men marching to the rear, as they had been ordered to do. 'Holding his pistol to my head he shouted and cursed at us for being deserters and cowards,' he recalled, adding that Gal insisted that he and another volunteer were immediately locked up. The story had, however, a happy ending when Gal called them to his dugout the following morning. 'There he stood before us an abject figure, tears in his eyes and asking our forgiveness. He told us he was ashamed of his actions and promptly made up for them by providing us with what we considered at the time to be the finest things in the world – food, hot and appetising and plentiful. The question can be posed: in what other army would a high-ranking officer bow his head and apologise to two ordinary soldiers? This is why the International Brigade was different.'[14]

The Brigades were also different amongst themselves, especially when it came to punishments. The British, for example, refused to think of those who were merely absent without leave as traitors and did not shoot deserters since this was seen as 'absolutely catastrophic' for morale. 'Many of them claimed, I think honestly, that they had been told when they joined up in England that they were signing on for only a limited period of some months and would then be able to return home,' admitted John Angus, a British commissar at one of the prison camps set up for their own men by the International Brigades in 1937. When it became clear that this was not the case, men began to complain 'that from volunteers we have become conscripts ... to be kept here until we are wounded or killed'.[15] The fact that some men were allowed home, either definitively or on leave, while others were not, simply enraged volunteers further. Rumours that officers and senior Communist Party cadres were being treated preferentially were sometimes, but not always, correct.[16]

Desertions were just one disciplinary problem and, like the others, fell into the remit of the political commissars. Refusing to obey minor orders, arguing with officers (or commissars), brawling, harassing civilians and – above all – getting drunk were issues that the Brigades, like almost all army units in history, had to deal with. More serious cases inevitably arose amongst the 35,000 men. Thieves, thugs, conmen and rapists were found in all ranks. Pillage, espionage, treason, incitement to mutiny and 'other cases of a characteristic gravity' could all bring the death sentence, though the first of these was widely tolerated. When jury members from the British Battalion were asked by a prosecutor to hand down a death sentence to an ammunition-truck driver who had taken men away from the Jarama battlefield, they instead sent him to a labour battalion for fifteen days.[17]

Guardhouses, labour camps, jails and Pioneer units (sometimes called 'labour', 'fortification', 'disciplinary', or 'engineering' units) coped with most troublemakers. According to a set of instructions issued to XV Brigade in March 1937, volunteers could spend between fifteen days and three months in Pioneer companies for crimes such as 'disorder without conscious will to sabotage, violations of ordinary law, desertion, repeated drunkenness'.[18] Anything less than that simply required a few days cooling off in the guardhouse. These units were amongst the most dangerous to belong to, since they were often required to dig or repair trenches and observation posts or lay barbed wire along – or ahead of – the front line at night, where they were targeted by snipers and enemy night patrols. 'You may last a week or you may last a month. But just by the law of averages, you're bound to be knocked off,' complained one survivor. That was an exaggeration, and such units were a common feature of most armies, but fear of them helped maintain discipline. Men sent to these units were not allowed, in principle, to bear arms to defend themselves as they carried out 'work at the front, in the first lines or elsewhere under very rigorous discipline ... and under good guard'.[19] Nor did they receive wages, wine or cigarettes.

One way for volunteers to avoid the Pioneer units was, ironically, to commit a more serious crime, such as 'conscious disorder', 'serious violations of ordinary law', or to be 'suspected of espionage (without formal evidence)'.[20] The latter category was, obviously, open to abuse and at least one of the camps set up to hold men who were deemed 'undesirables'[21] turned into a nightmarish place of sadistic abuse and torture.[22] These camps came into being after the spring of 1937, with one located at Chinchilla and another, 'Camp Lukács', near Albacete, run by Vladimir Ćopić's brother Emil.[23] As many as one in ten Brigaders are believed to have passed through Camp Lukács, where John Angus was a commissar, as punishment for fairly minor misdemeanours. Most men seem to have been treated decently, but abuses were also committed by some of the more hard-line guards. If Camp Lukács was sometimes tough, it was not nearly as terrible as the camp eventually set up in the run-down medieval castle at Castelldefels, just south of Barcelona, which at any one time housed between 255 and 400 International Brigade prisoners.[24] Inmates here could be starved, beaten and left without water, with the jail becoming so infamous in the town that rumours about it spread as far as Barcelona. Those living near the castle sometimes would pass water over the wall and International Brigade officers would be stopped in the street by locals complaining about the abuses happening there.[25]

The Castelldefels terror reached its peak under the sadistic command of an alcoholic and dictatorial French lieutenant called Marcel Lantez, known as 'the Hyena'.[26] Even the guards were scared of Lantez, who threatened them with his machine pistol and locked up those who argued with him. When an officer called Alfredo Vinet was sent to investigate the conditions in which the Brigade prisoners were being kept, he was disgusted. After mornings at the beach and long lunches, Lieutenant Lantez would return to the jail in a bullying mood. He had surrounded himself with a gang of thugs who applied his rule of terror to both inmates and guards – with one, an illiterate Belgian called Charles Werstappen, reasoning that this was reasonable since the inmates were 'enemy agents who had come to Spain to damage our cause'.[27] Werstappen, who signed documents with a thumbprint, was not the only guard who had been infected by the 'spy mania' of the Brigades, with others claiming that any 'agents of Hitler and Mussolini' deserved their beatings (though, if this had been proven, they would have been shot as traitors). Some of the worst violence was reserved for those deemed to be helping deserters or working with a man known as Le Flem Gaston (who had replaced Blue Nose at the French consulate).

Rations at the castle jail were minimal, mass punishments common and a small group of prisoners were systematically subjected to beatings, terror and torture. Vinet found a group of ten men locked away in a dungeon 'similar to those used in the Middle Ages', one of whom had been there for seventy-five days. 'The physical situation of this detainee was pitiful. When I asked the rest how many days they had spent inside that dungeon and the reason they were locked up, they all gave different

dates and said they didn't know the reasons.'[28] Danish volunteer Poul
Erik Dreyer was sent together with an Italian and an Englishman to a
tiny, windowless punishment cell squeezed into a hole under the stone
staircase of the castle, where there was room for three men and bucket.
'The ceiling was so low that we had to crouch ... the Englishman went
mad. I don't know how long we were there before they let us out, but
the Englishman was a shadow of his former self, a walking cadaver.'[29]

Rumours abounded about men who had been taken out and shot at
Castelldefels, and of a mysterious Chinese prisoner, Sen Sen Semfley,
who was routinely humiliated, being forced to walk on all fours or
drink water laced with urine.[30] It was not until September 1938, when
the castle housed 400 prisoners, that Marty finally admitted that
something needed doing about it and, saying 'that his great error had
been to ignore what was going on in Castelldefels', sent a senior Serbian
officer, Svetislav Djordjevic, to sort it out. His instructions were to tell
the men they could either rejoin the Brigades or go home. He arrested
Lantez, who was tried and imprisoned.[31] Djordjevic's claim that all but
one man returned to their units does not hold up to the evidence given
by those who were there.

Commissars also imparted political doctrine – some treating
political grumbling as a major sin – and gave lengthy morale-rousing
lectures and speeches that were often so laced with falsehoods that
the volunteers chafed against them. British Brigader John H. Bassett
recalled his moaning comrades being forced by one commissar to listen
to a public reading of *Frente Rojo*, a newspaper that relentlessly claimed
the Republic was winning, even when the men were clearly retreating.
'After the interpreter had made translations in four or five languages,
questions were invited. The British gave one concerted roar: "When are
we going home?" '[32] Such talk was considered bad for morale; attempts
were made to stifle a marching song that became popular amongst the
English-speaking units:

Oh, I wanna go home,
I don't wanna die,
Machine guns they rattle,
The cannons they roar,
I don't wanna go to the front any more.
Oh, take me over the sea,

Where Franco can't get at me,
Oh! My! I'm too young to die,
I wanna go home![33]

British humour and irreverence were not always appreciated. When the Polish Red Army officer and International Brigade commander General Walter attended a May Day celebration in which the Spaniards danced, the Poles sang beautifully and the Germans produced a serious cultural display, he was amazed that the British were allowed to shout out a song that began, 'In our quartermaster's stores there are very big rats, as big as wounded cats ...', and that their political commissars laughed along with them. Even the British tendency to stop at 5 p.m. and sit around in groups, muttering over cups of tea, provoked a degree of suspicion in the Polish general.[34]

It is hard to calculate the overall rate of desertion in the International Brigades. This was obviously more tempting for the French, whose homeland lay just across the Pyrenees, than for volunteers who had come from further afield or were political exiles with no home to return to. One list of those waiting for repatriation in the French consulate in Barcelona in January 1937 contained 117 names.[35] French police kept files on more than 500 men sent home via the country's consulates in Spain. Rémi Skoutelsky, the historian of the French volunteers, believes that, while not all were International Brigaders, the vast majority were deserters. Not all went via the consulates. Others escaped as stowaways or, dressed as civilians, travelled in the backs of trucks taking oranges across the border.[36] Many more would have been caught before reaching a consulate, meaning that desertion was, in Skoutelsky's words, 'a mass phenomenon'.[37]

A very conservative estimate suggests that at least a thousand men deserted the International Brigades – or roughly an average of one man for each platoon of thirty-five men.[38] That tallies with figures the Brigades themselves held on file, though the records are unreliable since the term 'deserter' was a catch-all that also covered those who were simply absent without leave and had missed three consecutive daily roll calls.[39] Some of those listed as 'missing in combat' were likely also deserters. Amongst the worst offenders appear to have been the British – with 129 deserters listed and fifty-three men reaching the UK in the first six months of 1937. The fact that most of them arrived around the same time as the fracas at the French School in Valencia, suggests that this made British consular officials decide to get volunteers out quickly.

The official line on deserters was harsh. Allegations that Marty routinely had them shot would lead to him being given the nickname 'the butcher of Albacete'. He was certainly involved in the court martial and shooting of Delasalle, but there is little hard evidence that he deserved the nickname. The local civil governor later reported that at least nine Brigaders had been executed in Albacete, while Marty is also on record as complaining that he had been sent a group of 'Nazi spies' discovered in Valencia who needed shooting, when this simply was not something that he could do.[40] Indeed, he can sometimes be found trying to relax the rigidity, or excessive independence, of attitudes among some national groups, particularly the Germans. The latter operated their own security service, based on a pre-existing German Communist Party structure, and had a reputation for unbending strictness.[41] At least one volunteer, Heinz Weil, appears to have been killed as a suspected Trotskyist. Exaggerated rumours spread amongst the other nationalities that the Germans were even prepared to shoot volunteers who contracted venereal diseases.[42]

Shootings of deserters and cowards certainly happened during battle, just as they did in the rest of the Republican army.[43] In that respect, the much-admired General Walter was a far bloodier character than the blustering, bullying Marty – who was rarely to be found at the front line. Specific instructions were also given to deal with those who, seeking a way home, chose to shoot themselves through some non-vital part of the body. 'From today all soldiers with self-inflicted wounds will be considered as traitors to the people and will be punished according to the military law of Spain – death by shooting,' read one order issued to XV Brigade in March 1937.[44] The basic rules, however, were set by the government and applied to all soldiers, whether volunteers or not. A decree signed by the Republic's president Manuel Azaña on 19 June 1937, for example, allowed the death penalty to be passed on those found guilty of desertion, mutiny, disobeying orders during battle or for being the first man in a unit to turn and run.[45] It also, however, allowed for twelve- to twenty-year prison sentences, which could be served in the Pioneer companies.

By those terms, the actual punishments meted out in the International Brigades were not usually severe, since they often handed down six-month prison terms and then sent deserters into Pioneer units. That did not stop some more sadistic individuals in the Brigades' own intelligence, police and prison units from treating them in a more violent, and sometimes lethal, fashion. American Tony DeMaio – a SIM (Spanish military intelligence) agent – was one of the most notorious. A Lincoln veteran called William C. McCuistion, who later gave evidence to an inquiry in the United States, claimed DeMaio shot two international deserters, one American and one British, at a cafeteria in Barcelona. 'The American ... had a State Department passport issued under the name of Aronofsky ... The other fellow wasn't quite dead. His name was Moran, an Englishman. He was taken away to the hospital.'[46] This may have happened during a rebellion by suspected deserters who had been picked up in and around the city and were being kept in a Brigades' building in the Horta neighbourhood.[47] Close study of the Abraham Lincoln Battalion, however, appears to show only two men shot for desertion (one of whom, Paul White, was sentenced to death by his own comrades[48]), while another probably died in prison. Other allegations point to a maximum of seven other cases amongst the Americans.

The deserters from XIV Brigade whom Auguste Lecoeur had discovered and sent back to the Pioneer units in the spring of 1937 soon had more serious things to worry about. They were to see action in the International Brigades' next major engagement, high in the Guadarrama mountains between Madrid and Segovia, where Ernest Hemingway would later set his celebrated Spanish Civil War novel *For Whom the Bell Tolls*.

31

Hemingway: Men and women in war: Brihuega, Madrid, March–April 1937

Ernest Hemingway was late. Circumstances had kept him away from the war for the first seven months, despite his love of both Spain and the Republic.[1] He had just missed the action at Guadalajara and little had happened since then. Although already famous as a novelist, he was also a journalist and Spain was the biggest news story of the day. He was also, or so he thought, an expert on war, having been wounded while serving as an eighteen-year-old volunteer ambulance driver (after being turned down by the US Army because of his 'bad eye') on the Italian front in the First World War, and winning Italy's Silver Medal for Valour.[2] Finally, he was in love. His marriage to his second wife Pauline Pfeiffer continued, but Martha Gellhorn, a bold, outspoken and courageous war correspondent-in-the-making, was now his main interest. Gellhorn was an equally ardent supporter of Republican Spain. They both found assignments there, she with *Collier's* magazine and he with the NANA news agency, in order to live the excitement of the world's most important war, seek inspiration for their writing and be together.

'Me, I am going to Spain with the boys,' Gellhorn wrote to a friend as she left to board her ship to Europe. 'I don't know who the boys are, but I am going with them.'[3]

Each, in their own way, also became cheerleaders for the International Brigaders. In other respects, their relationship mirrored that of Gerda Taro and Robert Capa, who combined their undoubted talents as war photographers with an unabashed desire to help the Republican cause. Hemingway had visited Republican Spain before the war and,

THE INTERNATIONAL BRIGADES

even before travelling, had been heavily involved in fundraising for an American medical unit, contributing his own money.[4] On a later trip to the Teruel front, he was photographed showing a young militiaman how to use his rifle. He had interviewed Mussolini in the 1920s, spotted him as the 'biggest bluff in Europe', and become an anti-fascist after Mussolini's men killed socialist Giacomo Matteotti to silence him in 1924. He saw no need to be even-handed and impartial in a war against fascism.[5] Gellhorn was even clearer about not needing 'all that objectivity shit'.[6]

Like any journalist, Hemingway wanted scoops. Other, more literary, reasons explained his desire to be here. The thirty-seven-year-old writer had not published a novel for seven years[7] and some saw an attempt to breathe life back into a waning talent, perhaps by rediscovering the spark of truth that had brought him literary fame in the first place. It was a quest that had become more difficult as he increasingly and obsessively put himself at the centre of all that happened. 'I think it was the only time in his life when he was not the most important thing there was. He really cared about ... that war. I believe I never would've gotten hooked otherwise,' Gellhorn said later, after she had transformed herself from another unreliable witness (who had faked a famous eyewitness account of the lynching of a Mississippi sharecropper) to a serious war correspondent.[8] He was going through several crises – in his writing, popularity and marriage – and Josephine Herbst, a fellow writer and journalist, believed he was seeking answers in the heightened experiences of war. 'It wasn't only that he was giving up his wife for Martha Gellhorn. He had answered a definite call when he came to Spain. He wanted to be *the* war writer of his age, and he knew it and went toward it,' she wrote. 'War gave answers that could not be found in that paradise valley of Wyoming where he had fished or even in the waters of Key West when the tarpon struck. What was the deepest reality *there* was in an extreme form *here*, and to get it he had to be in it, and he knew it.'[9]

Hemingway's relationship with the International Brigaders was complex. He loved their apparent disdain for death, their cosmopolitan officers and the rugged company of soldiers – though this was usually over whiskey in his room at the Hotel Florida rather than in a front-line trench. In Madrid, the front was close to hand but rarely very active. A quick tram ride and short stroll took them to University City or

West Park. 'Ten blocks from the hotel, fifteen blocks, a good brisk walk in the rain, something to circulate your blood,' wrote Gellhorn. 'No matter how often you do it, it is surprising just to walk to war, easily from your own bedroom where you have been reading a detective story or a life of Byron.'[10]

Hemingway also appeared to envy the volunteers' commitment to action, as if they were somehow bigger, better men than he because they were risking their lives. Sometimes this brought out a particularly vicious streak in him. He deemed Taro, for example, a 'whore'. It was a viperous reaction probably due to the fact that she routinely got closer to the real war than he did.[11] Hemingway reserved some of his worse bile for Jim Lardner, a twenty-three-year-old Harvard-educated junior *Herald Tribune* correspondent who swapped reporting for service with the Lincoln Battalion.[12] Hemingway described him as 'a superior little snot', admittedly months before Lardner was killed in action.[13] A need to measure himself against the Brigaders was also apparent. Milton Wolff, the last Lincoln commander, was especially damning in his assessment. After he first met Hemingway in Madrid, the twenty-one-year-old wrote: 'Ernest is quite childish in many respects. He wants very much to be a martyr. So much for writers. I'd rather read their works than be with them.' Hemingway, he later added, was a 'tourist' and a 'prick'.[14]

On visits to the British Battalion Hemingway was told to 'piss off' by Fred Copeman and almost shot by sentries when he began sifting through the anti-tank battery's weapons one evening.[15] Lincoln Brigader Alvah Bessie later described him as a 'man who could be loyal, generous, warm and modest to those he considered his friends [and] could also be (and much too often was) cruel, petty, a braggart, a bully, an anti-Semite and a permanent adolescent.'[16] The writer's love of the Republic was, nonetheless, sincere and provoked a boyish enthusiasm for the International Brigades – though he was far more interested in the officers than the men on the ground.

Hemingway's first major novel after the civil war was *For Whom the Bell Tolls*, with fictional Lincoln Brigader Robert Jordan as its protagonist. Several real behind-the-lines guerrilla fighters remembered meeting Hemingway during his time in Spain,[17] though none recalled the writer ever taking part in their operations. This, however, is what Hemingway claimed to Edwin Rolfe, in a note he sent the poet and former Lincoln Battalion commissar shortly after he had finished his novel. 'O.K. Once

I had to go to a town will not name to check personally (knew many people there) on effect of something that happened from the air and it's [sic] true effect. Also on possibility of rising there. How much dough. And to carry dough. Was scare[d] pissless all the time, really scared, woof [sic] because there is an indignity in that kind of finish that scares long in advance,' he wrote. 'On return had to report that (1)-hate our guts. 2. It would be pouring dough down a rathole. 3-Didn't trust the bastard[s w]ho were handling what there was. O.K. Report was considered defeatism of the deepest dye. Only was true and save [sic] much lives and money.'[18]

It is impossible to verify his version of events – and Hemingway had a definite tendency towards hyperbole – but his commitment to the Republican cause was always clear. He had arrived in Spain with a contract from NANA to write articles, but he also made a documentary film, *The Spanish Earth* (July 1937), with the leftist Dutch film-maker Joris Ivens.[19] Gellhorn's friendship with Eleanor Roosevelt meant the film was shown in the White House, where the president was sufficiently moved to call Spain 'a vicarious sacrifice for all of us' (but not moved enough to engineer the end of non-intervention).[20]

On seeing a draft of the screenplay of *For Whom the Bell Tolls*, Hemingway was adamant the enemy be called 'fascists' throughout (although the Francoists termed themselves Nationalists). 'Unless you make this emphasis the people seeing the picture will have no idea what the [Spanish] people were really fighting for,' he said. He was deeply admiring of XI Brigade, which was full of 'true worthy Germans: Germans as we love them,' though he sometimes found them overly serious. 'They nearly all had military training or fought in the [world] war. They were all anti-Nazis. Most of them were Communists and they marched like the Reichswehr. They also sang songs that would break your heart,' he wrote.[21] Their austere version of communism turned him off, but the worldly, sophisticated and womanising Hans Kahle he found perfect company, observing: 'Hans is a book to himself. We have too much together for me ever to risk losing any of it by trying to write about it.'[22] That 'too much together' suggests that, when in Madrid, Hans was a regular at Hemingway's late-night, whiskey-fuelled gatherings at the Hotel Florida – where the writer displayed what Josie Herbst called his 'splurging magnificence', and his room was often filled with International Brigade officers playing poker, talking politics,

literature and war.[23] Kahle could also be found at the Hotel Gran Vía –
where Barea discovered him intensely engaged with a film critic – or at
the Russian delegation's home in the Gaylord Hotel.[24] Gustav Regler
was amongst those who were charmed by the distinctly bourgeois tastes
of the otherwise orthodox communist Kahle. 'He wore silk shirts and
during lulls in the fighting he went to Madrid where he slept in the
Empire bed of a film star who had fled, swam in her pool and slowly
drank her cellar dry,' he recorded. 'During critical periods he scorned
all female consolations, but as soon as things eased up he was to be seen
again in the Gaylord or at the theatre.'[25]

The Florida was famous for what Virginia Cowles called its 'diverse
assembly of foreigners … idealists and mercenaries; scoundrels and
martyrs; adventurers and *embusqués*; fanatics, traitors and plain down-
and-outs.'[26] At the Gaylord one was more likely to run into Koltsov,
International Brigade officers, a Russian guerrilla warfare advisor or a
visiting literary luminary from Britain or France deemed to have the
correct political credentials. It was also where goodbye parties were
given for the departing 'Mexicans' including, famously, a boisterous
one for an engineering officer called Gorkin that was attended by
Regler. This ended up with tearful speeches from his fellow officers and
toasts in champagne. Koltsov later confided that everybody expected
Gorkin to fall victim to Stalin's purges on his return to Russia. 'We all
knew. That is why we gave him the party … The French give a man
rum before leading him out to the guillotine. In these days we give him
champagne.'[27] Koltsov told British journalist Claud Cockburn that he
himself feared becoming a victim. 'Everyone gets his turn – why not
me?' he said, employing his gift for mordant, dark humour. 'Guilty
of telling bad jokes in the people's tribunal!' As an observation, it was
unfortunately prescient.[28]

Of all the international units, Hemingway's greatest love was for XII
Brigade, whose victory at Guadalajara he praised lavishly after visiting
the battlefield late in March, after the main fighting had finished. He
called it 'the first battle in this war fought on a World War scale', and
claimed that 'Brihuega will take its place in military history with the
other decisive battles of the world.'[29] Hemingway identified so absolutely
with the Brigaders that he talked of deaths amongst their ranks in the
first person plural. 'I can truly say for all those I knew as well as one

man can know another, that the period of fighting when we thought the Republic could win the Spanish civil war was the happiest period of our lives,' he wrote. 'We were truly happy then for when people died it seemed as though their death was justified and important.' And he regarded Lukács, Regler and brigade doctor Werner Heilbrun as part of a broader mix of 'men of all political beliefs'.[30]

Hemingway's friendship with them had started at Guadalajara, when he drove back with Regler and Heilbrun, and continued to the extent that one of his goodbye parties (he made four visits of between two and six months to Spain during the civil war[31]) was held at Heilbrun's medical headquarters, with Hemingway eventually passing out drunk on his operating table.[32] The doctor was a particular favourite and Hemingway preferred his 'slanting smile, the cap cocked on the side, the slow, comic Berlin Jewish drawl' to the mostly ardent German communists who he found 'a little serious to spend much time with'.[33] With Lukács and Regler he was, of course, in the company of other writers and the former was 'beside himself with pleasure' whenever he saw Hemingway, even though Eisner had to interpret. 'Lukács would take him by the elbow, sit him down, serve him the tastiest bits of the meal and pour his drink. In a word, he acted like a nanny. Hemingway, meanwhile, looked at him with satisfaction and insistent curiosity.'[34]

Though Hemingway was prone to exaggeration, he did not consciously fabricate things quite as much as photographers Capa and Taro, who, when they visited XIII Brigade, were determined to show the world the 'forgotten' brigade. Thirteenth Brigade had moved to Peñarroya in Córdoba at the beginning of April with its two international battalions (Chapaev and Henri Vuillemin) after six weeks of hardship, but relative quiet, in the mountainous Alpujarras. There it enjoyed considerable success. With the help of an international section of sixteen T-26 tanks,[35] they took a series of small villages – Valsequillo, La Granjuela and Los Blázquez – near the border between Andalusia and Extremadura, capturing some 900 prisoners. They then established a line in the rugged terrain of the Sierra Noria, preventing any further Francoist advances.[36] They also successfully incorporated two completely Spanish battalions – the Juan Marco, made up of railway workers who came equipped with brand new Russian weapons – and the Otumba.[37] Both of the new battalions functioned well, but after months of putting up with daily bombardments and the local fauna – which one volunteer listed as 'snakes, lizards, scorpions, spiders, beetles, wasps, flies, mosquitos, lice, gnats and more' – the international volunteers were desperate for a rest.[38]

Thirteenth Brigade's impressive successes, however, took place too far away from Madrid to catch the eye of the world's media.[39] 'News about the heroic fights of the XI and other brigades around Madrid filled us with pride, but also envy. Who knew anything about the XIII Brigade? Journalists from all over the world went to Madrid – Egon Erwin Kisch, Willi Bredel, Hans Marchwitza, Bodo Uhse and many more. Erich Weinert wrote battle poems and Ernst Busch his songs. But what about us?' German volunteer Rudolf Engels asked.[40] His list included many of the best-known German-language writers amongst the International Brigades' cheerleaders and propagandists. Kisch did eventually visit and praised the brigade for 'defending Spanish liberty in the most south-eastern corner of Europe, far from Madrid, far from the rest of the world'.[41] In the end, however, it was Capa and Taro's 're-enactments' that rescued the XIII Brigade from anonymity.

In July 1937, the photographers appeared at Peñarroya with their new Eyemo movie camera and fulfilled instructions to provide the 'fakery in pursuit of the truth' – which *Time* owner Henry Luce insisted was part of the mix of his successful *March of Time* newsreels – by re-enacting the battle at La Granjuela,[42] as 'a real attack wouldn't have seemed as authentic as this', Capa told the German writer Alfred Kantorowicz.[43] The pair had originally come across XIII Brigade after arriving too late to see the fall of Málaga. Jan Kurzke's girlfriend, Kate Mangan, who shared a car with the couple while translating for a British journalist, remarked on the way they 'talked about Spain and the beautiful sunshine quite as if they were on holiday ... but they did not neglect their work. They were always ready to leap from the car to take significantly grim pictures and were merely personally detached from their subjects.'[44] Taro's mere arrival at XIII Brigade's Castell de Ferro headquarters provoked huge excitement amongst the volunteers there. Taro was 'a ripe beauty', wrote Mangan, 'with a tanned face and bright orange hair cropped like a boy's ... The natural tint of her hair was copper, she had the warm brown eyes that go with it, but the sun had bleached it orange and the effect was startling ... [She] wore a little, round, Swiss cap on the back of the astonishing hair. She had small feet and was a model of Parisian sportif chic.'[45]

If Hemingway enjoyed the company of Brigaders, the feeling was sometimes – but not always – mutual. He 'had the calming effect of a buffalo straying shaggily over the tundra, knowing its water-holes and its pastures', wrote Regler, who became one of Hemingway's great Brigader friends. 'For him we had the scent of death, like the bullfighters, and because of this he was invigorated by our company.'[46] Regler could see, too, his 'deep' affection for both Kahle and Lukács. He 'would have been hard put to say which he loved more, the towering German or the thick-set Hungarian, Lukács, who mingled war and peace, self-sacrifice and pleasure, in quite other ways'.

The unbridled, male-dominated world of war that Hemingway found so appealing could, however, present additional risks for women. Martha Gellhorn recalled one late-night journey to Madrid in the back of Italian politician and brigade commander Randolfo Pacciardi's car, during which the Garibaldi leader 'kept trying to get me to put my hand on his privates which filled me with terror and horror'. Pacciardi treated it as a tremendous joke. 'He laughed merrily at me and all my scruples. So brave about rifle and machine gun fire, so frightened of sex!'[47] Gellhorn, outwardly at least, was dismissive of the episode, quipping that 'determined Italians are something serious to beat off in no-man's-land in the middle of the night'. Pacciardi's behaviour did not seem to dim her view of the volunteers as a whole. 'Shock troops, now: you can tell a brigade is fine when they move from front to front, in trucks, fast, to wherever the danger is,' she wrote in *Collier's* after meeting Robert Merriman and the Lincoln volunteers. 'I thought: I'm proud as a goat that the Americans are known in Spain as good men and fine soldiers. That's all there is to it: I'm proud.'[48]

Marion Merriman's experience was more traumatic. Like some other trusted partners of prominent Brigaders, she took part in the vetting of suspicious-looking characters. On one mission, she was sent south to Murcia to look over two British women who were 'creating trouble amongst the American volunteers'.[49] She and 'two pleasant Slav officers' set off from Albacete one morning. 'As we drove through the barren lands, I caught up on my diary, writing entries as we motored along', she wrote:

> We reached Murcia about noon, went on to Orihuela for lunch
> then went for a swim, my first in the Mediterranean. Later I jotted

in my diary: 'A sandy beach, warm caressing water. Hold life, hold
life so close.'

We had dinner the two officers and I, on a terrace overlooking a
sleepy village caught on the arm of a cove. We marvelled at the rosy
grey of the sea dotted with slow-moving fishing boats. And, during
dinner, I noted that the atmosphere, the swim, the moonlight,
the pure beauty of where we were, seemed to give one of my
companions romantic ideas. In woman-less war, I'd seen the look
before. I dismissed it.

That evening we checked into the hospital at Socorro Rojo.
Weary from the long, if enjoyable, day. I fell quickly to sleep. But,
suddenly and sharply, I was wide awake. The man whose 'look' I'd
noted at dinner was holding me down, one hand clamped over my
mouth. I fought him, clawing, kicking. I couldn't scream. He raped
me. I kicked him away. He fled the room.

Terrified and sobbing, Marion Merriman dragged herself to the
bathroom and, since there was no hot water, filled a tub with icy water.
She felt filthy, and washed herself 'for hours', but never felt clean. She
scrubbed, shivered and wept in the dark.

The next morning I didn't know what to do. What could I do?
Should I try to find a way back to Albacete? Should I somehow get
hold of Bob? Should I try to reach Ed Bender? What should I do?
I had to calm myself. This is war, I told myself. Men are dying and
maimed. This is my burden. As horrible as the rape was, the worst
that could happen would be a pregnancy. If that happened, I steeled
myself, I would go to the hospital's doctors or to Paris and have an
abortion.

But should I tell Bob? I asked myself, over and over. I searched
and searched for the answer and finally concluded: I must not hurt
Bob with this. If I tell him, I reasoned, Bob might kill the man. Or
one of the other Americans would, for sure. There would be great
trouble. No this must be my secret burden. I cannot tell anyone –
ever. What has been done cannot be undone.

I went down to the commissary where the two officers were
eating breakfast. One was, as always, cheerful and friendly. He
seemed confused when I didn't sit with them. The rapist was brazen,

arrogant. We continued the mission. I ignored the rapist, but I could not get the rape off my mind. But I went on with my work.[50]

It became common knowledge, amongst wives, girlfriends and women journalists, that they were not welcome at the International Brigades base in Albacete, a view promulgated by Brigades chief André Marty, who saw women as a permanent threat.[51] Romances or 'fraternisation' between volunteers were inevitable, however, no matter how hard Marty campaigned to keep men and women apart. This failed, most obviously, in the medical services. Soldiers routinely fell in love with their female nurses, and sometimes vice versa. More complex situations arose when the medical staff fell for one another. Doctors Theodor Balk and Maya Guimpel, for example, conducted an affair while working alongside her husband Janik. All three knew about this and Balk talks of holding hands in the back seat of the car that (his close friend) Janik was driving, and of his jealousy when the married couple went off to bed in a house they all shared in El Escorial. 'Yes, we were rivals, Janik and me. But stronger than our rivalry was that feeling of togetherness,' he wrote later. This 'was something else ... animated by the same idea of freedom, without the egoism of being number one or two, without the sting of ambition, without the purse of vanities, a great brotherhood, a militant solidarity. Yes, we were rivals. But that did not count ... in Spain.'[52]

If men found it difficult to leave the International Brigades, women found it difficult to join them. Marty had purged many women from the medical services in December 1936, proclaiming that a more thorough selection was required. 'Among them will be the many women of central or southern Europe, who have infiltrated Spain with a pseudo-diploma of nurse or others ... you will stop this influx of political or other parasites, who have fallen on Spain like locusts,' he stated.[53] In fact, most of the twenty-three hospitals with 6,000 beds now being run by the Brigades were not in Albacete. They, and the 1,500 personnel – many of them women doctors and nurses – were spread across the country, with the beach town of Benicàssim and the city of Murcia two of the main nuclei.

Evelyn Hutchins, a tough former burlesque dancer from New York, was one of the few women who broke into one of the roles usually reserved for men in the International Brigades when she became a truck and ambulance driver for the medical service. She had been active in organising aid for Spain from the US, and sent her brother and husband to the Brigades before her. 'Some fellows thought it was very funny that I should be there driving. I am little but I never made any attempt to swagger or act mannish. I acted just the way I always acted,' she explained later. 'But the important thing was that the fellows who understood why I wanted to be there, why I had taken the job of driving which was the only possibility of getting as close as I could to the actual fighting – they didn't think a girl should want to fight and have a machine gun instead of driving a car. These fellows were the fellows who took the thing seriously.'[54]

Hutchins was a rare exception. Otherwise, the pecking order for acceptable women began with a small number of trusted party workers, often with Comintern pedigree, followed by a smattering of doctors and, then, downwards through the nurses, propagandists, friendly journalists and hangers-on. The latter categories often found themselves under suspicion of spying, as if each of them was a potential Mata Hari. Even in Murcia, where her boyfriend Kurzke was recovering, Kate Mangan found herself being interrogated by the British communist journalist Claud Cockburn, for exactly that reason:

> For a few minutes Claud persevered in trying to elicit from me what I was doing in Spain, what I was doing in Valencia and, finally, what I was doing in Murcia, but I gave him no satisfaction. Eventually I lost patience: 'In a civil war lots of strange types come to the surface; people you would never come across in normal circumstances; I'm one of them.'
> Claud's Party Line had not entirely obliterated his sense of humour and he was forced to laugh.
> 'Do you think I'm a spy?' I asked,
> 'All women are potential spies,' he said.[55]

The International Brigades were not the only people obsessed with spies. The term 'fifth columnists' had been coined to describe those who the Francoist General Emilio Mola had claimed were ready to rise against the Republic in Madrid if the four columns of troops that approached the city late in 1936 had conquered it. Indeed, enemies, infiltrators and saboteurs were suspected to be lurking everywhere. Nowhere was this more so than in Barcelona.

32

Damage in Catalonia: Barcelona,
late April 1937

Eric Arthur Blair had spent three months fighting boredom, cold, lice and hunger with a militia unit on the mostly dormant Aragonese front. The British writer known as George Orwell was fed up and determined to join the by now famous International Brigades in order to do some real fighting. He had made a first attempt at this before leaving for Spain the previous year, but an interview with Harry Pollitt, head of the Communist Party of Great Britain, had ended badly. Pollitt had 'evidently decided that I was politically unreliable [and] refused to help me'.[1]

Orwell turned, instead, to the Independent Labour Party (ILP), which backed the anti-Stalinist POUM, and which he would join after returning from Spain, declaring it to be the only party 'which aims at anything I should regard as Socialism'.[2] As a result, he had spent a period of frustrating inaction with an international POUM section. His opportunity to finally join the International Brigades appeared to have come when, at the end of April 1937, he was sent to Barcelona on two weeks' leave.[3] A communist friend in the city offered to arrange the transfer, urging him to bring other British fighters from his POUM militia unit with him. But Orwell delayed. He wanted to enjoy his time with his wife, Eileen, whom he had married the previous year, and who was staying at the Hotel Continental at the top end of the Ramblas. After almost three months in the trenches, the gangly writer also needed to recover his health. American novelist John Dos Passos ran into him at the hotel and found Orwell refreshingly honest, though 'his face had

a sick drawn look' and he seemed 'inexpressibly weary'.[4] The decision
to wait for his transfer to the International Brigades ironically nearly
cost him his life.

When he had first reached Barcelona three months earlier, Orwell
had been delighted to see the streets full of boiler-suited revolutionaries,
although he had been surprised to find an army divided up between
different parties and trades unions. 'Aren't we all socialists?' the author of
Down and Out in Paris and London had asked naively.[5] The Barcelona he
encountered when he returned from the front in his dirty, ragged clothes
in April 1937 was very different. The counter-revolution had ebbed, war
seemed far off and suspicion abounded. He described his disillusionment
in *Homage to Catalonia*, a book published eleven months later, that has
coloured many people's view of the Spanish Civil War.[6]

'The tide had rolled back,' he wrote:

> Once again it was an ordinary city, a little pinched and chipped
> by war, but with no outward sign of working-class predominance.
> The change in the aspect of the crowds was startling. The militia
> uniform and the blue overalls had almost disappeared; everyone
> seemed to be wearing the smart summer suits in which Spanish
> tailors specialise. Fat prosperous men, elegant women, and sleek
> cars were everywhere …
>
> … it dismayed me a little, and brought it home to me that some
> queer things had been happening in the last three months. During
> the next few days I discovered by innumerable signs that my first
> impression had not been wrong. A deep change had come over the
> town. There were two facts that were the keynote of all else. One
> was that the people – the civil population – had lost much of their
> interest in the war; the other was that the normal division of society
> into rich and poor, upper class and lower class, was reasserting itself
> … Everyone who had been in Madrid said that it was completely
> different there. In Madrid the common danger forced people of
> almost all kinds into some sense of comradeship. A fat man eating
> quails while children are begging for bread is a disgusting sight, but
> you are less likely to see it when you are within sound of the guns.[7]

Swollen by refugees, the population of Barcelona, already one of the
mostly densely packed cities in Europe, had increased by 40 per cent.

That had provoked bread riots,[8] but the most vicious battles were political. Orwell was only just beginning to realise that his POUM companions were in the thick of that. 'Politically conscious people were far more aware of the internecine struggle between Anarchist and Communist than of the fight against Franco,' he wrote in *Homage to Catalonia*.[9]

Conflict between the communist-backed Republican government and the anarchists (with their POUM allies) had been building almost since the first day of the war. The government clearly needed much fuller control of its resources and territory if it was to counter Franco. Crucial to this was to have a unified, centrally commanded and obedient Republican army. That meant forcing the powerful anarchists and others who were busy governing themselves and running their own militias in Barcelona, parts of Catalonia and much of Aragon, to bend to state discipline. The anarchists had already shown signs of rebellion. At Guadalajara, for example, the Teruel Battalion had demanded to be allowed to go to Valencia to debate its orders with the government. Ludwig Renn had ordered the International Brigades' military police to fire on the anarchist battalion's trucks if the threat was carried out. Eventually, they had to be disarmed. Since then, 800 anarchists had abandoned the front near the Aragonese town of Gelsa,[10] taking badly needed rifles and machine guns with them. It was estimated, indeed, that anarchists and others held 60,000 rifles in Barcelona alone, twice as many as on the Aragon front. Even Durruti, the anarchist martyr, had been infuriated by this.[11]

Orwell's POUM colleagues agreed with many anarchists that revolution and fighting fascism were inseparable.[12] Orwell did not join the POUM party, not least because he believed that winning the war took priority over implementing a revolution.[13] That was one reason why he wanted to join the International Brigades (and at least eight more of those on leave with him planned to do the same). Perhaps more importantly, Orwell's companions were also virulently anti-Stalinist: in December their leader Andreu Nin had been sacked from the Catalan government because he was jeopardising the support of the Republic's only reliable arms supplier, the Soviet Union.

On the streets of Barcelona these political differences were increasingly visible, as tension grew between the powerful socialist trades unions – allied with the government and the communists – and those of the anarchists.[14] Tit-for-tat killings were taking place, here and elsewhere.[15]

Orwell feared that violence would erupt on May Day, when the two sides celebrated the great workers' holiday. 'To be marching up the street behind red flags inscribed with elevating slogans, and then to be bumped off from an upper window by some total stranger with a sub-machine-gun – that is not my idea of a useful way to die,' he said.[16] The marches were eventually banned, and 1 May was conveniently declared to be a working day in order to 'increase war production'.[17] Orwell was relieved, but aware of the irony. 'Barcelona, the so-called revolutionary city, was probably the only city in non-Fascist Europe that had no celebrations that day.'[18]

Two days later Orwell was walking up the Ramblas when he heard rifle shots. Armed youths with red and black anarchist scarves around their throats were firing at what appeared to be a church tower down a side street. 'I thought instantly: "It's started!" But I thought it without any very great feeling of surprise – for days past everyone had been expecting "it" to start at any moment.'[19] An anarchist phone operator was reported to have interrupted a call made by the Republic's president, Manuel Azaña, who was in Barcelona.[20] The government's Assault Guard police had reacted by attempting to take control of the main telephone exchange building on the central Plaza de Cataluña, which was run by the anarchists. Shots were fired and events spiralled from there.

Orwell ran to the Hotel Falcón on the Ramblas, where foreign POUM fighters and sympathisers had gathered since the first days of the war. There he was handed a rifle and a few clips of ammunition. Armed men kept watch at the windows. Outside, an anarchist car bristled with weapons and 'a beautiful dark-haired girl of about eighteen' nursed 'a sub-machine-gun across her knees'.[21] Soon cobbles were being ripped up and barricades built. Men, women and children were hauling sandbags across the Ramblas. Orwell recalled that a German POUM woman fighter 'in a pair of militiaman's trousers whose knee-buttons just reached her ankles', looked on with a smile. Elsewhere in the city up to 7,000 anarchists and POUM members, including groups of German and Italians, were now manning the barricades.[22]

Orwell was sent further up the street to the roof of the Poliorama theatre, in order to defend the POUM headquarters on the opposite side of the boulevard. By now he had simplified the conflict in his mind. It was police – that is, the Assault Guards – against the poor.

'When I see an actual flesh-and-blood worker in conflict with his natural enemy, the policeman, I do not have to ask myself which side I am on,' he reasoned.[23] He spent three nights on the Poliorama's roof. The only shot he took was to try to explode a hand grenade that had rolled loose onto a pavement. His group reached an agreement with the Assault Guards on the roof of the building opposite them, promising not to be the first to shoot. Beer, and even a rifle, were swapped. 'We don't want to shoot you. We're only workers, the same as you are,' one of the Assault Guards shouted. 'He made the anti-Fascist salute, which I returned. I shouted across: "Have you got any more beer left?" "No, it's all gone." '[24]

While Orwell had hurried to the Hotel Falcón, German Friedrich 'Fritz' Fränken was one of half-a-dozen Brigaders who gathered at the grand Hotel Colón, headquarters of the Catalan communist party, PSUC. Barcelona was not an important base for the International Brigades, but they had offices in the city and volunteers were always passing through. Fränken and the others spent the first night of the uprising there, but when a temporary ceasefire was observed the following day and the streets filled up again, they judged it safe enough to cross the corner of the square to the Hotel Victoria for lunch. The hotel, however, was reserving its food for guests and they turned back.

Their outing in a part of the city where almost every street corner was occupied by a barricade manned by riflemen (and, on the anarchist side, women) or machine-gunners with an enemy on the opposite corner, was at best naive. Every significant building belonging to a party, union, militia group or Catalan government department was now barricaded. Many of these lay in the triangle between the Plaza de Cataluña, the Plaza de la República (now Sant Jaume) and the broad Via Laietana (running parallel to the Ramblas, and temporarily renamed after Durruti) and were within shooting distance of one another. Fränken, in other words, had ventured into the most violent part of town.[25]

As Fränken returned with fellow German Brigader Max Better, who was on leave, shouts came from behind a barricade: '¡Manos arriba!' ('Hands up!'). The two unarmed Germans were led into the anarchist CNT trades union building at gunpoint. Their clothes and hands were scraped and sniffed for traces of gunpowder. According to Fränken, they passed the test but were still accused of having manned a machine

gun that had been firing at the CNT building. A chaotic 'hearing' –
apparently conducted in Catalan, which they did not understand – at
first seemed to end with orders for them to be shot. 'It was enough
[for the anarchists] that we were International Brigaders,' assumed
Fränken.[26] However, after Fränken delivered an impassioned appeal,
they were kept in custody. 'We are communists and volunteers of
the International Brigades who consider all anti-fascists our fighting
partners,' he declared. 'The winner of a fratricidal struggle among anti-
fascists can only be Franco and fascism. If you kill us here, then two anti-
fascists – two opponents of Franco – who are your fellow combatants,
will fall.'[27]

The anarchists eventually handed the two men over to police officers
of some sort (Fränken does not seem sure who they were), who took
them away and promised to release them quickly. When that did not
happen, Fränken and Better jumped out of a bathroom window and
then went to a nearby bar to calm their nerves with some wine. By
now, the trouble in the streets was effectively over – though they were
chastised by Karl Mewis, their superior in the German communist party
(KPD), for jumping out of the window. Mewis helped run the PSUC's
foreigners department and was in charge of the KPD's Barcelona office.[28]
The police, he explained, were meant to be on their side. It was the kind
of comical, if potentially lethal, episode that led many observers to view
the May events as a mere repetition of Barcelona's regular outbursts of
political violence. An Italian journalist quipped that the city's paving
stones should be numbered, since this would 'save such a lot of trouble
in building and demolishing barricades'.[29]

Meanwhile, George Orwell managed to creep up the Ramblas on
occasions to visit his wife at the Continental. On one occasion he
encountered two International Brigaders who were recovering from
wounds. 'If they had been good party-men they would, I suppose,
have urged me to change sides, or even have pinioned me and taken
away the bombs of which my pockets were full,' he wrote. 'Instead they
merely commiserated with me for having to spend my leave in doing
guard-duty on a roof. The general attitude was: "This is only a dust-up
between the Anarchists and the police – it doesn't mean anything." In
spite of the extent of the fighting and the number of casualties I believe
this was nearer the truth than the official version which represented the
affair as a planned rising.'[30]

Orwell admitted that his was a partisan account and he was wrong in at least one important aspect. While POUM leaders such as Andreu Nin and Julián Gorkin loudly applauded the rebellious anarchist factions,[31] the anarchists' own leaders – four of whom were in the government – were desperately trying to calm their people down. 'Even if I had a rifle or a bomb in my hand, I would not know against whom to fire, because all those fighting are my brothers,' anarchist justice minister Juan García Oliver proclaimed when he arrived in the city from the temporary Spanish capital in Valencia.[32] He went on to claim, rather bizarrely, that he also felt obliged to kiss the corpses of dead policemen, since they were his allies; some anarchists reportedly shot up their own radio sets when they heard that.[33] García Oliver and his fellow ministers eventually imposed themselves on the 'purist' rebels who had formed sub-groups with names such as 'the Friends of Durruti' (with 5,000 members)[34] or 'the [Don] Quixotes of the Ideal'. The latter group proclaimed that its Dulcinea (Don Quixote's imaginary 'lady') was 'libertarian revolution'.[35] The contrast in the behaviour of the anarchist movement leaders and the POUM leaders was remarkable, since the latter effectively poured fuel on the fire.[36] Both they and their militia fighters – up to 10 per cent of whom were foreign – would eventually pay for that.

Five days after the violence erupted, the government in Valencia flooded the city with smart, well-armed Assault Guards. Their arrival, agreed to by the anarchist ministers, brought the whole affair to an end.[37] The government also took charge of the army of Catalonia, which had previously answered to the Catalan government, the Generalitat.[38] At least 218 people,[39] however, had been killed in the clashes in Barcelona alone, and it was clear that the impact would be lasting. Orwell returned to the Hotel Continental, but still found himself reaching for his pistol every time someone banged on the bedroom door.

> On the Saturday morning there was an uproar of shots outside and everyone cried out: 'It's starting again!' I ran into the street to find that it was only some Valencian Assault Guards shooting a mad dog. No one who was in Barcelona then, or for months later, will forget the horrible atmosphere produced by fear, suspicion, hatred, censored newspapers, crammed jails, enormous food queues and prowling gangs of armed men.[40]

Orwell was especially upset by a cartoon circulating that showed a POUM figure slipping off a hammer and sickle mask to reveal 'a hideous, maniacal face' painted with a swastika. 'Evidently the official version of the Barcelona fighting was already fixed upon: it was to be represented as a "fifth column" Fascist rising engineered solely by the POUM,' Orwell reported.[41]

When at the Hotel Continental he was approached again by the British friend with whom he had originally discussed joining the Brigades, he refused:

> 'Your papers are saying I'm a Fascist,' I said. 'Surely I should be politically suspect, coming from the POUM.'
>
> 'Oh, that doesn't matter. After all, you were only acting under orders.'
>
> I had to tell him that after this affair I could not join any Communist-controlled unit ... He was very decent about it. But from now on the whole atmosphere was changed. You could not, as before, 'agree to differ' and have drinks with a man who was supposedly your political opponent.[42]

Orwell was aware, though, that only fate had kept him on the POUM side of this confrontation. He had come tantalisingly close to becoming an International Brigader, a path followed by at least forty-four other foreign POUM volunteers.[43] That would have placed him – at least metaphorically – on the opposite rooftop during the stand-off in Las Ramblas. 'It is hard to say now what difference this would have made,' he wrote. 'Quite possibly I should have been sent to Albacete before the Barcelona fighting started.'[44]

Three days later, with his leave over, Orwell returned to the Aragon front. His hatred of the real enemy remained undimmed. He knew this was a fight against fascism, even as he realised that those shooting at him were often 'merely wretched conscripts'.[45] As dawn broke over the trenches on 20 May, however, he was careless taking cover and was hit through the neck by a sniper's bullet. Had the 6 foot 2 writer been a bit shorter, it might have gone through his head. Had he been the height of the Spanish militiamen who dug these trenches, it would have missed altogether. He later recalled 'no pain, only a violent shock, such as you get from an electric terminal; with it a sense of utter weakness, a feeling

of being stricken and shrivelled up to nothing'.[46] Convinced that he
was dying, he felt – just like the wounded Bernard Knox at Boadilla –
a 'violent resentment at having to leave this world which, when all is
said and done, suits me so well'. It was the volunteer's lament at not
just offering one's life for the cause, but actually having to give it up.
Remarkably, Orwell survived. Sent back to hospital in Barcelona, he
made plans to leave Spain as soon as possible. 'I had an overwhelming
desire to get away from it all,' he wrote. 'Away from the horrible
atmosphere of political suspicion and hatred, from streets thronged by
armed men, from air-raids, trenches, machine-guns, screaming trams,
milkless tea, oil cookery, and shortage of cigarettes.'

By now, however, Orwell himself was being spied on. Amongst those
tracking him were several International Brigaders working for Stalin's
sinister secret service, the Narodnyi Komissariat Vnutrennikh Del
(NKVD, or People's Commissariat of Internal Affairs), whose bosses
in Spain were Alexander Orlov and Naum Eitingon.[47] Both the
NKVD and the Soviet Union's GRU military intelligence (which was
running guerrilla training camps for Republican soldiers, including
many Brigaders) viewed the International Brigades as a rich, long-
term recruiting ground. Within their diverse ranks, after all, was the
world's largest international concentration of convinced – and often
multilingual – communists, skilled in fighting and prepared to sacrifice
their lives for the cause. It is not surprising that a chosen few were also
happy to spy, lie or assassinate for exactly the same ideal.

Recruitment would become systematic and formally known as the
'New Enrolment' initiative.[48] It made use of the fact that the Brigades'
personnel department was led by Comintern veterans and often staffed
by people already working for the NKVD, the GRU, the Republic's SIM
military intelligence service (founded later) or the German Communist
Party's internal security apparatus. Many would be sent to the guerrilla
warfare schools that the GRU helped run in Barcelona, Benimàmet
and the Sierra de La Mujer Muerta.[49] One such recruit was the white
Russian émigré Kirill Khenkin who, when he first arrived in Spain, was
called to see Alexander Orlov at his seventh-floor room in the Hotel
Metropol in Valencia. Young, tanned, blond men sat in cabriolet cars
outside – suggesting that some of the twenty-nine German Brigaders
recruited by the NKVD were in Orlov's personal security detail – and a

group of armed Serbians sat in the lobby. A white-jacketed waiter served breakfast, while Orlov smoked Lucky Strikes, carried a James Bond-style Walther-PPK 7.65mm and smelled strongly of eau de cologne. Khenkin was sent to enrol in the Brigades and later joined a guerrilla detachment, together with a Spaniard called Ramón Mercader. The latter would become famous as Trotsky's assassin, killing him with a blow from an ice pick in an operation organised by Eitingon in Mexico City in August 1940.

One of the NKVD's first International Brigade recruits was, like the old Etonian Orwell, a British public school-educated leftist, David Crook. Also like Orwell, whose *The Road to Wigan Pier* had been published while the writer was in Spain, Crook, a Jewish Londoner, had been shocked by his contact with poverty – in this case, while studying at Columbia University in New York, in the city's Bowery flophouses and on trips to visit striking Kentucky coalminers. He had been one of the few machine-gunners to escape when the British Battalion was forced to retreat at Jarama – thanks, in part, to his unlikely partnership with tough Manchester Irish merchant seaman Sam Wild. It was Wild who dragged himself back to the lines, and sent a stretcher to Crook, after they had lain wounded together in no-man's-land.

Recruiting Crook had been a simple business. 'Would you like to do some special work for the International Movement?' the French writer Georges Soria asked him. 'For the movement, of course, I'll do anything I'm asked,' Crook replied.[50] After a series of interviews with the Russians, Crook was ordered to return to the British Battalion and await instructions. These came shortly before the May events in Barcelona, when he was discharged from the Brigades on fictitious 'health grounds'. Arriving in the city at the same time as Orwell, he was briefed in 'a dimly lit room at a hotel on the fashionable Paseo de Gracia, with half-a-dozen shadowy figures discussing in three languages (Russian, Spanish and English) what I was to do'.

Crook posed as a disgruntled veteran-turned-journalist who thought the government and communists were selling out the revolution. This he did not find strenuous, since the anarchists in Barcelona who thought the same way – and constantly invited him to drinks – proved as friendly and generous as they had always been in Madrid. Crook even became a member of the Print and Graphic Arts section of the anarchist CNT union. He also could not resist occasional visits to the

International Brigades 'club' in the city, where he would bump into Sam Wild and others while pretending not to support their politics.[51]

Crook's hunting grounds were the Hotel Falcón – where he stole documents – and the Hotel Continental – where he befriended POUM-supporting journalists and others. Reports were written and passed over, in cafeterias or hotel bathrooms in the folds of newspapers, to his handler, an Irishman known as Sean O'Brien. One report on Eileen Blair, which made its way into the International Brigades' own security files, claimed that she was 'in an intimate relationship with [Georges] Kopp [Orwell's 'stout' Belgian commander]'.[52]

The British in the ILP office at the Hotel Falcón proved to be a simple target since they 'took easily to the long lunch hour of the Spaniards and perhaps even to the siesta habit'.[53] They often did not return until after 5 p.m., so Crook spent the extended lunch breaks stealing files and address books and taking them to the NKVD safe house run by a middle-aged German couple on Muntaner street. These were copied and replaced before the British returned from their siesta. A New Zealander known as Amy and a German called Alfonso were amongst the small group of NKVD operatives based at the two neighbouring apartments that made up the safe house. Other visitors, known only as 'ghosts', were kept out of sight.[54] They almost certainly included the young Polish International Brigades captain Leon Narwicz, another POUM infiltrator, and German Lothar Marx (or 'Joan'), whose photographs were used to identify the group's leaders. German Brigader Werner Schwarze, meanwhile, had joined its foreign militia, reporting back on the rival group of international volunteers. Narwicz would later be assassinated in Barcelona, in revenge for the killing of POUM leaders.[55]

When police started searching rooms in the Hotel Continental, David Crook was still undercover and joined those passing documents from balcony to balcony so that the papers could not be found. He was then 'arrested' and placed in a cell for nine days with some of Orwell's friends, including Kopp, in order to spy on them. He concluded that he could find no evidence of a major plot. He did not feel bad about it, however, since 'in the eyes of Stalin's followers (including myself) … the *poumists* were Trotskytes [sic]; and by opposing "war first, revolution later" and the Popular Front, the POUM was aiding fascism'.[56]

One of Crook's surveillance targets was Kurt Landau, the Austrian who acted as informal head of the fractious group of foreign anti-Stalinist communists whose offices were mostly at the Hotel Falcón, but who often slept at the Hotel Continental. Landau was rumoured to be living in a villa on the edge of town. This was only confirmed after Crook, posing as one half of a courting couple with a striking blonde NKVD agent known as 'Dolores', wandered past his house and confirmed that the man who sat out in the garden reading every day was, indeed, Landau. The latter was soon snatched by an NKVD squad. He never reappeared. 'Sean told me later he had been kidnapped, put in a wooden crate and loaded on to one of the Soviet ships bringing food or arms to the Republic. I was in those days in a state of blissful ignorance of Stalinism. How else could I have done the things I did in my twenties?' he recalled later.[57]

In fact, Landau and an unknown number of other victims may have ended up in an incinerator in a secret, private jail (or *checa*) run by the NKVD somewhere in the city. The oven was apparently constructed by Stanislav Alekseevish Vaupshasov, an experienced killer who took part in a series of NKVD assassinations in Spain and eventually became one of the Soviet Union's most highly decorated intelligence agents.[58] Other victims included Mark Rein, an itinerant socialist journalist who was well known across Europe. He was last seen rushing out of the same hotel 'without either his coat or hat',[59] shortly before Orwell arrived back in Barcelona late in April 1937. Brian Goold-Verschoyle, meanwhile, a twenty-four-year-old Irish NKVD radio operator, was lured onto a ship in Barcelona's harbour, locked into a cabin and taken to Russia. At around the same time as Orwell was sitting on the roof of the Poliorama theatre, Goold-Verschoyle entered Moscow's infamous Lubyanka prison, accused of Trotskyism. He would die in jail a few years later.[60] José Robles, a Spanish academic who had been teaching at Johns Hopkins University and was a friend of John Dos Passos and Hemingway, was probably another victim; the two writers eventually fell out over this, with Dos Passos outraged at the idea that Robles may have been murdered. 'Civil liberties shit,' Hemingway exclaimed to him. 'Are you with us or against us?'[61]

Orwell had to return to the Aragon front in mid-June to collect his discharge papers. When he walked back through the doors of the Continental Hotel in Barcelona, he was surprised to receive a theatrical hug from his wife Eileen, who hissed into his ear: 'Get out of here *at once!*'[62] In his absence, the POUM had been banned and many of its members locked up; offices and hospitals had been raided and shut down. Andreu Nin, having refused to sign a Moscow-style 'confession', was secretly shot. Bob Smillie, a twenty-year-old British POUM fighter, had already died in jail of peritonitis. Plain-clothes police had raided the Blairs' hotel room, taking away a diary and press cuttings; even Orwell's dirty laundry had been sequestered.

That night, Orwell slept in the ruins of a gutted church. By day he wandered the streets and even visited imprisoned colleagues like Kopp, but was conscious of 'the posters screaming from the hoardings that I and everyone like me was a Fascist spy'.[63] The following night he slept in an abandoned building with two other British POUM fighters. Days later he and Eileen crossed the French border by train, sitting in the first-class dining car – a recent reintroduction onto Spanish railways – in order to look like well-heeled British visitors. Their names were not yet on the police register at the frontier and, after six months, Orwell was back in France.

The selected NKVD assassination campaign in Spain was nothing like the vast purges in Russia, even if it was founded on the same ethos. Some writers feverishly claim the NKVD killed people in their 'hundreds' or 'thousands'. In fact, its victims numbered little more than twenty (though these were often prominent, including Nin, the Italian anarchist leader Camillo Berneri and his companion Francesco Barbieri). Spain was not the Soviet Union. It had its own government which believed in at least trying to apply a minimum level of due process of law. There were no mass trials; most of Orwell's foreign POUM companions were released and when the leadership was eventually tried in an open court, this declared them not guilty of espionage, and refused to bend to communist pressure for a death sentence. The Spanish experience, nevertheless, inoculated Orwell against totalitarianism of all kinds. It spawned not just *Homage to Catalonia* (which sold a mere 900 copies, before being reissued more than a decade later) but also *Animal Farm* and *Nineteen Eighty-Four*. It had a similar impact on Dos Passos, who left Spain in a hurry.[64]

For most International Brigaders, the 'events of May', as they became known, were no more than a distant rumour.[65] Many Brigaders had barely heard of the POUM, were clueless about what a Trotskyist might be and found the anarchists generous, congenial company. That did not stop the Brigades' own political commissariat from publishing a single-page leaflet with a picture of a volunteer about to be stabbed in the back, which warned volunteers to remain 'vigilant against provocateurs, POUM adventurers, splitters and stirrers of trouble in the rearguard'.[66] The Brigades' internal press (which included at least seventy-one publications in languages ranging from English to Yiddish) also gave lavish coverage to the arrest of one British POUM volunteer as an international art thief.[67] 'I had only a rather hazy idea of the nature of the crime of Trotskyism,' admitted Stephen Pollak, a Czech artist who had been studying in London. He nevertheless heard the word frequently. 'Trotskyite was the worst term of abuse in this army, and many political discussions in our battalion had ended with mutual charges of Trotskyism,' he added.[68] In fact, the term was used to settle petty scores and the Brigades' command eventually issued an order warning that those who made false accusations would be punished. This was ironic, given that one of the most paranoid Trotskyist witch-hunters of all was the Brigades' chief himself, André Marty.

The May events nevertheless had far-reaching consequences that would affect Brigaders directly. Prime Minister Francisco Largo Caballero refused to ban the POUM and was ousted from the government; the moderate socialist Dr Juan Negrín replaced him as prime minister.[69] Negrín hoped that he might finally persuade the British and French that the fascist coalition in Spain was a threat to them too.[70] Taming the more revolutionary workers organisations – be they unions, anarchists or revolutionaries like the POUM – was crucial to that strategy. The communists favoured that too.

The NKVD was not the only outfit spying on Brigaders. The German communists in charge of the PSUC Foreigners Service at the Hotel Colón – which included a 'Special Section' dedicated to intelligence, spying and policing – effectively ran a rogue outfit of their own.[71] 'The staff of this service have tended, on the one hand, to play at Sherlock Holmes, and, on the other hand, to play at German cadre politics – all without control by the party,' said an internal report in June 1937.[72] They were also rumoured to share use of the NKVD's oven.

The volunteers themselves were also spied on directly, with Briton Charles Oliver Green, for example, hired by the NKVD as their 'eyes' in the French-speaking Marseillaise Battalion.[73] The notoriously thuggish American Tony DeMaio was just one of several Americans to join the

Republic's own SIM military intelligence service, which the Russians helped set up in August 1937.[74]

The International Brigades' intelligence and cadre services, meanwhile, kept their own files. A carefully crafted document from those files, in which the author used a compass to produce circles within circles, shows Orwell's 'English group' as just one of several identified as dangerous to the Brigades. Amongst the names and groups on the document are a 'Scandinavian group' and – each on their own – the future Chancellor of Germany (and Nobel Peace Prize winner) Willy Brandt, and one of Holland's most famous writers, Jef Last. A separate diagram in the same file also casts doubt on Max Hodann, the German International Brigades doctor whose experiences in Spain would go on to inspire one of Germany's most important pieces of post-war writing, Peter Weiss's magnum opus, *The Aesthetics of Resistance*. Hodann's girlfriend, Norwegian journalist Lise Lindbaek, was the 'official' historian of the Thälmann Battalion. She, in turn, was part of a group of remarkable Scandinavian women war correspondents to gather in Spain – including Gerda Grepp, Norman Bethune's Swedish friend, the former marathon dancer Kajsa Rothman, and Barbro Alving (known by the pseudonym 'Bang').[75] Several of them also appear in the files as suspects.

Max Hodann's unnamed 'crime' may have been that he believed shell-shock victims were not cowards but men in need of careful rehabilitation. Perhaps, too, as a former sexual health campaigner, he could not be trusted to impose the slogans that Dutch writer Jef Last came across when touring the International Brigades' bases, that 'a communist must know how to suppress their sexuality'. This, Last said, was especially so for homosexuals who could be expected to receive 'punishments in Madrigueras of five weeks prison; [while] onanism carried a three-day sentence'.[76]

The list-making was prodigious in both extent and absurdity, with Marty himself claiming the organisations who wanted to infiltrate the Brigades included the Gestapo, Mussolini's OVRA, police units from Poland and France, French military intelligence, Trotskyists, anarchists, foreign socialists and the followers of Largo Caballero.[77] Amongst the names confidently registered as spies on another document are the head of the Abraham Lincoln Battalion, Robert Merriman, and American volunteer Robert Colodny – who went on to be an academic historian and one of the most loyal writers on the Brigades. Tom Wintringham's

American girlfriend Kitty Bowler, who was eventually expelled as a 'Trotskyist spy', is also on the list. Yet another document places Maria Osten, the German writer who was Mikhail Koltsov's long-term girlfriend, at the centre of a web of Trotskyist connections that includes Regler, Willi Münzenberg and Kantorowicz.[78]

It is difficult not to see in some of these documents, written in German, the forebear of what would eventually become the Stasi secret police force of communist East Germany. Certainly, they were the kind of allegations to jeopardise the future of anyone who – like the documents themselves – travelled to Moscow. In Osten's case that meant arrest and eventual death in 1942. It was a path also travelled by Koltsov, who was arrested just two days after he had been elevated to the rank of corresponding member of the Academy of Sciences. His carefree and clever attitude had probably cost him dearly, but a denunciation from the servile and suspicious Marty – a personal enemy – may have made things worse. Koltsov was executed in Moscow in February 1940. The true reason for Koltsov's death may, however, have been his success in arousing popular support for Spain across the Soviet Union. 'The cause of Spain aroused intense enthusiasm throughout Russia,' explained Louis Fischer, the well-connected American journalist who served as the International Brigades' quartermaster and knew Russia well. 'Many communists and non-communists hoped that the events in Spain might lend new life to the dying flame of the Russian revolution. Not Stalin. He had consented to sell the Spanish Republic arms. But not to make a revolution.'[79]

Although Stalin's purges provided a frightening political backdrop, their impact on the Brigaders was small. In practical terms, communist interference was mostly political rather than military – and the latter was far more important to the International Brigades' performance and the daily life of the volunteers. Commissars were a crucial party tool. Although only half the French volunteers in Spain were communist, for example, all but one of their forty-five commissars were party members. Amongst the British, apparently non-communist commissars would turn out to be clandestine party members. Even then, Marty and the other commanders were wary of excessively diligent party members overstepping the popular front line. Party meetings in each battalion had to be discreet, and Marty fretted that commissars might be seen as 'party inspectors', creating problems with the Spanish government. Political interference was sometimes chaotic, reflecting the fact that national communist parties were often in disarray, or tiny (Britain had 12,283 members in April 1937, a significant portion of whom were in Spain).[80] The Hungarian party, for example, was dissolved by the Comintern in 1936 and its leader Béla Kun arrested and, eventually, shot in Moscow in 1938. When the Polish party was also dissolved, General Walter got blind drunk and Szurek looked on as he wandered off, ranting to himself. With these two parties – along with the Germans and Italians – mostly in exile, Spain had become their effective base. 'We needed Spain more than the Republic needed us,' quipped one Italian. Nor did the Brigaders feel they were fighting to help impose a communist state in Spain, though many would have willingly done this if ordered to. As one Brigades' newspaper article stated, it was 'up to the Spaniards to choose the structure of the state'. They were here to stop fascism.[81]

Given that Stalin turned out to be one of the twentieth century's biggest ogres, Orwell can be forgiven for siding with the POUM, but the writer also displayed a wider ignorance about what was happening in Spain. Willy Brandt, a leading light amongst the foreigners gathered around the party, was much better informed and could see the enormity of the errors on both sides. He hated the Comintern but also viewed the POUM as absurdly dogmatic and failing to realise that only a popular front could win the war. 'First, the war must be won,' he said, before adding that 'victory is possible without carrying out the revolution, but in the end, you also cannot win by drowning the revolution.'[82]

Orwell was aware that he might be misleading his readers, and was honest about it. 'I believe that on such an issue as this no one is or can be completely truthful,' he said. 'It is difficult to be certain about anything except what you have seen with your own eyes, and consciously or unconsciously everyone writes as a partisan. In case I have not said this somewhere earlier in the book I will say it now: beware of my partisanship, my mistakes of fact and the distortion inevitably caused by my having seen only one corner of events.'[83]

Despite his terrifying experiences in Barcelona, Orwell had not lost his admiration for the volunteer unit that he had originally planned to join. He made that clear, two months after his return home, by stating, in an otherwise scathing review of a book by the early volunteer John Sommerfield: 'The International Brigade is in some way fighting for all of us – a thin line of suffering and often ill-armed human beings standing between barbarism and at least comparative decency.'[84]

33

Attack!: Guernica and Valsaín, April–June 1937

From his viewpoint in the hospital – where he was recovering from wounds sustained while fighting as a volunteer militiaman for the Republican army in the north – Canadian former sailor, lumberjack, welder and hobo Bill Williamson could not quite see the small town of Guernica on 26 April 1937. He understood, though, exactly what was happening to the ancient seat of Basque government, which was packed with refugees and the countryfolk who gathered there on market days. Wave after wave of aircraft were flying over it.

'You could see the bombs glinting in the sunlight as they fell, but you couldn't actually see where they fell because that was down in a little valley,' Williamson said later. 'But you could hear the explosions. And afterwards a whole bunch of Messerschmitts would come over and scream down (it sort of terrified you) dive-bombing the town. And then they'd go away and then another wave [would come].'[1] That night, with his arm in plaster, Williamson helped dig through the rubble for the injured, while the town itself was 'just a mass of flames and smoke'.[2] He may well have been the first foreign witness of the destruction of the emblematic town which was considered the spiritual heart of the now semi-autonomous Basque country. Parliaments of various kinds had gathered under an ancient oak tree here since the fourteenth century. Now it was mostly destroyed, and the grave of up to 1,645 people.

If thirty-year-old Williamson had understood what was happening, it was because he had experienced something very similar three weeks earlier, while at a hospital in the nearby town of Durango. This had suffered the first-ever blanket bombing of a civilian target in Europe, though, like previous aerial bombardments by the colonial powers in Africa or the Middle East, it had failed to provoke outrage.[3] Guernica's much higher death toll, however, garnered headlines across the world and inspired Pablo Picasso's iconic painting – with its screaming women, writhing animals and dead child.[4] The outrage was also used in the Republic's internal propaganda to try to galvanise the International Brigades – which Williamson transferred to the following month.[5] He carried with him considerable personal pain over the death of a militiawoman called Dolores whom he had fought alongside and whose photograph he conserved, showing her in regulation overalls with braided black hair scraped tightly back above dangling, triangular earrings.[6]

The discovery that it could raze a town by fire-bombing would be useful to the Luftwaffe in the long-term, but the campaign in the north provided other, more immediately practical lessons. Close cooperation between air and ground forces, Hitler's Condor Legion expeditionary force discovered, meant the former could be used to damage and demoralise infantry units with bombing and strafing, while the Francoist infantry mopped up behind them. Efficient communications, provided by new mobile command stations mounted on Krupp trucks, and the constant use of observer aircraft, were essential to that.[7]

The international outcry over the destruction of Guernica did nothing to temper Britain's enthusiasm for non-intervention. The British consul in Bilbao, Ralph Stevenson, visited the following day and provided foreign secretary Anthony Eden with a graphic report of 'many men and women erring through the streets searching in the wreckage of their houses for their dear ones'.[8] While Eden publicly admitted that 'if that kind of thing is repeated and intensified on a larger scale, it is going to mean a terrible future for Europe', the main concern was Germany's display of military might. In that sense, it only increased Britain's desire to pursue appeasement. Eden later admitted that Guernica had, indeed, been a harbinger – calling it 'the first blitz of the Second World War'. It was the kind of observation that Brigaders had begun to make in November 1936, as they watched Italian and German aircraft bombing civilians in Madrid.[9]

* * *

Ever since the Luftwaffe had airlifted the Army of Africa into Spain, Franco's army had proved that even if it did not always win, it knew how to attack. In the north, indeed, it had been refining its techniques. That is why it was now rolling the northern front back towards Bilbao. Elsewhere, the Republican army had demonstrated a growing sophistication and capacity for resistance. It had not, however, had much fortune with its own offensives, as the International Brigaders knew. The attempt to take Teruel had been a failure. So, too, had the assault on Lopera in December. The counter-attacks at Jarama merely served to prove the costliness, in the machine-gun era, of full-frontal attacks. There had been gains at Peñarroya and Motril, however, and Guadalajara had shown that the enemy could be thrown back. It had felt, indeed, like a turning point. The obvious next step was to launch an offensive.

If Bilbao was in danger, then a Republican offensive near Madrid would have the added benefit of forcing Franco to send troops and aircraft south from there. As a first test, the Republican command chose to attack Franco's positions between the snowy peaks of the Guadarrama mountain chain, north-west of Madrid, and the walled city of Segovia. This was the terrain, and the battle, where Hemingway would later place the action of *For Whom the Bell Tolls*. Aleksander Szurek accompanied his Polish chief, General Walter, to one of the highest points in this mountain chain to survey the terrain on 28 May 1937.[10] Walter now had his own division and had been given overall command of the operation, though only one of his seven brigades – the French-speaking XIV Brigade led by a hero of the University City fighting, Colonel Jules Dumont – was international.[11] In the distance sat Segovia and the vast, flat meseta plain of Castile. In between them lay a deep valley, through which the river Eresma descended towards Segovia. This was a potential gateway into Franco's hinterland. At its boldest, an offensive here might bring the conquest of Segovia, while a more modest advance would occupy the top of the Eresma valley, leaving the Republican army at the gates to the ancient, windswept Castilian city.

Earlier that month two new Russian-speaking officers had arrived to join General Walter's divisional staff. These were White Russians who had fought for the tsar against the revolutionaries and lost. One of them, Andre Escimontowsky,[12] had been a general, while the other, Theodore

Malkmus, had been a colonel. In the International Brigades, they were a captain and lieutenant, respectively. Walter and Escimontowsky became instant friends – like French and German veterans discussing their encounters in the world war, the White Russian and the Polish communist found they had been on the opposing sides in several battles, with both claiming to have escaped from the other, at some stage, in their underwear.[13] They shared a love of warfare as well as various traits born of Russian military culture, including wearing laced, calf-high riding boots and keeping their thinning hair closely cropped.[14] They both also believed that the battlefield was no place for half measures or weakness.

The wiry, white-haired Escimontowsky was sent up to one of the highest and chilliest peaks in the area, Peña Citores, as Walter's observer.[15] This rocky outpost was 2,182 metres above sea level and while, in the valley below, the volunteers sometimes sweated in the early summer heat, he and the half-dozen men with him often froze at night. The Russian jotted down concise, accurate and regular reports on the lined paper of a small notebook and sent them back to Walter. The quality of his observations reflects the mind of a former general used to understanding and analysing the movements on a battlefield. They would prove invaluable. Walter sent him brandy to get him through the cold nights, which the Russian consumed in large quantities. Walter understood men who drank. He was one himself.

The geometrical patterns of the ornamental gardens of the royal summer palace of La Granja – an eighteenth-century rococo masterpiece built in imitation of Versailles – could be seen clearly from Escimontowsky's position. Closer to him lay the tiny village of Valsaín, with its own ruined country palace and, in front of that, the Cerro del Puerco hill. Also visible, however, were the enemy aircraft that constantly took off from an airfield near Segovia and those that patrolled the ridges of the mountain range, knowing that Republican planes would be vulnerable as they flew back up over them on their return from the battlefield.[16]

Over the next few days, Escimontowsky tracked the movements of both sides and logged them in heavily Russified French in his ruled notebook (the first of many that he would fill over the coming months as Walter's eyes and head of his 'Operations Department'[17]). Those movements showed how much the Republican army and the International Brigades still had to learn.

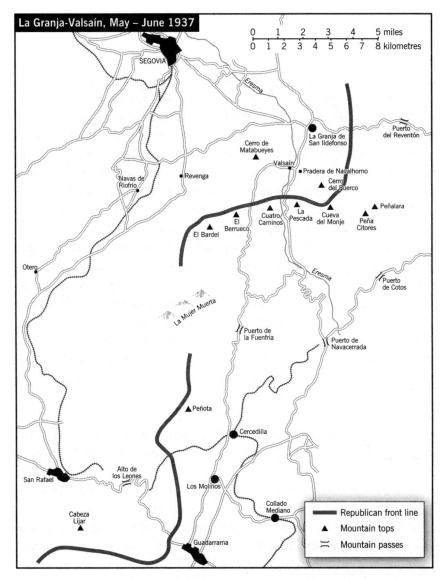

The attack plan for the morning of 30 May called for daring and surprise. Despite the fact that the tall pines which populated the valleys and mountainsides of the Guadarrama chain were perfect cover for a troop build-up, the Republican army failed to keep this secret. Deserters gave the Francoist commander General José Enrique Varela details of the plans and the night before the battle commenced the one hundred or more trucks carrying the troops into position through the pouring rain left their headlights on;[18] the snake-like pattern of lights progressing along the winding tracks that climbed and fell along the thickly forested – but usually empty – mountainside was definitive proof that those plans were about to be put into action.

Dumont's XIV Brigade arrived late, apparently because he had quibbled over the way in which his orders were delivered.[19] This left his men with little time to recover from their long march and meant he barely had time to send out reconnaissance patrols.[20] The men walked the last few kilometres, down a road that nobody appeared to have used for months and with a bright moon lighting up the last bits of snow in the treetops. Last-minute reconnaissance patrols achieved little. An unnamed Belgian led a patrol of three men straight into a position held by Franco's paramilitary *requetés* near the Cerro de Puerco hill, where he innocently asked directions to Dumont's headquarters. The three volunteers were disarmed and interrogated by a Francoist captain. At first, they refused to give any information but, according to the same captain, they eventually gave in to threats that they would be shot. 'They told me that 4,000 men were going to attack down the valley,' he reported.[21] Varela responded by sending three battalions as reinforcements.

The Francoists, then, were ready for the 'surprise' attack which began with a brief but intense aerial bombardment at 6 a.m. on the morning of 30 May.[22] The international volunteers of XIV Brigade had been assigned the task of assaulting both the village of Valsaín and the impressively fortified Cerro del Puerco hilltop. Those waiting for them were amazed to see that they did not even bother to take cover in order to creep up on them. Instead, they walked straight up to the barbed wire fences constructed fifty metres ahead of the main defensive positions and, still standing, began to cut them. Some sixty volunteers were immediately mowed down by machine-gun fire. Dumont had been told that the defences would be flimsy and poorly manned. 'The places that we expected to be unoccupied, turned out to be solidly fortified,' he complained in a later report.[23]

Losses in the first chaotic minutes were high and XIV Brigade could not get close enough to its targets to attack with grenades as it charged uphill towards solid bunkers equipped with machine guns.[24] The six available tanks had stayed some way back since it was feared that the

clanking of their tracks would give away the presence of the attack
force. When they arrived an hour later, it soon became clear that the
mountains here were too steep and rugged for the tanks to climb and
that, in effect, they could only be used as mobile artillery from the
roads. From his position, Escimontowsky could see that Dumont's
brigade had edged towards Cerro del Puerco, 'sans gran profit' while the
supporting artillery fire from nine guns was largely ineffective – with
one battery firing an estimated 60 per cent duds.[25]

At midday Dumont received an angry note from Walter, who wanted
to know why the attack had not succeeded. The note demanded that
he lead a fresh attack in person, and threatened to punish him for
failure. Szurek, who translated the written orders, realised immediately
that the tenor of the note would provoke a clash of military cultures.
Dumont was from the proud French officer class and had won both
the Croix de Guerre and the Légion d'Honneur during the First World
War, surviving wounds and gas attacks. Unlike the Poles, Bulgarians
or Russians that Walter was used to – who would have preferred to die
rather than accept the slightest hint of cowardice – Dumont could be
expected to respond badly. Szurek also realised, however, that Walter
was so furious that there was no point in contradicting him.[26]

When Dumont received the missive he was, as Szurek predicted,
outraged and declared that he was resigning. He gathered together his
battalion commanders, informed them that he was handing command
over to George Nathan, the ex-British army officer who was now a
senior staff officer, and then stormed off to Walter's headquarters to
present his resignation. 'I'm a soldier, and I won't accept it!' he shouted.
Walter refused to allow him to resign and Dumont claimed that he
agreed only 'to remain at my post until the end of the battle, but
asked to be relieved of my duties [after that]'.[27] The animus between
the two men would never abate, and Szurek noticed volunteers talking
openly of a 'French faction' and a 'Russian faction' within the Brigades.
(Something similar had already been mentioned in the letters found on
the deserters at the French College in Valencia.[28])

Dumont returned to the front where he failed to persuade the
inexperienced Spanish tankmen to do anything more than fire from
their hiding places, thereby using up all their ammunition. Elsewhere
the attack had not gone much better. Only one minor hill – the Cruz
de la Gallega – had been captured, though the Segovia road had been

successfully cut beyond La Granja, making it difficult for the Francoists to bring up reinforcements and supplies. The other important hilltops – Matabueyes and Cabeza Grande – remained in Francoist hands.[29]

From his mountain perch, Escimontowsky looked on as the next day's attack stalled at Valsaín, with XIV Brigade suffering 'heavy losses but making no headway'.[30] Frustration grew, sparking one of the strangest episodes of this short battle. It involved XIV Brigade's Pioneer, or 'disciplinary', unit, made up of French-speaking alcoholics and hotheads and which probably included deserters sent back from the French School in Valencia. The other White Russian officer who had arrived with Escimontowsky, Theodore Malkmus, was placed in charge of some of them. When a group of seven men got drunk and began to misbehave, he had them shot on the spot and then disappeared himself. Escimontowsky speculated that his friend may have 'shot himself in the head with his own revolver'.[31]

Fourteenth Brigade's Belgian cavalry commander Nick Gillain, a Lopera veteran and self-declared mercenary with the literary instincts of a pulp novelist, tells a different version of the story. He blames a French captain called Duchesne and his commissar, Binet, while limiting the dead to five. After the failed attack on Valsaín, he reported that Duchesne 'picked five men at random. He killed them Soviet-style, with a pistol shot to the back of the head, grabbing them by the neck with his left hand and shooting with the right ... The fifth man was only wounded and grabbed on to the captain's leg. Binet, the political commissar, knocked him back with a punch and then blew his brains out.'[32] Either way, it is clear that the episode, which does not appear in official reports, did actually take place. This was despite the fact that the Pioneers carried out some of the most dangerous tasks – with XIV Brigade doctor Theodor Balk witnessing them 'singing, cursing and encouraging one another' as they led an attack, charging across a meadow towards barbed wire and machine guns.[33] The company, indeed, suffered the worst casualties, including a French miner called Charlot who was reputed to drink up to five litres of wine a day, but could always be counted on to lead any assault.[34]

What, then, might have provoked the on-the-spot executions? Maurice Gillet, a battalion commander, gave a clue when he complained that those responsible for fortifying his battalion's positions (usually the Pioneers) had been useless, 'claiming that the dark night, the rain and the rocky ground … prevented them from doing their job'.[35] Gillain, meanwhile, said that 'caught under intense fire, the disciplinary section men suddenly weakened and ran'.[36] Whatever the reasons, it was a sign of growing frustrations within the Republican army.

Amongst the injured was the baby-faced architect and French army reserve officer Boris (Bob) Guimpel, who commanded the Domingo Germinal anarchist battalion whose men had been integrated into XIV Brigade (with their old name replacing that of the Vaillant-Couturier Battalion).[37] His appearance at the field hospital with a head wound shocked his sister, Maya, one of the brigade doctors. She was nevertheless relieved to see that he could still move his lips. 'I, as a doctor, understood that he wasn't dangerously wounded and didn't risk a stroke,' she said. The reactions of Guimpel's wife Manon, who had travelled with him from Paris and served as a nurse with XIV Brigade, is not recorded. This family of French picture framers was thoroughly middle class, but was also steeped in revolutionary tradition since both the parents had been forced to leave the tsar's Russia. Guimpel and the Pioneer company leader, a tough former French Foreign Legionnaire known as 'Coco' Vaillant, had earlier joked about how comfortable the ambulances seemed. Both ended up needing them.[38]

That evening Escimontowsky reported seeing hundreds of trucks bringing men and supplies to reinforce the Francoist side. The impact of that would be felt the following day. While one of the other brigades fought its way into the La Granja palace's ornamental gardens, XIV Brigade failed again at Valsaín. Overhead, meanwhile, the Francoist air force suddenly seemed to dominate the skies. The Republican air force – which was popularly called 'La Gloriosa', 'the Glorious' – was by now known in the division headquarters as 'the Invisible'.[39] That evening Escimontowsky's mountain-top position was blasted by a storm of snow, sleet and icy wind. 'No sign of [Lieutenant Theodore] Malkmus – probably dead,' he wrote.[40]

Escimontowsky left three men in his observation post the next day, and clambered down to visit Walter.[41] It was now clear that the attack had failed and on 2 June troops began to be pulled away. Fourteenth Brigade had lost at least 360 men, more than the other brigades involved in the operation.[42] Walter told the volunteers they had displayed 'an exceptional degree of combativity and awareness of the cause we are defending', but warned that the losses proved 'the superiority of the enemy in tactics and firepower [and] … have demonstrated to us our own deficiencies'.[43] These included insufficient knowledge of basic military tactics and how to use terrain. They still had to learn how to switch from defence to 'careful attack', while more training was needed 'to reduce casualties and protect our own lives'.[44]

In fact, the failure at Valsaín was not their fault. Inadequate artillery and air support, poor coordination and, above all, the lack of intelligence about the enemy's fortifications were mostly to blame.[45] In an angry meeting after the battle, François Vittori, XIV Brigade's political commissar, accused one of the Spanish generals in charge of the sector of treason.[46] There was no open criticism, however, of General Walter's role, or his plan of attack. Perhaps nobody dared. Walter insisted, somewhat absurdly, that it had all been worth it. 'Thanks to your heroism, Franco could not continue his march on Bilbao,' he told the volunteers. The city fell fifteen days later.

34

The Death of Lukács: Huesca, early June 1937

In early June, Hungarian communist and writer Máté Zalka – aka General Pavol Lukács of XII Brigade – travelled to Huesca to help lead yet another diversionary attack. The May bloodshed in Barcelona was fresh in everybody's minds and he was worried about the anarchist and POUM units who were meant to help him. The region around Huesca had belonged to the anarchist-controlled Council of Aragon[1] and served as a crucible for experiments in self-government and collectivisation. There had been relatively little fighting. The operation he was joining, indeed, was the first major one in the area since troops here had come under the central command of the Republican government in Valencia.[2]

After the victory in Guadalajara, the dapper and popular Lukács had been lobbying to form a division based around the now much-respected XII Brigade, which everyone associated with the victorious Italian Garibaldi Battalion. For the Huesca operation he was given what, in effect, was a full division, though this (45th Division) would not be formally named as such until after the battle.[3] It was made up of XII International Brigade, now with mixed Italian and Spanish battalions, and the new 150 International Brigade (reflecting a new numbering system in the Republican army, but sometimes referred to as 'XII *bis*' ['*b*']), based on the Polish Dombrowski and the French-speaking André Marty Battalions.[4]

Lukács was expected to follow a plan drawn up by the staff of local commander General Sebastián Pozas, a man who clearly disliked the International Brigades. This had been hurriedly put together over five days and assumed a level of coordinated action that Lukács decided was impossible.[5] As soon as one step went slightly wrong, it would fall to pieces, he thought. The government was in a hurry, however, and there was no time for changes or fine-tuning. Lukács was given instructions to send his men into the attack on the city of Huesca on 12 June, and to do so following Pozas's plan, which included frontal attacks on the two fortified villages, Chimillas and Alerre, that guarded the only passage out of the city. Lukács was furious. Not only would this prevent refugees from leaving, he said, but it would also prolong the battle unnecessarily by forcing those inside Huesca to fight to the death. 'Pure nonsense,' he complained.[6] There was, however, little else that could be done at such short notice (and this was mostly a last-ditch attempt to draw Francoist troops away from Bilbao) to conquer a city garrison that had been building defensive fortifications for nine months.

Struck down by migraines – the result of an old head injury – Lukács nevertheless pushed through with the help of some unidentified powders and whiskey. On the morning before the battle, his translator Eisner accompanied Lukács and his staff as they climbed to a hilltop overlooking Huesca from the north. The city's church towers were visible to the naked eye and through binoculars they could see laundry lines draped with clothes and the pre-Republican flag of Spain hanging from official buildings. Lukács confided his strategy to Eisner. He would ignore the plan to storm the city in a single day and, with the agreement of other divisional commanders, gradually creep up on it over five days. 'I'm not going to attack tomorrow, and that's it,' he told Eisner. When Regler and the Russian advisor Pavel Batov arrived at the same hilltop bearing a bottle of French lavender water and Russian newspapers as gifts, Lukács was delighted. The Russian had been, in many respects, the real military commander of Lukács's units – or so his rival Kléber believed[7] – whenever there was a battle to be fought. Batov pretended to have broken rules by abandoning his new post as an advisor in Teruel, but it is more likely he had been quietly ordered to be at Lukács's side, perhaps to stiffen his spine.[8] He agreed that the plan was poorly thought out, but does not appear to have suggested it be postponed.

Before returning to his headquarters in Apies on 11 June, Lukács inspected the two roads that led from there to the east. One was wide, straight and could be travelled quickly, but an 800-metre stretch was visible from Huesca and exposed to enemy artillery fire – though a screen had been built out of river reeds to disguise the traffic.[9] He

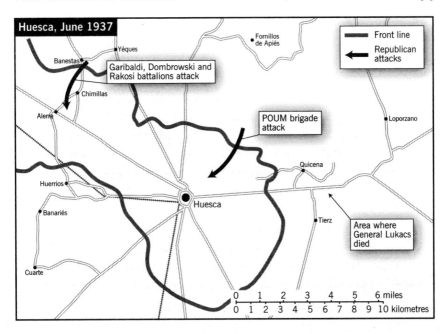

ordered that, from now on, all traffic should take the second route –
along a narrow, windy road with steep drops below it that nevertheless
remained out of sight of enemy eyes. His men would have to be moved
along this painfully bumpy route overnight, since slow-moving trucks
were too easy a target on the other road.

Returning to the same spot as they headed back later that afternoon,
Lukács was annoyed to see that the two cars that had preceded
them – carrying Dombrowski commander Józef Strzelczyck (alias Jan
Barwinski)[10] and the Garibaldi commander Randolfo Pacciardi[11] – had
swept past the checkpoint and on to the fast road. The sergeant in
charge reasoned that, while he intended to carry out orders, who was
he to stop senior officers from taking their own risks? The route was
twenty minutes shorter and preparation time for the following battle
was running out. Lukács now decided that his high-powered Peugeot
car would also get through. 'You'll be the first to disobey your own
instructions not to drive this way,' Batov pointed out.[12] 'But on the
other hand, if it's to avoid arriving late …' Batov shuffled into the back
seat beside him, while Regler rode up front with the Spanish driver,
Emilio. He revved the engine, floored the accelerator and the Peugeot
was travelling at between forty and fifty kilometres an hour as they

took the curve leading to the exposed stretch of road. At that speed, they would be out of danger in just over a minute. Regler recalled what happened next:

> The shell got us just as we were driving past the anarchist battalions. Our car was lifted into the air, to drop with a thud. I felt a savage blow in the back, and my hands were covered with splintered glass. The driver, beside me, was dead with his hand clutching the brake … Lukács was lying with his grey head against the upholstery; his brains were exposed. I tried to get the door open but it was jammed.
>
> '*C'est ça la fin*,' I said. I thrust an arm outside the car and, clutching the roof, dragged myself up. The sun was shining and a soft carpet of grass ran up the hillside. I was now conscious of the tepid pool of blood in which I had been sitting, but I went on pulling myself up. When I had managed to get halfway through the window I let myself fall. A shell whistled over me. '*Nous sommes les premières victimes de la division*,' I said, and gave a last glance at the groaning Lukács.[13]

Emilio had had time to throw the car towards the inside of the curve, in order to prevent it rolling off the road and down the hill, before passing out. Batov (also known as 'Fritz') recalled that Lukács had shouted the Russian diminutive of his name '*Frytsinka!*' before slumping on top of him. Batov scrambled out, leaving a trail of blood, before falling unconscious onto the hard road. When he regained consciousness, he saw that Lukács was hanging half out of the car. 'His head was touching the road, and everything was covered in blood,' Batov told the film-maker Roman Carmen. All four men were taken to hospital.[14] Shrapnel had penetrated Lukács's brain, and the surgeons decided there was nothing that could be done.[15] One visitor recalled that Lukács lay unconscious and heavily sedated, his body and face twitching.[16] He died the following day.

One eyewitness at the hospital claimed to have seen Lukács's legs peppered with bullet wounds[17] and rumours spread that anarchists had taken their revenge. The witness may have confused Lukács with the unit's German doctor, Werner Heilbrun, who also died when his car was strafed soon afterwards. In fact, it was haste that killed the elegant Hungarian spy, writer and soldier. Heilbrun's wife, Almuth, meanwhile, would remain in Spain – Hemingway was one of many captivated by her beauty.[18] These two deaths hit the American writer hard. 'I think I cried when I heard Lucasz [sic] was dead,' he recalled after the war.[19] 'I don't remember, I know I cried once when somebody died. It must have been Lucasz because Lucasz was the first great loss. Everyone else who had been killed was replaceable. Werner was the most irreplaceable of all.' Back in Moscow a nephew persuaded his family to destroy Lukács's diary because it contained commentary that would have been unpardonable in Stalin's time. Lukács had clearly been worried about something and had suffered from nightmares.[20]

Command was passed, temporarily, to the Bulgarian Belov and it was agreed that as few people as possible should be told. The news nevertheless slipped out. 'Imagine how terrible this was. The attack starts at dawn and our commander, General Lukács, is in the last few hours of life, dying from mortal wounds. For Lukács was more than a brigade commander. He was personally known and loved by all the brigade's soldiers and his loss was a deep blow to each fighter and each commander,' his Hungarian artillery commander, Szántó Rezső, recalled.[21]

Belov had barely a few hours to prepare for the next morning's attack. The assault turned out to be as disastrous as Lukács had predicted. Twelfth Brigade bravely attacked the concrete bunkers at Chimillas, as they tried to cut the road to Jaca. Before setting out, the Poles joked that they would be welcomed as the liberators of Huesca later that very day, just as they had been in Brihuega. First, though, they had to crawl along the bed of a stream below Chimillas and then attack uphill through fields of vines and unharvested wheat.

The Dombrowski and André Marty Battalions were accompanied by a new Rakosi international battalion, with only 288 men, which had just been established by the Hungarians and went into battle vowing to avenge the loss of their countryman Lukács. The latter's baptism of fire followed one of the more lamentable patterns of the International Brigades, where keen new 'national' battalions were routinely slaughtered as they tried to prove their valour. Battalion commander Dr Ákos Hevesi, a fifty-three-year-old veteran leader of the short-lived Hungarian Soviet Republic of 1919, and commissar Imre Tarr led from the front. Both died when the battalion became trapped by machine-gun fire. Rezső remembered it as 'the most tragic day in the history of our Brigade', with a quarter of its men lost.[22]

The Italians had more luck, with Giovanni Pesce amongst those tasked with securing the Jaca road north-west of Chimillas.[23] Many of the Garibaldi volunteers knew that their commander, Pacciardi, had also opposed the operation.[24] The communist Pesce was highly critical. 'What would Pacciardi think if half an hour before an attack a *garibaldino* or an officer wanted to argue over the plans?' he asked. 'Perhaps Pacciardi is tired of this hard fighting.'[25] Pacciardi's status as a non-communist brigade commander was becoming increasingly fragile, especially as new Italian recruits were now mostly being supplied by the Communist Party. He had also been complaining that recent changes had diluted the Italian nature of the Garibaldis, with some battalions now mostly Spanish. In fact, he now believed that the International Brigades had already completed their task by shoring up the defence of Madrid.[26]

It did not help that the Italians – as the most genuinely popular front international unit, with anarchists and many other non-communists in their ranks – had found the May events in Barcelona deeply disturbing. They had already been through the discomfort of being moved to the Aragonese town of Caspe, the heartland of anarchism – where one regional leader, José Mavilla, had claimed to 'prefer the sweet sound produced by the crash against the pavement of a saint's head fallen from a church to Beethoven's most harmonious sonata'.[27] Pacciardi believed they had been tricked, thinking they were preparing for an offensive, when they were actually on police duty in case the anarchists rebelled. Worse still, Russian advisors had tried to order Carlo Penchienati, the commander of one battalion, to take his men to Barcelona to help suppress the rebellion there in May.[28] 'Stay there! Don't move for any reason,' Pacciardi (whose adjutant was the anarchist Giorgio Braccialarghe) had said when Penchienati called to inform him. These uncertainties and internal tensions cannot have helped at Huesca. 'We are tired and nervous. It seems that something isn't working, and, what's more, the fascists have seen our movements,' said Pesce.[29]

When the dawn attack started, the Garibaldis advanced from the anarchist trenches across fields covered by waist-high vines. These provided scarce cover when the machine guns in the church towers at Chimillas and Alerre opened fire. The only option was to crawl. 'To advance in such conditions is like putting oneself before a firing squad,' observed Pesce.[30]

These two International Brigades now began to learn some of the lessons that XIV Brigade had been taught ten days earlier at Valsaín. Concrete bunkers could only be successfully attacked by artillery, aerial bombardment or surprise. Often they required all three. Crossing open ground towards such positions was fraught with danger. When the impetus of an attack ran out, those who had survived either had to seek cover or lie perfectly still for hours on end in order not to attract fire. This was torture to mind and body. The wounded groaned, cried for help or slowly died. Those who went to help them immediately attracted rifle and machine-gun fire, and frequently became yet another casualty. In the intense heat of June, water was a major problem. A single canteen might contain a litre, if it had not been left behind or nervously consumed early in the day. There was still water in the streams, but since retreat was often only possible after nightfall, many suffered dehydration or sunstroke.[31]

Pesce himself reached within about forty metres of the Francoist lines before realising that it was hopeless to go on, and stayed still until sundown, witnessing a final heroic attack by a battalion of Spanish soldiers from the Carlos Marx Division. 'They had guts, and we admired them,' he said. But they, too, were stopped.[32] Pesce crawled back and, that night, XII and 150 International Brigades picked up their dead and wounded under the cover of darkness.[33]

A surprise appointment was made to replace Lukács. Rumours of General Kléber's demise, or disappearance, were now proven false. Despite his often awkward character, some Republican leaders valued both his military experience and frankness. Since his minor role at Málaga, he had been courted first by Negrín to run the finance ministry's powerful Carabineros and then to take over the communist Carlos Marx Division in Catalonia.[34] His appointment meant both joining the battle halfway through and finishing the task of building a division based around the Garibaldis. Before he left for the front, however, he was sternly reminded that the best way to avoid repeating previous gaffes was by refusing to give newspaper interviews.[35]

Kléber arrived on 15 June to be told that his two International Brigades, XII and 150, were to carry out exactly the same assault that had failed a few days earlier. He complained energetically and demanded a delay. 'It was necessary to rework the plan and select another place for the attack,' he explained later.[36] That, he was told, was impossible. The reason, once more, was Bilbao – where XIV International Brigade's former commander, the Frenchman Joseph Putz, was holding out as commander of the First Basque Division.[37]

The next day's attack was another disaster, even though Spanish Republican troops on the north side of Huesca fought their way tantalisingly close to the city. The Dombrowski Battalion advanced more cautiously this time and, using tanks as cover, managed to place two machine guns within fifty metres of Chimillas, but got no further.[38] Worse still, according to Kléber, his men received little help or sympathy from the POUM fighters behind them. 'They were met with a hostile coldness and gloating over their misfortune from the Poumists sitting things out in their trenches,' he complained in a later report to Moscow.[39]

That was unfair. In fact, a POUM unit (with its own international volunteers) took a strategic hill, the Loma de los Mártires, while Kléber's battalions failed absolutely. Pozas praised 'the courage and brilliant behaviour' of POUM soldiers, while his chief of staff, Lieutenant Colonel Vicente Guarner, blamed the eventual loss of that same hill on Kléber, who had failed to send reinforcements. Guarner was critical of the International Brigaders, whom he claimed showed 'a lower level of discipline and combativity' than the Spanish troops who accompanied them.[40] Whatever the truth, all this happened on exactly the same day as the POUM was finally banned.[41]

More worrying was that, as at Valsaín, the previously indomitable International Brigades had failed. This was mainly because they had been given almost impossible missions whose real aim was simply to distract Franco from his campaign in the north. In both cases, however, brigade commanders – Dumont and Pacciardi – had argued with their superiors. In both cases, too, the volunteers had paid a high price in lives and casualties. They included two Italian battalion commanders, one of whom was dead and the other badly wounded.[42] If ever, in their eight-month history, the International Brigades had reason to complain about being used as cannon fodder, this was it. Huesca had not been taken and Bilbao fell on June 19, the same day that the attack was called off.

Walter also fretted that the International Brigades were losing effectiveness and fighting spirit. Dumont's brigade had 'heroically but passively allowed itself to be slaughtered over the course of five days at Valsaín ... [and] then there was Huesca, where the Lukács brigade was nothing like what it had been during earlier battles'.[43] There was every hope, however, that the Republic would learn from these two attacks. Changing the course of the war, or even just drawing a major part of Franco's army away from the north – where valuable industrial and mining areas around Santander still remained in Republican hands – required something much grander. A more ambitious operation, indeed, was soon being planned closer to Madrid. Almost all the International Brigades would be needed for that.

35

Brunete: Denmark, early summer 1937

Leo Kari was both worried and excited. The dark-haired, droopy-eyed, eighteen-year-old[1] apprentice had walked out of his home in Rødovre, a small village just outside Copenhagen, Denmark, turning back to wave at his mother every few steps, full of joy and optimism. The dull, mechanical factory job was forgotten and the three year apprenticeship, with only six months left, abandoned. He was on his way to Spain, where the famous International Brigades had already begun the task of defeating fascism with their victories at Jarama and Guadalajara. He would now help them complete the task. Even the familiar houses and trees that lined the road to the railway station suddenly seemed alive and beautiful – or so he wrote in a lightly novelised version of his memoirs.

When he reached Paris, Kari refused to accompany his fellow Scandinavian volunteers into a brothel, declaring the belief – not uncommon among Brigaders – that prostitution was slavery.[2] In Lyon, he had followed them sheepishly into a second one, determined not to be seen as aloof. He found the other volunteers were older, worldly and slightly bullying.

The train they had caught from Paris was known by some as the Red Express – since it had spent ten months carrying volunteers towards the frontier. Sympathisers along the route knew it, and would raise their fists in salute. By now, however, the French border was closed. Non-intervention was hampering the supplies of men and arms to the Republic (though ships carrying Soviet aircraft were still getting through), while Hitler and Mussolini broke their promises daily.

Reaching Spain by sea had become increasingly dangerous, especially after fifty-seven of the 255 Brigaders on the *Ciudad de Barcelona* died when it was torpedoed by a Francoist submarine just 400 metres off the Catalan coast on 31 May 1937. Many drowned after rushing below decks to find lifebelts, the ship sinking in just three minutes. 'As the rear end was going down, of course, the bow was coming up, and many comrades, from a false sense of security, or otherwise, kept climbing higher, which was suicide, as it was obvious what would happen when the ship plunged,' recalled Joe Gibbons, an Irish-American survivor.[3] Canadian Karol Fronczysty ended up clinging to a small jack mast that stuck out from the foredeck. He was sucked down with the rest of the boat a few seconds later. It was yet another flagrant breach of the non-intervention agreement by Mussolini, whose so-called 'pirate' submarines were sinking all kinds of Republican shipping.[4]

Now volunteers had to hike across the Pyrenees on foot, hiding from border guards. That had become the new rite of passage. Few of the thousands of volunteers who arrived this way would forget their first, dramatic sight of Spain after an exhausting day and night of clambering over the mountain range that separates it from the rest of Europe. 'The Pyrenees stood high behind us, white and hard, their peaks colouring to the rising sun,' recalled the English writer Laurie Lee, whose physical condition was so poor – and complicated by epilepsy – that his main task as a Brigader would be to play his fiddle for local children.[5] 'We looked far, far down into tiny valleys in which blue ribbons of water sparkled – beautiful Spain stretched out before us like on a wonderful canvas,' remembered Percy Ludwick, a British-Russian engineer.[6] At the outset of the trek, as thousands of volunteers had done already, and thousands more would do over the coming year, Leo Kari donned what seemed to him to be strange shoes – the rope-soled cloth sandals, or *alpargatas*, that were the footwear of local peasants. Some volunteers worried that these were too flimsy for the task, but they proved perfectly apt for the rugged mountainous terrain. Some of the group were caught by police before they could cross the border, and spent the next two weeks in police cells in France.

Thirty-six hours after setting out, a sore-footed Kari found himself in the same castle at Figueres where newly arrived volunteers had gathered since the early days of the war, before being sent out in batches to Albacete. Amongst those with him was a seventeen-year-old Norwegian boy – though those deemed underage were usually turned away.[7] The thick-walled, spartan castle smelt of age and mould. Kari spent much of his time exploring its dingy basements. By now the walls were covered in graffiti in more than a dozen languages, as volunteers scrawled and scratched their names or left messages for friends who were due to follow them. In its courtyards and canteen he found, 'Hungarian farmers, craftsmen from Switzerland, Scandinavian sailors, well-paid office workers from London, self-conscious Americans, loud Frenchmen, self-contained Finns and feisty Slavs.' More exotically, for a young man who had never left his own country, there was also 'a giant Icelander, a family from Poland – husband and wife and two adult sons – Negroes, Mongols, Jews, even a lone Abyssinian.'[8] Within days, most people had severe diarrhoea – another rite of passage – as stomachs struggled with olive oil and chickpeas.

Already Kari had noticed that things were not as utopian as he had hoped. Men drank, squabbled and exchanged blows. Locals looked at them warily. Even those who approved of the foreign volunteers were not sure what to expect from the men who actually arrived. By now they had discovered that individual volunteers could be good, normal, or varying degrees of bad. On the train ride to Albacete, Kari was disappointed to see none of the expected crowds of cheering locals. In the towns where the individual battalion training camps were located, people were even more watchful. Old men shared their wineskins, laughing at the foreigners' clumsiness as they tipped the liquid over their chins, but drank little themselves and said less. 'It's the war. Tomorrow will be better,' one told him.[9] Here, as in Barcelona, any early enthusiasm had worn off. It was beginning to feel like a long war. This was especially true for those early volunteers who had arrived nine months previously, many of whom were clamouring for permits to go home on leave, though these were scarce. As far as the Republican high command was concerned, however, the volunteers were full-time soldiers who were expected to fight until the end of the war. That meant the International Brigades could only send people home with permission from the war ministry.

Kari and a group of Scandinavian friends climbed the bell tower of a wrecked church and were amazed by the flat, parched and treeless landscape of La Mancha.[10] The heat was overwhelming, stoking tensions between the different Scandinavian groups training together to join XIII Brigade. A tattooed former Norwegian army corporal with a skull inked onto his chest vied with a Swedish former Foreign Legionnaire for a thuggish form of supremacy, swinging fists at other volunteers and locals alike. In the meantime, a laconic but respected English company commander, known only as Captain Smith, was replaced by a German determined to impose vigorous and rigid discipline on what he viewed as the unruly Scandinavians. 'Tell him that ... while Germans train endlessly to win at war and still lose, the English don't train more than necessary, but still win,' one angry Danish volunteer, referring to the Great War, told their translator, who refused to pass the comment on.[11] Like the Dutch, the individualistic Scandinavians bridled against such discipline.[12] This they associated with Prussians and the 'Mexican' party men schooled at Moscow's Lenin School or Frunze Military Academy.[13]

Kari's closest friends were working-class Danes who, like him, had left school and gone straight to menial jobs, unemployment or to sea. That did not stop them eagerly debating ideas, some of them profound. They wondered, for example, whether Christianity and socialism were not just two different forms of faith.[14] The Christians amongst them certainly thought so. Wasn't there also something stupid about having to use weapons to create a better society? And what happened, they wondered, when an ideal society was finally achieved? Would they all be happy, or immediately bored and looking for a new, higher ideal to struggle for?

One evening they sat in Pedro's fly-infested cafe in Madrigueras, where the olive-skinned owner who served rough red wine had finally warmed to them. Two Norwegian volunteers – Thälmann Battalion veterans blooded in the battles of Jarama and Guadalajara – walked in. The linguistic and geographical affinity of Scandinavians made them natural drinking partners, as well as often being placed in the same companies. Soon the Norwegians were telling them what to expect, lacing their stories with the world-weariness of military veterans throughout history – men who have already passed through the deeply transformative experience of even a single day in battle – talking to newcomers. It did not sound good. Málaga had been betrayed, they claimed, and the generals had failed to follow up the victory at Guadalajara. A useless government, meanwhile, had just allowed Bilbao to fall. Democratically elected politicians in Europe were even worse. The continent's social democrats expressed sympathy, but backed non-intervention, blocked Russian armaments and, rather than fight fascism themselves, allowed anti-fascist volunteers like them to die. The fascists had better arms, while Catalans in Barcelona hoarded weapons needed at the front. Some volunteers had been driven insane by thirst and hunger. The average lifespan on the front was three weeks, they said, though this was mainly because the stupid ones who had not learned to find cover usually died on the first day. These exaggerated assertions were made by men only partially aware of the bigger picture of the war and with their tongues loosened by alcohol, but there were degrees of truth in all of them.

On the final night before they left for the front, early in July 1937, Kari and the other new recruits in XIII Brigade's Chapaev Battalion danced with the same girls from Madrigueras who normally glanced furtively at them as they promenaded around town, though matronly chaperones were still on hand. Instead of shying away, mothers and elder sisters wished the men good luck and asked them to send love and greetings to their own brothers, husbands and boyfriends, if they encountered them. For people in Madrigueras, this was becoming a routine. They had already sent several batches of young foreigners off to war and knew that many would – like their own menfolk – die or return wounded. Pedro refused to charge Kari and his friends for their last evening's drinks. A final dilemma was whether the canteens they took to the front should be filled with brandy or lemonade. Kari argued for lemonade, because it quenched thirst. Someone pointed out that they might have to offer it to a dying comrade. They opted for brandy.

The recruits travelled by night towards the sierras overlooking an arid, sun-burnished plain north-west of Madrid, on which lay the small town of Brunete. The multilingual XIII Brigade accounted for just four of the eighty-eight battalions involved in the secret build-up to what was planned to be the fully reformed Republican army's first major offensive. Virtually all of the International Brigades were heading towards the hills above the plain. From here, a daring strike south was meant to encircle the Francoist forces to the west of Madrid while relieving pressure on the northern front, where port cities such as Santander and Gijón were holding out. Only XIV International Brigade, which had fought at Valsaín, was left out.

The scale of this battle was different to anything seen before. The International Brigades accounted for just under a fifth – or five of the twenty-seven brigades – of the estimated 70,000 Republican troops[15] who moved stealthily into the attack area during the first days of July. In all, the volunteer Brigades and a cluster of international artillery and tank units from the International Brigades provided some 14,000 troops. Only just over half of those were foreign, however, since Spaniards accounted for a growing number of the men in the Brigades' ranks, and sometimes formed entire battalions.

This was the first major attempt to turn the war around, building on the experience of eight months of fighting around the Spanish capital. 'The Army of Madrid is the best; if we can't achieve success with such elements, then we can't achieve it anywhere. If the operation works successfully, the military impact and, especially, the impact on morale, will be very large and we can start to breathe,' President Manuel Azaña, wrote in his diary.[16] If it failed, he added rather more glumly, then it was likely that nothing would work. Prieto, the fellow moderate socialist who was now defence minister, was even more melodramatic. 'The winner at Brunete will win the war,' he said.[17]

The excitement was immense. Haranguing his troops, one commissar claimed that this was a chance to avenge 'Bilbao and Guernica' – and, less logically, 'America'.[18] Kari's Chapaev Battalion – also known as the 'Twenty-One Nations' – had marched overnight to a gathering point in the steep, rock-strewn valley of the Aulencia river. Alfred Kantorowicz, the German writer who was now the battalion's political commissar, looked around him at the tanks, armoured cars and heavy artillery guns and decided that the tide was finally turning. Kantorowicz had previously edited one of the Brigades' many newspapers, so he also dreamed up a stirring imaginary headline to encapsulate the moment: 'The people's army is not just an anvil, it has become a hammer.' A new phase of reconquest and victory, he felt sure, was about to begin.[19]

While new volunteers like Kari – who had turned nineteen a few weeks earlier – were keen to see action, older veterans felt more cautious. Luigi Longo, or Gallo, the Inspector-General of the International Brigades,[20] observed that some, especially in Kari's brigade, had been fighting for months without rest. 'For eight or ten months, they have been on virtually all the fronts, taken part in all the harshest battles and have seen many of their comrades from the early days disappear,' he wrote. 'Some have been injured three or four times.'[21]

The victories at Guadalajara and Peñarroya, however, were part of a wider bolstering of morale. The change of government in Spain brought with it the sensation that political infighting was mostly over, while an increasing number of Spanish units were now able to match or outdo the International Brigades in preparation, courage and quality. One of the French founders of the Brigades, Vital Gayman, still estimated that they formed a quarter of the Republic's shock troops.[22] New arms and proper uniforms meant that the Republican forces, and the International Brigades, increasingly looked like an army of real soldiers.

A second American battalion, the George Washington, had been created and was about to be initiated in battle. Together with the Lincoln and British Battalions, this was part of a single 'regiment', while XV Brigade's other battalions – the Dimitrov, Six Février and Spanish-speaking Español – made up a separate 'regiment'. After the slaughter of its senior officers at Jarama, the Lincolns were now led by Oliver Law. The thirty-seven-year-old Texan was about to make history as the first black American commander to lead white troops into battle.

Law was a former US army soldier with six years' experience in uniform, whose coolness under fire in Jarama had impressed everyone. 'We came to wipe out the fascists ... some of us must die doing that job. But we'll do it here in Spain, maybe stopping fascism in the United States, too, without a great battle there,' he told an interviewer at Jarama.[23] Law had risen naturally up the ranks, and the choice for battalion commander had been between him and another black American, Walter Garland, who commanded the machine-gun company. While the International Brigades staff and commissars had consciously set out to appoint an African American, few protested about the choice. Both men were amongst the few American volunteers with military backgrounds, while Law's courage and coolness were indisputable. As a communist organiser of the unemployed during the Great Depression, he was also considered politically sound. His appointment was a further reminder that the Communist Party was a rarity in US politics, in that it both preached and tried to practise racial equality (at a time when lynching was still alive in the States, with fifty-seven black victims in the three previous years).[24] More than eighty African Americans passed through the Lincoln Battalion, and they shared a history of slavery with many of the Cuban volunteers in their brigade. Some, like the nurse Salaria Kea, cited Mussolini's war in North Africa as a reason for joining.

A handful of white volunteers, however, objected to taking orders from a black man. 'At least in the labor [punishment] company you are treated like [a] white man,' one volunteer spat. Others secretly whispered a sarcastic slogan: 'Restore the whites to equality with the negro.'[25] Colonel Stephen Fuqua, the American embassy's military attaché, who admired but was not permitted to help the volunteers, was surprised to see Oliver Law wearing an officer's uniform. An awkward conversation ensued:

> 'I see that you are in a captain's uniform.'
> 'Yes, that is because I am a captain ...'
> 'I am sure your people must be proud of you, my boy.'[26]

With the self-confident, extravagant and popular George Nathan as head of operations under the Yugoslav Vladimir Ćopić, XV Brigade was swept by a curious tide of euphoria. This had much to do with the fact that, after months of lice-infested tedium in the trenches at Jarama, the brigade had enjoyed a short period of rest. The orders to move to Brunete caught them preparing for a sports day in the village where they had been regrouping. 'We were tickled pink,' said an as yet untested volunteer called Milton Wolff. 'It was July 4th and we were really hepped up.'[27] Philip Detro, a Texan and non-communist, recalled a sudden outburst of camaraderie. 'Comrades who before hardly spoke to each other now became very friendly. Everybody opened up.'[28]

The only concern was that, for the Brunete operation, they had been assigned to a division led by the Hungarian János Gálicz, or Gal, the same man who had sent the Lincolns on their pointless and bloody advance during the attack on the Pingarrón.[29] Fifteenth Brigade spent the few days before the attack in an estate known as El Canchar, fourteen kilometres below the vast and imposing monastery at El Escorial, built by King Philip II in the sixteenth century as a place from which to run the world's first global empire. 'Encamped in a beautiful forest on the side of the mountains. We are about to enter a battle which will prove decisive in the war against fascism,' Peter O'Connor, an Irishman in the Lincoln Battalion, wrote in his diary.[30] The experience of night marches that week, when the heat subsided from fierce to merely uncomfortable, had already underlined to them one of the tortures of the coming battle – thirst.

Leo Kari and XIII Brigade, which made up the rest of Gal's 15th Division, were also at El Canchar.[31] The brigade had come almost directly from the front in Andalusia, picking up fresh recruits like Kari along the way. His Chapaev Battalion, the French-speaking Henri Vuillemin and the Spanish Otumba and Juan Marco Battalions had had little rest. A last-minute change saw the officers and commissar they had followed over the previous months replaced, to the irritation and anger of the men. The former Italian communist parliamentary deputy Vincenzo Bianco, known as Krieger, was made brigade commander just two days before they went into battle.[32] This change reflected the factional infighting amongst different communist groups. The previous commander, Zaisser, had committed the same crime of rank inflation as Kléber earlier in the war by allowing himself to be known as 'General Gómez'.[33] More importantly, he had complained vigorously that his exhausted brigade was not ready for battle.[34]

János Gálicz, or Gal, was part of the select group of (mostly Red Army) foreign officers, along with Walter and Kléber, to be handed an entire division, which usually contained two or three brigades, to command. Walter's 35th Division was also waiting in the hills above the Brunete plain. It included the German-speaking XI Brigade – with an Austrian February 12 Battalion now added to the Thälmann, Hans Beimler (formed in April) and Edgar André – and two Spanish battalions, one of which had been only recently formed.[35] Kléber's 45th Division was in reserve, with XII and 150 Brigades having an additional Spanish battalion commanded by the Bulgarian Malinov, also known as Christoff.[36]

Despite the presence of so many foreign volunteers, none of the International Brigades were involved in the first wave of the attack, which began overnight on 5 July, as thousands of men descended from the woodlands of the sierra and marched silently across the plain towards Brunete and other objectives. With a large initial advantage in men and munitions, Líster, El Campesino and José María Galán, a professional carabinero officer from a left-wing military family, led their divisions straight through the Francoist front line. The plan was to either surprise or sweep past the handful of well-fortified small towns and villages in order to take the ridges overlooking the plain before enemy reinforcements could arrive. From there they were to turn towards Madrid and meet up with a second, smaller Republican attack force advancing west from the southern tip of the Spanish capital,

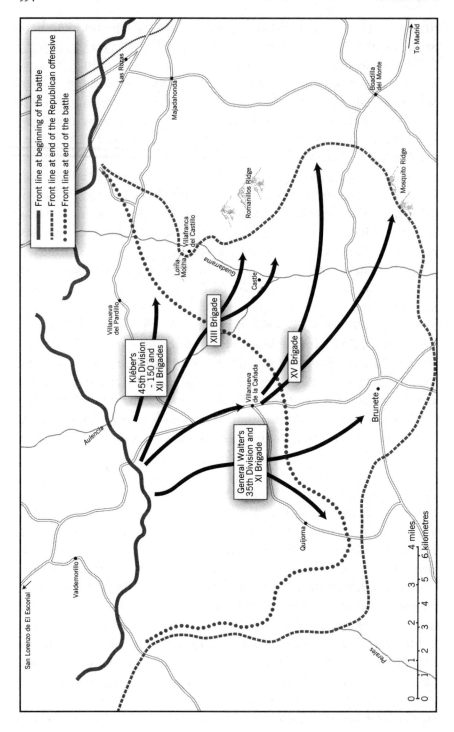

Front line at beginning of the battle
Front line at end of the Republican offensive
Front line at end of the battle

To Madrid

Las Rozas

Boadilla del Monte

Majadahonda

Mosquito Ridge

Romanillos Ridge

Villafranca del Castillo

Loma Mocha

Guadarrama

Castle

Villanueva del Pardillo

XIII Brigade

Kléber's 45th Division - 150 and XII Brigades

XV Brigade

Villanueva de la Cañada

Brunete

General Walter's 35th Division and XI Brigade

Aulencia

Quijorna

Perales

San Lorenzo de El Escorial

Valdemorillo

4 miles
6 kilometres

0 1 2 3
0 1 2 3 4 5

thereby encircling and reducing the forces harassing the city from the west. The attack plan, designed by the man who had so cleverly defended Madrid as Miaja's chief of staff, Vicente Rojo, depended as much on intelligent and successful manoeuvring as actual fighting. Speed and silence were equally vital since the aim was to attack the half-dozen fortified towns and villages on the plain before daylight, often from several directions, catching them unprepared in a massive, overwhelming assault.

A clear, star-spangled sky shed only slight light that night of the 5th, since the moon remained tucked away, and in the darkness thousands of boots tramping across the fields threw up a thin veil of dust.[37] For days, guerrilla units had been reconnoitring the terrain and observing the habits of enemy garrisons at night, and these now guided the units across the empty countryside – with locals having either left the area earlier in the war or asleep in their beds.[38] A vast, ghostly army walked through the darkness, along dirt tracks, dried-up streams and across the open countryside. On the plain the men soon noticed the softer, sandier soil of worked earth and the noise of crop stubble crunching underfoot. Occasional patches of vines, olives, chick peas and holm oaks dotted a plain that was scored by the gullies of dried-out streams and bordered by two rivers, the Guadarrama and the Perales.

The initial strike was startling in its success. The small Brunete garrison was barely able to get out of bed before the attackers were inside the town's narrow streets.[39] By 9 a.m. on 6 July, fighting there was already over, with only a handful of dead and injured amongst the attack force.[40] Prisoners included several officers and two Falange nurses who were siblings of the aristocratic sister-in-law of Falange leader Antonio Primo de Rivera.[41] Even General Varela's chief of staff, Lieutenant Colonel Gregorio López Muñiz, on the Francoist side, was impressed. 'It was an undeniably brilliant example of approximation by night march in order to attack by surprise. The lessons of La Granja had been well learnt,' he wrote later.[42] The plan, in other words, seemed destined for success.

Other settlements on the plain – such as Quijorna, Villanueva de la Cañada and Villanueva del Pardillo – did not fall immediately, but could be bypassed.[43] Most were well defended with barbed wire and trenches all around, and some had been strengthened with modest numbers of additional troops and anti-tank guns.[44] Some garrisons had been nervously expecting something to happen, though they were not sure what. The soldiers of Quijorna garrison, for example, went to bed fully dressed and were in their positions within minutes of hearing gunfire.[45]

Franco did not yet realise it, but by 10 a.m. on 6 July, a ten-kilometre-long wedge had been driven into a space behind his troops besieging Madrid. 'They have torn down my Madrid front,' he exclaimed a few hours later,[46] before giving instructions for preparations for an attack on Santander to be frozen.[47] One of the Brunete attack's objectives, in other words, was achieved instantly.

Much of the plain was now under Republican control. For those leading the attack, the urgent question was how far they should press their advantage. They were already well placed to move beyond the twelve kilometre-wide plain. It should now have been possible to strike south, cutting off the main road from Madrid to Talavera and Extremadura while also heading east for Boadilla. Units that advanced too far, however, risked being isolated and trapped. It was one thing, too, for the field commanders to follow precise, carefully made plans, and quite another for them to manoeuvre on their own initiative.[48] Líster eventually launched a timid push south that quickly ground to a halt.[49] Miaja and Rojo both preferred to consolidate.[50]

While Kléber's division remained in reserve, the other International Brigades were mostly part of a second wave that set out later on 6 July. Walter's division traipsed across the exposed plain to support the troops led by Líster and El Campesino while Gal's two brigades prepared for what was now a crucial task. On the eastern side of the plain stood the reed beds, low scrub and woodland that marked the course of the river Guadarrama. Beyond that a line of wooded hills rose upwards, separating the conquered territory from Boadilla, Aravaca and the La Coruña highway, where the International Brigades had fought in the final months of 1936. Beyond that lay the Casa de Campo, University City and Madrid itself. The attack plan gave Gal's brigades the task of storming the two main ridges, known as Romanillos and Mosquito. They would become famous for some, and infamous for others, over the coming days.

The obvious lesson from Jarama was that ridges like this should be attacked while they were still lightly defended. A British scout called Frank Graham roamed ahead of the advancing troops on his horse and found them almost deserted. He wished they had trucks to bring the men there quickly.[51] Several things happened, however, to slow them. One was a snarl-up in the approaches to the battlefield, as units poured down the steep, windy roads:[52] vehicles sat bumper-to-bumper, jerking forwards a dozen metres at a time. Thirteenth Brigade took five hours to cover the five kilometres to their start position in the hills two kilometres north of Villanueva de la Cañada, a small, elongated village that stood at the gateway to the plain, and which had been bypassed in the initial attacks.[53]

As the morning progressed and the battle to capture the village progressed, they enjoyed a ringside seat. Almost a dozen burned-out tanks already littered the fields in front of the village, where enemy anti-tank guns had stopped the first, early morning attack.[54] Now a second combined infantry and tank attack was being attempted.[55] 'It is unreal, like something we have seen on the screen in the cinema. But it is a thrilling sight,' recalled one British Battalion member. As the tiny dots that were Spanish infantrymen rushed towards the town, the volunteers played at armchair generals, criticising the sluggish way the units moved. 'Now, if we were down there, we could do it better,' they claimed.[56]

Gal's men were originally meant to bypass Villanueva, but the only decent road across the plain ran straight through it and supplies could only be moved properly once it had been taken.[57] The critics on the hill were right about the slowness of the infantry attack, which gave the defenders time to emerge from their bunkers after an artillery bombardment and return to their well-constructed network of trenches, concrete bunkers and foxholes.[58] General Walter considered it essential to attack such positions while an artillery bombardment was still going on. 'It's better to suffer losses from our own artillery by getting too close to the enemy than not to get the full benefit of the artillery fire,' he told Szurek (who nevertheless wondered who would be mad enough to actually do that).[59] The village was also ringed by barbed wire and attackers who tried to cut through that were mown down by machine-gun fire from the thousand-strong defenders.[60]

New orders came. Gal's brigades were to help take Villanueva de la Cañada and only then move on.[61] Their attack, the third of the day, began early in the afternoon. For newcomers like Leo Kari, it was an initiation into the sights, smells and sounds of real war. When the defenders' machine guns opened up, with their evenly paced rat-a-tat-tat, it sounded like someone banging a hammer on a tin roof. It also scared the newcomers, who threw themselves to the ground while the veterans walked nonchalantly on. The fire was not directed at them, but at the English-speaking XV Brigade, which had circled around to the south.[62] When they heard a buzzing noise that sounded like a swarm of bees, however, the old-timers dropped to their bellies and began crawling. That, Kari learnt, was the sound of bullets whipping through the air above them.

The village had been intelligently fortified, following a German system of circular trenches and barbed wire, and had just received reinforcements. On the plain, which fell gently away from the village on three sides, there were few places for the attackers to hide. The solid church tower offered a magnificent vantage spot for machine-gunners and a tiny walled cemetery outside the village provided another defensive strongpoint. A Moroccan unit held out there under intense artillery fire that sent the bones of the buried flying into the air.

The smouldering hulks of tanks were proof that the fascists had the latest German anti-tank weapons.[63] The International Brigades, however, had also just received the latest 45mm Russian anti-tank guns – three for each brigade. They were cumbersome, but devastatingly accurate.[64] The guns could be loaded with armour-piercing rounds, shrapnel rounds, or small grenade-like shells to destroy machine-guns nests.[65] The Garibaldis towed the rubber-wheeled weapons behind trucks, while the strong-muscled Scandinavian sailors of XIII Brigade's new anti-tank section often pulled them with ropes, nine men to a gun.[66] Fifteenth Brigade's new anti-tank section, manned by a group of intellectually minded British volunteers, some of them students, were kept out of this fight and chafed angrily, watching from the hills above, knowing that their weapons could save infantry lives.[67]

All afternoon men lay paralysed a few hundred metres from the town, as the sun burned their skin, the wounded cried out for help and the slightest movement drew fire. The British Battalion huddled 300 metres from the town in the ditches along the Brunete road, regretting that their water flasks had been taken off to be refilled (and not returned) just before they were ordered into the attack and that the streams on their maps were mostly dried out.[68] Unlike the other battalions, they were at least on a slope that rose gently out of the town, giving them the advantage of height. Even that, though, was not enough to risk rushing forward. They hugged the baking earth that lined the ditches, hid behind dung heaps and waited for nightfall.[69] The Americans in the Washington and Lincoln Battalions were also struggling under the glaring sun, and six out of eight men in one section collapsed from heatstroke.[70] Many of the Canadians in the American battalions – who called themselves 'the fighting Canucks' – lay out amongst the wounded, having failed to charge through the kill zone.[71] Kari's Chapaev Battalion, meanwhile, arrived two hours late. They had lost their way in the fog of dust thrown up by speeding vehicles and the bombs and shells that sent plumes of dry earth high into the air.[72]

George Nathan was sent to direct the attack personally but, as night began to fall, they had still not crossed the last few hundred metres to the village.[73] The final act of the battle for Villanueva de la Cañada came quickly, but was preceded by tragedy. Peering up from their ditches into the gloom of dusk, the British could see some forty people – led by women, old men and children – abandoning the village. They assumed that these were refugees fleeing the fighting during a lull and shouted at them to run. In the memory of one of those present, they instead remained 'closely packed together and casting fearful and anxious glances to left and right as they moved forwards'. Occasional shouts of '¡Camarada!' and '¡Comandante!' sounded like appeals for help and one British volunteer ran forward to guide them.[74] Only when the firing started did they realise that these people were leading a group of soldiers who crouched behind them. 'We had no alternative,' recalled the same witness, who never shook off the horror of what happened next.[75] The British Battalion's new commander,[76] Fred Copeman, turned to two machine-gunners beside him and gave his orders. 'Get ready to fire all you've got, and don't be sentimental,' he urged. At his whistle blast, he remembered, the machine-gunners 'let everything rip along the flat surface of the road ... Not a nice sight. One old lady was dead in front. Happily she did not know what had hit her. A few more women were wounded ... Only three men remained alive.'[77] Children also lay dead.[78]

This ghastly encounter appeared to galvanise the attackers and the final breakthrough came soon afterwards, on the western side of the village. One of XIII Brigade's Spanish battalions, the Juan Marco, rushed forward with grenades.[79] So too did the Bulgarians and Yugoslavs in XV Brigade's Dimitrov Battalion, whose courageous final dash brought heavy losses.[80] Soon both were inside the village. Encouraged, the British also rushed in. Once inside, the fighting was with bayonets and grenades, though the church's thick walls still provided valuable cover for the remaining defenders. By midnight, however, the battle was over.

The ferocity of the defence, the losses of their own men and the use of civilians as shields combined to strike fury into the volunteers. More than 140 prisoners were taken, but at least half a dozen were shot on the spot, including the mayor.[81] Copeman himself, enraged that a wounded fascist had shot a British volunteer who was apparently trying to help him, killed the artillery commander as he tried to surrender. 'All I saw was the Colt revolver he was waving around aimlessly. I was taking no chances, he dropped like a brick,' he recalled.[82] Some 350 members of the two International Brigades had been killed or wounded.[83] Amongst those to emerge from the rubble were two Belgians who had joined Franco's foreign legion and shouted 'Hello Ruskies!' at the International Brigaders.[84]

Villanueva de la Cañada was, by now, a smouldering pile of ruins littered with hundreds of corpses.[85] A similar fate had already struck, or awaited, the other villages on the plain – though this task took several days to complete. Thirteenth Brigade did not set out again until ten o'clock the following morning. By then, most of the dead had been found and buried. One of the last to be discovered was the brigade's brand-new Yugoslav commissar, Blagoye Parović, who had been amongst the first volunteers to reach Spain. The previous night, perhaps knowing that he had to prove himself to his new unit, he had insisted on helping lead the Juan Marco Battalion into the town. Political commissar Kantorowicz went through his pockets, removing his notepad, papers, a wallet, a watch and a cigarette case that were bundled up to be sent back to the brigade's HQ. At the last minute he flicked open the cigarette case, and helped himself to one of the fourteen elegant Gauloise Bleu there. He handed the rest out to the surprised group standing around him. 'This is his final gift to us,' he told the men, before Parović's corpse was taken off.[86]

Leo Kari and the fellow newcomers who had survived their first day of fighting felt curiously elated. They were now blooded soldiers, who had experienced victory. Wandering through the town that day, however, some began to realise that the heat was an enemy which provoked more than thirst. The corpses of Moroccan Francoist soldiers and their own companions were already blackened and bloated. Flies buzzed all over them.[87] The smell of decomposing flesh – at first sickly sweet, then rank – began to drift across the plain. It would remain there for the next few weeks, a nausea-inducing stench that new volunteers noticed immediately. Those tasked with shifting the bodies finally found a use for the bulky, hot, rubberised gas masks they were obliged to carry in case Franco was tempted to use the chemical warfare techniques employed by the Army of Africa in Morocco.[88] The volunteers wore them while picking up the dead, who were tossed into lime pits or taken away on trucks.

As the two brigades marched on towards the rivers at the bottom of the eastern heights that morning they were tormented by thirst. 'We marched in hilly, mostly shadeless terrain at temperatures that rose to fifty degrees in the sun during noon hours. Our cistern trucks had already been emptied by the time we left Villanueva at ten o'clock in the morning … The thirst makes you ignore the danger of death. It drives you mad,' wrote Kantorowicz.[89]

Some volunteers stripped to their shorts. Those with pale northern European skin turned a raw, violent red. Others studied the Moroccan captives with their hooded woollen cloaks, and took the opposite approach, leaving their baggy corduroy trousers, thick shirts and other clothes on.[90] 'That way you are well protected from the sun,' reasoned one Swedish volunteer. 'I would find Yanks who had ripped their shirts off. They had sunstroke and were usually beyond help.'[91] Steel helmets became a source of debate, since they both protected from and absorbed the sun. They would turn away a glancing bullet or flying debris, but explosive rounds killed a man if they just brushed against them.[92] Ludwig Renn, the famed war writer who helped lead XI Brigade onto the plain, never wore his. 'It doesn't protect you from anything at all, except for clods of earth,' he said.[93]

Neither clothing option – stripped or covered – defeated the heat. 'Clothes stuck to your body, faces became striped with sweat and your tongue felt like a wooden block. We thought only of water, fantasizing about the river,' said Kari. Reality was disappointing.[94] The Guadarrama river, which gave its name to such an impressive mountain range, turned out to be a meagre stream lined with rough vegetation and poplar stands.[95] 'The water was dirty and almost stagnant. But there was water. You laid your face to the surface and drank in deep, blissful gulps.'[96] Dysentery soon spread.

Above them, the men could see machine-gun nests being hastily set up. Were these friend, or foe? A patrol was sent up the slope to find out. The answer came in the form of raking machine-gun fire. 'Well, then,' said the Swiss Chapaev commander Otto Brunner, lying next to Kantorowicz. 'We'll give them a hiding tomorrow morning.'[97] By then, Franco's generals had had two days to prepare for their arrival.

36

The Romanillos and Mosquito Ridges: Guadarrama river, 8 July 1937

On the morning of 8 July, Leo Kari and Alfred Kantorowicz were with the rest of Gal's brigades in the irregular scrub of spiky ilex, low cork oaks and broom of the Guadarrama basin, looking up at the heights that they must now conquer. Rosemary, thyme[1] and other dried herbs crackled under foot, adding a perfume to this as yet unbloodied part of the battlefield. Red ants, which attacked en masse, were a surprise foe.[2] The shade and uneven nature of the terrain along the four-kilometre-wide stretch of woodland that they were occupying was welcome. The upward slope was not. Those who had been at Jarama recalled how easy it was to beat off attacks, and provoke carnage, from the top of a ridge. In addition, the Villanueva de la Cañada engagement had meant that they were a day late, doubling the time available for preparation of defensive positions above them.

A meagre force of chauffeurs and office workers from Franco's military post at Boadilla, along with some regular Moroccan and other soldiers, had been rapidly sent to Mosquito Ridge the previous day. These, like some of the Republican units on the plain, included city conscripts who had never held a gun or, in some cases, a spade in their lives. Even they, however, could see that their position was a good one. 'In order to attack us, the Reds had to advance almost two kilometres in sight of us, climbing a slope,' recalled one. 'We, on the other hand, had space behind us where we couldn't be seen and could move at will. The only inconvenience was that the ground was covered in trees and thick bushes, which were easy to hide in.'[3] The arrival of a *tabor* of Moroccans during the day added firepower to their position.[4]

Later that morning, the two International Brigades set off up the gentle, three-kilometre-long ramparts to the twin ridges of Romanillos – topped by a farm building – and Mosquito. Deer, rabbits and the occasional wild boar fled in front of them.[5] The first few folds in the hills proved easy to climb, with the enemy's forward posts retreating up the hill as XIII Brigade approached Romanillos, while the English-speaking XV Brigade climbed up towards Mosquito Ridge, which lay further south. The results of the day's attacks differed greatly between units, generating confusion about whether the assault had been successful, or not.

The Lincolns were amazed to find enemy soldiers fleeing before them. 'Some ran behind trees, stopped and fired at us. But mostly they just kept running. I couldn't believe my eyes. We weren't even shooting at them,' said one of Oliver Law's runners, Harry Fisher.[6] They also found that the enemy's retreat ended at the ridge, and they were eventually pinned down by fire from above.[7] In the meantime, at about 11 a.m., a separate group from XV Brigade followed several tanks all the way to the outskirts of Boadilla.[8] They had, in essence, achieved the aim of crossing the ridge but, for some reason, they turned around. The inexperienced Francoist soldiers on Mosquito Ridge were hiding in their newly dug foxholes, convinced that they had been surrounded. 'The Reds had got to the village without us noticing,' one said later. 'But they didn't live up to their reputation … [because], after a bit of shooting, they turned around and went back.'[9]

Reports reached Rojo's headquarters that the heights had actually been taken, provoking elation among staff there. It took two hours, and some misguided decision-making, before they realised they were wrong.[10] In fact, five separate attempts to take the highest peak of the Mosquito range were beaten back by the office clerks and other reinforcements above them, with the insect-like buzz of their bullets inspiring the 'Mosquito Ridge' nickname.

On the northern end of the ridge, Krieger's XIII Brigade felt that they, too, were about to triumph. 'We had won,' recalled Alfred Kantorowicz. 'As far as the eye could see … the fascists were running for their lives.'[11] A sense of reckless confidence overtook the men with him. This was paid for by 3 Company of the Chapaev Battalion. A tabor of Moroccan troops that had been rushed there from University City lay hidden behind rocks and in the thick undergrowth along one of the paths leading up a ravine towards Romanillos. These, or other Moroccans, ambushed the head of the company and an accompanying machine-gun section.[12] The attack was sprung so suddenly that the volunteers barely had time to use their weapons. Dead and injured fell to the ground and some men became trapped by their clothes in the thick, thorny undergrowth, while the rest of the company fled. 'Animals! Idiots! Dirty reds!'[13] the attackers shouted after them in Spanish.

The Moroccans, following the sadistic methods of the colonial Army of Africa, moved amongst the wounded, torturing and killing. 'The screams rose in nameless horror to the sky, through the night, going on and on, erasing everything else from the minds of those of us who were listening,' said Kari. 'I sank down ... and prayed to a God I did not know and did not believe in. Self-preservation drove me on, but the screams continued to ring in my ears.'[14] The exact details of what happened vary, but Kari – who later saw at least some of the bodies – talked of men burnt to death and others with their eyes gouged out, their ears, hands and feet sliced off or their genitals hacked off and stuffed into their mouths while they bled to death. If the aim was to strike terror into the volunteers, it worked. Kantorowicz, arriving later, smelled the charred human flesh. 'I looked away, wanting to vomit ... Nor did the comrades and friends of the desecrated speak of what they saw or felt. The horror had sunk too deep into us. It would never come to the surface,' he recalled.[15]

The Republican advance continued, however. All seemed to be going well until the brigaders reached the final 400 metres of ground that separated them from the well-fortified, if still relatively lightly defended, upper ridges. The Chapaev men now discovered what it was like to run up steep ground towards machine-gun and rifle fire, as an estimated seventy to eighty Francoist soldiers held them at bay from the central peak of the Romanillos heights.

Neither brigade, then, had conquered the last ridge. The Chapaev commander, Otto Brunner, installed his headquarters in a fortified white farmhouse with a circular trench all around it, which had been abandoned without a fight. Like the rest of the new line they were setting up, this suffered the marked inconvenience of being several hundred metres below the enemy. That evening Brunner wrote a report warning that his battalion was already down to 180 men. 'The sections are completely exhausted. They would like to carry out their orders well, but are physically not in a condition to do so. We urgently request at least two companies of reinforcements.'[16]

The following day, 9 July, the Chapaev Battalion dug in below the ridge, expecting a counter-attack which never came. The rest of Krieger's brigade showed a limited desire to attack. The horror of the previous day's ambush appeared to have had its desired effect.[17] The Lincolns, meanwhile, attacked their part of Mosquito Ridge, which had been reinforced by a Spanish Legion *bandera* early that morning. One attack set out from their lower ridge at exactly the same time as Franco's freshly arrived legionnaires decided to counter-attack, with both sides running down to the shallow fold between their positions.[18] Oliver Law led from the front. Earlier that day he had explained to his battalion that they would have neither artillery nor air support. Now he, like his men, admitted that he dreamed about little more than getting home in order to 'drink gallons and gallons of cool water'.[19]

Harry Fisher, Law's runner, wrote home describing the attack three weeks later. 'The Gods must have laughed when they saw us charge each other at the same time,' wrote Fisher, who had been following ten yards behind his commander:

> Once again Law was up in front urging us on. Then the fascists started running back. They were retreating. Law would not drop for cover. True, he was exhausted as we all were. We had no food or water that day and it was hot. He wanted to keep the fascists on the run and take the high hill. 'Come on, comrades, they are running,' he shouted. 'Let's keep them running.' All the time he was under machine-gun fire. [Later Fisher would write that it seemed every bullet was aimed at Law.] Finally he was hit. Two comrades brought him in, in spite of the machine guns. His wound was dressed. As he was being carried on a stretcher to the ambulance, he clenched his fist and said, 'Carry on boys.' Then he died.[20]

The Lincoln Battalion's commander was buried nearby. A simple wooden board read: 'Here lies Oliver Law, the first American Negro to command American whites in battle.'[21] The grave has never been found.

That evening the men of the Chapaev, Lincoln and other battalions on the lower ridges heard the deep rumble of engines and saw the lights of lorries bringing reinforcements onto the heights above them.[22] Despite this, the following day XV Brigade, now down to just 300 men – half a battalion – came surprisingly close to breaking through after sneaking up close to the enemy overnight and launching a well-coordinated attack with two Spanish brigades and fourteen tanks.[23] Defenders panicked and regrouped on a single peak under the command of a courageous Francoist captain, Estanislao Gómez Landero y Koch.[24] 'I myself had begun to think about how to escape,' one of the defenders recalled later. He was stopped by the sight of his captain running backwards and forwards giving calm instructions, then being shot but jumping off his stretcher to return to the fight before being shot again and killed. He had time to hurl one last insult. 'Let's show those English bastards who we are,' he shouted. 'Look, now they are retreating!'[25] By now, indeed, the attack had petered out. Fifteenth Brigade's volunteers never realised quite how close they had come to conquering a crucial position that might have changed the course of the Brunete battle.[26]

The Republican corps commander, meanwhile, was told that 'energetic pressure' was being applied by XIII Brigade to Romanillos and that 'this has not been taken, but it is hoped that it will be imminently'. This was a lie, since the brigade was down to 240 men and firmly stuck 500 metres from the Romanillos ridge top.[27] 'No one believed any more in the success of an assault,' said Kantorowicz as they went through the motions of attacking over the next two days. 'It had been nothing more than a pretence,' he noted.[28] Reports reaching corps headquarters of Gal's division spoke of weary men whose morale had been shattered. 'Many soldiers have had to be evacuated in a state of exhaustion and with symptoms of nervous stress,' the report noted.[29]

That evening, as if to confirm the fragility of their situation, Chapaev staff officers sat in the defensive ditches around the headquarters at the farmhouse, while artillery tried to destroy the building. Suddenly they noticed that someone was still inside, babbling incoherently and occasionally shouting out verses from 'The Internationale' and 'The Land of Tirol'.[30] An officer, whom Kantorowicz named only as 'X', tottered drunkenly out of the doorway. Like the rest of the battalion staff, and with water almost absent, he had quenched his day-long thirst with large quantities of wine. Adrenaline had neutralised the impact of the alcohol on everyone else, but this officer was either blind drunk, shell-shocked, or both. He lolled towards them as shrapnel flew around him, muttering incomprehensibly to himself before falling headlong into a ditch. 'It was the first time in the war that this brave and seasoned officer's nerves had failed,' commented Kantorowicz. 'God damn me, God damn me, we've to get out of here,' he heard Brunner mutter. No one argued.

Eventually, officers from several battalions agreed that commissar Kantorowicz should be sent to Madrid to complain about the way that Krieger was commanding them.[31] The latter was given to shows of bravura, including leading his men into fights with a sub-machine gun in his hands. In fact, his job was to direct them, worry about tactics and make sure they received proper tank or artillery support. He was also given to hurling drunken insults at both officers and men.[32]

The determination of the men involved in this small conspiracy was reinforced at a meeting the following morning. The French battalion commander, Robert Lhez, asked the captain who served as his adjutant (whom Kantorowicz called 'Captain Y', and was probably thirty-two-year-old Captain Roux[33]) to dash through the artillery fire to their own battalion headquarters and return with a map. Kantorowicz watched as he rose like an automaton and clambered out of the ditch:

Half a minute after he disappeared, we heard a sharp bang nearby, followed by a scream. We all reached for our pistols. An enemy rifle had to be within ten or twenty metres of our trench. We jumped up. We heard whimpering. We all rushed out of the trench. In the next hollow [Captain] Y lay with a head shot, his hand gripping a revolver. He was still alive. We leaned over him. He opened his eyes and wheezed, 'I couldn't do it again, I couldn't do it again … I'm not a coward, but I couldn't do it. I couldn't go through that any more.' He looked at Lhez: 'Don't say anything to our comrades. Don't tell my family. Promise.' Villette [the Henri Vuillemin commissar] knelt down beside him, and I ran to fetch a paramedic. When I came back with him, Y was already dead.

He had gone through hundreds of enemy fire barrages. This time he could not do it again. His nerves couldn't take it anymore. He preferred death. He preferred that to admitting that he couldn't endure the horror anymore. Otherwise one would have been able to scold him as a coward. He was a hero. When we were back in the ditch, the liaison officer of 'Juan Marco' was waiting for us with the message that the fascists were coming.[34]

The attacks on Romanillos and Mosquito by Gal's two International Brigades had failed. So, too, had the pincer movement meant to trap Franco's army outside Madrid. Land had been won, but the Republican army would now have to fight to keep it.

37

Resist: Brunete plain, 12 July 1937

It was around this time that the Norwegian writer Nordhal Grieg first came to the battlefield. He was one of more than one hundred writers and intellectuals from around the world who had gathered in Valencia on 4 July (and then visited Barcelona and Madrid) for what was perhaps the most illustrious literary gathering of the 1930s – the Second International Writers' Congress for the Defence of Culture, organised by the Alliance of Anti-Fascist Intellectuals.[1] All the attendees were prominent left-wingers, there to show their support for the Republic. They included one past and one future Nobel winner, the Spaniard Jacinto Benavente and Chilean Pablo Neruda. The closest most came to battle, however, was when three helmeted men burst onto the stage at their meeting in Madrid on 6 July with a Francoist flag captured that morning. 'The town of Brunete is now in our power!' they declared to rapturous applause. Gerda Taro, who had been taking photographs of the writers' congress, immediately jumped in a car – ignoring all prohibitions against journalists – and sped to the Brunete front, where she captured images of Republican soldiers that spread quickly around the world. She also stopped to join Kléber's men in a fist-raised rendition of 'The Internationale'.[2]

Few of the writers were prepared to run the risks that Grieg – one of the best Norwegian authors of his generation – was taking in his determination to experience war in person. As he descended onto the Brunete plain from the north, he found the battle entering an entirely new phase. With all the small towns and villages now taken, and the ridges to the east holding out, instructions had been issued for the Republican army to go on to what was deemed 'temporary' defensive mode. From the 'goblinesque oaks' of the sierra, Grieg could see a single, tarmac road running like a shiny, blue ribbon across the plain to Brunete.[3] On the mountains behind him, and despite the terrible heat on the plain, patches of snow still glinted teasingly against a pale blue horizon.

While the Republican army dug itself in, the Condor Legion, the Italians and the rest of the Francoist air force started a long, steady and nerve-shattering bombing campaign. Grieg saw fields burnt black by incendiary bombs. Fires crackled in the pine forests and brown columns of earth rose into the air wherever enemy shells landed. An American volunteer, schoolteacher John Cookson, paused to observe the battle-rent sky. 'Everything seems to have its opposite,' he wrote to his father. 'The dust thrown by bombs thousands of feet into the air drifts over the mountains and plains and the glorious golden Spanish sunsets are supplemented by an unrivalled red and purple against craggy mountains.'[4]

Grieg was looking for the Scandinavian volunteers serving with XI Brigade, which together with two Spanish brigades was under the command of General Walter.[5] Trouble had erupted as soon as XI Brigade commander Richard Staimer heard that one of these was led by a 'socialist'. To the sectarian Staimer, that automatically made the man a suspect and he ordered a Spanish officer to spy on him. The other brigade soon found out and all chances of harmony within the division were destroyed.[6] It was all part of what Ludwig Renn called Staimer's ability 'to show disdain for the Spaniards which, unfortunately, he was much better at than other, more useful, things'. Staimer had filled his brigade staff with careerist German communists, who often put political discipline and dogma above military common sense.[7] Szurek mistrusted these self-important officers who seemed to him to 'enjoy the limelight' excessively.[8] Renn, meanwhile, could never pardon for Staimer for disappearing whenever the fighting started. 'His way of doing things was, to me, incomprehensible,' he said.[9]

Grieg visited the village of Quijorna, where the Beimler and Austrian February 12 Battalions had helped overcome a stubborn defence and a rumour had spread that a lone machine-gunner perched in the church tower was a woman. On inspection, it was found to be the slumped corpse of a Moroccan soldier, surrounded by thousands of empty cartridge cases.[10] On the body of a dead Francoist soldier from Zaragoza, Grieg discovered a reminder that these, too, were men with homes and families. 'We have no food to send you, only some lettuce. But next week ... Benito will be here and then we can perhaps manage some sausage and cheese,' read a letter from the soldier's father.[11] Perhaps he was one of the many men buried alive as they took cover from intense Republican shelling in village cellars. A survivor recalled hiding in one of these with a hundred wounded men before the building crashed down on them. 'When the aircraft left, there was a tomb-like silence. Since nobody spoke, I thought I was the only one left alive,' he wrote. Then 'a ray of light – and hope of salvation – appeared and I realised I was not the only one ... We began to dig ourselves out with our hands, removing the earth that continued to fall on us, making a gap through which a single person could escape and pulling ourselves out. That is how a few of us survived, but no more than ten; the others would never get out.'[12]

Grieg found that, apart from the fight at Quijorna, XI Brigade had enjoyed a relatively quiet time in the south-west corner of the plain, taking part in the occasional poorly coordinated attack on the road running west out of Brunete.[13] Now it was in defensive mode. In later years, Republican generals would disagree over whether the failure of the larger plan was because they moved too slowly or because it had been overambitious.[14] In fact, the reason lay less with Republican errors and more with the rapid and efficient response of the enemy and, crucially, its pilots and aircaft from fascist Germany and Italy.

Brunete galvanised Franco. As one of his generals noted at the time, the advance threatened Franco's personal authority, since this 'depends on his [military] prestige'.[15] Historians do not agree on whether Franco's reputation as a brilliant general was actually deserved, but he certainly did not want to lose face at home or with Hitler and Mussolini.[16] Franco visited the battlefield himself on 8 July, just as the first reinforcements arrived from the northern front.[17] He became acutely aware of the danger that would ensue if the International Brigades broke over the ridges to Boadilla.[18] 'The Madrid situation requires our full attention,' he wrote in a cable that day. 'It is indispensable that all our aviation acts on this front and that other projects are postponed [in the north].'[19] Four days later, this final decision was paying off. Condor Legion commander General Hugo Sperrle – the fleshy gourmet who Hitler would rely on as a key air-force field marshal in the Second World War – insisted on moving his entire legion of eight squadrons and anti-flak batteries to Brunete and eventually took command of all enemy aircraft in the battle.[20]

The skies over Brunete, which had belonged to the Republic for the first two days of the offensive, soon hosted the greatest air battle the world had ever seen. Up to a hundred bombers and fighters were in the air at any one time, bombing, strafing and fighting duels. Below them, soldiers from both sides looked on mesmerised.

Francoist air dominance came down to numbers and the fraud of non-intervention. Most of Franco's air force was provided by Germany and Italy: Hitler and Mussolini sent 250 aircraft, together with pilots and groundcrews. A smaller number of aircraft were flown by Franco's own Spanish airmen. The new, speedy Messerschmitt 109 – which would become the backbone of the Luftwaffe's fighter force in the Second World War – was more than a match for the Soviet aircraft that had triumphed at Madrid and Guadalajara, though the Condor Legion was still sufficiently wary to wait several days before committing their precious new planes to the battle.[21] The Luftwaffe also applied the techniques it had been honing on the northern front, with reconnaissance aircraft permanently above the battlefield transmitting intelligence to mobile command vehicles. Their aerodromes were also closer, allowing them to react faster and remain above the battlefield longer. More important, however, were the calibre and number of pilots available to Franco. A first batch of newly trained Spanish Republican pilots had just returned from courses in the Soviet Union, but were not yet operational, which meant that part of the Republican air force – which already had fewer aircraft – had to stay on the ground.[22]

Brigaders quickly came to recognise the ponderous, throaty growl of the Junkers 52 engines, since these flew almost unmolested over the battlefield every night at a rate of up to one every ten minutes.[23] Ground troops eagerly followed the searchlights seeking out the bombers, praying that anti-aircraft gunners might reach them. That happened only rarely. Soon the smaller aircraft were also free to roam the battlefield almost at will during the day, practising the new and terrifying technique of continuous strafing known as 'the chain', or 'carousel', involving three or more aircraft revolving in a circle, taking turns to swoop down and attack troops on the ground while the others rose and circled before having another run.[24]

The damage on the ground was not great to begin with,[25] but the impact on morale and on the willingness of the Republic's soldiers to break cover and advance proved devastating.[26] The noise of exploding bombs was terrifying and, even without the shrapnel, the shockwaves knocked men unconscious. A Swedish volunteer was told to hide under trees and flatten his body against the ground. 'You're supposed to have a piece of wood in your mouth. I didn't,' he recalled after being injured in a bombing raid. 'I wasn't more than ten–twelve metre from the blast. The distance was enough for the shrapnel to fly above me, but the pressure wave took both my eardrums, since I had had my mouth closed. I lay unconscious almost an entire day before they found me.'[27] Volunteers spoke of their units miraculously surviving such bombardments. The terror, mental anguish and seemingly arbitrary physical damage was described by a XV Brigade volunteer after his unit, resting in a hollow below the lines, failed to camouflage itself properly and was attacked from the air:

Then they let loose. That awful whistle, scream and rush of the bombs, then the explosion. The whole earth was blasted into pieces. It heaved and rocked and swayed and roared and smoked, and the bombs kept coming down, and every time you heard that whistle and scream you knew there was a shaft pointing to the small of your back, the bomb would hit you right there and blow you to a million pieces … Then the bombing stopped and they began strafing. Everything was smoke and dirt and dark but you knew the machine guns would see through the dark, and everybody around you was killed, and you were left here alone and the next burst would catch you square across the back and you would be killed, too … Your ear was bursting, your head was splitting. Suddenly you didn't hear the roar at all. The planes were going, they were going away. You sat up, you looked around [expecting] to find everybody dead and you saw others sitting up and looking around – your whole group, your whole section, the whole Company, everybody alive, not a single one hurt.[28]

The battle scars incurred were often mental and doctors knew it, though some officers were inclined to suspect cowardice. Grieg saw one of XI Brigade's Spanish soldiers brought in to a field dressing station looking dead-eyed: 'He had a thick olive yellow face; it was totally without expression.' The man had been accused of pretending, but then the bombers came over: 'Suddenly he lifted his head listening; his features froze in a terrible fear, he started whimpering with little fearful sounds. It was a plane he heard. "You will get to go to the hospital," [Dr] Arco said to him. "Sit here with me." '[29]

Artillery bombardment was marginally less traumatic than attacks from the air, but still require those targeted to seek refuge. Fortunately, the German artillery ran like clockwork, to the extent that General Walter's HQ, based around his battered Matford truck, was targeted at between 2 and 3 p.m. every day for several days. When Renn spotted Walter wandering off to the bushes to relieve himself at just before 2 p.m., he warned him to be quick. Walter was caught with his trousers down, but soon rushed back.[30]

With most of the front lines fixed by 12 July, a tense, six-day stand-off began, while Franco's side prepared a counter-attack. On the ground, attention shifted to the north-eastern corner of the battlefield, where Kléber's division finally went into action, as the two sides tussled for control of the villages of Villanueva del Pardillo[31] and Villafranca del Castillo (held by the Francoists) over six days fighting.[32] The habit of constantly repeating failed attacks with fewer and fewer men (a practice on both sides) worked so badly that Kléber eventually refused to attack a hill called La Mocha, protected by a deep ravine and rings of barbed wire, for a fourth time. The bull-like 'general' confronted his old nemesis General Miaja personally about this.

I understand that there are cases when it is necessary to sacrifice entire divisions in order to break through the front in a designated sector, through which fresh reserves can then pass in order to develop a strike in depth. However, in this case I know that there are no reserves available for this purpose. Even if my division takes the hill – which given its present conditions is even less probable than at the start – there is no one behind it who could exploit the success. The slightest counter-attack by the enemy will force my weakened units back, and the enemy will exploit this in order to carry out a strike in depth on our rear. If the general's orders are that we repeat the attack, then I ... must warn him that I cannot encourage his hopes of our successfully carrying out the orders received.[33]

A thuggish Soviet advisor known as Ivon, or Ivan, threatened him with a court martial and would later disarm and beat another Red Army advisor from Finland who made similar arguments. Miaja was angry, but listened and did not order further attacks. Kléber had other problems too. His recently created 150 International Brigade, still had 'untrained recruits and poor cohesion'. Some Spanish conscripts deliberately inflicted wounds on themselves or deserted, leaving behind notes that read 'we do not want to serve or fight because we are commanded by foreigners'.[34] One Polish volunteer was even kidnapped and taken across the lines by deserters, who presented him to the Francoists as a trophy 'Russian'. An unknown number of troublemakers were shot on the spot, but mistrust between Spaniards and foreign officers reduced their effectiveness. Kléber also replaced brigade commander Fernando Gerassi, a Turkish-born painter of Sephardic origin, for disobeying orders.[35] Miaja wanted to court-martial him, but Kléber claimed Gerassi was ill, and kept him on his staff.[36] By 16 July, the stand-off that existed across the rest of the battlefield was established here, too, and Kléber's men were ordered to assume defensive positions for the expected grand counter-attack.[37] Everything was tensed, ready for the great assault.

38

The Coup that Lasted a Year: Brunete plain, 18–26 July 1937

Just before dawn on 18 July, the entire Brunete battlefield was awoken by the thunderous sound of heavy artillery. It was the first anniversary of the failed, fascist-backed coup d'état – and the day chosen for Franco's first major counter-attack. His Axis-led air force now enjoyed clear dominance and heavy bombers helped soften up Republican positions. The resulting cacophony could be heard in Madrid.[1] The principal target was the line in front of Brunete itself. Franco hoped that a thrust here could connect with assault troops storming down from the eastern ridges to the Guadarrama river.[2]

Over the previous week, Ćopić's XV Brigade had, intermittently, been able to rest and spend time in reserve positions by the dried-out Aulencia and Guadarrama rivers.[3] Water had to be dug for in the riverbeds, though rotting human and animals corpses threatened to poison it.[4] The two battered American battalions had been fused into one that inherited the Lincolns' name, bringing an end to the short, half-battle history of the Washington Battalion. To the considerable rage of officers and men, however, promises that Krieger's exhausted XIII Brigade would also be relieved were broken.[5] This meant that by the time the counter-attack started volunteers like Leo Kari, who had survived a week of futile attacks against the crests, spent a further six days coping with the thirst, sniping, aerial bombardment and strafing. 'The ten days at Romanillos had been hell … but the anniversary exceeded all of them,' he recalled. 'The noise deafened us, the dust blinded us and the stench was nauseous.'[6] The bombardments were often fiercer on the plain or at the bottom of the Guadarrama valley, where XV Brigade was resting.[7] 'Our previous concepts of hell have been thoroughly revised,' Kari added in his diary.[8]

Returning from Madrid, however, Kantorowicz thought he saw a transformation in the battered Chapaev Battalion, wrought by a fatalistic sensation that things could not get worse.[9] 'The surprising thing about suffering is its elasticity. You turn the lowest point into the norm and, from there, keep on living ... Those of the battalion who remained had acquired an impenetrable hardness ... They no longer wished to be replaced,' he said. Kari agreed. 'Here we are, and here we stay,' he jotted in his diary.[10]

The counter-attack spread to the hillside trenches occupied by Kari and his XIII Brigade comrades that afternoon.[11] With the heat pressing down on them, the Chapaev Battalion spotted distinctive white *rexa* turbans in the undergrowth, as Army of Africa troops crept towards them. As usual, the Moroccans used the folds in the terrain cleverly, coming ever closer and rushing forward in short bursts.[12] Even then, it seemed that the Chapaevs would hold them off, but an inexperienced company suddenly panicked and the contagion spread. The Juan Marco and Otumba soldiers abandoned their trenches unnecessarily, leaving their machine guns behind. Like all fleeing troops, they became easier targets as they ran. Other volunteers looked on aghast as they were mown down. When the Moroccans reach the forward line they found the positions empty and ready to be occupied, as they gained 600 metres of land.[13]

The battle was now to prevent the enemy taking control of the Guadarrama valley, a fight that continued for eight hard days.[14] When George Nathan appeared behind the Chapaev Battalion with reinforcements that night, rumours circulated once more that they would be allowed to rest.[15] Some hoped he might step in to command their entire brigade, replacing the despised Krieger, who was now ill. Kantorowicz's pleading for him to be removed had fallen on deaf ears in Madrid. He concluded that the men he had spoken to 'were responsible for the disaster' of appointing the Italian and did not want doubt cast on their own judgement.[16] Kantorowicz regarded Nathan as a 'fine English officer': the dapper Londoner maintained an aura of impeccable calm, together with a garrulous eccentricity. A British volunteer recalled bumping into Nathan one evening. 'I was plodding up under shell-fire when I saw under a shady tree a table neatly laid with a clean check table-cloth and an elegant person sitting smoking in an armchair. Shells were falling within not so very many yards of him. Naturally and inevitably it was Nathan,' he said. 'The meal I was invited to combined with Nathan's amusingly egotistical conversation was very reviving. Somehow it was almost impossible to be frightened when Major George Nathan was around.'[17]

However, Nathan did not take over the unfortunate XIII Brigade.[18] Kantorowicz claimed that, by now, all the Chapaev wanted was 'to make sure the enemy pays for what it has done.' In any case, he noted in his diary, they had realised they were as good as 'finished' as a unit.[19]

Over the next few days, the surviving battalions of Gal's division and other Republican brigades fought over, but slowly lost, the hillsides running up to the Romanillos and Mosquito ridges.[20] On the night of 19 July, the German speakers in the Chapaev Battalion became involved in a shouting match with what sounded like a group of drunken Germans in the trenches in front of them (possibly legionnaires or, less likely, Condor Legion gunners):

> They asked whether we were Germans. We shouted back: 'Red Front!'
> The Nazis on the other side began to jeer loudly at us: we were sons of bitches who would soon be hanging from the gallows, and that soon they would be on top of us. We answered that we were perfectly ready for them, asking why they didn't come over right away. Then they began to sing [the Nazi anthem] the Horst Wessel Song. Some of us wanted to answer back with The Internationale, but we decided it was better to stay quiet, that it would be shameful to use that song in a contest to see who could shout loudest. The Nazis finished with cries of 'Heil Hitler!' And then we felt free to shout back at the top of our voices: 'Death to Hitler!' After that we exchanged a few shots. The Nazis carried on and on with their shouting, insults and jeering. Nobody could even think of sleeping.[21]

The following morning a few dozen of the Chapaev men were allowed to withdraw.[22] Kantorowicz led them down to the Guadarrama, where, as he rested by the riverbank, an artillery shell knocked him unconscious. He awoke to the smell of sulphur and the cries of the men he had just led to the river, several of whom were dying of terrible injuries.[23] It was his turn to join the ranks of the shell-shocked. Instead of going to the nearby field dressing station, he set off in a trance back across the river, up the hill towards the farmhouse headquarters and the front line. 'I walked slowly, step-by-step, like an automaton; it was as if I had been frozen in ice. I had no idea what I was doing. I walked straight though the artillery fire without noticing anything that was going on around me,' he recalled. Having climbed the hill and crawled into the bomb shelter beside the farmhouse, he began to shake and weep uncontrollably. Barely able to talk, what he did say made little sense to those around him.[24] They sent him back down the hill, and off to hospital.[25] Kantorowicz's battle was over. So, too, was that of many of his comrades – with Brunner amongst the wounded and almost all the officers dead, missing or wounded.[26]

Gal's battered division carried out a gradual, fighting retreat.[27] Each day the Francoist assault troops advanced slowly down the slopes, 500 metres or a kilometre at a time, in attritional combat that left both sides exhausted. 'Each hut, hillock or rock, has been fought over hard,' Kari noted. 'Every tree, every shrub and every stone in the area has consumed blood.'[28] On 23 July, corps headquarters received the following message: 'The XIII Brigade has fallen to pieces, with its commanders lost and trying to reorganise in reserve. The XV has also … had to retreat 500 metres … The situation is very delicate.'[29]

The next day the remains of XIII Brigade were formally taken out of the front line, while Kléber's division was placed as a strategic reserve force to protect the south-eastern front. That night, the bulk of Gal's much-diminished division was told to cross over to a newly fortified second line above the west bank of the river, leaving just a few outlying units on the far side. It had been an orderly retreat and, bar a single moment of panic from XIII Brigade's Spanish battalions, a courageous and successful one that had sucked the energy out of a formidable enemy.[30]

Franco's men made less progress elsewhere. 'Our units are exhausted due to the high number of losses they have suffered and because of the intense heat, the lack of rest during seven days of continual movements and because they have not eaten a hot meal in all that time,'[31] a Francoist army report of 23 July read.

The battle, however, was not over. Franco could see that his grand plan of rolling the Republican army off the plain and then continuing to pursue and destroy it while conquering fresh territory had failed. Pride demanded, however, that he should at least recover some of the lost land. Anything less could be presented as a Republican triumph. On the night of 23 July, while Gal's battered division limped across the Guadarrama river, Franco was preparing another large push, hoping that the southern front of the plain might finally crack.

A heavy, pre-dawn artillery barrage announced that 24 July was to be another day of hard fighting. Franco's more limited objective permitted a greater concentration of firepower on a smaller area, around Brunete itself. The aim was to break through the defensive lines on either side and surround the town. For the remnants of XV Brigade that meant a morning of retreating and heavy fighting, with the first Francoist units finally crossing the Guadarrama in the morning. The men from XV Brigade also lost their stretch of the Brunete to Boadilla road, retreating in an orderly fashion to a new line 500 metres behind it. Among a group of twenty-five International Brigade prisoners, a Francoist officer looked down his nose at 'those Americans, with their Jews, and Negroes and democracy'. The Lincolns had, in fact, done much to contain the attack, especially after Walter Garland brought up their Maxim machine guns.[32]

Nordahl Grieg had picked this day to visit the front again. He hitched a ride to it in an ambulance, seeking out once more XI Brigade and the Norwegian and Scandinavian volunteers. Eleventh Brigade had stayed in its positions on the plain during the morning, coming to the rescue of a Spanish battalion with its anti-tank guns and sending the Edgar André Battalion on a successful counter-attack in which fifteen prisoners, a dozen rifles and a machine gun were captured.[33]

On arrival at the brigade's headquarters, housed in dugouts cut into the side of a shallow ravine, Grieg came across 'a strange character [who] ... was totally naked except for a white loincloth and alpargatas', sitting on a leather car seat under a tree. 'The friendly, learned, Gandhi-face with glasses bent over a map ... was Ludwig Renn.'[34] The tall, skinny and bespectacled Renn, who normally wore a tightly buttoned-up uniform, Sam Browne belt and officer's cap, was decidedly opposed to clothes in this heat. 'He was an eager nudist and reluctantly wore more than shorts out by the front,' reported Grieg (who exaggerated about the loincloth, since Renn wore shorts – admittedly with a bullethole through them). El Campesino joked that Renn should paint his rank insignia on his chest, since soldiers had no reason to know he was an officer.[35] Grieg also noticed that Renn usually referred to the enemy as *der gegner*, or 'the adversary', rather than the more common 'fascist' and never carried a weapon. 'I fired only two shots during the entire world war, and that was unnecessary and hysterical,' he explained. Staff officers, he meant, rarely had to fight.[36] His weapons were a map and a pair of field glasses.

Richard Staimer, XI Brigade's disciplinarian commander, had once more absented himself from the front, complaining of illness, and Renn was now commanding in his place. Under Staimer the normally courageous German battalions had been performing below their expected level. Some of the more experienced veterans of the Thälmann Battalion, for example, had asked to be given rearguard duties after their officers bungled a local attack on 18 July.[37] Renn had to reorganise their poorly placed defensive positions as soon as Staimer left. General Walter also became fed up with Staimer, issuing a written and public reprimand for abandoning the battlefield. 'No senior officer has the right to leave the sector covered by his units without my special permission,' Walter said in a note that, to Staimer's considerable embarrassment, was copied to the commanders of the division's other brigades.[38]

In contrast, Renn seemed undisturbed by the artillery shells landing fifty metres away, or the bullets that occasionally sang through the air above them. The great final push of Franco's counter-attack, indeed, did not yet seem to have perturbed Renn, or his men, in any way. A starstruck Grieg found the Saxon aristocrat spartan and unfussy, but was most impressed by how cool he was when they came under aerial bombardment. The Norwegian caught a brief sight of him while he himself was lying face down in a fresh crater. 'He lay on his back with his hands under his head and looked with interest through his glasses at every glimpse of the aircraft,' he remembered. 'Now and then he said with a caring voice: "Now hands in the ears." Then there was a loud bang right next to us and we got gravel in our noses and mouths. Suddenly Renn stood up and wiped the sand off himself; it looked as if he had stood up on the beach in Valencia. The planes were gone.'[39]

After the bombardment, the two men clambered to the top of the ravine to survey the battlefield, where most of the noise was coming from in and around Brunete, a few kilometres to the east. Renn peered through his field glasses and grunted in dismay: 'This is not sensible of them.' In the distance the plain was filling up with men retreating from the trenches in front of Brunete. They moved in large flocks, apparently unaware that this was far more dangerous than spreading out or staying put. 'All of a sudden, the fighter planes whizzed down low onto them. The soldiers ran, some suddenly stopped and fell; the others ran on,' wrote Grieg. 'The fighters played above them in wide turns, it was like an elegant show, they whizzed downwards shooting from their tails and then they triumphantly rose again. The men hung together like men sentenced to death; the mitrailleuses [machine guns] flew around them and mowed them down ...' The only consolation was that Renn told him he could also see 'fascist officers trying to drive their men up out of the trenches. They threaten with revolvers, beat them, no one obeys. This is great.'[40]

They were witnessing the first major, panicked Republican retreat at Brunete. The attack had caught the Republican army at a difficult moment. Líster's division, which held Brunete, was just starting the process of being replaced by Cipriano Mera's anarchists – a changeover that had to be halted once the attack started, but nevertheless disrupted attempts at defence. Those attempts were watched by Líster's Russian advisor Rodimstev who described the morning aerial and artillery bombardment as 'like the earth being torn apart'.[41] When tanks began rolling towards the forward trenches, he feared that they would carry the infantry following them straight into Brunete. He watched with amazement as a figure who Líster referred to as '*el Talento*', or 'the Talented One', emerged from his trench and strode towards, and then past, the tanks with a light machine gun. Once he had passed them, he sunk to the ground, and began firing at the advancing troops to separate them from the tanks, which also came under artillery fire.[42] It was not enough, however, to halt the attack. By midday most of Brunete was in Franco's hands.

The plain was now a mass of disorganised units, vehicles and individuals. The Condor Legion picked targets at leisure. Harro Harder – a German fighter pilot (and future Second World War air ace) who disobeyed Condor Legion rules on discretion by painting two large Nazi swastikas on either side of his Heinkel-51 – was amongst those who flew undisturbed above the battlefield. 'We shook up the enemy infantry so

badly that they ran from their positions in mindless flight,' he wrote in
his diary that day. Even after it ran out of ammunition, his squadron
kept diving at the running men. 'We didn't destroy anything,' he noted.
'We just increased the panic.'[43]

To the east of Brunete, in the sector defended by the ragged remains
of Gal's division, it also looked as if the front might crumble.[44] Some
men began to flee as a battalion of German-made tanks (trained by the
Condor Legion, whose own ground forces were mostly in seven anti-
flak batteries) made the situation worse by taking a hill overlooking
their positions.[45] That evening, Gal himself walked down the dried-
out bed of the river Guadarrama, gathering his scattered forces and
re-establishing his line. He could find only 300 men from Krieger's
XIII Brigade, but estimated he still had 800 soldiers in Ćopić's XV
Brigade, plus another 400 from a Spanish brigade attached to his
division.[46] Together they totalled half of a single, full-strength brigade.
That night, however, the remnants established a new, L-shaped line
along the river and north of the road leading out towards it from
Brunete.[47]

The Republican command was furious at the retreats. Late that day
it ordered a new line of defence to be established between Brunete and
Villanueva de la Cañada, with a second line behind the latter.[48] 'Any
attempt to abandon this must be countered with the utmost severity,'
ordered Rojo.[49] When Walter's division was mentioned in dispatches
for its good performance that day, it was one of his Spanish brigades –
rather than the Germans – that was singled out for special praise.[50]

Líster's battered division and Cipriano Mera's anarchists made a final,
failed attempt at retaking Brunete on 25 July.[51] The day started with
heavy bombardments, and while the battle for possession of the ruins of
Brunete continued, Renn watched with concern as other units retreated
around him and sent the Edgar André Battalion to cover part of this
widening hole.[52]

That afternoon the Condor Legion discovered Mera's anarchists
regrouping in a sparsely wooded area just north of Brunete.[53] These men
were closely packed together, and not dug in. Some seventy aircraft
unleashed the most devastating bombardment of ground troops seen
in the entire battle.[54] In groups of eight, the bombers created what one
pilot called 'passageways of destruction' half a kilometre wide. 'It is

not strange, therefore, that on the third such attack the Reds began to flee. The admirable thing is that they did not flee after the first one,' remarked one Francoist airman.[55]

The end result was panic of previously unseen proportions. As incendiary bombs set the stubble in the fields alight, dense black smoke drifted across the plain and much of an entire division began to run. Neither Republican armoured cars, which fired on their own men, nor the cavalry units who galloped madly around trying to shepherd them back together, could prevent the rout.[56] Above them, teams of Condor Legion aircraft set up their strafing carousels, bobbing up and down in turn to machine-gun those out in the open. Oberleutnant Harder found the plain full of easy targets – cars, tanks, horses, mules, and crowds of soldiers trying to hide and take cover by piling on top of one another in the small number of trenches. He later boasted of killing one hundred men in a single trench.[57]

39

The Price of War: Brunete plain, 25 July 1937

Early on the morning of 25 July 1937, Gerda Taro prepared to travel to the front with Ted Allan, a twenty-one-year-old Canadian reporter who was keen to witness one of the Polish photographer's famous Brunete outings.[1] Allan was infatuated with Taro: she was 'like a fox that is going to play a trick on you', according to one acquaintance.[2] She was shortly due back in Paris to be reunited with Capa, who was organising their next adventure: to cover the war that Japan – another Hitler's allies – had declared on China two weeks earlier for *Life* magazine.[3] Allan found a sleepy-looking Taro waiting beside a car in front of the three-storey, city-centre mansion known as the Palacio de Zabálburu, occupied by the poet Rafael Alberti and his 'Alianza de Intelectuales Anti-fascistas', which had become a second home to her. By now Taro had abandoned her French Riviera 'sportif chic' style of dress in favour of one more akin to a militiawoman – espadrilles and khaki overalls, her short hair dark, no longer neatly coiffured, a series of cameras slung around her neck. 'I must get some good pictures to take to Paris. If they are still fighting near Brunete, it will be my chance to get some action pictures,' Allan remembers Gerda telling him.

'Let's not go too close,' he replied.
'How do you want me to take pictures? Long distance?'
'That's an idea.'
'Are you frightened?'
'Yes. Aren't you?'
She laughed. 'Yes.'[4]

With an improvised front line and battle-shocked and panicked soldiers, the battlefield at Brunete was now very different to that experienced by Taro on previous visits. She and the reporter managed to drive past Villanueva towards the disintegrating front line, the hot morning sun quickly turning their car into an oven. General Walter was usually delighted to see his brave countrywoman, but this time he was furious. They must leave immediately, he shouted: 'in five minutes there will be hell'.[5] Taro refused.

A few minutes later the pair were sheltering with troops from Walter's 108 Brigade as Condor Legion aircraft bombed and strafed them. While Allan crouched at the bottom of their foxhole, Taro stood up to film with the Eyemo camera that they had begun to use for *Time*'s *March in Time* newsreels.[6] When then soldiers began to run, she jumped out to stop the panic, shouting for them to get back. By now she had switched to her Leica stills camera and when her film ran out, she and Allan set off for Villanueva by foot, hitching a ride part of the way on a tank. In Villanueva they spotted Walter's big black Matford staff car and waved it down. It was carrying three injured soldiers to hospital and there was no room inside, so she and Allan clung to the outside, balanced on the running boards.

Taro appeared convinced that the cameras carried some of her best work.[7] 'Tonight we'll have a farewell party in Madrid,' she shouted across at Allan, in his novelised version of events. 'I've bought some champagne.'[8] With enemy aircraft harassing them and the driver crouched as low as possible behind his steering wheel, the vehicle failed to move quickly enough out of the way of an out-of-control Republican tank. It smashed into them, flipping Taro and Allan off the car.[9]

A badly injured Taro was taken to the English hospital at El Escorial. She had sustained a serious wound to her stomach and there was little that the New Zealand doctor Douglas Jolly and his overworked team – who had already dealt with almost 10,000 wounded – could do.[10] The hospitals were so full, often with patients who clearly would not survive, that a group of French doctors went around at night covertly giving lethal doses of morphine to those who had been left on the grass outside, covered in dust and flies, to die.[11] A Hungarian doctor, Janos Kiszely, recalled Taro being 'more or less dead when she came into my hands'.[12] Her last, morphine-clouded words were to ask if her cameras were safe.[13] Unfortunately, those last pictures were lost for ever. She was such an unusual patient that somebody took a photograph of Gerda – the young woman with finely plucked, arched eyebrows lying on her deathbed, hands gently folded across her stomach, and the handsome Kiszely wiping away the blood that issued from her mouth and nose.

Not all was panic at Brunete. To the north-west, Líster's Russian advisor Rodimstev and an aide had set up and manned two machine guns, while Líster himself tried to turn his men back. When advancing enemy infantry appeared, the two men were only able to slow them down with short bursts of machine-gun fire. Suddenly, however, Renn's men from XI Brigade appeared on their right with a handful of tanks, and charged the attackers, stopping them in their tracks. 'I could scarcely believe my eyes,' said Rodimstev, who had mentally prepared himself for death.[14]

Rodimstev's sudden rescue showed that the breach was only in the centre of the southern front. The flanks were holding reasonably firmly, with Walter on one side and Gal on the other.[15] Even the supposedly demoralised and disintegrating XIII Brigade covered part of the breached zone with its fire.[16] When new officers arrived, however, and ordered Kari's Chapaev Battalion to shoot at retreating Republican soldiers, the men refused. 'At that moment,' the battalion 'died a death,' wrote Kari. 'Nobody fired, we had experienced that hell and knew those comrades felt they couldn't do anything else. Turned to stone, we observed the cavalry's attempt to stop the retreat, and still refused to fire. Who were these new commanders? They came from the division. They had not been in line ... No, we did not shoot our own companions.'[17]

On the other side of the breach, the shaven-headed Walter and bespectacled Renn were directing the defence of part of the south-western corner. While his Thälmann Battalion officers fretted that they could now be surrounded, Renn concluded that the situation was not as bad as those fleeing believed. They were being attacked and harassed from the air, but when he scanned the plain with his field glasses, looking for advancing tanks and infantry units, he could see none.[18] He did not retreat until late in the day, by which time the division's international battery – named after the imprisoned Romanian communist Ana Pauker – had run out of artillery shells. That evening they withdrew to the new defensive front line in front of Villanueva de la Cañada.[19]

As XI Brigade began to retreat, volunteer Harry Ericsson crawled back with two other Swedes to see what had happened to their anti-tank gun. It was still there, but abandoned. Confirming Renn's observation that only aircraft and artillery shells were pursuing the Republicans across the plain, they could see a mass of abandoned equipment, but no enemy troops. They were joined by a Spaniard and, between them, the four men set about hauling the gun back themselves. Its heavy iron shield protected them from bullets, and they found the whole exercise – which took more than twenty-four hours – welcome respite from their strict German officers. 'The Fascists never attempted any attack with their infantry or anything. We were left to our heaving and pulling in peace and quiet, basically,' Ericsson recalled. They were especially pleased at being able to report their officers for abandoning such a valuable weapon, though there is no record that any punishment was handed out to them.[20]

Kléber's two International Brigades, XII and 150, now appeared from their hiding place (as reserves) in the north-west corner of the battlefield and – while being harassed continually from the air – advanced along the road south of Villanueva towards Brunete. Rojo believed a far wider collapse had only been averted by the 'exemplary behaviour' of a few units, and because select cavalry groups had halted a large part of the fleeing army.[21] By evening, the new lines had been established. The Francoists had taken back Brunete, but most of the rest of the plain was still in Republican hands. Eleventh Brigade remained in the new line, as did Kléber's division.

The Republicans immediately prepared for a second day of Francoist attacks, with communist commander Juan Modesto ordering Walter and to 'install machine guns behind the front line, with order to fire on any group or individual who abandons their position'.[22] Kléber's internationals waited nearby, available to plug any gaps, while Gal's exhausted men handed their positions over to, amongst others, some Spanish marines. The Lincoln Battalion's commissar, Steve Nelson, at first welcomed their arrival but, after hearing the marines claim they were too tired to dig in, decided to set up his machine guns behind them.[23]

That night Renn climbed a small hillock from where he could observe the battlefield, which was lit up by fires caused by the incendiary bombs. A silver crescent moon cast its light from a cloudless sky, where bombers roared but could not be seen. Grieg watched as searchlights tried to find the bomber. 'Suddenly there was a crash up there in the dark ... A red bonfire was flaming down on the plain.'[24] Grieg thought he had seen two bombers crash into each other, but he had probably just witnessed something new in the history of aerial warfare. Soviet fighter pilots had decided to experiment with night attacks on the Junkers, using the flames from their exhausts to trace them. The fires raging on the battlefield enabled them to position themselves right above it. Having failed on his first attempt the previous night, the Russian air ace Mikhail Yakushin saw a Junkers 52 heading towards him. He let it pass, turned to follow, placed himself to its right in order to target an unprotected fuel tank – and opened fire. 'Almost at once the enemy gunner responded, but he was too late,' Yakushin recalled. 'His bomber was already going down in flames.' When he returned to his airfield the Republican air chief, Hidalgo de Cisneros, rang personally to congratulate him on becoming 'the first pilot in the world to have shot down a plane by night'. Republican propaganda – which claimed that no Russians were fighting – pretended that this magical feat had been carried out by its own pilots, Castejón and Montenegro.[25]

Franco was upset by the loss of this Ju 52 and two others in just twenty-four hours, but, overall, he had many reasons to be happy. His men had advanced several kilometres across the plain and recovered the emblematic, if physically almost non-existent, town of Brunete. For the devout, crusading general, it was a fitting end to the day of St James, patron saint of Spain's army. When his generals boisterously gloated over the impending conquest of Madrid at a meeting later that evening, Franco cut short the celebrations. 'Reinforce the defences in front of the conquered territory and stop the advance there,' he ordered. 'I need the reserves for the conquest of Santander ... Remember that I am in charge.'[26]

A combination of rugged Republican defence, the need to finish off the conquest of the north (thereby permanently releasing his forces there) and the loss of several valuable Junkers may all have weighed on General Franco's mind. Either way, the battle was all but over. The jittery Republicans, however, did not know this and the following morning, 26 July, they feared that there was still much fighting to do. Local skirmishes continued as Franco's commanders tried to improve their defensive positions. These immediately demonstrated the weakness of the Republican line. When the marines in front of the Lincoln Battalion were caught unawares, Nelson's machine guns helped contain the enemy, before the last remnants of Gal's division finally left the battlefield later that day.

Nerves were so frayed and the artillery barrages and aerial patrols over the battlefield so overwhelming that it took very little to make units retreat. By mid-morning waves of retreating troops were once more coming through Renn's lines. The Thälmann Battalion asked whether there was an order to retreat, but was told to hold their ground. Sometime later a sweat-drenched messenger asked to have a private word with Renn:

> *The Thälmann Battalion has shot the commander of the 108th Brigade.*
> That was such a terrible thing that, to begin with, I could not take it in.
> *By accident? By mistake?*
> No, on purpose.
> *How did that happen?*[27]

The unfortunate Spanish commander of 108th Brigade, now badly wounded, had been retreating with his men through the Thälmanns' lines. A terrible row had then broken out between his officers and Thälmann commander Bruno Hinz (aka Georg Elsner).[28] According to his commissar, Robert Weinand, Hinz ended up punching some of their officers, who declined to fight back. Then Weinand grabbed a rifle and threatened to bayonet them. It is not clear who, in the end, pulled the trigger. Renn was told that the 108 Brigade's commander (the same man Staimer had spied on, but whose brigade had been mentioned in dispatches for its bravery the previous day) had also tried to persuade the Spanish troops in the Thälmann Battalion to move back. That was when he had been shot. Renn did not seem concerned, and did not order any arrests. 'Those who provoke panic should be stopped, using violence,' he said. 'If things happened as you told me, I'm ready to defend him.'[29]

More troubling was the case of a Dutch volunteer who had been caught fleeing. Under the same rules, this was punishable by death. To Renn's amazement, the Dutchman agreed. He no longer cared about his life. One of the brigade's Spanish commissars argued that, since the deserter had come to Spain voluntarily and had hitherto behaved impeccably, it was wrong to punish him so severely. A court martial by his peers saw the Spaniards continue to argue against a death sentence while the Dutch volunteer's international comrades insisted, according to Renn, 'that they had not come to Spain to receive special treatment and even had to prove themselves more than their Spanish comrades'.[30] They sentenced the man to death. The Dutchman received the judgement calmly, telling them: 'I recognise that I have done wrong and that you have to shoot me.'[31] He then shook the hands of the men who tried him. They, in turn, gave him a glass of wine and a cigarette. The military policemen with him hung their heads and one of Renn's German staff officers asked to be spared the sight of the man being shot. 'I have suffered some rough interrogations at the hands of the Nazis, and I'm not a soft type. But what is about to happen to the Dutchman is not something that I can bear to see,' he said. The volunteer was marched out of sight and executed.[32]

This was yet another example of the International Brigades – and, especially, the German communists – demanding a degree of sacrifice not expected elsewhere in the Republican army. A similar incident in the 11th Division, where a Spanish communist sought out his political commissar and requested he be shot rather than forced to fight any more, ended up with him being sent home.[33]

At times, the only ground battle was between those fleeing and those trying to stop them. Kléber's sabre-waving cavalry squadrons, which patrolled the area between the first and second defensive lines on either side of Villanueva de la Cañada, were confronted by angry rifle fire. 'My cavalry squadrons occupied with restoring order had three men killed and 14 wounded in the "battle" with the panicked flood of armed people,' he reported.[34]

Such was the success of the small-scale, local enemy raids and the general state of nervousness on 26 July, that it raises questions about whether one more day of counter-assault by Franco's forces might have provoked a major collapse. During the day, however, Renn watched admiringly as Mera's anarchists flooded back onto the battlefield, ready to fight again. 'More than one of us will have to apologise to these anarchists,' he said.[35]

He was less happy with his own troops, with only the Austrian February 12 Battalion – led by a man he suspected of being an anarchist – meriting his complete trust.[36] Renn had by now concluded that, with the plain once again almost empty of enemy troops, the Francoist advance had halted. His battalion commanders, however, were nervous. They were now in the front line, being targeted by artillery fire and fretting that they were far ahead of everyone else. Thälmann commander Bruno Hinz even asked if he could retreat.[37] (Renn angrily informed his messenger that he could not.) Soon, Thälmann soldiers wounded in the artillery bombardment were reaching the dressing station at Renn's headquarters, each one accompanied by a suspicious number of perfectly fit companions.[38] The International Brigades' military police were also barring the way of a platoon of fleeing Edgar André soldiers and news reached Renn that the third German battalion, the Hans Beimler, was beginning to crack. All this contrasted with the reports that now reached him from the February 12 Battalion, which had sent patrols out and found no enemy troops within two kilometres of them. Renn had to drive around the other battalions, reprimanding their commanders for letting the wider panic affect them.[39] Their positions, indeed, would hold for most of the war.

As the battle of Brunete wound down to its close on the afternoon of 26 July, two disastrous losses struck the International Brigades. George Nathan had led the weary remnants of Gal's division back to the same valley from where, twenty-one days earlier, they had set out for the battle. The international part of the division – both XIII and XV Brigades – was half its original size, having lost 1,572 men out of 3,163.[40] Within this, the British Battalion had suffered the worst losses: just sixty-eight men were left standing out of an original 331, with the Dimitrov Battalion not far behind these figures. Nathan busied himself making sure that the survivors could now be fed in the peace and safety of their refuge, as the battle below them slowed in intensity. Overhead they could see a last wave of a dozen Ju 52 bombers, this time piloted by Spaniards, who wanted to pursue the retreating troops into the hills and planned to bomb Valdemorillo, the first major town north of the battlefield. With the Soviet fighters now largely absent, the Francoist airmen had assumed this would be easy, but a line of anti-aircraft guns were hidden nearby: one of the Junkers was shot down, two more were damaged, and the remainder decided to turn back.

First, however, the Junkers lightened their loads by releasing the bombs. One of these fell close to George Nathan. A piece of shrapnel hit him, piercing his liver, diaphragms and lungs, and killing him. He was the only casualty. For the men of the already decimated 15th Division, it was a ghastly and untimely death of a much-loved officer. At the funeral that night, hard men such as the fist-swinging Fred Copeman and the veteran communist 'General' János Gálicz, aka Gal, wept bitterly.[41]

This was the same day Rafael Alberti and María Teresa León, at the Alianza mansion, were woken up to take an urgent phone call from the English hospital at El Escorial. A woman photographer had just died there, the caller explained. 'All we know about her is that she's a photographer. We couldn't find any documents on her. She's dead. She was killed yesterday by a tank during the retreat from Brunete. Maybe you know her. If you don't come for her soon she'll have to be buried in an unmarked grave.'[42]

The following day Capa was still in Paris, awaiting Gerda Taro's arrival, when he read of her death. He had been flicking through *L'Humanité* in a dentist's waiting room. The newspaper was devoted mainly to the recent Japanese attack on Peking but, in a smaller piece on Spain, it announced that 'French journalist, Mlle. Tarot [sic]' was reported to have been killed.[43] Taro was buried in the French capital, with a mass funeral organised by the communist daily newspaper *Ce Soir*, with whom she had recently signed a contract. Her tomb was adorned with sculptures by Alberto Giacometti. A distraught Capa felt guilty for leaving her on her own. He would return to Spain later in the war and eventually became the world's most famous photographer. 'After her death, he would always talk about her with me, over and over again,' his friend Ruth Cerf said. 'She was the great love of his life.'[44]

The battle was over, but commanders on both sides still fretted that their opponents would try to launch another local raid or counter-attack. That night a motorbike messenger appeared at the camp where the surviving members of XIII and XV International Brigades were resting.[45] He brought orders for them to return to the plain and occupy a secondary line, in case there was an attack and breakthrough the following morning. The orders, given by Ćopić's second-in-command Major Hans Klaus, were received with indignation. British commissar George Aitken – a Moscow-trained Comintern man who, according to Jason Gurney, nevertheless 'suffered many struggles between his loyalty to the Communist Party and his sense of justice to the men' – went to argue with the corps commander. The reply was laconic: 'We may all be dead before morning.'[46] The order came just two days after Miko Markovicz had been stripped of command of the Lincolns for refusing an order to move forward again. Battalion commissar Steve Nelson recalled the conversation roughly as follows:

> 'Commander Klaus, this is a disastrous order. I will not order the American battalion to carry out this order because it will result in a disaster, like the one at Jarama,' said Markovicz....
>
> 'Markovicz, I gave you an order which I received from division. You and I are under military orders. This is not a debating discussion here. We must act, especially since we are International Brigades, whose role is to develop discipline,' said Klaus, standing up. 'I order you to carry out the order.'
>
> 'Colonel Klaus, I cannot carry out this order,' he replied.
>
> 'Markovicz, I order you to surrender your weapon,' said Klaus, stepping close and holding out his hand.[47]

The pistol was handed over and Nelson was given command. That order had eventually been rescinded, but just forty-eight hours later it was his task to tell the exhausted, broken troops that they must return to the battlefield. There were groans and complaints, while Nelson explained they would be protecting not just their Spanish comrades, but also themselves. The men agreed to go and had just gathered their equipment, when the orders were changed. 'Everyone felt not just good, but proud,' Nelson recalled.[48]

The reaction of XIII Brigade was more extreme. Krieger ranted and raved at his men, but they refused to move. When one officer loudly objected and refused to lead his battalion out, Krieger swung at him and ordered his arrest. The men then erupted in outrage. Krieger singled one Spanish soldier out:

> 'You will not fight?'
> 'No.'
> 'One, two, three! Your last word?'

Krieger then reportedly shot him in the head, though he would later deny it. Either way, only a cordon of officers prevented him from being lynched. Krieger was eventually arrested himself, while the remains of his two Spanish battalions, including their international officers, stood up, organised themselves and began to march towards Madrid. They were met in Torrelodones by a Spanish Republican unit which disarmed them. As with the Americans, the order to return to the line was eventually cancelled, but the damage was done.

Late that night of 26 July, to the amazement of survivors on both sides, silence reigned across the plain of Brunete. The battle really was now over. The Republic had gained land, while the recapture of Brunete gave Franco the propaganda victory he needed to preserve his personal reputation. This had been won for him, in large part, by aircraft and crews provided by Hitler and Mussolini – who were indeed convinced that the fascist air force had tipped the balance. Kléber agreed. 'The aviation question has become the Republic's biggest problem,' he said shortly afterwards. On its first attempt at a major offensive, the Republic had gained land while paralysing Franco's other operations. Optimists believed that, now it had experience of attacking, it could do even better next time.[49]

The battle had tested the volunteers, who spoke of the 'madness-inducing experience of Brunete', to the limit. 'We saw tough guys crack up and babble like babies, wild-eyed. We saw boys grow to resolute maturity in a day,' American machine-gunner David McKelvy White recalled.[50] The International Brigades had lost 3,700 men out of 11,700; of those, 1,259 were dead or missing. New volunteers were still crossing the French border at the rate of hundreds each week, however.[51] For once, the Brigaders had not borne the heaviest part of the suffering. Overall Republican losses were approximately 30,000 men, while Franco lost some 18,000 soldiers. It was evidence that, in the eyes of their commanders, many parts of the Spanish Republican army had now reached the same degree of trustworthiness as the Brigades themselves.

The Spanish government ordered the immediate dissolution of XIII International Brigade.[52][53] For the survivors, including Leo Kari and Alfred Kantorowicz, that was the worst possible punishment. A week later, the men of the Chapaev Battalion were instructed to pile their weapons in the middle of a farmhouse courtyard and these were taken away. The men were redistributed amongst the other brigades. That night Kari dreamt of wolves tearing at him, of the Moroccan soldiers charging and the screams of those they had tortured. Both he and Kantorowicz were transferred to other brigades.

40

Vengeance: Quinto, Aragon, 24 August 1937

In mid-August 1937, Alek Szurek and General Walter travelled away from the Madrid front towards the mostly peaceful front line in Aragon, to the east of Zaragoza. It was a change of environment in more than one way. The towns in this part of Aragon were bigger and had suffered less the hardships of war. Goods that were impossible to find in Madrid were sometimes plentiful here. Walter bought a collection of wineskins both to give away as gifts and in order to refine his own clumsy attempts at using them without tipping wine all over himself (he reportedly practised in the bath).[1]

The welcome usually accorded to International Brigaders in Madrid, where all doors opened to them, was not automatically offered by the local anarchists. They saw the Brigades as a mere extension of their bête noire, the Communist Party of Spain. According to Szurek, in one Aragonese town, which he did not name, local authorities were positively hostile. When they called on the town's anarchist leader and asked for a room at the handsome villa he occupied, they were turned away. 'The best I can do is put you up with the drivers,' he was told.[2] Perhaps the man was trying to make the point that, in the anarchist tradition, officers were worth no more than the men who drove them.

That night, Walter and Szurek slept on hard, bare beds with no mattresses. This slight was felt deeply by some on Walter's staff, especially the Russian émigré Karchevski who looked after the staff's security. He had already been locked up for twenty-four hours after punching a cook who mistakenly put salt in Walter's coffee before the Valsaín battle.[3]

When he was sent ahead to the small town of Grañen to set up Walter's headquarters for the coming operation in Aragon, he strode around with two revolvers and hand grenades hanging from his belt, terrorising the townsfolk. These he harangued for failing to show loyalty to the Republic. He also placed two machine guns pointing into the town square and a nearby yard. A furious Walter wanted to know why he was being so heavy-handed. 'Comrade General, anarchists …' came the apparently self-explanatory reply. Walter ordered him to change his attitude or accept that, as a White Russian, he would never be allowed home.[4]

The icy reception experienced by Walter and Szurek was part of a wider mistrust of the International Brigades as they moved into Aragon. 'We met closed windows and barricaded doors. Beautiful young brunettes did not come out to meet us with flowers in their hair. Only old women dared venture out of their homes,' recalled Szurek. 'We were not used to that.'[5] Hostility was mutual. In the folklore of the Brigades, the anarchists were already considered hopeless fighters. Amongst the many rumours was that, on this static front, they even played football matches against their opponents.[6]

Walter and Szurek were in Aragon to inspect the terrain for the next great offensive. This time, instead of descending on a single city or valley, the Republic planned to punch through various points on a 130 kilometre line. This stretched from the painter Francisco de Goya's birthplace at Fuendetodos all the way north to Tardienta. The troops who broke through were then to march on towards one of the biggest prizes in Francoist hands, the Aragonese capital of Zaragoza. With its high density of army barracks and training schools, Zaragoza had fallen during the failed coup a year earlier but workers in the city were now reportedly set to launch an armed rebellion of their own, coinciding with the offensive. As one of the six largest cities in Spain, its capture would help to balance out the loss of Bilbao.[7] As at Brunete, Huesca and La Granja, a secondary objective was declared: to relieve pressure on the ever-shrinking northern front. The Republican territory left there was now just a narrow strip of mostly coastal land, with the port city of Santander still holding out.

The overriding sensation in this region was of vast emptiness. The parched, bare lands and unwelcoming, rocky highlands reminded many visitors of the dusty Badlands they had seen in Hollywood films. Troops were few and positioned at occasional outposts. 'We reached one of the forward command posts but could easily have carried on into enemy territory without anybody noticing,' Rojo recalled,[8] after arriving on a baking hot August afternoon to inspect the area. At another post he was greeted by a shirtless lieutenant who had painted the bars of his rank above his left breast. The scattered observation points could not even watch the entire front. The army's reforms, he concluded, had not made it to this front and soldiers here could not be trusted.

The enemy appeared to have arranged themselves in a similarly slipshod fashion. 'We were able, without the slightest bother, to observe what was known as the enemy's defensive line and our impression was that with even a small force of soldiers one would be able to go anywhere,' said Rojo.[9] Real soldiers, properly organised, would cause havoc – or so he thought – especially if they attacked along such a broad front that they were impossible to contain. That meant bringing troops hardened in the fighting around Madrid, like the International Brigades.[10] He later regretted, however, that he had not valued more highly the men who knew this line best. 'Events [on the ground] proved later that those other troops … would turn out to be rather more useful,' he said.[11]

As the Republic's ambition grew, so too did the size of the armies it gathered. This offensive required even more troops than Brunete, with some 80,000 men in a hundred battalions.[12] Eighteen of these came from the International Brigades.[13] Only Dumont's XIV Brigade, still out of favour after La Granja, was left behind (and would help see off an attack on the Cuesta de la Reina, near Madrid, in October).[14] That the offensive should happen so soon after Brunete was, perhaps, a display of overconfidence. It certainly caught the International Brigades, as a whole, at a bad moment. The dismantling of XIII Brigade after Brunete had damaged their reputation and encouraged critics who saw them as communist interferers. 'Certain, even influential, circles in the [war] ministry did not refrain from expressing their political views, in the sense that they said the Italian and German intervention had been caused by … the existence of the International Brigades,' commented Kléber. 'In other words, if there had been no International Brigades, there would also not have been any Italian or German forces on the side of Franco.'[15]

This was clearly false and, given the non-intervention situation, a dangerous idea. The accusations of communist interference were,

however, both true and false. Many of the brigades were now mostly
Spanish and the recruits reaching them often came from a broad political base. Amongst the foreign volunteers, the Communist Party was
tightening its grip. Nowhere was this more so than amongst the Italians,
where Pacciardi had been arguing that the Garibaldis were no longer
either really international nor a proper popular front organisation.[16]
His anarchist adjutant Braccialarghe had been forcibly replaced, without consultation, and an ineffectual communist called Felice Platone
foisted on him. As a result, Pacciardi left, taking with him a group of
the original, non-communist volunteers.[17] In an army were most people
would have been accused of desertion, this was allowed – presumably
to avoid damaging the Brigades' reputation abroad. Kléber considered
him 'an extremely proud and capricious fellow' but could also see that
'sectarian' Italian communists were 'losing their comradely contacts
with the Socialists and anarchists and alienating them'.[18] Another non-
communist, Penchienati, was given command in an attempt to preserve
the Garibaldis' unique popular front structure.

Foreign volunteers were now a minority in many brigades. Seven
out of ten soldiers in the German-speaking XI Brigade were Spanish,[19]
for example, along with half of XV Brigade.[20] This caused yet another
layer of friction. Since most officers and commissars were foreign, while
most soldiers were Spanish, language created constant problems.[21] The
superior airs and national chauvinism of some – especially ardent
'Mexicans' like XI Brigade commander Richard Staimer – made
things even worse. They were, some volunteers confided and Kléber
confirmed,[22] behaving like the imperialists and colonialists whom
they routinely denounced. Kléber countered this by appointing more
Spanish officers, and claimed this immediately improved morale and
made his troops better fighters.[23] He nevertheless met with opposition
from Marty and the Albacete base, who grumbled that this would bring
'destruction of the International Brigades as such'.[24]

It was not just the Italians who were in turmoil. Kléber thought the
three oldest surviving brigades – including the German-speaking XI
Brigade and the French-speaking XIV Brigade – were all going through
crises that damaged their 'combat capabilities'. The older volunteers,
he realised, were increasingly in need of a rest. 'With a background
of general fatigue and great losses … they began to ask themselves
questions: "How long will we continue to suffer and bear our losses?

We have been fighting for a year, and that is enough. Let some others come and take our places."' He blamed, in part, letters from wives in France. These were, he claimed, increasingly filled with messages along the lines of: 'If you don't come back soon, I won't be able to stand it any longer and will give myself to another.'

Kléber's concerns may sound far-fetched, but Alek Szurek was confronted with a similar situation while on leave in France in 1937. His wife Berta told him that she could not bear life without a man and had asked her doctor for sedatives. 'Before I returned to Spain, I begged her to have no inhibitions and to let herself be seduced,' he wrote. 'She was young and pretty; she certainly could find suitors. However, it was impossible for her to even consider such a thing in Rouen since everyone knew her. News of her betrayal would be spread.'[25] In any case, there was a high chance that Szurek would be killed in Spain and never come back. In the end Berta moved to Paris, where she found a lover. 'So what?' said Szurek later. 'After the Spanish War, Berta told me who her close friend was. He was handsome, charming, had great intellectual values, and was an actor in the theatre. I had heard about him and held him in high esteem.' Later on they bumped into him in Paris. The actor seemed 'surprised and pleased' and wanted to go home with them. 'I did not want this man to be part of our life, and I told him,' said Szurek.[26]

Given the turmoil, it may have been overly optimistic to expect the International Brigades to perform well so soon after Brunete. Kléber's 45th Division, for example, had been promised a rest as it reorganised its 8,400 men.[27] It was also tasked with creating an entirely new version of XIII Brigade based on battalions from the now suppressed 150 Brigade – who were angry at inheriting that distinctly unlucky, and inglorious, number.[28] This new, mostly Slavic, brigade was, however, the biggest and most international of all. It brought together the Polish Dombrowski and Palafox Battalions (with the latter including the Jewish Botwin and Ukrainian Shevchenko companies) with the Hungarian Rakosi and the Yugoslav Djuro Djakovic Battalions.[29] Walter's 35th Division now combined the 'German-speaking' XI and 'English-speaking' XV Brigades,[30] which were below their full numbers, with 2,245 and 1,400 men respectively.[31]

The Zaragoza attack plan called for the swift advance of four different columns. Kléber's division and the Catalan communists of the Carlos

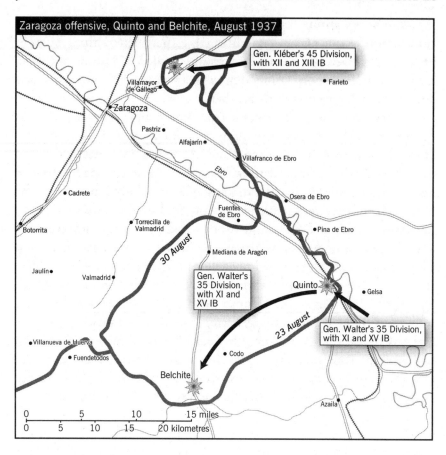

Marx 27th Division were, separately, to break through at various spots
north of the river Ebro[32] and descend on Zaragoza together on the
evening of the first day of battle, 24 August. Since the line here was
mostly made up of widely spaced hilltop forts and gun emplacements,
it was assumed they could creep past these or surround and attack them
in the dark.[33] The rest of the attacking army was to push through a more
densely populated area (in relative terms) to the south of the Ebro. The
largest column of all was based on Modesto's Vth Army Corps and
included Walter's 35th Division with his two International Brigades.[34]
The aim was to skirt around the more difficult spots in order to reach
Zaragoza as soon as possible. Having rushed past them, Modesto's men
would then have to besiege and take several heavily fortified positions,
including the towns of Quinto and Belchite.

According to Walter, his division's instructions for the first day of the battle were simple and clear. They were to take Quinto.[35] Studying the map, this had appeared a reasonable task. When he and his staff had crept up to the top of his designated observation and command post, a hill known as El Cornero with a sweeping view of the town and its surroundings, two days before the attack, he realised that it would not be so easy. Renn, who had been sent on a pro-Republican propaganda tour of the United States, was no longer with him, but the former White Russian general, Escimontowsky, was. So, too, was his loyal adjutant, Szurek.[36] From their hilltop they could see lines of trenches, individual fire holes and concrete pillboxes for up to twenty-five machine guns. The town spilled down a steep hillside overlooked by a robust, Mudejar church. It was surrounded by barbed wire and garrisoned by 1,500 of Franco's toughest troops, including *falangistas*, *requetés* and the Civil Guard. Although, in numerical terms, the attacking force was not much bigger, Walter had five times as many machine guns and far greater artillery power. He was not sure, however, that this was sufficient to overcome a well-fortified town whose approaches consisted of steep slopes or dusty stretches of flat, open land that were well covered by machine guns and small artillery pieces. A cemetery, once more, and a row of low fortified hills to the south provided additional obstacles close to it that would need to be overcome.[37]

Secrecy was crucial to the entire attack.[38] The anarchists, who had held the position outside Quinto since the beginning of the war, were lied to and told that Walter's visit was part of a wider, long-term reconnaissance of the Aragon line. They proved friendly and helpful. To Walter's amazement, they did not even bother to find out who the newly arrived men were. 'They seemed to enjoy explaining to a group of unknown officers who didn't even speak their language not just the positions of the enemy, but also for their own subordinate groups,' he said.[39] A return trip the following day, again with the help of the anarchists, persuaded him to attack from the north and west. Taking the cemetery, which lay above the town, would be a first crucial step. The neighbouring hills could be encircled and the enemy trapped there while the town was taken.[40]

Preparations during the twenty-four hours before the attack were fraught and chaotic. A lack of fuel led to a lack of trucks which, in turn, meant that men could not be moved into position. 'A more discouraging night I have never spent,'[41] Robert Merriman noted in his diary. Staimer's staff refused to lend trucks even after Merriman (now XV Brigade's chief of staff[42]) had jumped on a motorcycle and gone to beg them.[43] As a result, only the Dimitrov and Spanish Battalions were in place and ready to join the attack by dawn on 24 August.[44]

An hour and a half before the dawn assault was due to begin, the artillery commander informed Walter that he was not ready.[45] Walter ordered him to start by firing whatever guns he had, but this was done so badly that when the Dimitrov and Thälmann Battalions attacked the cemetery[46] they could only approach to within fifty metres.[47] Walter decided to experiment. Rather than hiding his artillery behind faraway hills and hoping they could lob shells accurately from there, he decided to bring a single 75mm artillery gun up to fire from point-blank range. This was anathema to the gunners – for whom the loss of such an exposed gun would have spelt disaster – and the artillery commander had to be bullied into it.

When the dozen international gunners who had volunteered to bring the artillery piece up opened fire from just 400 metres way, they quickly took out machine-gun posts and part of the cemetery wall.[48] Even then, a first infantry attack failed before the Lincoln Battalion took the cemetery in just a few minutes later that afternoon. Soon they were in the town itself, with help from eight T-26 tanks, while the Austrian February 12 Battalion entered from the other side. Tom Wintringham, who had spent the previous six months training new officers but had returned to XV Brigade's staff the previous week, was impressed. 'It was a beautiful piece of work,' he said.[49]

Overnight the enemy organised itself around three main resistance points in the church (with two heavy machine guns in the belfry[50]), at the town's cement factory and in a small hospital. Early in the morning, however, the machine-gun posts in the church belfry were, at least temporarily, put out of action by Walter's anti-tank guns, and at 9 a.m. the civilian population asked permission to leave.[51] Street-fighting continued all day as the defenders were beaten back to the church and a handful of other buildings. There, Walter and XV Brigade commander Ćopić personally directed the attack by the Thälmann and Lincoln Battalions (while Staimer, once more, stayed away).[52] The metre-thick walls provided strong protection, however, and the Brigaders repeatedly failed to enter through a hole opened up the previous day, so orders were given to burn down the church, where 150 Francoists were holding out.[53] Wintringham went looking for a neighbouring house that could be set ablaze, in the hope that the flames might spread. 'I was just having a good look round, nipping round corners and doors very quickly so they couldn't shoot me, when WHACK – a bullet hit me on top of the shoulder,' he wrote. Wintringham now recalled, with shame, that he had spent the previous months teaching pupils at the International Brigades' officers school how not to expose themselves to fire. The bullet smashed a bone and he had to be sent straight to hospital. He would not fight again.[54]

Eventually, sacks stuffed with hay and grenades, along with curtains, clothes and bedlinen, were soaked in gasoline, set alight and thrown into the church, filling it with dense smoke. A group of forty-two men jumped out through the windows and surrendered, but when the smoke cleared the rest were still holding out.[55] A 75mm gun was, once again, brought up close to knock down the belfry and fire through the church's doors and windows. Over a hundred shells were launched through the church doors from just 200 metres away, but still the defenders refused to surrender. They retired to the altar and choir stalls, keeping the internationals at bay with grenades and machine-gun fire. Later that night, fifty would escape through a side door.[56]

The following day, 26 August, Walter decided to clean out Quinto with the Dimitrov and Thälmann Battalions and then launch XV Brigade's British and Spanish battalions (which, as an experiment, included a mostly American company)[57] to finish the attack on Purburell Hill, where around 500 demoralised and thirsty enemy soldiers had been encircled and their water supply cut off.[58] Defenders in both places soon realised that there was no escape and began to surrender in small groups.[59] An hour later the town was taken and 240 prisoners were led out towards Walter's command post at El Cornero hill, while the Lincolns and Dimitrov joined the attack on Purburell Hill.[60]

Anti-tank guns targeted trenches and machine-gun emplacements with their devastating, rapid fire and, after half an hour a white flag was raised. An American machine gun opened up on the surrendering men, however, driving them back into their trenches, where they started to fight again.[61] The Republicans eventually had to send an officer to negotiate and apologise. Given a second opportunity, most were happy to raise their arms.

A group of Francoist officers nevertheless held out on a corner of the hill. Felix Kusman, a Russian-born American volunteer, was surprised to find that two of these officers were tsarist Russians. The first one he encountered screamed 'Red Pigs! Red Pigs!' at them in Russian. When it looked like he might be captured, he turned his gun on himself and, in Kusman's words, 'blew his brains out'. The other Russian also died. Kusman found a sword and a Bible on one body.[62] Closer investigation revealed that they were a former White Russian general called Fonk and a captain called Poluchin. Walter was delighted. 'They both met their deserved end,' he commented.[63] In all 1,060 prisoners were taken and 450 defenders killed, while the two International Brigades lost 330 men, including around seventy dead.[64]

Walter later wrote an academic dissertation for Moscow's Frunze Military Academy on his division's role in the Zaragoza offensive, putting the success of the attack on Quinto down to several things.[65] First of all, by attacking in stages and at different points, he had been able to build numerical advantages for each attack. Secondly, the use of artillery at point-blank range worked well. Thirty shells fired close up against the cemetery proved far more effective than hundreds fired from four kilometres away. 'It was perfectly possible, and beneficial, to fire from open positions,' he said.[66] Walter also claimed that another significant factor had been his own self-belief. 'The slightest doubts or vacillation at any level of command inevitably provokes apathy and indecision in the units,' he wrote.[67] This was his victory, he felt, and he furiously ejected a contingent of anarchists who arrived with a black and red flag and a photographer.[68]

The Zaragoza offensive had been launched in the belief that the workers in the city were about to rebel and would help eject the Francoists. In fact, rumours of an uprising there had been heavily exaggerated. The liberators of Quinto hoped, at least, that they would receive a welcome similar to the one they received in Brihuega after the Guadalajara battle, but the town had been in fascist hands for too long. Republican supporters had mostly been killed or forced out a year before. It was also close to the villages where anarchists had carried out their own 'red terror'.[69] Afterwards, Szurek recalled meeting the eyes of a young girl 'sitting proudly beside her father, her head held high as she combed her lovely, long, dark hair... When our eyes met, I saw a certain uneasiness and hostility in them towards Reds and even more towards Internationals. My God, what can be more terrible?' he asked.[70]

The young girl had good reason to mistrust the international volunteers. The desire for revenge was widespread. 'We just grabbed those guys, lined them up and shot them right there,' said one American. An argument over whether an injured prisoner should be killed was settled by a volunteer known as Crazy O'Leary, reputed to be a former mobster, who shot the man in the head.[71] Amongst the Brigades' own dead was one of Walter's favourites, his medical chief, Dr Dubois-Domanski, also known as Mietek, who had been shot by a sniper after sneaking up to the front line to watch the action. Szurek recalled Walter's anger:

> The General came to me, hugged me, and said, 'We'll avenge Mietek.' Amongst the prisoners brought from Quinto to the observation post were sharpshooters from the belfry. They did not go very far. The General ordered them shot, the executions were done by the soldiers who had escorted them. The condemned prisoners, either of their own accord or ordered by the corporal in charge of the execution, turned their backs. One prisoner raised his fist in the Republican salute … I could not reconcile myself to what happened, nor could many others. I saw one Republican staff officer walk with a drawn revolver behind a fascist officer after having interrogated him. The fascist officer cried before he died, the Republican officer's face was contorted by his moral dilemma over what he was forced to do. I knew the man. He was well-educated and polite; he would not hurt a fly.[72]

There was nothing spontaneous or uncontrolled about the killings. Walter himself shot several prisoners while Merriman accepted the executions, which had become an established part of this war, but was angry with a German volunteer who humiliated a young fascist officer first. 'Prisoners came in in droves wanting water, etc. Haggard, bad-looking lot,' the American noted in his diary. 'Selected officers questioned them and finally shot them … our men started to loot the town – bad but a fact.'[73] Merriman recorded a later decision to punish looters by shooting them, if necessary, but nothing was said about disciplining men who shot prisoners – while those who were not snipers, officers or non-commissioned officers were left alive.[74]

41

Conquest: Belchite, 31 August 1937

Elsewhere, the Zaragoza offensive had not gone well. The lightning strike on Aragon's biggest city from the south ground to a halt twenty-five kilometres short of its target, at the riverside town of Fuentes de Ebro after the 'surprise' attack ran, quite literally, out of fuel. The petrol arrived so late, along with many of the trucks, that an exasperated Líster ended up ordering his men to start marching to the front.[1] Their vehicles caught up with them later and Szurek saw them heading towards their target late that morning, kicking up a huge dust cloud above the ravine they were travelling through. 'It looked like a scene from a western movie,' he recalled.[2] According to the attack plan, Fuentes de Ebro – a gateway town that stood on the road to Zaragoza – should have been taken by surprise early in the morning. Even after the delayed start, Walter thought they should still have made it to the gates of Zaragoza that night. 'On August 24th, an opportunity to change the strategic situations of the war in favour of the Republic was, once again, wasted,' he wrote.[3]

To the north, some of Kléber's troops initially did much better. With trucks also scarce on his side of the river Ebro, and Zaragoza little more than twenty kilometres away, he ordered his men to march into battle. More controversially, he also changed the attack plan, ordering both his brigades – the Slav-led XIII and the Italian-led XII – to stay on the southern side of the road leading towards the city, rather than following the original plan for the Italians to advance on the north side.[4] They set out at night without local guides, no maps and poor knowledge of the terrain.[5] The Polish-led Dombrowski and Palafox Battalions found little in their way before reaching the lightly defended town of Villamayor de Gállego, just seven kilometres from Zaragoza.[6] Out of the one hundred battalions used in the offensive,[7] these two Polish battalions were the only ones to reach anywhere near the city. That night they could see its lights and hear the pealing of church bells, which they assumed were being rung to warn of their approach.[8] Kléber later claimed they had also caught the command staff of a Francoist unit by surprise, taking 150 POWs, most of them officers. These allegedly included four Germans and their translators.

The Poles paid dearly for their daring. The following morning tanks came out of Zaragoza and pushed them back. They found themselves isolated in enemy territory and without support. Over the next two days, starved of food and short of water, they had to fight their way out, pursued all the way. Part of the Palafox Battalion became trapped in a ravine known as the Barranco de las Casas, where it was wiped out. Survivors returned in dribs and drabs, bringing a handful of prisoners. Kléber claimed that around one hundred of these had been killed after they 'refused to go with them and tried to escape under the cover of night'.[9] The two Polish battalions lost 300 men and villagers had to dig mass graves in the Barranco de las Casas for all the bodies.[10]

Their fate would have been different if the Italians or the other northern column (which would have included Muriel Rukeyser's athlete boyfriend Otto Boch) had not been halted much further north at the town of Zuera.[11] Kléber claimed that the Italian units ignored his instructions and lost their way.[12] Some allegedly headed north, away from Zaragoza, while Walter reported that one battalion turned a full circle in the dark and marched into the Republic's own rearguard.[13] The Garibaldinis recalled it differently, claiming that they had simply been pinned down by fire from various hilltops as soon as it got light and were soon suffering from thirst and exhaustion. They had been sent into unfamiliar terrain without maps, they added, while the Poles had exaggerated the extent of their advance.[14]

The boldness of the Dombrowski and Palafox commanders revealed the dangers inherent in encouraging units to infiltrate enemy territory, bypassing forts or towns that might resist them. If everyone did the same and a new front line could be formed, then the enemy in their rearguard could be slowly worn down. If that did not happen and units ended up behind enemy lines on their own, they could be hunted down and destroyed. Kléber blamed the Italians, claiming that he also had to sacrifice his divisional reserve battalion[15] – the newly formed Djuro Djakovic Battalion of Bulgarians, Yugoslavs and Spaniards – which lost all but fifty of its members over the coming days.[16] If true, and Kléber liked to exaggerate, that meant they suffered the worst casualties of any international battalion at any time in the Spanish Civil War.

On the southern side of the river, meanwhile, there were repeated attempts to take Fuentes de Ebro and continue the advance, but it soon became clear that Zaragoza was beyond their reach. More limited objectives were set and it was now that the so-called battle for Zaragoza would change its name, even to historians, becoming the 'battle of Belchite'.[17]

This large country town in the middle of the harsh, dusty landscape to the west of Quinto had held out against the initial attack and was still in Francoist hands when Walter received a telegram from General Pozas on 31 August. 'You have been appointed commander of all the forces acting against Belchite, including armoured cars and artillery and with the right to request aviation support,' it read. 'Belchite must be taken today.'[18] It was his task, in other words, to take the largest remaining prize within reach.

Following the principle of bypassing the strongest points of resistance, Belchite had been surrounded while the front line was pushed up to Fuentes de Ebro in the north and Puebla de Albortón to the west.[19] By the time Walter received his telegram it had been under siege for a week. To Walter's fury, his two International Brigade commanders, Staimer and Ćopić, were nearly killed together when they went to survey the objective. They had ignored the most elemental rules for avoiding strafing attacks from the air by travelling in a tight convoy of two cars. The two men found a town of solid houses, factory towers and church spires, surrounded by dried-out fields and handsome olive groves. It had been turned into a fortress.[20] Pillboxes with half-metre thick concrete walls reinforced by iron rods studded the approaches, giving cover to anti-tank and machine guns. In front of these, lines of trenches and barbed wire made any approach by infantry extremely hazardous. It was far more daunting than any town they had taken so far, which explained why progress had been slow.[21]

Walter was not so impressed. He thought the pillboxes were badly designed, poorly camouflaged and too close to the town.[22] With the proper combined use of artillery, aerial bombardments and infantry, they should have been easy to put out of action. Such coordinated activity, however, was often beyond the abilities of the Republican army.[23] More importantly, Belchite also contained thick-walled buildings that were easy to defend, including a large fifteenth-century church with elegant, patterned Mudejar brickwork and a large seminary, as well as the narrow streets and cellars for storing country produce that made Spanish country towns such natural fortresses. These had been reinforced with sandbags and barricades. The quality and quantity of the defenders added to Walter's problems. The 3,000 or so soldiers in the town included battalion-sized units of legionnaires and Moroccans, as well as *requetés, falangistas* and Civil Guards.[24] It was a far tougher proposition than Quinto.

Walter had some 5,000 men available to him, from his own division and a number of anarchist brigades. The latter outnumbered his own men, since the German speakers of XI International Brigade were soon sent to reinforce the line north of Belchite, around the town of Mediana.[25] The regular army commander on the spot, Colonel Pedro Sánchez Plaza, was as unhappy about command being handed to Walter as the anarchists were. There had been no real plan of attack and each of the four brigades involved had been acting on its own initiative, but they had slowly been tightening the noose and taken several concrete pillboxes, the cemetery and various hills around the town. The defenders, however, were being resupplied from the air, receiving food, ammunition and spare parts that floated down under parachutes.[26] Francoist radio stations, meanwhile, broadcast stirring messages of support, telling them that they were about to be rescued, while priests, family members and military officers praised them over the airwaves and urged them to keep fighting. The defenders' hoped to emulate the heroes of the Alcazar at Toledo and hold on long enough for the Francoist counter-attacks to break through the new front line at Mediana and rescue them.[27]

Walter decided it could all be done much better, but Belchite could not be taken in a day. Instead, he adapted the strategies used at Quinto by trying to conquer it in stages.[28] He brought the English-speaking XV Brigade and the anarchists of the 116 Brigade to join the attack. As at Quinto, he decided to use the artillery close up, where their accuracy, destructive power and ability to damage the morale of the defenders would be far greater. 'You're shit! You'll carry your cannons across the stream on your backs,' Walter shouted at one reluctant artillery officer. 'I'll be here at 5 a.m. If the order is not carried out, you'll be held responsible and will pay with your head.'[29]

The attack started at 7 a.m. the following day, 1 September, from four different directions, with XV Brigade leading from the north. The British Battalion was held in reserve, while the Lincoln, Dimitrov, Spanish and Thälmann (on loan from XI Brigade) Battalions attacked. The close-up artillery fire knocked out machine-gun posts in church towers and destroyed much of the town centre, where the defenders' command post was positioned. The attackers took five of the fifteen concrete bunkers that morning, as well as the train station, a mill and several other important buildings. All this was managed at a relatively low cost, but Walter claimed he could feel 'the experienced hand' of the Italian and German commanders[30] in the enemy air force, which bombed his troops whenever the Republic's own aircraft disappeared.[31]

The attack continued the next day, 2 September, with Walter's Spanish brigade creeping up overnight with heavy machine guns to within a hundred metres of a crucial bunker, to start a daring early morning raid. It was a technique, he commented, that should have been used more frequently.[32] Another Spanish unit took the imposing, thick-walled seminary building. Shells continued to rain down, with Bob Merriman describing 'a spectacle – a city gradually smashed to bits by persistent artillery' before noting that 'they hide in underground passages and only in this way does the place hold'.[33]

By the evening, XV Brigade and others were in the town and house-to-house fighting began. Pressure built on the Mediana front, however, where a slowly retreating and jittery XI Brigade had lost what Walter called 'the calm spirit that had characterised the brigade in previous battles'.[34] The brigade's medical chief claimed it had already reached its physical and psychological limit and that, as a result, 'the soldiers won't be able to hold on to their positions for much longer'.[35] By now, the British and Thälmann Battalions had both been sent to help,[36] since Walter's main concern was that the Francoists would break through and lift the Belchite siege.

The Brigaders advanced slowly through the town on 3 September, placing machine guns on rooftops. Anti-tank guns, once more, were crucial for blasting through walls or eliminating machine-gun posts, with the Brigades' three guns firing a thousand shells each over two days, and one of them bursting its barrel.[37] That evening they watched hopelessly, however, as new gun parts and munitions reached the defenders by parachute.[38]

Walter pledged that the first five soldiers to reach the centre of Belchite would be promoted to lieutenant, while the first five officers would also be guaranteed promotion.[39] As the street-fighting continued, junior and non-commissioned officers took command of different groups, often mixed up from various units, who stormed buildings one by one with grenades. The fighting was now room-by-room, with grenades lobbed through holes knocked in the walls between them.[40]

In the baseball jargon used by the Americans, 'good pitchers' such as Merriman showed their prowess by hurling grenades from a distance through doors and windows.[41] For Merriman this was the 'greatest fun [yet] in Spain' and he played a prominent part, earning a fierce rebuke from Ćopić for abandoning his duties as the brigade's chief of staff.[42] The defenders, meanwhile, had established a warren of underground passageways by knocking holes through the walls of the cellars in each house. These, in turn, provided refuge to the frightened families who remained in the town.

Progress was slow, with the town's churches – including one that held up the Dimitrov and Lincoln Battalions – particularly hard to conquer.[43] It may have been now that the commander of one brigade that was meant to be attacking the town made the mistake of visiting Walter at his command post. Dr Len Crome witnessed the scene:

> 'Where is your Brigade?'
> 'I left them two hours ago. They were lying a kilometre from the town.'
> 'And where are they now?'
> The commander began to stutter: 'My general, I cannot tell you precisely ... but...'
> 'You cannot tell me! You ...' Walter was in a rage. He hit out at the officer with fists, the butt of his revolver, and then, when he fell, with his boots. Then: 'Budkovskyl.'
> 'Yes, comrade general.'

'Go with him to the Brigade and see that he takes the church. I hold you responsible. Shoot him if he hesitates, and take over command yourself. But remember, don't come back without the church.'

'Yes, comrade general.'[44]

Harsh words were exchanged with Sánchez Plaza,[45] whom Walter accused of deliberately trying to provoke clashes between internationalist volunteers and the anarchists.[46] That night the defenders regrouped in the city centre, leaving a lone machine-gun post in the cathedral tower. Earlier in the day, however, General Pozas gave a press conference announcing that Belchite had been taken. As a result, foreign newspaper correspondents began to visit. Many decided they had been duped. Walter was not surprised.[47] The following morning, Barcelona's *La Vanguardia* newspaper carried a headline claiming Belchite had fallen.[48] In fact, some 1,300 men were now defending a very small area – making the attackers' task much easier, but allowing the Francoist commanders to prevent partial surrenders.[49] Walter was admiring. 'The groups of *falangistas* and *requetés* resisted until they had used their last bullets,' he said.[50] The bodies of the dead, meanwhile, were being stacked and burnt in the main plaza or thrown into an empty underground well designed to store olive oil.

That night the defenders were given an ultimatum, to surrender or be destroyed. Over the radio, their commanders in Zaragoza now gave them permission to break out and a large group managed to do exactly that, flinging grenades as they ran through the dark into the olive groves. Some 160 made it through and their own side welcomed them back as heroes.[51] At least some of those trying to escape attempt were civilians, including women and children. A Spanish officer in XV Brigade remembered it like this:

Suddenly, a few yards in front of us, we heard voices and distinguished a mass of people coming toward us. Some were women. There were shouts of '*Camaradas!*' We thought they were more of the people who had been liberated ... Our commander called on them to halt. The answer was a shower of grenades ... it was impossible in the bad light to distinguish anything clearly.

We noticed that some of the civilians were firing at us. They were
officers in disguise, as we found out afterwards ... Some succeeded
in slipping past us, but the Dimitrov Battalion rounded them up
and disposed of them ... It was terrible fighting for the time it
lasted. But every one of the officers met his fate.[52]

The following morning a loudspeaker truck was drawn up. 'Fascist
soldiers, those of you who are Spaniards, listen! Your leaders are lying
to you. Quinto is in Republican hands. You will get no reinforcements.
The relief column sent from Zaragoza has been smashed at Mediana.
There is no relief for you in Belchite, there is only death!' they were
told. 'Come over to us and live. If you don't, you will all be wiped
out.'[53] The remaining 1,200 men surrendered en bloc and, finally, on 6
September, the Republican flag flew over Belchite.[54]

The anarchists of 153 Brigade were given command of the ruins and the
internationals were hurriedly moved out. That did not prevent looting,
at least for souvenirs of the battle. Amongst the trophies carried away
were Italian fascist flags and Nazi swastikas. Posters found on the walls
instructed women to dress modestly, with long skirts and long sleeves,
claiming, according to one shocked female visitor, that 'sin is woman's
because she tempts man'.[55] Merriman had time to wander through what
he called 'a very rich and beautiful place, now in ruins'.[56] The stench of
death was so strong that many wore scarves over their faces as masks.[57]
Merriman would return a few days later to find looting still going on.
'I even picked up a nice present for Marion which I sent back with the
things to Albacete. They are two beautiful red bedspreads,' he wrote.[58]

The capture of Belchite was by no means the work of XV International
Brigade alone, or just of Walter's division. In the scramble to 'claim'
Belchite, indeed, it was the anarchists who boasted that they had raised
a flag on the main church tower. Fighters from the former Tierra and
Libertad Brigade had been promised home leave if they were the first
to reach the centre, and when this was denied them (and, after a row
with Walter, their commanders agreed to withdraw from Belchite)
'there were disturbances', according to one report which did not state
exactly what the disgruntled troops did.[59] Anarchists started a false
rumour that the International Brigaders had been kept in reserve, and
out of danger, until the last moment. 'How can we expect obedience
from the troops unless commanders provide a good example?' they

asked in one report.[60] Walter was furious. 'Most of the successes in the Zaragoza operation belonged to our division,' he countered.[61] Fifteenth International Brigade had suffered the worst losses, he argued, with eighty dead, forty-seven disappeared and 203 wounded, though their companions in his Spanish 32nd Brigade had suffered almost as badly.[62] Losses of 600 men were, he claimed, entirely reasonable in exchange for the killing or capture of over 3,000 opponents.[63]

To Szurek's dismay, another member of the close-knit group of staff officers around Walter, the Polish captain Vladek Butowski, had died in the street-fighting. The former French Foreign Legionnaire (now repentant at having served as a 'slave to fascism') had written to his mother in Poland a few days earlier. It was the first letter since he had informed that he was leaving for Spain. Butowski told of his engagement to the volunteer nurse who cared for him after his men had dragged what they initially assumed was his bullet-ridden corpse off the battlefield at Jarama. 'I have the intention to be married, and will do it very soon, to a young Spanish schoolteacher whose name is Carmen. I am in love up to my ears. I liked Berta [his former girlfriend] as a sister, but I am in love with this woman, a comrade in life and war.'[64] It was one of the many passionate – if often truncated – relationships born out of the drama, heat and intensity of the war.

Szurek watched as selected prisoners were interrogated. Civilians were being inspected to see if they had bruising on their shoulders from firing a rifle. This time Szurek tried not to allow himself to lose his own calm. Instead he pitied the 'poverty and despair' of the prisoners. 'Their clothes were torn; they were dirty and hungry. Perhaps in spite of all they suffered, they were happy that they survived, that the sun was shining, and that it was all over.'[65] But when someone pointed out a suspected police informer, he was struck by a sudden rage – which he put down to his own experience of informers while he was an underground activist in Poland – and attacked the man with his fists. 'I walked away panting and ashamed. Belchite's citizens looked at me wordlessly,' he recalled. A Spanish colleague was more direct. 'Why did you beat him? It would have been better if you had shot him.' Up to 170 other prisoners – mostly military officers but also up to thirty local rightists – were shot.[66] If Walter claimed the victory, then responsibility for this was also his.

Szurek drove to Modesto's headquarters, where he found the victory being toasted with 'excellent French cognac'. Walter was drunk, and he and Modesto were behaving like little boys. They climbed a fig tree together to pick fruit before Walter ordered his driver to take him to Belchite, down the still-dangerous road that connected it to the town of Azaila. Polish volunteer doctor Jeanette Oppman, who had sent men back to the line at gun point in Brunete, and Koltsov's long-term girlfriend Maria Osten, were drinking with them, and asked to go along for the ride.[67] Szurek felt he had no choice but to get in the car as well:

> 'General, that road isn't free yet,' I ventured.
> 'Mr Alek shits in his pants,' the elated general replied. The women laughed and I raved. We kept on riding; I was very restless.
> 'Jadzka [Walter] stop it, for God's sake!' I shouted angrily. 'This is serious.'
> 'Well, let's go back,' the general decided. 'Mr Alek doesn't want to go this way.'[68]

The following day, with Francoist bombers already attacking the town, Szurek was surprised to see the usually fearless Walter and Modesto looking panic-stricken. The reason was that La Pasionaria, who had tried to drive straight into the still-occupied town a few days earlier after believing reports that it had already been taken, was visiting. Walter explained later that he had feared he might become responsible for La Pasionaria's death. 'I was worried about *madre* [mother],' he said, using his personal nickname for the powerful woman to whom he was always deferential.[69]

Walter was delighted. The volunteers and Spaniards under his command had been disciplined and, when left to their own devices in the street-fighting, had shown initiative and courage. They had defeated an enemy that showed 'great persistence and capacity for resistance'.[70] His own decision to bring the artillery close up had been crucial, he concluded, with XV Brigade's use of 45mm cannon in the street-fighting particularly successful.[71]

The wider offensive, however, had failed. Kléber was aware that this reflected poorly on the communists in the army. 'The entire operation, conceived for purposes of drawing the enemy away from Santander, was considered by the general staff in Valencia to be an operation that was directed and carried out by the forces of the communists,' he wrote. 'The Zaragoza operations had great internal significance for the Communist Party, because it presented the opportunity to put an end to the anarcho-Trotskyist-FAI domination in Aragon. It is no wonder that the party demanded the utmost exertion of effort from all its members. It is also understandable that the party could not be satisfied with the results.'[72] The communists' well-earned military reputation had been seriously dented, threatening their power and status within the Republic. They had previously done much to impose organisational discipline on the army, with French military attaché Henri Morel noting that 'out of fear of disorder, the moderates went over to the communists, who presented order'.

Walter's final conclusions were mixed. They had captured 900 square kilometres of territory but failed to save Santander, which Franco conquered on 26 August, the third day of the offensive.[73] If the original objective had been to take Zaragoza or, as the orders read, to get close enough 'to place the Aragonese capital under artillery fire',[74] this had also not happened. However, the operation was an improvement on Brunete in terms of land won, losses caused and losses suffered.[75] The greatest successes had been at Quinto and Belchite. The International Brigades had, once more, suffered more than their share of losses, accounting for almost 20 per cent of the total of 7,700 dead, wounded or missing in action.[76] Kléber claimed that his Polish XIII Brigade had suffered worst, losing 800 men, while the Italian XII Brigade was missing 250.[77] The English-speaking XV Brigade had lost 330 men (including 127 dead or missing) and a further 207 (with forty-seven dead) were gone from the German XI Brigade.[78] It can be assumed that more than half those losses were Spaniards fighting under the banner of the International Brigades.

Overall, though, Walter felt the battle showed significant improvements in the Republican army, which was more coordinated and worked better under fire than previously. The defence of the Mediana line by the Germans of XI Brigade and others, for example, had eventually succeeded because of support from the air. Over-optimism and the erroneous belief that a popular uprising was under way in Zaragoza had not helped. The plan of attack on Zaragoza itself – originally with just three and a half brigades and twelve artillery guns – against a heavily militarised city bounded on one side by the wide river Ebro, had never been realistic.[79] Fuentes de Ebro could and should have been bypassed, Walter thought.

A belated and disastrous attempt to take the town in October, as a Russian tank commander experimented with sending infantry units into battle on heavy BT-5 tanks that sank in the mud and became trapped in narrow streets, saw XV Brigade take heavy casualties. Its 'Spanish Battalion' (the Español, or 24th), which included Spanish and Portuguese speakers from Latin America, was virtually wiped out.[80]

The decision to move from '*No Pasarán!*' to '*Pasaremos*' (we shall pass), after Guadalajara had, Walter believed, been a difficult one to carry out. 'Offensive warfare with limited resources is more complex and requires that soldiers and officers display greater will-power, initiative and training than in static defence,'[81] he wrote. The Republican army was still not good enough for that.

Emilio Kléber, meanwhile, paid for his division's failure. The general had none of Lukács's charm or tact and, under his command, the division had been torn apart by one of the endemic failings of the International Brigades – the tensions between nationalities. The Poles (and Kléber himself) of XIII Brigade claimed the Italian XII Brigade had shirked its duties, abandoning them to be slaughtered. The latter accused the Poles of lying, or at least exaggerating, about 'taking' Villamayor.[82] All this exacerbated the tensions between the communists and non-communists in the Italian brigade.[83]

The prickly and outspoken Kléber was called to a hearing at the Communist Party headquarters in Valencia to defend himself against the accusation that he had deliberately set Poles against Italians, with La Pasionaria amongst those grilling him. His sacking was presented as a personal decision but, amongst other sins, he was criticised for letting 'people in your division became attached to you personally'.[84] Hans Kahle replaced him. Maximov, the latest head of the Russian military delegation, put a gloss on Kléber's departure. 'He worked for more than a year, longer than all the rest, and it was time to go home. They need people with experience at home,' he said.[85] In fact, after his recall to Moscow during Stalin's purges, Kléber – Manfred Stern – would be sent to spend the rest of his days in the Gulags.

42

The North Pole: Teruel, December 1937

On the evening of 14 December 1937, four of some of the most invisible characters in the International Brigades – American guerrilla war experts Irving Goff and Alex Kunslich along with two Finns – slipped out into the snow to cross the rugged countryside of Teruel, together with eight Spanish soldiers. With moonlight reflecting dangerously off the snow, the dozen men walked for twenty kilometres, skirting the high spots from which the enemy secured its line around the city. Their target was a small, unprotected bridge that crossed the Guadalaviar and linked the semi-besieged city to the town of Albarracín, set in a spur above the river.[1] The group had been trained by Russian experts, one of whom, Ilya Starinov, was also out that night. 'An amazing feeling arises when you cross the front line at night. It is as if you are walking on a narrow bridge over an abyss,' he said.[2]

Arriving shortly before dawn, they set their explosives and a timer, and then left hurriedly. By the time the charge exploded and the bridge tumbled into the ravine below, they were already on a distant hilltop. 'I've blown bridges,' Goff explained later, scoffing at the romanticised depiction of international guerrillas in Hemingway's *For Whom the Bell Tolls*. 'You put a detonator in the thing and then you'd better be twenty miles away.' They then cut telephone lines and, on their way back, bumped into an enemy cavalry patrol which harassed them as they moved towards their own lines before the main attack on Teruel began a few hours later.[3]

Early in December 1937 it had become clear, with forces amassing near the Guadalajara front, that Franco was planning yet another assault on Madrid.[4] If the war in the south and centre of Spain had turned into a draw in which the Republic had gained the initiative, this had partly

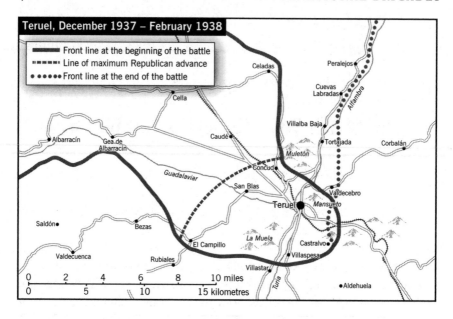

been because Franco was concentrating on the north. His recent victory there now released large numbers of troops and brought a dramatic increase in his army's ability to strike elsewhere.

The Republican army decided to hit first, in order to disrupt plans that might bring the war to a sudden and dramatic end. A pre-emptive offensive, it was hoped, would demonstrate to the world that the Republic was still vigorous and viable, while stretching out the war until an increasingly likely wider European conflagration started. The symbolic value of holding major cities, even where this outweighed their actual strategic value, continued to obsess both sides. That is why the Republic now turned its attention, once more, to modest Teruel, sitting on a mound beside the river Turia and overlooked by higher hills. The lines here had barely changed since XIII Brigade received its baptism of fire as part of the failed attempt to conquer it a year earlier.

The city occupied a salient of Francoist territory in the southern part of Aragon. This made it, in theory, a simpler target than other cities, and explains why it was chosen ahead of another fully planned option in Extremadura.[5] The Teruel salient contained around 8,000 of Franco's soldiers, so when the Republic gathered eighty-nine battalions (almost 80,000 men) to attack it,[6] the odds of winning were already promising. If Teruel could be surrounded before reinforcements arrived, then it seemed likely that the city would fall. For the first time, however, the International Brigades were not to be given a prominent role. There were two main reasons for this: first, the overall quality and morale of the Republic's regular army had improved, making the Brigades less 'special'; secondly, the Republic wanted to keep the Brigades, who were always the first stop for foreign reporters, out of the headlines. The capture of Teruel without them would help the Republic in its drive to use the non-intervention policies of Britain, France and the United States against Franco, who was far more reliant on foreign fighters. Finally, there were still politicians and generals who did not like the International Brigades, either because they were foreigners or because they were considered part of the 'communist' bloc within the army.[7]

Only General Walter's 35th Division, still with the German and English-speaking XI and XV International Brigades, was called upon to take part and then, initially, to remain in reserve in and around Alcañiz.[8] The only Brigaders to play a significant role in the first phase of the offensive were those – like Goff and Kunslich – who had joined the guerrilla units that specialised in behind-the-lines sabotage. They were part of a mixed guerrilla unit of highly trained men which was mostly Spanish, known as the 14th Corps.[9]

Unlike the attempts to take Zaragoza, Huesca or Segovia, the Teruel offensive proved a spectacular success. The element of surprise proved crucial.[10] Launched on 15 December, and accompanied by a heavy snowfall, it took just two days to encircle a city which – rather like Huesca – had survived with only one main route out, by both road and rail, to Zaragoza.[11]

Hemingway, Capa and other reporters gathered excitedly in the railway wagon parked inside a tunnel at Puerto Escandón that served as a rearguard Republican command post, before venturing out to the front.[12] Hemingway, who was used to the dramatic and harsh weather of America's mountain states, called this 'a country cold as a steel engraving, wild as a Wyoming blizzard or a hurricane'.[13] He and the other correspondents were able to drive down to Valencia most evenings to file reports, or send photographs, of the expected Republican victory.[14] Peering at Teruel through a periscope from a rocky outcrop, the American novelist described the city as sitting below a 'flat-topped, steep-flanked hill [the Mansueto] with a shiplike prow rising from the plain to protect the yellow brick-built town clumped above the river bank' set against a 'fantastically eroded background of red sandstone'.[15] His soldier's eye also saw, however, how difficult it might be to take. It was not just the dramatic hills that surrounded the city like sentinels, but also the weather. This became so cold that doctors found themselves having to amputate soldiers' frostbitten hands and feet.[16] After Teruel was surrounded, it took a further two weeks to oust the last defenders from the city centre. The international volunteers most involved at this stage were from the French and Romanian-led Ana Pauker artillery battery, which poured shells onto the buildings where the defenders grouped for their last stand – though the Asturian miners who placed charges of up to 1,500kg of dynamite in tunnels underneath them were more effective in persuading them to surrender.[17]

Festivities began long before the last defenders finally surrendered on 8 January, since it became clear before Christmas that the fascists could not hold out.[18] Walter's German- and English-speaking brigades, who were still in reserve, found themselves caught up in the celebrations. The Germans marched through a village they called La Codinera (probably La Codoñera), firing bullets into the air. Wine flowed freely everywhere. The commander of a new XV Brigade Canadian battalion – the Mackenzie-Papineaus, or Mac-Paps – marched his men through the snow the following day to clear their heads.[19] The wave of optimism that swept across the Republic made the white Christmas of 1937 – for some Brigaders – 'easily the most pleasant days ever to be experienced … in Spain'.[20] Toys were gathered and distributed to local children, dances held and victory toasted. Hershey bars, candies and French cognac appeared in the American camp. After so many months without fighting, and having replenished with new recruits and had time to train with them, morale among the International Brigades was as high as it had ever been. The British were given signed personal photographs by British Communist Party leader Harry Pollitt, which were probably not as well received (especially by the non-communists) as the letters and Christmas puddings he brought from home, or the pork, wine and nuts produced by the quartermaster.

The only dampener, for some, was the way a formal statute for the International Brigades, that was finally published on 23 September, was used to mark a difference between ordinary soldiers and officers. This statute cemented their role as 'front-line' shock troops and made them roughly equivalent in status to Franco's legionnaires. The new set of rules came as part of the Republican government's continued attempts to both improve organisation across the army and reduce the power of Marty and the Comintern cadres in Albacete, where they now occupied forty buildings. As a reminder that they, too, were under the command of the Spanish war ministry, Marty and his staff were publicly reprimanded for not yet having provided a proper list of their men.[21]

In many ways the statute simply formalised existing practices, but in others it was deliberately interfering. Marty formally lost control of the men trained at Albacete as soon as they left to join their battalion. They now belonged to the larger unit – a division or corps – of the Spanish army which their brigade had joined. The rules, pay, rights and obligations were the same as other soldiers in the regular Spanish army, and the defence ministry reserved the right to appoint half of its officers directly. The latter now became a superior class, much as they were in both the Red Army and 'imperialist' armies.[22] When officers and other ranks were separated for their Christmas meals that December, there were complaints. 'When the shit was being served up [at the front], we were all together, weren't were?' observed one political commissar.[23] There was no equality in pay, either – with a captain, for example, receiving twice the salary of a private soldier.[24]

Shortly after, the British were visited by Paul Robeson and listened to his rich, bass baritone renditions of spirituals, though by now he routinely changed the words of the famous *Show Boat* musical song 'Ol' Man River' from 'I'm tired of livin' and feared of dying', to the more rousing and hopeful 'I must keep fightin' until I'm dying.'[25]

There would be no such celebrations at New Year, for it was one thing to take Teruel and quite another to hold on to it. Most of Franco's generals, along with his German and Italian advisors, believed the city was unimportant or, rather, that it was not worth distracting them from the planned operation against Madrid.[26] Franco, however, hated to lose. So he now turned Teruel from a short, minor battle into a major, long-term one, which would last until the end of February. He suspended preparations for the Madrid attack four days before Christmas, meaning that one of the Republic's main objectives had been accomplished.[27] Its secondary objective – to draw the war out further, just as a full-scale European conflagration became increasingly likely – was also being met.

While the Republicans were mopping up the remaining Francoist units in the city, the enemy had already launched a counter-attack designed to take a series of surrounding hilltops. 'Whoever controlled those hills, controlled the city,' said Walter.[28] When Hemingway had climbed one of these early in the battle, he looked down at a 'pretty, peaceful' little city, with its 'church steeples and neatly geometrical houses', surrounded by sugar-beet fields. To one side lay 'red cliffs, sculptured by erosion into columns that looked like organ pipes, and beyond ... a devil's playground of red, waterless badlands'.[29] The grandest hill of all was the flat-topped Mansueto, protecting Teruel from the east.[30] To the west lay La Muela, the most impressive of 'several thimble-shaped hillocks thrusting up from the plain like geyser cones'.[31] This, and another hill to the north called the Muletón, provided the main 'balconies' overlooking the city for any attack force wanting to dominate it with artillery and machine-gun fire, and were Franco's primary targets.

The Republican generals had not realised with what determination Franco would set about trying to recover Teruel and had already withdrawn many of their best troops when a fierce counter-attack started on 29 December.[32] With almost total control of the skies and a big advantage in artillery, Franco's troops began pounding their way back towards Teruel. The combined firepower available to him was formidable. Used correctly, with concentrated attacks on small areas, it could thoroughly destroy or demoralise a particular sector of the front.[33] His units advanced rapidly towards La Muela, provoking panic inside Teruel itself.[34] The Francoist advance was only stopped by thick fog and a blizzard on the afternoon of 31 December,[35] reportedly the worst in living memory, as temperatures sank to minus 22 degrees Celsius, provoking frostbite and killing off many of the injured.[36]

Francoist boasts that they had taken back the city were quickly revealed to be lies. Four foreign correspondents following his troops set out together for the supposedly 'recaptured' city on New Year's Eve, only to have their car blown off the road by Republican artillery. Only one reporter survived. This was *The Times* of London correspondent and communist spy Kim Philby, who had previously tried to organise Franco's assassination.[37] Ironically, Franco would now award him the Red Cross of Military Merit. 'My wounding in Spain helped my work, both journalism and intelligence, no end,' he admitted later.[38]

Walter's two International Brigades were finally mobilised that day, joining the attempts to prevent the enemy reaching El Muletón. Placed near the town of Concud,[39] the German-speaking XI Brigade was forced to give up ground,[40] before being moved to La Muela, where some of the toughest fighting would take place. By now the snow was so thick on the steep-sided hills that the tanks attached to XI Brigade often slid back down the slopes they had climbed, tipping over when they hit the bottom.[41] Over the first few days, 340 of the brigade's men had to be withdrawn, suffering frostbite.[42] Machine-gun locks and rifle bolts had to be warmed by hand, or tucked inside clothes to stop them freezing. Hands sometimes stuck to exposed metal, frozen into place. Even the lice that inhabited the seams of every soldier's clothing found it too cold to move.

Fifteenth Brigade was also put into trucks on New Year's Eve and driven along the snowbound mountain roads, with icy winds throwing swirls of snow against windscreens or through the edges of their tarpaulin covers. The sight of so many wrecked vehicles lying in the ravines below them was proof of just how treacherous the roads had become, though the poor driving skills of former city taxi drivers from Madrid and Barcelona (unaccustomed to snow and ice) were also blamed. The volunteers were taken to a series of exposed defensive peaks twenty kilometres north of Teruel in the inhospitable Sierra Palomera, part of a long chain of sierras that ran northwards – and which the Americans dubbed 'the North Pole'.[43] With fingers and limbs stiffened by the cold, they dug in to the snow-covered fields and hillsides, though at night many were brought back to sleep in the semi-abandoned villages behind them.

Soon one in ten of XV Brigade's men also had frostbite or were complaining of numbness. Since there was no continuous line to defend, the battalions were distributed along a row of strongpoints from which to prevent an enemy breakthrough. The Mac-Paps were installed at Argente, the Lincolns moved on to Fuentes and the British and Spanish Battalions were placed near the village of Cuevas Labradas.[44] An unfinished tunnel there became both the brigade headquarters and a night shelter to which most men would retire every evening. This was considered 'the epitome of misery', since the fires lit to (unsuccessfully) warm the tunnel filled it with choking smoke, melted the icicles and created a carpet of slushy mud that soaked through leather boots.[45]

The young anarchists who had been holding these positions still had not dug proper trenches or machine-gun posts, but were quick to follow the example of the more experienced Brigaders. Once more, the suspicions, grievances and jealousies of the rearguard disappeared under shared danger. 'They had a good opinion of the International Brigades, and with our example they started to clean their rifles,' recalled one American sergeant. 'When we began to improve the trench and to make firing holes with sandbags, they imitated us. They were good soldiers and tried to do their best but did not know how.'[46] Elsewhere the volunteers were impressed by how the regular Spanish units now maintained discipline, putting up with artillery barrages or aerial bombardments and returning to their positions as soon as they were over.[47]

With no continual line of trenches blocking the enemy, the Francoists managed to infiltrate between the Spanish and Lincoln Battalions. This provoked a Lincoln counter-attack which proved how much they had learned in ten months. 'The guys who just a short time ago had been the biggest beefers against the snow, the cold ... were now coolly giving volley fire on order,' recalled the scrawny, bird-like poet Edwin Rolfe, who was now working on the International Brigades' *Volunteer for Liberty* newspaper and, occasionally, as an American commissar. 'They deployed beautifully, spread like a fan across the plateau under heavy fire, infiltrated as though on a training manoeuvre.'[48]

If the snow and cold were the most direct threat to both life and limb, it soon became apparent that another potent enemy was above them. On 3 January the sound of what seemed like more than a hundred enemy bombers paralysed many of the volunteers with fear. These flew over their positions and on to a town fifteen kilometres behind the front line, Perales del Alfambra, leaving it partially destroyed.[49] It was a sign of how Franco meant to proceed.

Republican attempts to push the nationalist advances back brought only limited successes, with XI Brigade involved in the continual attempts to retake positions on and around La Muela at bayonet point on 5 and 6 January. On one of its most successful charges it captured 240 prisoners,[50] but the cost was high. When XV Brigade was moved in to replace it on 14 January, at what Ćopić told his men was the 'post of honour' (where the fiercest fighting was), the new Canadian Mac-Pap Battalion found the trenches and no-man's-land on a spur of land to the north side of La Muela still full of semi-frozen corpses. Behind them lay a sharp, twenty-metre drop that blocked any attempt at escape. The British machine-gun company, meanwhile, was placed on the Santa Barbara hill, from where it could provide deadly, sweeping fire against approaching forces trying to drive their way down the Concud valley, five kilometres west of the city.[51]

Fifteenth International Brigade was now close enough to Teruel itself for the headquarters of the Lincoln Battalion, which acted as the brigade's reserve, to be established in the cellars of a series of properties owned by a Dominican convent on the outskirts of city, which also housed a psychiatric asylum. The nuns had believed Francoist propaganda that labelled international volunteers likely to inflict 'rape, mayhem and general disaster', but were eventually evacuated to Valencia.[52] One American volunteer likened the captured city to 'a blackened, Goya etching ... a city frozen and stark, surrounded by burnt, bomb-blasted hills'.[53] Miraculously, hot food could be prepared and delivered every day.[54] Most of the Americans retired at night to sleep in the warmth of these buildings and the city's shops were ransacked for warm clothes. Eccentric, improvised uniforms now reappeared, with one commissar wearing what looked like striped morning-suit trousers and a wide-brimmed black sombrero.[55]

A few days of calm – or what one American called 'an ominous lull'[56] – followed as the weather cleared, with the sun glittering off the melting snow and snipers exchanging fire from trenches that were sometimes a mere fifty metres apart. On this sector the fighting had temporarily become, one volunteer recalled, 'a closer approximation to the trench warfare of World War I than any other action' since Jarama.[57] By now it was also clear that the two armies had switched roles. The Republicans were fighting to hold on to Teruel, while the Francoists tried to recover it. With the latter's air supremacy, that now seemed wholly possible.[58]

The Francoists resumed their counter-attacks with renewed vigour on 17 January, aiming to occupy the major hills north and west of Teruel. Eleventh Brigade was given the task of defending one of these, El Muletón, while XV Brigade remained in various positions on or near La Muela, above the river Alfambra and just outside the western side of the city. The rocky peaks of El Muletón were the key to Teruel since they formed a natural fortress which, in theory, was difficult to assault. The Edgar André Battalion scrambled up through the snow to the peak to find only half-metre-deep trenches, already semi-destroyed and affording poor protection from artillery and air bombardment.[59]

For two days the German-speaking Republican volunteers battled over the small peaks on the south side of El Muletón.[60] They knew, however, that they were still not receiving the main force of the Francoist attack since they could also see the Alto de las Celadas hills to their north being pulverised by Franco's artillery and the air force provided by Hitler and Mussolini. By night, groups of German Minenwerfer mortars took it in turns to continue the bombardment. Hundreds of enemy aircraft appeared, while the Republican air force was almost completely absent. 'They must have had more important things to do,' Walter's chief of staff Putz scribbled sarcastically in his diary.[61] There was only one brief let-up, when the evening sky was lit up by what one volunteer called 'a vast sheet of cherry-coloured, mauve-red fire ... [while] faint bars of white striations moved through it'.[62] It was a freak phenomenon – similar to the aurora borealis – which mesmerised parts of the battlefield. The Alto de las Celadas hills fell in what one observer called 'the greatest attack of the war', with a preliminary bombardment that left them shrouded in smoke.[63] When this cleared, the German volunteers saw lines of attackers silhouetted against the snow as they stormed the hilltops. The two Republican brigades there suffered 50 per cent losses.[64]

The men of XI Brigade knew it would be their turn next. The Edgar André Battalion was already exhausted after two days of bombardment and battling over the small peaks on the south side of El Muletón.[65] The following day their positions came under even more intense attack, and the Austrians of the February 12 Battalion were sent in to replace them.[66] Enemy aircraft circled the hilltop constantly, 'like mosquitos around a light', swooping in to strafe or drop small bombs that sent rocks and stones skimming across the surface of the mountain.[67] A furious attack on 19 January filled the dense, damp air on top of El Muletón with a choking cloud of acrid smoke, lit up by the green and red bursts of shrapnel released overhead by time-fused shells.[68]

Part of XV Brigade watched helplessly from the distance as the February 12 Battalion slowly retreated, fighting its way backwards with little or no support from the air or Republican artillery. 'There were no real positions there,' recalled a member of Walter's headquarters company, which was sent in to help protect the last remaining patch of rock on the Muletón overnight on the 19/20 January.[69] 'We just lay straight on the mountain – or sometimes among the rocks. There was hardly any soil, no more than some twenty or thirty centimetres. We had no chance of digging positions in the cold. We were right up on the peak.'[70] Every square metre of land had been impacted by shrapnel.

Between them, the Edgar André and February 12 Battalions slowly ceded terrain, while fighting off eleven different attacks over five days.[71] It became an epic piece of resistance which so impressed the Republican high command that they considered minting a special medal to commemorate it.[72] One of the onlookers described having seen 'the remnants of the German anti-fascist battalions being destroyed as they tried to hold against an impossible hail of fire'. They eventually had to be ordered to relinquish their last defensive positions on the south face of the Muletón and by the evening of 20 January, this was under enemy control.[73]

Those who had climbed the Muletón convinced by the Brigades' slogan 'the [quality of the] fighter always wins over material of the enemy' had been proven tragically wrong.[74] Hemingway declared that it had been 'a position that they sold as dearly as any position was sold in any war'.[75] Much of that price was paid not by Germans or Austrians, but by a company of young Catalan anarchists who had joined XI Brigade, arriving at the snowy front with just rope-soled *alpargatas* on their feet and demanding that they be allowed to name their company after Buenaventura Durruti.[76] Most were still teenagers, but they proved to be ferocious fighters. Even the anarchist-allergic Germans recognised their bravery, especially after they ignored battalion commanders to carry out a daring raid in order to rescue seven of their own men who had been left behind defending a small hut.[77] 'The companies of Spanish recruits (from Catalonia and Madrid) proved themselves for the first time, showing their finest face,' an admiring Walter, who had installed his headquarters in some peasant cave houses dug into a nearby cliff, agreed afterwards. In all, the brigade had lost 900 men, including 300 to the cold.

The English-speaking XV Brigade prepared itself to be next, as it manned positions straddling the valley (where the river Guadalaviar becomes the river Turia) that runs towards Teruel from the west. Their instructions were 'to stand firm, and to be worthy of the sacrifice' of the German-speaking XI Brigade on El Muletón. By 19 January – as the

Germans were fighting over the last patch of the Muletón – many of the British and Canadians had moved onto the valley floor. There they were subjected to the combined barrage of shelling, bombing and strafing that preceded an attack.[78] The carousels of aircraft stacked above them, taking turns to dive and strafe their positions. Men claimed that the aircraft came so close that they could see the pilots at their controls, picking their targets.[79]

On the following day, 20 January, an attempt to burst through their lines was stopped, but only after both the British and the Canadians – who bore the brunt of the fighting – had retreated some distance. Their machine guns, positioned on the slopes above, created carnage. 'The XV Brigade is holding its position, and reserves are arriving,' Putz wrote in his diary.[80]

The most alarming episode of the day, however, came when the Mac-Paps saw half of one of their companies – some forty men – dash across no-man's-land to the enemy trenches. They were deserting. This was a Spanish company, made up of raw young conscripts from Valencia who had lost their officers and, amid rumours that a white flag had been raised, were easily persuaded by the enemy that they were already surrounded.[81] It was a traumatic event – especially as the deserters had taken two machine guns and twenty-five rifles that could now be used against their battalion. The Canadians were forced to fire on them, and it was, as one chronicler put it, 'an ominous thing, new in the history of the International Brigades'. This phenomenon was not unique to the Canadian battalion. Spaniards were also deserting from XI Brigade, with one commissar blaming this on the ferocious discipline enforced on them 'which bordered on terror', though the departure of Staimer as XI Brigade commander early in the battle and his replacement by Heinrich Rau appears to have improved things.[82] For the volunteers, these were cases of the people they had come to defend deciding that they would rather fight on the other side.

With the trenches so close to one another, Spaniards were able to have shouted conversations, which only a handful of volunteers understood. At one stage, the British looked on with alarm as their own Spanish recruits rose out of their positions for a no-man's-land meeting with troops from the trenches in front of them. Londoner Frank West, a former union shop steward turned commissar, broke it up by firing over their heads. 'You don't sit and talk with an enemy that's done what the fascists had done to you under any circumstances,' he said. 'We opened up over the top first until they were separated, and then the fascists got what they had coming to them.'[83] The Spanish recruits complained, seeing the British reaction to their sociable temporary truce as entirely dishonourable.

The gap left by the deserters had to be filled by a motley collection of clerks and administrators from the battalion's staff, including the paymaster. These, nevertheless, held on with the rest of XV Brigade until 23 January, when the attack petered out. The Francoist high command, always keen to exaggerate the numbers of international volunteers, claimed to have decimated three entire International Brigades, which they called the Lincolns, the Washingtons and the 'Walter Brigade'.[84] Eleven days later, on 3 February, the battered XV Brigade was relieved and sent back towards Madrid and the town of Belmonte de Tajo.[85]

As the battle-weary men travelled towards Belmonte de Tajo, American communists contrived to create a situation of such over-whelming presumptuousness that it was fortunate not to provoke permanent rifts within the Lincoln Battalion. The American-led battalion had left Teruel on a painfully slow-moving train that was taking it towards Valencia. The train was overtaken by a car carrying Earl Browder, the visiting head of the Communist Party of the USA. The train was stopped and the men, still hungry and in filthy clothing, were forced to listen to a series of speeches. Amongst other things, they learnt that Roosevelt had become the first world leader to challenge the wisdom of non-intervention and appeasement, with a famous 'quarantine' speech of 5 October 1937, in which he warned that a new era of terror was eroding international law, order and justice and paving the way for something far worse. 'Without a declaration of war and without warning or justification of any kind, civilians, including vast numbers of women and children, are being ruthlessly murdered with bombs from the air. It seems to be unfortunately true that the epidemic of world lawlessness is spreading,' Roosevelt declared, as Hitler, Mussolini and their allies in Japan continued to rip up post-First World War global peace treaties like the Kellogg–Briand Pact. 'And mark this well,' the president continued, 'when an epidemic of physical disease starts to spread, the community approves and joins in a quarantine of the patients in order to protect the health of the community against the spread of the disease.'[86] Nobody, however, in the international community was prepared to follow him.

Earl Browder also took it upon himself to admonish men who had just been through weeks of hard fighting about so-called 'unhealthy attitudes' and griping. He was probably referring to a small group of men who, angry at having to drill, had declared that they were now anarchists. When, however, he threatened that 'if some of you don't straighten out you just may be sent home', he was jeered. Laughter, catcalls and booing showed that, whatever his power over the communists, a good number of the men regarded this as a bad joke. 'Save me the first boat!' someone shouted. 'I'm grumbling, I'm grumbling – when do I go home?' spat someone else.[87] The rebellious-minded seafarers who made up the Lincolns' machine-gun company, despite many being communists, were amongst those who loudly demanded to know 'when the next boat was leaving'.[88]

It was a reminder that not all communists were blindly obedient, and that not all Lincoln volunteers were Americans or party members. Browder's arrogance, indeed, reflected the distance that separated those communists (including the ones not in uniform) who saw the party as proprietor of the International Brigades from those who simply wanted to fight fascism. The MI5 spy agency, which kept files on many British volunteers, later ruled that it had failed to leverage this division between so-called 'true believer' communists and those who were primarily anti-fascists. Arthur Landis, a volunteer who wrote a masterful history of the American volunteers, compared the Brigades to the Continental Army in the American War of Independence, 'which was, above all else, political'.[89] He also meant, however, that the views inside it were diverse – regardless of the Communist Party's role as the prime organiser and recruiter. 'The seamen, some of the Canadians and others of independent beliefs resented a situation in which views other than those of the CPUSA reached them but seldom,' he explained. 'That is not to say that they were in opposition to the British or American Communist Parties. They simply desired to hear opinions and ideas from other progressive and left sources too.'[90]

After an overnight stop in Valencia, the train set off again but sometime the following night a telegram was received. The men were needed back at Teruel.[91] Yet another counter-attack on 5 February had broken through, threatening the city from the north. Walter's International Brigades were wanted for an urgent diversionary attack at Segura de los Baños, some seventy-five kilometres north of Teruel.[92]

They faced, once more, sub-zero temperatures, icy winds, sleet and snow. There, against a largely unprepared enemy, they took a series of hilltops with surprise attacks, capturing a considerable quantity of prisoners, machine guns and other arms, along with luxuries such as Portuguese cigars and canned octopus. They then dug in to resist the expected counter-attacks, fulfilling their role as bait for a 'diversion', while again being subjected to constant bombing and artillery fire. Walter once more set up his headquarters in one of the many cave houses in the region. When his Russian advisor, Colonel Shevchenko, stepped out to watch a squadron of bombers arriving, he was killed by a bomb that fell a few metres from the cave. Had it fallen a short time later, it might have killed another Russian visitor – the chief advisor, Rodion Malinovsky, and deprived the Red Army of one of the men who would lead the epic defence at Stalingrad during the Second World War (and go on to become Soviet defence minister).[93]

The diversionary attack did little to blunt Franco's drive on Teruel. This was launched again on 17 February,[94] under the protection of Hitler and Mussolini's aircraft.[95] Within four days the city was all but encircled, with only a narrow escape path left along the banks of the river Turia. On the night of 22 February, with the Francoists already in parts of the largely ruined city, those defenders who could still walk crept out along the dark riverbanks to safety. Walter estimated the losses amongst them at 40 per cent.

Eleventh Brigade had lost many men at Teruel but, just as it was now mostly Spanish, so too were its dead – the young boys from Madrid and Catalonia accounted for perhaps three quarters of battle losses.[96] Once again, a new International Brigades battalion – in this case the Canadian Mac-Paps – had suffered badly, with an estimated 150 to 250 losses. Amongst the dead was twenty-four-year-old former University of Rochester track star John Field, whose fifty-eight-year-old engineer father Ralph Higbee Field had given up a teaching job and joined the Brigades pretending to be John's elder brother. He was working in the Canadians' kitchens, where he was told of his son's death.[97] The British Battalion had lost a third of its men and the Lincolns were now down by eighty.[98]

The battle of Teruel had lasted two and a half months. Walter saw the prime error as not having followed up the original success by advancing some forty kilometres further, a move which – by closing the entire

Teruel salient – would have shortened the front line and cut the railway line to Zaragoza. In Marty's bloated rhetoric, however, the heroism of Teruel was deemed certain to provoke a fresh wave of support from workers around Europe. 'Without doubt, tomorrow it will begin to prove its fruits. Tomorrow more food and more footwear will reach Spain just as there will be more people who realise that in Spain the future of the peoples of Europe is being decided,' he declared.[99] Elsewhere in the Brigades, men were told that the fact that it had taken Franco ten weeks to recover a city that the Republic had captured in 'five days' (it was, in fact, twenty-three days) was proof that the latter was ahead in the war.[100]

It was now late February, however, and the attack that Franco had been planning on Madrid had still not happened. Overall losses on both sides at Teruel had been staggeringly large – later historians would call this battle the Stalingrad of Spain, not just because of the cold and the extent of the slaughter, but because it appeared to mark a turning point in the war. With the Republican army now almost matching Franco's forces on the ground, in terms of skill, if not equipment, mastery of the air was proving to be his decisive advantage. He also had large reserves of foreign troops – the Italian CTV, now free from its duties on the northern front – that made the International Brigades pale into insignificance. During their attacks around Segura de los Baños, XV and XI Brigades had been only about twenty kilometres away from the Italians' new base. The balance of power, in other words, was increasingly tilting away from the Republic and the volunteers who had come to defend it.

43

Blitzkrieg: Belchite, 9 March 1938

At 6.30 a.m. on the morning of 9 March, over 35,000 troops from Mussolini's CTV fascist militia waited anxiously behind their start lines for a new assault.[1] The Republic's leaders had expected this to come at Guadalajara, with Franco finally bending to Italian and German frustration by launching the attack to capture Madrid that he had postponed in response to the loss of Teruel. Instead, the Italians were massed along a four-kilometre stretch of the line near Rudilla, halfway between Teruel and Belchite.[2] They were just one of three army corps preparing to smash through the Aragonese front. Stretched along a 100-kilometre-wide attack line, or waiting in reserve, were twenty-seven Francoist divisions. They had been rapidly resupplied and readied for action while the Republican units slowly mended their own battered forces.[3] With 150,000 men, 700 guns and 600 aircraft, this was to be an offensive of as yet unseen proportions, along a front stretching south from Fuentes de Ebro to Vivel del Río Martín.[4] The orders spoke of 'taking advantage of the superiority in material and morale' after Teruel.[5]

'This time the campaign was to be conducted along the blitzkrieg lines advocated by the Germans,' noted the Cambridge University graduate Peter Kemp,[6] one of a small number of British volunteers fighting on the other side, who had recently transferred from the *requetés* militia to the Spanish Legion. He and his fellow legionnaires were lined up just north of the Italians as part of the 45,000-strong Army Corps of Morocco.[7] The attackers outnumbered defenders by five to one.[8] Their aim was to split Republican Spain in two, driving a wedge through Aragon and Catalonia to the Mediterranean Sea. Fleets of sturdy new

American-built trucks,[9] part of 12,000 sold to Franco by Ford, General Motors and other US manufacturers, were there to help transport them. The arms embargoes did not cover these, or the fuel being sent by oil giant Texaco.[10] 'Without American petroleum, American trucks and American credit, we would never have won,' a Francoist official admitted later.[11]

For the first time, the International Brigades were being gathered into two separate and entirely international divisions, commanded by General Walter and the popular German Hans Kahle. Walter was delighted to welcome his fellow Poles and other Slavs from XIII Brigade into 35th Division, where they joined the German and English speakers of XI and XV Brigades. He saw in them the nucleus of a future army for his Polish homeland – a dream that, as later events would show, was not entirely misplaced. They were glad to leave their previous division, where they had been arguing with the Italian-speaking XII Brigade ever since they accused it of abandoning them at the gates of Zaragoza. They had spent most of their time since then in Extremadura, where they again blamed a failed attempt at capturing the town of Campillo de Llerena on a panicked retreat by one of the Italian battalions.[12] The Italians, meanwhile, maintained their 'popular front' spirit under yet another non-communist commander, the socialist Arturo Zanoni – though he faced considerable internal criticism from communists.[13]

A recently formed International Brigade, known as 129 Brigade, was the latest – and would be the last – new major international unit to be formed. It was due to join 45th Division, which Kahle had inherited from Kléber following its poor performance at Zaragoza.[14] This now also included the French-speaking XIV International Brigade which was resting at El Escorial[15] (and to which the Franco-Belgian André Marty Battalion was finally moved) as well as the Italian XII Brigade.[16] While the other brigades had gradually gathered together volunteers who spoke the same language (though Spanish was now the native tongue of most of the soldiers), the new brigade was a fresh Tower of Babel with a large proportion of foreign volunteers. These came from forty countries, though central Europeans and Slavs were predominant. Poles, Czechs and Yugoslavs – some of them fresh arrivals from the Lenin School in Moscow – occupied many of the most important posts. Bickering between the latter two groups – or, to be more precise, between their two national communist parties – was a problem to begin with. This was resolved by giving command to the fiercely disciplinarian Pole, Wacław Komar (using the name Roman Watcek). His attitude to military matters was much like that of his countryman Walter, with the same expectation of absolute obedience and the iron will of a disciplined '100 percenter'.[17] This was the same man who had boldly led the Polish battalions that came closest to Zaragoza. He also had a violent past as a teenage communist enforcer and assassin in Poland and, then, as a trainee and operative of the Soviet Union's Red Army, its OGPU (later NKVD) secret police and Comintern.[18]

The experienced Dimitrov and Yugoslav-led Djuro Djakovic Battalions formed the new brigade's core, while an entirely new battalion was named after the former Czech president and national hero Thomas Masaryk, who had guided his country to independence after the disintegration of the Austro-Hungarian Empire, and had died the previous year.[19] A Paraguayan communist called Emilio Païva served as the formal link to the Spanish Communist Party.[20] The enthusiastic new brigade lived a short, halcyon period of training in the town and fertile surroundings of Chillón, where local men worked in the strategically vital mercury mines of the region and had not been sent to war. Even a former right-wing mayor reputedly vied with the rest of the townsfolk in an informal competition to be the best host to these foreign visitors.

As Franco's army set out to force its way through the Republican front line on 9 March, Walter's brigades were amongst the few reserve units within easy reach of the line – though XIII Brigade had only arrived the previous day from Extremadura.[21] Fifteenth Brigade had moved back to the area around Belchite two days earlier, and the others were spread out in separate towns and villages across this thinly populated region.[22] Little else had been done to reinforce the area, although the dramatic bombings of rearguard towns over previous days – with the partial destruction of Alcañiz and death of more than 250 civilians rivalling the massacre at Guernica – were a signal that an attack might come soon.[23] A Lincoln company commander, Frank Bonetti, said they were 'not expecting anything serious', however.[24] This was partly because they were not on the front line – which lay twenty kilometres west, just past Fuendetodos[25] – and when the sky thickened with bombers and the sound of distant artillery fire rumbled across the land, they were not sure what this meant.[26] A twenty-year-old Spanish conscript with the Lincoln Battalion, Fausto Villar, recalled counting 120 aircraft in the sky at one time. 'It was an enormous display by Franco's Germans, telling us that the sky was theirs,' he wrote later.[27]

The initial bombardment was furious and intense. The Republican front-line troops positioned here were inexperienced and, crucially, with minimal reserves behind them. They were terrified by a menacing new aircraft, fresh out of the Junkers factories of Dessau and Bremen, that dived straight at them, dropping well-aimed bombs. This was the recently designed Stuka dive-bomber, or Ju 87, which fell hawk-like from the sky to unload bombs with such precision that the Luftwaffe deemed them capable of hitting to within five metres of their target.[28] There were only a few of these, but it was a first real test for the gull-winged aircraft that, with its shrieking sirens, would strike terror into the countries that Hitler began invading in the world war that started the following year. German-trained tank units and Condor Legion 88mm anti-aircraft guns – also with legendary precision and often used against targets on the ground – joined in what became a first proper trial of real blitzkrieg.[29] In fact, the opening bombardment was so intense that the Spanish Legion was able to just walk through some lines, bayoneting dazed men.

Amongst the first to realise what was happening was an outlying section of the Canadian Mac-Paps on the road from Belchite to Letux.[30] By first light, fleeing soldiers of all kinds were passing through its positions, muttering about breakthroughs and treason.[31] Walter hurried towards the front while Merriman, temporarily in charge of XV Brigade, prepared to defend the hard-won pile of semi-destroyed houses at Belchite by establishing what everyone assumed was still only a secondary line six kilometres to its west. The English-speaking volunteers moved forward slowly that night, unaware of the speed of the advancing enemy. This was not surprising, since the 45,000-strong Army Corps of Morocco had punched through a fifteen-kilometre stretch of line defended by 6,500 men, while, to the south, the 35,000-strong Italian corps had attacked a section of the front defended by just 3,000.[32] The Canadians were sent closer towards the advancing army near Azuara, with orders to arrest retreating soldiers and shoot their officers, but ended up waving their weapons at men who simply ignored them.[33] The British and Spanish Battalions remained nearby in reserve.[34]

The brigade that advanced to meet the enemy was by now reasonably well-equipped and trained. New recruits from Albacete had been sent to fill the gaps left by the punishing experience of Teruel, and they were nearly up to full strength.[35] The recruitment of foreign volunteers had continued apace (with February the second highest month for new volunteers since the previous June). Those arriving now were fully aware of how those who preceded them had suffered and, as a result, had few illusions about what they might face.[36] Many senior officers, however, were on leave – underlining the fact that nobody was expecting the attack.[37]

The speed and brutality of the assault that reached them early on 10 March was far beyond previous experience. Since there were so few reserve outfits available to form a second line, Walter's division was distributed in separate, often isolated, pieces. The advancing army swept through them like a tsunami. An angry Merriman, already looking exhausted and unusually shabby, had appeared overnight and demanded to know why the Lincolns were not in position already. The battalion's acting commander, David Reiss (filling in for officers on leave), insisted that an earlier order had not reached him. Reiss was a balding, older man from New Jersey who appeared tired of the fighting.[38] As they walked through the pre-dawn darkness, he told those with him: 'This is crazy. The only thing I had to do with war before this were the anti-war demonstrations I took part in back home.'[39] The brigade did not even reach their destination. Instead, they walked into machine-gun fire just after passing the medieval hilltop sanctuary[40] of Pueyo, four kilometres from Belchite. They rushed back to take up positions in and around the sanctuary's brick-patterned Mudejar tower, finding the caves below it packed with inexperienced Spanish troops, huddled in fear.[41]

These hilltop positions were pounded by artillery and the Brigaders watched aghast as the new Stuka dive-bombers descended on Belchite.[42] The blitzkrieg-style attack saw them rapidly forced into retreat as tanks and truckloads of men[43] rolled towards, and around, them.[44] As they raced back towards Belchite, Condor Legion aircraft swarmed, strafing the moving figures.[45] The sensation of being hunted prey was such that men once more claimed they could see the faces of the pilots trying to kill them. One Brigader recalled that the feeling was not 'of despair or fear, but ... of stupefaction' as, in the gloating words used by the attackers, they were 'decimated by our aviation'.[46] Amongst the first to die was Reiss, the eleventh Lincoln commander in its eighteen-month history, and one of five of that group to die (the others had all been wounded, two of them twice).[47] Fausto Villar, the young Spanish observer, held one corner of the blanket on which they tried to carry Reiss away after he was caught by the blast of an artillery shell,[48] but they eventually gave up. An American who stayed behind holding his hand and tried to prevent Reiss's innards from spilling out was one of many to fall prisoner.[49] For the first time, as they were overwhelmed by the speed of the attack, international volunteers began to be captured en masse.

The Lincolns ran back to take up positions in the town, but the fast-moving attack did not slow down.[50] The British Battalion were less exposed and retreated in an organised fashion, line by line, through the olive groves outside Belchite.[51] They had little to fire back at, however, since these attacks were motorised, with tank units manoeuvring rapidly to outflank them.[52] A lone anti-tank gun tried to slow the tanks down,[53] while aircraft pursued individual men as they ran. One Irish volunteer jumped onto the road and danced a defiant jig after one group of planes left and before the next wave arrived. In an exact reverse of the battle fought in these streets during the Zaragoza offensive, Belchite's battered church and handful of thick-walled factory buildings now served, temporarily, as a refuge, as did new concrete fortifications built to Russian plans.

Belchite, which had taken almost two weeks to capture, fell in just twelve hours, and was abandoned that afternoon. 'There is nothing sadder in a soldier's life than to abandon the towns and villages he fought for and won so dearly,' remarked Walter's aide-de-camp, Aleksander Szurek.[54] The Canadians, meanwhile, were left to their fate. They helped slow the attack further south and west before one of their officers bumped into Walter, who ordered them to withdraw early the following morning.[55] Two machine-gun crews who had been placed on a cliff wall could not be informed of the order, but held up the advancing troops for several hours. The Spanish and Finnish-Canadian machine-gunners fought until they ran out of ammunition and were caught. Only one was spared execution.[56]

The panicked retreat from Belchite was so hasty that XV Brigade began to break up. After heated discussion amongst the officers, some 300 men who had fled Belchite – mostly Spanish and British – set up a defensive line around a hill two hours' walk from the town.[57] That night they were amazed to see enemy campfires spring up on three sides of them and set out again in the dark before they were surrounded.[58]

Almost everywhere the story was the same. A defensive line or point would be established by an isolated group, which immediately discovered it was almost surrounded and was forced to move again. The sensations of disorientation and abandonment were new and terrifying. 'I had no idea what was going on, where we were, or what was going to happen next,' admitted one American who joined a column of several hundred men on a three-day cross-country march – avoiding the advancing enemy – through the dry, rugged woodlands of scrubby pine trees, rocky outcrops and sandy soil towards Caspe, sixty kilometres away.[59]

While the fragmented XV Brigade fled south and east on 11 March, Walter's two other International Brigades took up positions covering roads leading from Belchite to Azaila and Lécera. Patrols were sent out to search for what was left of XV Brigade, but little was found. The enemy had moved so swiftly into Belchite, however, that it appears to have stopped for a day so that the attack line further south could draw level.[60]

It was not until the morning of 12 March that twenty tanks were spotted, zigzagging across the flat, open land towards the position occupied by the Edgar André on either side of the road from Belchite to Azaila and stopping occasionally for infantry to catch up or be delivered by truck. The well-plotted movements of Willi Benz, commander of the Edgar André Battalion, give some idea of how chaos, improvisation and the will to survive became the driving characteristics of the days ahead as Walter's international division was broken up. This happened so quickly that it is impossible to piece together the movements of the groups of men who joined and separated continually over the next five days – often not knowing where they, or the enemy, were.

The twenty tanks that rolled across the flatlands outside Belchite – almost certainly the same ones that had ousted XV Brigade from this emblematic town – were heading straight for the Edgar André's positions. Benz, whose real name was Heinrich Schürmann,[61] urgently requested anti-tank guns. He was sent just one and, instead, opened a carefully guarded case of Russian-made armour-piercing rifle rounds that he carried with him, distributing them to his marksmen.[62] The

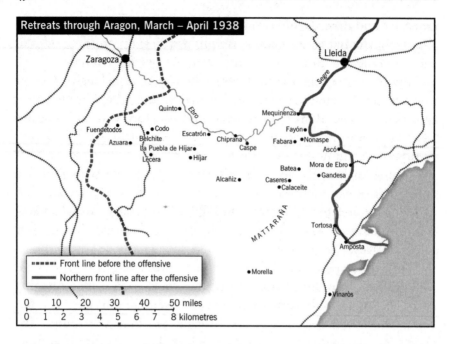

advancing armoured column, however, did not seem concerned when his men opened fire. 'It was clear that they knew we had no artillery or tanks,' recalled Benz, whose battalion was just above half-strength. They were easy prey, sitting alone on the road to Azaila with no protection on either flank. Nobody had informed the Edgar André that the other XI Brigade battalions had already moved south-west to protect Vinaceite.[63]

Even then, the approach was slow and cautious, with Benz surprised that the tanks did not just bulldoze straight through his lines. Instead, they waited for a short artillery barrage later that morning, which was immediately followed by tanks breaking through at three different points of their line. With the enemy looping around his position, Benz could see that this was lost.[64] He burned the documents he had on him (and hid others inside a pile of straw) as he prepared to flee. He then ran through the olive groves towards the Aguasvivas river with half-a-dozen men, zigzagging to avoid machine-gun fire from the Moroccan Army Corps' light tanks. Neither Benz nor most of his men – many of them miners or factory workers – knew how to swim, so they ran as fast as possible along the riverbank towards Azaila, where they eventually crossed a mill dam. A hillock on the other side of the river gave Benz a perfect view of the armoured column now heading towards Azaila, and he could see Francoist troops planting flags on each hilltop to guide the Condor Legion aircraft above them. The enemy column soon reached the town and took the bridge, since the volunteers did not have explosives to blow it up. That allowed the enemy to cross the river and head south towards Híjar in a race to cut off the remains of Walter's division. A column of tanks also turned north towards Quinto and the river Ebro, pushing the Austrian-led February 12 Battalion, which had been in reserve, away from the rest of XI Brigade.[65]

The scattered groups of German-speaking and Spanish soldiers from the Edgar André Battalion, meanwhile, walked or limped across the fields or down roads gouged with strafing marks and past the hulks of burned vehicles, some of them occupied by corpses of men they recognised. Most headed towards the town of La Puebla de Híjar, where Walter's famous 'mobile headquarters' (basically his voluminous staff car, now a large black Chevrolet) was parked.[66] Given the dangerous situation, however, Walter decided to move further back along the retreat route. With no room in the car, Benz found himself walking alone to the next town, Híjar, where he found 'desperate confusion, with scattered units readying to move, but not knowing what it was they were meant to do'.[67] He looked on as valuable heavy machine guns were abandoned, since there were no vehicles to drag them away. The small town's streets were full of bomb craters, wrecked buildings and confused soldiers. A local cafe was full of drunken men in uniform – some of them Americans – who were emptying the wine barrels.

The enemy was delighted. 'This flight is turning into a general rout; panic reins amongst those fleeing, commanders abandon their troops and the latter throw away their arms and equipment ... nothing has happened today to suggest that anyone is in charge,' a Republican reported on 12 March.[68] The glee on Franco's side was increased by its minimal losses, since infantry were only needed to mop up the dazed men who had already, in effect, been defeated by the combined might of tanks, artillery and aircraft. The upper reaches of the Republican army, meanwhile, had little idea about what was happening on the ground, and the local army corps commander admitted he had lost most of his units.[69] Walter, too, began to lose contact with his battalions.

For the volunteers scrabbling to make sense of what was happening, it was clear that they were bearing the brunt of a major offensive.[70] By 12 March, the retreat had become a series of disasters – large and small – in which Walter's brigades, or disconnected groups of men belonging to them, stumbled through territory that was increasingly occupied by advance units of the enemy. Each attempt at organising a line, or sometimes just halting to rest, would end with the appearance of yet another enemy unit on their flank or behind them.[71] One historian of the Irish volunteers, who were mostly in XV Brigade, compared the climate of haste and confusion to the Grimm brothers' tale of the hedgehog and the hare, in which Republican units rushed backwards and forwards only to find that the enemy already waiting for them at their destination.[72]

Later that day, Benz joined some of Walter's staff officers who were stopping fleeing troops – known as 'rabbits' in their jargon – and trying to organise new defensive positions. Soldiers from other units argued with them, however, declaring that resistance was useless. These were disarmed and sent on their way, though there were also reports of some being shot. At one stage Szurek came across a blond-bearded volunteer with a broad, heavyweight boxer's physique walking down the road with a machine gun over his shoulder. He invited the man to leave the gun and continue. 'And what will you do without the [machine-gunner] man?' enquired the gunner – who turned out to be the brother of a famous Jewish boxer from Warsaw called Rotholc – and joined the troops gathering to resist.[73] Elsewhere, however, vehicles were being hijacked at gunpoint by those desperate to flee. Weapons were even drawn to force soldiers to share water bottles as daytime temperatures rose, while men who had shed their blankets shivered in the cold nights.[74]

A cool-headed but hyperactive Walter drove around trying to make sense of the chaos. All his brigades were now in flight, leaving multiple paths towards the Mediterranean unprotected. 'A sixty-kilometre front was absolutely open for a push towards the coast,' noted Vicente Rojo, the mastermind of Madrid's defence who would soon be called in to try to restore order.[75]

Although a disaster was unfolding before him, Walter relished the proximity of battle.[76] At Híjar, he ordered Benz to gather a night-time patrol to see if the bridge over the river Martín was under enemy control. Walter himself joined them and Benz led what he called 'a patrol the likes of which must never have been seen in this war: it was made up of a general commanding a division, a brigade commander [Heinrich Rau,[77] now commanding XI Brigade], a battalion commander [Benz] and six lieutenants and sergeants'.[78] He might have added that, in Rau, it also included a future leader of communist East Germany. When they received machine-gun fire, Benz pushed Walter to the ground, making him tumble down the hill. 'His attack of fury and curses left me cold,' recalled Benz.[79] Walter followed his custom of not hiding from bullets at night (since the chances of being hit were slim) and, instead, sprinted down the road,[80] while his staff jumped into a ditch. He was not, however, nearly as fit as the younger Szurek, who ended up physically pushing him along the road.[81]

The following morning, 12 March, Benz helped organise a defensive line on the Alcañiz road, where two groups of survivors from XV and XI Brigades had gathered. Even with remnants of the Thälmann Battalion and others also now appearing, this ad hoc group boasted only 300 men with two tanks and a single anti-tank gun.[82] It was, however, one of the few organised fighting units left from two brigades which forty-eight hours earlier had boasted up to 4,000 soldiers. Much of the rest of Benz's brigade, for example, was already miles away, having fled beyond Caspe.[83] Others had not stopped there and stragglers from the International Brigades were already being picked up as far away as the coast. 'The XI Brigade did not create a particularly good impression on those days,'[84] Walter commented later. It did not help that, during the day, those who still followed his orders were fired on by their own artillery.[85]

On 13 March, much of what remained of Walter's division had either reached Alcañiz, or was on its way there – being harassed along the roads leading from the west. By now, some men had been retreating for three days and were exhausted. Szurek recalled infuriating Walter by falling asleep while interpreting a conversation with some Spanish officers. Attempts at rest, however, were often fruitless, with volunteers awoken by yet another wave of panicked men spilling through their positions. By day, the heat became unbearable. 'None of us who took part in the dreadful march will ever forget it,' recalled one British volunteer. 'We were in the middle of a rout. Thousands of men from other brigades were also on the march and mixed with them went the fleeing civilian population. The scene beggared description. As the long black column climbed wearily up the steep rocky hillsides, enemy planes came swooping and machine-gunning their helpless victims.'[86]

Their sense of despair might have grown had they known that the Italians and Spaniards on Franco's side were competing to see who could reach Alcañiz first. This meant that while Benz's column limped towards the town overnight with the two tanks ferrying those too exhausted to walk, the Italians were racing towards it from the south-west in trucks and tanks along virtually undefended roads. Benz's column met up with what was left of XIII Brigade after its battalions were forced back from Letux, Lécera and Muniesa.[87] This was now the largest organised group in Walter's division, but when they reached Alcañiz in the morning the Italians were already there. They had covered thirty-seven kilometres overnight, arriving at dawn on 14 March and beating the Moroccan Army Corps to take one of the most important early trophies in the offensive. They later claimed to have taken 2,000 prisoners.[88]

Some of Walter's staff were momentarily captured after approaching what they assumed was a Republican roadblock. Romanian artillery commander Walter Roman raised his hands and was led off towards a ditch just as Walter's 'head of services' Captain Karchevski arrived and turned his machine guns on the enemy. That allowed Roman and the others to flee, but Karchevski died, apparently while flinging his fists against those trying to capture him. As with many White Russian recruits, including the now hospital-bound and terminally ill Escimontowsky, his dreams of returning to the homeland died with him. Soon the Italians were ringing the town's church bells to announce their victory. Szurek wept, convinced that all those left behind them would be captured and shot.[89]

In fact, many escaped, but Walter was now cut off from most of his division and had to drive a long, circular route to the next major town on the retreat route, Caspe. The hundreds of men approaching Alcañiz from Híjar, meanwhile, were forced to strike north-east across the rugged Sierra de Vizcuerno to reach Caspe. The hungry, exhausted men fretted that the place they were now heading for – which had been the capital of the anarchist Council of Aragon – might also have been taken by the time they reached it. Eventually, however, they saw campfires lit up on the hillsides as troops of all kinds gathered to defend the city. Here, at last, they had an opportunity to make a stand.[90]

The following day, 15 March, the Italian-led XII Brigade reached the area by truck and train from Extremadura, with one battalion immediately sent to help defend Caspe – which Rojo, who that day took command of this part of the front, had identified as the critical defensive point. By this stage, the other International Brigade battalions in the area were ragged, fractured units, rarely with more than a third of their men. All now nevertheless set about defending Caspe, a large town on a hill close by the river Ebro.[91]

The defence, however, was fragmented. Walter, for example, sent Benz's group back towards a bridge near the village of Chiprana in order to block the enemy forces approaching along the southern banks of the Ebro. They did not make it that far. First their ammunition truck was blown up in an air attack and then a Scandinavian section which had been sent ahead clashed with the enemy vanguard and struggled back with just eleven men. Hidden in the woods, the few dozen volunteers from Benz's battalion harassed the enemy as it built up its forces for a final push. 'If they had known that there were only two dozen of us, the day might have ended very differently,' said Benz.[92]

The defence of Caspe was chaotic. A proper defensive line was never formed. In barely coordinated groups, positions were established, acts of bravery, cowardice or foolishness registered, positions outflanked and men lost, captured or forced into flight. Where resistance was strong, or small counter-attacks launched, there was always a gap that the enemy could use to infiltrate its troops closer in towards Caspe. The best weapons, especially anti-tank guns, were now scarce. Some men simply threw rocks, hoping the enemy would take them for grenades and duck into their trenches.[93] The advance, nevertheless, slowed for the first time. This was partly because Franco's army needed to draw breath, though the will to resist of the volunteers and other units in Caspe helped.[94]

Eventually, they were driven back into the town itself. Szurek wandered the burning streets with the commander of the Hungarian Rakosi Battalion, inspecting machine-gun positions. 'We did not know where our troops were, or where the enemy was,' he admitted.[95] The volunteers had, nevertheless, been read an order from Rojo explaining that anyone who panicked would be shot. He had, in his own words, decided 'to impose sacrificial missions' on some of his best units.[96] These included almost all of what remained of Walter's division, plus part of Hans Kahle's 45th Division, which was creating a defensive line behind the town. Even the new Masaryk Battalion of 129 Brigade was sent to join the fight, though the other international units did not seem to realise.[97]

The attack that came was much like that seen at Quinto or Belchite earlier in the war, but with the volunteers on the defensive side of the house-to-house fighting. Ragged groups of volunteers and Republican Spaniards occasionally defended themselves at bayonet point. 'I abandoned any attempts to give orders to what remained of my company: it was simply a case of each man for himself,' recalled British company commander, Walter Gregory. 'No longer were we organised in battalions, now we were simply the remnants of the XV International Brigade.'[98] His battalion commander, Sam Wild, only escaped after one of his men threw a punch at the Francoist soldier who thought he had captured them.[99] One moment remembered vividly by those who saw it came when an Italian tank drove into a square – and was initially greeted as friendly – but then opened fire on a group of two dozen Lincolns. The injured were then deliberately run over with its heavy tracks as more tanks poured into the square.[100]

This courageous attempt to hold the town was doomed to failure, but did slow the blitzkrieg advance for the first time. By 16 March, however, the defenders were holding on to little more than the town's railway station. A heavy aerial bombardment put many to flight and the last Brigaders abandoned the city the following night.[101] Caspe was fully in enemy hands by 18 March. Once more, international volunteers fell prisoner in dozens. Thirteenth Brigade, and within it the Naftali Botwin Jewish company, was all but wiped out. It had, nevertheless, been an epic fight. 'During those three days, the obstinacy with which the arbitrarily grouped troops improvised the defence, thanks to the will power of their commanders and the enthusiasm of some groups of men, helped the army recover, stopped the advance and fixed a line that would only be overrun twelve days later, after much sacrifice by the enemy,' said Rojo.[102] The new line was partially held by Hans Kahle's 45th Division, which had moved into position behind the city. The main objectives, however, of the first part of the Francoist attack had been reached. The price paid by the Brigaders was enormous. At one stage the British Battalion could only find twenty of its 607 men as, once more, groups of stragglers wandered through the woods beyond Caspe.[103]

Kahle's division now took over the fighting, initially holding a line along the river Guadalope. As long as that line held, Walter's shattered division could set about the difficult task of reorganising. It was sent to regroup in reserve positions on the eastern side of the Matarraña river, and then further back at Batea.[104] His battalions had been thoroughly defeated, and one volunteer recognised that they had been 'no match for the huge steel juggernaut'.[105] By now, the same volunteer saw that his fellow soldiers were 'stunned, sullen, hungry and dispirited'.[106] They were angry, too, wanting to know who to blame for a thousand or more lost 'comrades who they had come to know and love, with whom close friendships had been forged and tested'.[107]

The battle, however, was not over and the shattered International Brigades had to be rebuilt quickly into proper fighting units. Reinforcements were found from wherever they could. The guiding spirit of the Irish volunteers, senior IRA man Frank Ryan, reappeared from his office job in Madrid. Hospital patients deemed to have almost recovered from their wounds were sent to them along with recently arrived, half-trained volunteers from Albacete and prisoners from Camp Lukács.[108] Benz found Walter's headquarters full of hobbling and bandaged men. 'Some had to be sent straight back to hospital, because they were in no state to fight,' he recalled.[109] More young Spanish draftees also appeared as the battalions were rapidly reconfigured. By 26 March the British Battalion, for example, had been brought back to strength, though there were hardly enough English speakers to fill a company.[110]

The confusion of the previous days, meanwhile, produced accusation and counter-accusation within the Republican army. Walter had been happy for his men to shoot fleeing anarchists from 153 Brigade – his old rivals from Belchite – while the latter accused the volunteers of 'unauthorised retreats' and claimed to have halted fleeing German Brigaders at gunpoint.[111] There was even quarrelling within the Brigades, with British Battalion commander Sam Wild accusing the Lincolns of deserting their positions at Belchite.[112] (In fact, they had been ordered to withdraw.[113]) Similar accusations were made against Benz of the Edgar André Battalion, who would be formally chastised, and XII Brigade's socialist commander Arturo Zanoni was also replaced later in the month, amid communist complaints about his role in Caspe.[114] Brigadier General Juan Modesto was much closer to the truth when he later accused XVIII Army Corps commander Enrique Fernández Heredia of sacrificing Walter's men unnecessarily 'by sending battalions out on their own to defend places that, basically, were already in the enemy's hands'.[115]

Walter launched a witch-hunt within his division, convinced that defeat automatically suggested incompetence, cowardice or sabotage. Major Ivan Szwerda, a former White Russian guard who had been with the International Brigades since their first battles in Madrid, had panicked during the fighting in Caspe, shouting: 'Save yourselves if you can!' It was claimed that he had also torn off the insignia of his rank (to avoid being shot as an officer if captured) and had disappeared when sent to organise a defensive line.[116] Walter ordered Szurek to shoot him. The two men had met several times before. 'He was a happy, agreeable, frank man ... It was hard for me to carry out the order,' Szurek recalled later. That did not stop him. He formed a small firing squad and shouted 'Fire!' while the victim looked at him and cried 'Alek, why? Why? Why?'[117]

Szwerda was not the only man placed before a firing squad. 'One Major ... two lieutenants and one sergeant were shot yesterday for cowardice,' a freshly arrived American volunteer, the Brooklyn writer Alvah Bessie, noted in his diary.[118]

Again, the Spaniards serving with the International Brigades found this sort of discipline excessive for men who had travelled from far away to defend them. When a drunken Irish volunteer kept rushing into the division's field hospital, insisting that it should pack up and flee, the Spanish doctor on duty simply told him to calm down. Asked later whether he wanted the man punished, the doctor said no: 'He was an international and he was drunk,' he reasoned.[119] Walter disapproved.

Rumours also circulated about 'fascist provocateurs' in the ranks, and some of the more rigid Communist Party commissars now felt free to discipline not just grumblers but also political dissenters.[120] One of them, American Pat Reid, was sent on enforced sick leave, just as his brigade was filling up with men from the hospitals. 'He's talked against the [Communist] Party now for a year now, ever since he's been with the Lincolns [but] ... He's probably the best soldier in the battalion ... and a good anti-fascist. He hasn't changed the position of a single communist soldier,' argued one of his friends in an attempt to change the mind of a notoriously inflexible American commissar, Dave Doran. Reid was still sent away.[121] Others who were deemed to have fought badly were demoted.

An added difficulty to the task of rebuilding the broken brigades was that some men had fled with no intention of ever returning. Spanish recruit Fausto Villar found himself being ferried 200 kilometres away to the International Brigades beachside hospital in Benicàssim by two lieutenants who commandeered a series of trucks to take him there and talked openly about going on to the French border, having decided that the war was lost.[122] Villar was exhausted, bruised and battered after being chased by tanks, getting stuck in mud and falling headlong into a ditch at Belchite, but he was not wounded. Doctors gave him two injections and kept him in for a night, but then discharged him. He noticed that many other patients were in a similar state, suggesting that relatively minor injuries were being used as an excuse to abandon the front. The following day the doctor warned all three men that they had to report immediately to the International Brigades offices in Valencia. Instead, they went to Villar's home, a small garret flat in the city, to be greeted joyfully by his mother and girlfriend, who gave them a far more frugal meal than those served at the front:

Afterwards, the pair [of lieutenants] get up together, collect their greatcoats and thank me for the attentions they have received in our household. Then, telling me that their mission is complete as far as I am concerned, they leave.

I am left at a loss, for I had been expecting that tomorrow morning all three of us would be reporting together to the International Brigades office here in Valencia. Now, though, they have disclosed their real intentions and told me not to be so silly; I am back home now and the best course for me would be to keep indoors until the war is over, which will not be long now.

As for themselves, they are off to try to arrange a passage out of Spain before the war ends in our losing, as it surely must. They know that if they are captured, they will be shot; Martínez for being an officer of the Lincoln Battalion who has come over from America as a volunteer to fight fascism and Camacho, not just for being an officer, but also a runaway from the Francoist zone.

I tell them that ... I will be reporting to the International Brigades office because I think that, although we know that this war of ours is lost, I have a duty to fight on to the finish. They make no reply.[123]

Villar's tale was more than just a reminder that courage and cowardice lived side by side in the International Brigades. It was also a sign that the Spanish Civil War had reached a watershed moment, where the profound differences between the two sides in terms of equipment, international support and the training of soldiers had allowed Franco to deliver a devastating blow. Fascist firepower, with the Luftwaffe overhead and Mussolini's own troops and tanks on the ground, was a crucial part of that. For the first time the Brigades had felt the full force of a rapid and overwhelming blitzkrieg-style attack. It was far from over, but the juggernaut could only be slowed and halted by continuing the fight.

44

Boy Soldiers: Guadalope river, 19 March 1938

While Walter's men were regrouping, Kahle's division was fighting. For the first few days they managed to hold their positions on the Guadalope river, not least because Franco's army was now concentrating its efforts on extending the offensive to the north side of the Ebro, towards Huesca. There, having started on 23 March 1938, it was also advancing at a dizzying speed. Franco sought the psychological blow of crossing into Catalonia – where a fortified line of defence, like a small-scale version of France's Maginot Line, had been constructed along the river Cinca. This proved as ineffective as the real Maginot Line would in 1940. On 27 March, Franco's generals announced the capture of their first Catalan town, Massalcorreig.[1] Those volunteers who had joined Spanish units in Aragon at the beginning of the war and stayed – like Muriel Rukeyser's German athlete boyfriend Otto Boch – were amongst those bulldozed into submission by this new blitzkrieg campaign. Boch would, reportedly, die in his machine-gun nest overlooking the Segre.[2]

Benz, whose men had crossed the river Guadalope, watched with admiration as Kahle's soldiers fought to defend a bridge. 'It was one of the most magnificent battles that I have ever seen,' he wrote. 'Our forces pushed the enemy back on to a hill, with the help of two tanks and two armoured vehicles, but behind them came another attack group. The battle went backwards and forwards, with hand-to-hand fighting.' The Francoists 'were slowly forced to withdraw and our comrades were right against their hill when the tanks ran out of ammunition. The enemy took advantage of that to advance again, but did not get very far as our people remained firmly in possession of a small hillock and, thanks to that, the bridge was saved.'[3]

Much of the fighting was now being done by teenagers. With conscription reaching nineteen-year-olds the previous year,[4] most of the Spanish recruits – men like Fausto Villar – had yet to reach twenty. As the number of international volunteers decreased, and as the more experienced Brigaders were increasingly given jobs away from the front line, the weight of these youngsters in the ranks grew. Many were illiterate farm boys; a significant proportion were anarchists. The Spaniards, however, were not the only teenagers. In Caspe, a fresh-faced nineteen-year-old American called Rudy Haber, who looked even more youthful than his real age, had been left in charge of a machine gun covering the retreat of the last men to leave the town. He had commanded a section at Teruel, 'looked as innocent as a baby' and was never seen again.[5] The youngest of the Garibaldini, gawky-looking Carlo Sans, also died in the town.[6] Over the next few days the commander of XIV Brigade, Marcel Sagnier, would rely on an even younger boy – a seventeen-year-old Spaniard known as Navarro – to man the machine gun covering his men as they withdrew and, in the front line, to destroy an attacking enemy company.[7]

Another youth, Frenchman Pierre Georges, was amongst those in XIV Brigade trying to prevent the Francoist forces from crossing the river Guadalope and continuing their rush for the sea. In International Brigade terms he was already a veteran, having joined as a seventeen-year-old with the first men who arrived in October 1936. For someone so young, and given the intensity of the experience, that must have seemed a very long time ago. Georges was capable, however, and appreciated in the Brigades, where talent and courage (as well as political conformity) were quickly noticed. Initially, given his tender age, he was kept away from the front line and worked as an assistant with the French brigade's headquarters staff. At the age of eighteen he had been sent to the non-commissioned officers' school set up at El Escorial. Now he was in charge of a section, placing his men in positions on a spur of land above the river Guadalope near the bridges of El Vado and Masatrigos.

The French youngster had been sent here by Rabah Oussid'houm, an Algerian-born taxi driver and graduate of the Comintern's Far East University in Moscow,[8] whom Szurek had initially met when Rabah was behind bars having been accused of trying to rape a Spanish woman. Oussid'houm was now commanding the Commune de Paris Battalion[9] – one of approximately 500 Republican volunteers from French Algeria – and had recently taken on responsibility for looking after a twelve-year-old Spanish boy whose troubled life reflected his own difficult childhood.

Georges recalled running along the line of men who had dug themselves shallow dips and small buttresses using helmets and bayonets. He checked their positions, finding one flank protected by a light machine gun equipped with valuable anti-tank rounds in the hands of another teenager. 'He is a youngster from Marseilles,' wrote Georges. 'Eleven months in the front line and two wounds already. I know that, with him, the light machine gun is in safe hands.'[10] Their position was separate from the rest of the battalion and their orders were 'to hold it down to the last man'. The inevitable then happened. Tanks appeared and, behind them, groups of enemy infantry. His section fought all day, with Georges scanning the attacking force from behind a bush with his field glasses in order to pick out targets. The tanks were now less than a hundred metres away, with machine-gun bullets ricocheting off the stones around him; one piece of shrapnel hit him in the stomach, sending him tumbling into his trench. Half-conscious, he then heard his men hurling packages of explosives under the tracks of the tanks. The position was lost, though Georges would somehow escape. Most of his men were captured and many were shot. Oussid'houm died here.

The snapshot provided by Georges – who would later have a Paris Métro station named after him, or rather his Second World War French Resistance pseudonym of Colonel Fabien – showed how the line held by Kahle's men was slowly pushed back at great expense to both sides until it too broke. After that, a rout similar to that already suffered by Walter's brigades began.[11] Only the new 129 Brigade would escape this, having been sent further south, where it would spend months attached to a variety of larger Republican units – to the dismay of its volunteers, who wished to be with their international comrades.[12]

Benz and his Edgar André Battalion were amongst the first of Walter's battalions to be called back to duty and to realise how desperate the Republic's position was becoming. They were sent to help prevent the offensive on the north side of the Ebro river breaking through near the town of Mequinenza. This lay just across the Ebro, at its junction with the ample river Segre. It was also the site of a large bridge spanning the Ebro. Benz's men found the army here in tatters, with soldiers lying forlornly around the town. Mequinenza fell the day after they arrived, 28 March. All that could be done was to retreat back over the bridge and blow it up.[13] This cut off Republican troops on the other bank, some of whom had to be ferried back on boats. Walter himself came to check the demolished bridge, ignoring warnings that he would face enemy machine-gun fire. It was so thoroughly destroyed that he deemed too much explosive had been used, but he was satisfied that nobody could now cross and that this flank was safe.

Amongst the units now on the far side of the river was XIII Brigade, which had been sent to Lleida, a city that would fall the following week with Republican troops blowing up the two major bridges that crossed the river Segre in the city.[14]

'They acted as they [the International Brigades] always did; tough resistance, followed by counter-attacks, day and night,' wrote the Francoist military historian Manuel Aznar, echoing the reputation the Brigades had gained with the opposing army.[15] Thirteenth Brigade was pushed back and destroyed the river bridges further north at Corbins and Vilanova de la Barca,[16] as a new, permanent defensive line was established along the Segre. Franco, who hated Catalan nationalism, immediately abolished the six-year-old semi-autonomous government in this part of the region as he swiftly set about reversing the progressive reforms of the Republic.

On 28 March, a reinvigorated Francoist army definitively broke through Kahle's lines, at first north of Caspe and then gradually further south. Soon Mussolini's Italians were rampaging their way towards the rearguard areas where Walter's men had been regrouping and over the next two days these were all sent back into battle. The Germans from XI Brigade helped set up a first reserve line – roughly following the course of the river Matarraña – but, by the following evening, found the Italian volunteers retreating through their positions.[17]

The pattern of panic, uncontrolled flight and sporadic, poorly coordinated defence recommenced. At one stage the puce-faced figure of André Marty himself appeared in the middle of the road, angrily berating members of the Commune de Paris Battalion as they retreated. He was, he reminded them, a hot-blooded Catalan himself (since he had been born in French Catalonia, in the county of Roussillon) and would defend his land against the attackers while blowing out the undeserving brains of all cowards who abandoned their units.[18] As usual, he was more bluster than action.

By now, the entire administrative structure of the International Brigades was also beginning to fall to pieces. The base at Albacete was emptied of staff, while hospitals were scaled down, merged and hurriedly moved to Catalonia. Some 1,200 office workers, instructors and the last batch of fresh volunteers joined the drunks, thieves and other prison inmates who had been sent as reinforcements. One motley group, gathered together in the Vaillant-Couturier Battalion,[19] was blamed for starting a panic near Fabara, pulling part of XII Brigade into flight with it.[20] Amongst those who stood uselessly, pistol in hand, trying to force the men back was the Brigades' medical chief, Dr Henri Chretien. By 30 March, the Brigades had given up on Maella, Nonasp and Fabara – the last Aragonese towns before the border with Catalonia. Volunteers listened, crestfallen, as Italian fascist chants rang out from recently captured Nonasp, to be followed by cries and pistol shots, which they took to be the executions of captured comrades.[21]

Early that day, XV Brigade was rearmed and ordered back to the front.[22] For newcomers like Alvah Bessie, the experience was remarkably like that of those who had arrived to the initial chaos of November 1936. 'We were lined up and marched down toward the road, where there were cases and cases of unused Russian rifles, packed in grease. These were issued to the men, and as we had not rags with which to clean them, we tore strips off our underwear,' he wrote.

My rifle, whose metalwork bore the stamp of the Russian Imperial Eagle, was numbered 59034. Under the partly obliterated imperial emblem was a new stamp, the hammer and sickle of the Soviet Union.

There was no time to clean the arms adequately; we cleaned and wiped them as we marched. We halted for a moment to receive little paper packs of cartridges, which the men stuffed into their pockets and packed into their blanket rolls. We halted again to take on a load of hand grenades ... None of us had ever tossed a live grenade. We went on to the main road and marched in artillery formation ... It was ... impossible to realise that the training period was over and that within a few hours you would meet what you had come 4,000 miles to meet.[23]

A fresh breakthrough had by now forced the front back towards a line that roughly followed the main road leading from Calaceite, via Caseres and Gandesa, to Corbera d'Ebre.[24] The volunteers had their backs to the Sierra de Pàndols, part of a stretch of rugged sierras that ran parallel to the river Ebro as it turned and flowed south-west. The sierra would, at least, serve as a useful defensive buttress. Beyond that, as a second and more extensive natural barrier to Franco's advance, lay the Ebro itself, which grew in intensity as it flowed ever closer to the Mediterranean Sea.

Fifteenth Brigade's battalions were not, however, informed before they set out for this line on 30 March that the enemy had broken through again. Nor were they told that the positions they were meant to defend no longer existed.[25] The International Brigades as a whole were now charged with defending a significant part of the line. On paper, this was an impressive array of battalions whose names echoed the glories of Jarama and elsewhere. In practice, they were now pale imitations, led by foreign volunteers, but mostly with untrained Spanish conscripts and short of men, arms and support. There were other major differences. At Jarama, Russian tanks and aircraft had protected them. Now it was German and Italian hardware, often piloted or driven by Axis soldiers, that ruled the skies and led the skirmishing troops against a defensive line which, in the case of XV Brigade, no longer even had an anti-tank battery.[26]

Some of the international battalions would barely survive the following forty-eight hours. One of the worst disasters befell the British, who were called on to link up with Líster's 11th Division and prevent the enemy entering the village of Calaceite. Many of the soldiers in this rapidly reconstituted battalion were untried in battle. The high turnover amongst the officers meant that they, too, were relatively inexperienced.[27] Before dawn on 31 March, a Spanish liaison officer led them through the village towards the positions they were meant to occupy, unaware that Líster's men had already withdrawn. Rounding a corner on the road, they ran into two groups of tanks, one of which was coming straight along the road towards them while the other emerged out of a hollow to one side. 'We took it for granted that, as we were being guided into position still a kilometre ahead, they were our own tanks,' recalled one company commissar. In fact, they were Italians from Mussolini's CTV, who immediately drove between the two British columns and opened fire.[28] Battalion commissar Wally Tapsell, still assuming these were friends, shouted frantically at them. 'You bloody fool! Do you want to kill your own men?' he cried. The officer in the leading tank turret aimed his pistol and shot him dead, just as the rest of the men began to scatter.[29]

Other Italians quickly emerged from the woods along the roads, shouting and charging through the grey, pre-dawn light. With no hand grenades, the British Battalion was poorly prepared for close-quarter fighting or disabling tanks. Some men resorted to hurling tin cans or pretending to pull grenade pins out of rocks they picked up, hoping to fool the Italians into diving for cover.[30] All the men could really do was run into the hills. Irishman Frank Ryan, who had joined them, was captured almost immediately, becoming the most senior International Brigades prisoner.[31]

It was, wrote one American, 'the most humiliating defeat an English force ever suffered at the hands of Italians'.[32] More than one hundred Britons were captured in the space of a few minutes.[33] Wintringham, who heard about this later, was scathing, saying that it was not enough to claim that they did not know the enemy had advanced so far. 'This and the weariness that follows weeks of heavy fighting, and the fact that many men were new recruits who had only just joined the unit, cannot excuse the disastrous slackness,' he wrote.[34] Víctor Ruiz Albéniz, the same pro-Franco journalist who had first encountered the volunteers at University City in Madrid, saw them shortly afterwards. He claimed to be shocked by the aspect of the feared and respected International Brigaders. 'Most are manual workers and there is only one book-keeper, a mechanical engineer and a painter. Many are "pure race" Jews and, in general, they look terrible, with thin bodies and hungry faces.' Of the 607 men in the reformed British Battalion, only seventy managed to meet up the following day.[35] Another estimate spoke of 334 men who had disappeared permanently.[36]

By 1 April the entire line defended by the International Brigades had given way, and decimation of their ranks continued as they fled towards Gandesa, only to find it occupied. As small, scattered groups attempted to make their way through hostile countryside that night, one ragged bunch of a dozen Americans bumped into the rear of a column of Mussolini's Italian troops marching down a road. 'There was no doubt they were fascists,' recalled Harry Fisher, who had witnessed Oliver Law's death at Brunete. 'The soldiers were in high spirits, maintained good order, had clean uniforms, and marched in formation; their officers rode on horses.'[37] Rather than run and draw attention to themselves, they chose to march along behind them, pretending to be part of the advancing army. This ruse fooled the Italian officers who looked them over before they slunk off again into the woods.[38] By now, he said, the best way to distinguish Republican soldiers from Francoist ones was that the former 'were all in torn and tattered uniforms'.[39] Elsewhere, the Mackenzie–Papineau commissar Carl Geiser was surprised to be urged to surrender by someone calling in a Brooklyn accent: 'Come on over. Don't be afraid. We are your friends!' The voice belonged to an Italian CTV officer who had lived in New York.[40] Geiser eventually became the most senior American prisoner. His life was saved only because passing officers explained to his captors that they needed some international volunteers to survive, so that they could be swapped for Italian soldiers.[41]

Bob Merriman, meanwhile, realised that the remaining German- and English-speaking battalions from Walter's division had been all but encircled and ordered the entire 35th Division to do what it could to escape. 'We will get out of here if we can,' he said.[42] They made a failed attempt to fight their way into Gandesa, which had already been taken, but an Italian cavalry charge on their positions ended with appalling losses inflicted by the volunteers' heavy machine guns. At night, they walked silently past the enemy camps, seeking a way out. 'There wasn't a man who made that trip who didn't feel death walking by his side,' one survivor recalled.[43] At one stage, Merriman had led a group comprising several hundred Lincolns and others into a ravine, where they were trapped by machine-gun fire as they ran through a field of low vines. 'The Americans and Canadians, big strong men, fell en masse,' one Swiss volunteer observed. 'Most died and others fell prisoner.'[44]

Amongst those to escape the ambush was Fausto Villar. He met up in the woods with five other Spaniards from the battalion, four of whom were paunchy 'grandads' – as the prematurely aged peasants in their thirties who had been drafted were known. They warned him that they intended to surrender if confronted by enemy troops. On 2 April, Villar's group was discovered asleep in a sheep pen by a Francoist cavalry squadron, and joined a group of more than a hundred Lincoln prisoners. The American volunteers were weeded out and marched off:

LA UNIDAD *del* EJERCITO *del* PUEBLO SERA EL ARMA DE LA VICTORIA

PARRILLA

TODOS LOS PUEBLOS DEL MUNDO ESTAN EN LAS BRIGADAS INTERNACIONALES AL LADO DEL PUEBLO ESPAÑOL

Political divisions damaged the Republican army. Here a volunteer wearing the International Brigades' triangular symbol and a soldier with the Republic's purple, yellow and red flag send the message: 'Unity of the People's Army will be the Weapon of Victory'.

While western democracies appeased Hitler, Mussolini and fascism in Spain, the Comintern-led far left wanted to show that the Republic was not alone, with the International Brigades as proof, while also sending a message of racial equality. This poster reads: 'In The International Brigades, The Peoples of the World stand with the Spanish People'.

Robert and Marion Merriman: Abraham Lincoln commander and his wife, who was raped by another officer but did not report the crime.

George and Nan Green: a British brigader and a medical assistant who left their children behind to fight in Spain and were reunited at the hospital in Huete. George is playing the cello and Nan is on the accordion, with a Bavarian violinist and Spanish guitarists.

Ernest Hemingway (far left) was an avid Brigade admirer and supporter of the Republic. He is pictured with his close friend the German Brigade commander Hans Kahle, Ludwig Renn and (on the far right) Dutch filmmaker Joris Ivens. He and Ivens made the pro-Republican documentary *The Spanish Earth*.

George Orwell, photographed here (far left, at the rear, standing head-and-shoulders above the rest) was a POUM volunteer who planned to join the International Brigades, but fled Spain when POUM was purged.

Belgian volunteer nurses, including Lya Berger (third from right) and Vera Luftig (centre, with spotty scarf), partners of the deceased Akkerman brothers, Piet and Emil, in Barcelona's Plaza Catalunya on May Day 1937, just before factional violence erupted. Stalin's face adorns the communist headquarters behind them. Luftig became a World War II resistance fighter.

This leaflet warning Brigaders against being stabbed in the back by POUM members was published after the May 1937 violence between Republican factions in Barcelona. George Orwell's *Homage to Catalonia* explains events from the side of his defeated, and ultimately outlawed, POUM group – which demanded instant revolution as well as resistance.

Pierre Georges, aka Colonel Fabien (front right), joined the Brigades as a teenager, was injured and became a key figure in the French Resistance movement during the Second World War II, carrying out the first assassination of a German soldier in Paris. He is pictured here with Brigade members in July 1937.

Alvah Bessie: the novelist, journalist and screenwriter was jailed and blacklisted as one of the Hollywood Ten during the McCarthy era. He joined the Lincoln Brigade in 1938.

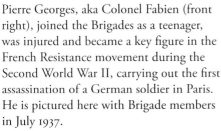
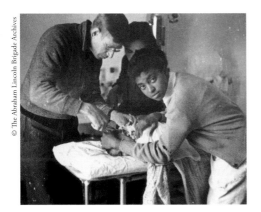

African American nurse Salaria Kea had protested against Mussolini's invasion of Ethiopia before serving in Spain and marrying injured Irish Brigader John Patrick O'Reilly, who later emigrated to the US.

George Nathan, a brave and popular Jewish British officer, who died on the final day of the Battle at Brunete, is in the centre of this photograph. Jock Cunningham (left) helped lead the battered XV Brigade back into the line at Jarama. British company commissar Ralph Campeau (right) died there.

General Walter with fellow officers, including Aleksander Szurek, beside him on the right. Italian Vittorio Vidali (left) and Juan Modesto (right) appear to be lying in front of them.

General Walter interrogating prisoners.

Oliver Law, the first African American to command white troops as head of the Lincoln Battalion, wearing his captain's stripes before Brunete – where he died. Pipe-smoking battalion commissar Steve Nelson has an arm over his shoulder.

Crossing the river Ebro, July 1938.

Adolf Hitler welcomes the returning Condor Legion, with Luftwaffe Commander-in-Chief Hermann Göring in white cap and Condor commander Wolfram von Richthofen on the far right. They had destroyed Guernica, refined Blitzkrieg, improved weapons and seen Britain, France and the US opt for appeasement.

British battalion members captured at Jarama are marched off by Franco's tricorn-wearing Civil Guard. International Brigaders who fell prisoner were often shot, but some were kept for propaganda purposes or to be swapped for Italians from Mussolini's Corpo Truppe Volontarie (CTV), who fought for Franco.

Later, albeit at some remove, there is the ratatat of machine-guns. We fear and reckon with some sadness that they must have liquidated all of the Internationals that were taken away earlier, although we cannot say so, because from time to time we can still hear scattered shots.

Not that that is the end of it. The eternal Judas, a lad from Buñol [Valencia], whom I never liked, either to show himself in a good light or because he himself is a fascist – God alone knows for sure – wastes no time in denouncing two out of the five or six American Brigaders whom I know to be still in our line posing as Spaniards, having weathered the questioning.

The squalor of the actions of the fellow from Buñol makes my stomach heave but, by way of a counter-point to the actions of this Buñolense, I am even more disturbed by the conduct of one of the Americans betrayed who throws himself to the ground, prostrate at the feet of the Francoist officer, to plead for mercy.[45]

Villar's evidence matches that of Priscilla Scott-Ellis, a British volunteer nurse serving Franco's forces, who was nearby when she noted in her diary that 'there are 85 prisoners here of the International Brigade, mostly American and some English. They will all be shot as the foreigners always are'.[46]

Villar was convinced that Merriman had died, but he may have survived, only to run straight into an enemy camp – where he was captured and executed.[47] Locals later talked of having witnessed a small group being held captive, interrogated and shot in batches over several days. One group included a tall officer (possibly Merriman) who initiated a loud argument with the firing squad so that the others could try to escape – though all were shot.[48] The Americans had lost their most charismatic officer. He had persuaded his wife to travel back to the United States some weeks earlier and Marion was at home alone when a journalist friend from San Francisco rang. Had she heard? 'The reporter eased himself out of the conversation, saying he was awfully sorry to give such news to me,' she recalled later.[49]

The situation was now even more chaotic and disastrous than it had been during the flight from Belchite to Caspe.[50] Part of the Italian XII Brigade continued to flee along a separate road towards the city of Tortosa and the coast, where they found their path blocked by Marty.

He had barricaded one of the escape roads with trucks and, helped by a group of Republican Assault Guards, managed to rally 300 men and send them back towards Gandesa. Most were caught there and their officers shot.[51]

The road out of Gandesa was full of soldiers and refugees, their carts piled high with mattresses, chairs, rattling pans and sacks of food. 'There were no group formations, there was no discipline. Officers were not giving orders; everyone was just heading toward the Ebro,' recalled Harry Fisher. Mostly that meant going to one place – the bridge at Móra de Ebro. The column was strafed, soldiers and civilians alike. When an American truck appeared and Fisher tried to help a woman on to it, she cried out for her baby. 'The baby was lying on the road lifeless,' he recalled. 'Sully [Lincoln volunteer Marty Sullivan] approached the woman and tried to explain that her baby was dead. But she still called out for it. I watched Scully carry the little bundle to the truck and put the baby in the mother's lap. The mother cuddled the baby as if it was alive.'[52]

At the Ebro, a few hours later, they bumped into Ćopić organising a line of resistance, while the buzzwords 'No Pasarán!' began to circulate again. Soon, however, it was recognised that the chances of preventing the enemy reaching the river were non-existent. Only the waters of the Ebro could halt them.

Fisher was sent on to the new XV Brigade gathering point near Móra la Nova. Only about one hundred members of the entire brigade of 2,000 soldiers were there. Benz's men were also told to cross the bridge, early on 3 April, and helped place explosive charges. Amongst those also setting the charges were General Walter himself and a sapper unit led by Briton Percy Ludwick.[53] A few hours later Fisher heard the bridge being blown. 'For the first time in a month I felt a sense of relief,' he recalled later. 'The Ebro river was wide and fast-flowing, the fascists were on the west side of it, and we were on the east.'[54]

Many had been left behind. The legendary Thälmann Battalion had just eighty men remaining from 450. The Lincolns could muster only sixty men.[55] Hundreds of volunteers were dead; many more had been captured. The Italian CTV militia army, for example, was by now holding a group of 480 international volunteers, who were described in a Paris newspaper as being made up of 141 British, 70 Americans, 42 German, 42 French, 31 Poles, 24 Australians, 24 Portuguese, 12 Swiss,

9 Italians, 7 Irish, 6 Norwegians, 2 Chinese and a Russian.[56] Fausto Villar, meanwhile, was marched off to be questioned by a German officer:

It is apparent from what he is saying that he is very well briefed about the sort of forces he has facing him. He goes on to ask me if there were Germans in my Division and I tell him that I do not know, that I can only speak for my own battalion, the Lincoln.

Now he asks me about the Brigade and about Merriman, for the fellow seems quite well-informed about everything connected with us and I tell him that I know nothing about Merriman since he is an officer and I am a common soldier. He returns to the subject of Merriman, asking me if he was with us when we were surrounded ... [then] he rips off the three pointed star of the International Brigades that I wear on my chest ... [and] we are walked down the plateau to the flat ground stretching in front of us, seemingly strewn with numerous lines of artillery, one beside the other, like some huge field planted with cannons instead of vines ... there are contingents of black-shirted Italian troops who, when we come level with them, wave cudgels and call out to us 'Any Italians among you?' while others threaten us at rifle-point as we pass through them.[57]

The majority of the International Brigade survivors were now safely across the Ebro, though others were still trapped and wandering around the countryside, waiting for an opportunity to swim the river. The battle, however, was not over. Franco was determined to reach the sea, and if he could not get there across the river, then he would do so elsewhere. Líster's troops continued to put up the most effective resistance to his attacks and between 4 and 17 April they ceded just eight kilometres of ground on the front between the sierra peaks at Les Armes del Rei and Peña Galera.[58]

Much further south, where the line of sierras that reached up towards Gandesa softened and became passable near the town of Morella, the new 129 Brigade had also been retreating as the thrust towards the Mediterranean continued along a separate path. Here, the men of Komar's brigade were swallowed up by the same sort of panicked flight that only the river Ebro had stopped further north. By 1 April they had already spent a week retreating along the roads that led from Alcañiz to Morella and, from there, to the sea at Vinaròs. By this stage the brigade had lost all contact with Kahle and had fallen in with the army group defending this sector of the front. It fought with the typical enthusiasm of a new unit keen to prove itself, and even managed one of the few victories during the retreats when they took a peak near the monastery at the Tozal de San Joaquín on 30 March. But this was a momentary episode and as they continued down the roads towards Morella, the volunteers found them full of abandoned arms, munitions, uniforms and food.[59]

A narrow valley outside Morella was chosen as a rallying point, with a truck load of rifles arriving and 129 Brigade's cavalry trying to stop the retreating men. Back up the road, a small group attacked with tanks but all they could manage was to slow the advance for a few hours. While commander Wacław Komar and his men held out in Morella – a walled town tucked against a massive rocky outcrop topped by an imposing twelfth-century castle – panic spread further down the road. Some Republican officers hijacked vehicles at pistol point, while others were shot on the spot for abandoning their men. Eventually, on 4 April, his men were surrounded, and Komar broke out with a hundred of them. The road they fled down, accompanied by five Spanish brigades, led to the seaside town of Vinaròs.[60] This was crowded with ambulances, armoured cars, mules and anything else that could carry men or armament.

Komar was a bloody-minded, argumentative commander, as likely to upbraid his own officers as he was to confront those above him. He railed against being separated from the other International Brigades, complained furiously when his battalions were loaned out to other brigades and divisions, was threatened with arrest by one division commander and argued with Lieutenant Colonel Juan Ibarrola, the loyalist Civil Guard officer who commanded another division. 'I told him that his way of treating my brigade was nothing more than a display of military ignorance,' he explained later.[61] 'Instead of leaving in my hands a brigade which I know well, whose men I know and whose officers have an extremely high morale, it had been taken from me, breaking up a unit with strong morale, mixing it with other panic-ridden ones.' Ibarrola ordered him to 'shut up and obey'.[62] In conspiratorial fashion, Komar then went on to suggest that Ibarrola could not be trusted because of his Catholicism and that this knowledge was also sapping the morale of the Brigaders. 'The international volunteers saw in him … an enemy of the International Brigades who deliberately tried to ensure their physical liquidation,' he wrote.[63] This was more a reflection of Komar's own, rigid dogmatism and the flights of paranoid fantasy that went with it.

Despite the dislike of the Republic displayed by the Roman Catholic Church hierarchy around the world, there were practising Catholic volunteers within the International Brigades, especially amongst the Poles and Irish.[64] Komar may, indeed, have been demoralising his own men by encouraging such opinions about Ibarrola. By now, in any case, their spirits had hit rock bottom since the road leading to the coast at Vinaròs could no longer be crossed, cutting his men off from the rest of the Brigades. 'The feeling [amongst the men] was that all was now lost,' he added.[65] With his volunteers demoralised and his Spaniards likely to desert, Komar became the fiercest disciplinarian in the Brigades. He had a Canadian sergeant shot for requisitioning a mule and then selling it (but did not dare mete out the same punishment to the Spanish sergeant with him, who was merely stripped of his rank). The head of the shock group in the Dimitrov Battalion – a volunteer called Bende – was executed, this time for pulling a gun on his superior. Komar also imposed a strict code of shared retribution. 'For every soldier who deserts from a section, his corporal will be tried and executed,' he announced. 'For a deserting corporal, the platoon sergeant will be tried and executed. For a sergeant it will be his lieutenant and for a lieutenant it will be his captain.'[66] This, he claimed, put an immediate end to all desertions.

Nothing was quite so demoralising, however, as the news that reached them on 15 April. It was Good Friday and the devout Carlist *requetés* who finally reached the beach at Vinaròs waded into the tranquil Mediterranean Sea as if it was the river Jordan. General Alonso Vega crossed himself with the salt water and those who believed that this really was a crusade saw something deeply significant in the date. The following day a rebel newspaper proclaimed: 'The victorious sword of Franco has sliced into two parts the Spain that is still occupied by the Reds.'[67]

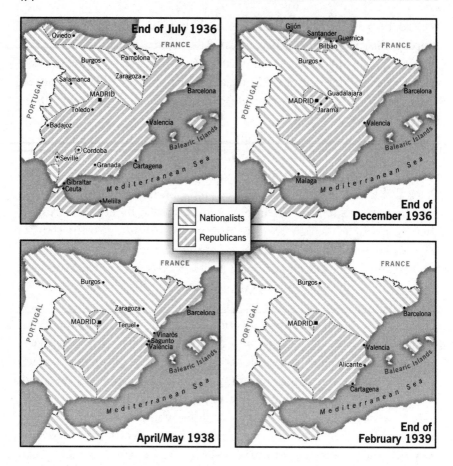

End of July 1936

Oviedo
Burgos • Pamplona
Salamanca
Zaragoza •
MADRID ■
Toledo •
Badajoz •
Valencia •
Cordoba
Seville • Granada • Cartagena
Gibraltar
Ceuta
Melilla
FRANCE
PORTUGAL
Barcelona
Balearic Islands
Mediterranean Sea

End of
December 1936

Gijón
Santander Guernica
Bilbao
Burgos •
MADRID ■ Guadalajara
Jarama
Valencia •
Malaga
FRANCE
PORTUGAL
Barcelona
Balearic Islands
Mediterranean Sea

Nationalists
Republicans

April/May 1938

Burgos •
Zaragoza •
MADRID ■ Teruel •
Vinaròs
Sagunto
Valencia
FRANCE
PORTUGAL
Barcelona
Balearic Islands
Mediterranean Sea

End of
February 1939

Burgos •
MADRID ■
Valencia •
Alicante •
Cartagena
FRANCE
PORTUGAL
Barcelona
Balearic Islands
Mediterranean Sea

45

Defeat, Despair, Hope: Móra la Nova,
4 April 1938

Once more, Franco decided to halt. After reaching the sea he had taken a further sixty kilometres of coast,[1] while the Republicans retreated to the far side of the Ebro, blowing up the bridges. Most experts, and Franco's German advisors, agreed that he could have rolled up through Catalonia easily over the next few weeks, taking advantage of the chaos in the Republican ranks and claiming final victory. He seemed, however, to be in little hurry to finish his war.

Nor, however, was he interested in negotiating its end, given that he sought total and absolute victory, with the consequent annihilation of any future opposition to his dictatorship. There was work to be done behind the lines, where death squads from the Falange wreaked revenge and those who had served the elected government, regional assemblies and town halls of the Republic before the war were pursued, jailed or shot. So, too, were those who had indulged in the massacres of priests and rightists, irrevocably dirtying the name of the Republic and limiting its outside support as a result. One group of wells at a remote spot in Francoist territory near Teruel had already filled up with the bodies of more than a thousand of his opponents, just as the ravines and gullies outside Granada had done earlier in the war.[2] 'The terror practised at the moment in the nationalist zone by Martínez Anido is unbearable even to the Falange,' the German ambassador commented.[3]

Franco's foreign advisors were furious at his leisurely approach to conquest. Many questioned whether he was really a good general, or just an unimaginative plodder who constantly fumbled the opportunities presented to him by the great advantages in military hardware or by political divisions within Republic.[4] The latter had erupted again during the retreats, with Negrín sacking defence minister Indalecio Prieto the week before Franco's troops finally reached the Mediterranean.[5]

Franco must, however, have felt emboldened by advances being made in the wider assault on Europe by the fascist powers and their authoritarian, reactionary allies across the continent. The spring of 1938 was a season of decisive gains, and not just in Spain. The 12 March Anschluss saw Hitler annex Austria with little effort and only timid reproaches from Britain, France and the other Western democracies, freeing him to start the next steps in his expansionist plans. For the Austrians of the February 12 Battalion this had added insult to injury on the same day that they were pushed back by Franco's advancing troops and Hitler's Condor Legion aircraft near Belchite. Seven weeks earlier, to help prepare the repression inside Austria itself, Franco's army had ordered the 'severe and thorough' interrogation of any Austrian volunteers captured at Teruel in order to discover 'where in Austria and by whom' they had been recruited.[6]

The only cheering news had been that, on 17 March, the new but short-lived French government of Léon Blum had reopened its frontiers to arms. The ferocity of German and Italian naval activity, especially Italian 'pirate' submarines, had been seriously impairing the arrival of armaments from the Soviet Union.[7] The opening of the border would, in theory, allow what remained of the Republic to rearm and drag the war out until it merged with the greater Europe-wide conflict that many now expected. In that case, the Republic might finally become a formal ally of Britain and France, dramatically altering the balance of forces. This was, indeed, the Republic's final hope. For Negrín, whose determination not to give up on victory contrasted with the pessimism of President Manuel Azaña (whose diaries show him arguing with Negrín about whether the Republic should simply surrender), this was worth the inevitable further losses in lives.[8] Franco's timidity about pushing north and taking Catalonia was also guided by a fear that the presence of his troops on the frontier might finally drive France into reacting.[9]

The door was slammed shut again on 13 June, by a new government led by Edouard Daladier. The following day, Franco's forces, driving south, took the important coastal city of Castellón. The bombing and sinking of a British steamship, the *Dellwyn*, in the port of Gandia did nothing to change the non-interventionists, who were now preparing for Hitler to take control of the Sudetenland from Czechoslovakia.[10] The contrast with Franco's fortunes was notable, since regular supplies of arms or men continued to arrive from Italy and Nazi Germany.[11] 'Notwithstanding all committees, Italy will not abandon Spain until the Nationalist flag is flying from the loftiest towers of Barcelona, Valencia and Madrid,' Mussolini's foreign minister, Count Ciano, said early in June.[12] Recruitment of new international volunteers slowed dramatically. A total of 1,298 men had arrived in February 1938, but only a few more than that would join the international units over the entire five months from April to August.[13] By 1 May, there were 12,614 volunteers left, and one in seven of those were being treated in hospitals. Fourteenth Brigade still boasted 1,479 French speakers, but the Italian XII Brigade was down to just 762 foreigners, of whom 104 were officers.[14]

Worse still, Stalin's interest was flagging. Even General Walter was packing to go home. His final report on the state of the International Brigades and the Spanish war was damning but, characteristically, blamed fifth columnists and spies for many of its failings. The disastrous retreat from Aragon had, he said, happened 'despite the presence of precise data that we had well in advance about the impending offensive' and even Russian advisors had been 'hypnotised by Guadalajara' and the expectation of a Francoist offensive there.[15]

Walter was delighted, nevertheless, to receive the Republic's 'Placa Laureada', or Silver Plaque, medal. Szurek, his devoted aide-de-camp, was less impressed. 'In spite of my attachment to him, I was taken aback by his elation. In my imagination I saw him, like many other generals, with a chest laden with so many medals that there was no empty space,' he recalled. 'I am convinced that people who pride themselves on medals, despite the pride of past heroic accomplishments, carry with them not only the nostalgia and love for a rich past full of life experiences but also, unfortunately, love of war itself.' Before he left on 8 May, Walter wanted to take his Spanish flamenco dancer girlfriend, Isabelita, back with him – though, since he was already married, that might have been tricky. A few weeks earlier he had caught her weeping in front of a photo of his daughters, begging their forgiveness. He was told, in any case, that Isabelita would not be allowed to leave. Instead, she and Szurek accompanied him to the frontier, and Isabelita wept all the way back. 'I'll never meet such a good man again in my life,' she reflected.[16]

Many volunteers had become lost behind enemy lines, and some managed to return. A small group from the British Battalion led by Lewis Clive, a former Grenadier Guards officer and gold medallist rower at the 1932 Olympic Games in Los Angeles, wandered the countryside for ten days before crossing the river.[17] Franco's men had captured so many prisoners during the retreats that it could not control them all. Some Brigaders escaped, including Ćopić, who was able to use his knowledge of both Spanish and Catalan to convince soldiers in Franco's side that he was a lost peasant who needed feeding. Others were able to take advantage of the remarkable similarities between uniforms to merge with their captors and then flee.[18]

Writer Alvah Bessie was sent out with a truck to look for men who might have crossed further downstream. He came across XV Brigade assistant commissar John Gates, together with Americans Joe Hecht and George Watt, drying themselves on a riverbank, naked under their blankets. 'They told us they had swum the Ebro early that morning; that other men had swum and drowned,' he said.[19] 'You could see they were reluctant to talk, and so we just sat down with them. Joe looked dead.'

Hemingway and Herbert Matthews of the *New York Times*, travelling together in a new Matford roadster, also reappeared at this time. Bessie was grateful for their gift of Lucky Strikes and Chesterfields. Matthews seemed to him to be permanently bitter, while Hemingway was still 'eager as a child':

> He asked questions like a kid: 'What then? What happened then? And what did you do? And what did he say? And then what did you do?' Matthews said nothing, but he took notes on a folded sheet of paper. 'What's your name?' said Hemingway; I told him. 'Oh,' he said, 'I'm awful glad to see you; I've read your stuff.' I knew he was glad to see me; it made me feel good, and I felt sorry about the times I had lambasted him in print; I hoped he had forgotten them,

or never read them. 'Here,' he said, reaching in his pocket. 'I've got more.' He handed me a full pack of Lucky Strikes.²⁰

Hemingway, in turn, recalled 'standing in the dusty brush beside a nervous-making road' as he listened to the three barefooted survivors, who had only just been clothed, tell their stories of how six companions had drowned. They described 'having to break across an open field toward the Ebro bank and being sniped at by artillery controlled by an observation plane overhead; finally the desperate swimming of the Ebro and wandering down the road, not to desert and not to try to reach the frontier, but looking for the remainder of the battalion'.²¹

Those who managed to cross the Ebro to safety often did not stop there. One of the last volunteers to make it across the bridge at Móra de Ebro met an American artillery officer who advised him that 'there is no Brigade – no division – no army. It is all over. The best you can do is get out of this country as fast as you can.'²² With so many soldiers wandering the Catalan countryside, it was never clear whether they were deserting, or simply lost. Many automatically headed for the French border, knowing that the further north they went, the more likely they were to escape a Francoist advance. Others sneaked onto the quays at Barcelona or Valencia, waiting for a boat to stow away on. Merchant marine vessels such as the *Essex Judge* and the *Kellwyn* threw them back out. In towns as far north as El Masnou, Ripoll, Ribes de Freser, Camprodon, Canet de Mar and Calella, Republican police arrested foreign volunteers heading for the French border and sent them back to their units. Often, they travelled in small groups. Nine French and Belgian members of XIV Brigade, for example, along with two Bulgarians from 129 Brigade and an Englishman from XV Brigade, were caught at Masnou over just a few days in mid-April.²³

In the Catalan seaside town of Cambrils, the Brigades set up their own control post, to bring together those who were lost or deserting. 'When we arrived, one hundred stragglers of all nationalities were gathered in the patio of a factory; they had lost their arms, some were wounded, hungry and in a dire physical condition,' recalled battalion commander Penchienati.²⁴ 'André Marty harangued them, hurling insults.' He also claimed that Marty personally shot four of them after they answered him back. There is no confirmation of that, and Penchienati was already on his way to becoming one of the Brigades' harshest and least trustworthy post-war critics. The degree of violence employed on the men was contentious at the time and for long afterwards. Andreu Castells, the best historian of the International Brigades (and a young Catalan recruit serving with 129 Brigade), claimed that a total of sixty-five men were shot for cowardice, mostly in the Italian, French, American and British battalions. Some of his sources are suspect and the most reliable ones give a total of around two dozen executions altogether, though it is safe to assume that more went unreported.[25] Either way, there was enough shooting for the Brigaders themselves to speculate as to how some of their comrades might have met their deaths.[26]

The whole structure of the Brigades had been disrupted by the retreats. On 19 March, Marty had formally ordered the closure of the International Brigades base in Albacete[27] – where 225 volunteers and 509 Spaniards were still working – along with the destruction of many documents and the removal of as much as possible to Barcelona. The training bases in towns such as Madrigueras and La Roda were hurriedly shut down. All was done in a rush, with one training camp at Quintanar de la República – run by Penchienati – given just four hours to destroy documents and put the remaining men into trucks.

The network of international hospitals also had to be rebuilt, with five new hospitals set up in Catalonia and the patients moved. A new Brigades base was set up in Horta, one of the poorer outskirts of Barcelona, but it was a shadow of the once proud base at Albacete.[28] It also seems, originally, to have taken over a half-built barracks where several hundred disgruntled deserters were held and some appear to have rioted.[29] Those International Brigade prisoners considered beyond recovery were also sent into Catalonia, with Ćopić's brother setting up the new jail in Castelldefels castle, where their graffiti is still conserved on the walls of a small chapel.[30] Some are roughly scribbled names and dates, or sketches of naked women. Others are large, carefully drawn scenes of the countryside or portraits of famous politicians. One, of two dogs looking wistfully out of a window, speaks poignantly of captivity and a desire for freedom.

Restoring morale was a problem, even amongst the officers. 'The strain has been terrific and our boys are not in very good shape,' one British communist wrote home. Their commanders were initially prepared to refuse any orders to go back into the front line: Captain

Clifford Wattis 'wanted to pull out immediately for Barcelona and said he had *camions* [trucks] already fixed, [battalion commander Sam] Wild was for refusing to go into the line again and Bob [Cooney, commissar] was wobbly'.[31] Those not tied to the discipline of the Communist Party were more likely to have reached the conclusion that the war was lost and further effort useless. In the British case, for example, the communists now declared that they mistrusted the admittedly 'brave man and excellently trained officer' Wattis, who had taken command in the field during the retreats.[32]

Eventually, however, the majority of the volunteers were persuaded that the war was not over and that, as one left-leaning British newspaper told them: 'If they should fail, not they alone, but all of us would be losers.'[33] It was an uphill task, but there was time to heal wounds, restore pride and return the Brigades to the condition of proper fighting units. With so many losses, and so few new international volunteers, they were now refilled almost entirely with Spaniards. It dawned on some Brigaders that they were now fulfilling a role that the original organisers had always wanted – to train, and provide example to, the new Republican army. This exercise was both paternalistic, since some Brigaders still clung to feelings of national superiority, and paternal, given that the recruits who now included seventeen- and eighteen-year-old Catalans.[34] They were, in other words, little more than children.[35] A handful were idealistic young communists who had asked to join the Brigades. Most were ordinary conscripts – illiterate farm boys, anarchist city kids or petit bourgeois Catalans, enamoured of their homeland or, in some cases, of the other side. The need to prepare and harden these teenagers alarmed the prematurely aged veterans, who fretted that they would never make real soldiers or learn how to protect themselves. Either way, the task was enormous and absorbing. The young recruits experienced the harsh love of some of their instructors, and the sadism of others.

With Austria gone, Hitler eyeing up the Sudetenland in Czechoslovakia and Mussolini pouring new troops into Spain to finish off the task there, it looked like the enemies of fascism were already the losers. The Spanish Republic, meanwhile, was punch-drunk, but still alive. With Negrín in control, it was also determined to hold out as long as it could. To do that, it needed not just to defend itself, but also to return to the attack. Only this, Negrín thought, would convince the world that the shattered remnants of Spanish democracy were still worthy of support. Spain's communists were similarly determined to fight back. They knew that they would be amongst those most vigorously repressed and punished by a Francoist Spain (though anarchists were in a similar position). For many of the volunteers, too, there was no question of giving up. This was especially so for the Germans and those from other dictatorial or authoritarian countries, who had nowhere to go back to. For them, Spain gave meaning to their lives and remained both a place of freedom and the front line of the fight against fascism at home. That explains why so many were happy to keep fighting in a war which, by most measures, the Republic now looked likely to lose.

46

Prisoners: The monastery at San Pedro de Cardeña, autumn 1938

Chen Agen had prepared his message carefully. It was written in Latin letters, but these did not go across the page. Rather, he had placed them going down, as he was used to doing with the Chinese script learned in his native Shanghai. When the Spanish propaganda men arrived with their camera to film Agen and his fellow international captives in the squalor of the monastery at San Pedro de Cardeña, the Chinese fighter held it up to the cameras. For those used to reading down, rather than across, the message was simple: '*Viva España. Arriba España. Chen Agen, Shanghai.*'

Agen's journey to this monastery-prison near to the Castilian city of Burgos had started in China itself, when he enrolled on a French boat, the *Girto Mora*, as a kitchen boy in 1937. He was running away from the nationalist Kuomintang of Chiang Kai-shek, which was pursuing him for organising a communist trades union. On board was a Vietnamese chef, a cultured man who Agen admired enormously. The chef, whose name was never recorded, told him of a huge battle that had broken out in a country called Spain. That battle pitted troops provided by fascists like Italy's Benito Mussolini and Germany's Adolf Hitler against democrats, communists and other left-wingers. These were allies of Japan, the same country that had invaded parts of China. People from around the world were travelling to Spain to help defend it against the right-wing generals led by General Francisco Franco who had risen against an elected, left-wing popular front government. Agen, the chef said, should join them. If Hitler and Mussolini were sending troops, then it was the responsibility of all anti-fascists to fight against them. He himself could not go, as the chef – a fellow communist – was due to travel to Moscow for political training. Like another Vietnamese ship's chef who would rise to fame, Ho Chi Minh, he was also already committed to the ideology that had fired the Russian revolution two decades earlier.

So Agen jumped ship when it docked in Spain. Trapped in the northern pocket of the Republic, he became one of those 8,000 or so international volunteers who joined the Spanish army directly, in his case fighting with a group of Asturian miners until he was captured. If he had been able to cross into France and make his way back to Spain, like the Canadian volunteer Bill Williamson, then he would probably have joined the International Brigades. More than a dozen other Chinese, most of them already migrants to Europe or the Americas, had already done so.[1] A similar number of Vietnamese, Filipinos and other East Asians had also volunteered, with the Vietnamese captain Lucien Tchen commanding a company in XIII Brigade.[2]

Agen's encounter with the Brigaders had finally taken place in jail, where all foreigners were treated as part of the same mass of dangerous foreign 'Reds'. The vast majority of the 600 other international volunteers now living amidst the filth of the San Pedro Monastery – where the medieval warrior El Cid Campeador had famously deposited his family for safekeeping – were International Brigaders. These were mostly from XI and XV Brigades, captured during the retreats from Aragon and would have included the 'two Chinese' who appeared in a Paris newspaper report.[3] While the majority of captured Brigaders were executed,[4] some were not. The reasons were various.

The international volunteers could be used for propaganda purposes, as both evidence that the other side was breaking the non-intervention treaty and to show how poor these international 'Red' soldiers (who became something of an obsession for Franco himself) really were. That is why Chen Agen was being filmed. Finally, they could also be exchanged for Italian soldiers and German airmen held by the Republic. Some 400 Italians, for example, had been captured in Guadalajara alone. Most of the British, Canadian and Swiss prisoners would be swapped for 110 Italians in 1939.[5] Some of those released earlier on returned to fight – with five of the twenty-three Britons captured at Jarama (who had passed through camps in Talavera and Salamanca, as well as being subjected to show trials in which some were nominally sentenced to death) back in Spain within six weeks.[6] One of them, Jimmy Rutherford, was captured a second time, taken to San Pedro and, after several weeks, removed and executed.[7] Other prisoners remained for years, either here or in larger camps like that at Miranda de Ebro. Those most likely to stay often had nowhere to go, since their countries (including Italy, Germany, Austria and various Balkan nations) did not want them. Some 150 international prisoners were sent to a work camp at Belchite, where their task was to help build a new town to replace the one destroyed by two separate battles.[8] Some of those helping to rebuild the town had once helped to conquer it or, later, had escaped when it was recaptured.

Conditions in the huge, open dormitory cells of San Pedro were ghastly. They were also a place of torture, degradation and death. There was one tap for 600 men, starvation rations and only a few toilets. Dysentery, boils, lice and fleas plagued the prisoners. A group of sadistic sergeants regularly beat the prisoners, especially those who were ill or slow, with five-foot long wooden sticks. A separate *sala de torturas* was used to mete out even tougher beatings.[9] One sergeant, who kept breaking his wooden sticks, eventually made a pizzle stick out of a dried bull's penis, weighted with a lead slug that raised welts on the prisoner's backs.[10] He was so keen on using this that the English speakers nicknamed him 'Sticky'.

Days often started with early morning beatings as the men were forced out onto the parade ground to be counted. 'As we went down the two flights of stairs, the guards along with Sticky would be waiting at the bottom door to lay into us as we came out,' recalled Bob Doyle. 'The return journey was the same.'[11] Doyle was taken into the *sala de tortura* after sitting down instead of eating his food standing up, as required. 'Four of them closed in and began raining blows on my back shouting "*¡Rojo! Rojo!*" ["Red! Red!"] and in their frenzy they sometimes missed their target and hit each other instead.'[12] The batterings lasted for ten minutes. Those who fell ill because of the poor conditions and beatings were treated by Basque nuns, who were also prisoners – a reminder that not all of the Catholic Church in their part of Spain had backed Franco.[13] Occasionally, the prison was visited by an unnamed bishop, who turned to the Spanish prisoners (mostly Basques and Asturians) and then pointed to the Brigaders, shouting: 'Look at them, the scum of the earth!'[14]

As a condensed version of the International Brigades themselves, the prisoners also formed a fresh Tower of Babel. One propaganda photograph, perhaps taken to shock Franco's own conservative backers, shows a group of twenty men, of whom five are probably either Afro-American or Cuban and three appear to be East Asian.[15] A camp committee was set up to help organise the prisoners and, when necessary, defend them against the worst abuses – though several much-hated volunteers also offered their services as 'helpers' to the guards. A so-called 'San Pedro Institute of Higher Education' was set up, with prisoners giving lectures on their areas of expertise.[16] They also found a way to print a newspaper, the *Jaily News*, on stolen 8.5 x 14-inch pieces of paper (a single copy of each edition was typed up and circulated). They sang to keep up their spirits, and after he left Spain one of the Americans made a record of their songs in various languages.[17] The slight, moustachioed Indian volunteer Gopal Mukund Huddar entertained people by reading their hands. Huddar still claimed to be from Iraq, used the name John Smith and had been captured with other members of the XV Brigade at Gandesa.

The senior prisoner, along with the Mackenzie–Papineau commissar Carl Geiser, was the charismatic Frank Ryan. He and the 140 men captured at Calaceite were saved because their captors were Italians, who shooed away a Civil Guard execution squad.[18] When asked who was in command, Ryan stepped forward immediately – despite the fact officers were more likely to be shot.[19] Perhaps he knew his uniform would give him away. When they were taken to the San Gregorio General Military Academy in Zaragoza, they were ordered to give the fascist salute and shout '*Fran-co!*' at the end of every parade ground headcount. 'Sir, to give that salute would signify we pledge our loyalty to Franco. I call upon all my fellow soldiers to refuse,' said Ryan, claiming that the Geneva Convention meant they could not be forced. After some discussion (and given that those who refused were beaten) the men agreed to give the salute, but did so in as messy a fashion as possible. The Francoists 'explained that foreigners were treated exactly like the Spanish prisoners', the *New York Times*'s William Carney reported after visiting.[20] That may have been true for those taken prisoner, but many had already been executed. Peter Kemp, the British *legionario* fighting for Franco, confirmed as much to the US vice-consul Charles Bay in April 1938. '[Kemp] said that, in general, any foreigners captured were executed by the troops taking them, without any kind of trial ... He said that feeling against foreigners was very bitter on the part of the Spaniards he had fought with ... he tried to save an Englishman who he thought worthy, but was ordered to execute him himself,' he reported.[21] Kemp told a friend that the man was a British sailor who had actually been trying to desert.[22] One calculation for the American volunteers who were captured, gives 173 men out of 287 executed.[23] Similar proportions can probably applied to all International Brigade prisoners.

Frank Ryan was eventually recognised by all as the natural leader.[24] After they were visited by foreign journalists, news that he was being held reached Ireland and prime minister Eamon de Valera himself tried to arrange his release. Ryan felt free to upbraid Carney for his pro-Francoist articles. He was eventually removed from San Pedro and subjected to a trial that saw him sentenced to be executed, though this was later commuted to thirty years in jail.[25] Ryan would, in any case, remain in Spanish prisons until after the end of the war.

At San Pedro, there were constant reminders of Hitler's backing for Franco. Gestapo agents were often in the prison, seeking out German Brigaders and looking for intelligence of all kinds.[26] German prisoners apparently suffered the worst beatings, and some were sent straight on to camps in Germany itself.[27] The most daring escape saw six Germans take two months to saw through a window bar before breaking out at night and walking almost as far as France before being recaptured. They spent the next month (or three months, in one case) crammed together in a dingy, dungeon-like cell.[28]

Gestapo and Nazi agents at San Pedro also conducted interrogations and medical examinations of volunteers from Britain, the United States, Portugal, Canada, Cuba and a handful of other Latin American countries. Callipers were laid out on a table in a field and a queue of prisoners were told to strip. Heads were measured. So were limbs.[29] Questionnaires asked them about everything from their drinking habits and sex lives to their political convictions. The Brigaders' answers were given half in jest and half in seriousness, but the earnest Spanish doctors assisting took each reply literally. They included Lieutenant Colonel Antonio Vallejo-Nágera, a German-trained military psychiatrist and avowed eugenicist.

He was the head of the so-called 'Military Psychological Studies Unit', with a special remit to pursue what he and Franco called 'Marxists' – a group that, in their definition, included almost all supporters of the popular front coalition that had won the 1936 elections. He was helped by two intellectual-looking young *falangista* doctors whose task was to prove that all Marxists were, by nature, either mad, psychotic or congenitally subnormal. '*A priori*, it seems probable that psychopaths of all types would join the Marxist ranks,' Vallejo-Nágera reasoned before starting the project. 'Since Marxism goes together with social immorality ... we presume those fanatics who fought with arms will show schizoid temperaments.'[30] Marxism was clearly an illness, so the eugenicist also considered it his duty to seek a cure or, at least, ways to prevent the infection from spreading.

'We supposed they thought it would be useful if the fascists ever invaded Britain,' said Bob Doyle.[31] 'An assistant ... called out the length, breadth, and depth of his skull, the distance between his eyes, the length of his nose, and described the skin colour, body type, wound scars and disability,' recalled American Carl Geiser, who was photographed with just a small cloth over his penis. 'Each prisoner was instructed to stand in front of a camera for a front and side view, and a close-up of the face. We were now "scientifically" classified.' The most bizarre questions, many Brigaders found, were about their sex lives: 'Where did you have your first woman? Was she a prostitute . . .?'[32]

After analysing his results, Vallejo-Nágera concluded that his original hypothesis had been right. His report claimed that 58 per cent of English prisoners were 'single men with sexual experience outside prostitution', that 7 per cent were recruited 'by charlatans in Hyde Park', that 17 per cent had signed up in 'employment agencies'. All (three) Welsh prisoners were 'alcoholics', he found. He classified almost a third of the English prisoners as 'mental retards'. Another third were deemed to be suffering from degenerative mental illnesses that were turning them into schizoids, paranoids or psychopaths. Their fall into Marxism was, in turn, exacerbated by the fact that 29 per cent were 'social imbeciles'. 'Once more we see confirmed that social resentment, frustrated aspirations and envy are the sources of Marxism,' the psychiatrist-eugenicist wrote. 'The persistence of the ideological attitude of the English Marxists is the result of their closed minds and lack of culture.'[33]

The results were hardly scientific, but did not prevent Vallejo-Nágera from becoming Francoist Spain's most important psychiatrist, producing proposals for the purification of a Hispanic race that, he claimed, had lost vigour from five centuries of intermingling with Jewish converts to Catholicism. As a devout Catholic, he could not back the kind of mass sterilisation favoured by some German colleagues but proposed, instead, the pre-selection of suitable breeding candidates to restore 'nobility' to the national bloodstock of Spain.

Vallejo-Nágera was, of course, wrong to assume that all the prisoners were avowed Marxists. 'Some of us were democrats, anarchists, some were communists,' said Geiser.[34] 'The thing we learned was that we all had to stick together.' The Spanish psychiatrist's testing produced one fascinating result, however. Despite the pressures of jail, 85 per cent of the foreigners refused to express regret for fighting to save Spain's Republican government. They could no longer fight, but had not lost their political principles. 'The immense majority remain firmly attached to their ideas,' Dr Vallejo-Nágera concluded.

47

The Last Charge: Ebro river, 24 July 1938

On the evening of 24 July, many of the remaining international volunteers in Spain found themselves creeping through the dark towards the banks of the river Ebro, which flowed through Catalonia and into the Mediterranean Sea. At Amposta, the last major town before the Ebro spreads into a large delta formed by centuries of deposits laid down by the river, the French-led XIV Brigade was at one end of an attack line that stretched 105 kilometres upriver. In fact, the attack they were preparing here was a feint, with the main offensive beginning twenty-five kilometres further upriver at Xerta and stretching eighty kilometres north beyond Fayón, where Republican brigades were also crawling through the mud and reeds on the riverbank.

The aim was to attack back into the territory lost during the retreats, strike at Gandesa, and either advance further from there or dig in to the rocky sierras and draw Franco's troops towards them. That, it was reasoned, would halt Franco's offensive towards the acting capital Valencia (in the southern part of the now divided Republican territory) and might also extend the war until something major happened to change the international situation. Morale was surprisingly high. 'The men knew there was little chance for a total defeat of the enemy,' wrote one American volunteer. 'They thought specifically in terms of seizing territory, entrenching and then holding it.'[1] They also knew, from their nightmarish retreats on the Aragon front, that the line of rugged sierras – with the Sierra de Pàndols at their centre – which lay just fifteen kilometres on the other side of the river from the main attack points between Xerta and Asco, provided a perfect defensive line from which to do battle.

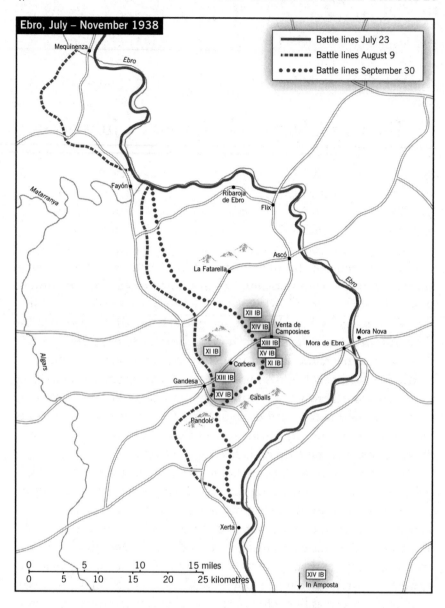

On rickety pontoon bridges, in boats with muffled oars,[2] canoes and rafts of all sizes, the five International Brigades all began to cross (or tried to cross) the river that morning, starting at just after midnight. They accounted for a fifth of the attacking brigades, suggesting that they were, once more, in favour as shock troops. The great majority of their soldiers were now Spaniards and the senior commanders for the operation were young Spanish communists, such as Merino or twenty-five-year-old Manuel Tagüeña, who was in charge of the entire XV Army Corps with 70,000 men, including part of the International Brigades.[3] The crossing began at fifteen minutes past midnight, just as the calendar moved into 25 July.

The Hungarian Rakosi Battalion of XIII Brigade led 35th Division across near Asco.[4] The Poles in the same brigade sat in silence, waiting their turn, listening to the first bursts of machine-gun fire on the other side of the river and wondering whether the Francoists had been waiting for them. 'Nobody knew if the first boats had managed to get across,' one man recalled.[5] The guns quickly fell silent, however, and Szurek – who was now a XIII Brigade staff officer – reassured them that the enemy was fleeing.[6] Soon the Poles, too, were across, and marching along hilly tracks as, at the head of the advancing army, they bypassed points of resistance in an attempt to take possession of the sierras before the enemy discovered them.

Those who crossed that night generally fared well. Those who tried the following day, during daylight, had more difficulty, since enemy aircraft were soon flying along the Ebro, picking targets at will, destroying pontoons and boats. The German-speaking XI Brigade, for example, were slower to the other side, but still able to seize Asco with the help of part of XV Brigade that day.[7] The Poles and Hungarians, meanwhile, marched on relentlessly. Small groups of enemy troops surrendered, scarcely able to believe what was happening. As dawn broke, they saw roads already strewn with abandoned backpacks, blankets, clothes and even arms as the scattered Francoist defenders began to flee. Confused peasants did not know whether to raise their arms in a fascist salute or clench their fists.[8] Two local women driving a cart found themselves joining the advance, transporting the heavier machine guns. They did not ask which side they were doing this for.

By shortly after 11 a.m.,[9] the Brigaders had already broken through the sierras to the crossroads at La Venta de Camposines, where the roads from Ascó to La Fatarella and Móra de Ebro to Gandesa met. The Mickiewicz Battalion reached this spot first, finding a few red-capped Moroccans standing around with their horses; trucks carrying soldiers retreating from Móra de Ebro trundled past and a battalion of men casually sat around preparing food. The battalion was quietly surrounded, attacked and captured – including its officers, some of whom tried to dash for their horses. 'No one shot back,' recalled one of their officers, Zygmunt Molojec.[10] By midday they were already in front of the sierras and marching along the road towards Corbera d'Ebre, its church tower emerging gradually as the Jewish Naftali Botwin company of the Palafox Battalion took the lead. The company commander, a tough former Foreign Legionnaire from Poland called Israel Halbersberg, had to rein in his overenthusiastic men after they exposed themselves to fire by moving too quickly over open ground.[11]

Eventually, the defenders retreated and the Brigaders were ushered into an abandoned Corbera by the former mayor, amid Catalan cries of '¡Visca Catalunya! ¡Visca la República!' By now the Poles had met up with the British Battalion.[12] That evening they reached within grenade-throwing distance of Gandesa, the main town of Tarragona's Terra Alta region, where a considerable garrison was camped out and defensive fortifications were more sophisticated. In under twenty-four hours, they had advanced twenty-five kilometres on foot, leading the Republican army in a surprise attack that had already achieved its most important targets. Other parts of 35th Division mopped up behind them, as parallel advances took place to the south and north.[13]

It should have been a moment of glory for Red Army officer Mijail Khvatov, alias Charchenko, a Ukrainian who was commanding XIII Brigade under the guise of a volunteer.[14] He did not, however, accompany the brigade on its advance. Szurek, who had become his aide, was unimpressed. Charchenko was determined to stay away from the front line, he concluded, because he was due to return home to the USSR within a month. The contrast with General Walter was enormous.[15]

Downstream, in the flatlands near Amposta, a very different sort of battle was taking place. The French brigade had successfully placed a pontoon bridge across the Ebro at Campredó and the entire Commune de Paris Battalion had crossed, establishing a bridgehead in the few hundred metres of land that separated the river from an irrigation canal. Their pontoon was quickly destroyed, however, and the Henri Barbusse, which crossed further downstream near Amposta, was the only other one to make it to the far shore. The battalions suffered radically different fates. The Henri Barbusse held on during the day, but was able to withdraw overnight back across the river. The Commune de Paris – now led by the Algerian-born communist

René Cazala – found itself trapped, unable to return and attacked by artillery and the machine guns of a Moroccan colonial regiment.[16] It is a violent and deadly combat we face in this small redoubt where we find ourselves entrenched,' wrote one battalion member. 'We all know it will be necessary to resist until nightfall; before that, we can expect no reinforcements. In front of us the enemy, at our backs the river; the situation is therefore quite clear and tragic.'[17] It was a massacre in which the battalion lost 80 per cent of its men. With the pontoon and boats destroyed, guns jamming and ammunition running short, one of Cazala's messengers, François Roche, swam the 400-metre-wide river to request fresh ammunition. When he swam back again, the situation was already disastrous. 'Groups of men could no longer do anything to defend themselves. Those who knew how to swim threw themselves into the river. Many drowned, others were killed by machine-gun fire.' Fewer than 200 out of 650 men made it back.[18] Seriously wounded, Cazala put a gun to his head and killed himself.[19] Pierre Landrieux of the Henri Barbusse recalled this day as the worst of the war:

> The most terrible sight of this battle ... was seeing in the mists of the emerging dawn and over the muddy and undulating waters of the Ebro, the bodies of our brothers in arms, fallen upstream during the crossing of this river, passing by.
>
> Helmeted or in their caps, they passed in front of us, one after another, still carrying their cartridges or their grenades, sinking and bobbing up, their heads and busts emerging from the water ... parading before our positions, as if for a last goodbye! Together with our Spanish brethren, how many of our own and other internationals were swept into the main delta of the Ebro and to the bottom of the Mediterranean?
>
> My most heartfelt memory of the day was that I could not cross this river and help our comrades on the other bank, who called for us, in vain, as reinforcement. Their cries, their shouts, resounded for a long time in my mind.[20]

Franco's initial response to this lightning attack was limited by the fact that most of his troops were further south, advancing on Valencia.

Others had been sucked into the fighting at Amposta. Panic had also overtaken some of his units and reports arrived of soldiers fleeing as far as Zaragoza.[21] On 25 July, however, he was able to use Condor Legion aircraft to bomb and strafe the pontoon bridges. The locks of several dams on tributaries further upstream were opened, sending water flooding down the river at three times its normal rate of flow – to the terror of the Brigaders, many of whom could not swim – and sweeping away much of what it encountered as levels were raised by two to four metres.[22]

Militarily, the river crossing was a huge success for the Republicans. The thinly defended terrain had been thoroughly investigated in the preceding weeks by partisan units, with everything from the position of machine guns to the identity of battalion commanders carefully mapped out. The noise of triumphant soldiers shouting and singing in a dozen different languages must have sounded strange, but the villagers in this rugged patch of Catalonia welcomed the volunteers as their liberators. The British Battalion carried the flags of both Catalonia and Spain, provoking spontaneous demonstrations of joy. 'As we turned a bend in the road we were surprised to find quite a large number of peasants, men and women, lining by the side who cheered us on. One old chap seemed overcome with emotion at the sight of the Catalan flag at the head of the battalion ... Rushing forward towards the standard, he clutched it passionately and smothered it with kisses,' recalled a British Brigader.[23]

Initially, Franco's troops surrendered without offering much of a fight. They were, like many of those now serving in the International Brigades, mainly teenage peasants and young working-class draftees who had little appetite for war. One American International Brigade officer who was captured, along with his Spanish Republican driver, eventually persuaded his scared young captors to surrender instead. 'They stacked their rifles, made a pile of their grenades, returned my pistol and turned themselves over,' he remembered. 'They then seemed happy for the first time – I had explained that prisoners of war were not harmed by our side – they sang songs and explained that all of them, except one, had relatives on our side, whom they were anxious to see.'[24] After the hardship and defeats of the previous six months, it was a glorious moment.

Within two days Republican forces had captured 800 square kilometres, an area the size of New York City, including eleven towns and numerous villages.[25] This covered the large loop in the river Ebro that ran north from Xerta to Fayón and an additional smaller bulge from there almost to Mequinenza, including a small stretch of territory in Aragon.[26]

More importantly, behind them stood the Sierras of Pàndols and Cavalls – an inhospitable territory of impenetrable gullies, rocky ridges and imposing, craggy crests. Beyond that lay the river itself. These were two magnificent natural defensive lines. Gandesa remained in Franco's hands, but it was half surrounded and the roads from there to the Ebro had been cut. Franco's attempts to take Valencia were halted instantly, as troops were directed to the new front. The Republic had not enjoyed such success since its advance on Zaragoza.[27]

The price paid was, so far, relatively small. 'Practically no resistance,' noted Alvah Bessie, as the Lincoln Battalion advanced on the first day. 'That, I should say, will come later when the fascists have gathered their material for a counter-attack.'[28] The Republic was fighting back. It was, as one historian put it, 'the last throw of the dice'.[29]

48

Resist, Fortify and Be Vigilant: La Cova Hospital, La Bisbal de Falset, July–September 1938

Nan Green had already seen some of the worst hospitals in Republican Spain, where rats crept into men's beds to nibble at the gangrenous limbs of amputees, and surgical refuse was simply thrown out of windows. She knew, however, that her job was to run such places, providing cures and care for wounded International Brigaders and those they fought alongside. This was why she had been tasked with helping to set up a hospital for the 35th Division in the most unlikely of places – a large, open cave that lay under a massive overlying lip of exposed rock amongst the almond trees, vines and pine scrub of the Priorat region, just across the river Ebro from the battlefield.[1] It was here that those who survived ghastly, bone-shattering trips from the front-line dressing stations in ambulances or on mules could finally be operated on.

The Cova de Santa Llúcia – as the cave was known to locals – was a hundred-foot wide space, open at the front, which curved inwards under the massive rock ledge. It was a place of miracles and refuge for the villagers who lived in houses perched above other rounded outcrops in the nearby village of La Bisbal de Falset. The broad front of the cave looked out over neat rows of trees on the terraced fields below, one of which now housed the large marquee tent that acted as the triage centre. Above the thick layer of rock lay another wooded field, making the cave invisible from the air. The cave itself provided a deep, hidden home for an operating theatre and 120 beds.[2] These were laid out in a higgledy-piggledy fashion, reflecting the uneven floors and walls, and causing the volunteer nurses to constantly bash into them in the gloomy interior.[3] This is where the men were carried in on stretchers after they had been divided into one of the three categories that British nurse Patience Darton described as 'serious', 'medium' and 'wait, it can go back'.[4]

By the time thirty-three-year-old nurse-administrator Nan Green arrived at La Cova Hospital, on or around 24 July 1938 – along with many of the other volunteer nurses and doctors[5] – she had already been in Spain for a year. Her relationship with the war had begun earlier than that, though, when her husband George, a jobbing cellist, guitarist and banjo player in London clubs and cinemas, had announced that he was going to Spain. It had not been a long talk. Although her own father was a chartered accountant and paid-up capitalist, Nan and George had been swept up together in a genuine, joyous and naive enthusiasm for equality, social change and the Soviet Union.[6] Such was their conviction that their poet son Martin Green wrote, looking back on his childhood: 'An infant revolutionary wheeled in a pram/ Speakers' Corner meant more to me/ Than did the statue of Peter Pan.' There was little questioning about the figureheads of global communism. 'Lenin and Stalin were nursery gods,' said Martin.[7] For his parents, the dilemma posed by the Spanish war was simple: 'The world was at the crossroads, democracy and peace or fascism and war.'[8]

The news that George was going to Spain had come during a family shopping outing in London, where Nan helped run a bookstall.[9] 'I've got to go to Spain,' George said suddenly. Her reply, she recalled later, was a straightforward 'yes'. When he asked if she could 'keep the home fires burning', her answer was exactly the same, even though they had two young children aged four and five.[10] The Greens were not conventional. She worked, they both looked after the children, and his musician father provided a useful and enlightened extra pair of hands. A Methodist nursery school provided happy day care. Sexual fidelity was not a required part of their relationship. Nan only once felt jealousy, an emotion 'so humiliating that I trod it down after a short struggle'.[11] George always told her about his sexual liaisons, including those on the horizon. Nan's response was often to invite the woman to tea. That put paid to any long-term threat to the relationship.

The blue-eyed and blond-haired George was, in the words of the poet Stephen Spender, 'fat, frank, bespectacled and intelligent', while his wife, another observer noted, was 'a brisk, efficient, dedicated no-nonsense woman of beauty and intellect'.[12] In the year and a half before she arrived at La Cova, they saw each other just five times.[13] Of greater importance to both of them was their shared belief in the communist cause – a belief that, later in life, would require Nan to 'unlearn' her personal 'blind spots' about both Stalin and the Soviet Union. When a brother-in-law chided George for abandoning his family, it was Nan who wrote back. 'Listen,' she said. 'George and I are thinking of more than our own children, we are thinking of the children of Europe, in danger of being killed in the coming war if we don't stop the Fascists in Spain.'[14]

George had driven to Spain in February 1937, delivering a truck loaded with supplies to British Medical Aid, which had become part of the International Brigades' medical services, initially attached to XIV Brigade, in January 1937.[15] As an ambulance man and all-round hospital assistant, he ferried the dying away from Valsaín, worked as an impromptu anaesthetist, risked the strafing runs at Brunete and, after burning himself on some frozen petrol, was sent to recover at the 'English hospital' in a twelfth-century monastery at Huete, 120 kilometres east of Madrid.[16] There, thanks to his quiet conviction, charm and soothing cello-playing, he soon became a political commissar. Nan heard little from him. What she did find out, in his letters, was either censored or came with gruesome descriptions of injured soldiers having gangrenous limbs chopped off. When George's friend and fellow ambulance man, the aristocratic artist Wogan Philipps, was invalided back to Britain, the latter suggested that she go to Spain as well as an hospital administrator. Philipps even offered to pay for her children to go to boarding school. She paced up and down all night. 'Would the separation (however temporary) from both parents make them unhappy?' she recalled asking herself. 'Was I rationalising a desire to escape from the heavy responsibility I was burdened with?'[17]

By morning, Nan's mind was set. 'If George has gone, he's gone because our children are no more important than the other children in Europe and we're trying to stop the war,' she said.[18] By September 1937, her children were at the Summerhill progressive boarding school (chosen, in part, because the headmaster supported the Spanish Republic) and Nan was in an open-topped truck on her way to Huete, where she was amazed to find her husband. They had not met for eight months; he was initially accused of 'monopolising this new woman', until people discovered they were married.[19] George had already decided that he wanted to fight and left to join the British Battalion, where he became a sergeant[20] and was placed in charge of a group of rebellious young Catalan anarchists. He also joined the so-called 'activist' movement, by which 'model' soldiers aimed to serve and educate by example.[21]

Nan was strict, kind, efficient and dedicated to her work.[22] There were many obstacles, apart from the dearth of supplies, horrific nature of the injuries and pressure of the job. She found herself dealing with anti-communist grumbling amongst the international nurses at one hospital and then, at another, was accused of Trotskyism and robbery by a paranoid, sexually jealous and morphine-addicted German doctor. The latter allegation came after a brief and much-regretted affair with a British patient, William Day, who later deserted. Her lover became a problem for all who met him. The affair a typical release of passion within the adrenaline-fuelled world of the war and the Brigades. Nan described being in an 'over-charged atmosphere [that] had exploded … like a rocket' and blamed the relationship on a form of 'mountain sickness' which put them all into 'a permanent state of mild excitement'.[23]

The British Communist Party was as prone to witch-hunts as any other and Nan was dubbed a '[sexually promiscuous] adventuress' in one secret report home.[24] The Brigades' medical services, which had a much lower proportion of communists, seemed to arouse special suspicions amongst hard-line party loyalists. Even André Marty was informed about Nan Green, further fuelling his paranoid misogyny. ('You have come to this country to work, to obey orders and not to whore about,' he had already warned twenty-two-year-old French-Spanish volunteer nurse Rosa Cremón, though only after asking her to sit on his knee.[25]) Sent to a filthy hospital at Uclés, the normally stoical and self-disciplined Nan was eventually found weeping uncontrollably, in part because she had not heard from George for six weeks. These were the chaotic days and aftermath of the retreats in Aragon, during which so many volunteers died, but she eventually received a letter from him. He now requested fidelity. 'I know we don't give or extract promises, and all that, and I know that it was precisely when you were in your front line that I betrayed you [referring to the one infidelity that had hurt her], but whilst I am here, would you like to be faithful to me? Please love me.'[26]

Nan was appointed secretary to Len Crome – the Latvian-born, Edinburgh-based doctor who had served under General Walter and was now head of medical services in the 35th Division (which included George's British Battalion).[27] The cave hospital at La Bisbal de Falset was just one of several under his command.

George, by now serving in an anti-tank unit, had crossed the Ebro with the rest of XV Brigade early on 24 July. The advance was so swift that Nan crossed the next day, since the 35th Division was setting up an advanced hospital at a farmhouse on that side of the river. Her job there included using watercolours to produce charts classifying the number and types of injuries treated at each dressing station on the front line, which were then used to work out supply needs. She knew, of course, that she ran the risk of seeing her own husband's name on the lists that she scoured every day. Instead, she received a letter from him dated 6 August 1938, boasting about the success but warning of the heavy toll on his company, which had been named after Labour Party leader Clement Attlee – whose party had finally shed its support for non-intervention the previous October.[28] 'What do you think of the Army of the Ebro eh? Losses very heavy. Major Attlee Column crossed the river with 105 men and we've only got 32 left. Everything missed me up to date. Have they bombed you yet? I believe you're this side of the river … Crossing the river itself was a beautiful operation.'[29]

George Green's letter summed up the best of the events of the previous two weeks, while glossing over the rest. The Ebro river crossing had been successful and the advance over the first seventy-two hours was spectacular but then, as expected, Franco had reacted. As he threw in reinforcements and Republican troops continued to cross the river, the battle became more heated and the lines stagnated.[30] Soon tens of thousands of men were fighting across a thirty-kilometre front in the Terra Alta, a land of 'rocky hills, deep ravines, bare cliffs, villages of farm labourers and cereal crops, vineyards, almonds, olives, Aleppo pines and fruit trees, which that summer registered temperatures of almost sixty degrees Celsius in the sun', according to novelist Javier Cercas.[31]

The advance of the 35th Division had halted just a few hundred metres away from Gandesa, the biggest town in the *comarca*.[32] The speed of the initial attack was not quite sufficient to overcome the well-designed defences before Franco filled up the town and the heights to the south of it with reinforcements.[33] That left the Brigaders fighting over the lower slopes and first bumps of the sierra.[34]

The British Battalion tried to take a small but crucial hilltop called 'the Pimple' (formally known as Puig de L'Àliga, or Hill 481[35]) overlooking Gandesa from the east. The German-speaking battalions of XI Brigade, which also tried to take this and neighbouring hilltops, would rename it 'Death Hill'.[36] Once more, men charged up steep slopes only to be mown down by machine-gun fire. At night, they watched the serpentine patterns of truck headlights moving towards them as enemy reinforcements arrived. A dip between the British and Lincoln positions (the Barranc d'En Pou[37]) became known as the 'Valley of Death' and, this being high summer, soon stank of rotting corpses.[38] Jack Jones, a young British Labour Party councillor and union activist,[39] remembered running up the hill time and time again until, on one charge, he felt his right arm go numb and saw blood gushing from his shoulder. Around him lay the dead and injured – some of whom crawled back later under the cover of darkness. The field hospital at Móra de Ebro, he recalled, was 'like an abattoir; there was blood and the smell of blood everywhere'.[40]

A week later, the British were still attacking the same hill, which was so small that there was room for just a dozen or so men on the summit.[41] The British were decimated. So, too, were the Canadian Mac-Paps, when the task was handed to them. The enemy suffered just as badly, if not worse, but were able to bring in fresh troops continually.[42] Lewis Clive, the British gold medal Olympic rower, was amongst those to die, just weeks short of his twenty-eighth birthday. 'He really was one of the comparatively few people who put into practice what they preach, which is a pretty difficult thing to do at the age of twelve at Eton,' a boyhood friend recalled later in their school magazine. 'He was incorrigibly idealistic, and I have often laid siege to his castle, at lunch in the City, but never with the slightest success.'[43]

The final attempt to take Death Hill came on 3 August. It failed. Similar results, at the cost of high casualties, were obtained up and down the line. From his new position on the staff of XIII Brigade, Szurek saw his fellow Poles and fresh Spanish draftees cut to pieces – with 60 per cent losses rising to 75 per cent amongst the mainly international officers (the Lincolns lost more than 300 of their 700 men).[44] The Catalan teenagers, however, proved their worth. 'We knew that the recruits would be able to advance, but not that they would attack day after day, resist the accurate fire of mortars – the more devastating weapon for morale – without panic or any weakening of their morale,' noted the Palafox commissar, Eugeniusz Szyr. 'We had not imagined that they would know how to respond to the cross-fire of machine guns without retreating, finding cover from the rocks, trees and terrain; that they would dig trenches with their bare hands; that the wounded would argue about being evacuated,' he continued, '... that the machine guns would pass from one set of hands to another ... though there were sometimes mistakes [and] unnecessary losses caused by exaggerated heroism.'[45] The idea that, in addition to front-line fighting, the International Brigades could serve to train up an army, or part of one, had finally come to fruition.

By the time George Green wrote to Nan on 6 August, employing the forced bravado of an *activista* soldier, attack had become defence. That day, the British Battalion was pulled back after thirteen days fighting, with just 150 men left out of 558.[46] The rest of the 35th Division joined them the following day.[47] As an anti-tank man, in a special unit, Green had so far been spared what one comrade called 'the worst any man can face in war – to be called upon time after time to go "over the top" under intense and deadly fire'.[48]

As the Republican army turned to defence, the slogan repeated continuously by the commissars was: 'Resist, Fortify and Be Vigilant'.[49] There were some similarities to Jarama, for they were now defending a line of hills against the approaching Francoist troops. The similarities, however, ended there. The destructive power of Franco's forces had multiplied several times since then. The capacity for resistance had increased almost as much and the volunteers knew exactly how to dig fire holes that could resist everything but a direct strike. They also defended in depth, so that any position won by the Francoists was immediately followed by a (normally higher) one, where the battle would have to start again and, usually, produced a counter-attack that attempted to retake it.[50] 'Hill lost, hill retaken,' became the slogan.[51]

Hemingway, quoting Clausewitz, was convinced that this was all worthwhile, since defence was also a way to win. 'Yes, this negative intention, which constitutes the principle of the pure defence, is also the natural means of overcoming the enemy by the duration of the combat, that is, of wearing him out,' he wrote on 11 August. He also noted that the Spanish war was now two years old and that the Japanese had attacked China a full year before. 'War is due in Europe by next summer at the latest. It nearly came on 21 May. It is possible that it will come now, in August. Or it may be delayed until next summer. But it is coming.'[52] It was worth, in other words, trying to hold on until then.

The psychological strain of endless hours of bombardment, however, was tremendous. It was as if all the worst experiences suffered by the volunteers over the previous twenty months had been kaleidoscoped together on this front. Intense barrages of shrapnel bombs and mortars kicked up a fog of dust, laced with spinning shreds of steel, while the ground shook and the continual blasts left many concussed. Water, again, was scarce. Uniforms turned to rags. Boots were shredded.[53] Typhus and dysentery added to the losses.[54] The injured lay crying out in no-man's-land and often could not be recovered. There were too few ambulances to ferry away the injured, so the task was often carried out by mule, with stretchers strapped to each flank.[55] Those who survived this stage would be sent to an old railway tunnel while they waited to cross the river to the cave hospital at La Bisbal de Falset.

The Catalan teenagers fought valiantly, but some were ill-prepared for the relentless psychological onslaught. The 'vigilance' called for by the commissars was both against the enemy and against deserters crossing towards their lines. Few units could stand more than ten days at the front without morale hitting rock bottom. When Alvah Bessie and the Lincolns marched back through Corbera d'Ebre to rest for a few days after the initial attack, they found very little left of the town. It was silent, bombed out and reeked of death.[56] One international volunteer admitted that this was the first time they began to come to terms with the idea that 'we could lose the war ... [with] the complete extermination of the International Brigades'.[57]

49

Dreams of Home: Sierra de Pàndols: early August 1938

For Nan Green these were days of frantic activity, as she sorted through the reports coming back from dressing stations established in roadside ditches.[1] Like the men, she was filthy and smelly, wearing a cut-down pair of overalls and, in her words, a 'too-short shirt'. 'How dirty I am!' she wrote to her sister Mem. 'My hair needs cutting – it has gone into tight dust curls like a Woolworths doll – the bandages around my infected feet are black – my one sandal goes flap-flap when I walk – everybody is dirty.'[2] She painted her charts, establishing an injury classification system that so impressed one of the New Zealand surgeons in the division, Douglas Jolly,[3] that he would copy it for the Allied forces in Africa and Italy in the Second World War. She made endless cups of tea – that great British cure-all – and sometimes gave direct blood transfusions of her own blood. 'Many people don't know how lovely it is to lie down beside the man whose face has gone ghastly white and your blood goes into him and you see the colour come back into his face and you begin to see him breathe,' Nan recalled later.[4] She remained awed by the 'indescribable feeling of comradeship',[5] and, after moving to a field station on the far bank of the Ebro, was able to visit George and the British Battalion. She found 'a raggle-taggle bunch of weary men, scattered over a hillside. George was there unharmed. We spent two evenings and one whole night on a louse-infected sofa.'[6]

News finally reached the volunteers that those with XV Brigade who had been there since June 1937 (before Brunete) could apply for leave. This had become a contentious issue, since the rules allowing thirteen days leave for every six months at the front were clearly not being observed.[7] Dreams of returning home, however, were cruelly dashed. Leave would only last six days and be for thirty men at a time. There was also an attempt to protect prominent political figures and four British volunteers who were due to stand at town hall elections in the UK in November were ordered home. Of the four, Lewis Clive, a Labour councillor in South Kensington, had just died; another of the candidates would be killed by friendly fire, and only Jack Jones and one other made it back to Britain.[8] On 15 August, just nine days after they had been pulled out of the front line, XV Brigade was sent back to the Sierra de Pàndols, to a position beside the French-led battalions of the 45th Division.[9] These had moved across the river to join the main attack force nineteen days earlier and suffered badly on a peak known as Hill 626.[10] Once more, briefly, an International Brigades line was formed in the heart of the battle, even if most of its soldiers were Spanish.

Franco had launched another major counter-attack and XV Brigade was to defend an infamous pile of bare rock known as Hill 666.[11] The volunteers' experiences of the worst of warfare now reached Dantean dimensions. They scrambled up mule paths on the steep, rocky Sierra de Pàndols to find the patchy covering of scrub oak, hawthorn and pine[12] turned into 'a blackened, war-torn and destroyed land ... burnt to a crisp'.[13] It was littered with the stinking bodies of dead men and animals, since there was no soil in which to bury them. 'God never made a more desolate stretch of territory, and man never contributed more to its further desolation,' Alvah Bessie observed.[14] Since the volunteers could not dig into the rock, they piled shale in front of them to form rudimentary parapets.[15] The Spaniards they were replacing left silently and, according to Harry Fisher, 'seemed to be in a state of shock'.[16]

By now, the British anti-tank unit had handed over its last gun to the Thälmanns and George Green was sent to join the brigade's machine-gun company. This was traditionally one of the most dangerous deployments, since machine guns were lethal to the enemy and, hence, more frequently targeted. He would have been amongst those called to a meeting of XV Brigade officers, commissars and 'activists', to insist on almost suicidal tactics. They were to counter-attack continually, the brigade commander said, even if cut off. Hill 666 simply had to be held. 'The whole purpose of the Ebro offensive depended on us holding,' recorded one American. The men wore camphor bags around their necks or urinated into their neckerchiefs to ward off the smell of the dead, both friend and foe.[17] The natural aromas of the region, of thyme and rosemary, had long been drowned out.[18]

On one occasion, Fisher and his companion Marty Sullivan were sent to get more transmission equipment and decided to go through a 'safe' valley where a battalion appeared to be resting. 'Soldiers were lying all over the ground. We realised they were not "at rest"; there was an awful stench, and insects were buzzing around the men. They were all dead, as many as 200, very possibly soldiers from both sides.'[19] Cuban volunteer Gerardo Sampedro encountered a similar scene, with a few remaining injured men asking for water, or for weapons to kill themselves with. On that occasion there was time for the men with him to replace tattered boots and uniforms with those, from the dead, that were in a better condition.[20]

For those who had lived through Teruel and the retreat from Aragon, the firepower lined up against them was both tragically familiar and terrifying in intensity. German and Italian aircraft, once more, roamed freely, bombing at leisure and in quantities of over 5,000kg per day.[21] Artillery shells poured down for hours at a time, usually followed by an enemy attack and a brief exchange of grenades.[22] A thin mist of dust – a mixture of cordite and blasted rock – hung almost permanently in the air. At night the men emerged from their holes, crawled towards the enemy positions to hurl grenades or tried to recapture a high point, then frantically dug to improve hideaways or rebuild the ones obliterated by the previous day's bombardment.

At Hill 666 the Lincolns ended up singing 'The Internationale' simply as a way of recovering their sanity after a day of bombardment.[23] They nevertheless kept hold of the hill, handing it over to the British on 24 August.[24] Further along the chain of spiky sierras, crests were lost and retaken as the story was repeated for all the volunteer units in the front line.[25] Franco's own artillery commander was frustrated by their resistance. 'The enemy goes back to refuges on the other side of the crests, which are hard to target … and then runs back as soon as the bombardment is over,' he complained.[26]

Sometime late in August, George Green joined the list of wounded. He had been caught by shrapnel, had a few stitches and then ordered to stay in hospital while suppurating sores on his legs were cured. 'The principal thing I feel is relief that he is away back from that hell for a while and I don't suffer the tension of wondering if he is alive which, with every boom I hear, comes,' Nan wrote to her sister.[27] She wasn't the only one who had been worrying about a husband at the front. Another English nurse at the cave hospital, Patience Darton, had married a German communist that February. ('What will you do with a German husband who has no passport?' someone had asked her. 'There will always be work for nurses and machine-gunners. Have you thought of that?' she replied.[28]) Patience's husband died in the first week of the battle.

Although they were in different hospitals, George could now pass notes to his wife. He wrote to his mother with undimmed enthusiasm, explaining that he 'came to war because we love peace and hate war ... [and] to hold the line here and now means that we can prevent this battle being fought again later on Hampstead Heath or the hills of Derbyshire'.[29] He admitted, however, that he would rather be back home. 'My idea of a good time is not being shot at, but is connected with growing lettuce and spring onions, and drinking beer in a country pub, and playing quarters with friends and having my children about,' he told her.[30]

If the line held at Sierra de Pàndols and elsewhere it was, in part, because the rugged sierras of Tarragona's highlands were so difficult to attack.[31] Further north across the Gandesa road, however, in the hills that led up towards the twisting Fatarella road, the countryside softened slightly and the attackers enjoyed more success. Part of XIII Brigade found itself retreating slowly here and then acting as a police force to prevent others from fleeing after a breakthrough captured a small amount of Republican territory at great expense on 19 August.[32] Enemy progress remained slow, despite the imbalance in firepower. Franco had been lured into a stubborn fight where he was forced to hammer away at relatively small positions, pouring vast amounts of explosives on to them and sacrificing troops for meagre results. Once more, this looked like mulish pride – and poor military leadership – to his allies. 'Write down in your journal that today, 29 August, I predict the defeat of Franco. This man either does not understand how to wage war, or does not want to,' Mussolini raged at foreign minister Ciano, who dutifully wrote the words down in his diary. 'The Reds are true fighters, Franco is not!'[33]

Franco, however, insisted that – however long it took, and regardless of his own losses – this was an opportunity to pummel the enemy. 'They don't understand,' he said. 'I have the best of the Republican army shut into an area [along a front] of thirty-five kilometres.'[34]

A second push on 3 September proved slightly more effective, as Franco's troops tried to move out of Gandesa towards Corbera d'Ebre and, beyond that, to the crossroads at La Venta de Camposines that would allow them to press on towards the river. It was a ten-kilometre stretch of road that his men had captured in barely more than two days during the Aragon retreats, but which the next three weeks of fighting yielded only part of.[35] There was no sudden panic, but gaps gradually opened up as different hilltops covered with slabs of limestone rock and charred vegetation were fought over. It was now that the Italians of XII Brigade, with two-thirds of their troops Spanish, finally crossed the river.[36] They were taken straight to poorly fortified positions on the far side of the Gandesa road and suffered unreasonably on the first two days, with almost a third of one of their battalions out of action.[37] They fought on bravely, however, only slowly ceding territory. Often a single small rocky outpost would be lost and taken two or three times in a day.

Another major attempt to break through the defences began with an intense bombardment, including six air attacks, on 13 September. 'It was the worst we had ever seen,' Italian commissar Blas Bonzano wrote. They were still able to hold some positions, after one company fought almost to the death before the survivors could be rescued with a counter-attack.[38] By now Franco was watching the battles with his own eyes.[39] The description he gives of one – in which 'one of our most brilliant units had the mission to break the front' – fits that of the assault on the Italian positions (or near them) on 13 September, but could just as easily have described similar attacks repulsed later by the Polish or German brigades, or other Republican units. 'More than 2,000 artillery pieces were lined up for that battle on a two kilometres front,' observed Franco:

> from our observatories we would see the efficiency of our artillery
> and mortar fire, evicting the enemy from its positions and forcing
> it to retire to the other side of the hill; our aviation amplified the
> destructive and morale-breaking impact; then the moment to attack
> arrived; brilliantly, our forces prepared to cross the great gully that
> separated them from the enemy positions, but when they were
> halfway up the slope, the fire of a number of machine-guns hidden
> behind the rocks in the gully ... stopped them without our batteries
> being able to locate and destroy them ... which annulled the effect

of our intense preparation [by bombardment] and brought about the failure of that day's operation.[40]

By now, the Commune de Paris was back in action with the rest of XIV Brigade. After its disastrous first day during the Ebro campaign, it had been rebuilt almost from scratch and was now led by Théophile Rol, one of the few surviving veterans from the Madrid battles. As a stretcher-bearer in late 1936, the former metalworker and amateur rugby player had thrown himself down a hill to try to save Hans Beimler when the legendary German communist had been shot in University City. Since then he had progressed through the ranks and, having suffered frostbite at Guadalajara and shrapnel wounds at Caspe, was now a captain noted for his risk-taking.[41] Rol did not survive the battle. It was assumed that, when he disappeared on 8 September, he had been wounded, caught and then executed.[42] (His close friend Henri Tanguy, the brigade commissar, later joined their names and used 'Rol Tanguy' for his nom de guerre as a Paris Resistance leader during the Second World War.[43])

For the English-speaking XV Brigade, meanwhile, the new counter-attack also meant a sudden return to the craggy sierra peaks on 6 September, this time in the neighbouring Sierra de Cavalls, where the British eventually established themselves on yet another three-digit hilltop, Hill 356.[44] It is impossible to track all the fights over so many small piles of limestone rock, but George Green and the British anti-tank men – now in the Brigade machine-gun company led by an American – rushed and captured several outcrops.[45] Amongst those killed trying to dislodge them was a fascist Irish volunteer called Daith Higgins, from the 18th Bandera of Franco's Spanish Legion, which was almost destroyed. At least one of Franco's officers wondered whether the twenty-one square kilometres gained over the first four days of this counter-attack had been worth the lives of so many men.[46]

The volunteers were also prepared to kill deserters from their own side, and when men from one of Líster's brigade tried to raise a white flag and cross over to the enemy, Afro-American volunteer Tom Page shot two of them on the spot.[47] Harry Fisher, meanwhile, recalled seeing an infamously sadistic American called Alex Pratt holding a gun to the head of a weeping Spanish recruit who was begging not be sent back into the front line. 'Pratt was once again using the bullying tactics of our enemy, the tactics we had come to Spain to put an end to,' he wrote.[48]

This counter-attack also ran out of steam and overnight on 11 September, XV Brigade was pulled back for a rest and its positions occupied by the Slavs of XIII Brigade, joining the German, French and Italian brigades on the front line. The Italians had already lost half their brigade of 2,764 soldiers but, in the words of one commissar, 'never lost their spirit of resistance'.[49] The International Brigades had performed a valuable role by defending the mountaintops, but they were by no means the only protagonists of the battle. 'It must be remembered too in terms of a proper perspective, that simultaneously with the movements of defence and attack of the limited units of the International Brigades, whole divisions of Spanish troops were suffering identical circumstances,' wrote Arthur Landis, an American Mac-Pap veteran.

The losses on both sides were, by now, terrible. The pool of potential reserves, however, was as imbalanced as the stock of munitions and armament. While Franco could drain the population of much of Spain and import fresh troops from Morocco or Italy – however unwillingly – the Republicans' Ebro army basically now relied on Catalonia. To the dismay of the volunteers, the reserves now reaching the International Brigades were often men in their thirties who had avoided being called up, or been driven back to the front after deserting.[50] It was by no means clear that they would fight as well as the teenage recruits who had crossed the river at the start of the battle.

On 16 September, two days after the bruised but unbeaten XV Brigade descended from the Sierra de Cavalls for a rest, hopes that a wider European war would force Western democracies to come to the Republic's aid were dashed. British prime minister Neville Chamberlain flew to Berchtesgaden to negotiate the handover of the Sudetenland to Hitler. Tension had been increasing over the previous weeks and rumours had reached the Brigaders that France was cancelling leave for its troops and reinforcing the Maginot Line.[51]

While the Brigaders were fighting fascists in Spain, Chamberlain had written to the British king, George VI, explaining that Britain and Nazi Germany were 'the two pillars of European peace and buttresses against communism'.[52] Ever the activists, the American volunteers telegrammed

President Roosevelt, reportedly warning that it was now clear that 'the bombs that were falling on Madrid would surely fall on London, Paris and New York' and demanding assistance for the Republic. 'Will the French and English cabinets fall as a result of popular indignation?' Alvah Bessie wrote in his diary.[53] The developments were a reminder, however, that the Brigaders saw themselves as fighting two battles: one, to defeat Franco and save the Republic; the other, to persuade the world that fascism would only be defeated by arms.

Hemingway had been less hopeful about Chamberlain in a piece he published in *Ken* magazine in July, after Britain signed a naval agreement with Italy.[54] 'He is not a fool, and when he makes a deal with Italy, it is a deal for the immediate best interests of the shareholding class he represents,' he wrote in July 1938. 'One thing you have learnt in the last 15 months is that when a politician cries you are bitched … They cry for history. But they act for expediency and for profit and loss; and above all they act to hold their jobs … They know how right they were, how good their hearts were, and for a minute they see themselves as statesmen and as historic figures; not as the pitiful, conniving, frightened people that they really are.'[55]

While XV Brigade rested, their friends from the foreign press came to visit.[56] Fisher was full of admiration. 'A car stopped at the foot of the hill. Bullets flew all around it. Two men got out and … climbed frantically and laboriously until they reached our resting place; they were exhausted. The two men were Herbert Matthews and Ernest Hemingway.'[57] A handful of volunteers were now sent on leave. They included Fisher, who was one of just seven Americans. He was told that he was going 'to Paris for a week or so, and that I had to be ready to head out in two hours'. He could not work out how, given that the frontier was closed, he was expected to get back. He looked quizzically at the Lincoln commander, Milton Wolff. 'He smiled at me and winked, and I knew that I was on my way home.' There was only a brief moment to say goodbye to his companion in fatigues, Marty Sullivan. 'I'll miss you, but I'm glad you're going,' he said before Fisher walked off, biting back tears.[58]

Not everyone, of course, waited for permission to leave. By now, fifteen American and Canadian volunteers in the Mackenzie–Papineau were, in Bessie's words, deemed to have 'fucked off' permanently.[59] At least two Lincoln and two Thälmann volunteers were also arrested for desertion.[60] Commissars in units where men deserted were now themselves threatened with immediate punishment, while the idealistic Germans had, a few weeks earlier, recommended 'singing revolutionary songs' as a means of prevention.[61]

Rumours also spread that the International Brigades were going to be pulled out permanently, that their task was done and the government wanted to do something that might force Hitler and Mussolini to remove their men too. Away from the action, many now dreamed simply of going home. In the case of one British volunteer this dream was of 'tea in my mother's house in suburbia, of pints of mild and bitter in oak-beamed pubs, and I could not help wishing I had never come'.[62]

50

The Last Fight: Barcelona, 16 September 1938

For weeks now, Mussolini's aircraft had been targeting Barcelona, their random bombing-runs over civilian parts of the city designed to cower the population and damage morale.[1] 'Terror is the most effective weapon of the air force,' one of his generals had reported, as raids on the city killed 3,000 people. 'It should be launched against enemy populations, destroying cities, their centres and all means of life, submitting it to a nightmare that forces surrender.'[2] Mussolini's foreign minister, Ciano, was shocked by one bombing report that urged Il Duce to greater efforts. 'I have never read such a terrifying document,' he said. 'There were only nine S-79 [aircraft] and it lasted just a minute and a half. Buildings reduced to dust, traffic stopped, panic that turned to madness.'[3]

From the windows of the city's Hotel Majestic, India's future prime minister Jawaharlal Nehru had watched the bombs fall on and around Barcelona in June: 'Five nights to the accompaniment of aerial bombardment. Five days and nights, crowded with events, and impressions, the memory of which will endure.'[4] He saw in those falling bombs a link between the fight against fascism and Indian resistance to colonialism. 'There, in the midst of want and destruction and impending disaster, I felt more at peace with myself than anywhere else in Europe. There was a light there, the light of courage and determination and of doing something worthwhile,' he wrote later. The previous month he had visited the British Brigaders. 'Reluctantly I came away from these gallant men of the International Brigade, for something in me wanted to stay on this inhospitable-looking hillside which sheltered so much human courage, so much of what was worthwhile in life,' he said.[5]

On 16 September 1938, Alvah Bessie, now also working as a commissar, was in Barcelona when, in one of their most notorious raids, Italian bombers flew over from their base on the island of Majorca, killing thirty women queueing at a fish market. He also picked up the first solid rumours that the volunteers were going home. It was being said that Marty had been to Moscow, where the Comintern had approved the withdrawal and that those leaving hospital were no longer being sent to the front. When Bessie returned to the Ebro two days later, it was already the main point of discussion. He also noted that the official Republican press, perhaps in preparation for this moment, had been playing down the International Brigades' role in the Ebro operation.

The volunteers, meanwhile, were beginning to feel a 'persisting superstition and fear of being killed "just before" going home', according to Bessie.[6] George Green, however, reacted in the opposite fashion. The men were likely to be called back for a final fight at any moment, so he discharged himself from hospital, and delivered the discharge document himself to the medical headquarters where Nan was working. They spent two hours eagerly talking about how they would soon be back in Britain with their children. 'We were expecting orders to return home,' explained Nan. 'We knew we would have to make our way out separately, so we made a pact that the first one out would not see the children until the other arrived. We wanted the double joy of reunion by sharing it with each other.'[7]

The Brigaders, meanwhile, had no option but to fight on. Franco, by now following events through his binoculars from a viewing point on the Coll de Moro hill west of Gandesa, launched yet another assault on the sierras on 18 September, starting with a day of intense artillery bombardment on a five-kilometre front.[8] The Germans of XI Brigade and the Poles of XIII were sent back into the line, while XV Brigade was left behind, knowing that it, too, would soon be needed. On the second day of the attacks, Franco targeted the hills in the Sierra de La Fatarella being defended by Hans Kahle's French- and Italian-speaking volunteers. This began with one of the longest bombardments of the war and continued with the usual insistence on frontal assault, regardless of the cost in human lives. In this case the lives were, once more, of young Moroccans. One hilltop was taken, then recovered, before Kahle was given an entire Spanish machine-gun battalion to help defend the most important peak in his area, Hill 496. He decided, however, to spread the machine guns out and, later that day, the Moroccans stormed it successfully.[9]

By this stage, Franco's attention was increasingly fixed on Czechoslovakia and the crisis being provoked by Hitler, which put his own army under serious threat. France, after all, had a treaty that obliged it to defend Czechoslovakia. If France and Germany suddenly went to war, then Republican Spain would be an ally of the former and troops or arms could be marched into Catalonia to defend it (though Mussolini had also pledged to send one or two extra divisions if that happened[10]). All depended on how French premier Daladier reacted. A declaration of war would undoubtedly have been welcomed by the French volunteers, who spent that day recomposing the line broken the previous evening in the Sierra de La Fatarella.[11]

It was clear, too, that if Hitler was allowed to proceed, and his friends in other countries were emboldened, the Jews of continental Europe would face further persecution.

The Naftali Botwin company of the Palafox Battalion prided itself on providing living proof that, as fascism and anti-Semitism grew, some Jews were already fighting back. Together with the rest of XIII International Brigade, they were now forcing Franco's troops to pay a high price as they struggled to advance up the road from Corbera d'Ebre (which had fallen on 4 September).[12] Like the rest of the volunteers, they suspected withdrawal was coming but, since they were already in the front line, they had more urgent tasks to think about. The Botwin company was placed in one of the most exposed positions on the front, shattered daily by artillery and mortar fire.

Emmanuel Mink, the Polish Olympiad sportsman who had been a founding member of the International Brigades, arrived to take over command. He brought with him a large group of recent recruits, mostly made up of Jews who had arrived from Paris in January. By this time, much of the original company was already dead. 'It was a suicidal position, in open country and surrounded by fascists,' he recalled.[13] They received fire from three sides and, each night, emerged from their holes to rebuild their trenches. Mink himself was immediately wounded by shrapnel and taken to hospital. On 21 September,[14] the position was finally overrun and they fought at bayonet-point against the Moroccan troops of the 5th Tabor of Regulares. Finding themselves surrounded, the Botwin survivors raised their hands. When the foreigners in the

Botwin company were ordered to step out, their nineteen-year-old Spanish anarchist commissar, Diego Mula, stopped one of them – Lieutenant Mischa Skorupinski – from joining the rest. Both men look on helplessly as the others were shot.[15] Khamhi Alcalaj, the Yugoslav who had temporarily replaced Mink, died. Skorupinski somehow managed to escape, while Mula was also eventually shot. Only three men appear to have escaped.

Just as the battle reached a fresh pitch and the Botwin company was annihilated, the volunteers' dreams of being sent home became reality. On 21 September, Negrín announced, in a speech to the League of Nations in Geneva, the immediate repatriation of all foreign volunteers. It was a move designed to shame the appeasers and make them either insist that Hitler and Mussolini's fascist powers leave Spain, or start helping the Republic and slowing the spread of Axis power. 'In her desire to contribute to the pacification and "restraint" which we all desire,' the Spanish prime minister declared,

and in order to eliminate all pretexts and possible doubts about the genuinely national character of the cause for which the Republican army is fighting, the Spanish Government has decided to withdraw immediately and completely all non-Spanish combatants ... It is with a feeling of great sorrow that we regard the idea of separating ourselves from this group of brave and self-sacrificing men who, led by a generous impulse that will never be forgotten by the people of Spain, came to our aid in the most critical moments in our history. I want to proclaim here the heroism and the high moral value of their sacrifice they voluntarily undertook not to safeguard petty selfish interest, but solely to serve and defend the purest ideals of justice and liberty ... I feel safe in saying without equivocation that their own countries will feel proud of them and this is the highest moral compensation they can receive.[16]

In truth, there were not that many international volunteers left, or not in fighting condition, especially after the previous few weeks of slaughter. In all, scattered around the country, they accounted for some 7,000 fit fighters – just enough for a small division. As a result, Negrín argued privately, their 'military efficiency has fallen off'. Rojo had already informed him that losing the volunteers would not hamper the Republic's now well-organised, if heavily outgunned, army.[17] This was not ingratitude, nor lack of respect. Negrín's real objective was to jolt the appeasers into insisting that Franco also withdraw his foreign units.[18] Without Mussolini and Hitler's aircraft, artillery and motorised divisions, after all, his army would lose the main parts of its superiority. The Ebro battle had already shown that, in other respects, the Republic had finally caught up in terms of military discipline, training and strategy.[19]

News of the immediate repatriation reached front-line officers the following day, but – at least in the case of XV Brigade – they decided not to pass it on to the men. All mail and newspapers were stopped.[20] Official orders to withdraw had not been received. They were about to return to the battle and needed every man to be on their best fighting form. 'We were simply going back into action again,' said one volunteer. 'We had no inkling that we were about to embark on our final fight with the Fascists.'[21] Some, however, did know and, having seen so many comrades fall over the previous two months, wondered whether they would survive. 'It was a cruel test,' one admitted.[22] Model activists such as George Green, however, did not feel much conflict about returning for one last fight. To them, it was a moral duty.

The news did not reach the Polish trenches. The men here were still defending a near impossible position straddling the road from Corbera, where they were constantly shelled, bombarded and sprayed with machine-gun fire. It was an important position and, against considerable odds, they stayed loyal to the slogans of 'resist' and 'build'. 'Here comes our sun!' the Mickiewicz Battalion commander Franek Ksiezarczyk would joke when night fell and the moon came out.[23] His commissar, Mieczyslaw Schleyen, agreed.[24] 'He was right. Life in our lines began at night. By day the sight of just two or three of our men would provoke a downpour of steel. After dark you could stretch, eat, chat to comrades and … above all, repair and build.'[25]

Every day the Mickiewiczs dug another hundred metres of trench, created another machine-gun nest or two and laid out fifty more metres of barbed wire. Szurek recalled watching with Merino and Caubín, the 35th Division's commander and head of operations, as the surviving members of the Mickiewicz Battalion re-emerged, ghost-like, from the dust and smoke after six hours of enemy bombardment.[26] They then immediately repulsed a tank attack. 'Those Poles!' Caubín shouted. 'They could hardly believe that our men were still in position,' Szurek recalled with pride.[27] The battalion's Ukrainian volunteers, meanwhile, prepared for their last major fight by building primitive anti-tank mines made out of bundles of grenades resting on two sticks, which in turn were attached to a string which, when pulled, would make them explode.

The attack that day on the positions held by XI and XIII Brigades began with yet another artillery bombardment which saw them disappear into a cloud of smoke and dust, 'so that it appeared impossible that anyone might survive'.[28] It was followed by attacks with tanks and cavalry and saw a heroic defence in which many of the Mickiewicz battalion's best men died.[29] They were still holding on to many of their positions when the order came to withdraw, since a neighbouring peak had been lost, leaving them exposed. Some initially refused to move, claiming that they could hold out for longer. They did not know that withdrawal meant, in all probability, survival and an end to their participation in the war.

Edwin Rolfe had rushed excitedly to the front with a huge pile of morning newspapers on 22 September. The front-page story was Negrín's speech, and he wanted to share it. He found XV Brigade's headquarters deserted. Everyone had gone back up to the line the night before.[30] The remains of the British, Lincoln, Mac-Pap and Spanish Battalions had moved up to support XIII Brigade overnight,[31] and spent much of the day huddling behind the hill defended by the Poles, listening to the battle rage just 300 metres ahead of them. As the front line rolled slowly back, and the battered Poles were sent into reserve, George Green and the rest of the English-speaking volunteers moved into the front line.

That night, meanwhile, at a field station near the front, Nan Green scoured the list of dead and wounded, and was relieved to see that George's name was not amongst them. The real fighting would begin in the morning, by which time the men of XV Brigade were amongst the few people in the world who did not know they were due to be withdrawn (though the news had seeped through to some). The Polish trenches – carefully built by men whose civilian jobs had often been as miners – had been destroyed the previous day and they spent the night frantically trying to construct new fortifications.[32]

Next morning the shelling was so intense that the volunteers felt their brains reeling from concussion. Bessie was nearby listening to the battle, tortured by the knowledge that men had been dying 'last night and today, at the very last moment of their participation in the Spanish war'.[33] On 23 September, as he waited for the men to be withdrawn, he watched a dogfight, ending with a Republican pilot plunging to the ground. 'In his death, [it was] difficult to avoid seeing the symbol of the end of the International Brigades,' he noted in his diary. 'For never before has there been a spontaneously gathered volunteer army like this one.'[34] He was only too aware of the cruelty of making the men fight for one more day. 'There will be bitterness among those who survive for the loss of those who died after it had been decided by the government to "immediately and completely" evacuate all foreign troops.'[35]

It was not a glorious last fight. According to Bessie, the new Spanish troops who had been press-ganged or brought from punishment camps soon 'raised white flags, fucked off to the rear or deserted to the enemy'.[36] It was, however, symbolically fitting that the final fight had not been against Spaniards, but against Franco's foreign troops. From the very beginning of the war, these had always been far more numerous than the 35,000 volunteers who eventually passed through the ranks of the International Brigades. It was also typical that, when XIII Brigade volunteers from Poland and the other Slavic nations – who now knew they were to be relieved – were told to march back into the second line of defence during the day, they did so without complaint. 'If the fascists attack then you have to fight. That's all there is to it,' remarked one of their commissars, perhaps putting a gloss on what, for some, must have been a wretched decision.[37]

Over the next twenty-four hours all the International Brigades were finally withdrawn from the front, and almost all the volunteers had crossed back over the river Ebro thirty-six hours later. Over two hundred men from the British Battalion had died, been wounded or had disappeared on the previous day. Some battalions had lost half, or more, of their men.[38] That night, two Brigaders woke Nan Green to tell her that George was amongst the missing. 'I pulled the sheets around my suddenly icy-cold shoulders, trying to grasp the thunderbolt. It must not, it could not be true,' she recalled.[39] Nan hoped that, like Green's company commander Walter Gregory, her husband had simply been captured. But Gregory himself had witnessed what, most probably, were the final minutes of her husband's life. He had placed George in a defensive position with his machine-gun crew before they were attacked by five tanks and infantry who captured their trench, forcing them to surrender. 'I kept looking behind me in the hope of seeing George and his crew, but they never came. I doubt if they ever left the trench, since the fascists had made it a policy to shoot machine-gunners on the spot,' he said.[40] Nan spent months looking for him in hospitals, and his death was not confirmed until the following year, by which time she had returned to Britain.

The last five days of fighting had been particularly bloody. For the men who survived them, they felt like tragedy. For those who watched and directed the fighting from the command posts of the Republican army, however, it looked more like a miracle. They saw one of Franco's army corps disintegrate as it tried to fight its way through them. Modesto said they had turned the site into 'a place of honour and glory' for the entire Republican army.[41] A great defensive victory had been won, with the division giving away just 500 metres of land in September, while Franco's Maestrazgo Army Corps lost 10,000 men. 'The fascists needed eight days rest before they could attack again,' Merino said. Manuel Tagüeña, the twenty-five-year-old mathematician who commanded an entire army corps, gave a goodbye party for the fifty unwounded survivors from amongst the 400 internationals he had put into a 'special battalion' belonging to his XV Corps. He lamented the sudden loss of '6,000 first class soldiers' but added that 'we were very happy to see them leave alive, and with honour, from a battle in which they had fought heroically'.[42]

For the volunteers, the final twelve hours had been especially cruel. Of the 106 British Brigaders who went into battle, only 58 returned. Overall losses for the battalion were 204 men out of 377, while the Lincolns lost 247 out of 440.[43] 'Nothing can compare with the end,' wrote one of the International Brigades' first British recruits, Glaswegian Peter Kerrigan, who had been through everything from Lopera to Jarama.[44] Alvah Bessie agreed. 'An inglorious page marks the end of the glorious XVth – a page of retreat, panic, desertion,' he wrote in his diary.[45]

Each nation had its tragic tale of last-minute loss. Szurek and the Poles mourned Josef Kolorz (aka Koletski), a much-loved communist organiser in France, who had been their final recruit. He had arrived a few days previously and was reportedly last seen shouting: 'I'll show them how a communist dies!'[46] Szurek was perplexed by this last-minute sacrifice in the name of a creed he himself would eventually lose faith in. 'Who needed it? And why? I still can't explain it,' he said later. The British had also lost young Ivor Hickman, a Cambridge graduate and mathematical engineering apprentice in Manchester, who had married the 'love of his life', psychology graduate Juliet MacArthur, immediately before leaving for Spain. 'I stand [only] a moderately good chance of going back to England (that's quite honest) but somebody's got to be killed and this death business isn't dealt out fairly or honestly,' he had written home. 'Anyway ... it's important to me because I have so many things to do yet.'[47] Others suffered slower deaths, at the cave hospital, or elsewhere. When he finally died of his injuries on 4 October 1938, Chaskel Honigstein of the Polish Botwin company officially became the International Brigades' final martyr.[48]

The Ebro battle, especially the suicidal thrust against Amposta on the first day, had accounted for 10 per cent of all deaths of French volunteers – even though these had been the first to arrive in Spain in force, twenty-two months earlier.[49] As they left the carnage behind them and stepped onto the pontoon bridges across the Ebro, it was not surprising that the volunteers experienced mixed feelings. Relief, sadness and exhaustion could not prevent them dwelling on whether it had all been worth it. 'People walked deep in thought without uttering a word,' recalled Szurek. 'We survived the war, but we were leaving the front at a difficult moment when the fight was for every metre of land.'[50]

Nan Green might have been expected to see her husband's death as tragic, but she knew he would not have seen it that way. 'He was killed almost in the last hour of the last day. But I've never felt able to be sorry for him because he was doing the right thing, he was doing his thing and it was the right thing, we all feel that,' she recalled. It had been a privilege for them to march 'right straight down the high road of history in the right cause and there hasn't been anything like it since, so flawless and so black and white and so good and so wholesome, and he was doing that and he was sure that we would win, and he was sure that the French were going to send the things over and he was with the battalion and I think that that was his last [thought] – that's how he died, he died flying as it were, you know, like a bird dies.'[51]

51

Farewell to Arms: Northern Catalonia,
24 September 1938–8 February 1939

The Brigaders were gathered in rearguard towns in Catalonia with their units but separated from their Spanish colleagues, who marched back to the front a few weeks later. Relief at surviving the war, and pride at having taken part, were tinged with bitterness over their final fight and a sense that they were abandoning Republican Spain at its most difficult moment. The last day had been 'the most painful of my period in Spain' said Milton Wolff, the Lincoln Battalion commander, after watching many men – especially the latest, unwilling Spanish recruits – disappear down a ravine that had provided an easy escape route from their position.[1] 'Many Brigaders, deep in their hearts, knew that one reason why they had been cast out was that collectively they no longer possessed the strength or enthusiasm of the early days,' observed Andreu Castells, the Catalan veteran of 129 Brigade. 'Their finest were already buried under Spanish soil.'[2]

Some 5,000 men, or one in seven, had died. A similar number were missing, either dead, imprisoned or had deserted. Around 6,000 had already been sent home, many of them injured, and a further 3,160 were in hospital.[3] The chances of returning home unscathed, then, had been somewhere below 50 per cent. Most of the earliest volunteers – those who had fought in the first few days at Jarama in February 1937, at University City or at Boadilla and the other battles to defend the La Coruña highway before and after Christmas 1936 – had almost certainly died.[4] Those who had survived, usually did so because they had been wounded and sent home or spent time in hospitals away from the battlefield. They had been an almost unique phenomenon for the time – an international volunteer army – and had paid a high price for what, to all intents and purposes, was a military defeat. Only time would tell if they had won a moral victory by arguing correctly that the only way to stop fascism was with a gun in your hand. Proof that they were right would come the following year, in Poland and elsewhere.

Henry Buckley, the British *Daily Telegraph* journalist who had followed the entire war from the Republican side, viewed the dissolution of the International Brigades as a Quixotic gesture 'which received little publicity because the world was watching Prague, not the Ebro'.[5] Sure enough, a week later, Chamberlain returned to Britain waving an infamous piece of paper containing his agreement with Hitler. This granted Nazi Germany a large part of Czechoslovakia and would ensure that the rest of the country was either taken over by authoritarian neighbours or, in the Slovakian half of the country, by a pro-Nazi regime. 'Peace for our time,' Chamberlain declared to a cheering crowd outside his Downing Street home.

Alvah Bessie saw the renewed Francoist offensive after the withdrawal of the International Brigaders as an extension of that, pointing out how simple it had been for Hitler to take control of a major arms producer like Czechoslovakia. 'Both he and Mussolini, having received carte blanche and with nothing to worry about in central Europe for the moment, can afford to turn all their attention to liquidating the Spanish war and dividing the spoils,' he wrote in his diary on 5 October 1938.[6]

Half-a-dozen Catalan towns now found themselves playing host to volunteers who no longer had much to do. They were 'restless and bored', according to Bessie, who heard rumours that – with Franco launching his fresh offensive on their old positions near Corbera d'Ebre at the end of September – they might be asked to volunteer again.[7] That rumour soon died. 'Men began thinking of their wives, children, and other dear ones; they pulled out family pictures; they yearned, as is understandable, to return to normal life.'[8] They also yearned for other things. In rest towns like Calella there were more than a dozen weddings of Brigaders to their Spanish girlfriends.[9] One whirlwind romance, between Czech volunteer Bruno Niesner and local girl Nuria Rebull in the beach town of San Feliu de Guíxols, produced a marriage that lasted just three days.[10] The mood of those who had come from the Ebro battle was not improved by the other Brigaders who joined them. They included those who had been working far from the front and others who had been in the Castelldefels jail.[11] Renn found himself in charge of a whole battalion of officers – specialist engineers, artillerymen and others – who suddenly appeared from offices and different parts of the army.[12] He was also disturbed by the former jailbirds, who now mocked their colleagues, got drunk, dropped their trousers in front of the local women and gave the Brigaders a bad reputation in host towns.[13]

Even the normally brisk André Marty admitted that the volunteers were entering a 'delicate and difficult' moment. 'Many of the soldiers are physically exhausted. They are all worried about their futures, some because of partial military call-ups [in their countries, as Europe sensed a wider war approaching] and others in case they have to go home to a fascist country,' he said. The French government had begun to put its people on a war footing and, as a result, had closed the border. That had prevented 300 wounded men from leaving Spain on 27 September, while a further 300 were waiting to go on 4 October.[14] This was a grave matter, since more than 3,000 men were in hospital and some were still dying of their wounds or various diseases, most commonly typhus. At least two dozen died in rearguard hospitals in Vic, Olot and Mataró over the next few weeks.[15]

Propaganda efforts concentrated on the young Polish Jew Honigstein, with a mass funeral procession through the streets of Barcelona headed by a banner in Catalan reading: 'Chaskel Honigstein, defender of Spain's independence, who shall remain forever in the land of free men.'[16] Leaflets carrying a poem by José Herrera Petere rained down on the crowd, praising: 'Your blood/ the last drop added to that torrent which/ from heights all around the world/ ran generously down to Spain.' The unit's own *Botwin* newspaper claimed that 'the internationals will leave with troubled hearts, like a workman who has not been able to finish his task … "What will you do now?" the internationals are asked. Everyone answers the same: "We will look for work and wait for the next opportunity to fight fascism." '[17]

A series of farewell ceremonies started on 17 October, with an exhausted Negrín himself travelling to a small country resort at Les Masies, near the monastery at Poblet. Thousands of men gathered in an arcaded courtyard, while Capa and Matthews looked on.[18] Alvah Bessie jotted down notes on the speakers: Negrín was a 'fine intellect, forceful speaker, very tired'; Modesto was 'visibly overcome with emotion – strong, male guy'; while Marty was 'the demagogue, old and flabby'.[19] Many had come to hate the Frenchman. Others still admired his commitment to them and to the cause.[20]

A League of Nations committee was formed to oversee their departure,[21] commanded by officers from various European armies, many of whom were intelligence agents trying to work out whether these 'Reds' were going to be a danger when they got home.[22] The committee registered a total of 12,673 foreigners in the Republican army. A separate government report stated that these included some 7,102 fit International Brigade soldiers, a further 3,160 who were in hospital and 1,964 other foreigners spread out in different Republican army units.[23] A further thousand or more would have been medical personnel. Repatriation centres were set up in towns and villages on the railway lines heading north towards France.[24] First, however, came the biggest farewell ceremony of all, through the streets of Barcelona on 28 October.

André Marty, Hans Kahle, Luigi Longo and Ludwig Renn led the marching men through the pale sunshine of an autumn afternoon.[25] Barcelona, a city mistrusted by militant communists like Renn, turned out en masse. Some 200,000 people lined the streets, throwing flowers while paper leaflets were hurled from windows and balconies were decorated with flags and red banners.[26] Even here the different military traditions between nations were obvious. The André Marty and Rakosi Battalions of French and Hungarians were smartly dressed in new uniforms, the Germans and Poles knew how to march, while the Americans appeared in mismatched uniforms or civilian clothes. Lincoln commander Milton Wolff admitted: 'We've never been what you call good at parade marching, and when we got on those streets with flowers up to our ankles I guess we did a kind of shag.'[27] The *New York Times*'s Herbert Matthews was more generous: 'They could not seem to keep in step or line, but everyone who saw them knew that these were true soldiers.'[28]

As it threatened to grow dark and rumours spread that the Italians were coming to bomb them, the crowds broke through the security lines and buried the men in flowers, hugs and kisses.[29] Men recalled being forced onto their knees by the weight of these embraces. 'The women and children were jumping into our arms, kissing us, calling us son, brothers, calling "come back", weeping,' recalled one volunteer. 'I never had such an experience, because these men, such tough fighters, every last one of them was crying.'³⁰ Bessie, who had been sick, wished he had been there. One wounded Brigader, watching from a balcony, felt both 'proud and sorrowful'. Another simply felt guilty. 'We, who were leaving the fight were yet receiving the heartfelt homage of the Spanish people,' he said.³¹

Dolores Ibárruri – La Pasionaria – lived up to the 'passion' in her nickname, leaning out from the podium and delivering a fiery speech to the crowd in Barcelona:

> It is very difficult to say a few words in farewell to the heroes of the International Brigades, both because of what they are and what they represent. A feeling of sorrow, an infinite grief catches our throat – sorrow for those who are going away, for the soldiers of the highest ideal of human redemption, exiles from their countries, persecuted by the tyrants of all peoples – grief for those who will stay here forever mingled with the Spanish soil, in the very depth of our heart, hallowed by our feeling of eternal gratitude.
>
> From all peoples, from all races, you came to us like brothers, like sons of immortal Spain; and in the hardest days of the war, when the capital of the Spanish Republic was threatened, it was you, gallant comrades of the International Brigades, who helped save the city with your fighting enthusiasm, your heroism and your spirit of sacrifice. And Jarama and Guadalajara, Brunete and Belchite, Levante and the Ebro, in immortal verses sing of the courage, the sacrifice, the daring, the discipline of the men of the International Brigades.
>
> For the first time in the history of the peoples' struggles, there was the spectacle, breath-taking in its grandeur, of the formation of International Brigades to help save a threatened country's freedom and independence – the freedom and independence of our Spanish land.
>
> Communists, Socialists, Anarchists, Republicans – men of different colours, differing ideology, antagonistic religions – yet all profoundly loving liberty and justice, they came and offered themselves to us unconditionally.
>
> They gave us everything – their youth or their maturity; their science or their experience; their blood and their lives; their hopes and aspirations – and they asked us for nothing. So, yes, they

wanted a place in this battle, they aspired to the honour of dying for us.

Banners of Spain! Salute these many heroes! Be lowered to honour so many martyrs!

Mothers! Women! When the years pass by and the wounds of war are staunched; when the memory of the sad and bloody days dissipates in a present of liberty, of peace and of wellbeing; when the rancour has died out and pride in a free country is felt equally by all Spaniards, speak to your children. Tell them of these men of the International Brigades.

Recount for them how, coming over seas and mountains, crossing frontiers bristling with bayonets, sought by raving dogs thirsting to tear their flesh, these men reached our country as crusaders for freedom, to fight and die for Spain's liberty and independence threatened by German and Italian fascism. They gave up everything – their loves, their countries, home and fortune, fathers, mothers, wives, brothers, sisters and children – and they came and said to us: 'We are here. Your cause, Spain's cause, is ours. It is the cause of all advanced and progressive mankind.'

Today many are departing. Thousands remain, shrouded in Spanish earth, profoundly remembered by all Spaniards. Comrades of the International Brigades: Political reasons, reasons of state, the welfare of that very cause for which you offered your blood with boundless generosity, are sending you back, some to your own countries and others to forced exile. You can go proudly. You are history. You are legend. You are the heroic example of democracy's solidarity and universality in the face of the vile and accommodating spirit of those who interpret democratic principles with their eyes on hoards of wealth or corporate shares which they want to safeguard from all risk.

We shall not forget you; and, when the olive tree of peace is in flower, entwined with the victory laurels of the Republic of Spain – return!

Return to our side for here you will find a homeland – those who have no country or friends, who must live deprived of friendship – all, all will have the affection and gratitude of the Spanish people

who today and tomorrow will shout with enthusiasm: 'Long live
the heroes of the International Brigades!'[32]

Buckley felt it had been a 'wonderful and dignified' send-off, but it
also brought on a sense of gloom. 'It seemed, somehow, the beginning
of the end,' he wrote, as if the Republic was being abandoned by its
last remaining friends.[33] Two days later Franco launched his definitive
offensive on the Ebro pocket.

Ernest Hemingway was distraught by the news of the Brigaders'
departure, especially when he and Martha Gellhorn met a dejected
Pacciardi – the same man who had sexually harassed her – who seemed
broken by the experience and was, like many volunteers, now both
stateless and poor. 'All of a sudden I heard Ernest, leaning against the
wall, on the steps, and crying. I never saw him cry before or since,'
Gellhorn recalled later. 'They can't do it! They can't treat a brave man
that way!' he said.[34] One biographer claims this was the moment
Gellhorn decided to marry Hemingway. 'I really did love E. then and it
had a long influence on me,' she remembered.

The novelist seemed to think that many volunteers had travelled
from America because of him. 'I always felt responsible for you being
here,' he told Bessie when he met him at XV Brigade's departure camp
in Ripoll. 'You know that speech I made at the Writer's Congress?'
he asked, referring to a meeting in New York in June 1937. 'I know
that speech was responsible for a lot of guys coming over.' Bessie was
perplexed.[35] Hemingway, once more, had put himself at the centre.
The core part of a later and unusually tender prose poem to the dead
American volunteers expressed his sincere regard for the men whose
willingness to act had provoked a certain envy in him:

> The dead sleep cold in Spain tonight and they will sleep cold all this
> winter as the earth sleeps with them. But in the spring the rain will
> come to make the earth kind again. The wind will blow soft over
> the hills from the south. The black trees will come to life with small
> green leaves, and there will be blossoms on the apple trees along the
> Jarama river. This spring the dead will feel the earth beginning to
> live again.

For our dead are a part of the earth of Spain now and the earth of Spain can never die. Each winter it will seem to die and each spring it will come alive again. Our dead will live with it forever ...

The dead do not need to rise. They are a part of the earth now and the earth can never be conquered. For the earth endureth forever. It will outlive all systems of tyranny.

Those who have entered it honorably, and no men ever entered earth more honorably than those who died in Spain, already have achieved immortality.[36]

Getting the men home was a complex task. It required France to accept its own volunteers and also allow others to cross its territory on their way home. There were fears that, as political tension grew across Europe, the mere presence of International Brigade veterans might provoke rightist or pro-fascist protests and some of the first to cross the frontier found themselves jeered by hard-right French activists. Passports that had been handed in to the International Brigades' office had disappeared, though most were later found.[37] Many men were economic migrants or political exiles who could not always prove that they had been living in the countries that they now wished to return to.[38] Some, according to the Brigades' own internal archives, were deemed to have no nationality at all.

The first major rail convoy left Calella on 18 November, carrying French volunteers in a train adorned with flowers and laurel wreaths in remembrance of the dead.[39] Tears were shed, once more, as the trains left Spain, the country which they had failed to save from Franco's reactionary generals and fascist allies.[40] Two days earlier, the last Republican troops had been thrown back across the Ebro. The operation had been a success, in that it extended the war by four months, but the best of the Republican army had been destroyed.[41] The Republic still held Madrid, most of Catalonia and a large swathe of land in southern and central Spain, but its resources had dried up. Franco's victory appeared inevitable, unless foreign powers intervened. After the shameful abandonment of Czechoslovakia, that was unlikely.

The bulk of those who could leave (and not everyone could) were home for Christmas. There were mass receptions at Austerlitz Station in Paris, London's Victoria Station, in the Swedish port at Malmö and at the 48th Street pier in New York.[42] The British were greeted by Labour leader Clement Attlee with a fellow future prime minister, the young Conservative and anti-appeasement campaigner Edward Heath (who had visited the British Brigaders in Spain),[43] spotted in the crowd. He had struck up friendships, including with the future trades union leader Jack Jones, when visiting the Brigaders before the Ebro offensive. Forming up behind the flags of the countries in the International Brigades, they marched straight from Victoria Station to the prime minister's residence at 10 Downing Street, with a letter demanding an end to non-intervention. They had no permission to march, but police decided to let them through.[44] Having lost their war, it was yet another attempt to win the argument against appeasement.

After months, or years, of warfare, the returning Brigaders had to face the harsh realities of getting back to 'normal' life. This was particularly difficult for the injured, whom the Spanish described with a word of shocking crudity, that was also harshly accurate about what war had done to their bodies – *mutilados*. The satisfaction of having answered the call of conscience and performed their 'duty' as anti-fascists was a solace for some. Numerous national committees raised money and held events to honour their bravery, but the volunteers were soon back on their own. 'Glory is ephemeral and epic moments only survive in books, and then solely for those who read them,' reflected Henri Tanguy, one of the French commissars.[45]

In most countries, the political right viewed the veterans as dangerous revolutionaries. Many intelligence agencies and police forces did as well. Even some anti-militarists on the left looked down on them, while those communists who returned to Moscow often found themselves under suspicion in the paranoid world left by the million deaths of the Great Purge of 1936–38. This was encouraged by reports from Marty, Walter and others about how the Brigades had supposedly been riddled with spies and so-called Trotskyists. Some of the senior Red Army personnel they had come to know and respect were Purge victims, who had been shot, or sent to the Soviet work camps. Of their own commanders, Kléber would not survive the Gulags and Gal, like Vladimir Ćopić, was shot.

Those volunteers who simply could not go home became known as 'the Dispossessed'. One report on patients at the hospital in Vic listed those with nowhere to go as Germans, Hungarians, Poles, Czechs, Yugoslavs, Estonians, Lithuanians and Finns.[46] As a result, some 3,200 men remained in Spain, their future entirely uncertain.[47] For the conservative Catalans of Sant Quirze de Besora, where the Germans of XI Brigade were quartered, this meant a strange Christmas in which their own Catholic celebrations were shared with mostly communist, atheist Germans who nevertheless sang their traditional seasonal songs.[48]

Just before Christmas 1938, Franco launched a fresh offensive on Catalonia and on 23 January, as his troops approached Barcelona, the remaining International Brigaders were called on to volunteer once more.[49] Meetings were held and stirring speeches made. 'We'll repeat Madrid; we'll make Barcelona another Madrid,' they were told, but the reception was not unanimously enthusiastic. 'We did not believe it possible,' recalled Szurek. 'A heavy silence enveloped the hall.'[50] The Communist Party, however, had decided. Then someone shouted out the words of the Dombrowski anthem: 'Our answer is one: to the Front, Dombrowski Brigade!' Only one of the surviving Botwin company members refused to go back.

It is unclear how many men returned to arms. Some reports spoke of more than a thousand. Tagüeña, who had commanded volunteers at the Ebro, now reported receiving 700 of them.[51] Renn was amongst those opposed to the idea, though most of the 1,360 Germans and Austrians with him were in favour – with 902 signing up. 'I wasn't at all enthusiastic. Was it reasonable to remobilise the Brigades?'[52] If Catalonia could not be saved, he reasoned, why sacrifice so many seasoned fighters? He was horrified to hear that Marty, who had no experience, was to command the unit and, worse still, that it had been suggested that Renn should accompany him to provide military expertise.[53] Fortunately, Marty did not want him or his battalion of 270 'technical' officers.

The Italians were amongst the least keen. Only twenty men appear to have rejoined the army in their rest town of Torelló.[54] Likewise, only a handful of the 300 Canadians who were about to leave Spain agreed to return to the fight. They included their senior officer Edward Cecil-Smith, though they were also not needed in the end. Marty berated the others, claiming they were now only interested in spending time with their Spanish girlfriends. 'If you rabbits want to run out of Spain with your *putas*, whores, go ahead,' one volunteer recalled him saying – though, like many Marty stories, this may have been apocryphal.[55]

Szurek became commissar of a Slav group which joined up with the German speakers at Granollers. They were handed rifles and light machine guns, but were immediately forced to retreat and he had to threaten to shoot a forester who refused to guide them through the woods. The volunteers were back on an unpredictable front line, carrying out a fighting retreat that often felt more like a guerrilla action than a last stand.[56] To begin with, they operated independently before being absorbed by the 35th Division under their old commander, Merino.[57] The newly formed units fought, or at least carried weapons, for just two weeks.[58] They do not seem to have made an important contribution, and certainly did not prevent the Francoist army from rolling up towards the French border. Barcelona fell on 26 January. The dream of turning it into another Madrid lasted less than one day. Within twenty-four hours of the first Francoist troops appearing on the slopes of the Tibidabo Hill, their officers were in the city hall and the Catalan government's palatial headquarters, making speeches from the balconies. Resistance had been negligible.

On 30 January 1939, Henry Buckley stood at the border a few kilometres from La Jonquera, in the north-east corner of Catalonia, and watched as French soldiers forced wounded Republican soldiers back across the frontier they had just crossed. It was a story he wished he had never had to cover. 'Sorry general, we have our orders,'[59] a French major replied when British Brigadier A. L. M. Molesworth, part of the League of Nations evacuation commission,[60] complained.

On 1 February, the Spanish parliament met in the cellars of the same castle in Figueres where many International Brigaders had begun their time in Spain. Only a fraction of the elected members were able to take part in the meeting. They could do little more than make plans for continuing resistance in the larger section of Republican Spain, including Madrid and Valencia, that lay south of the Ebro valley. 'This place is like a tomb,' Buckley confided to the Russian journalist Ilya Ehrenburg as the meeting started. 'My friend, this is the tomb not only of the Spanish Republic but of European democracy,' he answered. Buckley could not help but agree.[61] The meeting did nothing to stop the inevitable. A few days later the French border opened and the full exodus of refugees and a defeated army began.[62]

Military units of all kinds were, by this time, marching towards the frontier. The following day Renn and his group of around 600 men – which now included the Cubans and other Latin Americans left over from other brigades[63] – marched from La Bisbal d'Empordà to

Palafrugell, where they encountered the Poles who had not volunteered to fight. The latter stole from the food stores. 'All the good ones had gone to fight, only the scum were left,' he sniffed.[64] They had to find weapons so that they could police their own men. The Polish International Brigades doctor, František Kriegel, meanwhile, became the empty town's acting mayor. Renn's men then marched to the border, reaching it on 5 February, where they met up with Szurek and the other volunteers who had gone back to fight.[65] A final parade was held at the frontier on 8 February in front of Negrín, La Pasionaria and Modesto, before the men formed up and marched smartly across the border inland from Port Bou, their determination to maintain their military bearing and discipline making them stand out amongst the chaos.[66] 'With closed ranks and heads high we marched onto French soil. We sang, the gendarmes yelling, "Singing prohibited!" They brought us back to reality,' Szurek recalled.[67]

Dignity and discipline were maintained in the final moments. 'We surrendered our arms, adding them to the big pile in front of us. After so many lost battles, this act was very sad and utterly tragic,' said Szurek. Those same weapons had, he said, been a 'symbol of our freedom' and letting them go was more than just an admission of their defeat in a war that dragged on for two more months in the remaining Republican part of Spain, with Franco declaring absolute victory on 1 April 1939.[68] 'When we [first] took them in our hand, we were convinced that, thanks to them, we would win a better world,' Szurek explained.

The volunteers had lost a war, but – with the outbreak of the Second World War a mere five months away – they would soon be proved right about the dangers posed to all nations by the unchecked rise of fascism. That undoubted truth anchored their pride in later years and established their legend. They did not yet know, however, that their victory would finally come with the defeat of fascism five years later. For the moment, they only felt distraught that they were leaving the people of Spain at the hands of a merciless dictator and that, as W. H. Auden had observed in his 1937 poem 'Spain', 'History to the defeated/ May say Alas but cannot help or pardon'.[69] A few hours after the last volunteers crossed into France, Franco's army reached the border.

52

'Premature Anti-Fascists': Paris, 21 August 1941

Pierre Georges arranged to meet his two pistol-carrying colleagues at the Paris Métro station of Barbès-Rochechouart, at 8 a.m. on 21 August 1941. The former teenage International Brigader, injured while commanding a section during the retreats through Aragon and repatriated in August 1938, was now a twenty-two-year-old married man. He had escaped from a detention camp in occupied France and begun secretly training communist youths in guerrilla warfare.[1]

Germany had invaded Georges's country in May 1940, sweeping past the Maginot Line, and France, which was also attacked by Mussolini, capitulated the following month. Paris was now full of uniformed soldiers of the Wehrmacht, but the period of occupation had been relatively bloodless. Violence against the Germans was considered taboo, especially since Hitler was already infamous for responding, in occupied Poland and elsewhere, with the mass shootings of prisoners. The city was still cowed and a small anti-German demonstration eight days earlier had seen several young communists arrested. Two of them, Henri Gautherot[2] and the Jewish Polish immigrant Samuel Tyszelman, had been taken to the woods at Vallée-aux-Loups and executed. Georges wanted to do two things: to exact revenge, and to start a violent, underground struggle against the occupiers. Under the nom de guerre Colonel Fabien, he was destined to play an important role in that resistance.

'We spotted a magnificent naval commander strutting on the platform,' recalled Gilbert Brustlein, one of the young fighters with Georges in the Métro station. 'Fabien said, "That one." The train arrived, the officer got into the first-class carriage and at that moment Fabien fired two shots, turned around, and sprang up the steps leading to the exit … We ran as far as Sacré-Coeur.'³ They had killed a naval warrant officer, Alfons Moser.

It was, to all effects, the start of the French Resistance movement, in which veterans of the International Brigades were destined to play a major part – as they also would in partisan movements across occupied Europe. It was also an opportunity for the communists to begin erasing the shame of the Nazi-Soviet pact, which had finally collapsed when Germany attacked Russia on 22 June, exactly a year after France capitulated. That mutual non-aggression pact had been signed in front of Stalin by foreign ministers Vyacheslav Molotov and Joachim von Ribbentrop just a week before Germany began the Second World War by invading Poland on 1 September 1939. The agreement, and its consequences, had a devastating impact on many former International Brigaders. The more disciplined communists clung to the belief that Stalin's decision was forced on him by the need to build up his own army and because Britain and France had spurned an alliance. The rest recalled that they had gone to Spain to fight fascism, rather than collude with it.

This was especially difficult for the Poles who saw their country overrun in just five weeks. Germany annexed or took control of most of it, while Russia also invaded. Stalin went on to attack Finland in November and annex Estonia, Latvia, Lithuania and parts of Romania the following June. As a result, some Brigaders found themselves fighting against the same Red Army advisors who had been on their side just a year or so before.⁴ In the meantime Germany grabbed Denmark and Norway before invading Belgium, Holland and France in May 1940. Greece and Yugoslavia fell the following year. By the time Fabien carried out his attack, the Axis powers controlled all of Western Europe bar Britain, the neutral states of Switzerland and Sweden and the two Iberian countries of Spain and Portugal. Everything east of that, meanwhile, was under Stalin's control.

This dizzying succession of events in the two years after they left Spain, saw many Brigaders sink into disillusion. Bernard Knox, who had travelled with John Cornford to Madrid and Boadilla, stepped away from communism. 'The Nazi-Soviet Pact of 1939 was understandable; the Western betrayal of Czechoslovakia was a clear signal to Stalin that if Hitler turned against Russia [as he repeatedly announced that he would in his book *Mein Kampf*], the West would not raise a finger to help,' he said. 'But the brutal annexation of the Baltic states and still more the aggressive war against Finland were harder to accept.'⁵ Knox emigrated to the United States where, after a period in which Brigaders were viewed as suspect, he and several other veterans were eventually recruited by General 'Wild Bill' Donovan's OSS (Office of Strategic Services), the covert wartime intelligence agency with outposts across the world.

The Nazi response to Fabien's Paris Métro attack was ferocious. By the end of the following month fifty-eight communists had been executed. With Paris increasingly dangerous, the fledgling communist Resistance movement decided to move its campaign elsewhere. The next assassination of a German soldier was carried out in Nantes on 20 October by Brigades veteran Spartaco Guisco, accompanied by Gilbert Brustlein. They assassinated Lieutenant Colonel Karl Hotz, the city's military governor, and a fellow officer. Many French people were horrified and the Germans furious. Two days later the occupiers executed forty-eight prisoners in retaliation, apparently after Hitler personally insisted on instant revenge.⁶ Two of those killed were International Brigade veterans and two more died in a further round of executions later that week.⁷ The Free French leader Charles de Gaulle, who had escaped to Britain, responded with a radio broadcast on the BBC. 'War should be undertaken by those whose business it is,' he said. 'I am giving an order to those in the occupied territory not to kill Germans.'⁸

De Gaulle eventually changed his mind and many International Brigade veterans joined the Resistance in France, including women who had served in Spain as nurses and doctors. At least 105 were killed, with twenty of them amongst the hostages shot by the Germans in reprisals. Pierre Rebière, the stocky commissar who had carried the wounded Jan Kurzke off the battlefield at Boadilla, was one of the dead.⁹ One-third of those executed had been born outside France, with a single unit of twenty-three Resistance fighters who were caught and shot in 1944 including five Brigaders, none of whom were French.¹⁰

On 19 August 1944, Henri Rol-Tanguy ordered the umbrella Resistance organisation created earlier that year, the French Force of the Interior (FFI), to rise against the German troops in Paris. The former International Brigades political commissar had become regional commander of the Resistance movement.[11] The uprising forced the Allies to divert their offensive towards the city. A few days later, when half-tracks from General Philippe Leclerc's 2nd Armoured Division reached the centre of Paris they bore the names of Spanish Civil War battles – including Guadalajara, Ebro and Teruel – since they were mostly manned by Republican Spaniards from a company known as La Nueve, who were fighting for the Free French. As a result, it was a Spanish officer who first walked into the city hall to meet the Resistance leaders there.

The following day, 25 August, Rol-Tanguy and Leclerc co-signed the formal rendition of Paris by General Dietrich Von Cholitz.[12] Both Rol-Tanguy and Georges are today feted as Resistance heroes, and the Colonel Fabien Métro station in Paris is a reminder of the historical importance of the young Resistance leader who was killed in an explosion, possibly caused by someone mishandling a mine, on 29 December 1944.

If the war in Spain had been an act of resistance against fascism, then it was natural for International Brigade veterans to return to that battle by creating or joining partisan units across Europe, or joining their national armies. Initially, most of those who marched across the border from Catalonia had ended up in the windswept, wire-enclosed rudimentary camps set up on beaches in southern France. Of the 5,948 foreigners in these camps in March, from fifty countries, 5,736 were International Brigade veterans – with Italians and Poles forming the largest contingents, followed by Germans.[13] The number of Portuguese (a total of 316 Brigaders), Cubans and Argentines (with more than 200 each) proves that these groups – mostly from XV Brigade's Spanish-speaking battalion or the Italian-led XII Brigade – played a far more important role in the International Brigades than historians have previously acknowledged. The thirty-four Brazilians and twenty-five Greeks on a separate list suggest that these were not welcome home either and, as the Second World War began that September, there were still 3,500 Brigaders languishing in camps because, as Comintern leader Georgi Dimitrov wrote to Stalin, they were people 'whom no bourgeois government wishes to receive'.[14] Stalin showed little interest, however, in shipping them to the Soviet Union.[15] The Brigaders formed well-organised national groups, though some preferred to live outside their carefully controlled and sometimes politically paranoid groupings. They posed a serious dilemma for the collaborationist authorities of Vichy France and the more troublesome or senior veterans often ended up in a special camp at Vernet, which also served as a club for future partisan leaders.

It is remarkable, indeed, just how prominent they became. In Yugoslavia, for example, all four of Tito's partisan armies were led by Spanish veterans. A later secret report for the CIA acknowledged that 'the military organisers of the Partisan movement were the "Spaniards" – the pre-war Communists who had served in the International Brigades'.[16] When Knox tried to coordinate with partisans in Italy, he found his past with the International Brigades a useful passport. He mixed up his languages by mistake, occasionally using Spanish words such as *fuego* or *frente*, instead of *fuoco* and *fronte*. 'After another such fumble, the division commander stood up, smiling, walked over to me and patted me on the shoulder. "*Spagna*, no?" he said. He had been in the Battaglione Garibaldi that had fought next to us in the Casa de Campo. From that point on, relations with the partisans were no problem,' he recalled.[17]

Half of the Garibaldi veterans who returned to Italy joined the partisans, including Giovanni Pesce, who found that he preferred the old kind of warfare to the clandestine life of an urban guerrilla in Turin. 'I missed the comrades running alongside me, with one hundred men shouting out loud, rather than operating in silence,' he recalled. 'But here we have to fight terror with terror.'[18] Another Garibaldi veteran, Aldo Lampredi, was one of the three partisans who executed Benito Mussolini and his lover Claretta Petacci on 28 April 1945. The couple were finished off with Lampredi's Beretta pistol.

Knox was one of the Brigaders who went on to serve directly in Allied armies – though some were initially looked on with suspicion. Those who ended up in Britain often drifted into the Free French, Polish, Czech or other 'exile' armies that were being formed. Some Germans such as the writers Erich Weinert and Willi Bredel sided with the Red Army, shouting propaganda slogans at their invading countrymen from the rubble of Stalingrad.[19] Esmond Romilly, nephew of Winston Churchill, ran a cocktail bar in Miami before joining the Canadian air force, and was amongst the many to die in that war when his aircraft failed to return from a raid on Hamburg in late 1941.[20] Others, like the

Danish veteran Leo Kari, would never recover from the post-traumatic stress disorder that is now accepted as a widespread condition amongst returning combat soldiers.

Tom Wintringham, meanwhile, became one of the guiding lights in converting Britain's Local Defence Volunteers into the armed Home Guard. He had already been expelled from the Communist Party for refusing to break up with his girlfriend, and future wife, Kitty Bowler (whom Marty had deemed a Trotskyist spy). With an invasion of Britain likely in 1940 and Churchill proclaiming that 'if you've got to go you can always take one with you', Wintringham both lobbied for and initiated the teaching of guerrilla tactics and street-fighting. When the government dragged its feet, he even arranged special arms imports and set up a popular private guerrilla training centre, with several International Brigade veterans as instructors and the surrealist painter Roland Penrose teaching camouflage at what newspapers approvingly dubbed a school of 'ungentlemanly warfare'.[21] Trained guerrilla fighters from the Brigades were particularly highly valued. 'What do I know of guerrilla warfare? I learned everything in Spain,' American Brigader Irving Goff would declare years later after he had been recruited by OSS.[22] Edward Carter, one of the African American volunteers, served so magnificently as a US army sergeant that a US navy vessel was named after him.[23]

Suspicion of communists and mistrust of certain nationalities meant that some veterans found their desire to fight frustrated. The wounded Jan Kurzke, who had returned to London with his girlfriend Kate Mangan, was interned as a German 'alien' for thirteen months – to his profound disgust.[24] Many of the Poles, meanwhile, completed a long journey home via camps in French North Africa and on to the Soviet Union. There they joined a Soviet-organised Polish army, helping to form and lead a unit whose members were parachuted into occupied Poland.[25]

Those who survived Spain often did not survive the next war. Around half of the 250 Yugoslavs (out of 350 who made it back to their country) who joined their partisan movement would die, though twenty-nine eventually reached the rank of general – an extraordinary number that reflects the prominence given to Spanish fighters in Tito's regime (and fifteen years after the war, a CIA report on the key military figures said one-third of them were Brigade veterans).[26] Of the eighty-four surviving veterans from Latvia, twenty-five died fighting in the Red Army.[27] Since Jews and communists were Hitler's enemies, many veterans were killed at extermination or prison camps. They included at least 200 from just France, Italy and Austria.²⁸

A group of seven Romanian Jewish veterans, who had been picked out for especially brutal treatment, sought to add a degree of dignity to their inevitable deaths at Mauthausen. This was one of the worst camps, where International Brigade veterans were known as '*die rote Spanier*' (the 'Red Spaniards') and required to wear a red triangle (as well as a yellow star, if Jewish).²⁹ 'If any one of you survives this hell, tell our people where and how we died,' one of them announced to the Spanish inmates the night before.³⁰ The following day they marched straight towards one of the guard towers singing 'The Internationale' until they were machine-gunned to death.³¹

Perhaps inevitably, many became involved in the small rebellions and acts of resistance within the camps. One group broke out of Natzweiler concentration camp – which was specifically designated to house, amongst others, former German International Brigaders – and made it to, of all places, non-belligerent Spain (though Franco clearly supported Hitler, sending a division of volunteer troops to the Russian Front).³²

The Austrian Brigader Rudolf Friemel, confined at Auschwitz, had less luck. He persuaded the authorities to allow him to marry Margarita Ferrer, his girlfriend from Spain and mother of his son, in March 1944. It was the only wedding to be held at Auschwitz and the couple were serenaded by an orchestra before being allowed a single night together, in a room at the camp brothel (where non-Jewish female prisoners were turned into sex slaves for selected 'favoured' non-Jewish prisoners), before Margarita was sent back to Friemel's family's home.³³ That December he was hanged with other members of a group who had been caught planning to break out. 'I hoped to see you and my beloved little boy again, but I could never give up the fight. That was impossible for me,' Rudolf wrote to Margarita the night before he was due to be hanged. 'Now my hour has come. I don't feel sad, and nor should you, my sweet girl. When the war is over, you will return to Spain. Look after our son. Make a man and a fighter out of him. And look ahead in order to forget these unfortunate times. My final thoughts will be of you.'³⁴

International Brigaders were also amongst the sick and severely undernourished inmates who rose against the Auschwitz guards just before liberation. 'It is also stated that a band of prisoners – most of them veterans of the Spanish International Brigade – broke out of the compound and exchanged fire with the SS guards, as a result of which three of their own number were killed,' reported an American officer who arrived two days later.[35]

Emmanuel Mink, the sportsman who travelled to compete at the Barcelona Olympiad, stayed to fight and survived the Botwin company, was one of the survivors of a forced march of prisoners away from Auschwitz in the days before liberation.[36] Like many Jewish veterans, he ended up living in Israel, where International Brigaders were initially accused of abandoning their own people during the Great Revolt of the Palestinian Arabs, which coincided with the war in Spain. They were finally praised by President Chaim Herzog in 1986 for combatting the fascism that had claimed millions of Jewish lives.[37] Brigaders were, similarly, amongst the leaders of the resistance at Buchenwald, which ended with the capture of 200 SS men.[38]

Those Jewish volunteers who were not sent to the camps often, if not usually, lost family members. Aleksander Szurek would forever regret asking his wife, Berta, to keep their daughter Helena[39] close to her after he was arrested by the Germans in occupied France in 1941. 'I begged her to be brave and never to separate herself from the child,' he recalled later. 'My entreaty tortured me all through my life. I could not foresee that separation might have saved them. They perished together.'[40] Both died at Auschwitz.[41] Aleksander Szurek, who had obtained Russian papers, survived camps in France and Germany before eventually returning to Poland.[42]

Not everyone behaved with such courage. Some, indeed, changed sides or became informers. They included André Heussler, commissar with XIV Brigade, and his brigade companion Jacques Vaillant, the former French Foreign Legionnaire who ran the Pioneer companies.[43] The traitorous quartermaster Dupré sided, unsurprisingly, with the German invaders and was executed for treason in 1951.[44] A Lithuanian volunteer was also later spotted wearing a German Wehrmacht uniform by an International Brigades veteran who joined the Resistance in Paris.

One of the most curious figures was Frank Ryan, the bold, left-leaning IRA man who had been captured during the retreats. He was one of those who remained in the camp at San Pedro de Cardeña until after the outbreak of the Second World War. He was eventually freed by the Abwehr (German military intelligence) who organised a mock 'escape' for him in July 1940, and spirited him away to Berlin. There he seems to have worked with other Irish Republicans who thought that the war offered a unique opportunity to bring about a reunification of Ireland – especially if Hitler should invade Britain. There is still bitter debate over whether this meant the avowed anti-fascist who had persuaded XV Brigade to return to the line at Jarama became a Nazi collaborator, placing Irish nationalism above all else and losing the right to be considered a socialist. With his health failing, Ryan tried to return to Ireland, but was refused permission as his country did not want to jeopardise its position of neutrality. He suffered a stroke, and died in a German sanatorium in June 1944.[45]

As the full horrors of the Nazi regime and the Holocaust were revealed, some politicians in Western democracies looked back at the war in Spain and recognised that they had failed in their duty to defend the free world. Roosevelt admitted that his Spanish policy had been a 'great mistake', and Hoover's former secretary of state, Henry Stimson, had long before realised 'what a disaster the non-intervention agreement [regarding Spain] had been and how it played into the hands of the Axis powers'.

After the Second World War, Franco's Spain was not admitted into the United Nations. Shortly before his death in April 1945, Franklin Roosevelt had written that 'having been helped to power by Fascist Italy and Nazi Germany, and having patterned itself along totalitarian lines, the present regime in Spain is naturally the subject of distrust by a great many American citizens.' He continued: 'We do not forget Spain's official ... assistance to our Axis enemies at a time when the fortunes of war were less favourable to us, nor can we disregard the activities, aims, organizations and public utterances of the Falange ... These memories cannot be wiped out.' The Cold War and an American desire to set up military bases across Europe, would eventually produce a thawing of relations in the 1950s.[46]

Even more remarkable was the important role played by International Brigaders in Soviet bloc countries immediately after the Second World War. When these fell under Russian control, Stalin sought out communists who had proven themselves as loyal militants and partisans. Surviving Brigaders often fitted both categories. In the immediate post-war years they rose to prominence all over Russian-dominated Europe – running ministries, commanding armies and police forces and representing their countries as ambassadors. In fact, given that the cohort of surviving members from these countries cannot have numbered more than 9,000 people, the power they came to wield was remarkable. Even the alumni of the world's most prestigious universities would have had trouble competing with that degree of establishment success. The same regimes they helped to found would, however, also eventually devour many of them and are now widely scorned in the countries which suffered more than four decades of communist rule after the Second World War.

Nowhere were the Brigaders more powerful than in East Germany, as the Soviets struggled to find people they could trust who could help them construct a narrative of historic anti-fascism, cleansed of Hitler's Nazi legacy. They turned to former XI Brigade commissar and commander Heinrich Rau to run the first de facto government of their occupied zone, the German Economic Commission (DWK). Hundreds of German veterans eventually rose to the upper ranks of the regime, with at least six becoming government ministers.[47] Thirteen were in the central committee, eight in the Politburo and there would be at least one ex-Brigader on the all-powerful secretariat for all but a few years up to 1984. The new German state also needed armed forces and police, often to repress its own people. Brigaders took prominent positions there too, providing seventeen generals, forty colonels and numerous other officers. 'The German-speaking units of the International Brigades represented the nucleus of the armed forces of the future GDR,' the country would eventually certify.[48] Considering that there were barely more than a thousand veterans in East Germany, their importance is outstanding.[49]

Some German Brigaders became notorious oppressors, with veterans providing more than a dozen senior members of the feared Stasi secret police, while a hundred more joined the ranks of various police forces.[50] The infamous Stasi, indeed, was founded by Wilhelm Zaisser (aka General Gómez) with the help of Brigader Karl Heinz Hoffmann. The 85,000-strong Stasi 'People's Police' force and its network of 175,000 informers was led by Brigade veterans for all but four years until the fall of the Berlin Wall in 1989. By that time it had become East Germany's most notorious and hated tool of state repression. Erich Mielke, its head for thirty-two years and a veteran of the Brigades' internal security services, became known as 'the Master of Fear'. He was the ruthless architect of what one writer called 'the most perfected surveillance state of all time', which held files on millions of citizens.[51] When the Berlin

Wall finally fell, much of the popular hatred against the communist regime was channelled directly at him. He was eventually tried, and found guilty, of murdering two policemen in the pre-Nazi Weimar Republic days. Richard Staimer, meanwhile, became chief of police in the Brandenburg state (which contains Berlin), before moving to even more senior positions, while Hans Kahle had a more discreet role as police chief in Mecklenburg. At one stage, veterans were in charge of all three branches of the security services – including the army, the interior ministry's police and the Stasi.[52]

Much the same would happen in Yugoslavia – where thirty Brigaders eventually reached the rank of general – and, to a lesser degree, in Poland and Bulgaria.[53] In the decade immediately after the war, almost all the Eastern bloc countries had government ministers who had served with the International Brigades in Spain. A former machine-gunner with XII Brigade, Mehmet Shehu, was prime minister of Albania for twenty-five years.

A particularly vicious round of trouble started after Yugoslav leader Tito refused to accept submission to Stalin and the Soviet Union in 1948. Since the Stalinist mindset believed in contamination by proximity, and given that Yugoslavia's armed forces were being run by International Brigaders, veterans automatically became suspect. Hungarian foreign minister László Rajk, for example, was detained with six other Brigaders in September 1949.[54] Rajk was found guilty of spying at a show trial and executed the following day. Of the ninety-seven defendants declared guilty in the Hungarian trials, sixteen were former Brigaders. Two were executed and the rest went to jail while many more lost their jobs – though brigader Ferenc Münnich became prime minister in 1958.

Much the same happened in Czechoslovakia, where the Brigades would provide two interior ministers and half-a-dozen deputy ministers.[55] In what became known as the 'Slánský trial', senior party official Otto Sling was hanged and deputy foreign minister Artur London was imprisoned. Both were Brigade veterans. 'I was a treacherous enemy within the Communist Party,' Sling was forced to declare. 'I am justly an object of contempt and deserve the maximum and the hardest punishment.'[56] Osvald Závodský, another volunteer who had become head of the National Security Corps (NSB), was executed later, in 1954. Dimitrov Battalion commander Josef Pavel's career summed up the entire communist history of Czechoslovakia, since he was also imprisoned, then exonerated, became interior minister during the brief reformist Prague Spring in 1968 and was sacked and expelled from the Communist Party after Russian tanks appeared on the streets of the Czech capital. London's book, *The Confession*, became a classic denunciation of the Orwellian turn taken by Stalinist parties. In all these cases, the Spanish connection was deemed an important reason for suspicion.

All across the Soviet-controlled side of Europe, veterans found themselves being interrogated to see if they, too, had been contaminated by their contact with the outer world and the supposedly spy-ridden International Brigades. The Germans were indignant, since these interrogations reminded them of their treatment by the Gestapo (despite the fact that other Brigaders were amongst those ordering that these new interrogations be carried out). One Brigader, Willi Kreikemeyer, died mysteriously in a secret police cell and even the previously mighty Zaisser was amongst those to lose their jobs. 'I hear it rumoured that at the moment speaking about Spain is unwanted, and that everything connected with it is cancelled,' the loyal communist Ludwig Renn wrote in 1952. 'Supposedly this is happening because there were too many traitors in Spain. I don't understand such points of view.'[57] Perhaps the fact that the career-minded Staimer had by now married the daughter of President Wilhelm Pieck helped in preventing show trials in Germany too.[58]

There were also arrests in Poland, including of 129 Brigade commander Wacław Komar, though he was later reinstated.[59] Further trouble came for him and other Jewish veterans in 1967, however, with a burst of Polish 'socialist' anti-Semitism that followed the Six Day War between Israel and its neighbouring states. For men like Szurek, who had fought fascism and lost family in Hitler's camps, this was a devastating end to their dream. Many Jewish Brigade veterans lost their jobs. Emigration, to Israel, the United States, Canada or – in Szurek's case – to France, became the only solution. Cast initially into poverty, Szurek later became famous amongst veterans for his response to a Polish general who tried to kiss him on the cheek at a reunion. 'Not here,' he said. 'But here,' pointing at his backside.[60]

Although the Polish Brigaders did not reach the same prominence in the country's administration as their comrades elsewhere, they were honoured with monuments and street names. Under the virulently anti-communist right-wingers of the Law and Justice party, Poland's sometimes controversial Institute for National Remembrance has recently called for these to be torn down. It claims that the Polish Brigaders 'fought for the construction of the Stalinist state' and that 'relativising their activities [e.g. that not all were communists] will not change the fact that as a group they served the criminal communist ideology'.[61]

The political passions of the Cold War era saw some Brigade veterans on the other side of that conflict also pay a heavy price. American communists and their friends, for example, became the focus of suspicion and witch-hunts in the United States. Alvah Bessie, by then an Oscar-nominated screenwriter, became the most famous of them all as one of the 'Hollywood Ten' who refused to give evidence to the House Un-American Activities Committee (HUAC). 'I will never aid or abet such a committee in its patent attempt to foster the sort of intimidation and terror that is the inevitable precursor of a fascist regime,' he famously told HUAC, which saw him sent to jail for contempt. He was blacklisted by studio bosses and imprisoned for ten months. Amongst those to give evidence were embittered Brigade veterans such as William McCuistion who claimed to have witnessed the shooting of fellow deserters in a Barcelona bar. 'God knows, Hitler and Mussolini can be very little worse than the ruling clique of the communist bureaucrats and political commissars,' another deserter, Edward Horan, told the committee.[62]

The theatrical goings-on at the HUAC hearings overshadowed a more subtle and serious condemnation of those who had fought fascism before it became fashionable. They had been, some were told, 'premature anti-fascists'. Bernard Knox first came across the term when, after a distinguished Second World War career, he was interviewed by the chairman of the Yale Classics Department to study for a doctorate. He recalled that interview much later:

> To jazz my application up a bit, I had included my record in the
> US Army, private to captain 1942–45. The professor, who had
> himself served in the US Army in 1917–18, was very interested,
> and remarked on the fact that, in addition to the usual battle-stars
> for service in the European Theatre, I had been awarded a Croix
> de Guerre a l'Ordre de l'Armée, the highest category for that
> decoration. Asked how I got it, I explained that, in July 1944, I had
> parachuted, in uniform, behind the Allied lines in Brittany to arm

and organize French Resistance forces and hold them ready for action at the moment most useful for the Allied advance.

'Why were you selected for that operation?' he asked, and I told him that I was one of the few people in the US Army who could speak fluent, idiomatic, and (if necessary) pungently coarse French. When he asked me where I had learned it, I told him that I had fought in 1936 on the northwest sector of the Madrid front in the French Battalion of XIth International Brigade. 'Oh,' he said. 'You were a premature anti-fascist.'

I was taken aback by the expression. How, I wondered, could *anyone* be a *premature* anti-fascist? Could there be anything such as a premature antidote to a poison? A premature antiseptic? A premature antitoxin? A premature anti-racist? If you were not premature, what sort of anti-fascist were you supposed to be?[63]

It was not until the Vietnam War, when Lincoln Battalion veterans found themselves feted as they joined protest marches behind their own banners, that International Brigaders became particularly visible again in the United States. That did not stop future president Ronald Reagan from claiming they had fought 'on the wrong side'.[64] Western European veterans, if they survived the Second World War (and lists of former members held by, amongst others, Dutch police found their way to the Gestapo), were amongst the few not to suffer immediate consequences, though communist infighting would eventually see even André Marty shunned by his former ideological comrades. The famous denouncer of spies and internal enemies was himself denounced as 'an agent of the enemy … who imposed narrow-mindedness and sectarianism'.[65] More than a dozen senators and deputies in France, Norway and Italy (including two ministers, the Republican Randolfo Pacciardi and the socialist Pietro Nenni, while Giuseppe Di Vittorio headed the country's largest trades union) were veterans.[66]

Jack Jones, who survived the Ebro battle, became head of Britain's mighty Transport and General Workers Union. It has been suggested that he may even have been a Soviet informer, though this was something he vigorously denied. If it were true, however, Jones would have been just one of at least a dozen Brigade veterans in Western Europe who served communist Moscow's spy machine.[67] The most famous, or infamous, of these was Morris Cohen, who recruited a scientist at the Los Alamos testing centre in New Mexico to pass on blueprints of the first American nuclear weapons in 1945.[68] Jones, meanwhile, was at one time considered to be Britain's most powerful man – 'more powerful than the prime minister' – according to a Gallup poll in 1977.[69] That pitted him directly against another Brigade veteran, Sir Alfred Sherman, who became Margaret Thatcher's most trusted advisor when she was elected prime minister and began a ferocious battle with the trades unions two years later. Sherman and Thatcher had jointly co-founded the radical (for its times) right-wing think tank, the Centre for Policy Studies. Sherman had been expelled from the Communist Party for attacking Stalin over Yugoslavia, but never regretted his participation in the fight against fascism. 'Spain was a special case; a few more good divisions and I still think the tide could have been turned against Franco,' he said decades later.[70] He did, however, feel betrayed. 'We were given no real picture of Stalin's motives. We were pawns in many ways.'

Although veterans' associations kept the International Brigades spirit alive, many Brigaders returned to their lives without forming any part of that – especially where they suspected Communist Party control. It is clear, however, that most were deeply marked by the youthful, idealistic, dangerous and frightening trip to Spain. Many of those who, as journalists or observers, watched or cheered for them, also carried the flame of the Spanish cause for ever. Muriel Rukeyser, the poet who had fallen in love with German volunteer Otto Boch in the first days of the war, published an 'in Remembrance' note to her 'Bavarian, runner, cabinet-maker, fighter for a better world' in German newspapers during the 1972 Munich Olympics, asking his family to get in touch – though there was no answer. That moment in Spain, she said, had ignited something 'whose fires would not stop'.[71]

Indeed, for many of those who fought, Spain was the defining event of their lives. Regler, despite his own fall-out with communism, summed it up as the place 'where the light shone and the new geography began'.[72] Even after he had turned his back on communism, Stephen Spender was clear about the war's place in history. 'The resistance of the Republic became the cause of democracy, and that of the rebels the cause of Fascism. Whatever a great many Spaniards on both sides may have been fighting for, this was the issue being fought out by Italy, Germany, Russia and the International Brigades on Spanish soil.'[73]

The last of the International Brigaders are dead, or close to it. Over the two decades before writing this book, I met a number of them, men like Virgilio Fernández, who died in Guanajuato in December 2019. Direct experience of the Brigades will soon go to the grave. There was nothing perfect about the Brigaders and attempts to paint them as saints only serve to highlight their failings. These were (mostly) men at war. They killed and were killed. Some fought bravely, others did not. Some were noble and brave in their actions, others were cruel, cowardly or callous. Some fought for an ideal, others for adventure. And, for some, those ideals would take them on a journey of oppression that placed them closer, in their behaviour and blind defence of Stalinist communism, to the fascists whom they declared as their enemies than to the democratic Republic that they defended. All fought, however, against the most destructive and malevolent force unleashed by twentieth-century Europe's violent politics and history. As that distinguished Yale classics professor Bernard Knox pointed out, there could be nothing 'premature' about anti-fascism.

Franco was not a pure 'fascist' himself. He lacked the imagination for that. But it was fascism that rescued the botched coup attempt of his generals and made sure he won his war and could impose his reactionary, thirty-six-year dictatorship. His Spain was a place of political and social repression, where tens of thousands were placed before firing squads, women lost their basic rights, and death penalties were carried out into the 1970s. It was no coincidence that Hitler and Mussolini became so heavily involved in what, despite a continued unwillingness in Spain to view it as such, was patently the opening battle of the Second World War.

The Spanish Civil War, indeed, was not just fascism's first great, emboldening victory. It was also its longest-lasting one. That triumph, and the politics of appeasement by Western democracies that began in Spain, emboldened Hitler to extend his war and launch the Holocaust. Anyone who fought against Franco, then, was also fighting against that. War, as I have argued, is mostly binary. It obliges all but the most ardent pacifists to take sides. Few people living in Western democracies today would, with the benefit of hindsight, struggle to decide who to support. One of the tragedies of contemporary Spain is that this is not clear to all Spaniards. During his four decades of dictatorship, Franco frequently harked back to the 'great crusade' – the coup and civil war that cost the country half a million dead,[74] hundreds of thousands cast into jail or exile, and nearly forty years without basic freedoms. Some 150,000 people were killed by Franco's own firing squads and associated right-wing death squads alone.

John McCain, the decorated American military pilot, Vietnam prisoner of war, Arizona senator and Republican presidential candidate, could never have been called a 'fellow traveller'. In 2016, Senator McCain wrote an opinion column in the *New York Times* that highlighted the sacrifice of the International Brigade volunteers. It was inspired by the death that year of Delmer Berg, who is thought to have been the penultimate American Brigader to pass away. McCain admitted that his respect for the Brigades had begun when he read Hemingway's *For Whom the Bell Tolls* as a twelve-year-old:

> Not all the Americans who fought in the Lincoln Brigade [as it became known popularly, though it was really a battalion] were Communists. Many were, including Delmer Berg. Others, though, had just come to fight fascists and defend a democracy. Even many of the Communists, like Mr Berg, believed they were freedom fighters first, sacrificing life and limb in a country they knew little about, for a people they had never met. You might consider them romantics, fighting in a doomed cause for something greater than their self-interest. And even though men like Mr Berg would identify with a cause, Communism, that inflicted far more misery than it ever alleviated – and rendered human dignity subservient to the state – I have always harbored admiration for their courage and sacrifice.[75]

On 2 April 1953, Franco oversaw the opening ceremony of his future tomb at the Valley of the Fallen – an enormous underground basilica dug out of the rock below a granite ridge in the Sierra de Guadarrama. Franco died in 1975. In a fraught, fast and successful transition, Spain returned to democracy within three years. It also tried to bury the memory of the civil war, preferring to look forward – while electing moderate left-wing governments for fourteen of the next nineteen years.

A socialist government finally removed the dictator's body from the mausoleum in 2019, but the 150-metre high cross above it can still be seen from the outskirts of Madrid. It is an arrogant reminder of victory, although nominally this monument was meant to commemorate all the dead. In his inauguration speech, Franco had referred only to 'our fallen' and recalled 'the heroism and enthusiasm with which they engaged in those ferocious battles in which the International Brigades were forced to bite the dust of defeat'.[76] He was then into the fifteenth year of his four decade-long dictatorship, but was obviously still irked by the foreign volunteers who had defended the Republic. He did not mention the more numerous foreign fascist contingents of Axis-power soldiers and aviators, or African colonial troops, that had ensured his victory.

This was by no means his only mention of the Brigaders. Franco often referred to them in his speeches as, having been shunned by Western democracies immediately after the Second World War, he tried to reposition himself during the Cold War as an anti-communist rather than anti-democrat. It is now too late to ask them, but it is reasonable to assume that veterans felt some satisfaction at angering him so many years later.

In 2000, a group of Spanish hikers came across a crumbling, three-tier block of concrete in the otherwise wild and rugged surroundings of the Sierra de Pàndols, where much of the final fighting had taken place. Chipped and weathered, the knee-high memorial bore the names of thirty-five volunteers from XV Brigade – including men who had travelled from the United States, Canada, Britain, Palestine, Finland, Latvia and the nearby Spanish province of Valencia. Amongst the names of those commemorated on the memorial were former Lincoln Battalion commander Bob Merriman and the old Etonian Olympic rower Lewis Clive. At the time of its rediscovery, this was the only surviving 1930s monument to the International Brigades in Spain – though a dozen more have been erected since Franco's death. Hundreds of other memorials can be found spread across the world, from Seattle to Stockholm and as far east as the Volga river town of Samara. At least one hundred such memorial plaques or monuments are spread around just the United Kingdom and Ireland, from London's Jubilee Gardens to Aberdeen, Portsmouth or Waterford.

A memorial plaque bearing poetry by Nordhal Grieg and the names of four young men who died in Spain, was unveiled on the Norwegian island of Utøya by teenagers attending a summer camp run by the Labour Party's Workers' Youth League in July 2011. Two days later, far-right gunman Anders Behring murdered sixty-nine of those young people in the country's worst massacre since the Second World War.[77]

In November 1996, some 700 surviving Brigaders from twenty-eight countries[78] had gathered for their last major reunion in Madrid. They were by now mostly in their eighties or above. Eighty-five-year-old British nurse Patience Darton, who worked with Nan Green and whose marriage to the young German Brigader Robert Aaquist lasted just two months before she was widowed, was warned by her doctors that she was too frail to travel to Spain for the event. She was, however, determined to return to a country that meant so much to her, and which she had not visited since the war. Patience attended an evening concert in homage to the Brigaders, but later felt unwell and was taken to hospital. She died the following day with her son – from her second marriage to British Brigade veteran Eric Edney in the 1950s – at her bedside. Historian Angela Jackson, who has written extensively on women in the International Brigades, was also with her. 'She had heard the cheers of the crowd and the songs she remembered from the civil war. Without doubt, she would have thought her obituary published in Spain under the heading *Morir en Madrid* – *To Die in Madrid* ... was a fitting way in which to record the close of her life,' she said.[79]

It was an emotional reunion. Spain's political right wing had recently been elected to head a democratic government for the first time since the 1930s, with the People's Party (founded by Francoist minister Manuel Fraga Iribarne) in power under Prime Minister José María Aznar. The previous year, while in opposition, his party had joined a unanimous petition from the Spanish parliament calling for Spanish nationality to be offered to all former International Brigaders. 'At the very least, they should be allowed to consider as their home the same country [Spain] that occupies such a large place in their hearts,' one deputy argued.[80] That had been put into law earlier in 1996, fulfilling a promise made by President Negrín before the bulk of the Brigaders departed in 1938.

The special nationality law helped settle debate over whether there had been something 'premature' about their anti-fascism. The volunteers had fought 'for liberty and democracy' in Spain, it said, and they were 'deserving of the gratitude of the Nation'.[81]

Abbreviations

AAN	Archiwum Akt Nowych, Warsaw
AGMAV	Archivo General Militar De Ávila, Ávila
AHN	Archivo Histórico Nacional, Madrid
BL	British Library, London
BNE	Biblioteca Nacional de España, Madrid
CDMH	Centro Documental de la Memoria Histórica, Salamanca
HIL	Hoover Institution Library, Stanford University, California
IISH	International Institute of Social History, Amsterdam
IWM	Imperial War Museum, London
LoC	Library of Congress, Washington
MML	Marx Memorial Library, London
NA	National Archives, Kew
NYPL	New York Public Library, New York
PR	Pavelló de la República, Barcelona
RGASPI	Rossiisky Gosudarstvenny Arkhiv Sotsialno-Politeskoi Istorii (Russian State Archive for Social-Political History), Moscow
SAPMO	Stiftung Archiv der Parteien und Massenorganisationen der DDR im Bundesarchiv (Foundation Archives of the Political Parties and Mass Organisations of the GDR in the Federal Archive), Lichterfelde, Berlin
SM	Severiano Montero, personal digital library of the former president of AABI, Asociación de Amigos de las Brigadas Internacionales (author's copy)
TL	Tamiment Library, New York University, New York
WU	Warwick University Digital Collections

Notes

INTRODUCTION

1 Richard Baxell, *Unlikely Warriors: the British in the Spanish Civil War and the Struggle Against Fascism*, London, 2012, p. 6.

2 http://www.albavolunteer.org/2019/08/geoffrey-servante-1919-2019/.

3 John McCain, 'Salute to a Communist', *New York Times*, 24 March 2016.

4 Andreu Castells, *Las Brigadas Internacionales de la guerra de España*, Ariel, Barcelona, 1974, pp. 378–83.

5 RGASPI 545.2.108, p. 37; RGASPI 545.2.131, pp. 30–37.

6 Fernando Rodríguez de la Torre, *Bibliografía de las Brigadas Internacionales y de la participación de extranjeros a favor de la República (1936–1939)*, Instituto de Estudios Albacetenses, Albacete, 2006.

7 Vincent Brome, *The International Brigades*, Heinemann, London, 1965; Verle Bryant Johnston, *Legions of Babel*, Pennsylvania State University Press, London, 1967; R. Dan Richardson, *Comintern Army: The International Brigades and the Spanish Civil War*, Lexington, 1982; Michael Jackson, *Fallen Sparrows: The International Brigades in the Spanish Civil War*, Philadelphia, 1994.

8 RGASPI 545.6.1 to 545.6.61. I am indebted to Severiano Montero's trawl through these archives, which produced the figure of 62; RGASPI 545.2.108, pp. 55–6 provides two more countries: Iceland and Andorra. Tiny San Marino must also be added. I have not been able to confirm the reports in Andreu Castells, *Las Brigadas Internacionales*, pp. 379–80, of volunteers from Haiti, Jamaica or 'Arabia' – though Canute Frankson, a black American volunteer, emigrated from Jamaica and Dr Arnold Bennett Donawa was born in Trinidad.

9 Yvonne Scholten of the Dutch International Brigades foundation Stichting Spanje 1936–1939 pointed Bik out to me. There is more on him at the foundation's website, spanje3639.org.

10 RGASPI 545.2.108, pp. 55–6.

11 RGASPI 545.2.108, pp. 137, 208. My estimate, based on May 1938 figures and overall attrition rate.

12 Rémi Skoutelsky, *L'Espoir guidait leurs pas*, Paris, 1998, pp. 334–6, gives twenty-five percent dead for French (and one in ten of those at the Ebro battle); Michael Petrou, *Renegades*, Vancouver, 2008, pp. 22–3, 190–241, gives twenty-two percent killed and seven percent missing in action for the Canadians; Richard Baxell and the IBMT have recorded 540 deaths for an estimated 2,365 British, Irish and Cypriot Brigaders, with fifteen percent at the Ebro – see www.richardbaxell.info/where-killed/ for the dead by battle. The 2,365 figure is from my correspondence with Baxell; Ernest Hemingway's prose poem, 'On the American Dead in Spain', was published in *New Masses*, 14 February 1939.

13 Peter N. Carroll, 'The Spanish Civil War in the 21st Century', *Antioch Review*, Fall 2012, Vol. 70, No. 4, p. 651; https://www.theguardian.com/theguardian/2012/sep/27/roosevelt-franco-letter-archive-1945.

14 Arthur Koestler et al., *The God that Failed*, Hamish Hamilton, London, 1950, pp. 324–5.

15 The Jack Jones Trust, http://www.jackjonestrust.com/jack-jones/; Jack Jones 'worked for KGB' claim: http://news.bbc.co.uk/2/hi/uk/8289962.stm; Jonathan Glancey, 'It was never a black and white affair', *Guardian*, 10 November 2000; *The Campaign Guide 1977*, Conservative and Unionist Central Office, London, 1977, pp. 20, 771.

16 Boletín Oficial del Estado, Real Decreto 39/1996, de 19 de enero, sobre concesión de la nacionalidad española a los combatientes de las Brigadas Internacionales en la guerra civil española.

I WELCOME TO THE GAMES

1 Rukeyser papers, Boxes I–1, Folder 2 and I–3, Folder 2, LoC.

2 Rukeyser papers, 'Spanish diary', Box I–1, Folder 2, LoC.

3 Muriel Rukeyser, 'Mediterranean', *New Masses*, September 1936, pp. 18–20; Arno Lustiger, *¡Shalom Libertad!, Judíos en la guerra civil española*, Flor del Viento, Barcelona, 2001, p. 79.

4 Muriel Rukeyser, 'We Came for Games', *Esquire*, October 1974, pp. 192–4.

5 Rukeyser papers, 'Spanish diary', LoC.

6 *La Vanguardia*, 18 July 1936, p. 4.

7 https://datosclima.es/Aemethistorico/Meteosingleday.php.

8 *La Vanguardia*, 18 July 1936, p. 7.

9 https://www.olympic.org/news/jesse-owens-and-the-greatest-45-minutes-in-sport.

10 Rukeyser, 'We Came for Games'.

11 Bernard N. Danchik Papers, TL.

12 Ibid.

13 Daniel Katz, *All Together Different: Yiddish Socialists, Garment Workers, and the Labor Roots of Multiculturalism*, New York, 2011, p. 189; Peter N. Carroll, *The Odyssey of the Abraham Lincoln Brigade*, Stanford, 1994, p. 56.

14 Rukeyser papers, Boxes I–1, Folder 2, and I–3, Folder 2, LoC.

15 Yvonne Scholten, *Fanny Schoonheyt, Een Nederlands meisje strijdt in de Spaanse Burgeroorlog*, Amsterdam, 2001, pp. 115–18.

16 http://historiavibrant.cat/wp-content/uploads/2017/07/cartell1422.jpg.

17 George Orwell, 'The Sporting Spirit', *Tribune*, 14 December 1945, https://www.orwellfoundation.com/the-orwell-foundation/orwell/essays-and-other-works/the-sporting-spirit/.

18 Gabriel Colomé and Jeroni Sureda (eds), *Esport i relacions internacionals (1919–1939): l'Olimpíada popular de 1936*, Centre d'Estudis Olímpics (CEO-UAB), Barcelona, 1994, p. 14.

19 Danchik Papers, TL.

20 Chris Ealham, *Class, Culture and Conflict in Barcelona, 1898–1937*, Oxford and New York, 2004, pp. 140, 169.

21 Manu Valentín, 'El exilio judeoasquenazí en Barcelona (1933–1945): un rompecabezas que pide ser esclarecido', *Entremons* 6, Universitat Pompeu Fabra, Barcelona, No. 6, June 2014, pp. 8–10.

22 Kurt Blachstein, *¡Jóvenes que rompieron con todo!* http://www.mozaika.es/avanti-popolo-jovenes-que-rompieron-con-todo/; Valentín, 'El exilio', p. 12.

23 Fundació Pau Casals at http://www.paucasals.org/?idIdioma=es&idSeccion=-PAU-CASALS-cronologia&id=4.

24 https://www.lavanguardia.com/cultura/20160717/403269007262/golpe-de-estado-1936-pau-casals-novena-beethoven-palau-de-la-musica.html.

25 Clive Bush, *The Century's Midnight: Dissenting European and American Writers in the Era of the Second World War*, Peter Lang, Bern, 2010, pp. 401–2.

26 Scholten, *Fanny*, p. 41.

27 Jozef Winkler in Michał Bron et al., *Polacy w wojnie hiszpańskiej 1936–1939*, Warsaw, 1967, pp. 82–3; Valentín, 'El exilio', v.s. Mink.

28 Winkler, in Bron et al., *Wojnie Hiszpańskiej*, pp. 82–3.

29 Wohlrath, in Hans Maassen (ed.), *Brigada Internacional ist unser Ehrenname*, Vol. 1, Berlin, pp. 57–9.

30 Pelai Pagès i Blanch, *War and Revolution in Catalonia, 1936–1939*, trans. Patrick L. Gallagher, Leiden, 2013, pp. 20–5.

31 Carroll, *Odyssey*, p. 57.

32 Richard Rhodes, *Hell and Good Company*, New York, 2015, p. 6; Carroll, *Odyssey*, p. 57.

33 Pagès i Blanch, *War and Revolution*, pp. 26–9; Rhodes, *Hell and Good Company*, p. 6; Carroll, *Odyssey*, p. 57.

34 Max Friedemann, *Brigada Internacional ist unser Ehrenname*, Vol. 1, pp. 51–4.

35 Scholten, *Fanny*, pp. 38–9.

36 Felicia Browne, 'Drawings and Papers of Felicia Browne', Tate Gallery, Correspondence, TGA 201023/2; Tom Buchanan, 'The Lost Art of Felicia Browne', *History Workshop Journal*, 54, 2002, pp. 181–90.

37 Buchanan, 'Lost Art', pp. 180–201.

38 Rukeyser, 'We Came for Games'.

39 James W. Cortada, *A City in War*, Scholarly Resources, Wilmington, 1985, pp. 10–14.

40 Browne, 'Drawings and Papers', Tate Gallery.

41 Danchik Papers, TL.

42 Wohlrath in *Brigada Internacional ist unser Ehrenname*, Vol. 1, p. 58; Valentín, 'El exilio', p. 18.

43 Rukeyser, 'We Came for Games'.

44 Ibid.

45 http://bibliotecadelaevasion.pimienta.org/uploads/2010/11/lamodelo1.pdf.

46 Carroll, *Odyssey*, pp. 55–6.

47 Ange Cassar, 'Le dramatique récit de quatre jours se sang et mort vécus à Barcelone', undated, in the newspaper *Bourguignon*, at http://doczz.fr/doc/233779/sommaire-----auxerre-tv

48 Castells, *Brigadas*, p. 21; Hans Landauer, *Diccionario de los voluntarios austriacos en la España republicana 1936–1939*, Madrid, Asociación de Amigos de las Brigadas Internacionales, 2005.

49 Rukeyser, 'We Came for Games'.

50 Danchik Papers, TL.

51 Rukeyser, 'Death in Spain: Barcelona on the Barricades', *New Masses*, 1 September 1936.

52 Winkler, in Bron et al., *Wojnie Hiszpańskiej*, pp. 82–3; Tom Wintringham, *English Captain*, London, 1939, p. 18; Gerben Zaagsma, *Jewish Volunteers, the International Brigades and the Spanish Civil War*, London, 2017, p. 70.

53 *Le Maitron Dictionnaire Biographique, Mouvement Ouvrier-Mouvement Sociale*, Editions de L'Atelier, online http://maitron-fusilles-40-44.univ-paris1.fr/spip.php?article18053.

54 Felicia Browne, letter to Elizabeth Watson, 31 July 1936, Tate Gallery, TGA 201023/2/6.

55 *Diario de la Republica*, 30 August 1936.

56 Rukeyser, 'We Came for Games'.

57 German Resistance Memorial Center, http://www.gdwberlin.de/en/recess/biographies/indexofpersons/biographie/view-bio/willy-brandt/?nocache=1

58 http://georgeorwell.org/SpanishCivilWar.htm; Paul Preston, 'Lights and Shadows in George Orwell's Homage to Catalonia', *Bulletin of Spanish Studies*, 1–29.

59 Pavel and Clara Thälmann, *Combats pour La Liberté*, La Digitale, Baye, 1997, pp. 107–9.

60 Muriel Rukeyser, 'For O.B.', in *'Barcelona, 1936' and Selections from the Spanish Civil War Archive*, Lost and Found, CUNY, New York, 2011, p. 25.

2 THE WORKERS AND THE ARMY

1 Mika Etchebéhère, *La Meva Guerra d'Espanya*, Ediciones de 1984, Barcelona, 1987, p. 11.

2 Henry Buckley, *The Life and Death of the Spanish Republic*, London, 2013, p. 195.

3 José Luis Ledesma, La 'primavera tragica' de 1936, in Angel Viñas, ed., *Los Mitos del 18 de Julio*, Barcelona, 2013, p. 328; Paul Preston, *The Spanish Holocaust: Inquisition and Extermination in Twentieth-Century Spain*, London, 2012, pp. 122, 159–82.

4 Antony Beevor, *The Battle for Spain: The Spanish Civil War 1936–1939*, London, 2007, pp. 50–1.

5 Preston, *The Spanish Holocaust*, p. 25.

6 Mola, *El objetivo, los medio y los itinerarios* in Viñas, ed., *Los Mitos*, pp. 347–8.

7 Fernando Hernández Sánchez, *Con el cuchillo entre los dientes: el mito del 'peligro comunista' en España en julio de 1936*, in Viñas, ed., *Los Mitos*, p. 286.

8 Beevor, *Battle*, p. 46; *El Socialista*, Madrid, 21 de abril de 1934.

9 Beevor, *Battle*, p. 46; Preston, *Spanish Holocaust*, p. 115.

10 Angel Viñas, *La Conspiración del General Franco*, Barcelona, 2011, p. 150.

11 Hernández Sánchez, *Con el cuchillo*, pp. 289–90.

12 Ibid.

13 Fundación Francisco Franco, https://fnff.es/historia/390489769/manuel-aznar-entrevista-a-francisco-franco.html.

14 Viñas, ed., *Los Mitos*, p. 346; Preston, *Spanish Holocaust*, pp. 38–40.

15 Eduardo G. Calleja y Julio Aróstegui, *La Tradición Recuperada: El Requeté Carlista Y La Insurrección*, Historia Contemporánea 11, pp. 51–3.

16 Preston, *Spanish Holocaust*, p. 235; Maximiliano Barrio Gozalo, *El clero en la España moderna*, Madrid, 2010, p. 49.

17 Preston, *Spanish Holocaust*, pp. 131–2.

18 Preston, *The Spanish Civil War, Reaction, Revolution and Revenge*, London, 2016, p. 96; for original text see http://www.generalisimofranco.com.

19 Fundación Francisco Franco, https://fnff.es/historia/114323443/la-famosa-carta-que-dirigio-franco-a-casares-quiroga.html.

20 Sebastian Balfour, *Deadly Embrace: Morocco and the Road to the Spanish Civil War*, Oxford University Press, 2002, p. 267.
21 Preston, *Spanish Holocaust*, p. 133.
22 Thomas, *The Spanish Civil War*, 4th edition, 2012, p. 120; Balfour, *Deadly Embrace*, p. 267.
23 Beevor, *Battle*, p. 41.
24 Ian Winchester, 'So[u]ldiers for Christ and Men for Spain: The *Apostolado Castrense*'s Role in the Creation and Dissemination of Francoist Martial Masculinity', RUHM Vol. 4/8/2015, pp. 143–163.
25 Buckley, *Spanish Republic*, p. 205.
26 Ibid., p. 206.
27 Angel Viñas, *La conivencia fascista con la sublevación y otros éxitos de la trama civil*, in Viñas, ed., *Los Mitos*, pp. 92–4.
28 Preston, *The Spanish Civil War, Reaction, Revolution and Revenge*, p. 98.
29 Thomas, *Civil War*, Kindle pos. 3464.
30 Preston, *Spanish Holocaust*, p. 133; Beevor, *Battle*, p. 56; Thomas, *Civil War*, p. 120.
31 Preston, *Spanish Holocaust*, p. 133.
32 Thomas, *Civil War*, p. 134.
33 'Nuestro día más largo', from *La muerte de la esperanza* (G. del Toro, 1973; El Garaje, 2006), Quoted in http://www.Jesúsaller.com/nuestro-dia-mas-largo-relato-autobiografico-de-eduardo-de-guzman-sobre-la-lucha-en-madrid-del-17-al-20-de-julio-de-1936/
34 Eduardo de Guzmán, *Madrid Rojo y Negro*, Madrid, 2004, p. 37.
35 Preston, *The Spanish Civil War, Reaction, Revolution and Revenge*, p. 101.
36 Buckley, *Spanish Republic*, p. 212.
37 Arturo Barea, *The Clash*, London, 1984, pp. 109–10.
38 Buckley, *Spanish Republic*, p. 211.
39 Ibid., pp. 211–14.
40 Beevor, *Battle*, Kindle pos. 1598. Fundación Francisco Franco online at https://fnff.es/memoria-historica/553423062/joaquin-fanjul-alzamiento-en-el-cuartel-de-la-montana.html.
41 María Teresa León (ed.), *Crónica general de la Guerra Civil*, Centro de Estudios Andaluces, Sevilla, 2007 (original Alianza de Intelectuales, Madrid, 1937), pp. 13–14; Beevor, *Battle*, Kindle pos. 1598; Julius Ruiz, *The 'Red Terror' and the Spanish Civil War: Revolutionary Violence in Madrid*, New York, 2014, p. 50.
42 David Mathieson, *Frontline Madrid: Battlefield Tours of the Spanish Civil War*, Oxford, 2014, p. 68.
43 Etchebéhère, *La Meva Guerra d'Espanya*, p. 11.
44 Buckley, *Spanish Republic*, p. 216.

45 Barea, *The Clash*, p. 129.
46 Mathieson, *Frontline Madrid*, p. 72; Pietro Nenni, *España*, Barcelona, 1977, p. 119.
47 Preston, *Spanish Holocaust*, p. 260.
48 Interview with the author.
49 Manuel Vicente González, *El verano revolucionario de 1936 en Madrid*, Kindle pos. 837.
50 Viñas, ed., *Los Mitos*, pp. 347–8.
51 Vicente González, *El verano revolucionario de 1936 en Madrid*, Kindle pos. 788.
52 Buckley, *Spanish Republic*, pp. 214–5.
53 Barea, *The Clash*, pp. 120–1.
54 Buckley, *Spanish Republic*, pp. 214–5.
55 Etchebéhère, *La Meva Guerra d'Espanya*, pp. 17–19.
56 Marco Puppini, 'Le Brigate Internazionali E La Politica Italiana', in Josep Sànchez Cervelló and Sebastià Agudo Blanco (eds), *Las Brigadas Internacionales: nuevas perspectivas en la historia de la Guerra Civil y del exilio*, Tarragona, 2015, pp. 78–9. Álvaro López (ed.), *La Colonna Italiana*, Quaderno No. 5, Aicvas, Roma, June 1985.

3 AMATEUR WARRIORS

1 Scholten, *Fanny*, pp. 128–9.
2 Ibid., p. 128.
3 Isabel Esteve, *Los Primeros Voluntarios Alemanes En La Guerra De España (Julio–Noviembre 1936), Grupo Thälmann Y Centuria Thälmann*, unpublished; Valentín, *El exilio*, p. 18; Scholten, *Fanny*, pp. 128–9.
4 Renée Lugschitz, *Spanienkämpferinnen, ausländische Frauen im spanischen Bürgerkrieg, 1936–1939*, Berlin, 2012, p. 40.
5 Otto Boch letter, 8 January 1938, Rukeyser papers, Box I–4, Folder 11, LoC.
6 Rukeyser papers, Box I–4, Folder 1, LoC.
7 Rukeyser, 'We Came for Games'; Bush, *The Century's Midnight*, pp. 401–2.
8 Puppini, *Garibaldini in Spagna, Storia della XII Brigata Internazionale nella guerra di Spagna*, Udine, 2019, p. 199; Carlo Rosselli, *Oggi in Spagna, domani in Italia*, http://www.storiaxxisecolo.it/antifascismo/Guerraspagna1.htm.
9 Felicia Browne, letter to Elizabeth Watson, 31 July and 7 August 1936, Tate Gallery, TGA 201023/2/6–7.
10 Buchanan, 'Lost Art', pp. 180–201.
11 Esteve, *Los Primeros Voluntarios Alemanes*.

12 Buchanan, 'Lost Art', pp. 180–201; http://www.tate.org.uk/context-comment/who-was-felicia-browne.

13 Valentín, *El exilio*, p. 18.

14 Hans Maassen, ed., *Brigada Internacional ist unser Ehrenname*, Berlin, 1974, 2 vols, pp. 77–80.

15 Bron et al., *Wojnie Hispańskiej*, pp. 32, 33.

16 Maassen, ed., *Brigada Internacional ist unser Ehrenname*, p.60; Esteve, *Los Primeros Voluntarios*, p. 25, citing Karl Jung; https://elpais.com/elpais/2017/06/19/album/1497880143322667.html#fotogal3; http://www.oxfordtimes.co.uk/news/opinions/firstperson/14283809.FirstPersonHonouringthefightagainstfascism/

17 Antoni Mrowiec in Bron et al., *Wojnie hiszpańskiej*, pp. 84–5; Rémi Skoutelsky, *L'espoir guidait leurs pas, Les volontaires français dans les brigades internationales, 1936–1939*, Paris, 1998, p. 112; Lustiger, *Shalom*, pp. 80–1, 420; Castells, *Brigadas*, p. 600.

18 Louis Delaprée, *Morir en Madrid*, Raíces, Madrid, 2009, pp. 202–3.

19 Beevor, *Battle*, p. 89.

20 La mujer en la producción, *Juventud*, 29 de agosto de 1936, p. 6.

21 Etchebéhère, *La Meva Guerra d'Espanya*, pp. 73–4.

22 Ibid., p. 74.

23 Ibid., p. 85.

24 María Gómez Escarda, 'La mujer en la propaganda política republicana', *Barataria, Revista Castellano-Manchega de Ciencias Sociales*, No. 9, 2008, pp. 83–101.

25 Lugschitz, *Spanienkämpferinnen*, pp. 41–42, 49, 51.

26 Ibid., p. 44, citing *La Vanguardia*, 23 October 1936.

27 Ibid., p. 36.

28 Beevor, *Battle*, Kindle pos. 1455, 1766, 1789.

29 Thomas, *Civil War*, Kindle pos. 3883, citing *El Socialista*, 21 July 1936.

30 Beevor, *Battle*, pp. 71–4; Pedro Maria Egea Bruno, 'Entre La Historia Y La Propaganda: Las Dos Sublevaciones Del Acorazado Jaime I En Julio De 1936', *Ebre 38*, 2010, No. 4: 31–47; see also Michael Alpert, *La guerra civil española en el mar*, Madrid, 1987.

31 Joan Serrallonga i Urquidi, 'El aparato provincialdurante la Segunda Republica. Los gobernadores civils, 1931–1939', *Hispania Nova* 7, 2007.

32 http://www.jotdown.es/2011/10/sevillanas-i-el-radiofonista-queipo-de-llano/.

33 Thomas, *Civil War*, Kindle pos. 4082; *El Socialista*, 22 July 1936, at http://guerracivildiadia.blogspot.com/2018/11/la-muerte-de-sanjurjo.html; José María Carretero, *El general Sanjurjo: su vida y su gloria*, Ediciones Caballero audaz, 1940, p. 279.

34 Ian Gibson, *Queipo de Llano: Sevilla, verano de 1936 (con las charlas radiofónicas completas)*, Barcelona, 1986, pp. 77, 132.

4 THE FASCISTS ARE HERE

1 Gerald Howson, *Arms for Spain: The Untold Story of the Spanish Civil War*, London, 1998, p. 17; Preston, *Spanish Civil War, Reaction, Revolution and Revenge*, p. 118.

2 Howson, *Arms*, p. 18; Preston, *Spanish Civil War, Reaction, Revolution and Revenge*, pp. 118–19.

3 Preston, *Spanish Civil War, Reaction, Revolution and Revenge*, p. 119; Beevor, *Battle*, p. 117.

4 Preston *Spanish Civil War, Reaction, Revolution and Revenge*, pp. 118–21.

5 Arturo Barea, *Struggle for the Spanish Soul*, 1941, his 1941 pamphlet for George Orwell's Searchlight Books; Barea, *The Clash*, p. 115.

6 Preston, *Spanish Holocaust*, p. 84.

7 Howson, *Arms*, p. 19.

8 Preston, *Spanish Civil War, Reaction*, pp. 116–17.

9 Scott Ramsay, 'Ensuring Benevolent Neutrality: The British Government's Appeasement of General Franco during the Spanish Civil War, 1936–1939', *International History Review*, 2018.

10 Beevor, *Battle*, Kindle edition, Orion, pos. 3303–4; Thomas, *Civil War*, Kindle pos. 6163, 8917; Skoutelsky, *Novedad en el frente: Las brigadas internacionales en la guerra civil*, Madrid, 2006, pp. 66–8.

11 Arthur Koestler, *The Invisible Writing*, London, 1954, 2005 edn, pp. 336, 388–91.

12 Puppini, *Garibaldini*, p. 199; Enrico Acciai, *Antifascismo, coluntariato e guerra civil in Spagna*, Milan, March 2016, pp. 66–9.

13 Antoni Mrowiec in Bron et al., *Wojne hiszpańskiej*, pp. 86–92.

5 A PROFESSIONAL VIEW

1 Hugh Purcell and Phyll Smith, *The Last English Revolutionary*, Eastbourne, 2012, pp. 113–16.

2 Wintringham, *English Captain*, p. 17.

3 Tom Buchanan, *Britain and the Spanish Civil War*, Cambridge, 1997, pp. 102–3.

4 *International Brigade Memorial Trust*, Issue Ten 2005; https://www.theguardian.com/lifeandstyle/2016/dec/17/i-had-three-dads-they-all-betrayed-me; Purcell and Smith, *Last English Revolutionary*, pp. 105–6.

5 *The Volunteer*, http://www.albavolunteer.org/2011/12/queen-of-the-machine-gun-fanny-schoonheyt-dutch-miliciana/; José Fernando Mota, *Milicians,*

reclutesicomissarisaSantCugat.Elcampamentmilitaril'EscoladeComissarisdePins del Vallès (1937–1939), https://historiasantcugat.wordpress.com/2018/06/27/ milicians-reclutes-i-comissaris-a-sant-cugat-del-valles/#sdendnote33sym.

6 Eduard Jordá, 'Weil y la Guerra Civil', *Fronterad Revista Digital*, 2009, http://www.fronterad.com/?q=weil-y-guerra-civil.

7 Simone Weil, *Diario de España, Escritos históricos y políticos*, Madrid, 2007, pp. 509–21; Niall Binns, *La llamada de España: escritores extranjeros en la guerra civil*, Montesinos, 2004, pp. 121–2.

8 Weil, *Diario de España*, pp. 509–21; Binns, *La llamada de España*, pp. 121–2.

9 Baxell, *Unlikely Warriors*, pp. 82–9.

10 Wintringham, *English Captain*, p. 18.

11 Ibid., pp. 18–22.

12 Ibid., p. 20.

13 Ludwig Renn, *La Guerra Civil Española, Crónica de un escritor en las Brigadas Internacionales*, Madrid, 2016, p. 61.

14 Delaprée, *Morir en Madrid*, p. 186.

15 http://www.kz-gedenkstaette-dachau.de/literaturetipps.html.

16 Lise London, *Roja Primavera*, Guadarrama, 1996, p. 405; Boris Volodarsky, *Stalin's Agent, the Life and Death of Alexander Orlov*, Oxford, 2015, pp. 251–2, 260.

17 London, *Roja Primavera*, p. 405; Volodarsky, *Orlov*, pp. 251–2, 260.

18 Renn, *La Guerra Civil Española*, pp. 94–9.

19 Ibid., pp. 7–11.

20 Buchanan, *Britain and the Spanish Civil War*, p. 102.

21 Kowalsky, *USSR and the International Brigades*, p. 684–7; Skoutelsky, *The Volunteer*, March 2002, pp. 9–11.

22 Wintringham, *English Captain*, pp. 18–22; Purcell and Smith, *The Last English Revolutionary*, p. 107.

23 Robert Colodny, *The Struggle for Madrid: The Central Epic of the Spanish Conflict 1936–1937*, New York, 1958; Esteve, *Los Primeros Voluntarios*; http://www.alba-valb.org/volunteers/robert-colodny.

24 Pedro José Barrachina Bolea, José Angel Viñuales Alcubierra, *En el Frente de Tardienta 1936–1938*, Tardienta, 2013, Madrid, 2015, pp. 32–5.

25 Colodny, *Struggle for Madrid*, 2009, p. 60.

26 Lisa Lindbaek, *Bataljon Thälmann*, Oslo, 1938, pp. 33, 37–8.

27 Purcell and Smith, *English Revolutionary*, p. 107.

28 Wintringham, *English Captain*, p. 23.

6 CREATING THE BRIGADES

1 RGASPI 545.3.401, Rebière report, 'Sur Le Bataillon Commmune de Paris', pp. 1–105.

2 RGASPI 545.3.158; Manuel Espadas Burgos, Manuel Requena Gallego, *La Guerra Civil Española y las Brigadas Internacionales*, Cuenca, 1998, p. 147; Skoutelsky, *Novedad*, p. 75.

3 Gustav Regler, *The Owl of Minerva*, New York, 1959, pp. 273–5.

4 RGASPI 545.2.32, Gayman report, p. 18; Mrowiec and Lino Novás in *Crónica general de la Guerra Civil* (ed, Maria Teresa León), originally *Alianza de Intelectuales Antifascistas*, reprint by Editorial Renancimimiento, Sevilla, 2007, pp. 96–100; Alvaro López, *La Centuria Gaston Sozzi*, Cuaderno 4, Aicvas, Roma, 1964, pp. 1–35; Puppini, *Garibaldini*, pp. 31, 199.

5 Renn, *La Guerra Civil Española*, pp. 108–9.

6 Michael Alpert, *The Republican Army*, Cambridge, 2013, pp. 43–9.

7 Skoutelsky, *Novedad*, p. 76; Longo, *Las Brigadas Internacionales en España*, México, 1966, p. 51; RGASPI 545.3.401, Rebière report, pp. 1–105.

8 Alpert, *The Republican Army*, p. 34.

9 Skoutelsky, *Novedad*, p. 76; Longo, *Las Brigadas Internacionales en España*, p. 51; RGASPI 545.3.401, Rebière report, pp. 1–105.

10 Georgi Dimitrov, ed. Ivo Banac, *The Diary of Georgi Dimitrov, 1933–1949*, New Haven, 2003, pp. 28, 32.

11 Skoutelsky, *Novedad*, p. 75.

12 Antonio Ramírez Navarro, *Pauline Taurinya, la mujer que abandonó a André Marty*, in Sànchez Cervelló and Agudo Blanco (eds), *Las Brigadas Internacionales*, pp. 500–513.

13 Pelai Pagis i Blanch, 'Marty, Vidal, Kléber y el Komintern. Informes y confidencias de la dirección política de las Brigadas Internacionales', *Ebre 38: revista internacional de la Guerra Civil (1936–1939)*, No. 1 (2003), pp. 11–26.

14 Longo, *Brigadas*, p. 47; Skoutelsky, *Novedad*, p. 78.

15 Longo, *Brigadas*, p. 48.

16 Ibid., pp. 48–9.

17 RGASPI 545.3.401, Rebière report, pp. 1–105; Puppini, *Garibaldini*, p. 28; AICVAS, *Quaderno 5*.

7 THE TOWER OF BABEL

1 Ronald Liversedge, *Mac-Pap: Memoir of a Canadian in the Spanish Civil War*, New Star, 2013, p. 171; Skoutelsky, *L'espoir*, pp. 111, 119; Skoutelsky, *Novedad*, pp. 116–19, 127.

2 London, *Roja primavera*, p. 325; Skoutelsky, *L'espoir*, p. 119.

3 John Sommerfield, *Volunteer in Spain*, London, 1937, p. 21.

4 Hansard, HC Deb 24 October 1935, Vol. 305, cc357–69.

5 Jessica Mitford, *Hons and Rebels*, London, 1978, Chapter 10.

6 Esmond Romilly, *Boadilla*, London, 1937, Kindle pos. 150.

7 Preston, *Spanish Civil War, Reaction*, pp. 142–3.

8 Romilly, *Boadilla*, Kindle pos. 323.

9 Ibid.; RGASPI 545.3.401, Rebière report, p. 7.

10 Preston, *Spanish Civil War, Reaction*, pp. 142–3.

11 Romilly, *Boadilla*, Kindle pos. 374.

12 RGASPI 545.3.401, Rebière report, pp. 1–105; Romilly, *Boadilla*, Kindle pos. 323; Longo, *Brigadas*, p. 49.

13 RGASPI 545.3.401, Rebière report,, pp. 1–105.

14 Baxell, *Unlikely Warriors*, p. 76.

15 London, *Roja primavera*, p. 375.

16 Skoutelsky, *Novedad*, p. 124.

17 Walter Gregory, *The Shallow Grave: A Memoir of the Spanish Civil War*, London, 1986, p. 22.

18 Alexander Szurek, *The Shattered Dream*, Boulder, CO, 1989, p. 86; RGASPI 545.3.401, Rebière report.

19 Skoutelsky, *Novedad*, pp. 128–30.

20 Ibid., pp. 120–1, 175.

21 Ibid.

22 Baxell, *Unlikely Warriors*, p. 84; Niall Binns, *La llamada de España*, p. 80.

23 Valentine Cunningham, ed., *Spanish Front, Writers on the Civil War*, Oxford, 1986, p. 328.

24 https://www.nytimes.com/2010/08/17/books/17knox.html.

25 Bernard Knox, 'Premature antifascist', *Antioch Review*, spring 1999, p. 141.

26 Sommerfield, *Volunteer*, p. 17.

27 Jan Kurzke and Kate Mangan, 'The Good Comrade', International Institute of Social History, Amsterdam, pp. 16–18.

28 James Yates, *Mississippi to Madrid: Memoir of a Black American in the Abraham Lincoln Brigade*, Greensboro, NC, 1989, p. 114.

29 Szurek, *Shattered*, p. 89.

30 Skoutelsky, *Novedad*, p. 79.

31 Longo, *Brigadas*, p. 50.

32 Romilly, *Boadilla*, Kindle pos. 412.

33 Szurek, *Shattered*, p. 88.

34 George Orwell, 'Looking Back on the Spanish Civil War', *New Road*, June 1943, at https://www.orwellfoundation.com/the-orwell-foundation/orwell/essays-and-other-works/looking-back-on-the-spanish-war/.

35 Sommerfield, *Volunteer*, p. 33.

36 Skoutelsky, *Novedad*, p. 79.

37 RGASPI 545.3.401, Rebière report, p. 20.

38 Ibid.

39 Puppini in Sànchez Cervelló and Agudo Blanco (eds), *Las Brigadas Internacionales*, p. 76; Puppini in Celada et al. (eds), *Las Brigadas Internacionales, 70 años de memoria histórica*, Salamanca, 2007, pp. 355, 359.

40 Skoutelsky, *L'espoir*, pp. 62, 95.

41 RGASPI 545.2.32, Gayman report, p. 14.

42 Ibid., p. 12; Longo, *Brigadas*, p. 55; Skoutelsky, *Novedad*, p. 85; Sommerfield, *Volunteer*, pp. 36–7.

43 RGASPI 545.3.401, Rebière report, pp. 107–8, 136–7.

44 Ibid., pp. 21–5.

45 Skoutelsky, *Novedad*, pp. 78, 81.

46 RGASPI 545.2.32, Gayman report, p. 19.

47 Howson, *Arms*, p. 278.

48 RGASPI 545.3.401, Rebière report, p. 20; Nick Guillain, *Mercenario*, Tangier, 1939, p. 10.

49 Radosh, *Betrayed*, New Haven, 2001, p. 44.

50 Longo, *Brigadas*, pp. 56–7.

51 Radosh, *Betrayed*, p. 443.

52 Longo, *Brigadas*, pp. 56–7.

53 Romilly, *Boadilla*, Kindle pos. 305; Radosh, *Betrayed*, p. 118.

54 Radosh, *Betrayed*, p. 448.

55 Castells, *Brigadas*, pp. 89, 452.

56 Various authors, *Los Rusos en la Guerra de España*, Madrid, 2009, see https://www.fpabloiglesias.es/exposiciones/historico/los-rusos-guerra-espana-1936-193929.

57 Michael Alpert, *Franco and the Condor Legion*, Bloomsbury, London, 2019, p. vii; Edoardo Mastrorilli, 'Guerra civile spagnola, intervento italiano e guerra totale' ('Spanish Civil War, Italian intervention, and total war'), *Revista Universitaria de Historia Militar, RUHM*, 6, Vol. 3, 2014, p. 74.

58 Skoutelsky, *Novedad*, pp. 451–4.

59 Skoutelsky, *L'espoir*, pp. 154, 288.

60 Radosh, *Betrayed*, p. 104; Skoutelsky, *Novedad*, p. 86.

61 Romilly, *Boadilla*, Kindle pos. 561–678.

62 Frederick S. Litten, 'The CCP and the Fujian rebellion', *Republican China*, Vol. XIV, No. 1, November 1988, pp. 57–74.

63 Romilly, *Boadilla*, Kindle pos. 561–678.

64 Skoutelsky, *L'espoir*, p. 113.

65 RGASPI 545.2.32, Gayman report, p. 12.

66 Skoutelsky, *Novedad*, pp. 86–7.

67 RGASPI 545.2.32, Gayman report, p. 16.

68 Baxell, *Unlikely Warriors*, p. 244.

69 Ibid.

70 RGASPI 545.2.32, Gayman report, p. 16.
71 Ibid.
72 Skoutelsky, *Novedad*, p. 85.
73 Howson, *Arms*, pp. 278–9.
74 Skoutelsky, *Novedad*, p. 84, *L'espoir*, p. 61; Radosh, *Betrayed*, pp. 180, 184, 270 for Russian 'preachers'.
75 Skoutelsky, *L'espoir*, p. 61; RGASPI 545.6.31, 545.6.37, 545.6.52, 545.6.347 for lists of non-Russian Mexicans.
76 César Covo, *La Guerre Camarade!*, Atlantica, 2005, p. 68.
77 Skoutelsky, *L'espoir*, p. 63, *Novedad*, p. 93.
78 Knox, 'Premature antifascist', p. 141; Sommerfield, *Volunteer*, p. 49.
79 Radosh, *Betrayed*, p. 306; Longo, *Brigadas*, p. 71.
80 Vital Gayman, 'La base des Brigades Internationales', *Estudios de Historia Social*, No. 50–1, Madrid, 1989, pp. 316–22; Skoutelsky, *Novedad*, pp. 84–5.
81 Longo, *Brigadas*, pp. 70–1.
82 Sommerfield, *Volunteer*, p. 49.

8 THE FIRST BRIGADE

1 Radosh, *Betrayed*, p. 307, citing Kléber at RGASPI 495.74.206; Geoffrey Cox, 'Eyewitness in Madrid', *Harper's* 175, 1936, p. 34; Sommerfield, *Volunteer*, p. 90.
2 Geoffrey Cox, *The Defence of Madrid*, London, 1937, p. 66.
3 Ibid., p. 67.
4 https://www.abc.es/abcfoto/revelado/20150611/abci-cibeles-madrid-guerra-201506101904.html 'la linda tapada'.
5 Reverte, *La Batalla de Madrid*, Barcelona, 2007, p. 227.
6 Renn, *Guerra Civil*, pp. 133–4.
7 Reverte, *Madrid*, p. 234.
8 Manuel Vicente González, *Madrid Militarizado*, Madrid, undated, Kindle pos. 2780.
9 Gijs van Hensbergen, *Guernica: The Biography of a Twentieth-Century Icon*, London, 2005, p. 43.
10 Sommerfield, *Volunteer*; Delaprée, *Morir in Madrid*, p. 170.
11 Delaprée, *Morir in Madrid*, p. 170; Buckley, *Spanish Republic*, p. 266.
12 Delaprée, *Morir in Madrid*, pp. 168–70, 214.
13 Claude Bowers, *My mission to Spain: Watching the Rehearsal for World War II*, New York, 1954, p. 320; Paul Preston, *We Saw Spain Die: Foreign Correspondents in the Spanish Civil War*, London, 2009, Little Brown, Kindle pos. 914.
14 Jackson, *Fallen Sparrows*, p. 57.

15 Javier Juárez, *Comandante Durán*, Barcelona, 2016, Kindle pos. 2206.

16 Radosh, *Betrayed*, p. 310.

17 Manfred Behrend, '"Retter von Madrid" und Opfer Stalins', review of Walerij Brun-Zechowoj, Manfred Stern, *General Kléber. Die tragische Biographie eines Berufsrevolutionärs (1896–1954)*, http://www.glasnost.de/autoren/behrend/rezen-stern.html (accessed 5 November 2019), originally *Arbeiterstimme*, Nuremberg, January 2001.

18 Volodarsky, *Orlov*, p. 239; Robert W. Pringle, *Historical Dictionary of Russian and Soviet Intelligence*, Lanham, 2015, p. 161; Skoutelsky, *Novedad*, p. 94.

19 Radosh, *Betrayed*, p. 295, citing RGASPI 495.74.206, 'Account by M. Fred [Kléber]'.

20 Ibid., pp. 298–30.

21 Richardson, *Comintern Army*, p. 58; Radosh, *Betrayed*, p. 305; http://www.alba-valb.org/volunteers/annibale-humberto-galleani/? searchterm= Umberto accessed 26 September 2019.

22 Radosh, *Betrayed*, p. 306; Vicente González, *Madrid Militarizado*, Kindle pos. 2808; RGASPI 545.3.401, Rebière report, and Dupont typed report.

23 RGASPI 545.3.401, Rebière report, p. 32.

24 Sommerfield, *Volunteer*, p. 81.

25 Knox, 'Premature antifascist', p. 144; http://chs.huma-num.fr/exhibits/show/marty-et-les-Brigades-internat/marty-et-les-Brigades/portraits-et-lettres-de-brigad; Sommerfield, *Volunteer*, p. 68; RGASPI 545.3.401, Jules Dumont report, 'Journal du 2eme bataillon', p. 137.

26 RGASPI 545.3.401, Rebière report, pp. 30–1.

27 Reverte, *Madrid*, p. 271.

28 Sommerfield, *Volunteer*, p. 87.

29 John Sommerfield, 'Volunteer in Spain – Part III', *The New Republic*, July 21, 1937, p. 153.

30 Radosh, *Betrayed*, pp. 297, 301.

31 Beevor, *Battle*, Kindle pos. 3170.

32 Howson, *Arms*, p. 279–81.

33 Radosh, *Betrayed*, p. 300.

34 Mijaíl Koltsov, *Diario de la guerra de España*, Barcelona, 2009, p. 214; Reverte, *Madrid*, pp. 257, 265.

35 Reverte, *Madrid*, pp. 257, 265.

36 RGASPI 545.1.401 Rebière report, pp. 30–4.

37 Cox, *Eyewitness*, p. 33.

38 RGASPI 545.3.401, Jules Dumont report, 'Journal du 2eme bataillon', p. 137; Gayman, *La base*, p. 322.

39 Sommerfield, *Volunteer*, p. 85.

40 RGASPI 545.1.401, Rebière report, pp. 32–3.
41 Sommerfield, *Volunteer*, p. 93.
42 Sommerfield, *Notebooks*, pp. 11–13 at http://www.andrewwhitehead.net/
   john-sommerfields-spanish-notebook.html, at Cadbury Research Library
   XMS873, University of Birmingham.

                              9 NO PASARÁN

 1 RGASPI 545.3.401, Jules Dumont report, 'Journal du 2eme bataillon',
   pp. 136–46; *Madrid, Plano de sus vías públicas*, Ayuntamiento de Madrid,
   Seccion de Estadistica, Mayo 1934.
 2 RGASPI 545.3.401, Jules Dumont report, pp. 136–46.
 3 Madrid, Plano de sus vías públicas.
 4 *Frente de Madrid* magazine edition 5, p. 4, and whole of edition 3.
 5 AABI, Batallón Edgar André in *La lucha por la defensa de Madrid*, AABI,
   https://brigadasinternacionales.org/.
 6 Esteve, 'Recuerdos de Brigadistas Alemanes', Academia.edu, parts 1 and 2,
   v.s. Retmann.
 7 AABI, Montero digital library, v.s. *Voluntarios Hungaros*.
 8 Esteve, *Recuerdos de Brigadistas Alemanes*, parts 1 and 2, v.s. Petros.
 9 Koltsov, *Diario*, p. 218; See also *Frente de Madrid* magazine, editions 4, 5,
   8, 14, 15, 16, 21 and 22.
10 Esteve, *Recuerdos de Brigadistas Alemanes*, parts 1 and 2, v.s. Retmann.
11 RGASPI 545.3.401, Rebière report.
12 RGASPI 545.6.394, André Marty report, 'Caracteristique de Steimer [sic]
   Richard' report, pp. 57–80; RGASPI 545.6.25, Gustav Szinda report, 'Die
   heroischen Kämpfer der XI. Internationalen Brigade', pp. 1–81.
13 *Frente de Madrid* 5, v.s. Bañuls.
14 Ibid.
15 Longo, *Brigadas*, pp. 73–4; Valter Roman, *Sub Cerol Spanieie*, Bucharest,
   1972, Chapter 1, trans. into Spanish at cierzorojo.blogspot.es.
16 *Frente de Madrid* magazine, editions 4, 5, 8, 14, 15, 16, 21 and 22; http://
   gefrema80.blogspot.com.es/2016/11/9-de-noviembre-la-batalla-de-
   madrid.html; Steven J. Zaloga, 'Soviet tank operations in the Spanish civil
   war', *The Journal of Slavic Military Studies*, 12:3, 1999, pp. 134–62.
17 Koltsov, *Diario*, p. 230; *Frente de Madrid*, edition 21; http://gefrema80.
   blogspot.com.es/2016/11/9-de-noviembre-la-batalla-de-madrid.html.
18 *El Liberal*, 10 November, 1936, p. 3.
19 Ronald Fraser, *Blood of Spain: An Oral History of the Spanish Civil War*,
   London, 1994, Kindle pos. 6326.

20 Esteve, *Recuerdos de Brigadistas Alemanes*, part 2, section 2, pp. 309–11.
21 Ibid.
22 Ibid., parts 1 and 2, v.s. Zajen and Retmann.
23 *Frente de Madrid*, 4.
24 RGASPI 545.3.73, pp. 2–4; Esteve, *Recuerdos de Brigadistas Alemanes*, part 2, section 2, pp. 309–11.
25 RGASPI 545.3.73, pp. 2–4, 21–4.

IO DEATH IN THE PARK

1 Sommerfield, *Volunteer*, p. 113.
2 RGASPI 545.6.25, Szinda report, pp. 1–81.
3 Norbert Kugler in *Brigada Internacional ist unser Ehrenname*,Vol 1, Berlin, 1974.
4 http://gefrema80.blogspot.com.es/2016/11/9-de-noviembre-la-batalla-de-madrid.html; Sommerfield, *Volunteer*, p. 115; Sommerfield, *New Republic* 3, p. 153.
5 RGASPI 545.3.401, Dumont report, pp. 136–46.
6 RGASPI 545.3.401, Rebière report, p. 37.
7 Buchanan, 'Shanghai–Madrid axis? Comparing British Responses to the Conflicts in Spain and China, 1936–39', *Contemporary European History*, 21, p. 535; SS 197, *The Tactical employment of Lewis Guns*, Stationary Service Collection, London, January 1918.
8 RGASPI 545.3.401, Rebière report, pp. 28, 37–9; Dumont report, p. 139; RGASPI 545.3.73, lists of dead and injured, pp. 1–28, 191–2.
9 RGASPI 545.3.401, Rebière report, p. 37.
10 Ibid., p. 32.
11 Reverte, *Madrid*, p. 489, fn 78.
12 Ibid., p. 496, fn 84.
13 RGASPI 545.3.401, Dumont report, pp. 139–140; Reverte, *Madrid*, p. 331.
14 Reverte, *Madrid*, pp. 336–7; Frank Thomas, *Brother against Brother: Experiences of a British Volunteer in the Spanish Civil War*, Stroud, 1998, p. 69.
15 Reverte, *Madrid*, pp. 336–7, 343–4.
16 Fritz Rettmann in *Brigada Internacional ist unser Ehrenname*, Vol. 1; Lech Wyszczelkski, ed., *Dabrowszczacy*, Warsaw, 1986, pp. 18–19; Knox, 'Premature antifascist', p. 143.
17 RGASPI 545.3.401, Rebière report, p. 47.
18 Cox, *Defence of Madrid*, p. 156; various German eyewitness testimonies in *Brigada Internacional ist unser Ehrenname*, Vol. 1.
19 Reverte, *Madrid*, p. 342, citing *El Liberal*, 14 November, 1936.

11 BULLETPROOF BOOKS

1 Kurzke and Mangan, 'Good Comrade', pp. 218–19.
2 Sommerfield, *New Republic* 3, p. 153.
3 Knox, 'Premature antifascist', pp. 142–3.
4 RGASPI 545.3.401, Rebière report, p. 53.
5 Kurzke and Mangan, 'Good Comrade', p. 84.
6 Sommerfield, *Volunteer*, p. 147.
7 John Cornford, *Understand the Weapon, Understand the Wound*, Manchester, 2016, p. 162.
8 Ibid., p. 187.
9 Kurzke and Mangan, 'Good Comrade', p. 92.
10 RGASPI 545.3.401, Rebière report, p. 60.
11 Fraser, *Blood of Spain*, Kindle pos. 6351.
12 http://www.madrid1936.es/universitaria/images/dscn6478.jpg 1.5kilometres.
13 RGASPI 545.3.401, Rebière report, p. 47.
14 Kurzke and Mangan, 'Good Comrade', p. 92.
15 RGASPI 545.6.394, André Marty report, pp. 57–80; RGASPI 545.6.25, Szinda report, pp. 1–81.
16 Howson, *Arms*, p. 279.
17 Esteve, *Recuerdos de Brigadistas Alemanes*, parts 1 and 2, v.s.Stank.
18 Josie McLellan, *Antifascism and Memory in East Germany: Remembering the International Brigades 1945–1989*, Clarendon, Oxford, 2004, pp. 107–8.
19 RGASPI 545.3.73.
20 Marcel Acier, ed., *From Spanish Trenches: Recent letters from Spain*, New York, 1937, p. 76.
21 Marcel Acier, From Spanish Trenches, p. 76.
22 Kurzke and Mangan, 'Good Comrade', p. 93.
23 Ibid.

12 A NEW BRIGADE

1 Skoutelsky, *L'espoir*, p. 67.
2 Sidbrint database, Universitat de Barcelona, http://sidbrint.ub.edu/ca/content/longo-luigi
3 Longo, *Brigadas*, pp. 75–6.
4 Covo, *La Guerre*, p. 71; Renn, *Guerra Civil*, p. 154.
5 Castells, *Brigadas*, pp. 378–83.
6 RGASPI 545.6.3, p. 20.
7 Romilly, *Boadilla*, Kindle pos. 421.

8 Ibid., Kindle pos. 533.

9 RGASPI 545.2.32, Gayman report, p. 19.

10 Romilly, *Boadilla*, Kindle pos. 687.

11 Longo, *Brigadas*, p. 75.

12 Alexei Eisner, *Chelovek s tremya imenami, Povest'o Mate Zalke*, Moscow, 1986, Chapter 9.

13 Alexei Eisner, *La 12 Brigada Internacional*, Valencia, 1972, pp. 67–8.

14 Romilly, *Boadilla*, Kindle pos. 698.

15 Renn, *Guerra Civil*, p. 149; RGASPI 545.3.155, pp. 1–3.

16 Eisner, *12 Brigada*, p. 72.

17 Eisner, *Zalke*, Chapter 1; Preston, *We Saw Spain Die*, Kindle pos. 4514.

18 Eisner, *12 Brigada*, p. 73.

19 Eisner, *Zalke*, Chapters 3, 4, 12.

20 AABI, *Paul Lukács. El general que aunó las armas y las letras*, https:// brigadasinternacionales.org/.

21 Eisner, *12 Brigada*, pp. 73–5.

22 Ibid., p. 77.

23 Romilly, *Boadilla*, Kindle pos. 738.

24 Longo, *Brigadas*, pp. 76–7.

25 RGASPI 545.3.175.

26 Renn, *Guerra Civil*, p. 169.

27 Ibid., pp. 168–9.

28 RGASPI 545.3.175, Raymond Hantz, 'Le Bataillon "André Marty" (XIII Brigade Internationale) de Noviembre 1936 à Février 1937', Memoire de Raymond Hantz, pp. 19–22; Renn, *Guerra Civil*, pp. 173–6.

29 Longo, *Brigadas*, pp. 81–2.

30 Eisner, *12 Brigada*, p. 97.

31 Ibid., p. 121; Longo, *Brigadas*, p. 82; Puppini, *Garibaldini*, p. 59.

32 Eisner, *12 Brigada*, p. 98.

33 Ibid., p. 100; Longo, *Brigadas*, p. 82.

34 Longo, *Brigadas*, p. 81; RGASPI 545.3.175, Hantz report, pp. 19–22.

35 Renn, *Guerra Civil*, pp. 174–80.

36 Ibid., p. 192.

37 RGASPI 545.3.175, Hantz report, pp. 19–22; RGASPI 545.6.394, Marty report, pp. 57–80.

38 Covo, *La Guerre*, p. 66.

39 Eisner, *12 Brigada*, pp. 102–5.

40 RGASPI 545.3.175, Hantz report; Eisner, *12 Brigada*, p. 116; Renn, *Guerra Civil*, p. 193.

41 Covo, *La Guerre*, p. 66; Longo, *Brigadas*, p. 83.

42 Eisner, *12 Brigada*; Skoutelsky, *Novedad*, pp. 100–1 gives this as rumour.

43 Skoutelsky, *Novedad*, pp. 99–100.

44 Eisner, *12 Brigada*, p. 114.

45 Regler, *Owl of Minerva*, p. 280.

46 Covo, *La Guerre*, p. 35.

47 Ibid., pp. 68, 98.

48 Ibid., p. 98.

49 Radosh, *Betrayed*, p. 312; RGASPI 545.6.394, Marty report, pp. 57–80.

50 RGASPI 545.6.394, Marty report, pp. 57–80.

51 Eisner, *12 Brigada*, p. 107.

52 Ibid., p. 127.

53 Eisner, *12 Brigada*, pp. 88, 127; Alexei Kochetkov, *Beyond the Pyrenees (I Am Coming Back to You* Book 2), T&V Media, Kindle pos. 1218–23.

54 Renn, *Guerra Civil*, p. 698; Eisner, *12 Brigada*, p. 127.

55 Radosh, *Betrayed*, p. 273.

56 Renn, *Guerra Civil*, p. 195; AABI, *Paul Lukács: El general que aunó las armas y las letras*, AABI, https://brigadasinternacionales.org/.

57 Romilly, *Boadilla*, Kindle pos. 1275.

58 RGASPI 545.3.175, Hantz report, p. 18.

59 Ibid., pp. 19–24.

60 RGASPI 545.3.401, Ribière report, p. 66.

61 RGASPI 545.3.175, Hantz report, p. 25.

62 Regler, *Owl of Minerva*, pp. 280–1.

63 Ibid., p. 279.

64 Manuel Vicente González, *Las Brigadas Internacionales y las Brigadas Mixtas en la Batalla de Madrid*, Marisol Kindelan, Kindle pos. 2018.

13 SAVE MADRID

1 RGASPI 545.2.145, Hans Kahle letter, 22/11/1936.

2 RGASPI 545.3.73; Various German testimonies in Various authors, *Brigada Internacional ist unser Ehrenname*, Vol. 1, pp. 18–21; Radosh, *Betrayed*, p. 308.

3 RGASPI 545.2.145, Kahle letter.

4 *Peuple en Armes*, 4, 25 November 1936, pp. 2–3.

5 Regler, *Owl of Minerva*, p. 297.

6 RGASPI 545.2.128; *Peuple en Armes*, 5, 15 December 1936, p. 5; http://vexi.cat/annasebas/bicementerio.htm.

7 Eisner, *12 Brigada*, pp. 158, 184.

8 There is confusion over the exact timing of handovers: RGASPI 545.3.158, pp. 8, 19; RGASPI 545.3.401, pp. 46–9; RGASPI 545.3.87, p. 60; RGASPI 545.3.73, pp. 6–7, 15–23, 28; RGASPI 545.6.25, p. 12; Longo, *Brigadas*,

p. 91–3; Puppini, *Garibaldini*, p. 59; Alvaro Lopez, AICVAS *Quaderno 7* 'Il Battaglione Garibaldi cronologia', Rome, May 1990, pp. 71–2; *Las Brigadas Internacionales y las Brigadas Mixtas*, Kindle pos. 1078, 2018, 1513, 4129; AABI, Sven Tuytens, *Piet Akkerman, Un Che guevara de Amberes*, AABI, https://brigadasinternacionales.org/.

9 Radosh, *Betrayed*, p. 311; Eisner, *12 Brigada*, p. 130; *Peuple en Armes* 4, 25 November 1936, pp. 2–3.

10 Radosh, *Betrayed*, p. 311.

11 Michel Lefebvre and Remi Skoutelsky, *Las Brigadas Internacionales, Imágenes Recuperadas*, Barcelona, 2003, p. 62.

12 Eisner, *12 Brigada*, pp. 153–4.

13 *New York Times*, 'Cornell Capa, Photojournalist and Museum Founder, Dies at 90', 24 May 2008.

14 Eisner, *12 Brigada*, p. 153.

15 Ibid., p. 154; Vaill, *Hotel Florida*, p. 83, p. 375 footnotes.

16 Regler, *Owl of Minerva*, p. 281.

17 Ibid., p. 282; Vaill, *Hotel Florida*, p. 84.

18 Regler, *Owl of Minerva*, p. 282; Vaill, *Hotel Florida*, p. 84.

19 Vaill, *Hotel Florida*, p. 85; Capa, *Death in the Making* (unpaged); Delapree, *Martyrdom of Madrid*, Madrid, 1937, p. 40.

20 *Regards*, 17 December 1936, pp. 1, 6–17 at https://gallica.bnf.fr/ark:/12148/bpt6k7654709m/f5.image.texteImage

21 Delaprée, *Morir en Madrid*, Madrid, 2009, pp. 185–8.

22 Longo, *Brigadas*, pp. 93–4.

23 Ibid., p. 93.

24 Eisner, *12 Brigada*, pp. 139, 141; Renn, *Guerra Civil*, p. 199; Longo, *Brigadas*, p. 94.

25 Eisner, *12 Brigada*, p. 138.

26 Ibid., p. 141.

27 Renn, *Guerra Civil*, pp. 202–4.

28 Covo, *La Guerre*, pp. 75–81, 88.

29 Eisner, *12 Brigada*, p. 142.

30 Renn, *Guerra Civil*, pp. 202–4.

31 Longo, *Brigadas*, p. 95.

32 Covo, *La Guerre*, pp. 88–9.

33 Regler, *Owl of Minerva*, pp. 284–5.

34 Covo, *La Guerre*, p. 89.

35 Sommerfield, *Volunteer*, p. 109.

36 Covo, *La Guerre*, p. 79; Eisner, *12 Brigada*, p. 145; Renn, *Guerra Civil*, p. 203.

37 *Ahora*, 14 November 1936, p. 11; Cabeza San Deogracias, José, 'Antonio Col como ejemplo del uso de la narrativa como propaganda durante la Guerra Civil española', *Revista Historia y Comunicación Social*, 2005, 10, pp. 37–50.

38 RGASPI 545.6.25, Szinda report, pp. 1–81.

39 Ibid.

40 Alpert, *Republican Army*, p. 249.

41 Renn, *Guerra Civil*, p. 200.

42 Thomas, *Brother against Brother*, p. 73.

43 AABI, Sven Tuytens, *Piet Akkerman, un Che Guevara de Amberes en la Guerra Civil Española*, AABI, https://brigadasinternacionales.org/; Thomas, *Brother against Brother*, p. 7; RGASPI 545.3.175, Hantz report; Longo, *Brigadas*, p. 102; Eisner, *12 Brigada*, p. 147; Skoutelsky, *Novedad*, p. 109.

44 RGASPI 545.3.174, Roasi report, pp. 140–3; Puppini, *Garibaldini*, p. 62; Renn, *Guerra Civil*, p. 211.

45 Eisner, *12 Brigada*, p. 158.

46 Romilly, *Boadilla*, Kindle pos. 1725.

47 Castells, *Brigadas*, pp. 526–94.

48 RGASPI 545.3.175.

49 RGASPI 545.6.25, Szinda report, pp. 1–81; Radosh, *Betrayed*, p. 313; Skoutelsky, *Novedad*, p. 140; Castells, *Brigadas*, p. 548.

50 Lindbaek, *Bataljon Thälmann*, p. 74; RGASPI 545.6.395, Marty report.

51 Radosh, *Betrayed*, p. 313.

52 Longo, *Brigadas*, p. 96.

53 RGASPI 545.2.108, p. 54; Skoutelsky, *L'espoir*, pp. 154, 339.

54 Skoutelsky, *Novedad*, pp. 108–9, citing Charles Jacquet papers.

55 Richardson, *Comintern Army*, p. 66; Sidbrint database, Universitat de Barcelona, http://sidbrint.ub.edu/en/content/vehlow-franz.

56 Covo, *La Guerre*, pp. 104–5; Skoutelsky, *Novedad*, p. 105; *Le Maitron Dictionnaire Biographique*, http://maitron-en-ligne.univ-paris1.fr/spip.php?article129465.

57 Eisner, *12 Brigada*, p. 167; Regler, *Owl of Minerva*, p. 285.

58 Regler, *Owl of Minerva*, p. 286.

59 'Ha muerto el comisario político Hans Beimler', *Ahora* (Madrid), 2 December 1936, p. 6.

60 Agnes Hodgson, diary entry, 6 December 1936, in Judith Keene, ed., *The Last Mile to Huesca: An Australian Nurse in the Spanish Civil War*, http://spartacus-educational.com/SPbeimer.htm, and http://spartacus-educational.com/JFKhodgsonA.htm.

61 Victor Hurtado, *Las Brigadas Internacionales, Atlas Guerra Civil Español*, Barcelona, 2013, p. 27.

62 Longo, *Brigadas*, p. 105.

14 HAIL, THE SAVIOUR OF MADRID!

1 Puppini, *Garibaldini*, p. 39.

2 *El Heraldo de Madrid*, 12 November 1936, p. 1; *Ahora* (Madrid), 12 November 1936, p. 8.

3 Marco Puppini, *Le brigate internazionali e la politica italiana*, in Sànchez Cervelló and Agudo Blanco (eds.), *Las Brigadas Internacionales*, pp. 76–91.

4 Puppini in Celada et al., *70 años*, p. 356; Puppini, *Le brigate internazionali*, pp. 76–9.

5 Acciai, *Antifascismo*, pp. 67–9; Puppini, *Le brigate internazionali*, pp. 76–91.

6 Puppini in Celada et al., *70 años*, pp. 356–7.

7 Puppini, *Le brigate internazionali*, pp. 78–9; full text in Álvaro López, *La Colonna Italiana*, Quaderno No. 5, Roma, 1985.

8 Puppini in Celada et al., *70 años*, pp. 357–8; Puppini, *Garibaldini*, pp. 42–3.

9 Puppini in Celada et al., *70 años*, p. 358.

10 Ibid.

11 Puppini, *Le brigate internazionali*, pp. 78–9.

12 Knox, 'Premature antifascist', p. 142; http://www.sar.org.ro/polsci/?p=1256.

13 Puppini, *Le brigate internazionali*, pp. 80–1.

14 *El Liberal*, 26 November 1936.

15 Vaill, *Hotel Florida*, p. 135; https://elpais.com/diario/2011/10/29/madrid/1319887463850215.html.

16 Rafael Alberti, *Poesía* (1924–44), Buenos Aires, 1946, p. 235.

17 Radosh, Betrayed, p. 309.

18 Radosh, *Betrayed*, pp. 309–10; *La Voz* (Madrid), 5 December 1936, p. 1.

19 *Mundo gráfico*, 2 December 1936; *La Voz*, 5 December 1936; *New York Times*, 13 December 1936.

20 Castells, *Brigadas*, p. 143.

21 Radosh, *Betrayed*, pp. 295–368.

22 *New York Times*, 13 December 1936, p. 41, and January 3, 1937, p. 120; Radosh, *Betrayed*, p. 310.

23 Vicente Rojo, *Así fué la defensa de Madrid (Aportación a la Historia de la Guerra de España, 1936–1939)*, Imprenta de la Comunidad de Madrid, 1987, pp. 252–4.

24 Radosh, *Betrayed*, pp. 314–15.

25 Ibid.

26 RGASPI 545.3.401, Rebière report.

27 RGASPI 545.6.394, Marty report, p. 4.

28 Eisner, *12 Brigada*, p. 189.

29 Ibid.

30 Alfred Kantorowicz, *Spanisches Kriegstagebuch*, Frankfurt, 2016, p. 41.

31 Romilly, *Boadilla*, p. 137.

32 Morris Riley, *Philby: The Hidden Years*, London, 1999, p. 131; see also Stewart Purvis and Jeff Hulber, *Guy Burgess: The Spy Who Knew Everyone*, London, 2016.

33 *New York Times*, 27 December 1936, p. 66.

15 THE BATTLE OF THE MIST

1 Romilly, *Boadilla*, Kindle pos. 2681.

2 RGASPI 545.6.25, Szinda report, pp. 16–17.

3 RGASPI 545.3.73, pp. 1–28, 191–2.

4 Kurzke and Mangan, *The Good Comrade*, p. 309.

5 Kantorowicz, *Spanisches*, pp. 45–6.

6 Knox, 'Premature antifascist', pp. 142–5; Romilly, *Boadilla*, Kindle pos. 2166; Baxell, *Unlikely Warriors*, pp. 111–12, 160; see also *Scottish Labour History*, 11 May 1977, p. 41. http://libraryblogs.is.ed.ac.uk/edinburghuniversityarchives/tag/spanish-civil-war/

7 Renn, *Guerra Civil*, pp. 232–3.

8 Kurzke and Mangan, 'Good Comrade', p. 308.

9 Renn, *Guerra Civil*, pp. 232–3, 243; Reverte, *Madrid*, pp. 419–23.

10 Knox, 'Premature antifascist', p. 144.

11 Knox, 'Premature antifascist', pp. 142–5; RGASPI 545.3.401, pp. 62–5.

12 Kurzke and Mangan, 'Good Comrade', p. 103.

13 Ibid., pp. 309–15.

14 Roderick Stewart and Sharon Stewart, *Phoenix, the Life of Norman Bethune*, Montreal, 2011, Kindle pos. 3246.

15 Kurzke and Mangan, 'Good Comrade', p. 314.

16 Kantorowicz, *Spanisches*, pp. 46–7.

17 AABI – Comuna de Paris 1, 'Louis' (trans. Ana Soler) at AABI online at https://brigadasinternacionales.org/

18 RGASPI 545.3.401, Rebière report, p. 65.

19 Javier M. Calvo Martínez, at http://frentedebatalla-gerion.blogspot.com.es/2009/01/intento-de-resumen-de-una-batalla-no.html; 'La guerra civil española mes a mes, nº 8', Biblioteca El Mundo, basados en los trabajos de J. M. Martínez Bande y en los croquis de de J. A. Hernández Serrano.

20 RGASPI 545.3.401, Rebière report, p. 69.

21 RGASPI 545.3.73, pp. 1–28, 191–2.

22 Castells, *Brigadas*, p. 583.

23 *Todos Unidos*, November, 1937, p. 15; RGASPI 545.3.73, pp. 1–28, 191–2.

24 CDMH Salamanca, Serie Militar 5491/3.

25 RGASPI 545.3.401, Ribière report, p. 66.

26 RGASPI 545.6.25, Szinda report.

27 RGASPI 545.3.401, Rebière report, pp. 67–8.

16 STALIN WAS STILL A SAINT

1 Regler, *Owl of Minerva*, p. 277.

2 Judith Thurman, 'Rules of engagement: writing, fighting, and André Malraux', *New Yorker*, 2 May 2005; see also Preston, *We Saw Spain Die*, Chapter 6.

3 Regler, *Owl of Minerva*, p. 278.

4 Andy Durgan, 'With the POUM international volunteers on the Aragon Front (1936–1937)', *Ebre 38*, 8, 2018, pp. 137–8; Andy Durgan, 'Marxism, war and revolution: Trotsky and the POUM', *Revolutionary History*, Vol. 9, No. 2, 2006; Regler, *Owl of Minerva*, p. 278.

5 Regler, *Owl of Minerva*, pp. 230–4.

6 Ibid.

7 Ibid., pp. 236, 241, 248–50.

8 Ibid.

9 Ibid., pp. 236–7, 260.

10 Ibid.

11 Helen Rappaport, *Joseph Stalin: A Biographical Companion*, Santa Barbara, 1999, p. 142; Robert Conquest *The Great Terror: Stalin's purge of the thirties*, Oxford, 1968, p. 169.

12 Regler, *Owl of Minerva*, p. 250.

13 Ibid., p. 271.

14 Ibid., pp. 248, 267.

15 J. V. Stalin, *On the Draft Constitution of the U.S.S.R*, Report Delivered at the Extraordinary Eighth Congress of Soviets of the U.S.S.R., 25 November 1936. See version at Marxist Internet Archive https://www. marxists.org/reference/archive/stalin/works/1936/11/25.htm (consulted 3 November 2019).

16 *Peuple en Armes*, No. 5, 15 December 1936, p. 12.

17 Peter Petroff, *New Constitution of the U.S.S.R.*, at Marxists.org/archive/ petroff/1936/Soviet-constitution, original source: *Labour*, July 1936, pp. 266–7.

18 Michael Petrou, *Renegades: Canadians in the Spanish Civil War*, Vancouver, 2008, p. 181.

19 RGASPI 545.3.401, Rebière report.

20 André Gide, *Return from the USSR*, New York, 1937, pp. 42, 49.

21 Ibid., p. 62.

22 Roger Codou, *Le Cabochard: Mémoires d'un communiste*, Paris, 1983, pp. 100–1.

23 Antonio Ramírez Navarro, *Pauline Taurinya. La mujer que abandonó André Marty*, in Sànchez Cervelló and Agudo Blanco (eds.), *Las Brigadas Internacionales*, pp. 500–13.

24 Regler, *Owl of Minerva*, p. 279; Ramírez Navarro, *Pauline Taurinya*, pp. 500–13.

25 Henri Dupré, *La Légion Tricolore En Espagne, 1936–1939*, Paris, 1942, p.13.

26 Sidbrint database, Universitat de Barcelona, http://sidbrint.ub.edu/ca/content/dupre-henri.

27 https://brigadasinternacionales.org/index.php?option=comcontent&view=article&id=976:comuna-de-paris-1&catid=44:croni-bi&Itemid=82.

28 Dupré, *Tricolore*, pp. 48–9, 62.

29 Ibid., pp. 7, 19, 44, 48–9, 52–3, 62, 69, 73, 103–4, 238.

30 Ibid., pp. 7, 19, 44, 48–9, 52–3, 62, 69, 73, 103–4, 238; Nicholas Atkin, *The French at War*, p. 71.

31 Dupré, *Tricolore*, pp. 7, 19, 44, 48–9, 52–3, 62, 69, 73, 103–4, 238; Atkin, *The French at War*, p. 71.

32 Castells, *Brigadas*, pp. 121–3; Manuel Requena Gallego, 'Albacete, base de reclutamiento e instrucción de las Brigadas Internacionales', *Al-Basit: Revista de estudios albacetenses*, Nº. Extra, 1996, pp. 78–9; Esteve, *Recuerdos de Brigadistas Alemanes*, part 2, pp. 229–31.

33 Esteve, *Recuerdos de Brigadistas Alemanes*, pts 1 and 2, v.s. Engel; Castells, *Brigadas*, p. 122.

34 Castells, *Brigadas*, p. 124; RGASPI 545.3.284, p. 5.

35 Pedro Corral, *Si me quieres escribir: la batalla de Teruel*, Barcelona, 2005, p. 21.

36 Esteve, *Recuerdos de Brigadistas Alemanes*, pts 1 and 2, v.s. Rau, Engel, Munschke and Michel; AABI, *La XIII BI en el frente de Granada*, http://www.brigadasinternacionales.org.

37 Esteve, *Recuerdos de Brigadistas Alemanes*, pts 1 and 2, v.s. Rau and Munschke.

38 AABI, *La XIII BI en el frente de Granada*, http://www.brigadasinternacionales.org; Sidbrint database, Universitat de Barcelona, http://sidbrint.ub.edu/en/content/becker-klaus.

39 *Time* magazine, 3 August 1953.

40 IWM, Aitken Reel 2.

41 RGASPI 545.3.284, Commissar Massin letter, pp. 7–8.

42 Longo, *Brigadas*, p. 145.

43 RGASPI 545.3.284, Massin letter, pp. 7–8.

44 Castells, *Brigadas*, pp. 125–6; Skoutelsky, *Novedad*, p. 270.

45 RGASPI 545.3.284, pp 5–6; AABI, *La XIII BI en el frente de Granada*, http://www.brigadasinternacionales.org.

17 SANS NOM AND THE POLES

1 William W. Hagen, 'Before the "final solution": toward a comparative analysis of political anti-Semitism in interwar Germany and Poland', *Journal of Modern History*, Vol. 68, No. 2, June 1996, pp. 377–8.

2 Szurek, *Shattered*, p. 85.

3 Hagen, 'Before the "final solution" ', pp. 353–6.

4 Ibid., p. 361.

5 Ibid., pp. 351–81.

6 Ibid., pp. 369–72.

7 Norman Davies, *God's Playground – A History of Poland*, New York, Vol. II, pp. 407–9, 426–9.

8 Centralne archivum komitetu centralnego polskiej zjednoczonej partii robotniczej 9.182/V–14 *Warsaw Krotka historia udzialu polskich ochotnikow w wojnie o niepodlegosc hiszpanii*, pp. 6–9.

9 Len Crome, Walter 1897–1947, 'A Soldier in Spain', *History Workshop Journal*, No. 9, Spring 1980, p. 128; Szurek, *Shattered*, p. 317.

10 Szurek, *Shattered*, pp. 86–8.

11 Ibid., pp. 90, 208; Thomas E. Sawyer, *The Jewish Minority in the Soviet Union*, New York, 2019 edn, see the Jewish Resettlement Initiative in Chapter 4.

12 Szurek, *Shattered*, p. 96.

13 Ibid., pp. 96–104.

14 Len Crome, 'A Soldier in Spain'.

15 Szurek, *Shattered*, p. 104.

16 Vladimir Iosifovich Pyatnitskiy and Ilya Grigorievich Starinov, *Razvedshkola No 005, Istoriya partizanskogo dvizheniya*, Kharvest, 2005, Chapter 5.

17 Len Crome, 'A Soldier in Spain', pp. 116–128.

18 Ibid.

19 Radosh, *Betrayed*, p. 448.

20 Ibid.

21 Castells, *Brigadas*, p. 128.

22 *Le Journal* (Paris), 24 May 1939; Sidbrint database, Universitat de Barcelona, http://sidbrint.ub.edu/es/content/delesalle-gaston; Jacques Delperrié de Bayac, *Las Brigadas Internacionales*, Júcar, Madrid, 1978, p. 162.

23 Katharine Bail Hoskins, *Today the Struggle: Literature and Politics in England during the Spanish Civil War*, Austin, 1969, p. 100.

24 Rob Stradling, *History and Legend: Writing the International Brigades*, Cardiff, 2003, p. 147; Joe Monks, *With the Reds in Andalusia*, London, 1985, online version at http://irelandscw.com/ibvol-Monks.htm, v.s. 'Of the thirteen'.

25 Baxell, *Unlikely Warriors*, p. 114.

26 http://theauxiliaries.com/men-alphabetical/men-n/nathan/nathan-gm.html.

27 Ibid.

28 Baxell, *Unlikely Warriors*, pp. 114–15, citing Joe Monks.

29 Radosh, *Betrayed*, p. 448; Miguel Vilches Giménez, 'La batalla del Cerro Telégrafo', *Adalid* 4.

30 Szurek, *Shattered*, pp. 92–6.

31 Antonio Pantoja Vallejo and José Pantoja, *La XIV Brigada Internacional en Andalusía. La Tragedia de Villa del Río y la Batalla de Lopera*, Jaén, 2006, p. 100.

32 Ibid., p. 99.

33 Antonio Marín Muñoz, *La Guerra Civil en Lopera y Porcuna (1936–1939) Vestigios de la Contienda*, Lopera, 2008, p. 25; Pantoja and Pantoja, *Tragedía*, pp. 97–102.

34 Szurek, *Shattered*, p. 93.

35 Pantoja and Pantoja, *Tragedía*, pp.103–17; Theodor Balk, *La Quatorzième*, *Éditions du Commisariat des Brigades Internationales*, Madrid, 1937, p. 47; Castells, *Brigadas*, p. 126.

36 RGASPI 545.3.410, Petrovitch report, pp. 6–7.

37 Ibid.; RGASPI 545.3.399, Heussler report, p. 22; Vilches, 'Cerro Telégrafo', pp. 151–3; Pantoja and Pantoja, *Tragedía*, pp. 103–17; Balk, *La Quatorzième*, pp. 48–9.

38 Vilches, *Cerro Telégrafo*, pp. 151–3; Pantoja and Pantoja, *Tragedía*, pp. 103–117, 151–2.

39 RGASPI 545.3.410, Petrovitch report, pp. 6–7; Castells, *Brigadas*, p. 129; Pantoja and Pantoja, *Tragedía*, pp. 103–17, 151–2.

40 Pantoja and Pantoja, *Tragedía*, pp. 103–17; Seweryn Ajzner, *La Base de las Brigadas Internationales en Albacete*, AABI, trans. from French by Ana Soler Espiauba, https://www.brigadasinternacionales.org/index.php?option=comcontent&view=article&id=684:base-albacete-aizner&catid=44:croni-bi&Itemid=82

41 Pantoja and Pantoja, *Tragedía*, pp. 103–17.
42 Ibid., pp. 113–14; RGASPI 545.3.410, Petrovitch report, pp. 6–7.
43 Gillain, *Mercenario*, pp. 10–18.
44 Pantoja and Pantoja, *Tragedía*, pp. 103–17; Balk, *La Quatorzième*, p. 56; RGASPI 545.3.399, Heussler report, pp. 18–24.
45 RGASPI 545.3.410, Petrovitch report, pp. 6–7; RGASPI 545.3.399, Heussler report, p. 23; Castells, *Brigadas*, p. 129; Pantoja and Pantoja, *Tragedía*, pp. 107-17.
46 Szurek, *Shattered*, p. 95; RGASPI 545.3.410, Petrovitch report, pp. 6–7; Pantoja and Pantoja, *Tragedía*, p. 117; Vilches, *Cerro Telégrafo*, p. 153; see also Balk, *La Quatorzième*.
47 RGASPI 545.3.410, Petrovitch report, pp. 6–7.
48 Szurek, *Shatttered*, p. 95.

18 MEN IN RUBBER COATS

1 Monks, *With the Reds*, v.s. Andújar.
2 RGASPI 545.3.399, Heussler report, pp. 21–2.
3 Pantoja and Pantoja, *Tragedía*, pp. 123–4.
4 Ibid., p. 153.
5 RGASPI 545.3.394, Guimpel report.
6 Balk, *La Quatorzième*, p. 70; Pantoja and Pantoja, *Tragedía*, p. 125.
7 *Diario La Union de Sevilla*, Numero extraordinario 1, 8 de julio 1938 in Pantoja and Pantoja, *Tragedía*, p. 286.
8 Joe Monks, *With the Reds*, s.v. 'firstest with the mostest'.
9 Pantoja and Pantoja, *Tragedía*, p. 153.
10 Balk, *La Quatorzième*, p. 71; Calleja and Aróstegui, 'La Tradición Recuperada', pp. 29–53.
11 AABI Montero personal digital archive, v.s. Collange.
12 *Diario La Union de Sevilla*, Numero extraordinario 1, 8 de julio 1938 in Pantoja and Pantoja, *Tragedía*, pp. 97, 286.
13 Balk, *La Quatorzième*, p. 75.
14 Ibid., pp. 71–2.
15 Gillain, *Mercenario*, pp. 14–15.
16 Pantoja and Pantoja, *Tragedía*, p. 157.
17 Monks, *With the Reds*.
18 Pantoja and Pantoja, *Tragedía*, p. 163.
19 Ibid., p. 166.
20 AABI Montero personal digital archive, v.s. Collange, pp. 49–53.
21 RGASPI 545.3.394, Guimpel report.
22 RGASPI 545.3.399, Heussler report, pp. 28, 30, 32, 34.

23 Pantoja and Pantoja, *Tragedía*, p. 169.
24 Szurek, *Shattered*, p. 96; RGASPI 454.3.399, Heussler report, p. 24.
25 Szurek, *Shattered*, p. 98.
26 IWM, Sydney Quinn, IWM 801, Reel 2.
27 RGASPI 545.3.399, Heussler report, pp. 18–36.
28 Szurek, *Shattered*, p. 101; RGASPI 545.3.399, Heussler report, pp. 34–5.
29 RGASPI 545.3.399, Heussler report, p. 31.
30 Pantoja and Pantoja, *Tragedía*, p. 176.
31 Ibid., p. 180.
32 Ibid., p. 176, citing Longo.
33 Ibid.
34 Gillian, *Mercenario*, pp. 17–20.
35 Baxell, *Unlikely Warriors*, p. 117.
36 Monks, *With the Reds*; RGASPI 545.3.399, Heussler report, pp. 34–8.
37 IWM, Szurek, *Shattered*, p. 103.
38 Pantoja and Pantoja, *Tragedía*, p. 179.
39 Ibid., p. 203.
40 Ibid., p. 181.
41 Ibid., pp. 179–181.
42 IWM 801, Reel 2, Sydney Quinn.
43 Pantoja and Pantoja, *Tragedía*, pp. 180–4.

19 JUSTICE AND A DIFFERENT KIND OF ARMY

1 Monks, *With the Reds*, v.s. jammed.
2 IWM Walter Greenhalgh 10356, Reel 3.
3 Gillain, *Mercenario*, p. 14.
4 Szurek, *Shattered*, p. 105.
5 RGASPI 545.3.399, Heussler report, pp. 36–8.
6 Szurek, *Shattered*, pp. 104–5; RGASPI 545.3.399, Heussler report, pp. 38–9; Gillain, *Mercenario*, 15; Pantoja and Pantoja, *Tragedía*, pp. 243–4; Delpierre, *Brigadas*, pp. 144–6; AABI Montero personal digital archive, v.s. Collange.
7 Pantoja and Pantoja, *Tragedía*, p. 241.
8 Gillain, *Mercenario*, p. 15; Szurek, *Shattered*, p. 105.
9 RGASPI 545.3.399, Heussler report, p. 40.
10 RGASPI 545.3.394, Guimpel report.
11 Pantoja and Pantoja, *Tragedía*, p. 168; RGASPI 545.3.399, Heussler report, pp. 20–2.
12 RGASPI 545.3.394, Guimpel report; Pantoja and Pantoja, *Tragedía*, pp. 244–6; RGASPI 545.6.31, p. 77.
13 Gillain, *Mercenario*, pp. 15–16.

14 Juan Pablo Calero, 'Vísperas de la revolución. El congreso de la CNT (1936)', *Germinal* 7, April 2009, pp. 97–132; Santos Julia, 'La ugt de Madrid en los años treinta: un sindicalismo de gestión', *Revista Española de Investigaciones Sociológicas*, 20, 1982, pp. 121–51.

15 Beevor, *Battle*, Kindle pos. 4161–72.

16 RGASPI 545.3.394, Guimpel report; Skoutelsky, *Novedad*, pp. 265–7.

20 MOTHERS AND JEWS

1 *Herdenkingsnummer gewijd aan de gebroeders Ackerman*, Antwerp, 1938, p.4; Rudi Van Doorslaer, *'Israël Piet' Akkerman, De Diamantzager (1913–1937). Een joodse militant van de Derde Internationale in Antwerpen*, BTNG–RBHC, XXII, 1991, 3–4, pp. 721–82; Sven Tuytens, *Piet Akkerman, un Che Guevara de Ameres en la Guerra Civil Española*, http://www.brigadasinternacionales.org/index.php?option=comcontent&view=article&id=755:piet–akkerman&catid=44:croni-bi&Itemid=82.

2 Sven Tuytens, 'Piet Akkerman, un líder sindical belga caído por la libertad en la Guerra Civil española', *Público*, 20 March, 2015.

3 Van Doorslaer, *'Israël Piet'*, pp. 726–30.

4 Rudi Van Doorslaer, 'Joodse Vrijwilligers uit België in de Internationale Brigaden, Een Portret van een Vergeten Generatie?', *Belgisch Tijdschrift voor Nieuwste Geschiedenis, BTNG (Revue Belge d'Histoire Contemporaine, RBHC)*, 1987, No. 18, p. 165; Rudi Van Doorslaer, 'Tussen wereldrevolutie en joodse identiteit: Joden Uit Belge in Spaanse Burgeroorlog', *Cahiers d'Histoire de la second guerre global*, XVII, 1995, 1, pp. 49–54.

5 Zaagsma, *Jewish Volunteers*, p. 2; Jan Rybak, 'Jewish volunteers, the International Brigades and the Spanish Civil War', *European Review of History (Revue européenne d'histoire)*, 2018.

6 IISG COLL00207, *Herdenkingsnummer gewijd aan de gebroeders Ackerman*, p. 4.

7 Ibid.

8 Jessica Mitford, *Decca: The Letters of Jessica Mitford*, p. 6, https://www.theguardian.com/books/2001/dec/20/londonreviewofbooks

9 Zaagsma, *Jewish volunteers*, September 2001, citing Jaff Schatz, *The Generation: The rise and fall of the generation of Jewish communists of Poland*, Oxford, 1991, p. 50.

10 Rudi Van Doorslaer, 'Joodse Vrijwilligers', pp. 171–2.

11 IISG COLL00207, *Herdenkingsnummer gewijd aan de gebroeders Ackerman*, p. 4.

12 Rudi Van Doorslaer, 'Joodse Vrijwilligers' p. 179; Sven Tuytens and Van Doorslaer, *Piet Akkerman*, pp. 138, 144.

13 RGASPI 545.3.175, Hantz report; Castells, *Brigadas*, p. 572.

14 RGASPI 545.3.175, Hantz report; *Le Maitron Dictionnaire Biographique*, http://maitron-en-ligne.univ-paris1.fr/spip.php?article120231; Sidbrint database, Universitat de Barcelona, http://sidbrint.ub.edu/ca/content/marie-jean.

15 RGASPI 545.3.175, Hantz report.

16 Ibid., p. 30.

17 Víctor Fernández Soriano, 'Bélgica y la guerra civil: el impacto del conflicto español en la política', *Cuadernos de Historia Contemporánea*, 2007, Vol. 29, pp. 219–33.

18 Longo, *Brigadas*, p. 155; Sven Tuytens, *Piet Akkerman, un Che Guevara*.

19 RGASPI 545.3.175, Hantz report.

20 Ibid.

21 Sven Tuytens at http://www.brigadasinternacionales.org/index.php?option=comcontent&view=article&id=755:piet-akkerman&catid=44:cronibi&Itemid=82 – though they would reconquer the village seventeen days later.

22 Zaagsma, *Jewish Volunteers*, p. 2, citing Carey Nelson as quoted in Jeffrey Sharlet, 'Troublemakers', *Pakn Treger*, Fall 1998; see also http://www.yiddishbookcenter.org/pakntreger/archiveFall98/feature.shtml.

21 THE FINAL BATTLE FOR MADRID

1 Cardona, 'De Madrid a la caída del Norte', in Edward Malefakis, *La Guerra Civil española* (2nd edn), Madrid, 2016.

2 Michael Alpert, 'La historia militar', in Stanley Payne y Javier Tusell (eds.), *La guerra civil. Una nueva visión del conflicto que dividió España*, Madrid, 1996, pp. 137–8.

3 RGASPI 545.6.395, Marty report, p. 5.

4 *Armor*, March–April 1999, p. 34; Thomas, *Civil War*, p. 540.

5 Acier, *From Spanish Trenches*, p. 82.

6 RGASPI 545.6.395, Marty report, p. 58.

7 Ibid., p. 57.

8 Ibid., p. 59; https://www.combatientes.es/BasedeDatosBrunete5.htm s.v. 'Hornung'.

9 RGASPI 545.6.395, Marty report, pp. 57–9.

10 Ibid.

11 Thomas, *Civil War*, Kindle pos. 7458.

12 Esteve, *Recuerdos de Brigadistas Alemanes*, pt 2, annex, pp. 49–50.

13 RGASPI 545.6.394, Marty report, pp. 57–8.

14 Ibid., pp. 61–2; Skoutelsky, *Novedad*.

15 Balk, *La Quatorzième*, pp. 94–6; RGASPI 545.3.394, Guimpel report, pp. 1–2.
16 Szurek, *Shattered*, pp. 109–110.
17 Ibid.
18 Ibid.
19 Ibid.; RGASPI 545.3.394, Guimpel report, pp. 1–2.
20 RGASPI 545.6.25, Szinda report, pp. 17, 25.
21 Reverte, *Madrid*, p. 595.
22 Javier M. Calvo Martínez, http://frentedebatalla-gerion.blogspot.com.es/2009/01/intento-de-resumen-de-una-batalla-no.html; 'La guerra civil española mes a mes'.
23 Thomas, *Civil War*, Kindle pos. 7607.

22 BETHUNE, BLOOD AND BOMBING

1 Stewart and Stewart, *Phoenix*, pos. 2809.
2 Ibid., pos. 2810–3005.
3 Ibid., pos. 3004, 3026.
4 Lugschitz, *Spanienkämpferinnen*, p. 51.
5 Stewart and Stewart, *Phoenix*, pos. 3021, 3104.
6 David Lethbridge, *Bethune in Spain*, Eastbourne, 2013, pp. 114–15.
7 Preston, *We Saw Spain Die*, p. 138.
8 RGASPI 545.6.542, p. 109; Lethbridge, *Bethune in Spain*, p. 115.
9 Stewart and Stewart, *Phoenix*, pos. 3116
10 Ibid., pos. 3365.
11 Ibid., pos. 3369.
12 Beevor, *Battle*, p. 200.
13 Stewart and Stewart, *Phoenix*, pos. 3463.
14 Ibid., pos. 3537.
15 Beevor, *Battle*, p. 199.
16 Stewart and Stewart, *Phoenix*, pos. 3541.
17 Andres Fernández Martín, María Isabel Brenes Sánchez, *1937. Éxodo Málaga Almería, nuevas fuentes de investigación*, Casabermeja, 2016, pp. 193, 210, 219.
18 Fernández Martín and Brenes Sánchez, *Éxodo*, pp. 223, 228, 258, 264–5.
19 Beevor, *Battle*, pp. 200–1.
20 Stewart and Stewart, *Phoenix*, pp. 187–8.
21 Fernández Martín and Brenes Sánchez. *Éxodo*, p. 24.
22 Stewart and Stewart, *Phoenix*, pos. 604, citing Worsley.
23 Dr Norman Bethune, *The crime on the road Malaga–Almeria narrative with graphic documents revealing fascist cruelty*, 1937.

24 T. C. Worsley, *Los Ecos de la batalla*, Salamanca, 2012, pp. 241–3.

25 Bethune, *The crime*; Stewart and Stewart, *Phoenix*, Kindle pos. 8317.

26 Fernández Martín and Brenes Sánchez, *Éxodo*, pp. 302–7, 340–417; Kurzke and Mangan, 'Good Comrade', p. 172.

27 Stewart and Stewart, *Phoenix*, pos. 3691.

28 Ibid.

29 Lethbridge, *Bethune*, p. 136.

30 Mao Tse-tung, 'In Memory of Norman Bethune', 21 December 1939, from *Selected Works*, vol II.

31 Esteve, *Recuerdos de Brigadistas Alemanes*, pts 1 and 2, v.s. Ewald Munschke.

32 Ibid.; AABI Montero personal digitial archive, v.s. Chapaev Otto Brunner, dated 17 February 1937.

33 Esteve, *Recuerdos de Brigadistas Alemanes*, pts 1 and 2, v.s. Ewald Munschke.

34 Ibid.

35 Ibid., v.s. Sierra Nevada.

36 *New York Times*, 'Crazy With Women, Lucky with Spain', 16 May 1993, Section 7, Page 12, https://www.nytimes.com/1993/05/16/books/crazy-with-women-lucky-with-spain.html.

37 Esteve, *Recuerdos de Brigadistas Alemanes*, pts 1 and 2, v.s. Sierra Nevada, v.s. Rudolf Engel.

38 Ibid., v.s. Rudolf Engel.

39 Knox, 'Premature antifascist', pp. 145–6.

23 A VALLEY CALLED JARAMA

1 Baxell, *Unlikely Warriors*, p. 138.

2 Luis Díez, *Jarama*, Madrid, pp. 78–9.

3 Ben Hughes, *They Shall not Pass! The British Battalion at Jarama*, Oxford, 2011, pp. 232–4.

4 Jesús González de Miguel, *La Batalla de Jarama*, Madrid, 2009, p. 762.

5 Baxell, *Unlikely Warriors*, p. 138.

6 Víctor Ruíz, writing as El Tebib Arrumi, *Jarama y Tajuña*, pp. 37, 51–2.

7 RGASPI 545.3.175, Hantz report, pp. 36–8 (see also Spanish translation at AABI-Montero 'RGASPI 545.3.175'); RGASPI 545.3.394, Maniou report, 'Le bataillon André Marty pendant la bataille du Jarama', pp. 8–18; Víctor Ruíz, writing as El Tebib Arrumi, *Jarama y Tajuña*, p. 40.

8 RGASPI 545.3.394 Maniou report, pp. 8–28.

9 RGASPI 545.3.175, Hantz report, pp. 36–8; RGASPI 545.3.394, Maniou report, pp. 8–12.

10 RGASPI 545.3.394, Maniou report, pp. 8–12.

11 Luis Díez, *Jarama*, p. 72.

12 Víctor Ruíz, writing as El Tebib Arrumi, *Jarama y Tajuña*, p. 14.

13 Ibid., p. 27.

14 RGASPI 545.3.394, Maniou report, pp. 8–12.

15 Ibid.

16 RGASPI 545.3.175, Hantz report, pp. 36–8; RGASPI 545.3.394, Maniou report, pp. 8–12.

17 Ibid.

18 Víctor Ruíz, writing as El Tebib Arrumi, *Jarama y Tajuña*, p. 32.

19 RGASPI 545.3.175, Hantz report, pp. 36–8; RGASPI 545.3.394, Maniou report, pp. 8–12.

20 RGASPI 545.3.175, Hantz report, pp. 36–8.

21 Ibid.

22 AABI-Montero, v.s. Dombrowski Jarama 18 enero.

23 RGASPI 545.3.394, Maniou report, pp. 8–12; Víctor Ruíz, writing as El Tebib Arrumi, *Jarama y Tajuña*, p. 60.

24 Luis Díez, *Jarama*, p. 77.

25 RGASPI 545.3.394, Maniou report, pp. 8–12.

26 RGASPI 545.3.175, Hantz report; RGASPI 545.3.394, Maniou report, pp. 8–18; Víctor Ruíz, writing as El Tebib Arrumi, *Jarama y Tajuña*, p. 33.

27 RGASPI 545.3.394, Maniou report, pp. 8–12.

28 Víctor Ruíz, writing as El Tebib Arrumi, *Jarama y Tajuña*, p. 34.

29 RGASPI 545.3.394, Maniou report, p. 13.

30 RGASPI 545.3.175, Hantz report, pp. 36–8; RGASPI 545.3.394, Maniou report, p. 13; Jesús González de Miguel, *Jarama*, p. 100.

31 RGASPI 545.3.394, Maniou report, p. 13.

32 Jesús González de Miguel, *Jarama*, pp. 104–5, 199; Alpert, *Republican Army*, p. 228.

33 Luis Díez, *Jarama*, p. 81; Víctor Ruíz, writing as El Tebib Arrumi, *Jarama y Tajuña*, p. 33.

34 RGASPI 545.3.394, Maniou report, p. 13.

35 Ibid., pp. 13–18.

36 Ibid.

37 Regler, *Owl of Minerva*, p. 288.

38 United Nations General Assembly, *Official Records of the Second Session of the General Assembly, Supplement No. 11*, A/364, 3 September 1947 https://unispal.un.org/DPA/DPR/unispal.nsf/0/07175DE9FA2DE563852568D3006E10F3

39 Regler, *Owl of Minerva*, p. 289.

40 Ibid., pp. 287–8.

41 Víctor Ruíz, writing as El Tebib Arrumi, *Jarama y Tajuña*, pp. 33, 39, 50.

42 Luis Díez, *Jarama*, pp. 100–10.

43 Víctor Ruíz, writing as El Tebib Arrumi, *Jarama y Tajuña*, pp. 33–50.
44 RGASPI 545.3.394, Maniou report, pp. 13–17.
45 AABI, 'El batallón Dombrowski en la batalla del Jarama', https://
    brigadasinternacionales.org/; Balk, *La Quatorzième*, p. 114.
46 Jesús González de Miguel, *Jarama*, p. 128.
47 RGASPI 545.2.402, Louis report, p. 29; AABI, IBS, 'La XI y la XV
    Batallones en la Batalla del Jarama', https://brigadasinternacionales.org/.
48 RGASPI 545.2.402, Louis report, p. 29.
49 Gina Medem, *Los judíos voluntarios de la libertad*, Madrid, 1937, pp. 43–4;
    AABI, 'La XI y la XV Batallones en la Batalla del Jarama', https://
    brigadasinternacionales.org/.
50 Skoutelsky, *L'espoir*, p. 119.
51 J. Eaden and D. Renton, *The Communist Party of Great Britain Since 1920*,
    Basingstoke, 2002, p. 18.

24 THE BRITISH

1   Baxell, *Unlikely Warriors*, pp. 68–9.
2   Ibid., p. 68; Gregory, *The Shallow Grave*, p. 24.
3   Jason Gurney, *Crusade in Spain*, London, 1974, p. 58.
4   Hughes, *Jarama*, p. 62.
5   Purcell and Smith, *The Last English Revolutionary*, p. 125.
6   George Aitken, IWM 10357, Reel 2.
7   A. J. Ayer, *Part of My Life*, 1977, spartacus-educational.com.
8   RGASPI 495.20.92, p. 35; Andrew Thorpe, 'The Membership of the
    Communist Party of Great Britain, 1920–1945', *The Historical Journal*,
    Vol. 43, No. 3 (September 2000), pp. 777–800.
9   Baxell, *Unlikely Warriors*, pp. 124–6.
10 Wintringham, *English Captain*, pp. 54–5.
11 Baxell, *Unlikely Warriors*, pp. 130–3.
12 Purcell and Smith, *The Last English Revolutionary*, pp. 122–6.
13 Kurzke and Mangan, 'Good Comrade', pp. 111–13.
14 Sidbrint database, Universitat de Barcelona, http://sidbrint.ub.edu/es/
    content/galicz-janos.
15 Carlo Penchienati, *Brigate Internazionali in Spagna: delitti della Ceka
    comunista*, Echi del Secolo, Milan, 1950, p. 52.
16 Jesús González de Miguel, *La Batalla de Jarama*, p. 133; Charlotte Haldane,
    The Truth Will Out, London, 1949, p. 135.
17 Fausto Villar Esteban, 'A Little Valencian in the Lincoln Brigade: An Anti-
    War and Anti-Heroic Symphony', trans. Paul Sharkey, Special Collections,
    University of Michigan Library.

18 Jesús González de Miguel, *Jarama*, p. 133.
19 Baxell, *Unlikely Warriors*, p. 137.
20 Ibid., p. 141.
21 Hughes, *Jarama*, p. 71.
22 Baxell, *Unlikely Warriors*, p. 142.
23 Hughes, *Jarama*, p. 66.
24 Wintringham, *English Captain*, p. 67.
25 Hughes, *Jarama*, pp. 69–71.
26 Ibid., p. 78.
27 Wintringham, *English Captain*, p. 62.
28 Hughes, *Jarama*, p. 74; Wintringham, *English Captain*, pp. 63–6.
29 Wintringham, *English Captain*, p. 63.
30 Ibid., p. 64.
31 Hughes, *Jarama*, p. 77.
32 Ibid., p. 79.
33 Baxell, *Unlikely Warriors*, p. 146.
34 Wintringham, *English Captain*, pp. 74–5.
35 Baxell, *Unlikely Warriors*, p. 144.
36 Hughes, *Jarama*, p. 94.
37 Baxell, *Unlikely Warriors*, p. 145; Hughes, *Jarama*, p. 90; RGASPI 545.3.471, Wintringham report.
38 RGASPI 545.3.471, *A Documentary History of the XV Brigade*; Hughes, *Jarama*, p. 88.
39 *La Batalla del Jarama*, documentary film, dir. Miguel Angel Nieto, Diagrama Producciones, Madrid, 2006.
40 RGASPI 545.3.742.
41 Baxell, *Unlikely Warriors*, p. 148.
42 Wintringham, *English Captain*, pp. 85–6; Hughes, *Jarama*, p. 112.
43 Hughes, *Jarama*, p. 65.
44 Baxell, *Unlikely Warriors*, p. 148.
45 Hughes, *Jarama*, pp. 68.
46 Ibid., pp. 96, 100–1.
47 Ibid., pp. 94–5.
48 Ibid., p. 108.
49 Ibid., pp. 109–11.
50 Ibid., pp. 109–10; RGASPI 545.3.471, *A Documentary History of the XV Brigade*.
51 Hughes, *Jarama*, p. 110.
52 Baxell, *Unlikely Warriors*, p. 149.
53 Hughes, *Jarama*, p. 111, notes 14 and 15.
54 Ibid., p. 112.

55 AABI, *La XI y la XV Batallones en la Batalla del Jarama*, https://brigadasinternacionales.org/.

56 Jesús González de Miguel, *Jarama*, pp. 104–5.

57 http://www.parquelineal.es/historia/guerra-civil/la-batalla-del-Jarama/puente-del-pindoque/.

58 Regler, *Owl of Minerva*, p. 292.

59 Hughes, *Jarama*, p. 111.

60 Ibid., pp. 71–2, 102, 104, 116.

61 Gurney, *Crusade*, p. 113.

62 RGASPI 545.3.471, *A Documentary History of the XV Brigade*.

63 Baxell, *Unlikely Warriors*, p. 151.

64 RGASPI 545.3.471, *A Documentary History of the XV Brigade*.

25 DISOBEYING ORDERS

1 David Crook, *Some essays by David Crook, gleaned from student magazines like* English Study, at davidcrook.net, undated, p. 161.

2 RGASPI 545.3.471, *A Documentary History of the XV Brigade*, pp. 12–14; Hughes, *Jarama*, p. 129; Wintringham, *English Captain*, pp. 102–3; Víctor Manuel Santidrian Arias, 'Enrique Líster: el antimilitarista que llegó a general', *Revista Universitaria de Historia Militar*, Vol. 7, No. 13 (2018), pp. 423–39.

3 Baxell, *Unlikely Warriors*, p. 152.

4 Ibid., p. 153.

5 Wintringham, *English Captain*, p. 151.

6 RGASPI 545.3.471, *A Documentary History of the XV Brigade*, pp. 17–18.

7 Ibid., p. 19.

8 Baxell, *Unlikely Warriors*, p. 153; Hughes, *Jarama*, p. 148.

9 Hughes, *Jarama*, p. 148, footnote 1.

10 Baxell, *Unlikely Warriors*, p. 175.

11 Beevor, *Battle*, p. 211.

12 Ian MacDougall, *Voices from the Spanish Civil War: Personal Recollections of Scottish volunteers in Republican Spain 1936-1939*, Edinburgh, 1986, p. 62.

13 Wyszczelkski (ed.), *Dabrowszczacy*, pp. 21–2; see also Jesús González de Miguel, *Jarama*; AABI, *El batallón Dombrowski en la batalla del Jarama*, https://brigadasinternacionales.org/.

14 José María Gárate Córdoba, *Mil Días de Fuego*, Barcelona, 1972, pp. 171–2.

15 Wyszczelkski (ed.), *Dabrowszczacy*, Ksiazka i Wiedza, Warsaw, 1986, pp. 21–2.

16 Gina Medem, *Los judíos voluntarios de la libertad*, pp. 43–4.

17 AABI, *El batallón Dombrowski en la batalla del Jarama*, https://brigadasinternacionales.org/.

18 Hughes, *Jarama*, p. 158; Wintringham, *English Captain*, p. 114.

19 Hughes, *Jarama*, p. 164.

20 RGASPI 545.3.471, *A Documentary History of the XV Brigade*.

21 Hughes, *Jarama*, p. 166.

22 RGASPI 545.3.471, *A Documentary History of the XV Brigade*; Baxell, *Unlikely Warriors*, p. 155.

23 Hughes, *Jarama*, pp. 53, 169, 184–5; Sidbrint database, Universitat de Barcelona, http://sidbrint.ub.edu/ca/content/hilliard-robert-m.

24 Frank Ryan (ed), Ryan, Frank (ed.), The Book of the XVth Brigade: Records of British, American, Canadian and Irish volunteers in the XV International Brigade in Spain 1936–1938, Madrid, 1938, p.57; Hughes, *Jarama*, pp. 170–1.

25 Baxell, *Unlikely Warriors*, p. 155; *Book of XV Brigade*, p. 58; Hughes, *Jarama*, p. 172.

26 Hughes, *Jarama*, pp. 172–4.

27 RGASPI 545.3.471, *A Documentary History of the XV Brigade*, p. 15.

28 Baxell, *Unlikely Warriors*, p. 156; Various authors, *Book of XV Brigade*, p. 58.

29 Various authors, *Book of XV Brigade*, p. 60.

30 Baxell, *Unlikely Warriors*, p. 88; Hughes, *Jarama*, pp. 175–6; Various authors, *Book of XV Brigade*, p. 60.

31 Baxell, *Unlikely Warriors*, p. 156, note 89.

32 Hughes, *Jarama*, pp. 175–6.

33 Baxell, *Unlikely Warriors*, p. 157.

34 Ibid., p. 159, note 1.

35 Thomas, *Brother against Brother*, p. 95.

26 THE YANKS ARE COMING!

1 Cecil Eby, *Comrades and Commissars, the Lincoln Battalion in the Spanish Civil War*, Pennsylvania, 2007, p. 25.

2 http://www.albavolunteer.org/2019/03/in-memory-of-the-city-college-of-new-york-alumni-students-and-teachers/ acessed 23 April 2019; http://www.albavolunteer.org/2017/09/an-analysis-of-american-and-canadian-volunteers-compiled-by-the-international-Brigades-in-spain/#ednref1.

3 RGASPI 545.3.455, 'General Report on 1745 people from the United States', pp. 144–52; Carroll, *Odyssey*, pp. 65, 88; http://www.albavolunteer.org/2017/09/an-analysis-of-american-and-canadian-volunteers-compiled-by-the-international-Brigades-in-spain/#ednref1.

4 Fraser Ottanelli, 'Anti-Fascism and the Shaping of National and Ethnic Identity: Italian American Volunteers in the Spanish Civil War', *Journal of American Ethnic History*, Vol. 27, No. 1, 2007, pp. 10–12; Puppini, *Garibaldini*, p. 200, gives the average age of Italian recruits in 1936 as thirty-three.

5 RGASPI 545.3.455, 'General Report on 1745 people from the United States', pp. 144–52; RGASPI 545.3.455, p. 156; Carroll, 'The Spanish Civil War in the 21st Century', p. 651.

6 RGASPI 545.3.455, 'General Report on 1745 people from the United States', pp. 144–52; Carroll, *Odyssey*, p. 18.

7 RGASPI 545.3.455, 'General Report on 1745 people from the United States', p. 144; Carroll, *Odyssey*, p. 65.

8 Carroll, *Odyssey*, p. 94.

9 Ibid., pp. 95, 97.

10 Ibid., pp. 96–7.

11 RGASPI 545.3.471, *A Documentary History of the XV Brigade*.

12 Ibid.

13 Carroll, *Odyssey*, p. 97.

14 Ibid. Much later, a Brigade firing squad executed Harris.

15 https://www.newyorker.com/magazine/2016/04/18/the-americans-soldiers-of-the-spanish-civil-war.

16 Carroll, *Odyssey*, p. 96.

17 Ibid., p. 97.

18 Carroll, 'Spanish Civil War in the 21st Century', p. 651.

19 Carroll, *Odyssey*, p. 93.

20 Robert Hale Merriman, ed. Raymond Hoff, *Merriman's Diaries, Exegesis*, self-published, 2018; copyright Tamiment Library, NYU, New York, http://digitaltamiment.hosting.nyu.edu/files/original/5434ae298184e90c2b45d6139c10f81d072d5c41.pdf, p. 76; Carroll, *Odyssey*, p. 93.

21 RGASPI 545.3.471, *A Documentary History of the XV Brigade*, p. 19; Arthur H. Landis, *The Abraham Lincoln Brigade*, New York, 1967, pp. 40–1.

22 Carroll, *Odyssey*, p. 98.

23 Eby, *Commissars*, p. 52.

24 Carroll, *Odyssey*, p. 99.

25 http://www.albavolunteer.org/2016/02/Jarama-series/.

26 Eby, *Commissars*, p. 54.

27 http://www.albavolunteer.org/2016/02/Jarama-series/.

28 Carroll, *Odyssey*, pp. 97, 99; *The Volunteer*, http://www.albavolunteer.org/2016/02/Jarama-series/#ednref4.

29 RGASPI 545.3.471, *A Documentary History of the XV Brigade*, pp. 26–8; Various authors, *Book of XV Brigade*, pp. 72–82; Carroll, *Odyssey*, pp. 99–100.

30 Ibid.

31 Ibid.; http://www.albavolunteer.org/2016/02/Jarama-series/; RGASPI
    545.3.471, *A Documentary History of the XV Brigade*, p. 26–8.

32 Carroll, *Odyssey*, pp. 100–3; http://www.albavolunteer.org/2016/03/
    Jarama-series-pingarron/; Landis, *Lincoln Brigade*, p. 77.

33 http://www.albavolunteer.org/2016/03/Jarama-series-pingarron/

34 Landis, *Lincoln Brigade*, p. 40.

35 RGASPI 545.3.471, *A Documentary History of the XV Brigade*, p. 32.

36 http://www.albavolunteer.org/2016/03/Jarama-series-pingarron/; http://
    www.albavolunteer.org/2016/03/Jarama-series-the-aftermath/.

37 Carroll, *Odyssey*, p. 101; RGASPI 545.3.471, *A Documentary History of the
    XV Brigade*.

38 http://www.albavolunteer.org/2016/03/Jarama-series-pingarron/.

39 Puppini, *Garibaldini*, p. 200; RGASPI 545.3.471, *A Documentary History
    of the XV Brigade*, pp. 32–3.

40 RGASPI 545.3.471, *A Documentary History of the XV Brigade*, p. 33.

41 *Le Maitron Dictionnaire Biographique*, http://maitron-en-ligne.univ-
    paris1.fr/spip.php?article150459, notice BARTHEL Jean

42 RGASPI 545.3.471, *A Documentary History of the XV Brigade*.

43 Ibid., pp. 34–7.

44 Carroll, *Odyssey*, p. 115, citing *Our Fight* newspaper; Eby, *Commissars*,
    p. 86; Richardson, *Comintern Army*, p. 78, citing *Notre Combat*, No. 7,
    15 March 1937, p. 1; RGASPI 545.3.471, *A Documentary History of the XV
    Brigade*, p. 36.

45 Eby, *Commissars*, p. 110.

46 Carroll, *Odyssey*, p. 106.

27 MUSSOLINI AT GUADALAJARA

1 Puppini *Garibaldini*, pp. 89, 204.

2 Ibid.

3 Giovanni Pesce, *Un Garibaldino en España*, Madrid, 2012, p. 109.

4 Ibid., pp. 107–8.

5 RGASPI 545.6.31.

6 RGASPI 545.2.108, pp. 210–11.

7 Castells, *Brigadas*, pp. 160–3; Jill Edwards, *The British Government and
   the Spanish Civil War, 1936–1939*, Basingstoke, 1979, pp. 53–5; RGASPI
   545.2.108, p. 211; Thomas, *Civil War*, Kindle pos. 8917.

8 P. I. Samoïlov, *Gvadalakhara (Razgrom ital'yanskogo ekspeditsionnogo
   korpusa)*, Voyenizdat, 1940, militera.lib.ru, pp. 41–4, 48–51.

9 Mastrorilli, 'Guerra Civile Spagnola', pp. 68–87; Ismael Saz, 'Fascism and empire, fascist Italy against republican Spain', *Mediterranean Historical Review*, 1 June 1998, Vol. 131–2, pp. 116–34; Ismael Saz, 'El fracaso del éxito, Italia en la guerra de España', *Espacio, Tiempo y Forma, Serie V, H. Contemporánea*, 1992, pp. 105–28.

10 John F. Coverdale, *Italian Intervention in the Spanish Civil War*, Princeton, 1976, pp. 224–5; Javier Rodrigo, 'Italian fascism and war experience in the Spanish Civil War (1936–39)', *War in History*, Vol. 26, issue 1, 1 January 2019, pp. 86–104; Ígor Médnikov, Los límites de una renovación: la historiografía actual rusa sobre la guerra civil Española', *Studia Historica*, Vol. 32, 2014.

11 Beevor, *Battle*, Kindle pos. 4609.

12 Pesce, *España*, p.120; Giovanni Pesce, *Un Garibaldino in Spagna*, Varese, 2009, p. 68.

13 Médnikov, 'Los límites de una renovación'; see Samoïlov, *Gvadalakhara* and Kiril Meretskov, *Na sluzhbe narodu*, Moscow, 1968, pp. 153–9.

14 Samoïlov, *Gvadalakhara*, pp. 37–41.

15 Ibid., pp. 34–5; Médnikov, 'Los límites de una renovación', p. 420.

16 Samoïlov, *Gvadalakhara*, pp. 37–43, 51–6.

17 Ibid., pp. 48–56; Colonel Antonio J. Candil, 'Soviet armor in Spain: aid mission to republicans tested doctrine and equipment', *Armor*, Vol. 108, Issue 2, March–April 1999.

18 Renn, *Guerra Civil*, p. 347.

19 AICVAS *Quaderno 7*, pp. 77–80; Renn, *Guerra Civil*, pp. 348–50; Esteve, *Recuerdos de Brigadistas Alemanes*, pts 1 and 2, v.s. Herbert Jander and Mayer; Samoïlov, *Gvadalakhara*, pp. 52–6.

20 Meretskov, *Na sluzhbe narodu*, pp. 153–9.

21 Ibid., p. 159; Esteve, *Recuerdos de Brigadistas Alemanes*, pts 1 and 2, v.s. Jander.

22 Renn, *Guerra Civil*, p. 351.

23 Ibid., pp. 343–4.

24 Ibid.; Meretskov, *Na sluzhbe narodu*, pp. 153–9.

25 Esteve, *Recuerdos de Brigadistas Alemanes*, pts 1 and 2, v.s. Mayer.

26 Meretskov, *Na sluzhbe narodu*, p. 153.

27 Samoïlov, *Gvadalakhara*, pp. 51–63.

28 Esteve, *Recuerdos de Brigadistas Alemanes*, pts 1 and 2, v.s. Emil Bleimehl.

29 Anders MacGregor-Thunell, *Spanish Civil War – Oral History*, http://educationforum.ipbhost.com/topic/897-spanish-civil-war-oral-history/ v.s. Emil.

30 Ibid. v.s. cognac.

28 THE ITALIAN CIVIL WAR

1 Samoïlov, *Gvadalakhara*, pp. 65–3; AICVAS *Quaderno 7*, pp. 78–9.

2 AICVAS *Quaderno 7*, pp. 78–9.

3 Renn, *Guerra Civil*, p. 353.

4 Pesce, *Spagna*, p. 61; Olao Conforti, *Guadalajara, la primera derrota del fascismo*, Barcelona, 1977, pp. 129–30.

5 Pesce, *España*, pp. 110–11; AICVAS *Quaderno 7*, pp. 78–9.

6 P. I. Samoïlov, *Gvadalakhara*, p. 60.

7 Renn, *Guerra Civil*, p. 354.

8 Pesce, *España*, p. 117; Puppini, *Garibaldini*, pp. 93–4.

9 Alberto Magnani, 'Entrevista a Giovanni Pesce', *Ebre* 38, 3, 2008.

10 Samoïlov, *Gvadalakhara*, p. 63.

11 Magnani, 'Entrevista a Giovanni Pesce', pp. 233–5; RGASPI 545.1.12, p. 14; Puppini, *Garibaldini*, p. 91.

12 Samoïlov, *Gvadalakhara*, pp. 67–71.

13 Ibid.

14 Renn, *Guerra Civil*, p. 348.

15 Pesce, *España*, p. 120.

16 Ibid., p. 121.

17 Pesce, *Spagna*, pp. 66–8; Samoïlov, *Gvadalakhara*, pp. 73–7.

18 Pesce, *España*, p. 115.

19 Aleksandr Ilích Rodimstev, *Bajo el cielo de España*, Moscow, 1981.

20 Samoïlov, *Gvadalakhara*, pp. 73–7; Esteve, *Recuerdos de Brigadistas Alemanes*, pts 1 and 2, v.s. Jander and Mayer.

21 MacGregor-Thunell, *Spanish Civil War – Oral History*.

22 Esteve, *Recuerdos de Brigadistas*, pts 1 and 2, v.s. Jander and Mayer; Pesce, *España*, pp. 122–3; Conforti, *Guadalajara*, p. 137; Samoïlov, *Gvadalakhara*, p. 76; AICVAS *Quaderno 7*, p. 80.

23 Pesce, *Spagna*, pp. 71–2; Pesce, *España*, p. 124.

24 Samoïlov, *Gvadalakhara*, pp. 78–86.

25 Ibid., pp. 73–86.

26 Kochetkov, *Beyond the Pyrenees*, pos. 1178–1196.

29 THE BATTLE OF THE LOUDSPEAKERS

1 Pesce, *España*, p. 132; Pesce, *Spagna*, p. 79; *Guadalajara* (leaflet), July 1937, Comisión de propaganda del Comisariado de Guerra y Ediciones de la Voz, p. 18.

2 Javier Rodrigo, 'Italian fascism and war experience'.

3 Pesce, *España*, pp. 134–45.

4 Regler, *Owl of Minerva*, p. 305.

5 Pesce, *España*, pp. 137–9.

6 Ibid., pp. 134–45.

7 Regler, *Owl of Minerva*, pp. 305–7; Pesce, *España*, p. 136.

8 Pesce, *España*, p. 129.

9 AICVAS *Quaderno 7*.

10 Samoïlov, *Gvadalakhara*, pp. 105–111.

11 Ibid., p. 117.

12 Ibid., pp. 118–23

13 Ibid., pp. 123–9.

14 Thomas, *Brother against Brother*, p. 101.

15 Rhodes, *Hell and Good Company*, p. 167.

16 Pietro Nenni, *España*, Barcelona, 2007, p. 208.

30 BLUE NOSE AND THE DESERTERS

1 RGASPI 545.6.1274, pp. 95–108; Auguste Lecoeur, *Le Partisan*, Paris, 1963, pp. 71–9.

2 Lecoeur, *Le Partisan,* pp. 75–9.

3 Skoutelsky, *Novedad*, p. 221, citing RGASPI 545.6.1274, pp. 95–108.

4 Lecoeur, *Le Partisan*, p. 77.

5 Ibid.

6 RGASPI 545.2.142a, pp. 9–15.

7 Lecoeur, *Le Partisan*, pp. 76–9.

8 Ibid.

9 Ibid., p. 79.

10 RGASPI 545.2.142a, p. 6.

11 RGASPI 545.6.1274, pp. 95–108.

12 RGASPI 545.2.142a, pp. 17–22.

13 Ibid.

14 Baxell, *Unlikely Warriors*, pp. 263–4.

15 Ibid., pp. 247–50.

16 Ibid.

17 RGASPI 545.3.451, p. 15.

18 Ibid., p. 12; Petrou, *Renegades*, pp. 128–30; Baxell, *Unlikely Warriors*, p. 255.

19 RGASPI 545.3.451, p. 12; Petrou, *Renegades*, pp. 128–30; Baxell, *Unlikely Warriors*, p. 255.

20 RGASPI 545.3.451, p. 12; Petrou, *Renegades*, pp. 130–1.

21 Alfonso López Borgoñoz, *Las Brigadas Internacionales en Castelldefels*, Castelldefels, 2015, p. 120.

22 Petrou, *Renegades*, pp. 130–1; *Gaceta de la República*, 133, 13 May 1937, pp. 675–9, Decreto of 13 May 1937.

23 Pedro Corral, *Desertores: La Guerra Civil que nadie quiere contar*, Barcelona, 2006, p. 472; Sidbrint database, Universitat de Barcelona, http://sidbrint.ub.edu/en/content/copic-emil.

24 Borgoñoz, *Castelldefels*, pp. 113–33; RGASPI 545.2.150, *Asunto del Preventorio de las B.I. en el castillo de Castelldefels* (1938); Peter Huber and Michael Uhl, 'Die Internationalen Brigaden, Politische überwachung und repression nach sichtung der russichen und westlichen archivatken', *Ebre 38*, No. 2, 2004, p. 27.

25 RGASPI 545.2.150, *Asunto del preventorio de las B.I. en el castillo de Castelldefels*, p. 14; Borgoñoz, *Castelldefels*, p. 132, citing Jules at RGASPI 545.2.102.

26 Sidbrint database, Universitat de Barcelona, http://sidbrint.ub.edu/en/content/lantez-marcel. *Le Maitron Dictionnaire Biographique*, http://maitron-en-ligne.univ-paris1.fr/spip.php?article115837, notice LANTEZ Marcel; Petrou, *Renegades*, p. 126.

27 RGASPI 545.2.150, *Asunto del preventorio de las B.I. en el castillo de Castelldefels*, pp. 19, 23, 25, 33.

28 Petrou, *Renegades*, p. 127.

29 RGASPI 545.2.150, p. 14; Josep Lladós and Mario Reyes, 'Le presó secreta de les brigades', *El Temps*, No. 667, 31 March 1997, pp. 48–55; Manuel González Moreno-Navarro, *Las Brigadas Internacionales (Guerra Civil española 1936–1939): su paso por Cataluña*, Barcelona, 2009, pp. 36–7.

30 Borgoñoz, *Castelldefels*, pp. 160–1; RGASPI 545.2.102, Castelldefels report, p. 162.

31 González Moreno-Navarro, *Las Brigadas Internacionales*, pp. 38–40.

32 Baxell, *Unlikely Warriors*, p. 240.

33 Petrou, *Renegades*, p. 108.

34 Len Crome, 'A Soldier in Spain', p. 125.

35 Skoutelsky, *Novedad*, p. 220.

36 RGASPI 545.6.487, p. 31.

37 Skoutelsky, *Novedad*, p. 222.

38 Alpert, *Republican Army*, p. 69.

39 RGASPI 545.6.487, pp. 4–47; RGASPI 545.6.359, pp. 145–9; RGASPI 545.6.649, pp. 30–4; RGASPI 545.2.143a; RGASPI 545.6.78, pp. 1, 27; RGASPI 545.6.1464, pp. 10–17; RGASPI 545.6.62, pp. 8–22; RGASPI 545.6.1560, pp. 1–4; RGASPI 545.6.99, pp. 10, 12–19; RGASPI 545.6.99, p. 10; RGASPI 545.6.64, *Bulletin des Commissaires politiques*, June 1937, pp. 51–3.

40 Skoutelsky, *Novedad*, pp. 344, 353–5.

41 Huber and Uhl, 'Die Internationalen Brigaden'.

42 Ibid.

43 Petrou, *Renegades*, pp. 132–7; Baxell, *Unlikely Warriors*, pp. 260–2; Carroll, *Odyssey*, pp. 181–8.

44 Petrou, *Renegades*, p. 124.

45 RGASPI 545.1.64, *Bulletin des Commissaires politiques*, June 1937, pp. 51–3.

46 *Investigation of un-American propaganda activities in the United States Hearings before a Special Committee on Un-American Activities, House of Representatives*, Seventy-fifth Congress, third session–Seventy-eighth Congress, second session, on H. Res. 282, Vol. 13, p. 7827, Washington, 1940; Volodarsky, *Orlov*, p. 258.

47 Moreno-Navarro, *Las Brigadas Internacionales*, p. 30.

48 Carroll, *Odyssey*, pp. 182–8.

31 HEMINGWAY: MEN AND WOMEN IN WAR

1 Alex Vernon, *Hemingway's Second War: Bearing Witness to the Spanish Civil War*, Iowa City, 2011, pp. 3–13.

2 Marcelina Hemingway Sanford, 'Hemingway Goes to War', *The Atlantic*, August 2014, https://www.theatlantic.com/magazine/archive/2014/08/hemingway-goes-to-war/373437/; 'Hemingway on War and Its Aftermath', *Prologue*, Vol. 38, No. 1, Spring 2006, https://www.archives.gov/ publications/prologue/2006/spring/hemingway.html

3 Caroline Moorhead, *Martha Gellhorn: A Life*, London, 2004, p. 129.

4 Vernon, *Hemingway's Second War*, p. 13.

5 'Hemingway on War and Its Aftermath'.

6 https://www.telegraph.co.uk/culture/film/9760815/Hemingway-and-Gellhorn-a-pairing-of-flint-and-steel.html.

7 http://www.newyorker.com/archive/2005/10/31/051031crbobooks#ixzz28 RYoy4jQ.

8 Vaill, *Hotel Florida*, p. 153.

9 Vernon, *Hemingway's Second War*, p. 14.

10 Martha Gellhorn, *Face of War*, Granta, London, 1986, p. 30.

11 Vaill, *Hotel Florida*, p. 172.

12 Eby, *Commissars*, p. 359; http://www.alba-valb.org/volunteers/james-philip-lardner.

13 Vaill, *Hotel Florida*, p. 306.

14 Carroll, *Odyssey*, p. 238.

15 Baxell, *Unlikely Warriors*, pp. 304–5.

16 http://www.alvahsbooks.com/alvah-bessie/review-by-alvah-bessie-ernest-hemingway-a-life-story-by-carlos-baker/, reviewed by Alvah Bessie, *Marin Independent Journal*, Saturday, 26 April 1969.

17 'Hemingway on War and Its Aftermath'.

18 Carroll, 'Spanish Civil War in the 21st Century', p. 647.

19 Hans Schoots, *Living Dangerously: A Biography of Joris Ivens*, Amsterdam, 2000, p. 4; L. Wagner-Martin, *Ernest Hemingway: A Literary Life*,

Basingstoke, 2007, p. 123; *New York Times*, Herbert Mitgang, 'Hemingway on Spain: Unedited Reportage', 30 August 1988.

20 Carroll, 'Spanish Civil War in the 21st Century', p. 647.

21 Ernest Hemingway, introduction to Gustav Regler, *Great Crusade*, p. viii.

22 Ibid.

23 Vaill, *Hotel Florida*, p. 172.

24 Ibid., p. 145.

25 Regler, *Owl of Minerva*, p. 297.

26 Vernon, *Hemingway's Second War*, pp. 22–3.

27 Regler, *Owl of Minerva*, p. 296.

28 Vaill, *Hotel Florida*, p. 324.

29 http://www.nytimes.com/books/99/07/04/specials/hemingway-brihuega.html.

30 Hemingway introduction to Gustav Regler, *Great Crusade*, p. viii.

31 Vernon, *Hemingway's Second War*, p. 31; http://www.albavolunteer.org/2016/06/the-earth-endureth-forever-ernest-hemingway-and-the-spanish-civil-war/.

32 Vaill, *Hotel Florida*, p. 182.

33 Ernest Hemingway, Introduction to Gustav Regler, *Great Crusade*, pp. viii–xi; Vernon, *Hemingway's Second War*, p. 87.

34 Eisner article from *Noviy Mir*, 1961 trans. at https://brigadasinternacionales.org/index.php?option=comcontent&view=article&id=1137:2017-05-18-17-41-15&catid=44:croni-bi&Itemid=82.

35 Esteve, *Recuerdos de Brigadistas*, pts 1 and 2, v.s. Franz Plura.

36 Ibid., v.s. Ewald Munschke.

37 Ibid., v.s. Rudolf Engels.

38 Ibid., v.s. Ewald Munschke.

39 Ibid., v.s. Rudolf Engels; Munschke.

40 Ibid., v.s. Rudolf Engels.

41 Ibid., v.s. Ewald Munschke.

42 Vaill, *Hotel Florida*, pp. 208, 213–15.

43 Ibid., pp. 213–15.

44 Kurzke and Mangan, 'Good Comrade', pp. 158, 162.

45 Ibid.

46 Reglar, *Owl of Minerva*, pp. 296–7.

47 Martha Gellhorn, *Selected Letters of Martha Gellhorn*, (ed.) Caroline Moorehead, New York, 2006, p. 222.

48 Martha Gellhorn, 'Men Without Medals', *Collier's*, 15 January 1938.

49 Marion Merriman Wachtel and Warren Lerude, *American Commander in Spain: Robert Hale Merriman and the Abraham Lincoln Brigade*, Reno, 1986.

50 Ibid., p. 149; Merriman, *Exegesis*, pp. 285–6.

51 Lugschitz, *Spanienkämpferinnen*, p. 50.

52 Theodor Balk, *Das verlorene Manuskript*, Frankfurt, 2016, pp. 104–7.

53 http://chs.huma-num.fr/exhibits/show/marty-et-les-Brigades-internat/marty-et-les-Brigades/les-femmes-de-la-xive.

54 http://www.alba-valb.org/volunteers/evelyn-rahman-hutchins; John Dollard manuscript collection, John Dollard Research Files for Fear and Courage under Battle Conditions, Tamiment Library, ALBA 122, transcript http://www.alba-valb.org/resources/lessons/document-library/interview-with-evelyn-hutchins.

55 Kurzke and Mangan, 'Good Comrade', p. 134.

32 DAMAGE IN CATALONIA

1 Preston, 'Lights and Shadows', p. 17.

2 George Orwell, 'Why I Join the I.L.P', *New Leader*, June 24, 1938.

3 Bill Alexander, in Christopher Norris (ed.), *Inside the Myth: Orwell: Views from the Left*, London, 1984, p. 91.

4 Preston, 'Lights and Shadows', pp. 22, 52.

5 George Orwell, *Homage to Catalonia* (Penguin Modern Classics), Kindle pos. 2497–8.

6 Mary Low and Juan Breá, *Red Spanish notebook: the first six months of the revolution and the Civil War*, San Francisco, 1979, p. 214.

7 Orwell, *Catalonia*, Kindle pos. 1265.

8 Preston, 'Lights and Shadows', p. 15.

9 Low, *Red Spanish Notebook*, p. 214.

10 Daniel Evans, 'The Conscience of the Spanish Revolution: Anarchist Opposition to State Collaboration in 1937', PhD thesis, University of Leeds, 2016, p. 74.

11 Agustín Guillamón, *Barricades in Barcelona: The CNT from the victory of July 1936 to the necessary defeat of May 1937*, pp. 206, 212, http://libcom.org/library/part-4-0; Preston, 'Lights and Shadows', p. 18.

12 Evans, 'The Conscience', p. 119.

13 Orwell, *Catalonia*, Appendix One (Chapter V in most editions), Kindle pos. 2775.

14 Reiner Tosstorff, *El POUM en la Revolució espanyola*, Barcelona, 2009, eBook edition at tagusboks.es, without page numbering, v.s. 'els fets de Maig'.

15 Preston, 'Lights and Shadows', p. 21; Evans, 'The Conscience' pp. 106–9.

16 Orwell, *Catalonia*, Kindle pos. 1327.

17 Guillamón, *Barricades in Barcelona*, pp. 212–3.

18 Orwell, *Catalonia*, Kindle pos. 1323.

19 Ibid., pos. 1327–39.

20 Preston, 'Lights and Shadows', p. 21.

21 Orwell, *Catalonia*, Kindle pos. 1391.

22 Evans, 'The Conscience' p. 119; Guillamón, *Barricades in Barcelona*, pp. 212–13, 230–2.

23 Orwell, *Catalonia*, Kindle pos. 1366–9.

24 Ibid., pos. 1503–4.

25 Guillamón, *Barricades in Barcelona*, pp. 230–2.

26 Max Schäfer, *Spanien – 1936 bis 1939, Erinnerungen von Interbrigadisten aus der BRD*, digital edition, 2018, p. 315.

27 Ibid., p. 316.

28 Ibid., pp. 314–17, Volodarsky, *Orlov*, p. 264, Esteve, *Recuerdos de Brigadistas Alemanes*, pts 1 and 2, v.s. Karl Mewis papers and pt 2 annex, p. 85.

29 Orwell, *Catalonia*, Kindle Pos. 1535.

30 Ibid., pos. 1534–9.

31 Preston, 'Lights and Shadows', p. 16.

32 Evans, 'The Conscience', p. 127, quoting *Ideas*, 20 May 1937.

33 Guillamón, *Barricades in Barcelona*, pp. 212–13, 230–2.

34 Ibid., pp. 212–3.

35 Chris Ealham, 'De la unidad antifascista a la desunión libertarian: los comités superiores del movimiento libertario contra los quijotes anarquistas en el marco del Frente Popular (1936–1937)', *Mélanges de la Casa de Velázquez*, nouvelle série, 41 (1), 2011, pp. 121–42.

36 Preston, 'Lights and Shadows', p. 16.

37 Ibid., p. 21.

38 Ibid., pp. 21–2.

39 Manuel Aguilera Povedano, 'Los hechos de mayo de 1937: efectivos y bajas de cada bando', *Hispania*, Vol. 73, No. 245, September–December 2013, pp. 789–816, citing Solé, Josep, y Villarroya, Joan, 'Les víctimes dels Fets de Maig', *Recerques*, 12 (Barcelona, 1982), pp. 197–206.

40 Orwell, *Catalonia*, Kindle pos. 1706–09.

41 Ibid., pos. 1671–5.

42 Ibid., pos. 1680–6.

43 Durgan, 'With the POUM', p. 156; see also Les Combattants du POUM, *Front de l'Est, Front d'Estremadura, Front du Centre*, July 1938, Biblioteca de la Republica, Barcelona, p. 75.

44 Orwell, *Catalonia*, Kindle pos. 1278–85.

45 Ibid., pos. 245.

46 Ibid., pos. 1810–13, 1830–2.

47 Volodarsky, *Stalin's Agent*, p. 168.

48 Ibid., pp. 323–4.

49 Christopher Andrew, *The Mitrokhin Archive: The KGB in Europe and the West* (Penguin Press History), pp. 95–6.

50 David Crook, *Hampstead Heath to Tian An Men – The autobiography of David Crook,* at davidcrook.net, 1990, chapters 3–17 to 18.

51 Ibid., Ch. 3–18 to 4–9; RGASPI 545.4.120, 'Betrifft: David Crook', pp. 79–80.

52 RGASPI 545.6.120; Orwell, *Catalonia*, Kindle pos. 266.

53 Crook, *Hampstead*, Chapter 4–4.

54 Ibid., Chapter 4–3 to 4–4.

55 Guillamón, 'Narwicz, Leon (hacia 1918–1938)', http://www.sbhac.net/ Republica/Personajes/Biografias/Guillamon/GCEPER[Guillamon] LeonNarwicz.pdf.

56 Crook, *Hampstead*, Chapters 4 and 5; Volodarsky, *Stalin's Agent*, pp. 240, 246–7.

57 Crook, *Hampstead*, Chapters 4–6.

58 Andrew, *The Mitrokhin Archive*, p. 97.

59 Volodarsky, *Stalin's Agent*, pp. 89, 245.

60 Ibid., pp. 242–5.

61 Vaill, *Hotel Florida*, p. 191.

62 Orwell, *Catalonia*, Kindle pos. 2085.

63 Ibid., pos. 2347.

64 Volodarsky, *Stalin's Agent*, pp. 168–71, 218–19 and 230–8; Vaill, *Hotel Florida*, p. 188; Durgan, 'With the POUM', p. 157; Burnett Bolloten, *The Spanish Civil War: Revolution and Counterrevolution*, Chapel Hill, 1991, pp. 516–20.

65 Aguilera Povedano, 'Los hechos de mayo de 1937', pp. 789–816.

66 PR, Pavello Republica DH 6(1)/11 (7).

67 Durgan, 'With the POUM', p. 158; Nuria Nuñez Días-Balart, 'La humanidad soñada:propaganda y realidad de las Brigadas Internacionales', in *Las Brigadas internacionales: el contexto internacional, los medios de propaganda, literatura y memorias*, Manuel Requena Gallego, Rosa Maria Sepúlveda Losa (eds.), Ediciones de la Universidad de Castilla-La Mancha, Cuenca, 2003, pp. 73–90.

68 Stephen Pollak, *Strange Land Behind Me*, London, 1951, p. 28.

69 Preston, 'Lights and Shadows', p. 22.

70 Helen Graham, *The War and its Shadow: Spain's Civil War in Europe's Long Twentieth Century*, Brighton, 2012, pp. 94–5.

71 Huber and Uhl, 'Die Internationalen Brigaden', p. 16.

72 RGASPI 545.6.3, pp. 1–3.

73 RGASPI 545.6.142, p. 60.

74 Volodarsky, *Stalin's Agent*, pp. 218–19, 257–8; http://www.international-Brigades.org.uk/content/list-volunteers.

75 RGASPI 545.2.147, pp. 302–6.

76 Jef Last, *The Spanish Tragedy*, London, 1939, p. 34; Carroll, *Odyssey*, pp. 163–4; Candido Polo, *La Confusión de babel*, in Manuel Requena Gallego, Rosa María Sepúlveda Losa (eds.), *La sanidad y las Brigadas Internacionales*, Cuenca, 2006, p. 163.

77 Skoutelsky, *Novedad*, p. 345.

78 RGASPI 545.2.147, pp. 302–6.

79 Preston, *We Saw Spain Die*, Kindle pos. 4929–84.

80 RGASPI 495.20.93, Report on some main tactical, organisational and cadres problems confronting the C-P.G.B, pp. 34–5.

81 Skoutelsky, *Novedad*, pp. 125, 297, 326, 331, 334, 350.

82 Walther L. Bernecker, 'Willy Brandt y la guerra civil española', *Revista de Estudios Políticos*, 29, 1982, pp. 6–7, 16–17 and 20–2, citing Willy Brandt, *Ein Jahr Krieg und Revolution in Spanien*; Volodarsky, *Stalin's Agent*, p. 246; Preston, *We Saw Spain Die*, Kindle pos. 4929–84.

83 Orwell, *Catalonia*, Kindle pos. 2456–64.

84 In *Time and Tide*, 31 July 1937, review of John Sommerfield's *Volunteer in Spain* ('tripe') and Franz Borkenau's *The Spanish Cockpit*, reprinted in *Orwell in Spain*, pp. 379–80.

33 ATTACK!

1 Michael Petrou, *Renegades*, p. 145, citing IWM 1238 and 1425.

2 Ibid.

3 Stefanie Schüler-Springorum, *La guerra como aventura*, Madrid, 2014, Kindle pos. 5530–2; Gijs van Hensbergen, *Guernica*, p. 42.

4 Gijs van Hensbergen, *Guernica*, p. 42.

5 RGASPI 545.3.467, Ćopić diary.

6 Michael Petrou, *Renegades*, plates section.

7 Montero, *La Batalla de Brunete*, Madrid, 2010, p. 224.

8 Thomas, *Civil War*, Kindle pos. 14527.

9 Ramsay, 'Ensuring Benevolent Neutrality'.

10 Hector Monterrubio Santín and Eduardo Juárez Valero, *La Batalla de La Granja*, 2008, Librería Icaro, San Ildefonso, p. 112.

11 Ibid., p. 111; RGASPI 545.3.21, pp. 25–6.

12 RGASPI 545.3.20.

13 Szurek, *Shattered*, p. 141.

14 http://arqueologiadeimagenes.blogspot.com/2013/06/guerra-en-el-pinar-fotografias-ineditas.html http://bidicam.castillalamancha.es/bibdigital/archivodelaimagen/i18n/consulta/registro.cmd?id=42886.

15 RGASPI 545.3.21, Observer's diary, pp. 26–30.

16 AABI, Montero digital archive, *Diario de Boris Guimpel*; AABI, *La XIV BI en la batalla de La Granja*, https://brigadasinternacionales.org/.

17 Karol Wacław Świerczewski, *W bojach o Wolność Hiszpanii*, Warsaw, 1966, p. 249.

18 Monterrubio and Juárez, *La Granja*, p. 157.

19 Ibid., p. 159.

20 Ibid.

21 Ibid., pp. 157–8.

22 RGASPI 545.3.21, Observer's diary, pp 26–7; RGASPI 545.3.397, Dumont, *Copie d'un rapport sur l'operationde front de la siere de Navacerrada*, pp. 65–71.

23 RGASPI 545.3.397, Dumont report, pp. 65–71.

24 Ibid.

25 RGASPI 545.3.21, Observer's diary, pp. 25–7.

26 Szurek, *Shattered*, p. 143; *Le Maitron Dictionnaire Biographique*, http://maitron-en-ligne.univ-paris1.fr/spip.php?article23330, 10 November 2018.

27 RGASPI 545.3.397, Dumont report, pp. 65–7.

28 RGASPI 545.3.397, Dumont report, pp. 65–71; Castells, *Brigadas*, p. 218; Gillain, *Mercenario*, pp. 58–9; Szurek, *Shattered*, p. 143.

29 RGASPI 545.3.397, Dumont report, pp. 65–71.

30 Ibid., pp. 65–71, 83; RGASPI 545.3.21, pp. 27–9; Szurek, *Shattered*, pp. 142–3.

31 RGASPI 545.3.397, Dumont report, pp. 65–71, 83; RGASPI 545.3.21, Observer's diary, pp. 27–9; Szurek, *Shattered*, pp. 142–3.

32 Gillain, *Mercenario*, pp. 58–9.

33 RGASPI 545.3.397, Maitre report, pp. 83–7; Balk, *La Quatorzième* (at RGASPI 545.2.402), pp. 198–200.

34 J. Delperrié de Bayac, *Brigadas*, p. 24.

35 RGASPI 545.3.397, Gillet report, p. 82.

36 Gillain, *Mercenario*, p. 58.

37 Castells, *Brigadas*, p. 588; Szurek, *Shattered*, p. 98; Le Maitron Dictionnaire Biographique, http://maitron-en-ligne.univ-paris1.fr/spip.php?article87195, notice GUIMPEL Boris dit Mailly.

38 AABI, Montero digital archive, *Diario de Boris Guimpel*.

39 Ibid.

40 RGASPI 545.3.21, Observer's diary, p. 28.

41 Ibid.

42 Monterrubio and Juárez, *La Granja*, pp. 222–4 citing AGMAV C. 2675 Cp. I/8 andAGMAV C. 475 Cp. 3.
43 RGASPI 545.3.21, Observer's diary, p. 29.
44 RGASPI 545.3.1, p. 9.
45 RGASPI 545.3.397.
46 J. Delperrié de Bayac, *Brigadas*, p. 243.

34 THE DEATH OF LUKÁCS

1 José María Maldonado Moya, *El Frente de Aragón: La Guerra Civil en Aragón*, Zaragoza, 2007, p. 157.
2 Ibid., pp. 159–164, 175.
3 Radosh, *Betrayed*, p. 334; RGASPI 545.3.155, p. 16; Alexei Eisner, *Chelovek s tremya imenami, Povest'o Mate Zalke*, Moscow, 1986, Chapter 14.
4 Maldonado, *Aragón*, p. 177.
5 Ibid., pp. 180, 189.
6 Eisner, *Zalke*, Chapter 14.
7 Radosh, *Betrayed*, p. 337.
8 Eisner, *Zalke*, Chapter 14.
9 Kochetkov, *Beyond the Pyrenees*, Kindle pos. 1223–8; http://www.victorjuan.net/Lukacs.htm citing Ehrenburg, *Gente, Años, Vida*.
10 Castells, *Brigadas*, p. 548; Sidbrint database, Universitat de Barcelona, http://sidbrint.ub.edu/ca/content/strzelczyk–jozef.
11 Pesce, *España*, pp. 161–3.
12 Eisner, *Zalke*, Chapter 14.
13 Regler, *Owl of Minerva*, p. 312.
14 Simonov Konstantin Mikhaylovich, *Raznyye dni voyny. Dnevnik pisatelya Sayt*, 1982.
15 Eisner, *Zalke*, Chapter 14.
16 Szántó Rezső in *Magyar Önkéntesk a Spanyol nép Szabadságharcában*, Kossuth Könyvkiadó, Budapest, 1959, p. 92.
17 Virgilio Fernández del Real to author.
18 Vernon, *Hemingway's War*, p. 141.
19 Regler, *Great Crusade*, pp. viii–xi.
20 According to his niece, Judit Löcsei, and my correspondence with her daughter, Jutka Kovacs.
21 Pesce, *España*, pp. 162–8.
22 RGASPI 545.3.284, pp. 11–12, 87–8; Szántó Rezső in *Magyar*, pp. 90–4; Bron et al., *Wojnie hiszpańskiej*, p. 24.
23 Szántó Rezső in *Magyar*, p. 91; Kochetkov, *Beyond the Pyrenees*, Kindle edition, pos. 1240–6.

24 Pesce, *España*, pp. 161–3.
25 Ibid., p. 163.
26 Puppini in Celada et al., *70 años*, pp. 356–62.
27 Evans, 'The Conscience', p. 81 citing José Luis Ledesma, *Los días de llamas de la revolución. Violencia y política en la retaguardia republicana de Zaragoza durante la Guerra Civil*, Zaragoza, 2003, p. 61..
28 Puppini in Celada et al., *70 años*, pp. 356–62; Pacciardi interview at *Avanti*, 18 February 1989, p. 16.
29 Pesce, *España*, pp. 160, 163–4.
30 Ibid., pp. 166–7.
31 Ibid., pp. 166–170.
32 Ibid., p. 172.
33 CDMH, Salamanca, FOTOGRAFÍAS EMIL VEDIN, 434.
34 Radosh, *Betrayed*, pp. 332–3.
35 Ibid., p. 334.
36 Ibid., p. 335.
37 Maldonado, *Aragón*, pp. 186, 194.
38 Bron, et al., *Wojnie hiszpańskiej*, p. 25.
39 Radosh, *Betrayed*, p. 336.
40 Maldonado, *Aragón*, p. 185.
41 Andy Durgan, 'With the POUM', pp. 154–6; Puppini, *Garibaldini*, pp. 361–2.
42 Puppini, Garibaldini, pp. 361–2.
43 Radosh, *Betrayed*, p. 436.

35 BRUNETE

1 Nationalmuseet online at http://modstand.natmus.dk/person.aspx?34934.
2 Leo Kari, *Bag Spaniens bjerge: en erindringsroman redigeret af Lenni Kari*, Copenhagen, 2017, p. 29.
3 http://irelandscw.com/ibvol-GibbonsLetter.htm; Sidbrint database, Universitat de Barcelona; http://sidbrint.ub.edu/ca/content/gibbons-joseph.
4 K. W. Watkins, *Britain Divided: The Effect of the Spanish Civil War on British Political Opinion*, Westport, 1976, pp. 79–80.
5 Laurie Lee, *A Moment of War*, Viking, London, 1991, p. 5.
6 Baxell, *Warriors*, p. 464.
7 RGASPI 545.3.451, p. 19.
8 Kari, *Spaniens*, pp. 38–9.
9 Ibid., p. 63.
10 Ibid., pp. 62–3.
11 Ibid., pp. 48–9.
12 MacGregor-Thunell, *Spanish Civil War*.

13 Ibid.

14 Kari, *Spaniens*, pp. 71–3.

15 RGASPI 545.1.1, p. 25; Montero, *Brunete*, pp. 48, 229.

16 Montero, *Brunete*, p. 52.

17 Ibid.

18 RGASPI 545.3.467, Ćopić diary.

19 Kantorowicz, *Spanisches*, Kindle pos. 4729–4766.

20 Sidbrint database, Universitat de Barcelona, http://sidbrint.ub.edu/es/content/longo-luigi.

21 RGASPI 545.3.284, pp. 20–3.

22 Skoutelsky, *Novedad*, pp. 237, 316.

23 Carroll, *Odyssey*, p. 136.

24 Tuskagee Institute figures, http://law2.umkc.edu/faculty/projects/ftrials/shipp/lynchingyear.html

25 Carroll, *Odyssey*, pp. 18, 135–7; Skoutelsky, *Novedad*, p. 198; Ryan (ed.), *Book of the XVth Brigade*, p. 156.

26 Adam Hochschild, *Spain in Our Hearts: Americans in the Spanish Civil War, 1936–1939*, London, 2016, Kindle pos. 3479–83.

27 Carroll, *Odyssey*, pp. 140–1.

28 Ibid., p. 140.

29 Richardson, *Comintern Army*, p. 85; Merriman and Lerude in Alvah Bessie and Albert Prego, *Our Fight: Writing by Veterans of the Abraham Lincoln Brigade, Spain 1936–1939*, New York, 1987, p. 110; Eby, *Commissars*, p. 65.

30 See Peter O'Connor diary, *A Soldier of Liberty: Recollections of a Socialist and Anti-fascist Fighter*, Dublin, 1996; Ernesto Viñas and Sven Tuytens, *Lugares de las Brigadas Internacionales en Madrid: Batalla de Brunete*, AABI, Madrid, 2015, p. 13; RGASPI 545.3.467, Ćopić diary.

31 Permaniaobra.blogspot.com, Viñas, *La XIII brigada internacional en la batalla de Brunete*.

32 Montero, *Brunete*, p. 229; RGASPI 545.3.467, Ćopić diary.

33 Richardson, *Comintern Army*, p. 68.

34 RGASPI 545.3.284, p. 12.

35 Castells, *Brigadas*, p. 530.

36 Radosh, *Betrayed*, p. 337.

37 Montero, *Brunete*, pp. 68–71.

38 Ibid.

39 Ibid., p. 75.

40 Ibid., p. 76.

41 Online at https://fnff.es/memoria-historica/901536334/hermanas-larios-fernandez-de-villavicencio-heroinas-de-la-seccion-femenina.html.

42 Montero, *Brunete*, p. 95.

43 Ibid., p. 94.

44 Montero, Ibid., p. 82.

45 Montero, Ibid., pp. 82–3.

46 Montero, Ibid., p. 92.

47 Montero, Ibid.

48 Montero, Ibid., p. 77; Rodimstev, *Cielo*, p. 272.

49 Montero, *Brunete*, pp. 78–81.

50 Juan Barceló, *Brunete: El nacimiento del Ejército Popular*, 2018, pp. 361–2.

51 Baxell, *Unlikely Warriors*, p. 229.

52 *La XIII brigada internacional en la batalla de Brunete* online at permaniaobra.blogspot.com; RGASPI 545.3.467, Ćopić diary.

53 Kantorowicz, *Spanisches*, Kindle pos. 4766–41.

54 MacGregor-Thunell, *Spanish Civil War*; Montero, *Brunete*, p. 85.

55 Montero, *Brunete*, pp. 85–6.

56 Ryan (ed.), *Book of the XVth Brigade*, pp. 139–40.

57 Montero, *Brunete*, p. 84; Rodimstev, *Cielo*, pp. 271–3.

58 Rodímstev, *Cielo*, p. 273; Barceló, *Brunete*, p. 128.

59 Szurek, *Shattered*, p. 138.

60 Montero, *Brunete*, pp. 85–6.

61 Barceló, *Brunete*, p. 361.

62 Baxell, *Unlikely Warriors*, pp. 225–6; Kantorowicz, *Spanisches*, Kindle pos. 4809; Ryan (ed.), *Book of the XVth brigade*, pp. 132, 141–2.

63 Kantorowicz, *Spanisches*, Kindle pos. 4803–41.

64 Baxell, *Unlikely Warriors*, p. 224; MacGregor-Thunell, *Spanish Civil War*, v.s. Conny Anderson.

65 MacGregor-Thunell, *Spanish Civil War*, v.s. Sixten Rogeby.

66 Ibid., v.s. Conny Anderson.

67 Baxell, *Unlikely Warriors*, pp. 221–5.

68 Ryan (ed.), *Book of the XVth Brigade*, pp. 139–40.

69 Ibid.

70 Harry Fisher, *Comrades: Tales of a Brigadista in the Spanish Civil War*, Lincoln, 1998, pp. 54–5; Carroll, *Odyssey*, p. 141, citing Wolff interview.

71 Ryan (ed.), *Book of the XVth Brigade*, p. 145.

72 Kari, *Spaniens*, Fronten chapter, section 5.

73 Aitken, IWM reel 2; RGASPI 545.3.467, Ćopić diary; Montero, *Brunete*, pp. 87–9.

74 Ryan (ed.), *Book of the XVth Brigade*, Jack Roberts, 'The Fascist Sortie'.

75 Baxell, *Unlikely Warriors*, pp. 226–7.

76 Ibid., p. 221.

77 Ibid., p. 227.

78 Ibid., pp. 226–7.

79 Kantorowicz, *Spanisches*, Kindle pos. 4803–62.

80 Montero, *Brunete*, p. 89.

81 Baxell, *Unlikely Warriors*, pp. 227–8; Kantorowicz, *Spanisches*, Kindle pos. 4841–62; Barceló, *Brunete*, p. 151; Montero, *Brunete*, p. 89.

82 Baxell, *Unlikely Warriors*, p. 228.

83 premaniobra.blogspot.com document, *XIII brigada internacional de la 15 división republicana*, v.s. Bajas habidas en la XIII brigada internacional durante la batalla de Brunete (220/15–IHCM).

84 Balfour, *Deadly Embrace*, LSE Online.

85 Kantorowicz, *Spanisches*, Kindle pos. 4841–62.

86 Ibid., Kindle pos. 4863–99.

87 Baxell, *Unlikely Warriors*, p. 228.

88 Barceló, *Brunete*, p. 109; Balfour, *Deadly Embrace*, pp. 82, 83, 87, 99, 196, 205 and 219.

89 Kantorowicz, *Spanisches*, Kindle pos. 4863–99.

90 MacGregor-Thunell, *Spanish Civil War*, v.s. Conny Anderson.

91 MacGregor-Thunell, *Spanish Civil War*, v.s. Elis Frånberg.

92 Nordahl Grieg, *Spansk Sommer* (*Verano español*), Arqueología de Imágenes, 2017, unattributed English translation at https://web.archive.org/web/20120208103212/http://www.bruneteenlamemoria.com/nordahlgrieg.htm, Chapter 9.

93 Ibid.

94 Kari, *Spaniens*, pp. 86–7.

95 Petrou, *Renegades*, p. 69.

96 Kari, *Spaniens*, pp. 86–7.

97 Kantorowicz, *Spanisches*, Kindle pos. 4899–4923; Kantorowicz, trans. Isabel Esteve, *Diario Español*, unpublished, p. 281.

36 THE ROMANILLOS AND MOSQUITO RIDGES

1 Kari, *Spaniens*, p. 88.

2 Fisher, *Comrades*, p. 59.

3 'El cerro del Mosquito', *Historia y Vida*, June 1972, No. 50, pp. 33–5.

4 http://pemaniobra.blogspot.com/ v.s. 17/3–IHCM, Relación de hechos destacados.

5 Kantorowicz, trans. Esteve, *Diario Español*, p. 285; Premaniobra.blogspot.com, *La XIII brigada internacional en la batalla de Brunete*.

6 Fisher, *Comrades*, p. 59.

7 Ibid.

8 Viñas and Tuytens, *Lugares*, p. 28; *Historia y Vida*, June 1972, No. 50, pp. 33–5.

9 *Historia y Vida*, June 1972, No. 50, pp. 28, 33–5.

10 Viñas, 'La XV brigada internacional en la batalla de Brunete', http://pemaniobra.blogspot.com/

11 Kantorowicz, trans. Esteve, *Diario Español*, p. 282.

12 Kari, *Spaniens*, p. 89.

13 Ibid.

14 Ibid., pp. 87–9, 93–7; Viñas at http://pemaniobra.blogspot.com/ v.s. 8/7/37 11 división, Relación de hechos destacados (17/3–IHCM); Kantorowicz, trans. Esteve, *Diario Español*, p. 288; Kantorowicz, *Spanisches*, Kindle pos. 4958–96, 5019–49.

15 Kari, *Spaniens*, pp. 87–9, 93–7; Viñas at http://pemaniobra.blogspot.com/ v.s. 8/7/37 11 división, Relación de hechos destacados (17/3–IHCM); Kantorowicz, trans. Esteve, *Diario Español*, p. 288; Kantorowicz, *Spanisches*, Kindle pos. 4958–96, 5019–49.

16 Kantorowicz, trans. Esteve, *Diario Español*, p. 288.

17 pemaniobra.blogspot.com v.s. 'XIII brigada internacional de la 15 división republicana', 'Ejército de Maniobra, XVIII cuerpo de ejército, v.s. Relación de bajas de la 15 división, XIII brigada internacional (37/4–IHCM)', and v.s. 'Bajas habidas en la XIII brigada internacional durante la batalla de Brunete (220/15–IHCM)'.

18 *Historia y Vida*, June 1972, No. 50, pp. 33–5; pemaniobra.blogspot.com v.s. 9/7/37 Diario de operaciones de la división Provisional del Guadarrama (81/6–IHCM) and v.s. División Provisional del Guadarrama del ejército franquista.

19 Harry Fisher letter dated 19 July 1937 cited by Grover Furr in *The Volunteer*, 1 June 2010, 'Anatomy of a Lie: The Death of Oliver Law'; Fisher, *Comrades*, p. 62.

20 Harry Fisher letter dated 29 July 1937 cited by Grover Furr in *The Volunteer*, 1 June 2010, 'Anatomy of a Lie: The Death of Oliver Law'; Fisher, *Comrades*, p. 62.

21 Fisher, *Comrades*, p. 62.

22 Baxell, *Unlikely Warriors*, p. 231; Kantorowicz, *Spanisches*, Kindle pos. 5050–62.

23 http://pemaniobra.blogspot.com/ v.s. 10/7/37 Diario de operaciones de la división Provisional del Guadarrama (81/6–IHCM), v.s. Sanidad del Ejército de Maniobra, Bajas habidas en la XV brigada internacional durante la batalla de Brunete (220/15–IHCM and 15–PCE), v.s. 10/7/37 XVIII cuerpo de ejército, Orden general no. 5, de las 5.30 horas (182/14–IHCM); 'El cerro del Mosquito', *Historia y Vida*, June 1972, No. 50, pp. 33–5.

24 http://pemaniobra.blogspot.com/ v.s. R. C. GETAFE – 43 – Iª v/393; v.s.10/7/37 Diario de operaciones de la división Provisional del Guadarrama (81/6–IHCM); *Real Academica de la Historia*, http://dbe.rah.es/biografias/69998/estanislao-gomez-landero-y-koch

25 'El cerro del Mosquito', *Historia y Vida*, June 1972, No. 50, pp. 33–5.

26 Pemaniobra.blogspot.com v.s.10/7/37 Diario de operaciones de la división Provisional del Guadarrama (81/6–IHCM).

27 Kantorowicz, *Spanisches*, Kindle pos. 5063–97; http://pemaniobra. blogspot.com, XIII brigada internacional de la 15 división, v.s. XVIII cuerpo de ejército, Parte de operaciones (75/5–IHCM); v.s. 10/7/37 Diario de operaciones de la división Provisional del Guadarrama (81/6–IHCM); Kantorowicz, *Spanisches*, Kindle pos. 5063–97.

28 Kantorowicz, *Spanisches*, Kindle pos. 5156.

29 Pemaniobra.blogspot.com v.s. XVIII cuerpo de ejército, Parte de operaciones (75/5–IHCM) and XVIII cuerpo de ejército, Estado Mayor, Informe de la observación efectuada en el sector de la 15 división, de las 20 horas (370/22–IHCM).

30 Kantorowicz, trans. Esteve, *Diario Español*, p. 299.

31 Kantorowicz, *Spanisches*, Kindle pos. 5156–91.

32 Ibid.

33 Skoutelsky, *Novedad*, p. 312.

34 Kantorowicz, trans. Esteve, *Diario Español*, p. 282.

37 RESIST

1 Robert. S. Thornberry, 'Writers take sides, Stalinists take control: the Second International Congress for the defense of culture (Spain 1937)', *The Historian*, 2000, Vol. 62(3), pp. 589–605; https://www.uv.es/republica/ plano/cultura/cultura2.htm; Luis-Mario Schneider, Inteligencia y guerra civil española, pp. 77–79.

2 Vaill, *Hotel Florida,* pp. 218–20.

3 Grieg, *Spansk Sommer*, unattributed English translation at https://web. archive.org/web/20120208103212/http://www.bruneteenlamemoria.com/ nordahlgrieg.htm

4 Cary Nelson and Jefferson Hendricks (eds.), *Madrid 1937: Letters of the Abraham Lincoln Brigade*, New York, 1996, p. 201, letter by John Cookson from Villanueva de la Cañada, 29 July 1937.

5 Montero, *Brunete*, p. 51.

6 Szurek, *Shattered*, pp. 153–5.

7 Renn, *Guerra Civil*, pp. 475, 478.

8 Szurek, *Shattered*, p. 153.

9 Renn, *Guerra Civil*, pp. 475, 478.

10 Ibid., pp. 471, 473; Baxell, *Unlikely Warriors*, p. 228.

11 Grieg, *Spansk Sommer*, unattributed English translation at https://web. archive.org/web/20120208103212/http://www.bruneteenlamemoria.com/ nordahlgrieg.htm.

12 Montero, *Brunete*, pp. 82–3; http://frentedebatalla-gerion.blogspot.com/2012/08/brunete-primera-parte-el-pasado-mes-de.html.

13 Barceló, *Brunete*, p. 382; Montero, *Brunete*, p. 70; Renn, *Guerra Civil*, pp. 476–8; premaniobra.blogspot.com, v.s. Helge Brännare, XI brigada internacional de la 35 división republicana.

14 Barceló, *Brunete*, pp. 317–31.

15 Montero, *Brunete*, p. 178.

16 Ibid.

17 Ibid., pp. 93, 178.

18 Ibid., p. 131.

19 Ibid., pp. 132, 131.

20 Ibid., pp. 93, 211.

21 Beevor, *Battle*, Kindle pos. 5890; Montero, *Brunete*, pp. 210–13, 222; Schüler-Springorum, *La guerra como aventura*, Kindle pos. 2423–36.

22 Montero, *Brunete*, pp. 157, 212, 220–1, 224, 226.

23 Ibid., p. 214.

24 Renn, *Guerra Civil*, p. 491; Montero, *Brunete*, pp. 224, 226.

25 Tuytens and Viñas, *Lugares*, p. 34.

26 Montero, *Brunete*, p. 225.

27 MacGregor-Thunell, *Spanish Civil War*, v.s. Conny Anderson.

28 *Book of XV Brigade*, p. 147.

29 Grieg, *Spanish Summer*, unattributed English translation of *Spansk Sommer* at https://web.archive.org/web/20120208103212/http://www.bruneteenlamemoria.com/nordahlgrieg.htm.

30 Renn, *Guerra Civil*, p. 158.

31 Tuytens and Viñas, *Lugares*, p. 48.

32 Radosh, *Betrayed*, p. 340; Montero, *Brunete*, p. 142.

33 Radosh, *Betrayed*, p. 340.

34 Ibid.

35 Ibid., pp. 337–42.

36 Montero, *Brunete*, pp. 140, 230; Tuytens and Viñas, *Lugares*, p. 50; Viñas, XII brigada internacional de la 45 división republicana, and CL brigada internacional de la 45 división republicana, at pemaniobra.blogspot.es.

37 Tuytens and Viñas, *Lugares*, p. 51.

38 THE COUP THAT LASTED A YEAR

1 Montero, *Brunete*, p. 152.

2 Renn, *Guerra Civil*, p. 478.

3 Tuytens and Viñas, *Lugares*, pp. 17–18.

4 Montero, *Brunete*, p. 237.
5 Tuytens and Viñas, *Lugares*, p. 33.
6 Kari, *Spaniens*, p. 90.
7 Kantorowicz, trans. Esteve, *Diario Español*, p. 305.
8 Kari, *Spaniens*, p. 90.
9 Kantorowicz, trans. Esteve, *Diario Español*, p. 305.
10 Kari, *Spaniens*, p. 90.
11 Tuytens and Viñas, *Lugares*, p. 36
12 Montero, *Brunete*, p. 171.
13 Kantorowicz, trans. Esteve, *Diario Español*, pp. 306–9.; Tuytens and Viñas, *Lugares*, p. 36.
14 Montero, *Brunete*, p. 171.
15 Tuytens and Viñas, *Lugares*, p. 34–5.
16 Kantorowicz, *Spanisches*, Kindle pos. 5287.
17 *Book of XV Brigade* pp. 174–5, Hugh Slater article.
18 Kantorowicz, trans. Esteve, *Diario Español*, p. 306; Tuytens and Viñas, *Lugares*, p. 37.
19 Kantorowicz, trans. Esteve, *Diario Español*, p. 309; Kantorowicz, *Spanisches*, Kindle pos. 5435.
20 Tuytens and Viñas, *Lugares*, p. 37.
21 Kantorowicz, trans. Esteve, *Diario Español*, p. 309; Kantorowicz, *Spanisches*, Kindle pos. 5435.
22 Kantorowicz, trans. Esteve, *Diario Español*, pp. 309–10;Tuytens and Viñas, *Lugares*, p. 37
23 Kantorowicz, trans. Esteve, *Diario Español*, p. 312.
24 Ibid., p. 314.
25 Ibid., p. 315.
26 Montero, *Brunete*, p. 172; Kari, *Spaniens*, p. 90.
27 Montero, *Brunete*, pp. 171–5.
28 Kari, *Spaniens*, pp. 91–2.
29 Tuytens and Viñas, *Lugares*, p. 38.
30 Montero, *Brunete*, p. 175.
31 Ibid., pp. 176–7.
32 Ibid., pp. 177–81, 186, 191–2.
33 Renn, *Guerra Civil*, pp. 482–3.
34 Grieg, *Spansk Sommer*, unattributed English translation at https://web.archive.org/web/20120208103212/http://www.bruneteenlamemoria.com/nordahlgrieg.htm.
35 Renn, *Guerra Civil*, p. 479.
36 Szurek, *Shattered*, p. 117.

37 Frank Hirschinger, 'Der Mythos um den Kommandeur des "Thälmann Bataillons", Bruno Hinz (1900–1937)', *Totalitarismus und Demokratie*, 8, 2011, p. 305; Renn, *Guerra Civil*, p. 479.
38 RGASPI 545.3.1, pp. 66–9.
39 Grieg, *Spanish Summer, Spansk Sommer*, unattributed English translation at https://web.archive.org/web/20120208103212/http://www.bruneteenlamemoria.com/nordahlgrieg.htm; Grieg, *Verano*, pp.132–40.
40 Grieg, *Spanish Summer, Spansk Sommer*, unattributed English translation at https://web.archive.org/web/20120208103212/http://www.bruneteenlamemoria.com/nordahlgrieg.htm; Grieg, *Verano*, p. 135.
41 Rodimstev, *Cielo*, p. 284.
42 Ibid., pp. 284–5.
43 Montero, *Brunete*, pp. 187–9; Peter Wyden, *The Passionate War: The Narrative History of the Spanish Civil War*, New York, 1983, p. 384.
44 Tuytens and Viñas, *Lugares*, pp. 39–41.
45 Montero, *Brunete*, p. 191; Patrick Laureau, *Condor: The Luftwaffe in Spain, 1936–39*, Lanham, 2010, p. 17.
46 Tuytens and Viñas, *Lugares*, pp. 39–41.
47 Ibid., pp. 38–41.
48 Montero, *Brunete*, p. 192.
49 Ibid.
50 RGASPI 545.3.1, p. 77.
51 Montero, *Brunete*, pp. 184, 193–4.
52 Ibid., pp. 194–5; Renn, *Guerra Civil*, pp. 486–7.
53 Montero, *Brunete*, pp. 194–5.
54 Ibid.
55 Ibid., p. 197.
56 Ibid., p. 196.
57 Ibid.; Wyden, *The Passionate War*, p. 385.

39 THE PRICE OF WAR

1 Vaill, *Hotel Florida*, p. 226.
2 Ibid., p. 223.
3 Ibid.
4 Ibid., pp. 223–7.
5 Ibid., pp. 226–7.
6 Ibid., pp. 208, 214.
7 Jane Rogoyska, *Gerda Taro: Inventing Robert Capa*, London, 2013, pp. 215–20.
8 Ibid.

9 Ibid.
10 IWM, John Kiszely, IWM 12934.
11 Ibid., Reel1.
12 Ibid., Reel 2.
13 Vaill, *Hotel Florida*, p. 228.
14 Montero, *Brunete*, p. 198.
15 Ibid., pp. 200–1.
16 Viñas and Tuytens, *Lugares*, pp. 41–2.
17 Kari, *Spaniens*, pp. 95–8.
18 Renn, *Guerra Civil*, p. 486.
19 Montero, *Brunete*, p. 201.
20 MacGregor-Thunell, *Spanish Civil War*, v.s. Harry Ericsson.
21 Montero, *Brunete*, pp. 201, 203.
22 Ibid., pp. 202–4; Viñas and Tuytens, *Lugares*, pp. 41–2.
23 Montero, *Brunete*, pp. 202–4; Viñas and Tuytens, *Lugares*, pp. 41–2.
24 Grieg, *Spansk Sommer*, unattributed English translation at https://web.archive.org/web/20120208103212/http://www.bruneteenlamemoria.com/nordahlgrieg.htm.
25 Szurek, *Shattered*, p. 159.
26 Montero, *Brunete*, pp. 199–202.
27 Renn, *Guerra Civil*, p. 491.
28 Hirschinger, 'Der Mythos', p. 305
29 Renn, *Guerra Civil*, pp. 491–2.
30 Ibid., pp. 499–500.
31 Ibid.
32 Ibid.
33 Montero, *Brunete*, p. 182.
34 Radosh, *Betrayed*, p. 341.
35 Renn, *Guerra Civil*, p. 495.
36 Ibid., pp. 488–9; Montero, *Brunete*, pp. 199–202, 205–8.
37 Sidbrint database, Universitat de Barcelona, http://sidbrint.ub.edu/ca/content/hinz-bruno accessed 11 November 2019.
38 RGASPI 545.3.57.
39 Renn, *Guerra Civil*, pp. 494–6.
40 RGASPI 545.3.284; premaniobra.blogspot.com v.s. 37/4–IHCM, 75/5–IHCM, 220/15–IHCM, 15 and 16–PCE; Montero, *Brunete*, p. 229–30.
41 Baxell, *Unlikely Warriors*, pp. 233–4; Viñas and Tuytens, *Lugares*, p. 43.
42 https://elpais.com/diario/2011/10/29/madrid/1319887463850215.html.
43 Rogoyska, *Taro*, pp. 215–20.
44 Ibid.
45 RGASPI 545.1.1, p. 25.

46 IWM, Interview with George Aitken, IWM 10357, Reel 2.

47 Carroll, *Odyssey*, p. 144.

48 Ibid., pp. 144–6; RGASPI 545.6.1011, Wendorf, pp. 55–6.

49 Eby, *Comrades*, p. 195.

50 RGASPI 545.1.1, RGASPI 545.3.284, RGASPI 545.3.57; Montero, *Brunete*, pp. 229–30, 213, 221; premaniobra.blogspot.com v.s. 37/4–IHCM, 75/5–IHCM, 220/15–IHCM, 15 and 16–PCE Rafael Casa de la Vega, *Brunete*, Madrid, 1967, pp. 279–80; Hochschild, *Spain in Our Hearts*, Kindle pos. 3508.

51 Hochschild, *Spain in our Hearts*, p. 228, citing David McKelvy White.

52 RGASPI 545.1.1, RGASPI 545.3.284, RGASPI 545.3.57.

53 Eby, *Commissars*, p. 195; Szurek, *Shattered*, p. 157; see also Aitken, IWM Reel 2; Viñas and Tuytens, *Lugares*, pp. 44–6.

40 VENGEANCE

1 Szurek, *Shattered*, pp. 187–8.

2 Ibid., p. 188.

3 Antonio Passaporte, *Memorias Da Guerra Civil Espanhola*, edited by Rodolfo Passaporte, unpublished.

4 Szurek, *Shattered*, p. 193.

5 Ibid., p. 191.

6 Ibid.

7 https://w3.grupobbva.com/TLFU/dat/cuadernosFBBVA51espanaweb.pdf

8 Maldonado, *Aragón*, p. 204.

9 Ibid.

10 Ibid., pp. 204–5.

11 Ibid., p. 205.

12 Radosh, *Betrayed*, p. 353; Karol Wacław Świerczewski with Fernando Martínez de Baños Carrillo and Agnieszka Szafran, *El General Walter*, Delsan, 2011, p. 29.

13 Świerczewski, Martínez and Szafran, *El General*, p. 22.

14 Castells, *Brigadas*, pp. 290–2.

15 Radosh, *Betrayed*, p. 348.

16 Puppini, *Le Brigate Internazionali*, in Sànchez Cervelló and Agudo Blanco (eds.), *Las Brigadas Internacionales*, p. 81.

17 Puppini in Celada et al., *70 años*, pp. 360–1 citing ACS (Roma) – Fondo Nenni – Serie Partito – b.86, f2177 Rapporto del Segretario del Partito alla Direzione, Valencia 9/37l.

18 Radosh, *Betrayed*, pp. 342–3.

19 Świerczewski, Martínez and Szafran, *El General*, p. 46.

20 Ibid., p. 47.

21 Radosh, *Betrayed*, pp. 344–5.

22 Ibid., p. 345.

23 Ibid.

24 Ibid., p. 346.

25 Szurek, *Shattered*, p. 297.

26 Ibid.

27 Radosh, *Betrayed*, p. 353.

28 Ibid., pp. 354, 348.

29 Karol Wacław Świerczewski, *W bojach o Wolność Hiszpanii*, Warsaw, 1966, pp. 25, 110–11.

30 Świerczewski, Martínez and Szafran, *El General*, p. 47.

31 Ibid., p. 67; Swierczewski, *Hiszpanii*, chart, p. 53. Four XV BI battalions remained, with Six Février & Washington gone. Full strength should be 2,400.

32 Maldonado, *Aragón*, p. 207, map.

33 Świerczewski, Martínez and Szafran, *El General*, pp. 78–9.

34 Szurek, *Shattered*, p. 194.

35 Świerczewski, Martínez and Szafran, *El General*, p. 74.

36 Ibid., p. 75.

37 Ibid., pp. 74–6.

38 Merriman, *Exegesis*, p. 476.

39 Świerczewski, Martínez and Szafran, *El General*, pp. 77–9.

40 Ibid., pp. 80–4, 88.

41 Merriman, *Exegesis*, p. 496.

42 Wintringham, *English Captain*, p. 110; Merriman, *Exegesis*, p. 548.

43 Świerczewski, Martínez and Szafran, *El General*, p. 99; Merriman, *Exegesis*, p. 496.

44 Szurek, *Shattered*, p. 194; Świerczewski, Martínez and Szafran, *El General*, pp. 87, 99.

45 Świerczewski, Martínez and Szafran, *El General*, p. 100.

46 Esteve, *Recuerdos de Brigadistas Alemanes*, Vol. 2, pp. 31–3.

47 Świerczewski, Martínez and Szafran, *El General*, pp. 102–4.

48 Ibid., pp. 100–9.

49 Wintringham, *English Captain*, p. 120; Landis, *Lincoln Brigade*, p. 263.

50 Świerczewski, Martínez and Szafran, *El General*, p. 114.

51 Wintringham, *English Captain*, pp. 110–11; Świerczewski, Martínez and Szafran, *El General*, p. 113.

52 Świerczewski, Martínez and Szafran, *El General*, pp. 114, 118.

53 Ibid., pp. 111, 115.

54 Baxell, *Unlikely Warriors*, p. 267; Wintringham, *English Captain*, pp. 110–11.

55 Świerczewski, Martínez and Szafran, *El General*, p. 116.

56 Świerczewski, Martínez and Szafran, *El General*, pp. 117–18; Baxell, *Unlikely Warriors*, pp. 266–9; Merriman, *Exegesis*, pp. 209, 507.

57 Merriman, *Exegesis*, p. 500; Świerczewski, Martínez and Szafran, *El General*, p. 119.

58 Gonzalo Lorén Garay, 'La batalla de Quinto de Ebro en la ofensiva republicana sobre Zaragoza', *Revista de Historia Militar*, 115 (2014), pp. 98, 118.

59 Michonneau, *Belchite*, p. 35.

60 Świerczewski, Martínez and Szafran, *El General*, p. 120; Merriman, *Exegesis*, pp. 507–8.

61 Świerczewski, Martínez and Szafran, *El General*, p. 120.

62 Merriman, *Exegesis*, pp. 510–11; http://www.alba-valb.org/volunteers/felix-kusman.

63 Świerczewski, Martínez and Szafran, *El General*, p. 120.

64 Lorén Garay, 'La batalla', p. 122.

65 Świerczewski, *W bojach o Wolność Hiszpaanii*, preface.

66 Świerczewski, Martínez and Szafran, *El General*, p. 124.

67 Ibid.

68 Ibid., p. 121.

69 Stéphane Michonneau, *Fue ayer*, Belchite. *Un pueblo frente a la cuestión del pasado*, Zaragoza, 2017, p. 48.

70 Szurek, *Shattered*, p. 195.

71 Baxell, *Unlikely Warriors*, p. 268; Petrou, *Renegades*, p. 72.

72 Szurek, *Shattered*, pp. 197–8.

73 Merriman, *Exegesis*, p. 505; Carroll, *Odyssey*, p. 156; Radosh, *Betrayed*, p. 365.

74 Szurek, *Shattered*, p. 198; Juan Modesto, *Soy del Quinto Regimiento*, Paris, 1969, p. 131.

41 CONQUEST

1 Maldonado, *Aragón*, 211.

2 Świerczewski, Martínez and Szafran, *El General*, p. 194.

3 Ibid., pp. 154–7; Maldonado, *Aragón*, p. 211.

4 Świerczewski, Martínez and Szafran, *El General*, pp. 142–8; Radosh, *Betrayed*, pp. 354–5.

5 Maldonado, *Aragón*, p. 212; Świerczewski, Martínez and Szafran, *El General*, pp. 142–8; Puppini, *Garibaldini*, pp. 134–6.

6 Maldonado, *Aragón*, p. 212; Świerczewski, *W bojach o Wolność Hiszpaanii*, preface; Radosh, *Betrayed*, pp. 354–8.

7 Świerczewski, Martínez and Szafran, *El General*, p. 29.

8 Ibid., pp. 146–7; Świerczewski, *W bojach o Wolność Hiszpaanii*, preface.

9 Radosh, *Betrayed*, pp. 356.

10 Świerczewski, Martínez and Szafran, *El General*, p. 150.

11 Ibid., pp. 125–31, 142–3; Maldonado, *Aragón*, p. 212.

12 Radosh, *Betrayed*, pp. 352–4; Puppini in Celada et al., *70 años*, pp. 79–80.

13 Radosh, *Betrayed*, pp. 354–6; Świerczewski, Martínez and Szafran, *El General*, pp. 142–3; Sanz, 'Durruti en Madrid', p. 160.

14 Puppini, *Garibaldini*, pp. 134–6.

15 Radosh, *Betrayed*, p. 364.

16 Ibid., pp. 357, 364.

17 Świerczewski, Martínez and Szafran, *El General*, pp. 165–8; Michonneau, *Fue ayer*, p. 31.

18 Szurek, *Shattered*, p. 199; Świerczewski, Martínez and Szafran, *El General*, p. 179.

19 Świerczewski, Martínez and Szafran, *El General*, pp. 79, 168–9, 178.

20 Merriman, *Exegesis*, p. 533; Archivo Histórico Nacional, AHN, DIVERSOS-VICENTE_ROJO, Car.8, N.6, 9 and 45 for maps.

21 Świerczewski, Martínez and Szafran, *El General*, p. 205.

22 Ibid., pp. 176–8.

23 Ibid., p. 176.

24 Ibid., p. 177.

25 Ibid., pp. 179–181; Merriman, *Exegesis*, pp. 533–5; Maldonado, *Aragón*, pp. 182–4.

26 Świerczewski, Martínez and Szafran, *El General*, pp. 181–4.

27 Ibid., pp. 182, 207.

28 Ibid., pp. 184–6.

29 Szurek, *Shattered*, p. 199; Świerczewski, Martínez and Szafran, *El General*, p. 186.

30 Świerczewski, Martínez and Szafran, *El General*, pp. 176, 191.

31 Ibid., pp. 187–190.

32 Ibid., p. 194.

33 Merriman, *Exegesis*, p. 538.

34 Świerczewski, Martínez and Szafran, *El General*, pp. 195–6, 220; Ryan (ed.), *Book of the XVth Brigade*, pp. 273–4.

35 Świerczewski, Martínez and Szafran, *El General*, pp. 217–19.

36 Ryan (ed.), *Book of the XVth Brigade*, pp. 273–4.

37 Baxell, *Unlikely Warriors*, p. 269.

38 Świerczewski, Martínez and Szafran, *El General*, p. 198; Merriman, *Exegesis*, pp. 538, 561–2.

39 Świerczewski, Martínez and Szafran, *El General*, p. 197; Merriman, *Exegesis*, p. 539.

40 Unpublished memoir of Joaquín Moreno, from copy owned by Eduardo del Campo, 'Tabique a Tabique', part published at https://www.elmundo. es/cronica/2014/03/30/5336b1beca47418d308b456d.html.

41 Merriman, *Exegesis*, p. 545.

42 Ibid., p. 547.

43 Ibid., pp. 541–2.

44 Len Crome, 'A Soldier in Spain', pp. 116–28.

45 Maldonado, *Aragón*, p. 218.

46 Radosh, *Betrayed*, p. 482.

47 Świerczewski, Martínez and Szafran, *El General*, p. 198; Merriman, *Exegesis*, pp. 538, 562.

48 Merriman, *Exegesis*, p. 562.

49 Świerczewski, Martínez and Szafran, *El General*, pp. 201, 207.

50 Ibid., p. 202.

51 https://www.elmundo.es/cronica/2014/03/30/5336b1beca47418d308b456d. html accessed 17 November 2018; Maldonado, *Aragón*, p. 218.

52 Ryan (ed.), *Book of the XVth Brigade*, pp. 284, 286; https://www.elmundo. es/cronica/2014/03/30/5336b1beca47418d308b456d.html

53 Merriman, *Exegesis*, p. 551.

54 Świerczewski, Martínez and Szafran, *El General*, p. 203.

55 Merriman, *Exegesis*, p. 557.

56 Ibid., p. 548.

57 Ibid., pp. 548–9.

58 Ibid., p. 556; Świerczewski, *W bojach o Wolność Hiszpaanii*, p. 100.

59 IISH CP–49A.3.

60 IISH CNT C61, IISH CP–49A.3.

61 Świerczewski, Martínez and Szafran, *El General*, p. 283.

62 Ibid., p. 203.

63 Ibid.

64 Szurek, *Shattered*, pp. 201–3.

65 Ibid., p. 205.

66 Stéphane Michonneau, *Fue ayer*, p. 46; Archivo Histórico Nacional, FC-CAUSAGENERAL, 1423, Exp. 62; Szurek, *Shattered*, pp. 205–6; Joaquín Moreno memoir at https://www.elmundo.es/cronica/2014/03/30/ 5336b1beca47418d308b456d.html.

67 Szurek, *Shattered*, pp. 204–5; Florence Gavras, *Le Sel de la Terre, Espagne, 1936–1938: des brigadistes témoignent de leur engagement*, Paris, 1999. pp. 134–6; Skoutelsky, *Novedad*, p. 321.

68 Szurek, *Shattered*, p. 204.

69 Ibid., p. 205.

70 Świerczewski, Martínez and Szafran, *El General*, p. 207.

71 Ibid., p. 206.
72 Radosh, *Betrayed*, p. 358.
73 Świerczewski, Martínez and Szafran, *El General*, pp. 174–5.
74 Ibid., p. 226.
75 Ibid., p. 222.
76 Ibid., pp. 222, 249.
77 Radosh, *Betrayed*, p. 359.
78 Świerczewski, Martínez and Szafran, *El General*, pp. 203, 221–2.
79 Ibid., pp. 223–7.
80 Castells, *Brigadas*, pp. 284–8; Landis, *Lincoln Brigade*, pp. 314–23; Steven J. Zaloga, *Spanish Civil War Tanks: The Proving Ground for Blitzkrieg*, Oxford, 2010, p. 36; Baxell, *Unlikely Warriors*, pp. 271–2.
81 Świerczewski, Martínez and Szafran, *El General*, p. 225.
82 Radosh, *Betrayed*, p. 359.
83 Ibid., pp. 342–4, 360, 364.
84 Ibid., p. 365.
85 Ibid., pp. 367–8; Thomas, *Civil War*, Kindle pos. 13694.

42 THE NORTH POLE

1   http://www.alba-valb.org/volunteers/irving-goff; Landis, *Lincoln Brigade*, p. 349.
2   Ilya Grigorievich Starinov, *Zapiski diversanta*, Moscow, 1997, Chapter 5.
3   Carroll, *Odyssey*, pp. 167–8; Helen Graham, 'The Wars of Bill Aalto: guerrilla soldier in Spain, 1937–39', in *The Volunteer*, 21 March 2014, http://www.albavolunteer.org/2014/03/the-wars-of-bill-aalto-guerrilla-soldier-in-spain-1937-39/.
4   Maldonado, *Aragón*, pp. 249, 251.
5   Ibid., p. 245.
6   Świerczewski, Martínez and Szafran, *El General*, pp. 251–2; Maldonado, *Aragón*, p. 246.
7   Castells, *Brigadas*, p. 298.
8   Maldonado, *Aragón*, p. 248.
9   Helen Graham, *The War and its Shadow*, pp. 75–101.
10 Świerczewski, Martínez and Szafran, *El General*, pp. 278–9.
11 Ibid., p. 258; Maldonado, *Aragón*, pp. 246, 251.
12 Buckley, *Spanish Republic*, p. 351; Castells, *Brigadas*, p. 298.
13 Ernest Hemingway, 'Hemingway Reports Spain', *The New Republic*, 12 January 1938.
14 Buckley, *Spanish Republic*, p. 347.
15 Hemingway, 'Hemingway Reports Spain', pp. 273–5.

16 Maldonado, *Aragón*, pp. 251–3; David Alegre Lorenz, *La Batalla de Teruel: Guerra total en España*, Madrid, 2018, Kindle pos. 3911, 4255, 4291, 6376.
17 Świerczewski, Martínez and Szafran, *El General*, pp. 257, 269; Castells, *Brigadas*, p. 298.
18 Ibid., pp. 257, 269.
19 RGASPI 545.3.7, Teruel report, p. 82.
20 Landis, *Lincoln Brigade*, p. 350.
21 Skoutelsky, *Novedad*, pp. 221–8.
22 Ibid., pp. 451–6.
23 Baxell, *Unlikely Warriors*, p. 278; Landis, *Lincoln Brigade*, p. 350.
24 RGASPI 545.2.131, p. 29.
25 Landis, *Lincoln Brigade*, p. 350; Castells, *Brigadas*, p. 299; Buckley, *Spanish Republic*, p. 347.
26 Maldonado, *Aragón*, p. 251.
27 Ibid., pp. 256–7.
28 Świerczewski, Martínez and Szafran, *El General*, p. 270.
29 Hemingway, 'Hemingway Reports Spain', p. 273.
30 https://batallate.es/project/val-9-2-valdecebro-mansueto/.
31 Hemingway, 'Hemingway Reports Spain', p. 274.
32 Świerczewski, Martínez and Szafran, *El General*, p. 259.
33 Ibid., pp. 266–7.
34 Ibid.; Maldonado, *Aragón*, p. 261.
35 Świerczewski, Martínez and Szafran, *El General*, pp. 266–7.
36 Darman, *Heroic Voices of the Spanish Civil War: Memories from the International Brigades*, New Holland, 2009, p. 128; Maldonado, *Aragón*, p. 263.
37 Preston, *We Saw Spain Die*, Kindle pos. 4037–56; see telegram at http://batallate.es/wp-content/uploads/2017/08/Telegrama-enviado-31-12-37.pdf.
38 Volodarsky, *Stalin's Agent*, p. 388.
39 Max Faber, 'Bataillon »Thälmann« vor Concud', in *Brigadas Internacionales*, 2, p. 93 f.
40 Castells, *Brigadas*, p. 299.
41 RGASPI 545.3.7, Teruel report, p. 95.
42 RGASPI 545.6.25, Szinda report, pp. 57–61.
43 Landis, *Lincoln Brigade*, p. 356–8; Baxell, *Unlikely Warriors*, p. 282.
44 Landis, *Lincoln Brigade*, pp. 356–7, 363.
45 Ibid., p. 358.
46 Ibid., pp. 359–60.
47 Ibid., p. 361.
48 Ibid., p. 359; Cary Nelson and Jefferson Hendricks, *Edwin Rolfe, A Biographical Essay and Guide to the Rolfe Archive at the University of Illinois at Urbana-Champaign*, Urbana-Champaign, 1990, pp. 1–30.

49 Landis, *Lincoln Brigade*, p. 357.
50 Ibid., p. 366; Castells, *Brigadas*, pp. 299–300; Maldonado, *Aragón*, p. 263.
51 Baxell, *Unlikely Warriors*, p. 282; Eby, *Commissars*, p. 276.
52 Landis, *Lincoln Brigade*, p. 370.
53 Ibid., p. 368.
54 Ibid.
55 Ibid., p. 369.
56 Ibid.
57 Ibid.
58 Maldonado, *Aragón*, pp. 265–7; Świerczewski, Martínez and Szafran, *El General*, p. 268.
59 RGASPI 545.3.7, Teruel report, pp. 97–9.
60 Castells, *Brigadas*, p. 301; RGASPI 545.3.7, Teruel report, pp. 97–104.
61 RGASPI 545.3.7, Putz report, pp. 133–8; Sidbrint database, Universitat de Barcelona, http://sidbrint.ub.edu/ca/content/putz-joseph accessed 4 October 2019.
62 Landis, *Lincoln Brigade*, pp. 373–5.
63 Ibid., p. 372.
64 RGASPI 545.3.7, Putz report, p. 137; Świerczewski, Martínez and Szafran, *El General*, pp. 270–1; Maldonado, *Aragón*, pp. 266–9; Landis, *Lincoln Brigade*, p. 383; Szurek, *Shattered*, pp. 217–18.
65 Castells, *Brigadas*, p. 301; RGASPI 545.3.7, Teruel report, pp. 97–104.
66 Castells, *Brigadas*, p. 301; RGASPI 545.3.7, Teruel report, p. 105.
67 RGASPI 545.3.7, Teruel report, p. 105.
68 Ibid., pp. 105–7; Świerczewski, Martínez and Szafran, *El General*, pp. 216–17; Eby, *Commissars*, p. 276.
69 MacGregor-Thunell, *Spanish Civil War*, v.s. Gösta Hjärpe; RGASPI 545.3.7, pp. 97–101.
70 RGASPI 545.3.7, Putz report, p. 137; Szurek, *Shattered*, pp. 217, 218.
71 RGASPI 545.3.7, Putz report, pp. 133–8.
72 Szurek, *Shattered*, p. 218.
73 Esteve, *Recuerdos de Brigadistas Alemanes* pts 1 and 2, v.s. Willi Benz; http://www.argus.bstu.bundesarchiv.de/sgy11/rightframe.htm?vid=sgy11&kid=2ea3ece7-e8e4-4c71-af60-4cfbadb26cb0; RGASPI 545.3.7, Teruel report, pp. 105–9; Szurek, *Shattered*, p. 218; Castells, *Brigadas*, p. 302.
74 RGASPI 545.3.7, Teruel report, p. 119.
75 Landis, *Lincoln Brigade*, p. 376.
76 Castells, *Brigadas*, p. 302, note.
77 RGASPI 545.6.25, pp. 57–61.
78 Baxell, *Unlikely Warriors*, pp. 282–3.
79 Ibid., p. 283.

80 Landis, *Lincoln Brigade*, pp. 378–82; Castells, *Brigadas*, p. 301; Peter Kemp, *Mine Were of Trouble*, London, 1957, p. 85; Christopher Othen, *Franco's International Brigades, Adventurers, Fascists, and Christian Crusaders in the Spanish Civil War*, London, 2013, p. 245; RGASPI 545.2.7, Putz report, p. 138.
81 RGASPI 545.3.433, pp. 170–1; RGASPI 545.3.434, p. 87.
82 RGASPI 545.3.8, p. 2; Sidbrint database, Universitat de Barcelona, http://sidbrint.ub.edu/en/content/rau-heinrich and http://sidbrint.ub.edu/en/content/staimer-richard.
83 Darman, *Heroic Voices*, p. 129.
84 Landis, *Lincoln Brigade*, p. 383.
85 Ibid., p. 384; Castells, *Brigadas*, p. 302.
86 http://www.vlib.us/amdocs/texts/fdrquarn.html v.s. 'epidemic'.
87 Eby, *Commissars*, p. 281.
88 Landis, *Lincoln Brigade*, p. 386.
89 CDMH *Aragón* 6/7,9,11; Landis, *Lincoln Brigade*, p. 385.
90 CDMH *Aragón* 6/7,9,11; Landis, *Lincoln Brigade*, p. 385.
91 Landis, *Lincoln Brigade*, p. 387.
92 Ibid., pp. 388, 396.
93 Szurek, *Shattered*, p. 220.
94 Castells, *Brigadas*, p. 303.
95 Maldonado, *Aragón*, p. 278.
96 RGASPI 545.3.184, pp. 91–2.
97 William Rust, *Britons in Spain: The History of the British Battalion of the XVth International Brigade*, Torfaen, 2003, p. 114.
98 Baxell, *Unlikely Warriors*, p. 283; Eby, *Commissars*, p. 279.
99 RGASPI 545.3.7, Teruel report, p. 81.
100 Alvah Bessie, *Alvah Bessie's Spanish Civil War Notebooks*, Lexington, 2001, Loc 1034; https://batallate.es/la-batalla-de-teruel/.

43 BLITZKRIEG

1 Beevor, *Battle*, p. 324; Landis, *Lincoln Brigade*, p. 410; Maldonado, *Aragón*, pp. 371, 372, 382.
2 Maldonado, *Aragón*, p. 380.
3 Landis, *Lincoln Brigade*, pp. 410–11.
4 Maldonado, *Aragón*, p. 298; Beevor, *Battle*, p. 324; Landis, *Lincoln Brigade*, p. 410.
5 Maldonado, *Aragón*, p. 298.
6 Baxell, *Unlikely Warriors*, p. 307.
7 Maldonado, *Aragón*, pp. 364–5, 374.

8   Baxell, *Unlikely Warriors*, p. 307; Maldonado, *Aragón*, pp. 346, 375.

9   Hochschild, *Spain in our Hearts*, Kindle pos. 2699.

10 Ibid.

11 Beevor, *Battle*, Kindle pos. 3098–100.

12 Castells, *Brigadas*, p. 304.

13 Ibid., p. 305.

14 Ibid., pp. 305, 494.

15 RGASPI 545.3.27, p. 60; Castells, *Brigadas*, p. 315.

16 Castells, *Brigadas*, pp. 305, 513, 504.

17 RGASPI 545.3.529, 'Rapport sur la 129 Brigade Internationale pour Roman Watcek' (Watcek report); Fisher, *Comrades*, p. 111; Castells, *Brigadas*, pp. 306–7, 521.

18 https://nowahistoria.interia.pl/prl/news-waclaw-komar-i-wszystkie-jego-tajne-misje-zaczynal-jako-part,nId,1581972.

19 Castells, *Brigadas*, pp. 306–7; see RGASPI 545.3.529, Watcek report.

20 Gerald Gino Baumann, *Los voluntarios latinoamericanos en la Guerra Civil española*, Cuenca, Servicio de Publicaciones de la Universidad de Castilla-La Mancha, 2009, p. 140.

21 Świerczewski, Martínez and Szafran, *El General*, p. 284; Castells, *Brigadas*, p. 311; Maldonado, *Aragón*, p. 346.

22 RGASPI 545.3.91, Willi Benz, Relato sobre la contraofensiva fascista, p. 2; RGASPI 545.3.281, p. 46; RGASPI 545.3.68, p. 243, pp. 244, 465 for maps; Castells, *Brigadas*, p. 311; Maldonado, *Aragón*, p. 396.

23 Maldonado, *Aragón*, pp. 383–4.

24 Landis, *Lincoln Brigade*, p. 407.

25 Maldonado, *Aragón*, p. 411.

26 Landis, *Lincoln Brigade*, pp. 408–9.

27 Fausto Villar Esteban, *4 kilometres en Belchite*, https://sites.google.com/site/gceformulario/4-kilometres-en-belchite 7.

28 Beevor, *Battle*, p. 324.

29 Ibid., p. 325; Maldonado, *Aragón*, p. 330; http://www.ejercito.mde.es/unidades/Madrid/riac61/Enlaces/FLAK36.pdf.

30 Castells, *Brigadas*, p. 311; Landis, *Lincoln Brigade*, p. 409.

31 Landis, *Lincoln Brigade*, pp. 404–10.

32 Maldonado, *Aragón*, pp. 368, 371.

33 Petrou, *Renegades*, p. 84.

34 Ibid.; Landis, *Lincoln Brigade*, pp. 409, 413–5; Castells, *Brigadas*, p. 312.

35 Baxell, *Unlikely Warriors*, p. 306; Landis, *Lincoln Brigade*, pp. 406–9.

36 RGASPI 545.2.108, pp. 210–11; Baxell, *Unlikely Warriors*, p. 306.

37 Fisher, *Comrades*, p. 102.

38 Eby, *Commissars*, p. 287.

39 Fisher, *Comrades*, p. 105.
40 https://www.turismodezaragoza.es/provincia/patrimonio/mudejar/santuario-virgen-del-pueyo-belchite.html; Landis, *Lincoln Brigade*, p. 418.
41 https://sites.google.com/site/gceformulario/4-kilometres-en-belchite.
42 Fisher, *Comrades*, pp. 101–5.
43 Maldonado, *Aragón*, p. 396.
44 Ibid.; Fisher, *Comrades*, p. 105.
45 Maldonado, *Aragón*, p. 303; Fisher, *Comrades*, pp. 106–7; Villar, 'A Little Valencian'.
46 Maldonado, *Aragón*, p. 396; Landis, *Lincoln Brigade*, p. 419.
47 Landis, *Lincoln Brigade*, p. 415; Castells, *Brigadas*, p. 561.
48 Villar, 'A Little Valencian'.
49 Fisher, *Comrades*, p. 183.
50 https://sites.google.com/site/gceformulario/4-kilometres-en-belchite
51 RGASPI 545.3.497, Sam Wild report, pp. 25–6.
52 Landis, *Lincoln Brigade*, pp. 420–1.
53 Ibid., pp. 418–20.
54 Szurek, *Shattered*, p. 226.
55 RGASPI 545.3.507, pp. 23–31; Petrou, *Renegades*, p. 85; Landis, *Lincoln Brigade*, p. 423.
56 Landis, *Lincoln Brigade*, pp. 423–4.
57 Fisher, *Comrades*, p. 111; Landis, *Lincoln Brigade*, pp. 418–27.
58 Fisher, *Comrades*, p. 110.
59 Bessie, *Notebooks*, p. 16; Fisher, *Comrades*, pp. 110–14.
60 RGASPI 545.3.91 Benz report, p. 2; RGASPI 545.3.281, p. 46; Esteve, *Recuerdos de Brigadistas Alemanes*, pts 1 and 2,v.s.Willi Benz.
61 Bundesarchiv, Berlín-Lichterfelde, SAPMO, SgY 11/ V 237/ 7/ 114, http://www.argus.bstu.bundesarchiv.de/sgy11/rightframe.htm?vid=sgy11&kid=2ea3ece7-e8e4-4c71-af60-4cfbadb26cb0.
62 Esteve, *Recuerdos de Brigadistas Alemanes*, pts 1 and 2, v.s.Willi Benz.
63 RGASPI 545.3.91, Benz report, p. 2; Esteve, *Recuerdos de Brigadistas Alemanes*, pts 1 and 2, v.s.Willi Benz.
64 RGASPI 545.3.91, Benz report, p. 2; Esteve, *Recuerdos de Brigadistas Alemanes*, pts 1 and 2, v.s.Willi Benz.
65 RGASPI 545.3.91, Benz report, p. 2; Esteve, *Recuerdos de Brigadistas Alemanes*, pts 1 and 2, v.s.Willi Benz.
66 Szurek, *Shattered*, p. 228; Esteve, *Recuerdos de Brigadistas Alemanes*, pts 1 and 2, v.s.Willi Benz.
67 Szurek, *Shattered*, p. 228; Esteve, *Recuerdos de Brigadistas Alemanes*, pts 1 and 2, v.s.Willi Benz.

68 Manuel Azar, *Historia militar de la guerra de España*, vol. III, 1969, pp. 39–40; Maldonado, *Aragón*, p. 406.

69 Ibid., pp. 402, 406–10.

70 Landis, *Lincoln Brigade*, pp. 422–3; Castells, *Brigadas*, p. 313.

71 Castells, *Brigadas*, p. 314.

72 Barry McLoughlin, *Fighting for Republican Spain, 1936–38, Frank Ryan and the Volunteers from Limerick in the International Brigades*, 2014,, p. 89.

73 Szurek, *Shattered*, p. 226.

74 Fisher, *Comrades*, pp. 99–110; Landis, *Lincoln Brigade*, pp. 422–5.

75 Maldonado, *Aragón*, p. 417.

76 Szurek, *Shattered*, p. 226.

77 Castells, *Brigadas*, p. 499.

78 Esteve, *Recuerdos de Brigadistas Alemanes*, pts 1 and 2, v.s. Willi Benz.

79 RGASPI 545.3.91, Benz report, p. 5.

80 Szurek, *Shattered*, p. 227.

81 Esteve, *Recuerdos de Brigadistas Alemanes*, pts 1 and 2, v.s. Willi Benz.

82 v.s.Ibid.

83 v.s.Ibid.

84 Świerczewski, Martínez and Szafran, *El General*, p. 284.

85 Esteve, *Recuerdos de Brigadistas Alemanes*, pts 1 and 2, v.s. Willi Benz; Castells, *Brigadas*, pp. 312–13.

86 Baxell, *Unlikely Warriors*, p. 309; Szurek, *Shattered*, p. 230.

87 RGASPI 545.3.281, p. 46.

88 Maldonado, *Aragón*, p. 414.

89 Szurek, *Shattered*, pp. 228–9; Thomas, *Civil War*, Kindle pos. 18529, footnote to 7597.

90 RGASPI 545.3.158, Garibaldi, Mes de Marzo, p. 40, RGASPI 545.3.91, Benz report, p. 3; Maldonado, *Aragón*, pp. 413–15; Szurek, *Shattered*, pp. 228–9; Castells, *Brigadas*, p. 314; Esteve, *Recuerdos de Brigadistas*, pts 1 and 2, v.s. Willi Benz.

91 RGASPI 545.3.158, Garibaldi, Mes de Marzo, p. 40; Pesce, *España*, p. 213; Fisher, *Comrades*, p. 114; RGASPI 545.3.497, Wild report, pp. 22–8.

92 Esteve, *Recuerdos de Brigadistas Alemanes*, pts 1 and 2, v.s. Willi Benz.

93 Fisher, *Comrades*, p. 116.

94 Castells, *Brigadas*, pp. 314–16; Landis, *Lincoln Brigade*, pp. 416, 425–30.

95 Szurek, *Shattered*, p. 230.

96 Maldonado, *Aragón*, p. 419.

97 RGASPI 545.3.529, Watcek report.

98 Baxell, *Unlikely Warriors*, p. 312.

99 Ibid.

100 Fisher, *Comrades*, p. 114–15; Landis, *Lincoln Brigade*, p. 342.

101 Castells, *Brigadas*, p. 316.

102 Maldonado, *Aragón*, p. 419.

103 Esteve, *Recuerdos de Brigadistas Alemanes*, pts 1 and 2, v.s. Willi Benz; Landis, *Lincoln Brigade*, p. 434; Maldonado, *Aragón*, p. 446; Baxell, *Unlikely Warriors*, p. 312; Fisher, *Comrades*, p. 119.

104 Baxell, *Unlikely Warriors*, p. 313.

105 See Percy Ludwick memoir at Marx Memorial Library, London.

106 Ibid.

107 Ibid.

108 Baxell, *Unlikely Warriors*, p. 313.

109 Esteve, *Recuerdos de Brigadistas Alemanes*, pts 1 and 2, v.s. Willi Benz.

110 Baxell, *Unlikely Warriors*, p. 313.

111 Castells, *Brigadas*, p. 313, citing José Peirats, *La CNT en la Revolución*, Ruedo Ibérico, Paris, 1971, p. 100.

112 RGASPI 545.3.497, Wild report, p. 22; Baxell, *Unlikely Warriors*, p. 308.

113 https://sites.google.com/site/gceformulario/4-kilometres-en-belchite; Landis, *Lincoln Brigade*, pp. 420–2.

114 Puppini, *Garibaldini*, pp. 149–53.

115 Juan Modesto, *Soy del Quinto Regimiento*, p. 228.

116 RGAPSI 545.3.8, p.8; Szurek, *Shattered*, p. 231.

117 Ibid.

118 Bessie, *Notebooks*, p. 17.

119 Szurek, *Shattered*, p. 231.

120 Castells, *Brigadas*, p. 314.

121 Fisher, *Comrades*, p. 119; Carroll, *Odyssey*, p. 165.

122 Szurek, *Shattered*, p. 231; Villar, *4 kilometres en Belchite*.

123 RGASPI 545.3.91, p. 5; Castells, *Brigadas*, p. 317.

44 BOY SOLDIERS

1 Castells, *Brigadas*, p. 317; Maldonado, *Aragón*, pp. 429, 439.

2 Castells, *Brigadas*, p. 317; Rukeyser, 'We Came for Games'; Muriel Rukeyser, '*Barcelona, 1936*' & *Selections from the Spanish Civil War Archive*, New York, 2011, p. 6.

3 Esteve, *Recuerdos de Brigadistas Alemanes*, pts 1 and 2, v.s. Willi Benz.

4 Michael Alpert, *Republican Army*, p. 157; James Matthews, *Reluctant Warriors, Republican Popular Army and Nationalist Army Conscripts in the Spanish Civil War, 1936–1939*, Oxford Historical Monographs, 2012; http://faustovillar.blogspot.com/2012/11/4-km-en-belchite.html.

5 Fisher, *Comrades*, pp. 116, 157.

6 Puppini *Garibaldini*, p. 150; http://www.antifascistispagna.it/?pageid=7&ricerca=139.

7 RGASPI file 545.3.27, pp. 59–60, 67.
8 *Le Maitron Dictionnaire Biographique*, http://maitron-en-ligne.univ-parisi. fr/spip.php?article157305, notice OUSSIDHOUM Rabah, HAMIDOU
9 Ibid., consulted 29 December 2018.
10 *L'Humanité*, 1 November 1996, trans. into Spanish at http://www. bajoaragonesa.org/elagitador/le-colonel-fabien-en-el-frente-del-guadalope/.
11 RGASPI 545.3.281, p. 46; RGASPI 545.3.2, 7, 14 brigada, Operaciones, Frente de Aragon, pp. 59–70.
12 See RGASPI 545.3.529, Watcek report.
13 RGASPI 545.3.91 Benz report; Castells, *Brigadas*, p. 318; Esteve, *Recuerdos de Brigadistas Alemanes*, pts 1 and 2, v.s. Willi Benz.
14 Castells, *Brigadas*, p. 318.
15 Aznar, Historia militar de la guerra de España, vol. III, p. 75.
16 RGASPI 545.3. 281, p. 47; Castells, *Brigadas*, p. 319.
17 RGASPI 545.3.159, p. 40; RGASPI 545.3.91, Benz report, pp. 5–6.
18 Castells, *Brigadas*, p. 319.
19 RGASPI 545.3.27, 14 brigada, pp. 59–60.
20 Castells, *Brigadas*, p. 319.
21 Ibid.; RGASPI 545.3.27, pp. 64–6; RGASPI 545.3.189, Brigada Garibaldi, pp. 9–14.
22 Castells, *Brigadas*, p. 321; Landis, *Lincoln Brigade*, p. 448.
23 Landis, *Lincoln Brigade*, pp. 446–7.
24 Castells, *Brigadas*, p. 320.
25 RGASPI 545.3.91, Benz report, pp. 5–6; Landis, *Lincoln Brigade*, pp. 447–9.
26 Baxell, *Unlikely Warriors*, p. 308.
27 Ibid., p. 318.
28 RGASPI 545.3.497, Bob Cooney report, p. 17.
29 Baxell, *Unlikely Warriors*, p. 316.
30 Ibid., p. 315.
31 McLoughlin, *Fighting for Republican Spain*, pp. 90–1.
32 Eby, *Commissars*, p. 324.
33 Castells, *Brigadas*, p. 322, citing Brome, citing Koeningsberg.
34 Wintringham quoted in Landis, *Lincoln Brigade*, p. 450.
35 RGASPI 545.3.497, Cooney report, p. 18.
36 Ibid., p. 21.
37 Fisher, *Comrades*, p. 126.
38 Baxell, *Unlikely Warriors*, p. 316.
39 Fisher, *Comrades*, p. 117.
40 Carl Geiser, *Prisoners of the Good Fight*, Westport, 1986, pp. 67–8; RGASPI 545.3.507, pp. 40–1.
41 Geiser, *Prisoners*, p. 75; Landis, *Lincoln Brigade*, pp. 458–66.

42 Landis, *Lincoln Brigade*, p. 463.

43 Ibid.

44 Castells, *Brigadas*, pp. 323–4.

45 Priscilla Scott-Ellis, *The Chances of Death: A Diary of the Spanish Civil War*, London, 1995, p. 52.

46 Ibid.

47 Chris Brooks, 'The Death of Major Robert Hale Merriman', http://www.albavolunteer.org/2016/03/the-death-of-major-robert-hale-merriman/.

48 Oral testimony, collected by Alan Warren.

49 Marion Merriman, American Commander, p. 219.

50 Landis, *Lincoln Brigade*, p. 465.

51 Puppini, *Garibaldini*, pp. 153–4; Castells, *Brigadas*, p. 324.

52 Fisher, *Comrades*, p. 128.

53 Baxell, *Unlikely Warriors*, p. 318; Esteve, *Recuerdos de Brigadistas Alemanes*, pts 1 and 2, v.s. Willi Benz.

54 Fisher, *Comrades*, pp. 129–30.

55 Landis, *Lincoln Brigade*, p. 468.

56 Castells, *Brigadas*, p. 323.

57 Villar, 'A Little Valencian'.

58 Castells, *Brigadas*, p. 332.

59 Ibid., pp. 325–32; RGASPI 545.3.529, Komar (Watcek) report.

60 Castells, *Brigadas*, pp. 329–31.

61 RGASPI 545.3.529, Komar (Watcek) report, pp. 28–34, 37.

62 Ibid., pp. 33–4.

63 Ibid.

64 *Carta colectiva de los obispos españoles a los obispos de todo el mundo con motivo de la guerra en España*, Pamplona, Gráficas Descansa, 1 July 1937, http://secviccentdocumentosoficiales.blogspot.com/2006/09/carta-colectiva-de-los-obispos.html.

65 Castells, *Brigadas*, pp. 331–2; RGASPI 545.3.529 pp. 34–5.

66 RGASPI 545.3.529, Komar (Watcek) report, p. 41.

67 *ABC, Sevilla*, 16 April 1938.

45 DEFEAT, DESPAIR, HOPE

1 Baxell, *Unlikely Warriors*, p. 319.

2 https://batallate.es/project/con-5-1-los-pozos-de-caude/

3 Landis, *Lincoln Brigade*, p. 511.

4 Baxell, *Unlikely Warriors*, p. 320.

5 Kim, Amor i Sagues, *La Última Batalla: derrota de la República en el Ebro*, Madrid, 2004, p. 48.

6   David Alegre Lorenz, *La batalla de Teruel*, Kindle pos. 3068–103.

7   Maldonado, *Aragón*, p. 361.

8   Amor, *Última batalla*, p. 50.

9   Ibid., p. 49.

10 Hansard, HC Deb 29 July 1938 vol 338 cc3484-92.

11 Amor, *Última Batalla*, p. 53; Landis, *Lincoln Brigade*, p. 504, fn 44.

12 Galeazzo Ciano, *Ciano's Diaries, 1937–8*, London, 1952 (ed. Muggeridge), p. 123; Thomas, *Civil War*, Kindle pos. 12258; Landis, *Lincoln Brigade*, pp. 504, 540–1.

13 RGASPI 545.2.108, pp. 208–10.

14 Ibid., pp. 137–43.

15 Radosh, *Betrayed*, pp. 477–79, 488–90.

16 Szurek, *Shattered*, pp. 242–3.

17 Baxell, *Unlikely Warriors*, p. 317.

18 Castells, *Brigadas*, p. 335; Baxell, *Unlikely Warriors*, p. 317.

19 Bessie, *Diary*, pp. 136–8.

20 Ibid., pp. 137–8.

21 Hemingway, 'American Volunteers Retreat From Gandesa', *North American Newspaper Alliance (NANA)*, 4 April, Barcelona.

22 Baxell, *Unlikely Warriors*, p. 319.

23 CDMH PS-Barcelona 604/3, ff2–6, 23, 25–6, 34, 37, 42, 52, 57, 60; PS-Barcelona 794/1, ff4, 6, 7, 14, 18, 22, 35, 43.

24 Carlo Penchienati, *I Giustiziati Accusano: Brigate Internazionali in Spagna*, Rome, 1965, pp. 137–64.

25 Castells, *Brigadas*, pp. 336–7; Gallego in RUHM Vol. 6/11/ 2017, p. 592; https://publicaciones.defensa.gob.es/media/downloadable/files/links/R/E/REVISTASPDF2568.pdf.

26 Penchienati, *I Giustiziati Accusano*, pp. 133–40, 153; Castells, *Brigadas*, pp. 335–8; J. Delperrié de Bayac, *Brigadas*, pp. 172–6.

27 Fred Thomas, *To Tilt at Windmills: a memoir of the Spanish Civil War*, East Lansing, 1996, p. 102; Manuel Requena Gallego, 'Albacete', p. 82.

28 Castells, *Brigadas*, p. 334; Baxell, *Unlikely Warriors*, p. 313.

29 Moreno-Navarro, *Las Brigadas Internacionales*, pp. 27–31; Penchienati, *I Giustiziati Accusano*, pp. 119, 131–3.

30 Castells, *Brigadas*, p. 333.

31 Baxell, *Unlikely Warriors*, p. 319.

32 Ibid.

33 Ibid., pp. 319–23.

34 Andreu Caralt Gimenez, *3.666 Biberons, La Lleva del Biberó-41*, Generalitat de Catalunya, Barcelona, 2017, p. 8.

35 Petrou, *Renegades*, p. 94.

46 PRISONERS

1 Hwei-Ru Tsou and Len Tsou, *Los Brigadistas Chinos en la Guerra Civil, La Llamada de España (1936–1939)*, Madrid, 2013, pp. 202–4.
2 Tsou and Tsou, *Los Brigadistas Chinos en la Guerra Civil*, pp. 230–72.
3 Castells, *Brigadas*, p. 323.
4 Geiser, *Prisoners*, p. 259.
5 jailynews.blogspot.com, v.s. 23 de Enereo de 1939.
6 http://www.international-Brigades.org.uk/content/captured-Jarama.
7 Baxell, *Unlikely Warriors*, p. 359; Geiser, *Prisoners*, p. 120.
8 Lidia Bocanegra, 'Španski borci: Herbert Fornezzi', University of Granada, http://digibug.ugr.es/bitstream/handle/10481/48152/BocanegraHerbert Fornezzi.pdf;jsessionid=D7BAB533613C825D49394600AD007577?seque nce=1.
9 Doyle, *Brigadista: An Irishman's Fight Against Fascism*, Dublin, 2006, p. 73; Geiser, *Prisoners*, p. 129.
10 Geiser, *Prisoners*, p. 129.
11 Doyle, *Brigadista*, pp. 72–3.
12 Ibid., pp. 74–5.
13 Ibid., p. 81.
14 Ibid., p. 77.
15 BNE, Campo de concentración de San Pedro de Cardeña, Burgos Prisioneros republicanos de las Brigadas Internacionales III, pp. 7–8, Grupo de prisioneros rojos de distintas nacionalidades, April 1938.
16 Doyle, *Brigadista*, pp. 78–9.
17 Geiser, *Prisoners*, p. 122.
18 McLoughlin, *Fighting for Republican Spain*, pp. 93–8.
19 Doyle, *Brigadista*, p. 66.
20 Geiser, *Prisoners*, pp. 94–7; BNE, Campo de concentración de San Pedro de Cardeña, Burgos Prisioneros republicanos de las *Brigadas Internacionales III*, pp. 37–9, 79–80; http://www.qub.ac.uk/sites/frankryan/ InterpretativeResources/HistoricalContext/FrankRyanArevolutionarylife/; http://thejailynews.blogspot.com/ v.s. Frank Ryan.
21 Geiser, *Prisoners*, p. 98.
22 Othen, *Franco's International Brigades*, pp. 217, 246.
23 Geiser, *Prisoners*, p. 259.
24 Seán Cronin, *Frank Ryan: The Search for the Republic*, Dublin, 1980, p. 145; Adrian Hoar, *In Green and Red: The Lives of Frank Ryan*, Dingle, 2004, p. 215.
25 McLoughlin, *Fighting for Republican Spain*, p. 99.
26 Geiser, *Prisoners*, p. 144.

27 http://thejailynews.blogspot.com/ v.s. Friedetzky; Geiser, *Prisoners*, pp. 146–7.

28 Geiser, *Prisoners*, pp. 175–8.

29 Ibid., p. 146.

30 Antonio Vallejo-Nágera, 'Psiquismo del fanatismo marxista', *Revista Semana Médica Española*, 6 (1939), pp. 173–80.

31 Ibid.; Giles Tremlett, 'Marxists are Retards', *Guardian*, 1 November 2002.

32 Geiser, *Prisoners*, p. 146; Doyle, *Brigadista*, p. 81.

33 Vallejo-Nágera, 'Psiquismo del fanatismo marxista', pp. 173–80.

34 Geiser, *Prisoners*, p. 259.

47 THE LAST CHARGE

1 Landis, *Lincoln Brigade*, p. 521.

2 Baxell, *Unlikely Warriors*, p. 325.

3 Manuel Tagüeña Lacorte, *Testimonio de dos guerras*, Barcelona, 1978, p xvi.

4 Szurek, *Shattered*, p. 254; Landis, *Lincoln Brigade*, p. 521.

5 RGASPI 545.3.286, XIII Brigade history notes, pp. 325–35.

6 Ibid., p. 325.

7 Landis, *Lincoln Brigade*, p. 523.

8 RGASPI 545.3.286, XIII Brigade history notes, pp. 325–50.

9 Ibid., pp. 330.

10 Ibid., pp. 328–33.

11 Ibid., p. 335; Arno Lustiger, *¡Shalom Libertad! Judíos en la guerra civil española*, Flor del Viento, Barcelona, 2001, pp. 361–4.

12 Baxell, *Unlikely Warriors*, p. 327; Landis, *Lincoln Brigade*, pp. 532–3.

13 Landis, *Lincoln Brigade*, pp. 528–9.

14 Castells, *Brigadas*, p. 506; TL, Tamiment Ersler papers ALBA 198, Box 1, Folder 17; Sidbrint database, Universitat de Barcelona, http://sidbrint.ub.edu/ca/content/kharchenko-mihail accessed 11 October 2019

15 Szurek, *Shattered*, pp. 254–30.

16 *Le Maitron Dictionnaire Biographique*, http://maitron-en-ligne.univ-paris1.fr/spip.php?article152727, notice CAZALA René, Marcel

17 Javier Cercas, *Lord of All the Dead*, 2019, p. 253.

18 Skoutelsky, *L'espoir*, p. 104; Amor, *Última Batalla*, p. 72.

19 Skoutelsky, *L'espoir*, pp. 104–5.

20 Ibid., p. 104.

21 Xavier Moreno Juliá, *Italia (Y Alemania) En La Guerra Civil Española: Una Aproximación Con La Batalla Del Ebro Como Eje De Análisis*, in Sànchez Cervelló and Agudo Blanco (eds.), *Las Brigadas Internacionales*, citing Galeazzo Ciano, *Diaries, 1937–1943*, pp. 167–9.

22 Amor, *Última Batalla*, p. 80.
23 Baxell, *Unlikely Warriors*, p. 327.
24 Landis, *Lincoln Brigade*, pp. 534–5.
25 Ibid., p. 516; Amor, *Última Batalla*, p. 79.
26 Bessie, *Notebooks*, p. 69; Landis, *Lincoln Brigade*, p. 539; Amor, *Última Batalla*, p. 73.
27 Landis, *Lincoln Brigade*, p. 516.
28 Bessie, *Notebooks*, p. 68.
29 Baxell, *Unlikely Warriors*, p. 324.

48 RESIST, FORTIFY AND BE VIGILANT

1 Nan Green, *A Chronicle of Small Beer*, Nottingham, 2005, pp. 69–71; Angela Jackson, *Beyond the Battlefield: Testimony, Memory and Remembrance of a Cave Hospital in the Spanish Civil War*, Torfaen, 2005, pp. 21–4; Linda Palfreeman, *Salud! British Volunteers in the Republican Medical Service during the Spanish Civil War, 1936–1939*, Brighton, 2012, p. 141.
2 Rhodes, *Hell and Good Company*, pp. 230–1.
3 Jackson, *Beyond the Battlefield*, p. 27.
4 Ibid.
5 Rhodes, *Hell and Good Company*, p. 230.
6 Preston, *Doves*, Kindle pos. 1882.
7 Martin Green, 'Heritage', *London Review of Books*, 7 August 1980, p. 15.
8 Preston, *Doves*, Kindle pos. 2083; Green, *Small Beer*, pp. 45–7; Martin Green, 'Heritage', *London Review of Books*, 7 August 1980, p.15
9 Preston, *Doves*, Kindle pos. 1882.
10 https://www.theguardian.com/books/2015/feb/11/martin-green
11 Preston, *Doves*, Kindle pos. 2016; Green, *Small Beer*, pp. 37–8.
12 Milt Felsen, *The Anti-Warrior: A Memoir*, Iowa City, 1989, p. 73.
13 Preston, *Doves*, Kindle pos. 2115.
14 Ibid., Kindle pos. 2101
15 Palfreeman, *Salud!*, pp. 49–50, 69–73; Preston, *Doves*, Kindle pos. 2137.
16 Preston, *Doves*, Kindle pos. 2165.
17 Green, *Small Beer*, p. 53.
18 Preston, *Doves*, Kindle pos. 2302.
19 Preston, *Doves*, Kindle pos. 2326.
20 Ibid., Kindle pos. 2352.
21 Ibid., Kindle pos. 2365.
22 Jackson, *Beyond the Battlefield*, p. 27.
23 Green, *Small Beer*, pp. 60, 67.
24 Preston, *Doves*, Kindle pos. 2516.
25 Palfreeman, *Salud!*, p. 51.

26 Preston, *Doves*, Kindle pos. 2502.

27 Ibid., Kindle pos. 2357.

28 Preston, *Spanish Civil War*, p. 143.

29 Preston, *Doves*, Kindle pos. 2576.

30 Landis, *Lincoln Brigade*, pp. 530–1.

31 Cercas, *Lord of All the Dead*, p. 249.

32 Castells, *Brigadas*, p. 352.

33 Baxell, *Unlikely Warriors*, pp. 328–9.

34 Cercas, *Lord of All the Dead*, pp. 253–63.

35 Castells, *Brigadas*, p. 356.

36 Ibid.

37 Ibid., p. 357.

38 Landis, *Lincoln Brigade*, p. 543.

39 http://www.spartacus.schoolnet.co.uk/SPjonesJ.htm.

40 Baxell, *Unlikely Warriors*, pp. 330–1.

41 Ibid., pp. 331–3.

42 Castells, *Brigadas*, p. 358.

43 Baxell, *Unlikely Warriors*, p. 333.

44 Landis, *Lincoln Brigade*, p. 539; Castells, *Brigadas*, p. 358.

45 RGASPI 545.3.286, p. 337.

46 Baxell, *Unlikely Warriors*, p. 334.

47 Castells, *Brigadas*, p. 359.

48 Baxell, *Unlikely Warriors*, p. 337.

49 RGASPI 545.3.189, Brigada Garibaldi, pp. 6–7; RGASPI 545.3.150, Emilio Suardi, Comisario, letter, p. 139; RGASPI 545.3.148, p. 135.

50 Jorge M. Reverte, *La Batalla del Ebro*, Barcelona, 2006, p. 260.

51 Cercas, *Lord of All the Dead*, p. 264.

52 Ernest Hemingway, *By-line*, New York, 2002, pp. 276–8.

53 Baxell, *Unlikely Warriors*, p. 334.

54 Castells, *Brigadas*, p. 358.

55 Landis, *Lincoln Brigade*, p. 548.

56 Ibid., p. 544.

57 Baxell, *Unlikely Warriors*, p. 335.

49 DREAMS OF HOME

1 Castells, *Brigadas*, p. 359.

2 Preston, *Doves*, Kindle pos. 2588.

3 Ibid., Kindle pos. 2571.

4 IWM 10361, Nan Green.

5 Preston, *Doves*, Kindle pos. 2588.

6 Ibid., Kindle pos. 2552; Green, *Small Beer*, pp. 68–73.

7 Skoutelsky, *Novedad*, pp. 451–6 for text of 23 September 1937 regulations.

8 Baxell, *Unlikely Warriors*, p. 337.

9 Castells, *Brigadas*, p. 360; Baxell, *Unlikely Warriors*, p. 335; Petrou, *Renegades*, p. 97.

10 Castells, *Brigadas*, pp. 357–61.

11 Baxell, *Unlikely Warriors*, p. 335.

12 Castells, *Brigadas*, p. 360.

13 Landis, *Lincoln Brigade*, p. 552.

14 Ibid.

15 Ibid., p. 551.

16 Fisher, *Comrades*, p. 150.

17 Landis, *Lincoln Brigade*, p. 555; Castells, *Brigadas*, p. 359.

18 Castells, *Brigadas*, p. 360.

19 Fisher, *Comrades*, p. 151.

20 Various authors, *Cuba en la Defensa de la Republica Española*, Editora Política, La Habana, 1981, p. 143.

21 Baxell, *Unlikely Warriors*, p. 338.

22 Landis, *Lincoln Brigade*, pp. 555–8.

23 Ibid., pp. 558–9.

24 Castells, *Brigadas*, p. 361; Reverte, *Ebro*, p. 208; http://www.international-Brigades.org.uk/content/ebro-offensive.

25 Castells, *Brigadas*, p. 361.

26 Reverte, *Ebro*, p. 219.

27 Preston, *Doves*, Kindle pos. 2597.

28 Jackson, *Beyond the battlefield*, pp. 46–7.

29 Preston, *Doves*, Kindle pos. 2588.

30 Ibid., Kindle pos. 2619.

31 Reverte, *Ebro*, p. 193.

32 Castells, *Brigadas*, pp. 362, 368.

33 Xavier Moreno Julía, in Sànchez Cervelló and Agudo Blanco (eds.), *Las Brigadas Internacionales*, p. 109 citing Galeazzo Ciano, *Diaries, 1937–1943*, p. 168; Reverte, *Ebro*, p. 222.

34 Reverte, *Ebro*, p. 219.

35 Castells, *Brigadas*, map IX.

36 Marco Puppini, Introduction, in Augusto Cantaluppi y Marco Puppini, *Ebro 1938: no pasarán: i Garibaldini caduti nella battaglia dell' Ebro!*, Milano, 2011, p. 158, trans. into Spanish by Carla Sevilla, https://brigadasinternacionales.org/index.php?option=comcontent&view=article&id=768:garibaldinos-ebro&catid=44:croni-bi&Itemid=82; Puppini, *Garibaldini*, p. 166.

37 RGASPI 545.3.189, Brigada Garibaldi, p. 29.

38 RGASPI 545.3.148, pp. 93–7.

39 Miguel Alonso Baquer, *El Ebro: La Batalla decisiva de los cien días*, Madrid, 2003, pp. 366–7.

40 Francisco Franco, *ABC de la Batalla Defensiva Por Generalísimo*, http://www.editorialfajardoelbravo.es/articulos/historia/ABCdelaBatalla Defensiva.pdf.

41 Castells, *Brigadas*, p. 363; *Le Maitron Dictionnaire Biographique*, http://maitron-en-ligne.univ-paris1.fr/spip.php?article129465, notice ROL Théophile dit ROLL D'ESPINAY.

42 http://Brigadesinternationales.fr/wiki/ROLTh%C3%A9ophile.

43 Gavras, *Le Sel*, pp. 141–2.

44 Baxell, *Unlikely Warriors*, p. 338; Reverte, *Ebro*, pp. 238–44.

45 Landis, *Lincoln Brigade*, pp. 570–1.

46 Reverte, *Ebro*, pp. 249, 252.

47 Bessie, *Notebooks*, p. 105.

48 Fisher, *Comrades*, p. 154. 'Pratt' is an alias, and a mystery.

49 RGASPI 545.3.150, brigada Garibaldi, p. 136; AABI, *Las Brigadas Internacionales en la Batalla del Ebro, 3a parte. Septiembre: resistencia y retirada*, brigadasinternacionales.org; Reverte, *Ebro*, p. 252.

50 Reverte, *Ebro*, p. 263.

51 Bessie, *Notebooks*, p. 103.

52 R. Gerald Hughes, *The Postwar Legacy of Appeasement: British Foreign Policy Since 1945*, London, 2014, p. 206; *The British Political Elite and the Soviet Union*, edited by Louise Grace Shaw, London, 2003, p. 18.

53 Bessie, *Notebooks*, p. 113.

54 Hansard, *Anglo-Italian Agreement*, HC Deb 02 May 1938, Vol. 335, cc. 533–669.

55 Ernest Hemingway, 'A Call for Greatness', *Ken* 2:1 (14 July 1938), p. 23, reproduced in Robert O. Stephens (ed.), *Hemingway's Nonfiction: The Public Voice*, Chapel Hill, 1968.

56 Landis, *Lincoln Brigade*, p. 574; Castells, *Brigadas*, p. 361.

57 Fisher, *Comrades*, p. 154.

58 Ibid., p. 156.

59 Bessie, *Notebooks*, p. 107, 8 September.

60 Castells, *Brigadas*, p. 367.

61 RGASPI 545.3.189, pp. 6–7; RGASPI 545.3.150, p. 139.

62 Baxell, *Unlikely Warriors*, p. 339.

50 THE LAST FIGHT

1 Edoardo Mastrorilli, 'Guerra Civile Spagnola', p. 79.

2 Mastrorilli, 'Guerra Civile Spagnola', p. 79; Skoutelsky, *Novedad*, p. 61.

3 Mastrorilli, 'Guerra Civile Spagnola', p. 80.

4 Jawaharlal Nehru, *Toward Freedom: The Autobiography of Jawaharlal Nehru*, John Day, New York 1941, pp. 358, 363.

5 Jawaharlal Nehru, 'Homage to Spain', in China, Spain and the War: Essays and Writings by Jawaharlal Nehru, Allahabad, 1940, p. 78.

6 Bessie, *Notebooks*, pp. 110–12.

7 Preston, *Doves*, Kindle pos. 2619.

8 Landis, *Lincoln Brigade*, p. 575; Bessie, *Notebooks*, p.111; Reverte, *Ebro*, p. 219.

9 Reverte, *Ebro*, pp. 280–3; Aldo Jourdan, 'Souvenirs de la guerre d'Espagne', online at http://bteysses.free.fr/espagne/Aldo_JOURDAN.html.

10 Ciano, *Diaries*, p. 162, in Xavier Moreno Juliá, in Sànchez Cervelló and Agudo Blanco (eds.), *Las Brigadas Internacionales*, p. 109.

11 Reverte, *Ebro*, p. 285.

12 Ibid., p. 237.

13 Lustiger, *¡Shalom Libertad!*, pp. 361–3: RGASPI 86. 545.3.286, p. 356.

14 Lustiger, *¡Shalom Libertad!*, p. 362.

15 Reverte, *Ebro*, p. 288; Lustiger, *¡Shalom Libertad!*, pp. 86–7, 362–3, 365; RGASPI 545.3.286, p. 356.

16 Marion Merriman, *Commander in Spain*, p. 232.

17 Radosh, *Betrayed*, p. 469, citing Rossiiskii gosudarstvennyi voennyi arkhiv (RGVA). [Russian State Military Archive], f 33987.3.1149, pp. 284–5; Baxell, *Unlikely Warriors*, p. 340.

18 Thomas, *Civil War*, Kindle pos. 12908.

19 Reverte, *Ebro*, p. 287.

20 Bessie, *Notebooks*, p. 114.

21 Baxell, *Unlikely Warriors*, p. 341.

22 Ibid.

23 RGASPI 545.3.286, p. 370; TL, Gabriel Ersler papers at Tamiment ALBA198, Box: 1, Folder: 10.

24 RGASPI 545.3.286, p. 385; Zaagsma, *Jewish Volunteers*, p. 126.

25 RGASPI 545.3.286, p. 370.

26 AABI https://brigadasinternacionales.org/index.php?option=comcontent&view=article&id=1306:ebro-septiembre-38&catid=44:croni-bi& Itemid=82.

27 Szurek, *Shattered*, p. 258; AABI https://brigadasinternacionales.org/index.php?option=comcontent&view=article&id=1306:ebro-septiembre-38&catid=44:croni-bi&Itemid=82.

28 Szurek, *Shattered*, pp. 257–8.

29 RGASPI 545.3.286, pp. 370–85; Pedro Mateo Merino, *Por vuestra libertad y la nuestra: El choque frontal de Camposines*, https://brigadasinternacionales.org/index.php?option=comcontent&view=article&id=1306:ebro-septiembre-38&catid=44:croni-bi&Itemid=82.

30 Landis, *Lincoln Brigade*, p. 576.

31 Bessie, *Notebooks*, pp. 113–14.

32 Baxell, *Unlikely Warriors*, p. 342.

33 Bessie, *Notebooks*, p. 114.

34 Ibid., p. 115.

35 Ibid.

36 Ibid., p. 116.

37 RGASPI 545.3.286, p. 385.

38 Bessie, *Notebooks*, p. 116.

39 Green, *Small Beer*, pp. 74–5.

40 Preston, *Doves*, Kindle pos. 2654.

41 AABI, https://brigadasinternacionales.org/index.php?option=comcon
    tent&view=article&id=1306:ebro-septiembre-38&catid=44:croni-bi&
    Itemid=82.

42 Tagüeña Lacorte, *Testimonio*, pp. 250–1.

43 Bessie, *Notebooks*, p. 116; Mateo Merino, *Por Vuestra Libertad*, pp. 365–72.
    The chief of staff of the 35th Division (home to the XI, XIII and XV
    International Brigades) gives 42 per cent losses for front-line units, with
    one XIII battalion virtually demolished: Julián Henríquez Caubín, *La
    Batalla del Ebro: Maniobra de Un División*, Guadalajara, 2009, p. 436.

44 Baxell, *Unlikely Warriors*, p. 345.

45 Bessie, *Notebooks*, p. 116.

46 Szurek, *Shattered*, p.261.

47 See John L. Wainwright, *The Last to Fall: The Life and Letters of Ivor
    Hickman*.

48 Castells, *Brigadas*, p. 367.

49 Skoutelsky, *L'espoir*, p. 105.

50 Szurek, *Shattered*, p. 261.

51 IWM 10361; Angela Jackson, *British Women and the Spanish Civil War*,
    London, 2002, p. 189.

51 FAREWELL TO ARMS

1 Eby, *Commissars*, p. 407.

2 Castells, *Brigadas*, p. 372.

3 Ibid., pp. 377–8; Skoutelsky, *Novedad*, p. 457.

4 *The Volunteer*, http://www.albavolunteer.org/2015/12/blast-from-the-past-
   new-Jarama-series/.

5 Buckley, *Spanish Republic*, p. 395.

6 Bessie, *Notebooks*, p. 124.

7 Ibid., p. 123.

8 Szurek, *Shattered*, p. 269.

9 González Moreno-Navarro, *Las Brigadas Internacionales*, pp. 142–7.

10 Ibid., p. 81.

11 Bessie, *Notebooks*, p. 127.

12 Renn, *Guerra Civil*, p. 632.

13 Ibid., p. 631.

14 González Moreno-Navarro, *Las Brigadas Internacionales*, p. 111.

15 Ibid., pp. 65–6, 77–8.

16 Ibid., p. 157; Lustiger *¡Shalom Libertad!*, pp. 446–9.

17 Lustiger, *¡Shalom Libertad!*, p. 448.

18 González Moreno-Navarro, *Las Brigadas Internacionales*, pp. 111–14.

19 Bessie, *Notebooks*, pp. 130–1.

20 Castells, *Brigadas*, p. 372.

21 Bessie, *Notebooks*, p. 129.

22 Ibid., p. 132.

23 González Moreno-Navarro, *Las Brigadas Internacionales*, pp. 101, 104.

24 Ibid., pp. 115–8.

25 Renn, *Guerra Civil*, p. 617.

26 Ibid., p. 618.

27 http://www.alba-valb.org/volunteers/milton-wolff.

28 Ibid.

29 González Moreno-Navarro, *Las Brigadas Internacionales*, pp. 158–60.

30 Eby, *Commissars*, p. 411.

31 Baxell, *Unlikely Warriors*, pp. 348–9.

32 Dolores Ibárruri, 'Farewell Address' (speech, Barcelona, Spain, 1 November 1938). http://www.english.uiuc.edu/maps/scw/farewell.htm.

33 Buckley, *Spanish Republic*, p. 395.

34 Vaill, *Hotel Florida*, p. 331; Gellhorn, (ed.) Moorehead, *Selected Letters of Martha Gellhorn*, p. 222.

35 Vaill, *Hotel Florida*, p. 334.

36 Hemingway, 'On the American Dead in Spain', *New Masses*, February 1939, http://www3.uah.es/saguado/OntheAmericanDeadinSpain.htm.

37 Bessie, *Notebooks*, pp. 134–7.

38 Petrou, *Renegades*, pp. 103–5.

39 González Moreno-Navarro, *Las Brigadas Internacionales*, pp. 142–7.

40 Petrou, *Renegades*, pp. 103–5.

41 González Moreno-Navarro, *Las Brigadas Internacionales*, pp. 142–7.

42 Castells, *Brigadas*, p. 388; Eby, *Commissars*, p. 417; Petrou, *Renegades*, p. 104; Benito Peix Geldart, in 'La Vuelta a Casa de los voluntarios suecos', in *Brigadas Internacionales*; Josep Sánchez Cervelló, and Sebastián Agudo

Blanco (eds.), *Las Brigadas Internacionales, nuevas perspectivas*, Tarragona, 2015, pp. 399–400.

43 Max Arthur, 'For us, Spain wasn't an adventure: it was the battle against fascism', *Observer*, 26 April 2009.

44 Baxell, *Unlikely Warriors*, p. 399; Bessie, *Notebooks*, p. 135.

45 Skoutelsky, *L'espoir*, p. 271.

46 González Moreno-Navarro, *Las Brigadas Internacionales*, pp. 65–6.

47 Renn, *Guerra Civil*, p. 650.

48 González Moreno-Navarro, *Las Brigadas Internacionales*, pp. 130–2; John Kraljic, 'New Material on Vladimir Copic', *The Volunteer*, Fall 1999, pp. 8–9.

49 González Moreno-Navarro, *Las Brigadas Internacionales*, p. 147.

50 Szurek, *Shattered*, pp. 270–6.

51 González Moreno-Navarro, *Las Brigadas Internacionales*, pp. 141, 162–3; Szurek, *Shattered*, pp. 270–6.

52 Renn, *Guerra Civil*, p. 633.

53 Ibid., pp. 634–5.

54 González Moreno-Navarro, *Las Brigadas Internacionales*, pp. 134–8, 161–4.

55 Petrou, *Renegades*, p. 101, citing RGASPI 545.6.537.

56 Lustiger, *¡Shalom Libertad!*, p. 445.

57 Szurek, *Shattered*, p. 273; Renn, *Guerra Civil*, pp. 637, 641–2.

58 Szurek, *Shattered*, p. 277.

59 Buckley, *Spanish Republic*, p. 416.

60 Baxell, *Unlikely Warriors*, p. 352; Bessie, *Notebooks*, p. 131; Petrou, *Renegades*, p. 101; Eby, *Commissars*, p. 411; Castells, *Brigadas*, p. 373.

61 Buckley, *Spanish Republic*, pp. 41–5.

62 Ibid., p. 417.

63 Renn, *Guerra Civil*, p. 635.

64 Ibid., pp. 635–6.

65 Ibid., pp. 638, 641; Szurek, *Shattered*, p. 267.

66 Szurek, *Shattered*, p. 276; Renn, *Guerra Civil*, p. 643.

67 Szurek, *Shattered*, p. 277.

68 Ibid.

69 W.H. Auden, 'Spain', Faber & Faber, London, 1937.

52 'PREMATURE ANTI-FASCISTS'

1 *Le Maitron Dictionnaire Biographique*, http://maitron-en-ligne.univ-paris1.fr/spip.php?article50415, notice GEORGES Pierre, dit Fredo, dit Colonel Fabien; Robert Gildea, *Fighters in the Shadows: A New History of the French Resistance*, London, 2015, Kindle pos. 1828.

2 *Le Maitron Dictionnaire Biographique*, http://maitron-en-ligne.univ-paris1.
   fr/spip.php?article50368, notice GAUTHEROT Henri and article157866,
   notice TYSZELMAN Samuel (Szmul)
3 Gildea, *Fighters,* Kindle pos. 1828.
4 MacGregor-Thunell, *Spanish Civil War,* v.s. Conny Anderson.
5 Knox, 'Premature Antifascist', p. 147.
6 Gildea, *Fighters*, Kindle pos. 1856.
7 Data extracted from *Le Maitron, Dictionnaire biographique*, http://
   maitron-en-ligne.univ-paris1.fr
8 Gildea, *Fighters,* Kindle pos. 576, 1879.
9 *Le Maitron, Dictionnaire biographique*, http://maitron-en-ligne.univ-paris1.
   fr/spip.php?article128316, notice REBIÈRE Pierre [REBIÈRE Philippe,
   Pierre] [Pseudonymes dans la Résistance: Émile RÉGNIER, ANDRÉ]
10 Data extracted from *Le Maitron, Dictionnaire biographique*, http://maitron-
   en-ligne.univ-paris1.fr; see also http://chs.huma-num.fr/exhibits/show/
   marty-et-les-Brigades-internat/nouveaux-combats/brigadistes-
   dans-la-r--sistanc.
11 *Le Maitron Dictionnaire Biographique*, http://maitron-en-ligne.univ-
   paris1.fr/spip.php?article50760, notice TANGUY Henri [TANGUY
   Georges, René, Henri]. Pseudonyme dans la clandestinité: ROL, dit
   depuis 1970 ROL-TANGUY.
12 Gildea, *Fighters*, Kindle pos. 6569; Roger Bourderon, 'Le colonel Rol-
   Tanguy', *Revue historique des armées*, No. 248, 2007, pp. 106-115; http://
   journals.openedition.org/rha/1043; *Le Maitron Dictionnaire Biographique*,
   http://maitron-en-ligne.univ-paris1.fr/spip.php?article50760,   notice
   TANGUY Henri [TANGUY Georges, René, Henri]. Pseudonyme dans la
   clandestinité: ROL, dit depuis 1970 ROL-TANGUY.
13 CHS, 'Camps', *Marty et les Brigades internationales*, accessed 24 February
   2019, http://chs.huma-num.fr/items/show/22.
14 Kowalsky, *USSR and the International Brigades*, p. 701.
15 Ibid., p. 702.
16 A. Ross Johnson, with the assistance of Jeanette A. Koch, *The Yugoslav
   Military Elite* (U), Office Of Regional And Political Analysis Central
   Intelligence Agency 1977, p. 5. at https://digitalarchive.wilsoncenter.org/
   document/208967
17 Knox, 'Premature antifascist', pp. 133–49.
18 Agudo Blanco, *Las Brigadas Internacionales*, p. 88.
19 McLellan, *East Germany*, p. 48.
20 Kevin Ingram, *Rebel: The Short Life of Esmond Romilly*, New York, 1985,
   pp. 205–30.

21 Purcell and Smith, *The Last English Revolutionary*, pp. 160–1, 192–6.

22 Studs Terkel, *The Good War: An Oral History of World War II*, New York, 1984, p. 491.

23 Peter Carroll, 'The Myth of the Moscow Archives', *Science & Society*, Vol. 68, No. 3, p. 341.

24 Soledad Fox Maura, 'Memorias de la XI brigada: The Good Comrade', in Celada et al., *70 años*, p. 160.

25 Celada et al., *70 años*, p. 426.

26 Vjeran Pavlakovic, *The Battle for Spain is Ours*, Zagreb, 2014, pp. 325–6, 331–2; Johnson and Koch, Yugoslav Military Elite, pp. 5–6, 87.

27 The Volunteer, Fall 1994, Vol XVI, No. 2, p. 21, letter from Percy Ludwick.

28 AABI, *Sobre los brigadistas deportados en Mauthausen*, AABI online, https://brigadasinternacionales.org/; see also M. Constante and M. Razola, *Triángulo azul. Los republicanos españoles en Mauthausen*, Zarazoga, 2008; Lustiger, *¡Shalom Libertad!*, pp. 439–41; Puppini, in Celada et al., *70 años*, p. 363.

29 *Encyclopedia of Camps and Ghettos*, 1933–1945, Vol. 1, p. 962; Constante and Razola, *Triángulo azul*.

30 Constante and Razola, *Triángulo azul*.

31 Castells, *Brigadas*, p. 411; see also Constante and Razola, *Triángulo azul*.

32 *Le Maitron Dictionnaire Biographique*, http://maitron-en-ligne.univ-paris1.fr/spip.php?article105826, notice CHRISTMANN Édouard. http://maitron-en-ligne.univ-paris1.fr/spip.php?article174425, notice CICHOSZ Joseph; *Encyclopedia of Camps and Ghettos*, 1933–1945, Vol. 1, p. 1004.

33 http://auschwitz.org/muzeum/aktualnosci/nieudana-ucieczka-z-auschwitz-61-lat-temu-w-auschwitz-stracono-pieciu-liderow-obozowej-konspiracji-,12.html.

34 Ibid.

35 William Harlan Hale, 'Dachau concentration camp (report on a two-day visit, 1–2 May)', Warwick University Digital Collections, Papers of Richard Crossman MP, 154/3/PW/1/1–3.

36 Lustiger; *¡Shalom Libertad!*, pp. 439–41.

37 Zaagsma, *Jewish Volunteers*, p. 2.

38 Castells, *Brigadas*, p. 411; David. A. Hackett, *The Buchenwald Report*, Colorado, 1995, pp. 4–5. At least seventy-six SS men were captured by them in nearby woods in the few hours after they abandoned the camp on 11 April 1945; https://asso-buchenwald-dora.com/le-camp-de-buchenwald/histoire-du-camp-de-buchenwald/la-liberation/. See also *Le Maitron Dictionnaire Biographique*, http://maitron-en-ligne.univ-paris1.fr/spip.php?article137279, notice HOLDOS Ladislav dit aussi Laszlo, pseudonyme Pedro, dit Radislav, dit Laco, dit Peter alias Pierre KALIARIK.

39 Szurek, *Shattered*, p. 317.
40 Ibid., p. 304.
41 Ibid., p. 317.
42 Ibid., pp. 304–12, 320.
43 *Le Maitron Dictionnaire Biographique*, http://maitron-en-ligne.univ-paris1.fr/spip.php?article74701, notice HEUSSLER André, Marcel.
44 Castells, *Brigadas*, p. 412.
45 *Frank Ryan: A Revolutionary Life*, http://www.qub.ac.uk/sites/frankryan/InterpretativeResources/HistoricalContext/FrankRyanArevolutionarylife/
46 Carroll, 'Spanish Civil War in the 21st Century', pp. 649–50; https://www.theguardian.com/theguardian/2012/sep/27/roosevelt-franco-letter-archive-1945.
47 Arnold Krammer, 'The cult of the Spanish Civil War in East Germany', *Journal of Contemporary History*, 39, No. 4, October 2004, p. 537.
48 Ibid., p. 535.
49 McLellan, *East Germany*, p. 43.
50 Krammer, 'The cult of the Spanish Civil War', pp. 538–9.
51 See Ana Funder, *Stasiland: Stories from behind the Wall*, London, 2011.
52 Krammer, 'The cult of the Spanish Civil War', pp. 535–8.
53 Vjeran Pavlakovic, *The Battle for Spain is Ours*, pp. 325–6, 331–5.
54 Ádám Ánderle, 'La sombra ee Ernő Gerő, La acusación de trotskismo a los brigadistas húngaros: Albacete (1938) Y Budapest (1949)', *Hispania Nova, Revista de Historia Contemporánea*, 13, 2015.
55 Jaroslav Bouček, 'Českoslovenští interbrigadisté jako zdroj politických elit po roce 1945', in I. Koutská and F. Svátek (eds.), *Politické elity v Československu 1918–1948*, Prague, 1994, pp. 147–80.
56 Myrna Kostash, *Bloodlines: A Journey into Eastern Europe*, Douglas & McIntyre, Vancouver, 1993, p. 27.
57 McLellan, *East Germany*, pp. 58–60, 64.
58 Ibid.
59 Szurek, *Shattered*, p. 327.
60 Ibid., p. 376.
61 https://gdansk.ipn.gov.pl/pl2/aktualnosci/38741,Opinia-Instytutu-Pamieci-Narodowej-wzgledem-Dabrowszczakow.html.
62 *Investigation of un-American propaganda activities in the United States Hearings before a Special Committee on Un-American Activities*, House of Representatives, Seventy-fifth Congress, third session–Seventy-eighth Congress, second session, H. Res. 282, Vol. 13, p. 7827; Carroll, *Odyssey*, pp. 186, 233.
63 Knox, 'Premature antifascist', pp. 133–49.

64 'Remark By Reagan On Lincoln Brigade Prompts Ire In Spain', *New York Times*, 10 May 1985; Carroll, 'Myth of the Moscow Archives', pp. 337–41.

65 http://chs.huma-num.fr/exhibits/show/marty-et-les-Brigades-internat/marty/marty---quelques-rep--res; http://chs.huma-num.fr/exhibits/show/marty-et-les-Brigades-internat/nouveaux-combats/marty-et-l-aver

66 Puppini in Celada et al., *70 años*, p. 363; 'Garibaldinos de la Guerra Civil Española, maquisards de la Résistance, partigianos de la Resistenza', in Sànchez Cervelló and Agudo Blanco (eds.), *Las Brigadas Internacionales*; Puppini, 'Le Brigate Internazionali E La Politica Italiana', in Sànchez Cervelló and Agudo Blanco (eds.), *Las Brigadas Internacionales*.

67 Volodarsky, *Stalin's Agent*, pp. 180–9, pp. 367–8.

68 Ibid., pp. 226–9.

69 The Jack Jones Trust at http://www.jackjonestrust.com/jack-jones/; 'Jack Jones "worked for KGB"' claim online at http://news.bbc.co.uk/2/hi/uk/8289962.stm

70 Jonathan Glancey, 'It was never a black and white affair', *Guardian*, 10 November 2000; *Campaign Guide 1977*, pp. 20, 771.

71 Rukeyser, '*Barcelona, 1936*', p. 7.

72 Regler, *Owl of Minerva*, p. 272.

73 Koestler et al., *The God that Failed*, p. 222.

74 Preston, *Spanish Holocaust*, pp. xi–xx.

75 John McCain, 'Salute to a Communist', *New York Times*, 24 March 2016.

76 *Discurso en la inauguración del Valle de los Caídos*, 2 April 1959, generalisimofranco.com/discursos/discursos/1959/00003.htm.

77 RGASPI 545.6.621; Online report, https://leksikon.fylkesarkivet.no/article/c0217ff3-6aec-4a8c-bc2b-0f1b2c6ff402/.

78 Ana Pérez, Julia R. Cela y Gemma Calatayud, *La memoria de las Brigadas ... Documentación de las Ciencias de la Información*, 2013, Vol. 36, 8, pp. 5–102.

79 Angela Jackson, 'For Us It Was Heaven', http://www.albavolunteer.org/2012/07/patience-and-the-americans-an-english-nurse-in-spain/.

80 Diario de Sesiones, Congreso de los Diputados, Pleno y Dip. Perm., núm. 186, de 28/11/1995, pp. 9873–8.

81 Boletín Oficial del Estado, Real Decreto 39/1996, de 19 de enero, sobre concesión de la nacionalidad española a los combatientes de las Brigadas Internacionales en la guerra civil española.

Bibliography

PRIMARY SOURCES

Contemporary newspapers

ABC, Madrid
ABC, Sevilla
Ahora, Madrid
Ce Soir, Paris
El Heraldo de Madrid
Le Journal, Paris
Juventud, Madrid
El Liberal, Madrid
Life and Letters Today, London
Manchester Guardian, Manchester
New Masses, New York
New York Times, New York
Peuple en Armes, Madrid
Regards, Paris
La Vanguardia, Barcelona

CONTEMPORARY MAGAZINE ARTICLES, LEAFLETS AND PAMPHLETS

Cox, Geoffrey, 'Eyewitness in Madrid', *Harper's,* 175, 1936, p. 34
Gellhorn, Martha, 'Men Without Medals', *Collier's,* 15 January 1938
'Guadalajara' (leaflet), Comisión de propaganda del Comisariado de Guerra y Ediciones de la Voz, July 1937

Hemingway, Ernest, 'Hemingway Reports Spain', *New Republic*, 12 January 1938

———'A Call for Greatness', *Ken*, 2:1 (14 July 1938), 23, reproduced in Robert O. Stephens, (ed.), *Hemingway's Nonfiction: The Public Voice*, University of North Carolina Press, Chapel Hill, 1968

Herdenkingsnummer gewijd aan de gebroeders Ackerman, Antwerp, 1938

Orwell, George, review of John Sommerfield's *Volunteer in Spain*, and Franz Borkenau's *The Spanish Cockpit*, *Time and Tide*, 31 July 1937, reprinted in George Orwell and Peter Davison, *Orwell in Spain*, Penguin, London, 2001

Rukeyser, Muriel, 'Mediterranean', *New Masses*, September 1936, pp. 18–20

NON-CONTEMPORARY NEWSPAPER AND MAGAZINE ARTICLES

Glancey, Jonathan, 'It was never a black and white affair', *Guardian*, 10 November 2000

Green, Martin, 'Heritage', *London Review of Books*, 7 August 1980

Hattenstone, Simon, '"Of the original 30, by mid-December only six were left": the comrade: Sam Russell', *Guardian*, 10 November 2000

McCain, John, 'Salute to a Communist', *New York Times*, 24 March 2016

Najati Sidqi, 'I Went to Defend Jerusalem in Córdoba: memoirs of a Palestinian communist in the Spanish International Brigades', *Jerusalem Quarterly*, 62

'Remark by Reagan on Lincoln Brigade Prompts Ire in Spain', *New York Times*, 10 May 1985

Rukeyser, Muriel, 'We Came for Games', *Esquire*, October 1974, pp. 192–4

OFFICIAL PUBLICATIONS

Boletín Oficial del Estado, Madrid, Spain, Real decreto 39/1996, 19 January 1996

Carta colectiva de los obispos españoles a los obispos de todo el mundo con motivo de la guerra en España, Pamplona, Gráficas Descansa, 1 July 1937 at http://secviccentdocumentosoficiales.blogspot.com/2006/09/carta-colectiva-de-los-obispos.html

Diario de la Republica, Madrid, Spain, 30 August 1936

Gaceta de la Republica, 133, 13 May 1937

Hansard, HC Deb, 24 October 1935, Vol. 305

———Anglo-Italian Agreement, HC Deb, 2 May 1938, Vol. 335, cc533–669

International committee for the application of the agreement regarding non-intervention in Spain: the legislative and other measures taken by the participating governments to give effect to the agreement regarding non-intervention in Spain, and by the Swiss government to prohibit the export, &c., of arms and war material from Switzerland to Spain; Report by Mr Francis Hemming ... presented by the Secretary of State for Foreign Affairs to Parliament by Command of His Majesty, November 1936, HMSO, London, 1936

Investigation of un-American propaganda activities in the United States Hearings before a Special Committee on Un-American Activities, House of Representatives, 75th Congress, third session; 78th Congress, second session, H. Res, 282, Vol. 13, p. 7827, US Government Printing Office, Washington 1940

Official Records of the Second Session of the General Assembly, Supplement No. 11, A/364, 3 September 1947, UN General Assembly, https://unispal.un.org/DPA/DPR/unispal.nsf/0/07175DE9FA2DE563852568D3006E10F3

UNPUBLISHED PRIMARY SOURCES, MEMOIRS AND DIARIES

Esteve Torres, María Isabel, 'Recuerdos de Brigadistas Alemanes', five volumes of translations into Spanish of individual memoirs, with translator's commentary from the Bundesarchiv, Berlin, online: Academia.edu

————'Los primeros voluntarios alemanes en la guerra de España' (July–November 1936), Grupo Thälmann y Centuria Thälmann

————'Recuerdos de brigadistas alemanes sobre la Guerra de España' (1936–1939), Partes 1/1, 1/2, 2/1, 2/2, Anexo a la primera colección, Anexo de la segunda colección, Índice de nombres de la primera colección, Índice de la segunda colección

————'España 1936–1939', Recuerdos de brigadistas alemanes residentes en la República Federal Alemana

Hoff, Raymond, 'Merriman's Diaries, Exegesis', self-published, 2018; copyright to this annotated version of Robert Hale Merriman's diary has been transferred to the Tamiment Library, NYU, New York: http://digitaltamiment.hosting.nyu.edu/files/original/5434ae298184e90c2b45d613 9c10f81d072d5c41.pdf

Kurzke, Jan and Mangan, Kate, 'The Good Comrade', manuscript at International Institute of Social History, Amsterdam

Merriman, Robert Hale, 'Diary', transcript: http://merrimandiary.com/

Moreno, Joaquín, unpublished memoir from copy held by Eduardo del Campo, part published at https://www.elmundo.es/cronica/2014/03/30/53 36b1beca47418d308b456d.html

Passaporte, Antonio Pedro, 'Memórias Da Guerra Civil Espanhola', edited
    by Rodolfo Leão Passaporte
Villar Esteban, Fausto, 'A Little Valencian in the Lincoln Brigade: an anti-
    war and anti-heroic symphony', trans. Paul Sharkey, Special Collections,
    University of Michigan Library, MI

PUBLISHED PRIMARY SOURCES

Abramson, Paulina and Adelina, *Mosaico roto*, Compañía Literaria,
    Madrid, 1994
Acier, Marcel (ed.), *From Spanish Trenches: Recent Letters from Spain*, Modern
    Age Books, New York, 1937
Alberti, Rafael, *Poesía* (1924–44), Editorial Losada, Buenos Aires, 1946
Allan, Ted, *This Time a Better Earth*, William Morrow & Co.,
    New York, 1939
Angus, John, *With the International Brigade in Spain*, Loughborough
    University, Loughborough, 1983
Antón, José García, *Un español en la XIV Brigada Internacional: vivencias de
    un lejano pasado*, Diego Marín, Murcia, 2004
Arthur, Max, *The Real Band of Brothers: First-Hand Accounts from the Last
    British survivors of the Spanish Civil War*, HarperCollins, London, 2009
Auden, W. H., *Spain*, Faber & Faber, London, 1937
Ayrton, Peter (ed.), *¡No Pasarán!: Writings from the Spanish Civil War*,
    Serpent's Tail, London, 2016
Azaña, Manuel, *Diarios completos*: *monarquía, república, guerra civil*, Crítica,
    Barcelona, 2000
Azcárate, Pablo de, *Mi embajada en Londres durante la guerra civil española*,
    Ariel, Barcelona, 1976
Balk, Theodor, *La Quatorzième*, Éditions du Commisariat des Brigades
    Internationales, Unión Poligráfica, Madrid, 1937
————*Wen die Kugel vor Madrid nicht traf, Tagebuch-Roman über
    den Spanischen Bürgerkrieg und das Los der Spanienkämpfer*, Röhrig, St
    Ingbert, 1995
————*Das verlorene Manuskript*, Fischer, Frankfurt, 2016
Barea, Arturo, *Struggle for the Spanish Soul*, Searchlight Books, London,
    1941
————*The Clash*, Fontana, London, 1984
————*The Forge*, Fontana, London, 1984
Bessie, Alvah, *Alvah Bessie's Spanish Civil War Notebooks*, University Press of
    Kentucky, Lexington, 2001

Bessie, Alvah, and Prego, Albert, *Our Fight: Writing by Veterans of the Abraham Lincoln Brigade, Spain 1936–1939*, Monthly Review Press, New York, 1987

Bethune, Dr Norman, *The crime on the road Malaga–Almeria narrative with graphic documents revealing fascist cruelty 1937*, Publicaciones Iberia, Madrid, 1937

Bodek, Adrián, *Brigadas Internacionales: Memorias vivas*, Oficina de Arte y Ediciones, Madrid, 2014

Borkenau, Franz, *The Spanish Cockpit: An eye-witness account of the political and social conflicts of the Spanish Civil War*, first published Faber & Faber, London, 1937; Kindle edition, ChristieBooks, 2016

Bowers, Claude, *My Mission to Spain: Watching the Rehearsal for World War II*, Simon & Schuster, New York, 1954

Brandt, Willy and Struve, Günter (eds.), *Draußen, Schriften während d. Emigration*, Dietz, Berlin, 1976

Breá, Juan and Low, Mary, *Red Spanish Notebook: The first six months of the revolution and the civil war*, City Lights, San Francisco, 1979

Bron, Michał, et al., *Polacy w wojnie hiszpańskiej 1936–1939*, Wydawnictwo Ministerstwa Obrony Narodowej, Warsaw, 1967
——————*Principio y continuación*, AABI, Madrid, 2004

Broué, P. and Témime, E., *La Revolución y la Guerra de España*, two volumes, Fondo de Cultura Económico-Colección Popular, Mexico City, 1977

Buckley, Henry, *The Life and Death of the Spanish Republic*, I. B. Tauris, London, 2013

Calandrone, Giacomo, *La Spagna brucia: cronache garibaldine*, Riuniti, Roma, 1962

Camus, Albert, *¡España Libre¡*, Júcar, Madrid, 1978

Chaves Nogales, Manuel, *Los secretos de la defensa de Madrid*, Espuela de Plata, Sevilla, 2017

Ciano, Galeazzo, *Ciano's Diaries, 1937–8*, Methuen, London, 1952

Codou, Roger, *Le Cabochard: Mémoires d'un communiste*, La Decouverte, Paris, 1983

Colodny, Robert, *The Struggle for Madrid*, Paine-Whitman, New York, 1958

Copado, Bernabé, *Con la Columna Redondo, Combates y conquistas, Crónicas de guerra*, Imprenta de la Gaviria, Sevilla, 1937

Cordón, Antonio, *Trayectoria: Memorias de un militar republicano*, Crítica, Barcelona, 1977

Cornford, John, *Understand the Weapon, Understand the Wound*, Fyfield, Manchester, 2016

Covo, César, *La Guerre Camarade!*, Atlantica, 2005

Cox, Geoffrey, *The Defence of Madrid*, Gollancz, London, 1937

Crook, David, *Hampstead Heath to Tian An Men: The autobiography of David Crook*, at davidcrook.net, 1990

—————*Some essays by David Crook, gleaned from student magazines like English Study*, at davidcrook.net, undated.

Cunningham, Valentine (ed.), *The Penguin Book of Spanish Civil War Verse*, Penguin, Harmondsworth, 1980

—————(ed.), *Spanish Front: Writers on the Civil War*, Oxford University Press, Oxford, 1986

Darman, Peter, *Heroic Voices of the Spanish Civil War: Memories from the International Brigades*, New Holland, 2009

De Guzmán, Eduardo, *Madrid Rojo y Negro*, Oberón, Madrid, 2004

—————*La Muerte de la Esperanza*, El Garaje, Madrid, 2006

Delaprée, Louis, *Morir en Madrid*, Edición de Martin Minchom, Raíces, Madrid, 2009

—————*The Martyrdom of Madrid: Inedited Witnesses (Le martyr de Madrid: témoignages inédits)*, NP, Madrid, 1937.

De La Torriente Brau, Pablo, *Aventuras del soldado desconocido cubano*, Colección Saeta, Editorial Letras Cubanas, La Havana, 1981

Dimitrov, Georgi, *The Diary of Georgi Dimitrov, 1933–1949*, Yale UP, New Haven, 2003

Doussin, Georges, *El Año de la Victoria*, G. Del Toro, Madrid, 1974

—————(ed.), *L'ARAC Association Républicaine des Anciens Combattants, 1917–2007, Combattants pour la vie, des voix pour l'espoir*, Le Temps des Cerises, Montreuil, 2007

Doyle, Bob, *Brigadista: An Irishman's Fight against Fascism*, Currach Press, Dublin, 2006

Duff, Charles, *No Angel's Wing*, Corbett Press, London, 1947

Dupré, Henri, *La Légion tricolore en Espagne, 1936–1939*, La Ligue Francaise, Paris, 1942

Ehrenburg, Ilyá, *Eve of War, 1933–41: Volume IV of Men, Years-Life*, Macgibbon and Kee, London, 1963

—————*Corresponsal en España*, Prensa Ibérica, Barcelona, 1998

Eisner, Alexei, *La 12ª Brigada Internacional*, Promoteo, Valencia, 1972

—————*Chelovek s tremya imenami, Povest'o Mate Zalke*, Izdatel'stvo politicheskoy literatury, Moscow, 1986

Elstob, Peter, *Spanish Prisoner*, Carrick and Evans, New York, 1939

Etchebéhère, Mika, *La Meva Guerra d'Espanya*, Ediciones de 1984, Barcelona, 1987

Felsen, Milt, *The Anti-Warrior: A Memoir*, University of Iowa Press, Iowa City, 1989

Firsov, Fridrikh, et al., *Secret Cables of the Comintern, 1933–1943*, Yale University Press, New Haven, 2014

Fisher, Harry, *Comrades: Tales of a Brigadista in the Spanish Civil War*, University of Nebraska Press, Lincoln, 1998

Fraser, Ronald, *Blood of Spain: An Oral History of the Spanish Civil War*, Pimlico, London, 1994

Funder, Anna, *Stasiland: Stories from behind the Wall*, Granta, London, 2011

Gárate Córdoba, J. M., *Mil días de fuego*, Luis de Caralt, Barcelona, 1972

Gavras, Florence, (ed.), *Le sel de la terre, Espagne, 1936-1938: des brigadistes témoignent de leur engagement*, Éd. Tirésias, Paris, 1999

Geiser, Carl, *Prisoners of the Good Fight*, Lawrence Hill, Westport, 1986

Gellhorn, Martha, *The Face of War*, Granta, London, 1998

—————*Selected Letters of Martha Gellhorn*, edited by Caroline Moorehead, Holt, New York, 2006

Gide, André, *Return from the USSR*, Knopf, New York, 1937

Green, Nan, *A Chronicle of Small Beer*, Trent Editions, Nottingham, 2005

Gregory, Walter, *The Shallow Grave: A memoir of the Spanish Civil War*, Victor Gollancz, London, 1986

Grieg, Nordahl, *Spansk sommer (Verano español)*, Arqueología de Imágenes, Granja de San Ildefonso, 2017

————— *Spanish Summer*, unattributed English translation at https://web.archive.org/web/20120208103212/http://www.bruneteenlamemoria.com/nordahlgrieg.htm

Guillain, Nick, *El Mercenario: diario de un combatiente de la guerra de España*, Editorial Tanger, Tangier, 1939

Gurney, Jason, *Crusade in Spain*, London, Faber & Faber, 1974

Györkei, Jenő (ed.), *Magyar Önkéntesk a Spanyol nép Szabadságharcában*, Kossuth Könyvkiadó, Budapest, 1959

Haldane, Charlotte, *The Truth Will Out*, Weidenfeld & Nicolson, London, 1949

Hemingway, Ernest, *For Whom the Bell Tolls*, Scribner, New York, 1940

—————*By-line*, Scribner, New York, 2002

—————*Hemingway on War*, Simon & Schuster, New York, 2004

————— *The Fifth Column and Four Stories of the Spanish Civil War*, Arrow Books, London, 2013

Henríquez Caubín, Julián, *La Batalla del Ebro: Maniobra de una división*, Silente, Guadalajara, 2009

Hodgson, Agnes with Keene, Judith (eds.), *The Last Mile to Huesca: An Australian Nurse in the Spanish Civil War: The diary of Agnes Hodgson*, New South Wales University Press, Kensington, 1988

Hoffmann, Heinz, *Mannheim, Madrid, Moskay, Erlebtes aus drei Jahrzehnten*, Militärverlag der Deutschen Demokratischen Republik, Berlin, 1982

Janka, Walter, *Spuren eines Lebens*, Rowohlt Repertoire, Hamburg, 2016

Jirku, Gusti, *We Fight Death: The work of the medical service of the International Brigades in Spain*, Madrid, date unknown

Kantorowicz, Alfred, *Spanisches Kriegstagebuch*, Fischer Digital, Frankfurt, 2016

————*Diario de la guerra civil española*, trans. Vicente Abella, Constraescritura, Madrid, 2018

———— *Diario español, Traducción de la edición de la Aufbau-Verlag Berlín de 1951*, trans. Isabel Esteve, unpublished.

Kapor, Cedo (ed.), *Španija 1936–1939: zbornik se'canja jugoslovenskih dobrovoljaca u španskom ratu*, five volumes, Inicijativni odbor-Udruzenje spanskih boraca, Beograd, 1971

Kari, Leo, *Bag Spaniens bjerge: En erindringsroman redigeret af Lenni Kari*, Lindhardt og Ringhof Forlag, Copenhagen, 2017

Kemp, Peter, *Mine Were of Trouble*, Cassells, London, 1957

————'I fought for Franco', in *History of the Twentieth Century*, A. J. P. Taylor (ed.), Purnell, London, 1968, pp. 1604-1609

Kochetkov, Alexei, *Beyond the Pyrenees: I Am Coming Back to You*, Book 2, T&V Media, Forest Hills, 2016

————*In Our Latin Quarter: I Am Coming Back to You*, Book 1, T&V Media, Forest Hills, 2016

Koestler, Arthur, *Spanish Testament*, Victor Gollancz, London, 1937

————et al., *The God that Failed*, Hamish Hamilton, London, 1950

————*Invisible Writing*, Collins, London, 1954

Koltsov, Mijaíl, *Diario de la guerra de España*, Planeta, Barcelona, 2009

Landau, Katia, *Los verdugos de la revolución española (1937–1938)*, Sepha, Málaga, 2007

Last, Jef, *The Spanish Tragedy*, Routledge, London, 1939

Lecoeur, Auguste, *Le Partisan*, Flammarion, Paris, 1963

Lee, Laurie, *A Moment of War*, Viking, London, 1991

————*To War in Spain*, Penguin, London, 1996

Leeds, Joseph, (ed.), *Let My People Know: The Story of Wilfred Mendelson 'Mendy', 17 August 1915, 28 July 1938*, publisher not stated, 1942

León, María Teresa, (ed.), *Crónica general de la Guerra Civil*, Centro de Estudios Andaluces, Sevilla, 2007 (original by Alianza de Intelectuales, Madrid, 1937)

Lindbaek, Lisa, *Bataljon Thälmann*, Tiden Nordsk Forlak, Oslo, 1938

Liversedge, Ron, *Mac-Pap: Memoir of a Canadian in the Spanish Civil War*, New Star, 2013

London, Artur, *España, España*, Artia, Prague, 1965

————*Se levantaron antes del alba*, Ediciones Península, Barcelona, 2010

London, Lise, *Roja primavera*, Ediciones del Oriente y del Mediterraneo, Guadarrama, 1996

Longo, Luigi, *Las Brigadas Internacionales en España*, Era, México, 1966

Maassen, Hans (ed.), *Brigada Internacional ist unser Ehrenname, Erlebnisse ehemaliger deutscher Spanienkämpfer*, Militärverlag der Deutschen Demokratischen Republik, Berlin, 1974, 2 vols

MacDougall, Ian, *Voices from the Spanish Civil War: Personal Recollections of Scottish Volunteers in Republican Spain 1936-1939*, Polygon, Edinburgh, 1986

Maisky, Ivan, *Spanish Notebooks*, Hutchinson, London, 1966

Mateo Merino, Pedro, *Por Vuestra Libertad y la Nuestra*, Disenso, Madrid, 1986

Matthews, Herbert L., *The Yoke and the Arrows: A Report on Spain*, Braziller, New York, 1957

————————*Education of a Correspondent*, Greenwood Press, Westport, 1970

Meretskov, Kiril, *Na sluzhbe narodu*, Politizdat, Moscow, 1968

Merin, Peter (pseud.), Bihalji-Merin, Oto, *Spain between Death and Birth*, Dodge Publishing, New York, 1938

Mitford, Jessica, *Hons and Rebels*, Quartet, London, 1978

Modesto, Juan, *Soy del Quinto Regimiento: Notas de la guerra española*, Editions de la Librairie du Globe, París, 1969

Monks, Joe, *With the Reds in Andalusia*, John Cornford Poetry Group, London, 1985; http://irelandscw.com/ibvol-Monks.htm

Mora, Juan Miguel de, *Sólo queda el silencio*, Servicio de Publicaciones de la Universidad de Castilla-La Mancha, Cuenca, 2005

Nehru, Jawaharlal, *China, Spain and the War: Essays and Writings* by Jawaharlal Nehru, Kitabistan, Allahabad, 1940

————————*Toward Freedom: The Autobiography of Jawaharlal Nehru*, John Day, New York, 1941

Nelson, Cary and Hendricks, Jefferson, *Madrid 1937: Letters of the Abraham Lincoln Brigade from the Spanish Civil War*, Routledge, New York, 1996

Nelson, Steve, *The Volunteers: A personal narrative of the fight against fascism in Spain*, Masses and Mainstream, New York, 1953

Nenni, Pietro, *España*, Plaza y Janés, Barcelona, 1977

Nieto, Miguel Angel (director), *La Batalla del Jarama*, documentary film, Diagrama Producciones, Madrid, 2006.

Nilsson, Göte, *Svenskar i spanska inbördeskriget*, Norstedt, Stockholm, 1972

North, Joseph, with foreword by Ernest Hemingway, *Men in the Ranks: The Story of 12 Americans in Spain*, Friends of the Abraham Lincoln Brigade, New York, 1939

O'Connor, Peter, *A Soldier of Liberty: Recollections of a Socialist and Anti-fascist Fighter*, MSF, Dublin, 1996

Orwell, George, *Homage to Catalonia*, Secker & Warburg, London, 1938
——————*Nineteen Eighty-Four*, Penguin Books, London, 2003, first
    published by Secker & Warburg, London, 1949
——————'Looking Back on the Spanish Civil War', in *England Your
    England*, Secker & Warburg, London, 1953
——————, (ed.) Davison, Peter, *Orwell in Spain*, Penguin, London, 2001
Parshina, Elizaveta, *La Brigadista*, La Esfera de los Libros, Madrid, 2002
Payne, Robert, *The Civil War in Spain, 1936–1939: History written by those
    who there*, Secker & Warburg, London, 1963
Penchienati, Carlo, *I giustiziati accusano: Brigate Internazionali in Spagna*,
    Arte della Stampa, Rome, 1965
——————*Brigate Internazionale in Spagna: Delitti della 'Ceka' comunista*,
    Echi del Secolo, Milan, 1950
Pesce, Giovanni, *And No Quarter: An Italian Partisan in World War II*, Ohio
    University Press, 1972
——————*Un Garibaldino en España*, Atenea, Madrid, 2012
——————*Un Garibaldino in Spagna*, Arterigere-Chiarotto Editore,
    Varese, 2009
Pitcairn, Frank, *Reporter in Spain*, Lawrence & Wishart, London, 1936,
    Kindle version, ChristieBooks, 2106
Pollak, Stephen, *Strange Land Behind Me*, Falcon, London, 1951
Pyatnitskiy, V. I. and Starinov, I. G., *Razvedshkola No. 005, Istoriya
    partizanskogo dvizheniya*, Kharvest, Moscow, 2005
Radosh, Ronald, Habeck, Mary R. and Sevonstiananov, Grigory, (eds.),
    Spain Betrayed: The Soviet Union in the Spanish Civil War, Yale University
    Press, New Haven, 2001.
Regler, Gustav, with preface by Ernest Hemingway, *The Great Crusade*,
    Longmans, Green and Co., New York, 1940
——————*The Owl of Minerva*, Farrar, Straus and Cudahy, New York, 1959
Renn, Ludwig, *La Guerra Civil Española, Crónica de un escritor en las
    Brigadas Internacionales*, Fórcola, Madrid, 2016
Rodimstev, Aleksandr Ilích, *Bajo el cielo de España*, Progreso, Moscow, 1981
Rojo, Vicente, *Así fue la defensa de Madrid Aportación a la Historia de la
    Guerra de España, 1936–1939*, Imprenta de la Comunidad de Madrid, 1987
Rolfe, Edwin, *The Lincoln Battalion: The story of the Americans who fought in
    Spain in the International Brigades*, Random House, New York, 1939
Roman, Valter, *Sub Cerol Spanieie*, Editura Militara, Bucharest, 1972, trans.
    into Spanish at cierzorojo.blogspot.es
Romilly, Esmond, *Boadilla*, Hamish Hamilton, London, 1937
Ruíz Albéniz, Victor, *Campañas del Jarama y el Tajuña (Las crónicas de El
    Tebib Arrumi II)*, Librería Santarén, Valladolid, 1938

Rukeyser, Muriel, *'Barcelona, 1936' & Selections from the Spanish Civil War Archive*, Lost and Found, CUNY, New York, 2011

Ryan, Frank (ed.), *The Book of the XVth Brigade: Records of British, American, Canadian and Irish volunteers in the XV International Brigade in Spain 1936–1938*, War Commissariat, Madrid, 1938

Saint-Exupéry, Antoine de, *Saint-Exupéry en la Guerra de España*, KEN, Mutilva, 2016

Samoilov, P. I., *Gvadalakhara, razgrom ital'yanskogo ekspeditsionnogo*, Voyenizdat, Moscow, 1940

Sánchez Cervelló, Josep and Agudo Blanco, Sebastián (eds.), *Las Brigadas Internacionales, nuevas perspectivas en la historia de la Guerra Civil y del exilio*, Universitat Rovira i Virgili, Tarragona, 2015

Sawyer, Thomas E., *The Jewish Minority in the Soviet Union*, Routledge, New York, 2019

Schäfer, Max, *Spanien – 1936 bis 1939, Erinnerungen von Interbrigadisten aus der BRD*, Neue Impulse Verlag GmbH, digital edition, 2018

Scholten, Yvonne, *Fanny Schoonheyt, Een Nederlands meisje strijdt in de Spaanse Burgeroorlog*, J. M. Meulenhoff, Amsterdam, 2001

Schoots, Hans, *Living Dangerously: A biography of Joris Ivens*, Amsterdam University Press, Amsterdam, 2000

Scott, Carl-Gustaf, 'The Swedish Left's Memory of the International Brigades and the Creation of an Anti-Fascist Postwar Identity', *European History Quarterly*, 39.2

Scott-Ellis, Priscilla, *The Chances of Death: A diary of the Spanish Civil War*, Michael Russell, London, 1995

Serrano, Caridad, *Recuerdalo tú: una historia sobre la estancia de la Brigadas Internacionales en Madrigueras*, AABI, Albacete, 2003

Simonov, Konstantin Mikhaylovich, *Raznyye dni voyny: nevnik pisatelya sayt*, Khudozhestvennaya literatura, Moscow, 1982

Sommerfield, John, *Volunteer in Spain*, Lawrence and Wishart, London, 1937

Sossenko, George, *Aventurero idealista*, Ediciones de la Universidad de Castilla-La Mancha, Colección La Luz de la Memoria No. 3, Cuenca, 2004

Sperber, Murray A., *And I Remember Spain: A Spanish Civil War Anthology*, Macmillan Publishing Co., New York, 1974

Stalin, J. V., *On the Draft Constitution of the USSR, Report Delivered at the Extraordinary Eighth Congress of Soviets of the USSR, 25 November 1936*, at Marxist Internet Archive, https://www.marxists.org/reference/archive/stalin/works/1936/11/25.htm

Stanton, Edward F., *Hemingway and Spain: A Pursuit*, University of Washington Press, Seatle, 1989

Starinov, Ilya Grigorievich, *Zapiski diversanta*, Al'manakh Vympel, Moscow, 1997

Stein, Sigmunt, *Ma Guerre D'Espagne, Brigades internationales: La fin d'un mythe*, Seuil, Paris, 2012

Świerczewski, Karol Wacław, *W bojach o Wolność Hiszpanii*, Wydawnictwo Ministerstwa Obrony Narodowej, Warsaw, 1966

——————with Fernando Martínez de Baños Carrillo, Fernando and Szafran, Agnieszka, *El General Walter*, Sirvió a Tres Banderas, Delsan, 2011

Szurek, Alexander, *The Shattered Dream*, East European Monographs, Boulder, CO, 1989

Tagüeña Lacorte, Manuel, *Testimonio de dos guerras*, Planeta, Barcelona, 1978

Terkel, Studs, *The Good War: An Oral History of World War II*, Pantheon, New York, 1984.

Thälmann, Pavel, and Thälmann, Clara, *Combats pour La Liberté*, La Digitale, Baye, 1997

Thomas, Frank, *Brother Against Brother: Experiences of a British volunteer in the Spanish Civil War*, Sutton, Stroud, 1998

Thomas, Fred, *To Tilt at Windmills: A memoir of the Spanish Civil War*, State University of Michigan Press, East Lansing, 1996

Tisa, John, *Recalling the Good Fight: An autobiography of the Spanish Civil War*, Bergin & Garvey, South Hadley, MA, 1985

Tse-tung, Mao, *Selected Works, Vol. II*, Foreign Language Press, Peking, 1965

Various authors, *The Tactical Employment of Lewis Guns*, General Staff, London, 1918

——————*The Campaign Guide 1977*, Conservative and Unionist Central Office, London, 1977

Weil, Simone, *Escritos históricos y políticos*, Trotta, Madrid, 2007

Wheeler, George, *To Make the People Smile Again*, edited by David Leach, Zymurgy, Newcastle, 2003

Wintringham, Tom, *English Captain*, Faber & Faber, London, 1939

Worsley, T. C., *Los Ecos de la Batalla*, Amaru, Salamanca, 2012

Yates, James, *From Mississippi to Madrid: Memoir of a Black American in the Abraham Lincoln Brigade*, Open Hand, Greensboro, NC, 1989

SECONDARY SOURCES

Unpublished secondary sources

Sugarman, Martin, 'Against Fascism: Jews who served in the Spanish Civil War', 2000. available at https://www.jewishvirtuallibrary.org/jsource/ History/spanjews.pdf

Published secondary sources

Acciai, Enrico, *Antifascismo, voluntariato e guerra civil in Spagna*, Edizioni Unicopli, Milan, March 2016

Ajzner, Seweryn, *Polska a wojna domowa w Hiszpanii, 1936–1939*, Państwowe Wydawnictwo Naukowe, Warszaw, 1968

Alcofar Nassaes, José Luis, *Los asesores soviéticos en la Guerra civil Española, Los mejicanos*, Dopesa, Barcelona, 1971

————————'Spansky', *Los extranjeros que lucharon en la Guerra civil española*, Dopesa, Barcelona, 1973

Alegre Lorenz, David, *La Batalla de Teruel, Guerra total en España*, La Esfera, Madrid, 2018

Alpert, Michael, *La guerra civil española en el mar*, Siglo XXI, Madrid, 1987

————————*A New International History of the Spanish Civil War*, Macmillan Palgrave, Basingstoke, 2003

————————*Franco and the Condor Legion*, Bloomsbury, London, 2019.

————————*The Republican Army in the Spanish Civil War, 1936-1939*, Cambridge University Press, Cambridge, 2013.

Álvarez, Santiago, *Historia política y militar de las Brigadas Internacionales: testimonios y documentos*, Compañía Libertaria, Madrid, 1996

Amor i Sagues, Kim, *La Última Batalla: Derrota de la República en el Ebro*, Oberon, Madrid, 2004

Atkin, Nicholas, *The French at War, 1934–1944*, Longman, Harlow, 2001

Aznar, Manuel, *Historia militar de la guerra de España*, 3 vols, Editora Nacional, Madrid, 1969

Balfour, Sebastian, *Deadly Embrace, Morocco and the Road to the Spanish Civil War*, Oxford, Oxford University Press, 2002

————————and Preston, Paul (eds.), *Spain and the Great Powers in the Twentieth Century*, Routledge/Cañada Blanch, Abingdon, 2009

Baquer, Miguel Alonso, *El Ebro, La Batalla decisiva de los cien días*, Esfera, Madrid, 2003

Barbieri, Pierpardo, *Hitler's Shadow Empire: Nazi Economics and the Spanish Civil War*, Harvard University Press, Cambridge, 2015

Barceló, Juan, *Brunete: El nacimiento del Ejército Popular*, Viento Céfiro, 2018

Barnett, Neil, *Tito*, Haus Publishing, London, 2006

Barrachina Bolea, Pedro José and Viñuales Alcubierra, José Angel, *En el Frente de Tardienta 1936–1938*, Ayuntamiento de Tardienta, Tardienta, 2013, La Esfera, Madrid, 2015

Barrio Gozalo, Maximiliano, *El clero en la España moderna*, CSIC, Madrid, 2010

Bauman, Gerold Gino, *Extranjeros en la Guerra Civil española*, Editorial de Guayacán, San José de Costa Rica, 1997

Baxell, Richard, *Unlikely Warriors: The British in the Spanish Civil War and the Struggle Against Fascism*, Aurum, London, 2012

Beevor, Antony, *Stalingrad*, Penguin, London, 1998

——————*The Battle for Spain: The Spanish Civil War 1936–1939*, Orion, London, 2007

——————*The Second World War*, Weidenfeld & Nicholson, London, 2012

Bernadac, Christian, *Dagore, le carnet secrets de La Cagoule*, Editions France-Empire, Paris, 1977

Binns, Niall, *La llamada de España: Escritores extranjeros en la guerra civil*, Montesinos, 2004

Blanco Escolá, Carlos, *La incompetencia militar de Franco*, Alianza, Madrid, 2000

Blas Zabaleta, Patricio and Eva de, *Julián Besteiro, Nadar contra corriente*, Algaba, Madrid, 2002

Bolloten, Burnett, *The Spanish Revolution: The Left and the Struggle for Power*, University of North Carolina Press, Chapel Hill, 1979

——————*The Spanish Civil War: Revolution and Counterrevolution*, University of North Carolina Press, Chapel Hill, 1991

Bosch, Aurora, *Miedo a la Democracia, Estados Unidos ante la Segunda República y la Guerra Civil Española*, Crítica, Barcelona, 2011

Bredel, Willi, *Spanienkrieg*, 2 vols, Aufbau Verlarg, Berlin, 1977

Brendon, Piers, *The Dark Valley: A panorama of the 1930s*, Vintage, London, 2000

Brome, Vincent, *The International Brigades*, Heinemann, London, 1965

Browne, Sebastian, *Medicine and Conflict: The Spanish Civil War and its traumatic legacy*, Routledge/Cañada Blanch, London, 2019

Brun-Cechowoj, Walerij, *Manfred Stern, General Kleber: Die tragische biographie eines berufsrevolutionärs 1896–1954*, Trafo-Verl, Weist, 2000

Buchanan, Tom, *Britain and the Spanish Civil War*, Cambridge University Press, Cambridge, 1997

Bullock, Alan, *Hitler and Stalin*, HarperCollins, London, 1991

Bush, Clive, *The Century's Midnight: Dissenting European and American writers in the era of the Second World War*, Peter Lang, Bern, 2010

Cacucci, Pino, *Tina Modotti: A Life*, St Martin's Press, New York, 1999

Calvo, Javier M. and Montero, Severiano, *Lugares de las Brigadas Internacionales en Madrid, Vol. 3 (Batallas del Jarama y de la carretera de La Coruña)*, AABI, Madrid, 2014

Calvo González-Regueral, Fernando, *La Guerra Civil en la Ciudad Universitaria*, La Librería, Madrid, 2019

Cantaluppi, Agosto and Puppini, Marco, *Sin haber empuñado nunca un fusil jamás, Antifascistas Italianas En la Guerra Civil Española*, Universidad de Castilla-La Mancha, Cuenca, 2016

Caralt Giménez, Andreu, *3.669 Biberons: La Lleva del Biberó-41*, Generalitat de Catalunya, Barcelona, 2017

Cardona, Gabriel, *Franco y sus generales*, Temas de Hoy, Madrid, 2001

Carr, Raymond, *The Spanish Tragedy: The Civil War in perspective*, Weidenfeld & Nicolson, London, 1977

Carretero, José María, *El general Sanjurjo: Su vida y su gloria*, Ediciones Caballero audaz, Madrid, 1940

Carroll, Peter N., *The Odyssey of the Abraham Lincoln Brigade*, Stanford University Press, Stanford, 1994

Casas de la Vega, Rafael, *Brunete*, Fermin Uriarte, Madrid, 1967

—————*El Terror, Madrid 1936*, Investigación histórica, Editorial Fenix, Madridejos, 1994

Castells, Andreu, *Las Brigadas Internacionales de la guerra de España*, Ariel, Barcelona, 1974

Celada, R. et al. (eds.), *Las Brigadas Internacionales: 70 años de memoria histórica*, Amar, Salamanca, 2007

Cercas, Javier, *Lord of All the Dead*, MacLehose Press, 2019

Cierva, Ricardo de la, *Leyenda y tragedia de las Brigadas Internacionales, Prensa española*, Madrid, 1971

Colomé, Gabriel and Sureda, Jeroni (eds.), *Esport i relacions internacionals 1919–1939, l'Olimpíada popular de 1936*, Centre d'Estudis Olímpics CEO-UAB, Barcelona, 1994

Conforti, Olao, *Guadalajara, la primera derrota del fascismo*, Oikos-Tau, Barcelona, 1977

Coni, Nicholas, *Medicine and Warfare: Spain, 1936–39*, Routledge, Abingdon, 2008

Conquest, Robert, *The Great Terror: Stalin's purge of the thirties*, OUP, Oxford, 1968

Constante, Mariano and Razola, Manuel, *Triángulo Azul: Los republicanos españoles en Mauthausen*, Gobierno de Aragón y Amical de Mauthausen, Zaragoza, 2008

Constantine, Mildred, *Tina Modotti: A Fragile Life*, Chronicle Books, San Francisco, 1993

Cooper, Mike and Parkes, Ray, *We Cannot Park on Both Sides: Reading volunteers in the Spanish Civil War 1936–39*, Reading International Brigades Memorial Committee, Reading, 2000

Corral, Pedro, *Si me quieres escribir: La batalla de Teruel*, Debate, Barcelona, 2005

————— *Desertores. La Guerra Civil que nadie quiere contar*, Debate, Barcelona, 2006

Cortada, James W., *Historical Dictionary of the Spanish Civil War*, Greenwood Press, Westport, 1982

—————————*A City in War*, Scholarly Resources, Wilmington, 1985

Coverdale, John F., *Italian Intervention in the Spanish Civil War*, Princeton Univesity Press, Princeton, 1976

Cronin, Seán, *Frank Ryan: The search for the Republic*, Repsol Publishing, Dublin, 1980

Davies, Norman, *God's Playground: A History of Poland*, Columbia University Press, New York, 1982

Delperrié de Bayac, Jacques, *Las Brigadas Internacionales*, Júcar, Madrid, 1978

Derby, Mark (ed.), *Kiwi Compañeros: New Zealand and the Spanish Civil War*, Canterbury University Press, Christchurch, New Zealand, 2009

De Vicente González, Manuel, *Los Combates por Madrid*, MK Editora, Madrid, 2014

—————————*Las Brigadas Internacionales y Las Mixtas en la Batalla de Madrid*, MK Editora, Madrid, undated

—————————*Madrid militarizado*, MK Editora, Madrid, undated

Díez Alvárez, Luís, *La Batalla del Jarama*, Anaya, Madrid, 2005

Dolan, Chris, *An Anarchist's Story: The life of Ethel Macdonald*, Birlinn, Edinburgh, 2009

Drath, Viola Herms, *Willy Brandt: Prisoner of His Past*, Hamilton, Lanham, 2005

Eaden, J. and Renton, D., *The Communist Party of Great Britain Since 1920*, Palgrave, Basingstoke, 2002

Ealham, Chris, *Class, Culture and Conflict in Barcelona, 1898–1937*, Routledge, Oxford and New York, 2004

Eby, Cecil, *Comrades and Commissars: The Lincoln Battalion in the Spanish Civil War*, University of Pennsylvania, Pennsylvania, 2007

Edwards, Jill, *The British Government and the Spanish Civil War, 1936–1939*, Palgrave Macmillan, Basingstoke, 1979

Espadas Burgos, Manuel et al., Manuel Requena Gallego (ed.), *La Guerra Civil Española y Las Brigadas Internacionales*, Ediciones de la Universidad de Castilla-La Mancha, Cuenca, 1998

Fernández Martín, Andrés and Brenes Sánchez, María Isabel, *1937: Éxodo Málaga Almería, nuevas fuentes de investigación*, Aratispi Ediciones, Casabermeja, 2016

García Candau, Julián, *El Deporte en la Guerra Civil*, Espasa, 2007

Garrard, Carol and John, *The Life and Fate of Vasily Grossman*, Pen and Sword, Barnsley, 2012

Gibson, Ian, *Queipo de Llano: Sevilla, verano de 1936 (con las charlas radiofónicas completas)*, Grijalbo, Barcelona, 1986

Gildea, Robert, *Fighters in the Shadows: A New History of the French Resistance*, Faber & Faber, London, 2015

González, Lucas et al., *Voluntarios de Argentina en la Guerra Civil Española*, Ediciones del CCC, Buenos Aires, 2008

González de Miguel, Jesús, *La Batalla de Jarama*, La Esfera de los Libros, Madrid, 2009

González Moreno-Navarro, Manuel, *Las Brigadas Internacionales (Guerra Civil española 1936–1939): Su paso por Cataluña*, Promociones y Publicaciones Universitarias SA, Barcelona, 2009

Graham, Helen, *The Spanish Civil War: A very short introduction*, OUP, Oxford, 2005

——————*The War and its Shadow: Spain's Civil War in Europe's Long Twentieth Century*, Sussex Academic Press, Brighton, 2012

Gray, Daniel, *Homage to Caledonia: Scotland and the Spanish Civil War*, Luath Press, Edinburgh, 2008

Guillamón, Agustín, *Barricades in Barcelona: The CNT from the victory of July 1936 to the necessary defeat of May 1937*, Barcelona, 2006, https://libcom.org/history/barricades-barcelona-cnt-victory-july-1936-necessary-defeat-may-1937-agust%C3%ADn-guillam%C3%B3n

Hamacher, Gottfried et al., *Gegen Hitler, Deutsche in der Résistance, in den Streitkräften der Antihitlerkoalition und der Bewegung, Freies Deutschland*, Dietz, Berlin, 2005

Heiberg, Morten, *Emperadores del Mediterráneo: Franco, Mussolini y la guerra civil española*, Barcelona, 2003

Hoar, Adrian, *In Green and Red: The Lives of Frank Ryan*, Brandon, Dingle, 2004.

Hochschild, Adam, *Spain in Our Hearts: Americans in the Spanish Civil War, 1936–1939*, Pan Macmillan, London, 2016

Hopkins, James K., *Into the Heart of the Fire: The British in the Spanish Civil War*, Stanford University Press, Stanford, 1998

Hoskins, Katharine Bail, *Today the Struggle: Literature and politics in England during the Spanish Civil War*, University of Texas Press, Austin, 1969

Howson, Gerald, *Arms for Spain: The untold story of the Spanish Civil War*, John Murray, London, 1998

Huber, Peter, *Los Voluntarios Suizos en la Guerra Civil Española: Diccionario Biográfico*, Silente, Guadalajara, 2009

Hughes, Ben, *They Shall not Pass!: The British Battalion at Jarama*, Osprey, Oxford, 2011

Hughes, R. Gerald, *The Postwar Legacy of Appeasement: British foreign policy since 1945*, Bloomsbury, London, 2014

Hurcombe, Martin, *France and the Spanish Civil War*, Ashgate, Farnham, 2011

Hurtado, Víctor, *Las Brigadas Internacionales, Atlas Guerra Civil Español*, Dau, Barcelona, 2013

Ingram, Kevin, *Rebel: The Short Life of Esmond Romilly*, Dutton, New York, 1985, pp. 205–30.

Irujo, Xabier, *El Gernika de Richthofen: Un ensayo de bombardeo de terror*, Gernikako Bakearen Museoa Fundazioa/Gernika-Lumoko Udala, Gernika, 2012

Isaia, Nino, Sogno, Edgardo et al., *Due Fronti: La grande polemica sulla guerra di Spagna*, Libri Liberal, Firenze, 1998

Jackson, Angela, *British Women and the Spanish Civil War*, Routledge/Cañada Blanch, London, 2002

———————*Beyond the Battlefield: Testimony, Memory and Remembrance of a Cave Hospital in the Spanish Civil War*, Warren and Pell, Torfaen, 2005

———————*Els brigadistes entre nosaltres. Pròleg i epíleg a l'última gran batalla de la Guerra Civil espanyola*, Cossetània Edicions, Valls, 2008

———————*For Us it Was Heaven: The passion, grief and fortitude of Patience Darton, from the Spanish Civil War to Mao's China*, Sussex/Cañada Blanch, Brighton, 2012

Jackson, Michael, *Fallen Sparrows: The International Brigades in the Spanish Civil War*, American Philosophical Society, Philadelphia, 1994

Johnson, A. Ross and Jeanette A. Koch, The Yugoslav Military Elite (U), Office Of Regional And Political Analysis Central Intelligence Agency, 1977

Johnston, Verle B., *Legions of Babel: The International Brigades in the Spanish Civil War*, Pennsylvania State University Press, London, 1967

Juárez, Javier, *Comandante Durán: Leyenda y tragedia de un intelectual en armas*, Debate, Madrid, 2016

Juliá, Santos et al., *Victimas de la Geurra Civil*, Temas de Hoy, Madrid, 1999

Katz, Daniel, *All Together Different: Yiddish socialists, garment workers, and the labor roots of multiculturalism*, NYU Press, New York, 2011

Kirschenbaum, Lisa, *International Communism and the Spanish Civil War: Solidarity and suspicion*, CUP, New York, 2015

Kostash, Myrna, Bloodlines: A journey into Eastern Europe, Douglas & McIntyre, Vancouver, 1993

Landauer, Hans, *Diccionario de los voluntarios austriacos en la España republicana 1936–1939*, Asociación de Amigos de las Brigadas Internacionales, Madrid, 2005

Landis, Arthur H., *The Abraham Lincoln Brigade*, Citadel, New York, 1967

Laureau, Patrick, *Condor: The Luftwaffe in Spain, 1936–39*, Stackpole, Lanham, 2010

Lefebvre, Michel and Skoutelsky, Remi, *Las Brigadas Internacionales, Imágenes Recuperadas*, Lunwerg, Barcelona, 2003

Lethbridge, David, *Bethune in Spain*, Cañada Blanch/Sussex Academic, Eastbourne, 2013

Levinger, Laurie E., *Love and Revolutionary Greetings: An Ohio boy in the Spanish Civil War*, Wipf and Stock, Eugene, 2012

Lines, Lisa, *Milicianas: Women in combat in the Spanish Civil War*, Lexington Books, Lanham, 2012

Little, Douglas, *Malevolent neutrality: The United States, Great Britain, and the origins of the Spanish Civil War*, Cornell University Press, Ithaca and London, 1985

López, Alvaro, *La Centuria Gaston Sozzi*, Quaderno 4, Aicvas, Roma, 1964

———— *Dalla Spagna alla Resistenza in Europa in Italia ai campi di sterminio*, Quaderno 3, Aicvas, Rome, 1983

————*La Colonna Italiana*, Quaderno 5, Aicvas, Rome, 1985

————*Il Battaglione Garibaldi cronologia*, Quaderno, 7, Aicvas, Rome, 1990

López Borgoñoz, Alfonso, *Las Brigadas Internacionales en Castelldefels*, Vol. I, *La Casa De Prevención Y Cuartel De Recuperación De Las Brigadas Internacionales En Castelldefels Marzo De 1938 A Enero De 1939*, Ayuntamiento de Castelldefels, Castelldefels, 2015

López Fernández, Antonio, *Defensa de Madrid*, A. P. Marquez, Mexico City, 1945

Lugschitz, Renée, *Spanienkämpferinnen, Ausländische Frauen im Spanischen Bürgerkrieg 1936–1939*, Lid Verlag, Berlin, 2012

Lustiger, Arno, *¡Shalom libertad! Judíos en la guerra civil española*, Flor del Viento, Barcelona, 2001

McDermott, Kevin, and Agnew, Jeremy, *The Comintern: A history of international communism from Lenin to Stalin*, Palgrave Macmillan, Basingstoke, 1996

McLellan, Josie, *Antifascism and Memory in East Germany: Remembering the International Brigades 1945–1989*, Clarendon, Oxford, 2004

McLoughlin, Barry, *Fighting for Republican Spain, 1936–38: Frank Ryan and the Volunteers from Limerick in the International Brigades*, 2014

————and McDermott, Kevin (eds.), *Stalin's Terror: High politics and mass repression in the Soviet Union*, Palgrave, Basingstoke, 2003

Maldonado Moya, José María, *El Frente de Aragón: La Guerra Civil en Aragón*, Mira, Zaragoza, 2007

Malefakis, Edward, *La Guerra Civil española*, Taurus, Madrid, 2016

Marín Muñoz, Antonio, *La Guerra Civil en Lopera y Porcuna (1936–1939): Vestigios de la Contienda*, A. Marín, Lopera, 2008

Mathieson, David, *Frontline Madrid: Battlefield Tours of the Spanish Civil War*, Signal, Oxford, 2014

Medem, Gina B., *Los judíos voluntarios de la libertad (un año de lucha en las Brigadas Internacionales)*, Comisariado de las Brigadas Internacionales, Madrid, 1937

Megargee, Geoffrey (ed.), *Encyclopedia of Camps and Ghettos, 1933–1945*, Vol. 1, Indiana University Press, Bloomington, 2009

Merriman, Marion and Lerude, Warren, *American Commander in Spain: Robert Hale Merriman and the Abraham Lincoln Brigade*, University of Nevada Press, Reno, 1986

Michonneau, Stéphane, *Fue ayer: Belchite: Un pueblo frente a la cuestión del pasado*, Zaragoza, Prensas de la Universidad de Zaragoza, 2017

Minchom, Martin, *Spain's Martyred Cities: From the Battle of Madrid to Picasso's Guernica*, Sussex Academica Press/Cañada Blanch, Brighton, 2015

Molero i Olivella, Esteve, *Les quintes del biberó*, Rúbrica, Barcelona, 1999

Møller, Morten, *De glemtes hær, Danske frivillige i Den Spanske Borgerkrig*, Gyldendal, Copenhagen, 2017

Montero, Severiano, *La Batalla de Brunete*, Raíces, Madrid, 2010

Monterrubio Santín, Hector and Juárez Valero, Eduardo, *La Batalla de La Granja: Historia de un enfrentamiento olvidado*, Ícaro, Segovia, 2008

Moorehead, Caroline, *Martha Gellhorn, A Life*, Vintage, London, 2004

Nelson, Cary and Hendricks, Jefferson, *Edwin Rolfe: A biographical essay and guide to the Rolfe Archive at the University of Illinois at Urbana-Champaign*, University of Illinois Press, Urbana-Champaign, 1990

Neugass, James, *War is Beautiful: An American ambulance driver in the Spanish Civil War*, edited by Peter N. Carroll and Peter Glazer, New York, New Press, 2008

Newnham, Tom, *Dr Bethune's Angel: The life of Kathleen Hall*, Foreign Languages Press, Beijing, 2003

Norris, Christopher (ed.), *Inside the Myth: Orwell: Views from the Left*, Lawrence & Wishart, London, 1984

Núñez Díaz-Balart, Mirta, *La disciplina de la conciencia: Las Brigadas Internacionales y su artillería de papel*, Flor del Viento, Barcelona, 2006

O'Keefe, Ken, *Places of the International Brigades in Downtown Madrid*, AABI, Madrid, 2012

————and Montero, Severiano, *Lugares de las Brigadas Internacionales en Madrid*, Vol. 2, *Ciudad Universitaria, Casa de Campo y otros*, AABI, Madrid, 2014

Othen, Christopher, *Franco's International Brigades, Adventurers, Fascists, and Christian Crusaders in the Spanish Civil War*, Hurst and Co., London, 2013

Pagès i Blanch, Pelai, *War and Revolution in Catalonia, 1936–1939*, Brill, Leiden, 2013

Palfreeman, Linda, *Salud!: British Volunteers in the Republican Medical Service During the Spanish Civil War*, 1936–1939, Sussex Academic Press, Brighton, 2012

Pantoja Vallejo, Antonio and Pantoja, José, *La XIV Brigada Internacional en Andalucía: la tragedia de Villa del Río y la Batalla de Lopera*, Diputación Provincial, Jaén, 2006

Pavlaković, Vjeran, *The Battle for Spain is Ours: Croatia and the Spanish Civil War, 1936–1939*, Sredjna europa, Zagreb, 2014

Payne, Stanley and Tusell, Javier (eds.), *La guerra civil: Una nueva visión del conflicto que dividió España*, Temas de Hoy, Madrid, 1996

Petrou, Michael, *Renegades, Canadians in the Spanish Civil War*, University of British Columbia Press, Vancouver, 2008

Philippou Strongos, Paul, *Spanish Thermopylae: Cypriot Volunteers in the Spanish Civil War, 1936–39*, Warren & Pell Publishing, Barcelona, 2009

Pike, D. W., *Spaniards in the Holocaust: Mauthausen, the Horror on the Danube*, Routledge/Cañada Blanch, London, 2000

Preston, Paul, *The Coming of the Spanish Civil War: Reform, reaction and revolution in the Second Republic, 1931–1936*, Macmillan, London, 1978

——————*Franco*, HarperCollins, London, 1993

——————*A Concise History of the Spanish Civil War*, Fontana, London, 1996

——————*¡Comrades!: Portraits from the Spanish Civil War*, HarperCollins, London, 1999

—————— *Doves of War: Four Women of Spain*, HarperCollins, London, 2002

——————*We Saw Spain Die: Foreign Correspondents in the Spanish Civil War*, Constable, London, 2009

—————— *The Spanish Civil War: Reaction, Revolution and Revenge*, William Collins, London, 2016.

——————*The Spanish Holocaust: Inquisition and Extermination in Twentieth-Century Spain*, HarperPress, London, 2012

Pringle, Robert W., *Historical Dictionary of Russian and Soviet Intelligence*, Rowman and Littlefield, Lanham, 2015,

Puigsech Farràs, Josep, *Nosaltres, els comunistes catalans*, Eumo, Vic, 2001

Puppini, Marco, *Garibaldini in Spagna: Storia della XII Brigata Internazionale nella guerra di Spagna*, Storia Kappa Vu, Udine, 2019

Purcell, Hugh and Smith, Phyll, *The Last English Revolutionary*, Sussex Academic Press/Cañada Blanch, Eastbourne, 2012

Purvis, Stewart and Hulber, Jeff, *Guy Burgess: The Spy Who Knew Everyone*, Biteback, London, 2016

Rappaport, Helen, *Joseph Stalin: A Biographical Companion*, ABC-Clio, Santa Barbara, 1999

Requena Gallego, Manuel, *La Guerra Civil española y las Brigadas Internacionales*, Ediciones de la Universidad de Castilla–La Mancha, Cuenca, 1998

————(ed.), *La Guerra Civil española y las Brigadas Internacionales*, Ediciones de la Universidad de Castilla-La Mancha, Cuenca, 1998

————and Sepúlveda Losa, Rosa María (eds.), *Las Brigadas Internacionales, el contexto internacional, los medios de propaganda, literatura y memorias*, Ediciones de la Universidad de Castilla–La Mancha, Cuenca, 2003

————and Sepúlveda Losa, Rosa María (eds.), *La Sanidad de las Brigadas Internacionales*, Ediciones de la Universidad de Castilla–La Mancha, Cuenca, 2006

———— (ed.), *La Despedida Española: Homenaje a las Brigadas Internacionales, 1938–2008*, Espuela de Plata, Sevilla, 2008

————and Eiroa, Matilde (eds.), *Al lado del Gobierno Republicano: Los brigadistas de Europa del Este en la guerra civil española*, Ediciones de la Universidad de Castilla–La Mancha, Cuenca, 2009

Reverte, Jorge M., *La Batalla de Madrid*, Booket, Barcelona, 2007.

————, *La Batalla del Ebro*, Booket, Barcelona, 2006.

Rhodes, Richard, *Hell and Good Company: The Spanish Civil War and the World It Made*, Simon & Schuster, New York, 2015

Richardson, R. Dan, *Comintern Army: The International Brigades and the Spanish Civil War*, University Press of Kentucky, Lexington, 1982

Riley, Morris, *Philby: The Hidden Years*, Janus, London, 1999

Rodrigo, Javier, *La Guerra Fascista: Italia en la Guerra Civil Española*, Alianza, Madrid, 2016

Rodríguez de la Torre, Fernando, *Bibliografía de las Brigadas Internacionales y de la participación de extranjeros a favor de la República (1936–1939)*, Instituto de Estudios Albacetenses, Albacete, 2006

Rogovin, Vadim Z., *Stalin's Terror of 1937–38: Political Genocide in the USSR*, Mehring, Oak Park, 2009

Rogoyska, Jane, *Gerda Taro: Inventing Robert Capa*, Jonathan Cape, London, 2013

Rojas, Carlos, *Por qué perdimos la guerra*, Nauta, Barcelona, 1971

Ruiz, Julius, *The 'Red Terror' and the Spanish Civil War: Revolutionary Violence in Madrid*, Cambridge University Press, New York, 2014

Rust, William, *Britons in Spain: The history of the British Battalion of the XVth International Brigade*, Warren & Pell Publishing, Torfaen, 2003

Sánchez Ruano, Francisco, *Islam y guerra civil Española*, La Esfera, Madrid, 2004

Schüler-Springorum, Stefanie, *La Guerra Como Aventura*, Alianza, Madrid, 2014

Shaw, Louise Grace, *The British Political Elite and the Soviet Union*, Routledge, London, 2003

Skoutelsky, Rémi, *L'espoir guidait leurs pas: Les volontaires français dans les Brigades internationales, 1936–1939*, Paris, Grasset, 1998

—————*Novedad en el frente: Las brigadas internacionales en la guerra civil*, Ediciones Temas de Hoy, Madrid, 2006

Spencer Carr, Virginia, *Dos Passos: A Life*, Northwestern University Press, Evanston, 2004

Stewart, Roderick and Sharon, *Phoenix: The Life of Norman Bethune*, McGill-Queens University Press, Montreal, 2011

Stradling, Robert, *The Irish and the Spanish Civil War 1936–39*, Manchester University Press, Manchester, 1999

—————*History and Legend: Writing the International Brigades*, University of Wales Press, Cardiff, 2003

Taube, Jakob, *Hans Kahle (1899–1947): Der vergessene Kommandeur der Thälmann-Brigade*, Leipziger Universitätsverlag, Leipzig, 2017

Taylor, A. J. P. (ed.), *History of the Twentieth Century*, Purnell, London, 1968

Thomas, Hugh, *The Spanish Civil War*, 4th edition, Penguin, 2012

Tosstorff, Reiner, *El POUM en la Revolució espanyola*, Editorial Base, Barcelona, 2009

Tsou, Hwei-Ru and Len, *Los Brigadistas Chinos en la Guerra Civil: La Llamada de España (1936–1939)*, Catarata, Madrid, 2013

Tuytens, Sven and Van Doorslaer, Rudi, *Israël Piet Akkerman: Van Antwerpse vakbondsleider tot Spanjestrijder*, ABVV Algemene Centrale, Antwerp, 2016

Uhl, Michael, *Mythos Spanien: Das Erbe der Internationalen Brigaden in der DDR*, Verlag J. H. W. Dietz, Bonn, 2004

Vaill, Amanda, *Hotel Florida: Truth, Love, and Death in the Spanish Civil War*, Farrar, Straus and Giroux, New York, 2014

Van Hensbergen, Gijs, *Guernica: The Biography of a Twentieth-century Icon*, Bloomsbury, London, 2005

Various authors, *Cuba en la Defensa de la Republica Española*, Editora Política, La Habana, 1981

—————*Los Rusos en la Guerra de España*, Editorial Fundación Pablo Iglesias, Madrid, 2009

Vernon, Alex, *Hemingway's Second War: Bearing Witness to the Spanish Civil War*, University of Iowa Press, Iowa City 2011

Vidal, César, *Las Brigadas Internacionales*, Espasa-Calpe, Madrid, 1998

Viñas, Angel, *La Conspiración del General Franco*, Crítica, Barcelona, 2011
————(ed.), *Los Mitos del 18 de Julio*, Crítica, Barcelona, 2013
————and Blanco, Juan Andrés, *La Guerra Civil Española: Una Visión Bibliográfica*, Marcial Pons Historia, Madrid, 2017
Viñas, Ernesto and Tuytens, Sven, *Lugares de las Brigadas Internacionales en Madrid: Batalla de Brunete*, AABI, Madrid, 2015
Vinyes, Ricardo, Armengou, Montse and Belis, Ricard, *Els Nens Perduts del Franquisme*, Proa, Barcelona, 2002
Volodarsky, Boris, *Stalin's Agent: the Life and Death of Alexander Orlov*, OUP, Oxford, 2015
Wagner-Martin, L., *Ernest Hemingway: A Literary Life*, Palgrave Macmillan, Basingstoke, 2007
Watkins, K. W., *Britain Divided: The effect of the Spanish Civil War on British Political Opinion*, Greenwood Press, Westport, 1976
Weiss, Peter, *La Estética de la resistencia: España, antesala de la tragedia*, Versal, Barcelona, 1987
————*The Aesthetics of Resistance*: Vol. 1, *A Novel*, Duke University Press, 2005
Wyden, Peter, *The Passionate War: The Narrative History of the Spanish Civil War*, Simon & Schuster, New York, 1983
Wyszczelkski, Lech (ed.), *Dabrowszczacy*, Ksiazka i Wiedza, Warsaw, 1986
Zaagsma, Gerben, *Jewish Volunteers: The International Brigades and the Spanish Civil War*, Bloomsbury, London, 2017
Zaloga, Steven Z., *Spanish Civil War Tanks: The Proving Ground for Blitzkrieg*, Osprey, Oxford, 2010

Chapters in secondary sources

Bouček, Jaroslav, 'Českoslovenští interbrigadisté jako zdroj politických elit po roce 1945', in I. Koutská and F. Svátek (eds.), *Politické elity v Československu 1918–1948*, Ústav světových dejin ČAV, Prague, 1994, pp. 147–80

SECONDARY MAGAZINE AND NEWSPAPER ARTICLES

Crain, Caleb, 'Lost illusions: the Americans who fought in the Spanish Civil War', *New Yorker*, 18 April 2016
'East Germany: soldiers of communism', *Time*, 3 August 1953
'Frente de Madrid', *Gefrema*, Nos 4, 5, 8, 14, 15, 16, and 21
'Hemingway on war and its aftermath', *Prologue*, Vol. 38, No. 1, spring 2006: https://www.archives.gov/publications/prologue/2006/spring/hemingway.html

Hemingway Sanford, Marcelina, 'Hemingway goes to war', *The Atlantic*,
August 2014: https://www.theatlantic.com/magazine/archive/2014/08/
hemingway-goes-to-war/373437/

Historia y Vida (Battle of Brunete issue), No. 50, June 1972

'Jack Jones worked for KGB': http://news.bbc.co.uk/2/hi/uk/8289962.stm

Lladós, Josep and Mario Reyes, Mario, 'Le presó secreta de les brigades',
El Temps, No. 667, 31 March 1997, pp. 48–55

Mitgang, Herbert, 'Hemingway on Spain: unedited reportage', *New York
Times*, 30 August 1988

Thurman, Jane, 'Rules of engagement: writing, fighting, and André
Malraux', *New Yorker*, 2 May 2005

Academic articles

Aguilera Povedano, Miguel, 'Los hechos de mayo de 1937: efectivos y bajas
de cada bando', *Hispania*, Vol. 73, No. 245, September–December 2013

Altarozzi, Giordano, 'Volontari romeni e italiani nella guerra di Spagna
(Romanian and Italian volunteers in the Spanish War)', *Editura
Universității Petru Maior*, September 2009

Ánderle, Adam, 'La sombra ee Ernő Gerő, La acusación de trotskismo a los
brigadistas húngaros: Albacete (1938) Y Budapest (1949)', *Hispania Nova,
Revista de Historia Contemporánea*, No. 13, 2015

Andreassi Cieri, Alejandro, 'El KPD en la Guerra Civil española y la
cuestión del Frente Popular: algunas reflexiones', *Hispania*, 2014, Vol. 74,
No. 246, pp. 177–204

Baxell, Richard, 'Myths of the International Brigades', *Bulletin of Spanish
Studies*, Vol. 91, Issue 1–2, 2014, pp. 11–24

Bensalem, Abdellatif, 'Los voluntarios arabes en las Brigadas Internacionales
(España, 1936–1939)', *Revista Internacional de Sociología*, October 1988,
Vol. 46, No. 4

Bernecker, Walther L., 'Willy Brandt y la guerra civil española', *Revista de
Estudios Políticos*, No. 29, 1982

Blachstein, Kurt, '¡Jóvenes que rompieron con todo!', *Mozaika*, http//www.
mozaika.es/avanti-popolo-jovenes-que-rompieron-con-todo/

Bourderon, Roger, 'Le colonel Rol-Tanguy', *Revue historique des armées*,
No. 248, 2007, http://journals.openedition.org/rha/1043

Buchanan, Tom, 'The lost art of Felicia Browne', *History Workshop Journal*,
54, 2002, pp. 181–90

————————"Shanghai–Madrid axis?" Comparing British Responses to the
Conflicts in Spain and China, 1936–39', *Contemporary European History*,
Vol. 21, Issue 4, 2012

Cabeza San Deogracias, José, 'Antonio Col como ejemplo del uso de la narrativa como propaganda durante la Guerra Civil española', *Revista Historia y Comunicación Social*, No. 10, 2005, pp. 37–50

Calero, Juan Pablo, 'Vísperas de la revolución, El congreso de la CNT (1936)', *Germinal*, No. 7, April 2009, pp. 97–132

Calleja, Eduardo and Aróstegui, Julio, 'La tradición recuperada: el Requeté carlista y la insurrección', *Historia Contemporánea*, No. 11, pp. 51–5

Candil, Antonio, 'Soviet armor in Spain: aid mission to republicans tested doctrine and equipment', *Armor*, March–April 1999

Carroll, Peter, 'The myth of the Moscow Archives', *Science & Society*, Vol. 68, No. 3, pp. 337–41

Crome, Len, 'Walter 1897–1947, a soldier in Spain', *History Workshop Journal*, No. 9, spring 1980, pp. 116–28

Daley, John, 'The theory and practice of armored warfare in Spain: an experiment reconsidered', *Armor*, March–April 1999

Durgan, Andy, 'Freedom fighters or Comintern army?', *International Socialism Journal*, No. 84, autumn 1999, pp. 1–16

—————'Marxism, war and revolution: Trotsky and the POUM', *Revolutionary History*, Vol. 9, No. 2, 2006

—————'With the POUM international volunteers on the Aragon Front (1936–1937)', *Ebre 38*, No. 8, 2018

Ealham, Chris, 'De la unidad antifascista a la desunión libertarian: los comités superiores del movimiento libertario contra los quijotes anarquistas en el marco del Frente Popular (1936–1937)', *Mélanges de la Casa de Velázquez*, nouvelle série, No. 41 (1), 2011, pp. 121–42

Egea Bruno, Pedro María, 'Entre la historia y la propaganda: las dos sublevaciones del acorazado jaime i en Julio de 1936', *Ebre 38*, No. 4, 2010, pp. 31–47

Fernández Soriano, Víctor, 'Bélgica y la guerra civil: el impacto del conflicto español en la política', *Cuadernos de Historia Contemporánea*, 2007, Vol. 29, pp. 219–33

Gayman, Vital, 'La base des Brigades Internationales', *Estudios de Historia Social*, Nos. 50–1, Madrid, 1989

Godicheau, François, 'El proceso del poum: proceso ordinario de una justicia extraordinaria', *Historia Contemporánea*, No. 29, 2005, pp. 839–69

Gómez Escarda, María, 'La mujer en la propaganda política republicana', *Barataria, Revista Castellano-Manchega de Ciencias Sociales*, No. 9, 2008, pp. 83–101

Grassia, Edoardo, 'Barcellona, 17 e 18 marzo 1938', *Diacronie: Studi di Storia Contemporanea*, 29 July 2011

Hagen, William. W., 'Before the "final solution": toward a comparative analysis of political anti-Semitism in interwar Germany and Poland', *Journal of Modern History*, Vol. 68, No. 2, June 1996

Hirschinger, Frank, 'Der Mythos um den Kommandeur des "Thälmann Bataillons", Bruno Hinz (1900–1937)', *Totalitarismus und Demokratie*, No. 8, 2011

Huber, Peter and Uhl, Michael, 'Die Internationalen Brigaden, Politische überwachung und repression nach sichtung der russichen und westlichen archivatken', *Ebre 38*, No. 2, 2004

Jordá, Eduard, 'Weil y la guerra civil', *Fronterad Revista Digital*, 2009, https//www.fronterad.com/weil-y-la-guerra-civil/

Juliá, Santos, 'La ugt de Madrid en los años treinta: un sindicalismo de gestión', *Revista Española de Investigaciones Sociológicas*, No. 20, 1982, pp. 121–35

Kennedy-Epstein, Rowena, '"Whose fires would not stop": Muriel Rukeyser and the Spanish Civil War, 1936–1976', *Journal of Narrative Theory*, Vol. 43, No. 3, Fall 2013, pp. 384–414

Knox, Bernard, 'Premature antifascist', *Antioch Review*, Yellow Springs, Ohio, spring 1999, pp. 133–49

Kowalsky, Daniel, 'The Soviet Union and the International Brigades, 1936–1939', *Journal of Slavic Military Studies*, No. 19, 2006, pp. 681–704

Krammer, Arnold, 'Germans against Hitler: the Thaelmann Brigade', *Journal of Contemporary History*, Vol. 4, No. 2, 1969, pp. 65–83

——————'The cult of the Spanish Civil War in East Germany', *Journal of Contemporary History*, Vol. 39, No. 4, October 2004, pp. 531–60

Kvam, Wayne, 'Ernest Hemingway and Hans Kahle', *Hemingway Review*, spring 1983, Vol. 2, No. 2

Litten, Frederick S., 'The CCP and the Fujian rebellion', *Republican China*, Vol. XIV, No. 1, November 1988

Loren Garay, Gonzalo, 'La batalla de Quinto de Ebro en la ofensiva republicana sobre Zaragoza', *Revista de Historia Militar*, No. 115, 2014

Mackenzie, S. P., 'The Foreign Enlistment Act and the Spanish Civil War, 1936–1939', *Twentieth Century History*, Vol. 10, No. 1, 1999, pp. 52–66

McLellan, Josie, '"I wanted to be a little Lenin": ideology and the German International Brigade volunteers', *Journal of Contemporary History*, Vol. 41, No. 2, April 2006

Magnani, Alberto, 'Entrevista a Giovanni Pesce', *Ebre 38*, No. 3, 2008

Marco, Jorge, 'Transnational soldiers and guerrilla warfare from the Spanish Civil War to the Second World War', *War in History*, pp. 1–21

Mastrorilli, Edoardo, 'Guerra civile spagnola, intervento italiano e guerra totale' ('Spanish Civil War, Italian intervention, and total war'), *Revista Universitaria de Historia Militar, RUHM*, Vol. 3, No. 6, 2014, pp. 68–87

Mednikov, Igor, 'Los límites de una renovación: la historiografía actual rusa sobre la guerra civil Española', *Studio Historica*, Vol. 32, 2014

Momryk, Myron, '"For your freedom and for ours", Konstantin (Mike) Olynyk: a Ukrainian volunteer from Canada in the International Brigades', *Canadian Ethnic Studies (Etudes Ethniques au Canada)*, Vol. 20, No. 2, 1 January 1988

Ottanelli, Fraser, 'Anti-fascism and the shaping of national and ethnic identity: Italian American volunteers in the Spanish Civil War', *Journal of American Ethnic History*, Vol. 27, No. 1, 2007, pp. 9–31

Pagis i Blanch, Pelai, 'Marty, Vidal, Kléber y el Komintern: informes y confidencias de la dirección política de las Brigadas Internacionales', *Ebre 38, revista internacional de la guerra civil 1936–1939*, No. 1, 2003, pp. 11–26

Perez, Ana, Cela, Julia R. and Calatayud, Gemma, 'La memoria de las Brigadas Internacionales a través de la Documentación recogida por la Asociación de Amigos de las Brigadas Internacionales (AABI)', *Documentación de las Ciencias de la Información*, Vol. 36, 2013, pp. 85–102

Pozharskaya, Svetlana, 'Comintern and the Spanish Civil War in Spain', *Ebre 38*, No. 1

Preston, Paul, 'Lights and shadows in George Orwell's *Homage to Catalonia*', *Bulletin of Spanish Studies*, 1–29, 2017

Puigsech Farràs, Josep, 'Entre el ejército del Comintern y la solidaridad antifascista: la trayectoria de Giuseppe di Vittorio en el debate sobre la naturaleza de las Brigadas Internacionales' ('Between the Comintern army and the antifascist solidarity: the trajectory of Giuseppe di Vittorio inside the discussion about the International Brigades'), *Studia Historica, Historia Contemporánea*, No. 28, 2010

Ramsay, Scott, 'Ensuring benevolent neutrality: the British government's appeasement of General Franco during the Spanish Civil War, 1936–1939', *International History Review*, 2018

Rein, Raanan, 'Echoes of the Spanish Civil War in Palestine: Zionists, communists and the contemporary press', *Journal of Contemporary History*, Vol. 43, No. 1, 2008, pp. 9–23

Requena Gallego, Manuel, 'Monográfico sobre la guerra civil y las Brigadas Internacionales en Albacete', in *Al-Basit: Revista de Estudios Albacetenses*, Instituto de Estudios Albacetenses de la Diputación Provincial de Albacete, 1996

Santadrián Arias, Víctor Manuel, 'Enrique Líster: el antimilitarista que llegó a general', *RUHM*, Vol. 7, No. 13, 2018, pp. 423–39

Saz, Ismael, 'Fascism and empire, fascist Italy against republican Spain', *Mediterranean Historical Review*, 1 June 1998, Vol. 131–2, pp. 116–34

——'El fracaso del éxito, Italia en la guerra de España', *Espacio, Tiempo y Forma*, Serie V, *Historia Contemporánea*, T. V., 1992, 105–28

Serrallonga i Urquidi, Joan, 'El aparato provincial durante la Segunda Republica: los gobernadores civiles, 1931–1939', *Hispania Nova* 7, 2007

Thornberry, Robert S., 'Writers take sides, Stalinists take control: the Second International Congress for the defense of culture (Spain 1937)', *The Historian*, 2000, Vol. 62, No. 3, pp. 589–605

Thorpe, Andrew, 'The membership of the Communist Party of Great Britain, 1920–1945', *The Historical Journal*, Vol. 43, No. 3, September 2000, pp. 777–800

Valentín, Manu, 'El exilio judeoasquenazí en Barcelona 1933–1945: un rompecabezas que pide ser esclarecido', *Entremons*, Universitat Pompeu Fabra, Barcelona, No. 6, June 2014, pp. 8–10

Van Doorslaer, Rudi, 'Joodse Vrijwilligers uit België in de Internationale Brigaden, Een Portret van een Vergeten Generatie?', *BTNG (RBHC)*, 1987, No. 18, pp. 165–85

—— 'Israël "Piet" Akkerman, de Diamantzager (1913–1937), Een joodse militant van de Derde Internationale in Antwerpen', *BTNG (RBHC)*, Vol. XXII, 1991, Nos. 3–4, pp. 721–82

——'Tussen wereldrevolutie en joodse identiteit: Joden uit Belge in Spaanse burgeroorlog', *BTNG (RBHC)*, Vol. XVII, 1995, No. 17, pp. 13–87

Vera Jiménez, Fernando, 'Cubanos en la Guerra Civil Española, La presencia de voluntarios en las Brigadas Internacionales y el Ejército Popular de la República', *Revista Complutense de Historia de América*, No. 25, 1999

Vilches Giménez, Manuel, 'La batalla del Cerro Telégrafo', *Adalid*, No. 4

Winchester, Ian, 'So[u]ldiers for Christ and Men for Spain: the *Apostolado Castrense*'s Role in the Creation and Dissemination of Francoist Martial Masculinity', *RUHM*, Vol. 4, No. 8, 2015, pp. 143–63

Zaloga, Steven J., 'Soviet tank operations in the Spanish Civil War', *Journal of Slavic Military Studies*, Vol. 12, No. 3, 1999, pp. 134–62

THESES

Evans, Daniel, 'The Conscience of the Spanish Revolution: Anarchist Opposition to State Collaboration in 1937', PhD thesis, University of Leeds, 2016

Fernandez, Jorge Christian, ' "Voluntários da Liberdade": Militares Brasileiros nas Forças Armadas Republicanas durante a Guerra Civil

Espanhola (1936–1939)', Master's Thesis, Universidade Do Vale Do Rio Dos Sinos, 2003

Piquero Cuadros, Enrique Santiago, 'Las crónicas de los corresponsales soviéticos durante la Guerra Civil española (1936–1939) como fuente para el estudio histórico-literario del conflicto', PhD thesis, Complutense University, Madrid, 2014

DATABASES AND WEBSITES

AABI, Asociación de Amigos de las Brigadas Internacionales, https://brigadasinternacionales.org/

André Marty and the International Brigades, Consortium Archives des Mondes Contemporains, http://chs.huma-num.fr/exhibits/show/marty-et-les-brigades-internat/accueil

Auschwitz Museum, http://auschwitz.org/muzeum/

Batalla de Teruel, https://batallate.es/

Bocanegra, Lidia, 'Španski borci: Herbert Fornezzi', University of Granada, http://digibug.ugr.es/bitstream/handle/10481/48152/BocanegraHerbertFornezzi.pdf;jsessionid=D7BAB533613C825D49394600AD007577?sequence=1

Brunete en La Memoria, http://pemaniobra.blogspot.com/, curated by Sven Tuytens and Ernesto Viñas

Combatientes.es, Archivos Históricos Militares y Civiles, Guerra Civil Española, curated by Natalia Lemos Geddo

Francisco Franco, archive of speeches, generalisimofranco.com/discursos/discursos/

Frank Ryan, 'A Revolutionary Life', http://www.qub.ac.uk/sites/frankryan/

Fundación Francisco Franco, fnff.es

Fundació Pau Casals, http://www.paucasals.org/?idIdioma=es&idSeccion=-PAU-CASALS-cronologia&id=4

Gefrema, Grupo de Estudios del Frente de Madrid, http://gefrema80.blogspot.com.es

German Resistance Memorial Center, www.gdwberlin.de

International Brigade Memorial Trust, UK, http://www.international-brigades.org.uk/

Intstytut Pamięci Narodowej, Institute of National Remembrance, Poland, https://ipn.gov.pl/

Istituto Nazionale Ferruccio Parri and Associazione Italiana Combattenti Antifascisti di Spagna (AICVAS), http://www.antifascistispagna.it/

Jack Jones Trust, http://www.jackjonestrust.com/jack-jones/

jailynews.blogspot.com, blog on San Pedro de Cardeña prison camp

La Cárcel Modelo De Barcelona, 1904–2004, at La Biblioteca de la Evasión, http://bibliotecadelaevasion.pimienta.org/uploads/2010/11/lamodelo1.pdf

Le Maitron Dictionnaire Biographique, Mouvement Ouvrier-Movement Sociale, Editions de L'Atelier, maitron.univ-paris1.fr

Les Amis des Combattants En Espagne Republicaine, http://www.acer-aver.fr/index.php

MacGregor-Thunell, Anders, *Spanish Civil War – Oral History*, online translations of Swedish memoirs, http://educationforum.ipbhost.com/topic/897-spanish-civil-war-oral-history/

Mota, José Fernando, *Milicians, reclutes i comissaris a Sant Cugat. El campament militar i l'Escola de Comissaris de Pins del Vallès (1937–1939)*, https://historiasantcugat.wordpress.com

National Museet, Denmark, http://modstand.natmus.dk/person.aspx?34934

Olympic Museum, https://www.olympic.org/

Sidbrint database, Universitat de Barcelona, http://sidbrint.ub.edu i

Sogn og Fjordane county archives, Norway (Fylkesarkivet i Sogn og Fjordane), https://resource.fylkesarkivet.no/article/c0217ff3-6aec-4a8c-bc2b-0f1b2c6ff402#

Sommerfield, John, 'Notebooks', http://www.andrewwhitehead.net/john-sommerfields-spanish-notebook.html

Tate Gallery, London, www.tate.org

The Volunteer, Abraham Lincoln Brigade Archives, www.albavolunteer.org

Acknowledgements

Historians, like scientists, sit on the shoulders of giants who come before them. This is certainly true for historians of the Spanish Civil War. I wish to express a special debt to Paul Preston, Richard Baxell and Peter N. Carroll – three historians who have been generous with their time and with their knowledge of the International Brigades and the war. The first two and Chris Brooks kindly read parts (or the whole) of early drafts of this book, along with Severiano Montero, the former head of the Asociación de Amigos de la Brigadas Internacionales (AABI) in Madrid, and probably the person with the most extensive knowledge of the International Brigades. Katharine Scott and Walter Donohue were, once more, early readers – their dedication is immense and their contributions crucial. I am very grateful to all for their time and thoughts. Any remaining errors are my responsibility. So, too, is the interpretation of events surrounding this unique transnational army in one of the twentieth century's most controversial wars.

The list of researchers who study the Spanish Civil War is too long to reproduce here, but two previous historians of the International Brigades must be acknowledged: Andreu Castells and Remi Skoutelsky. Their work – published in 1974 and 2006 respectively, and never translated into English – remains crucial. Otherwise, only a handful of serious historians have attempted global histories. In English, R. Dan Richardson's *Comintern Army*, published in 1982, like Vincent Brome's *International Brigades* and Verle Bryant Johnston's *Legions of Babel*, written in the 1960s, had limited resources. In *Fallen Sparrows*, Michael

Jackson produced an eloquent 140-page analysis as things stood in 1994. He memorably described the International Brigades as the 'kind of mystery where no-one really knows the answers to the naïve questions posed'. The opening of the Comintern archive in Moscow has changed that somewhat. I am fortunate that the International Brigades part of the archive is now online, allowing more extensive research than ever before. My special thanks, therefore, go to the Russian State Archive of Socio-Political History (RGASPI). I also want to thank staff at the libraries and archives I visited, including: Archiwum Akt Nowych (AAN) in Warsaw; the International Institute for Social History (IISH) in Amsterdam; the Centro Documental de Memoria Histórica (CDMH) in Salamanca; the Archivo General Militar in Avila; the CRAI library at the Pavelló de la República in Barcelona; the Biblioteca Nacional and EFE picture archive in Madrid; the Imperial War Museum, British Library and Marx Memorial Library in London; the Tamiment Library at New York University; the Manuscripts and Archives division of New York Public Library; and, finally, the Hoover Institution at Stanford University, Palo Alto. Matilde López Aguerre gave me family documents on Uruguayans while I was in Montevideo.

Spain's state institutions keep archives public and, where possible, online. Their PARES portal, the Centro de Estudios y Documentación de las Brigadas Internacionales (CEDOBI) at the University of Castilla La Mancha in Albacete and the Sistema de Información Digital sobre Las Brigadas Internacionales (SIDBRINT) run by Lourdes Prades and Teresa Abelló at the University of Barcelona, have been key. I relied on the transcription into Spanish of material at the Bundesarchiv in Berlin by Isabel Esteve, who graciously allowed me to use her work.

Many lagoons remain in the military history of important battles. A handful of Spanish journals fill the void – especially Ebre 38 and Revista Universitaria de Historia Militar (RUHM). Local history groups and individuals do much of the best research. My thanks go to: José Antonio Zarza, Antonio Morcillo, Ken O'Keefe and others at GEFREMA (Grupo de Estudios del Frente de Madrid); Ernesto Viñas and Sven Tuytens at Brunete en La Memoria; Jaime Cinca at Belchite; José Luis Pantoja at Lopera: Alfonso López Bogoñoz in Castelldefels; as well as Alan Warren in Aragon and Catalonia. Volunteers also publish and process archival documents at websites like combatientes.es, rutasbelicas.com, batallate.es and bruneteenlamemoria.es. My thanks, too, to Almudena Cros, Andrés Chamorro and those who research and organise events at AABI in Madrid.

Much research has been done by Brigaders' relatives and national support groups. As a result, I am indebted to AABI, the Abraham Lincoln Brigade Archives (ALBA), the International Brigade Memorial Trust (IBMT) in Britain, Les Amis des Combattants en Espagne Républicaine (ACER), the Associazione Italiana Combattenti Volontari Antifascisti Di Spagna (AICVAS), the Spanje 1936-39 Foundation and the Kämpfer und Freunde der Spanischen Republik (KFSR). AABI's brigadasinternacionales.org website and ALBA's albavolunteer.org continually produce fresh insights. The Documentation Archive of the Austrian Resistance (DöW) at doew.at and the Le Maitron Dictionnaire Biographique at Maitron.fr contain many Brigader biographies from Austria and France. I am grateful to Irene Filip at DÖW and Claude Pennetier at Maitron for guidance.

Historians, researchers, archivists and Brigader relatives in a dozen countries have responded to queries or let me see and sometimes publish memoirs or personal documents. They include Walther Bernecker, Irene Filip, Mark Derby, Milo Petrovic, Blanka Matkovic, Diliana Ivanova, Iwona Zielińska-Sąsiada, Jutka Kovacs, Judit Löcsei, Peter Crome, Yvonne Scholten, Rudi Wester, Coco Barreiro in Uruguay, Morten Møller, Lenni Kari, Rina Ronja Kari, Anders MacGregor, Sharon Stewart, Ainhoa Zufriategui, Isabel Barrionuevo, Aku Estebaranz, Jostein Moen, Rolf Saether, Serge Alternês, Bill Rukeyser, Randal Scamardo, Ian Moffat, Chris Ealham, Paul Sharkey, John Wainwright, Antonio Rodríguez Celada, Maurice Tszorf, Luke Stegemann, James Fernandez, Peter Brooks, Gijs van Hensbergen, Sarah Chadfield, Andre Gounot, Valerie Deacon, Martin Minchom, Jane Rogoyska, John Kiszely, Tom Buchanan, Chris Brooks, Soledad Fox Maura and Susana Grau at the Cañada Blanch Centre at the London School of Economics and Political Science (LSE). Susana, along with Paul Preston, has been generous with the centre's resources, and I am immensely grateful for access to their library and publications, and the LSE's other academic resources.

While I have relied on my own translations for Spanish, Portuguese, Catalan, Italian and French sources (with some assistance), the

International Brigades were a Tower of Babel that produced documents in two dozen languages, including Esperanto. Those who helped wrestle with everything from Dutch and Danish to Russian, Yiddish and Hungarian include Sebastiaan Faber, Gleb Zilberstein, Deborah Green, Jutka Kovacs, Andrea Wolfes, Mikkel Larson and Mary Mowbray.

At Bloomsbury, this project has been capably guided by Michael Fishwick, Lauren Whybrow, Sarah Ruddick, Bill Swainson, George Gibson and Lilidh Kendrick. Kate Johnson has been a fine editor. Jordi Aynaud's Spanish translation allowed for parallel reviewing in two languages. My thanks to Aynaud (also for editorial comments), as well as to Miguel Aguilar and Roberta Gerhard at my Spanish publisher, Debate, for organising this and handling the Spanish edition that appears at the same time as this one. My agent, Georgina Capel, has been a rock.

Lucas and Samuel Tremlett both helped research parts of this book and have patiently watched it grow over five years. Katharine Blanca Scott Ripoll remains my first – and finest – editor.

13 July 2020

Tables

Volunteer numbers by origin or language/regional groups

	TOTAL RECRUITS BY MARCH 1937 (AFTER JARAMA & GUADALAJARA BATTLES)	SNAPSHOT OF SECOND YEAR RECRUITS. OCTOBER 1937–JANUARY 1938, FIGUERES, CATALONIA	TOTAL RECRUITS PLUS WOUNDED, MISSING OR DEAD ON 26 DECEMBER 1937 (PRIOR TO BATTLE OF TERUEL)	TOTAL RECRUITS PLUS WOUNDED, MISSING OR DEAD ON 31 MARCH, 1938 (DURING ARAGON RETREATS)	VOLUNTEERS SERVING ON 1 MAY 1938 (AFTER RETREATS AND CLOSE OF ALBACETE BASE)	TOTAL RECRUITS IN WAR, OCTOBER 1936–SEPTEMBER 1938	VOLUNTEERS LEFT IN SPAIN ON OCTOBER 1938 DISBANDMENT
Franco-Belgian group			8,300				
German group			5,237				
Anglo-American group			4,265				
Italian group			2,343				
Slav group			7,619				
German	1,354	164			1,044	2,217	
American	733	174			739	2,341	
Austrian	231	134			437	872	
Balkan	1,184					2,895	
Baltic	659					892	
Belgian	1390	107			711	1,722	

Canadian	173	173	181	512
Czechoslovakian	284	226	610	1,066
Scandinavian	98			799
French	6,928	408	2,687	8962
Dutch	302	72	171	628
Hungarian	285	70	195	528
British/English	877	267	717	1,825
Italian	2,124	261	1,321	3,002
Polish	1,541	584	1,212	3,117
Portuguese	112	12		134
Swiss	275	50	110	408
Diverse	164		1,201	1,122
Finnish		26	81	
Danish		42	198	
Swedish		71	173	
Rumanian		62	109	
Russian		9	80	
Yugoslavian		122	387	
Albanian		2		
Argentinian		9		
Armenian		7		
Bulgarian		42	165	
Chilean		1		
Cuban		8		
Scottish		2		
Danzig		5		
Estonian		6		
Greek		15		
Irish		8		
Icelandic		1		
Latvian		6		
Lithuanian		12		
Luxembourgeois		1		
Moors (*sic*)		1		
Palestinian		13		
Norwegian		26		
Paraguayan		2		
Puerto Rican		1		
Turkish		1		
Andorran		1		
Chinese		1		
DEAD		15.7%	4,575, 15.1%	

MISSING/ DESERTED			11.9%	5,740, 18.3%			
REPATRIATED (injured or not)			Included with missing and deserted	5,062, 16.1%			
IN HOSPITAL			12.8%	2,361, 7.5%			
TOTAL	18,714	3,477	27,764	31,369	12,614	32,297	12,208–673
Source	Source: RGASPI 545.2.108 pp. 210–11	Source: RGASPI 545.2.108, pp. 55-6. 3,515 recruits reach Albacete, so most use this route (RGASPI 545.2.108 p. 208)	Source: RGASPI 545.2.108 pp. 52–4	Source: Zaisser Report in Rémi Skoutelsky, *L'Espoir guidait leurs pas*, pp. 329-331, using RGASPI 517.3.15	Source: RGASPI 545.2.108, p. 137	Source: RGASPI 545.2.108 pp. 210. August 1938 figures, when recruitment has almost dried up, but final total will be slightly higher.	Source: Manuel González Moreno-Navarro, *Las Brigadas Internacionales, Su Paso por Cataluña*, pp. 101–4, citing International Committee for Retirement of Volunteers (CIRV).

International volunteers on 26 December 1937, prior to second Teruel battle

	FRANCO-BELGIAN LANGUAGE GROUP	GERMAN LANGUAGE GROUP	ANGLO-AMERICAN LANGUAGE GROUP	ITALIAN LANGUAGE GROUP	SLAV LANGUAGE GROUP	FOREIGN TOTAL	SPANISH BRIGADERS SERVING IN I.B. UNITS
TOTAL	8,300	5,237	4,265	2,343	7,619	27,764	
DEAD	23.5%	13.5%	10.6%	12.8%	12.5%	15.7%	
INJURED, MISSING, REPATRIATED OR DESERTED	25.1%	5.9%	3.3%	10.7%	7%	11.9%	
CURRENT STRENGTH	4,268	4,221	3,671	1,793	6,136	20,089	26,725
PERCENTAGE IN FRONTLINE UNITS	41.3%	47.7%	32.8%	42.4%	46.4%	42.8%	77%
DESTINATION UNKNOWN	14.8%	4.8%	10.6%	11.6%	18.9%	12.9%	
PERCENTAGE IN REARGUARD & hospital	43.9%	47.5%	56.6%	46%	34.7%	44.3%	23%
Percentage in hospital	17.7%	21.3%	21.6%	21.1%	11.8%	17.7%	
Base reserves	10%	12.3%	22.5%	14.7%	13.4%	14.2%	
Base auxiliary services	11%	7.4%	7.3%	8.5%	4.8%	7.3%	
Medical personnel	1.8%	5.1%	5.1%	0.7%	4.3%	3.7%	
TOTAL medical personnel	75	213	188	13	263	752	
Working in industry	3.4%	1.4%	0.1%	1%	0.4%	1.2%	
POLITICAL AFFILIATIONS OF ACTIVE VOLUNTEERS							
Communists & young communists	55.6%	70.8%	63.9%	60%	50.7%	59.7%	

Socialists & other anti-fascist parties or groups	15.9%	8.7%	1.9%	1.2%	3.8%	6.8%	
No party or unknown	28.5%	20.5%	34.2%	38.8%	45.5%	33.5%	
Source:	RGASPI 545.2.108 pp. 52–4	RGASPI 545.2.108 pp. 52–4	RGASPI 545.2.108 pp. 52–4	RGASPI 545.2.108 pp. 52–4	RGASPI 545.2.108 pp. 52–4	RGASPI 545.2.108 pp. 52–4	RGASPI 545.2.108 pp. 52–4

Total numbers of foreign and Spanish brigaders
Distribution by units and ranks on 20 December 1937, before Battle of Teruel

	General	Colonel	Lt. Colonel	Comandante (Major)	Captain	Lieutenant	Alférez (2nd Lieutenant)	Brigada	Sergeant	Driver	Corporal	Private	TOTAL
XI Brigade			2	10	60	127		7	231	105	257	2199	2998
XII Brigade				6	35	84	23	6	203	58	25	2032	2472
XIII Brigade			1	11	34	100		3	225	28	189	2248	2839
XIV Brigade			2	12	46	47	19	62	185	89	140	2595	3197
XV Brigade			2	9	37	64	1	5	170	83	232	1837	2440
15 Division	1	1		5	12	14		12	58	51	36	768	958
35 Division	1	1		5	21	36	1	7	84	108	115	870	1249
45 Division		1	3	11	48	103	11	4	211	227	40	1973	2632
20 Battalion of 86 Brigade			2	3	11	27	3	3	24	57	82	1887	2099
Anti-aircraft battalion				5	19	51	1	18	179	44	165	1141	1623
Anti-aircraft artillery				1	4	16	2	11	40	17	32	189	312
1st heavy artillery				1	4	9	3	6	24	22		230	299
2nd heavy artillery					7	5	6	9	26	1	26	192	272
Madrid special service				6	5	7	3	7	15	167	7	249	466
Frontline transport					8	20	7	47	248	186	113		629
Frontline medical				10	42	88	31	48	137	82	135	1369	1942
Rearguard medical			1	12	35	66	19	25	80	74	94	997	1403
Rearguard transport				1	1	4	2	11	29				48
In hospital				4	57	151	18	17	189			4775	5211
At base	1		4	32	135	279	64	55	298	492	193	7805	9358

	General	Colonel	Lt. Colonel	Comandante (Major)	Captain	Lieutenant	Alférez (2nd Lieutenant)	Brigada	Sergeant	Driver	Corporal	Private	TOTAL
TOTAL	3	3	17	144	621	1298	214	363	2656	1891	1881	33356	42447
% FOREIGN/ SPANISH													45%/55%
TOTAL FRONTLINE FORCES	2	3	12	95	393	798	111	255	2060	1325	1594	19779	26427
TOTAL REARGUARD FORCES	1		5	49	228	500	103	108	596	566	287	13577	16020

(Source: Paymaster at RGASPI 545.2.108 p. 37 & 545.2.131, pp. 30–37)

Index

A Note on the Author

Giles Tremlett is a contributing editor to the *Guardian* and Fellow of the Cañada Blanch Centre, London School of Economics. He has lived in and written about Spain for over twenty years, and is the author of *Catherine of Aragon*, *Ghosts of Spain* and *Isabella of Castile*, winner of the 2018 Elizabeth Longford Prize. He lives in Madrid with his family.

A Note on the Type

The text of this book is set in Adobe Garamond. It is one of several versions of Garamond based on the designs of Claude Garamond. It is thought that Garamond based his font on Bembo, cut in 1495 by Francesco Griffo in collaboration with the Italian printer Aldus Manutius. Garamond types were first used in books printed in Paris around 1532. Many of the present-day versions of this type are based on the *Typi Academiae* of Jean Jannon cut in Sedan in 1615.

Claude Garamond was born in Paris in 1480. He learned how to cut type from his father and by the age of fifteen he was able to fashion steel punches the size of a pica with great precision. At the age of sixty he was commissioned by King Francis I to design a Greek alphabet, and for this he was given the honourable title of Royal Type Founder. He died in 1561.